D0911861

AN ARCHAEOLOGY OF THE SOUL

KNIGHT-CAPRON LIBRARY
LYNCHBURG COLLEGE
LYNCHBURG, VIRGINIA 24501

An ARCHAEOLOGY *of the* SOUL

North American Indian Belief and Ritual

Robert L. Hall

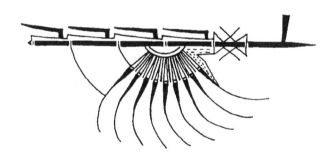

UNIVERSITY *of* ILLINOIS PRESS / URBANA *and* CHICAGO

KNIGHT-CAPRON LIBRARY
LYNCHBURG COLLEGE
LYNCHBURG, VIRGINIA 24501

© 1997 by the Board of Trustees of the University of Illinois
Manufactured in the United States of America
1 2 3 4 5 C P 5 4 3 2 1

This book is printed on acid-free paper.

Library of Congress Cataloging-in-Publication Data

Hall, Robert L.
    An archaeology of the soul : North American Indian belief and
ritual / Robert L. Hall.
        p.   cm.
    Includes bibliographical references and index.
    ISBN 0-252-02299-8 (alk. paper). — ISBN 0-252-06602-2 (pbk. :
alk. paper)
    1. Indians of North America—Religion. 2. Indians of North
America—Rites and ceremonies. I. Title.
E98.R3H16 1997
299′.7—dc20   96–8952
                                                                  CIP

For Barbara
pour toutes les années heureuses

KNIGHT-CAPRON LIBRARY
LYNCHBURG COLLEGE
LYNCHBURG, VIRGINIA 24501

CONTENTS

PREFACE

FOR 150 YEARS AND MORE museums have been collecting, curating, and exhibiting objects of material culture of the North American Indians. For 150 years and more scholars have been recording the languages, beliefs, and practices of the North American Indians. As a subfield of anthropology, archaeology has sought to straddle both lines of endeavor, using the evidence of the material culture of the past to reconstruct what it could of the social, political, and economic life in America before European contact. The motivation for all this activity has included some element of pure curiosity at all levels of concern, whether it be simply "to see what's there" or to pursue some more grandly defined programs envisioned by their authors to further the aims of social science.

Archaeology in particular has come under criticism from within and without. Beginning with Walter Taylor's 1948 *Study of Archaeology* archaeologists have become especially introspective, examining the theoretical basis for what it is they do as archaeologists. This has culminated in the 1990s with consideration of the question of whether it is really possible to know the past at all. Is our view of the past forever condemned to be merely a backward projection of the present, biased in this or that direction by special interests? For their part, American Indians have mounted their own criticism of anthropology, beginning with activities of the American Indian Movement (AIM) directed at stopping archaeological field projects and continuing with the broader-based campaign to reclaim Indian skeletons, sacred objects, and objects of tribal patrimony from museums.

It is an irony lost upon many that material objects of tribal patrimony often exist as such precisely because they did once become part of a museum collection. The objects of the three Sacred Tents of the Omaha are a case in point. There was a time a little over a century ago when tribal leaders were becoming very concerned over the fate of these objects. Care of the items was traditionally delegated to a line of hereditary keepers, but as the keepers advanced in years, no one was appearing to assume their roles. The objects were so sacred that only qualified persons could even touch them. The leaders were becoming reconciled to the conclusion that the objects would have to be buried with their keepers. Some of the sacred objects had

already been buried when Francis La Flesche, the son of a former principal chief of the Omahas, negotiated the transfer of the Sacred Pole to Harvard's Peabody Museum of Archaeology and Ethnology, where it has remained until recently repatriated to the Omahas.

Much the same situation holds for Indian intellectual property. Contrary to much popular and even some scholarly opinion, Indian property rights were well defined. A man might know every word of a song by heart yet be neither allowed nor willing to sing it himself unless he had purchased or earned the right along set guidelines. A person who repeated a sacred story to which he was not entitled was more than a literary thief subject to angry words and actions from his fellow tribesmen; he faced the prospect of supernatural retribution as well. So it was that many custodians of tribal tradition faced a dilemma their ancestors could not have anticipated—whether to make the words of the sacred literature known to outsiders or to allow those words to follow them into the grave. And so it came to pass, for instance, that the guardian of the Sacred White Buffalo Hide transferred his knowledge to Francis La Flesche in 1898.

La Flesche's life work became the recording of the oral traditions of the Osage tribe, a tribe whose language was closely akin to Omaha, of which La Flesche was a native speaker. What would we have lost if La Flesche had not pursued this task? What would the Osage have lost if La Flesche had not pursued this task? Margot Liberty estimates that a complete record of the War Rites and other ceremonies of the Osage—Osage language text, English literal translation, and English free translation of the songs and speeches for all kinship divisions of the tribe—would have occupied about forty thousand pages of print or fifty to eighty volumes, five hundred to eight hundred pages each, of the large size of the *Annual Report of the Bureau of American Ethnology*. And this would be for the Osage alone! Most of this has already been lost, of course. La Flesche was able to obtain and publish only a small representative sample in his lifetime, little more than 5 percent of the total Osage ceremonial record. The heart of this remarkable record has happily been made accessible to a wide readership in the form of a volume of La Flesche's writings edited by Garrick Bailey.[1]

Granting, for argument, that there are redeeming social benefits to Indians for the avid collecting policies of museums and ethnographers through the past century and a half, what are they? Museums can only exhibit so many objects, and the rest too often reside in cabinets as unstudied study collections. Much of the great body of textual materials published for the Osage and many other tribes remains unanalyzed. What purpose can it serve now that it has been saved? Just such a question was posed to his class by one of my former anthropology professors almost fifty years ago.

Professor C. W. M. Hart assigned my class the term paper topic of judging the usefulness of the many volumes of ethnographic 'texts' gathered during the formative years of American anthropology by its pioneers. I was not then able to come up with any special insights into the question on the grand scale that it was proposed, although I did find personal satisfaction in reading Leonard Bloomfield's *Menomini Texts*, one of the important contributors to which I discovered to be Jerome Lawe, a Menominee who had married the niece of my great-grandmother, who was Stockbridge Mohican. I knew well the families of Jerome's son Raymond and daughter Lizzie Lawe Worden and bought a copy of the volume to give to Raymond, who was fluent in Menominee.

Menomini Texts also contained stories related by Valentine Satterlee, one a version of the tale telling how he had tricked the anthropologists Alanson Skinner and Samuel Barrett into eating the beating heart of a giant snapping turtle. That was a story I had heard part of from my grandmother. I showed my grandmother the volume and she told me how one day Leonard Bloomfield overheard two Menominees in Keshena talking to each other in Menominee, one casting his eyes toward the University of Chicago linguist and asking in Menominee, "Who is that guy that's been hanging around here?" The friend shrugged and replied, "I don't know him," after which Bloomfield interjected jokingly, in their own language and much to their astonishment, "Why, I'm a Menominee, of course."

Nostalgia and literary value aside, it was twenty-five years before I really came to appreciate the utility of such texts. I found that texts were valuable for discovering mental associations between otherwise discrete classes of phenomena, associations that provided clues to patterns of thought and belief that might otherwise escape attention. The book that follows is a summation of much of the work that I began during the seventies exploring the resources of preserved traditions. Important parts were inspired by 'experimental archaeology', and much was inspired by objects in museum collections that I found to contain some feature that posed a riddle to me. I discovered that there was culture history to be extracted from museum collections and ethnographic records that I had not before even dreamed the existence of. I gradually redirected my career away from conventional scientific field archaeology toward a more humanistic, noninvasive archaeology emphasizing Native American spirituality. Because of the particular concern of this book for matters of the spirit, I have chosen the title *An Archaeology of the Soul*.

The use of the word 'archaeology' in my title is quite appropriate, because the book is not based so much upon fieldwork among contemporary Indian groups as upon records culled from the published literature—archaeological, ethnographic, and historical—which are, for the most part, buried and inaccessible to the average reader for reasons of distance or time. One of the long-standing criticisms of anthropologists by Indians has been the perception that anthropologists see their clientele as other anthropologists rather than the very Indians who provided their source material. This was true enough during the formative years of anthropology in the decades before and after the turn of the past century. It is much less true today. An anthropologist would have to be extremely naïve today to think that his or her publications would not be discussed critically by a concerned and informed Native American readership, and such readers are quite actively seeking out the older literature for assistance in discovering aspects of their Indian identities.

As the Lakota anthropologist Bea Medicine has observed, Indian participation in such revitalized rituals as the Sun Dance "transcends tribal affiliation and previous belief orientation" in that Ojibwas may today participate in the Sun Dance of their traditional Lakota enemies, or Canadian Micmacs from New Brunswick may feel "obliged to regain an Indian identity by making a pilgrimage to Pine Ridge."[2] In the early sixties I was invited to participate in a Memorial Day service at Greenwood, South Dakota, of the Native American Church during which the ritual was conducted in the tipi of a visiting Omaha delegation rather than in the wooden meeting house of the resident Yanktons, and the peyote was utilized in the minced form customary for the Yanktons rather than in the whole-button form preferred by the Omahas. More recently, I have participated in a sweat lodge ceremony in Texas led by an Apache instructed in South Dakota and attended by several Maya Indians, in which the fiercely hot and steamy interior of the lodge was incensed by the mingled odors of local kinnikinnick and Guatemalan copal gum, a virtual celebration of eclecticism in a revitalized ritual.

Mixing of this kind has certainly been accelerated and expanded by the efficiency of modern transportation and by the sharing of widely spoken languages, but I do not feel that diffusion and reintegration of elements should be considered to be a purely modern phenomenon. With this in mind I have selected Calumet ceremonialism as a theme around which to relate such seemingly unrelated phenomena as the Morning Star sacrifice of the Skiri Pawnees, the worship of Xipe Totec in Mesoamerica, the relationship of sacred pipes to spearthrowers, and the cosmology of the Aztec calendar stone. What I am promoting amounts to a doctrine of uniformitarianism for cultural processes today and in the past akin to the geological uniformitarianism that teaches that the processes of erosion and sedimentation observable today can explain the geology of continents in ancient times—hardly a unique approach, only uniquely applied. Sharing was an important cultural process in the past, as it is today. My contribution has been the insights that come from the pancontinen-

tal, deep-time perspectives of the archaeologist, complementing but not diminishing the contributions of investigators working intensively in a single contemporary community.

My hope is that this work will be seen as a resource facilitating a broader recognition of the continent-wide roots of many varieties of American Indian religious experience, much as the European rediscovery of classic Mediterranean civilization contributed new themes to contemporary art, philosophy, and literature. While this may be presumptuous for me as an individual, it is not so as a programmatic initiative with the potential of helping to give direction to a generation seeking ways in which to discover or express its Indianness.

ACKNOWLEDGMENTS

THIS BOOK has had a prolonged gestation period persisting through the last twenty-five years of my career, so that it would be difficult to acknowledge all those who have had some influence in its creation. Progressively fewer have had an opportunity to comment on its final form as it went through draft after draft, but all must be absolved of guilt for excesses of enthusiasm in which I may have indulged while pursuing this or that topic beyond the frontier of unchallenged consensus into the realm of intriguing prospect.

First I must acknowledge the sometime influence, assistance, encouragement, or kindnesses of Duane Anderson, Wendy Ashmore, Leonard Blake, Donald Blakeslee, Elizabeth Brandt, Johanna Broda, Ben Bronson, Joseph R. Caldwell, John B. Carlson, Michael Closs, Lawrence A. Conrad, Ella Deloria, John Douglas, Carol Diaz Granados Duncan, Munro Edmonson, Lu Ann, Elsinger, Thomas E. Emerson, Duane Esarey, Gary Feinman, Kent V. Flannery, Raymond Fogelson, Mary LeCron Foster, Melvin L. Fowler, Judith Franke, Jill Leslie McKeever Furst, Eloise Gadus, Merwyn S. Garbarino, James F. Garber, Guy Gibbon, William Green, James B. Griffin, Thomas Haberman, George Hamell, Alan D. Harn, Dale R. Henning, Frank Hole, Stephen D. Houston, Alice B. Kehoe, David H. Kelley, John E. Kelly, Janice Klein, Vernon James Knight, John Koontz, Edwin C. Krupp, George Lankford, Donald Lathrap, Floyd Lounsbury, Nancy O. Lurie, Joyce Marcus, Virginia Miller, Cheryl Ann Munson, Patrick J. Munson, Robert Neuman, Patricia O'Brien, Elizabeth Olton, David F. Overstreet, Douglas R. Parks, Max G. Pavesic, James L. Phillips, Jack Prost, Paul Proulx, Kent Reilly, Robert E. Ritzenthaler, James A. Robertson, Francis Robicsek, Courtney Schmoker, John Paul Staeck, Ellen F. Steinberg, James B. Stoltman, Andrea Stone, Melburn Thurman, Amy Trevelyan, Patty Jo Watson, Ronald Weber, Andrew H. Whiteford, Michael D. Wiant, and Larry Zimmerman.

During later stages of the writing I was especially aided by the comments of JoAllyn Archambault, James A. Brown, C. Randall Daniels-Sakim, N'omi Greber, Lawrence H. Keeley, Cecilia F. Klein, Bea Medicine, Robert J. Salzer, Bryan Stross, Stephen Williams, and my late life-long friend and colleague Warren L. Wittry. My wife, Barbara, was a conscientious and valued critic at all stages of the writing and our daughter, Susan, a motivating influence in the preparation of the computer graphics and a contributor to the freehand illustrations. I am particularly grateful for criticism of the final drafts of the manuscript by Garrick A. Bailey of the Department of Anthropology at the University of Tulsa and Raymond J. DeMallie of the American Indian Studies Research Institute at Indiana University, as readers for the University of Illinois Press. This book is appreciably better for their informed input and I thank them enthusiastically. I am equally grateful for the caring attention of the staff of the University of Illinois Press to all stages of the production of this book—Elizabeth G. Dulany at the acquisitions stage, Theresa L. Sears at the editorial stage, and the many less visible hands that help to pat, mold, prod, and coax a manuscript on its way. I thank also Louisa Castner, who as copy editor aided me in recognizing many fantasies of punctuation and syntax for which the world is not yet ready.

Preparation of the manuscript was facilitated generously by a fellowship with the Institute for the Humanities of the University of Illinois at Chicago and by a semester's sabbatical leave also awarded by the university. My period with the Institute for the Humanities was especially gratifying because of the intellectual stimulation provided by the other fellows—Susan Cole, Carolyn A. Edie, Sona S. Hoisington, Clark Hulse, Constance C. Meinwald, A. Lavonne Brown Ruoff, and Leroy R. Shaw—and by director Gene W. Ruoff and guest participants William G. Jones and Stephen E. Wiberley Jr. As bibliographer for the social sciences in the library of the University of Illinois at Chicago, Stephen deserves additional credit for developing the anthropology section of the library into the valuable asset that it is and the resource that it was for the writing of this book.

At the institutional level this book was greatly facilitated by the resources of several libraries: in Chicago, the Newberry Library, the library and archives of the Field Museum Department of Anthropology, the library of the University of Illinois at Chicago, as mentioned, and the library and archives of the Chicago Historical Society; in Libertyville, Illinois, the Cook Memorial Library; in Madison, Wisconsin, the library and archives of the State Historical Society of Wisconsin; and in Washington, D.C., the anthropology archives of the Smithsonian Institution. I was aided also by: the Midwest Archaeological Center of the National Park Service, Lincoln, Nebraska; the State Archeological Research Center of the South Dakota State Historical Society, Rapid City; the Illinois State Museum, Springfield; and the Dickson Mounds Museum of the Illinois State Museum, Lewistown, Illinois.

The illustrations appearing in figures 11.1 and 13.1 were reproduced with the permission of the President and Trustees of Harvard College and those in figures 14.10b–c with the permission of the Department of Anthropology of the University of Minnesota, Minneapolis. Permission to use a quotation from his cover story "Skeletons in Our Closet" in the Chicago *Reader* was kindly granted by James Krohe Jr. The calumet-pipe logo appearing on the title page is redrawn from that featured on the cover of the proceedings of the First Annual Conference for Tribal Judges held at the State University of South Dakota, Vermillion, March 2–6, 1959,[1] which was, in turn, based upon a painted detail from a Plains buffalo robe then on display in the university's W. H. Over Museum.

AN ARCHAEOLOGY OF THE SOUL

1 / Weeping Greetings and Dancing the Calumet

AFTER JEAN NICOLET, the first European to describe the upper Midwest was Pierre d'Esprit, Sieur de Radisson, whose travels took him and Médard Chouart, Sieur des Groseilliers, to several parts of Wisconsin, Minnesota, and neighboring territory. Groseilliers was the adventurer senior in experience and undoubtedly the leader, but it was his brother-in-law Radisson who left a written record of their travels and hence Radisson whose name is now honored by an international chain of luxury hotels and Radisson whose character in the film *Hudson's Bay* was, as I remember, played by the lean and handsome, Academy Award–winning actor Paul Muni, and Groseilliers's character who was the overweight comic companion.[1] Groseilliers's misfortune is something that the explorer Louis Jolliet could sympathize with. Returning from his 1673 journey of discovery on the Mississippi River it was Jolliet's journal that was lost in a canoe accident and his companion Jacques Marquette's journal that survived, and it is therefore Marquette's words that we remember.

Radisson's description of his and Groseilliers's experiences in northwestern Wisconsin in the years 1658–1660 includes incidents worthy of repeating because of what they tell us of Indian customs and the etiquette of intergroup relationships. Four days south of Chequamegon Bay on Lake Michigan Radisson and Groseilliers arrived at a village of Ottawas living there as refugees from the Iroquois wars. These Ottawas were on Dakota lands as guests of the Santee or Eastern Dakotas. As Radisson tells it, he explained that certain presents they gave to the Ottawas were for the purpose of assuring that Radisson and his companion would be remembered and spoken of for a hundred years if no other Frenchmen came among them and were as generous, which they thought unlikely.

One present was a kettle to be used by the Indians for calling their friends to the Feast of the Dead that was made each seven years, Radisson wrote, to renew friendships.[2] Two hatchets were given to encourage the young men to make their strength known to others, to protect their wives, and to show themselves to be men by knocking in the heads of their enemies. Six knives were given to show that the French were great and mighty friends and allies of the Indians, and a sword blade was given to show that the French were masters of peace and war, willing to help their allies and destroy their enemies. Sundry awls, combs, needles, red paint, mirrors, brass rings, bells, beads, and other objects were given to signify that the Indians would always be under the protection of the French and to assure that the Indians would remember the French favorably in later years.[3]

COUNCILS OF WELCOME

Following this, Radisson and Groseilliers were called to a council of welcome, to a feast of friendship, and then to a welcoming dance. Before the dance, it was necessary to "mourn for ye deceased." The dance that then followed served "to forgett all sorrow."[4] A very similar sequence of mourning and rejoicing was reported two centuries later by the artist George Catlin when arriving among the Iowas:

> This peculiar dance is given to a stranger, or strangers, whom [the Iowas] are decided to welcome in their village; and out of respect to the person or persons to whom they are expressing this welcome, the musicians and all the spectators rise upon their feet while it is being danced.
>
> The song is at first a lament for some friend, or friends, who are dead or gone away, and ends in a gay and lively and cheerful step, whilst they are announcing that the friend to whom they are addressing it is received into the place which has been left.[5]

While at the Ottawa village a delegation of Dakotas arrived. These Dakotas stripped Radisson and Groseilliers naked and redressed them in buffalo and beaver skin garments. After this the Dakotas honored the Frenchmen with a weeping greeting, crying over their heads until they were wet, then offering them their

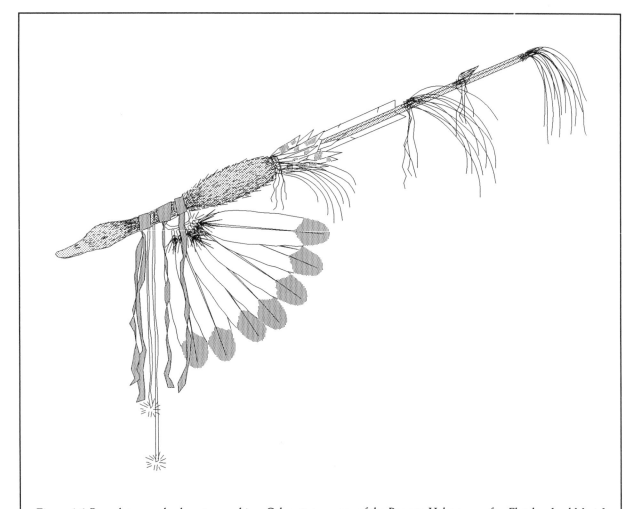

Figure 1.1 Round-stemmed calumet as used in a Calumet ceremony of the Pawnee Hako type, after Fletcher [and Murie] (1904, pl. 87) and Skinner (1926, pl. 37), revised from Hall (1977, fig. 2c). Not to scale.

pipes to smoke, and finally "perfuming" the French and their weapons with smoke from their pipes, not from common pipes but "pipes of peace and of the warrs, that they pull out but very seldom, when there is occasion for heaven and earth."[6]

The pipe was not an ordinary pipe but a calumet-pipe with a bowl of "a red stone, as bigge as a fist and as long as a hand." The stem was five feet long and as thick as a thumb. To it was tied the tail of an eagle painted with several colors and opened like a fan. On the top of the wooden pipe stem were the feathers of ducks and other birds.[7]

When Radisson and Groseilliers returned to Montreal in 1660, others learned that the way was open and the opportunity available for other Frenchmen to travel west into the area of Lakes Superior and Michigan. A peace negotiated in 1667 between the French and the Iroquois allowed many bands of refugee Indians to return from hiding and settle at locations in Wisconsin more easily accessible to traders. Green Bay became a

center of fur trading operations in the west. The first Frenchman to take advantage of the trading opportunities at Green Bay was Nicolas Perrot. While in the Lake Superior area in 1667 Perrot was invited by the Potawatomis settled on Green Bay to visit them, which he did in 1668. He arrived while many of the local Indians were away with a flotilla of canoes bringing furs to Montreal, challenging the monopoly claimed by the Ottawas for trading directly with the French at Montreal. At Green Bay Perrot was received with almost the same awe and honors as Jean Nicolet had been accorded thirty-four years earlier when Nicolet visited the tribes of the area.[8]

In the late fall of 1669 Father Claude Allouez became the first missionary to reach Green Bay. Arriving on December 2, the feast day of St. François Xavier, Allouez named his mission for the day and the saint. On April 16, 1670, he left the bay, traveling up the Fox and Wolf Rivers, to visit the village of the Outagamie or Fox Indians. While portaging up the Fox River on April 19, Allouez reports, the edge of the sun began to darken at noon and continued to darken until a third of the sun's disk was hidden by the moon. He says the eclipse lasted until two o'clock. This was a remarkably accurate description of the event. We can calculate that for Allouez's location near Appleton, Wisconsin, the sun began to disappear at exactly eight minutes before noon, that 32 percent of the face of the sun was eclipsed at the maximum, and that the eclipse ended at ten minutes before two in the afternoon.[9] Five days later Allouez arrived at the village of the Outagamies where he was received by crowds who had come to see the manitou or powerful spirit that was visiting them. True, the first Frenchmen to be seen in each area may often have been regarded as manitous, but it cannot have hurt Allouez's public relations to have arrived within days of a marvelous event.

The winter of 1685–1686 found Nicolas Perrot quartered in a fort he built at Trempeleau, Wisconsin, on the Mississippi River. There he was visited by a delegation of Iowas who honored Perrot, as the Dakotas had favored Radisson and Groseilliers a generation earlier, with a weeping greeting, approaching Perrot "weeping hot tears, which they let fall into their hands along with saliva, and with other filth which issued from their noses, with which they rubbed the heads, faces, and garments of the French; all these caresses made their stomachs revolt."[10] Several days later Perrot visited the Iowas in their own village nine leagues away and there:

> Twenty prominent men presented the calumet to Perrot, and carried him upon a buffalo-skin into the cabin of the chief, who walked at the head of the procession. When they had taken their places on the mat, this chief began to weep over Perrot's head, bathing it with his tears, and with the moisture that dripped from his mouth and nose; and those who carried the guest did the same to him. . . . Never in the world were seen greater weepers than those people; their approach is accompanied by tears, and their adieu is the same.[11]

After a winter hunt for beavers to trade with the French a party of Iowas returned to Perrot's fort. Perrot traveled with them to their village and there received the complete honors of a Calumet ceremony:

> [Perrot] sat down on a handsome buffalo-skin, and three Ayoes stood behind him who held his body; meanwhile other persons sang, holding calumets in their hands, and keeping these in motion to the cadence of their songs. . . . They told him that they were going to pass the rest of the winter in hunting beaver, hoping to go in the spring to visit him at his fort; and at the same time *they chose him, by the calumet which they left with him, for the chief of all the tribe.*[12]

This was the ceremony of the Calumet of the Captain (chapter 10), which did not in fact make Perrot the chief of the Iowas except in a symbolic sense. We know now that it meant that Perrot was being received as a reincarnation of a dead chief, much as George Catlin was welcomed by the Iowas of a much later generation by being received in the place of someone absent or mourned (above). The unusual weeping greeting that so disgusted the French very likely related in part to the same idea.

Wailing was a part of mortuary rites quite widely and among the Dakota, Iowa, Caddo, and Kiowa, to name just a few. The ritual of greeting included wailing, if not always the actual shedding of tears. The anthropologist James Mooney was told by the Kiowas of the southern Plains that they greeted friends this way after a long absence "because his coming reminded them of those who had died since his last appearance."[13] Precisely the same interpretation of their 'welcome of tears' was given to the anthropologist Charles Wagley when he revisited the Tapirapé Indians of Brazil after an absence because, they said, this traditional welcome "mixes emotions of joy at seeing an old friend with the sadness of the memory of those who died during the interim. Both the sadness and the joy are expressed ritually by crying."[14]

The comparison between the Brazilian greeting and that offered to Nicolas Perrot can be extended if one merely substitutes a cotton hammock or hanging bed for the buffalo skin on which Perrot was carried by the Iowas before their version of the welcome of tears. Wagley introduces his book *Welcome of Tears* with these descriptions from the period of 1556–1665:

> The traveler must sit down in a cotton bed hanging in the air and wait quietly for a while. Soon afterwards women appear, surround the hammock, squat on the ground and, covering their eyes with their hands, cry. With their tears they welcome the visitor whom they profusely praise.[15]

> When a visitor enters their home, they honor him by crying. As soon as he arrives, the visitor is seated in a hammock; and without speaking, the wife, her daughters and friends sit around him, with lowered heads, touching him with their hands; they begin to cry loudly and with an abundance of tears.[16]

> When any of them or their foreign friends arrive, they immediately offer him a cotton hammock. The women gather around the visitor and with their hands covering their eyes and grasping him by the legs, they begin to cry with shrieks and marvelous exclamations. This is one of the strongest signs of courtesy that they can show their friends.[17]

THE VULNERABLE HOST

The weeping greeting was actually more of an honor than it would seem because Indians did not lightly allow strangers to acquire tears, saliva, sweat, or other bodily effluvia that could be used for the purpose of black magic or witchcraft. The principle can be found worldwide among peoples who believe in magic. In his autobiography Louis Leakey explained that as a baby he was spat upon by members of the local Kikuyu tribe in Africa—as an honor! Leakey related the practice to another Kikuyu practice of spitting into the palm of one's hand before offering the hand to another in a greeting. The idea is that if you want to show your friendship to someone or to honor an influential person or "a stranger to whom you wish to show respect or humility," you offer that person your hand with your spit on it, thus transferring to the other person the magical means to make you vulnerable and put you at his mercy.[18]

We can believe that in their own minds, the Iowas or Dakotas who allowed their tears to flow on the French were making themselves vulnerable to the French even beyond the range of their firearms. In so-called contagious magic it was believed that an object such as a lock of hair or a driblet of saliva forever retained a mystical connection or contact (hence 'contagious' magic) with the person who was the source and that any action directed to that object would affect the person equally.[19] Under other circumstances an Indian might hide his saliva after spitting so that he would not be injured by anything that his enemies could do with the saliva. One army officer in the Southwest noticed that Indians off the reservation took pains to spit only on their blankets.[20] Clyde Kluckhohn has described the Navajo belief that a sorcerer intent on harming someone may obtain a nail clipping or a snip of hair or a bit of ground soaked in the urine of the intended victim, bury the object with a shred of flesh from a decaying corpse or a sliver of lightning-struck wood, and then recite a spell setting the number of days to pass after which the victim will die.[21]

The principle of vulnerability that I see in operation in the weeping greeting is recognizable even in our everyday greetings and symbolic acts of friendship. The friendly clinking together of drinking glasses was originally accompanied by a sloshing together of their contents to give assurance that none was poisoned. Offering the open hand in a handshake was originally a demonstration that the hand contained no weapon. The military hand salute survives from a time when warriors fought in armor; a friendly greeting included the raising of the visor of the iron helmet that enclosed the head. A warship entering a friendly harbor fired a cannon salute to show that its cannons were now empty.

The offering of a calumet-pipe to a stranger may relate in some part to the same principle of vulnerability because a calumet-pipe was more than just a sacred smoking pipe. The round-stemmed calumet, such as that used in the Calumet ceremony proper, was a symbolic arrow. In that sense the offering of a calumet-pipe was equivalent to the offering of an arrow in greeting, and Indians did, in fact, rather widely offer arrows in greeting. While on the Gulf Coast in 1528 the Spanish explorer Alvar Nuñez Cabeza de Vaca was given a gift of arrows as "a pledge of friendship" or "in token of friendship."[22] The Manahoac Indians of Virginia presented Captain John Smith with a quiver of arrows when the English and Manahoacs made their first friendly contact in 1608.[23]

That part of the calumet-pipe that was most sacred was the long feathered stem or calumet proper rather than the stone pipe bowl, and this has led to some confusion. In popular English usage today a calumet is any highly decorated Indian pipe with a long wooden stem. The word 'calumet' is not of Indian but of French origin. *Calumet* was the regional variation in Normandy of the literary French word *chalumet* derived from Old French *chalemel* and ultimately from the Low Latin diminutive *calamellus* of Latin *calamus* 'reed'.[24] These French words signified a tube, reed, pipe, or shepherd's flute. I say 'calumet-pipe' when I am talking about the combination of long stem and bowl but 'calumet' when I am talking about the long stem by itself. In his study of sacred pipes Jordan Paper uses the term 'sacred pipe' to refer to the whole class of pipes with detachable long stems.[25]

DANCING THE CALUMET

Calumet pipes may be divided into round-stemmed and flat-stemmed varieties. The round-stemmed calumets included those that explicitly symbolized arrows and that were used in the calumet ceremonies patterned on the Pawnee Hako ceremony.[26] The flat-stemmed calumet-pipes were commonly tribal and clan pipes, certainly equally sacred but with a different history and function. They symbolized the corporate identity of a group. I derive the flat-stemmed calumet-pipe from an inferred practice two to three thousand years ago of using a flat-stemmed atlatl or spearthrower of the single-hole variety as a holder for a cane (i.e., American bamboo) or stone tube pipe (chapter 14). The flat-stemmed calumet was always used in combination with a bowl as a calumet-pipe. The round-stemmed calumet was commonly used without the bowl in ceremonies and often was not even perforated. One other long-stemmed pipe had an even more complex history. That with a round, disk-shaped, red pipestone bowl originally represented a ceremonial club or "mace," as archaeologists have called it, which itself was of a form derived from that of a spearthrower of the twin-fingerloop variety (chapter 14).

Calumet ceremonialism involving visitors might be limited to the ritual offering of smoke to six directions—east, west, north, south, sky, and earth—plus the passing of the pipe from hand to hand and from mouth to mouth for smoking. The complete ceremony included the Calumet Dance, which was a choreographed mock battle scene, plus the ritual adoption of the honored guest, which in earlier years served to symbolically reincarnate someone prominent among the honored dead. The historical relationship of the ceremony to mourning was evident in some early historical accounts of calumet ceremonialism but was not explicit in nineteenth- and twentieth-century ethnographic descriptions of ceremonies such as the Hako.

Before his mission to the Indians at Green Bay Father Allouez had traveled in 1665 to Chequamegon Bay on the southern shore of Lake Superior, where among Indians of many other tribes he had met some of the Illinois nation who there had a village hundreds of miles north of their home territory. These Illinois told Allouez that out of fear of the Iroquois others of their tribesmen had taken refuge west of a great river they called the Messipi. This was the first recorded knowledge of the Mississippi River by that name.[27] It would have to be from these Illinois visitors to Lake Superior that Allouez learned in the period of 1665–1667 of the Calumet Dance:

[The Illinois] practice a kind of dance, quite peculiar to themselves, which they call "the dance of the tobacco-pipe." It is executed thus: they prepare a great pipe, which they deck with plumes, and put [it] in the middle of the room, with a sort of veneration. One of the company rises, begins to dance, and then yields his place to another, and this one to a third; and thus they dance in succession, one after another, and not all together.

One would take this dance for a pantomime ballet; and it is executed to the beating of a drum. The performer makes war in rhythmic time, preparing his arms, attiring himself, running, discovering the foe, raising the cry, slaying the enemy, removing his scalp, and returning home with a song of victory—and all with an astonishing exactness, promptitude, and agility.

After they have all danced, one after the other, around the pipe, it is taken and offered to the chief man in the whole assembly, for him to smoke; then to another, and so in succession to all. This ceremony resembles in its significance the French custom of drinking, several out of the same glass; but in addition, the pipe is left in the keeping of the most honored man, as a sacred trust, and a sure pledge of the peace and union that will ever subsist among them as long as it shall remain in that person's hands.[28]

Vernon Kinietz years ago noticed the similarity between the Calumet Dance as described above and the Discovery Dance, which was often performed in connection with the mourning of a warrior in the Midwest.[29] The "discovery" part of the Discovery Dance referred to the discovery of the enemy during the course of the raid dramatized in the dance. The Discovery Dance and adoption each figured in the mourning of the dead and in the full Calumet ceremony.

The first European to leave a written account of the upper Mississippi River was Father Jacques Marquette, who accompanied Louis Jolliet on his exploration of the Mississippi in 1673. The discoverer of the lower Mississippi River was Hernando de Soto. De Soto came upon the Mississippi in 1541, but it fell to others to actually describe the river. De Soto died and was buried in the Mississippi in 1542.

Jolliet and Marquette began their expedition at St. Ignace, Michigan, on May 17, 1673, accompanied only by five Canadian voyageurs—Pierre Moreau, Jean Plattier, Jean Tiberge, Jacques Largillier, and an unnamed youth.[30] Canoeing along the west shore of Green Bay several days later they met the Menominees, who tried to dissuade them from traveling down the Mississippi. The inhabitants of the area were warlike and unmerciful, they said, and the river full of dangerous places and horrible monsters that could devour men and canoes together. One was supposed to be a demon who could be heard from a great distance.

Continuing beyond Lake Winnebago the Frenchmen visited the Mascouten village on the upper Fox River. This village was inhabited also by the Miamis and Kickapoos. All three peoples were living in Wisconsin as refugees from their own territory in northeastern Illinois and northern Indiana from which they had fled to remove themselves from the reach of Iroquois war parties. On June 10 Jolliet and Marquette left the Mascouten village with two Miamis as guides who escorted them up the Fox River as far as the portage trail to the Wisconsin River. Once afloat on the Wisconsin they saw no more Indians for days. On June 17 they entered the Mississippi River, "with a joy that I cannot express," wrote Marquette.[31]

Several days later they observed that turkeys and "wild cattle" (buffalo) had begun to replace the kinds of wild game that had been familiar in Wisconsin. On June 25 they noticed a trail at the water's edge leading inland. With a courage that it is hard today to imagine, Jolliet and Marquette left the others of their party with their two canoes and followed the trail two leagues inland until they reached a community of three villages of the Illinois. This was a stroke of luck because Marquette had a familiarity with the Illinois language, which he had taken pains to acquire from an Illinois slave he had met at Chequamegon Bay in 1669. Marquette had prepared himself well for just such an opportunity as he was now taking advantage of.[32]

Arriving at the first village Jolliet and Marquette made their presence known to the Illinois who assigned four tribal elders to greet the strangers. Two of the Illinois men carried tobacco-pipes elaborately decorated with feathers, which they raised to the sun as if offering the pipes to the sun to smoke. The Indians identified themselves as Illinois and offered their pipes to the Frenchmen to smoke. Later, the Frenchmen received an invitation to visit the paramount chief of the Illinois in a neighboring village of three hundred lodges, and they did so. There the chief gave the visitors a small slave boy and a calumet as gifts and treated them to an enormous four-course feast of corn, fish, dog, and buffalo. The Europeans declined to partake of the cooked dog as politely as they could. The next day Jolliet and Marquette were escorted back to their canoes by nearly six hundred Indians. The brevity of the visit was balanced by the wealth of information that Marquette included in his journal on the customs of the Illinois:

There remains no more, except to speak of the Calumet. There is nothing more mysterious or more respected among them. Less honor is paid to the Crowns and scepters of Kings than the savages bestow upon this. It seems to be the God of peace and of war, the Arbiter of life and death. It has but to be carried upon one's person, and displayed, to enable one to walk safely through the midst of Enemies—who, in the hottest of the Fight, lay down Their arms when it is shown. For that reason, the Illinois gave me one, to serve as a safeguard among all the Nations through whom I had to pass during my voyage.

There is a Calumet for peace, and one for war, which are distinguished solely by the Color of the feathers with which they are adorned; Red is a sign of war. They also use it to put an end to Their disputes, to strengthen Their alliances, and to speak to Strangers. It is fashioned from a red stone, polished like marble, and bored in such a manner that one end serves as a receptacle for the tobacco, while the other end fits into the stem; this is a stick two feet long, as thick as an ordinary cane, and bored through the middle. It is ornamented with the heads and necks of various birds, whose plummage is very beautiful. To these they also add large feathers,—red, green, and other colors,—wherewith the whole is adorned. They have a great regard for it because they look upon it as the calumet of the Sun; and, in fact, they offer it to the latter to smoke when they wish to obtain a calm, or rain, or fine weather. . . .

The Calumet dance, which is very famous among these peoples, is performed solely for important reasons; sometimes to strengthen peace, or to unite themselves for some great war; at other times, for public rejoicing. Sometimes they thus do honor to a Nation who are invited to be present; sometimes it is danced at the reception of some important personage, as if they wished to give him the diversion of a Ball or a Comedy. . . . A large mat of rushes . . . serves as a carpet upon which to place with honor the God of the person who gives the Dance; for each has his own god, which they call their Manitou. This is a serpent, a bird, or other similar thing, of which they have dreamed while sleeping, and in which they place all their confidence for the success of their war, their fishing, and their hunting. Near this Manitou, and at its right, is placed the Calumet in honor of which the feast is given; and all around it a sort of trophy is made, and the weapons used by the warriors of those Nations are spread, namely: clubs, war-hatchets, bows, quivers, and arrows.

Everything being thus arranged, and the hour of the Dance drawing near, those who have been appointed to sing take the most honorable places under the branches; these are men and women who are gifted with the best voices, and who sing together in perfect harmony. Afterward, all come to take their seats in a circle under the branches; but each one, on arriving, must salute the Manitou. This he does by inhaling the smoke, and blowing it from his mouth upon the Manitou, as if he were offering to it incense. Every one, at the outset, takes the Calumet in a respectful manner, and, supporting it with both hands, causes it to dance in cadence, keeping good time with the air of the songs. He makes it execute many differing figures; sometimes he shows it to the whole assembly, turning himself from one side to the other. After that, he who is to begin the Dance appears in the middle of the assembly, and at once continues this. Sometimes he offers it to the sun, as if he wished the latter to smoke it; sometimes he inclines it toward the earth; again, he makes it spread its wings, as if about to fly; at other times, he puts it near the mouths of those present, that they may smoke. The whole is done in cadence; and this is, as it were, the first Scene of the Ballet.

The second consists of a Combat, carried on to the sound of a kind of drum, which succeeds the songs, or even unites with them, harmonizing very well together. The Dancer makes a sign to some warrior to come to take the arms which lie upon the mat, and invites him to fight to the sound of the drums. The latter approaches, takes up the bow and arrows, and the war-hatchet, and begins the duel with the other, whose sole defense is the Calumet. This spectacle is very pleasing, especially as all is done in cadence; for one attacks, the other defends himself; one strikes blows, the other parries them; one takes to flight, the other pursues; and then he who was fleeing faces about, and causes his adversary to flee. This is done so well—with slow and measured steps, and to the rhythmic sound of the voices and drums—that it might pass for a very fine opening of a Ballet in France.

The third Scene consists of a lofty Discourse, delivered by him who holds the Calumet; for, when the Combat is ended without bloodshed, he recounts the battles at which he has been present, the victories that he has won, the names of the Nations, the places, and the Captives whom he has made. And, to reward him, he who presides at the Dance makes him a present of a fine robe of Beaver-skins, or some other article. Then, having received it, he hands the Calumet to another, the latter to a third, and so on with all the others, until every one has done his duty; then the President presents the Calumet itself to the Nation that has been invited to the Ceremony, as a token of the everlasting peace that is to exist between the two peoples.[33]

Somewhere in Arkansas, Jolliet and Marquette reached a relocated village of the Mitchigamea branch of the Illinois. Like the Moingwena, Peoria, Kaskaskia, Tamaroa, and Cahokia—all branches of the Illinois Nation—the Mitchigamea feared attack from the League of the Iroquois. It was the Peoria-Illinois that Jolliet and Marquette had encountered on June 25 in their villages near the mouth of the Des Moines River in what is now Clark County, Missouri, many days travel by foot west of their homes on the Illinois River.[34] The Illinois did not have light, bark canoes like the northern Indians that could be easily portaged from stream to stream. While among the Peoria Marquette must have been told about the Moingwena-Illinois living farther inland on the river now named for them, the Des Moines, because that is where they appear on Marquette's map. The Mitchigamea are shown on the west side of the Mississippi River just upstream from the Arkansas River.

The sighting of Jolliet and Marquette's bark canoes created an alarm in the Mitchigamea village. Warriors armed themselves with bows and arrows, tomahawks, warclubs, and shields and prepared to attack the small party of Frenchmen from the shore and on water. Warriors scrambled into heavy wooden dugout canoes made from large logs and paddled themselves into positions upstream and downstream from the strangers. One warrior hurled his club at the intruders, but it sailed by without striking anyone, and all the while Marquette was anxiously holding high the sacred calumet without effect.

Finally, some older men standing on the shore recognized the calumet in Marquette's hands. They shouted to the young men who were positioning themselves to attack the canoes, and the attack was checked. Two of these elders then approached the canoes and threw their own bows and arrows at the feet of the Frenchmen, "as if . . . to reassure us," Marquette says.[35] The showing of the calumet by Marquette had generated a response from the Mitchigamea that was tantamount to a gift of arrows. The display of the calumet—the symbolic arrow—was returned in kind, and tensions were relaxed.

At the Mitchigamea village Jolliet and Marquette heard of another and larger village eight or ten leagues farther down the Mississippi. This was a village of the Arkansa or Quapaw tribe. By now the presence of the strange travelers on the river was known and their peaceful intentions clear. A half-league from the Quapaw town two canoes came out, in one of which was a leader who stood upright holding his own calumet in view and who then smoked with the Frenchmen. Once in the town they learned that they were within only days of the sea. At this point Jolliet and Marquette came to fear that they would fall into the hands of the Spanish if they continued farther, and they decided to return to Canada. They had accomplished their purpose: they had satisfied themselves that the Mississippi flowed into the Gulf of Mexico. They would have jeopardized their ability to report their findings if they had traveled among Indians who might turn them over to the Spanish. The chief of the Quapaws danced the calumet for the visitors and made them a present of it.

Jolliet and Marquette began their return journey on July 17, 1673, and arrived back at the mouth of Green Bay by the end of September. They traveled this time by a somewhat different route. They followed the Illinois and Des Plaines Rivers to a portage to the Chicago River and thence northward along the west shore of Lake Michigan. While still on the Illinois River near present-day Utica, Illinois, across from Starved Rock, they visited a village of seventy-four lodges of the Kaskaska-Illinois and Father Marquette left them with his promise to return soon to establish a mission. Marquette did keep his promise.

Marquette began his trip a year later to return to the Kaskaskias, but he was too ill to travel beyond the Chicago River. He wintered at the future site of Chicago until March 29, 1675, when he set out once more for the Kaskaskia town. There Marquette established the Mission of the Conception in a ceremony that lasted from Maundy Thursday, April 11, until Easter Sunday, April 14, 1675, but he knew he could not stay. He was too weak and close to death. On Monday he received a long line of his new Indian followers while lying on his bed and promised them that if he could not return someone else would to continue the mission.[36]

Marquette was placed on a buffalo robe held taut by

young men who carried him to his canoe. Near midnight on May 18, 1675, Father Jacques Marquette died and was buried in a grave at the mouth of the Marquette River near present-day Ludington, Michigan. Two years later his bones were returned to St. Ignace in a birch-bark box and reburied in the floor of the chapel. In 1705 the Jesuits were obliged to leave St. Ignace, but before leaving they burned the chapel over Marquette's grave.[37]

There was no later Catholic religious presence at the site of the St. Ignace mission until 1873. In that year a priest was again stationed at the location of the former mission, and to the new priest, almost two hundred years after Marquette's reburial, "some ancient Ottawa told the legend of a great priest who had been buried near the inlet now known as East Moran Bay."[38] The site of the burned mission chapel was discovered and below a fire-reddened floor strewn with ashes, charcoal, and rusting nails was found a pit containing only scraps of birch-bark. The grave was empty, opened years earlier, but eighteen fragments of human bone found next to the crude crypt were collected and saved. These relics are preserved in the Jesuit university in Milwaukee, Wisconsin, that keeps Marquette's name alive.

2 / La Salle Explores the Mississippi Valley

IN APRIL OF 1682 a small band of eastern Indians were dipping their paddles in the brackish bayous of the delta where the several mouths of the Mississippi River blended their sweet water with the brine of the Gulf of Mexico, more than seventeen hundred miles by canoe from their New England homeland. Later in the same year these New England Indians returned north and settled in a new village somewhere within or near present-day Starved Rock State Park in the upper Illinois River valley. Journeys of this magnitude hardly fell within the normal pattern of mobility of most Indians, even during the fur trade era. These were Indians forced out of New England in the aftermath of the Puritan victory in King Philip's War of 1675–1676.

Francis Parkman wrote that in December of 1681 a small band of "Abenakis and Mohegans" reached the Mississippi River in the company of the French explorer René-Robert Cavelier, Sieur de La Salle. Later writers sometimes assumed that these 'Mohegans' were New York.Mahicans.[1] Fortunately, La Salle's second in command on the journey, Henri de Tonty, left a written record not only of the tribal composition of La Salle's Indian allies but also of the names of most of them.[2]

LA SALLE'S MAHINGANS

The eighteen Indian men in Robert La Salle's party were described as *Sauvages Mahingan ou Abenakis et Sokokis* and the Indian women, as one *Huronne* [Huron], five *Abenaquises* [Abenakis], three *Nipissieriniennes* [Nipissings], and one *Ochipoise* [Chippewa/Ojibwa]. In other words, Tonty indicates that La Salle was accompanied not by Mahingans *and* Abenakis but by Mahingans *or* (i.e., who were) Abenakis and Sokokis, and by their women. Part of the problem stems from the triple confusion of Mohegan, Mahican, and Mahingan.

'Mahican' is the simplified English form of Muhheakunneuw (Mahican Indian) derived from the placename Muhheakunnuk, which referred to the ebbing and flowing waters of the Hudson River. The Hudson was subject to tidal action as far upstream from the Atlantic

Ocean as Albany, New York.[3] Albany was located within what was originally the home territory of the Mahicans. The Canadian Algonquins came to refer to these Mahicans as the Mahingans or Wolves as a pun on the name Mahican.[4] The French allies of the Algonquins followed suit by also calling the Mahicans Wolves, or Loups in French, but by 1662 the designation 'Loup' had become extended to apply as well to the Delawares and Western Abenakis, who were linguistic cousins of the Mahicans. This extension of meaning has added to the dismay of historians trying to disentangle the histories of the tribes of northeastern North America.[5]

The Sokokis were a Western Abenaki group who had lived in the middle Connecticut valley until forced out in the aftermath of the English victory of 1676. Gordon Day affirms that the eastern Indians on this Mississippi River exploration were Sokokis and Penacooks.[6] The following are the Indian men listed by Henri de Tonty for the Mississippi exploration:

Le capitaine Clance	Alimalman
Amabanso	Apexos
Hirguen	Chouakost
Ahos	Akiesko
Seneche	Maskinampo
Nananouairinthe	Miouema
Youtin	Ononthio
Sanomp	Pioua
Ouabaresmanth	[Ouiouilamec][7]

René-Robert Cavelier, Sieur de La Salle, was born in Rouen, France, in 1643, the son of a wealthy merchant. Cavelier was his family name. La Salle was the name of an estate near Rouen belonging to the Cavelier family and was the name that was later assumed by him as a *seigneur* or landowner to whom tenants were obligated by oaths and material tokens of fidelity. La Salle did not benefit, however, from his father's fortune. He began training to enter the Jesuit Order and under French law forfeited his rights of inheritance. When after a few years he decided to discontinue his course of study toward the priesthood, it was already too late. His father had died, and he had lost his right to any part of his father's estate.[8] With little to keep him in Rouen and with greater possibilities for an adventurous life in New France, La Salle left for Canada, where an older brother was already living. That was in the spring of 1666; La Salle was twenty-three years old. He twice was granted, developed, and sold profitable *seigneuries* or landed estates, either of which would have provided a comfortable life for a gentleman with less ambition.

In 1674 La Salle sailed to France to petition for himself a patent of nobility and the *seigneurie* of Fort Frontenac, which the governor of that name had constructed at the head of Lake Ontario on the site of present-day Kingston, Ontario. This fort controlled access to Lake Erie and provided a reminder of French presence within sight of the Five Nations of the Iroquois League. La Salle returned in 1675 with the royal privileges granted him and used them as the basis for still more planning. Louis Jolliet, accompanied by Father Jacques Marquette, had two years earlier, in 1673, traveled from Green Bay by way of the Fox and Wisconsin Rivers to the Mississippi but had stopped short of reaching the Gulf of Mexico by fear of capture by the Spanish. La Salle had no plans limited by fear of man or nature.

In 1678 La Salle received an additional royal privilege that gave him virtual control over the exploration, fortification, and trade—for buffalo hides, at least—of the whole of the interior of North America south of the Great Lakes, including the Ohio Valley and that part of French North America that came in time to be governed from New Orleans. La Salle called it Louisiana after his sovereign Louis XIV. To help finance this enterprise he sold his *seigneurie* of Fort Frontenac. He received additional financing from friends and relatives and soon traveled west with a company of adventurous compatriots to establish a base in the Illinois valley, which lay well south of the area regarded as Canada proper.

France's Sun King, Louis XIV, was pleased to know that France might benefit from additional trade with Indians in the interior of North America, but he did not feel that it was time to attempt an actual colonization of French settlers so far from the St. Lawrence valley and so remote from the seat of colonial government at Quebec. Long-established traders in Canada who were already jealous of the privileges granted the young La Salle with the *seigneurie* of Fort Frontenac found their noses completely out of joint when La Salle was not only raised to the ranks of the untitled nobility but was also given what was potentially the most lucrative trading license in French America, even though La Salle was forbidden to trade with the Ottawas and other Indians who traditionally took their furs to Montreal.

La Salle would not only fight cold and starvation in his travels but would also face frightened creditors, mutiny, sabotaged enterprises, and murder attempts by his employees in addition to schemes of entrapment and murder by his enemies. He accused Nicolas Perrot of putting poison hemlock in his salad. He suffered the loss of three sailboats constructed by him for trade and exploration in North America, and in 1687 he concluded his career with a lead ball through the brain fired by one of his own men.

Unlike the hopes and desires of the New England settlers, those of La Salle depended upon the presence and welfare of the native inhabitants in the region of his enterprises. The fur trade was secondary to the economy and long-range interests of the Puritans of New England; Indians were an obstacle to the pursuit of the dreams of the English farmers. Indians were an essential prerequisite for the fur trading empire that La Salle envisioned; he willingly and enthusiastically courted their friendship and association. Considering the proven and suspected untrustworthy character of many of La Salle's French friends and employees, La Salle undoubtedly found the loyalty of his Indian allies and companions a welcome counterbalance to his misfortunes in the choice of other associates. The New England Indians, La Salle's Mahingans, provided a palace guard of sorts, quite in addition to their usefulness for scouting and hunting.

LA SALLE RETURNS OUABICOLCATA TO LIFE

The winter of 1680–1681 found La Salle quartered in a fort he had constructed at the mouth of the St. Joseph River in southwestern Michigan. He arrived after an arduous overland trek of sixty leagues on snowshoes from the Illinois country and on the last day of a January that had seen snowfall on each of twenty days in succession. Because the fort and river were in the home area of the Miami Indians, the records of La Salle's activity there refer to Fort Miami on the Miami River.

Also at the mouth of the Miami, or St. Joseph, River was a village of Indians who had not long before arrived from the East Coast to hunt and trap beaver. These were twenty-five or thirty men together with their women and children, who had been driven westward by their hatred of the English, it was said, and the growing scarcity of beaver for trapping in the lands near the English colonies. In all, seven or eight tribes were represented, among them some from the borders of Virginia, some from "Manhattan or New Amsterdam," and still others from the neighborhood of Bristol, Rhode Island.[9] Bristol was the scene of the beginning and the concluding actions of the war of 1675–1676 between the English and the New England Indians that entered history books named for the Wampanoag chief Metacomet, whose Christian name was Philip—King Philip's War. The Mahicans, who lived in the upper Hudson valley and who were marginal to New England, did not participate in this war.

Located not far from Fort Miami in Michigan and the village of the New England Indians was the village of the Miamis. Here they lived as in their own land and not as refugees. When spring arrived and planting had begun, which would have been sometime in May of 1681, La Salle made a formal visit to the Miamis accompanied by a party of forty Frenchmen and New England Indians. These Indians had been persuaded by La Salle to settle locally rather than return east to live among the Five Nations Iroquois after their winter hunt, as had been their original intention. Indian formalities required that gifts be exchanged to validate statements made and to ratify agreements entered into, and Indian practice was to express such declarations in a highly figurative form. The following account of the proceedings of La Salle's council with the Miamis is from an official document presented to the French government with the title, in translation, *Relation of the Discoveries and Travels of the Sieur de La Salle, Lord and Governor of Fort Frontenac, beyond the Great Lakes of New France, and undertaken by the command of Monseigneur Colbert—1679–1681*. With the exception of certain lapses of accuracy that served La Salle's purposes, the document is a valuable ethnographic record:

> Presenting them with a roll of tobacco, [La Salle] told [the Miamis] he gave them this *petun* because it was their custom to take it when wishing to discourse upon any very important matter, in order to drive away the bad humors that might disturb the mind. . . . He then gave them a piece of blue cloth, saying that, as they were troubled by the loss of their relatives recently killed by the Iroquois, and as the sight of the half-roasted bodies might prevent their hearing with pleasure what he wished to say, he would cover them with this piece of cloth in order to turn away their eyes from the dead and direct them to the sky, which peace should make calm and which the sun should brighten more than ever.[10]

La Salle was, of course, not giving the Miami the blue cloth to literally cover the bodies of the Miami dead but only to figuratively cover them. The Miami had recently suffered a defeat in battle from a war party of Iroquois returning from a destructive raid against the Illinois. With these Iroquois were four hundred women and children captives of the Tamaroa-Illinois tribe, about half of the total taken by the combined Iroquois war parties after an attack on the Tamaroa village near the mouth of the Illinois River in the fall of 1680. Other contemporary French reports made the number of captive Tamaroas two or three times larger.[11]

The third gift was a piece of red cloth to cover the ground, so that they should no longer see the blood of their brethren, and in order to signify the color, with which they painted their faces for festal occasions, that they should henceforward live together in pleasure and good cheer.

The fourth gift was composed of twenty hoods—a kind of garment used alike by Frenchmen and Savages. He told them he gave them these hoods to dress their dead, not thinking with them that the dead had any need of clothing, but in testimony of his friendship for those who had been killed, and of his sorrow for their loss.

The fifth gift was of fifty hatchets, to be used for the erection of a magnificent tomb for the deceased kinfolk. The sixth gift was composed of necklaces, bracelets, and anklets of porcelain and glass beads, painted red, of rings and bells to adorn these Savages, who have no finer ornaments for their festivals in honor of their dead. The seventh gift was thirty sword-blades, which he thrust into the ground about the former gifts, saying that he was making an iron fence in order that the bodies of their deceased kinsmen should henceforth suffer no injury.[12]

In this wise M. de La Salle made use of all these first gifts to gain the good will of the Miamis, for nothing touches their hearts sooner than respect shown to their dead, just as nothing arouses them to vengeance more surely than outrage done to the dead. Then he continued in the following terms:—

"We have thus, my brothers, performed our duty to the dead, who must be satisfied, who now ask nothing except to be left in peace, and who desire to dry our tears, and to think of caring for their children left here in their places. But I mean to do more—*I will bring them to life again*. You daily mourn the loss of Ouabicolcata, the greatest of your chiefs. Think him not dead; I have his mind and soul in my own body; *I am going to revive his name and be another Ouabicolcata*; I shall take the same care of his family that he took in his lifetime; and that no one may mistake, I declare that my name is not Okimao (the name given [La Salle] by the Savages). *My name is Ouabicolcata; he is not dead; he lives still*, and his family shall want for nothing, since *his soul is entered into the body of a Frenchman*, who can provide his kinsmen abundantly with all things needful."

Here [La Salle] made an eighth gift of a piece of red cloth. This metaphor, as bold as it was new, yet thoroughly suited to the character of these people, to whom nothing is dearer than the memory of their dead, was received with such tokens of delight and such unusual applause as to interrupt for sometime the continuance of his speech.[13] He then caused the ninth gift, consisting of three great kettles, to be brought forward, saying that the dead man now brought to life must display his delight in a great feast, and that he gave these kettles for its preparation.

The tenth and eleventh gifts consisted of forty hoods, forty shirts, and forty blankets for men, for women, and for children, and a chest filled with knives, hatchets, and other goods highly prized by them, accompanied by the assurance that, coming back from the other world, and wishing to provide for his kinsmen, he [La Salle as the reincarnated Ouabicolcata] had brought what was most needful, in order to show them by this example that, so long as they would be ruled by his counsel, they should want for nothing.

The twelfth gift was six muskets. In presenting these he said:— "I have now a matter of great importance to propose to you. He who is the master of life and of the whole earth is a very great captain. He is potent and feared throughout the world; he loves peace and desires us to hear his words, which are for our preservation and our greatest good. This is the King of France, the greatest of those who bear sway on the other side. His kindness extends even to *your dead, whom his subjects have come here to bring again to life*; but he wishes to protect them, he wishes you to obey his laws and to undertake no war without the consent of Onontio, who commands in the King's name at Quebec and who loves all nations alike, because this is the King's will. You must live in peace with all your neighbors, especially with the Illinois. You have had dissensions,—but you are sufficiently avenged by their overthrow [by the Iroquois this past fall]. Although still able to do you harm, they desire to make peace: content yourselves with the glory of having forced them to ask it of you. You are interested in their preservation, since, were they destroyed, the Iroquois would not fail to renew their ancient feud with you. For my sake, at all events, do not attack them. I wish to obey the laws of that great captain to whom I owe it that *I have been brought to life again*, and whose protection will keep us in unbroken peace. Adopt my views, and make use of these guns only for hunting and for defense."

Here he gave them two porcelain necklaces, a usual gift among the Savages, and continued in the following words:— "Here, my brothers, are other Miamis come to take the places of my kinsmen who were slain by the Iroquois. They have the bodies of New England Savages, but the mind and heart of the Miamis. Receive them as your brethren; they will dwell with me and will share one lodge with you. They love peace as well as I, and you would drive us all away should you continue to make war upon the Illinois."

The Miamis listened with inexpressible delight to this continued figure of speech, and accepted with enthusiasm the role played by M. de La Salle in speaking continually as if he had been Ouabicolcata. The New England Savages were also well pleased with the manner in which he had introduced them and incorporated them into [the Miami] nation. They made, on their own account, four gifts, interpreting them with an allusion to the meaning given by M. de La Salle to his gifts. Ouiouilamec, who spoke fluently the Miami tongue, which M. de La Salle then understood but imperfectly, served as interpreter to them all.[14]

Ouiouilamec or Ouiouilamet was said to have been the son of the chief of a tribe near Boston. He had lived in the Midwest for four years, which means he would have left the Boston area just after the conclusion of King Philip's War (1675–1676). Ouiouilamec had served La Salle for two years up until the time of this council with the Miamis and was very useful because of the knowledge of the languages of the area that he had acquired. Parkman refers to him as La Salle's "Mohegan hunter, who seems to have felt towards him that admiring attachment which [La Salle] could always inspire in his Indian retainers."[15] The following day the Miamis gave to La Salle beaver robes as presents of their own along with their reply to his overture of friendship and alliance:

> We had never seen, O brother Ouabicolcata, the dead restored to life. He who has restored thine must be a good spirit, since he gives back life at the same time to all thy kinsmen. By this miracle he has made the sky fairer, the sun brighter, the earth greener. Along with life he has given the garments for all thy brethren, who had been used to go naked. Thus in losing thee we have gained all, since thy death has moved the great captain with pity for us. We are ashamed of having nothing to give him in return for all the good he has done us. But thou, Ouabicolcata, knowing our poverty, will excuse us, since thou art our brother and the cause of our being poor; for it was *to ransom thy bones* that we gave, this winter more than three thousand beaver skins to the Iroquois. We give thee what remains, hoping that we may be able in the spring to present to thee greater tokens of our gratitude, and through thee to make the Great King master of all the beaver of our streams.[16]

The Iroquois had committed a great breach of protocol by accepting the Miamis' gift of three thousand beaver skins for the return of Miami captives taken earlier during the winter of the same year and then not returning the captives. Custom demanded that if a gift were accepted, the request should also be granted. In this case it would appear that the Miami chief Ouabicolcata had been killed in the encounter with the Iroquois and that the beaver skins were meant also "to ransom his bones."

Although the Miamis are represented as saying that they had never before seen the dead restored to life in this symbolic way, I find this difficult to believe. Saying that the Miamis had not previously been familiar with symbolic reincarnation would naturally have enhanced La Salle's image in the official report of the transaction. As early as 1694, only several years later, the Illinois are known to have been adopting prisoners of war "to resuscitate the dead."[17] The Miamis were culturally quite closely related to the Illinois and spoke a kindred language:

> The second gift was again of ten beaver skins. "Here," continued the orator, "is something to spread upon the mat of our brother Ouabicolcata. He is not dead; for an entire year we shall taste the delight we have in seeing him once more. This thought will be pleasant to dwell upon during our hunting. O Ouabicolcata, we are under the watchcare of the Spirit that has brought thee to life, and we beg thee, since thou comest from him, to explain to him the meaning of these robes, by which we acknowledge him master of our land. This land will henceforth be dearer to us, nor will the fear of our enemies again compel us to forsake it, since even if they kill us, thy King has the power to restore our life."

The third gift was of ten beaver skins, accompanied by these words of Ouabibichagan:— "We are resolved to obey the voice of this Great Spirit. We lay down our arms, we break our arrows, we hide our tomahawks deep in the earth. The Illinois is our brother, since he acknowledges the King of France, who is at once our master and our father, having restored to life our brothers. But we pray this Great Spirit to give intelligence to our brother, the Illinois. He is accustomed to devour the Miamis, and will continue to slay them unless prevented by the Great King."

In this speech we have heard the metaphor of burying the hatchet for concluding peace, but also the often less figurative expression of devouring one's enemy for the act of war:

> The fourth gift, also of ten beaver skins, was meant to indicate the satisfaction of the Miamis. "My brother," said the orator to M. de La Salle, "we cannot express to thee all our joy. We are so delighted to see thee as to be incapable of speaking. We shall express ourselves more fully when we shall have been satisfied with the sight of thee. We cannot now say anything except that it is well, that it is very well, thou art not

dead! We thank thee, Great brother Ouabicolcata; how great a kindness! We shall cry out so loudly to thank thee that thou wilt hear us where thou dwellest! We have made thee master of our beaver and of our life. We make thee master also of our mind and of our body, for we owe to thee both life and the garments that cover us. Thou hast given back to us our brothers, but they will always be thine, having no other spirit than that which thou hast given them!"

> The fifth gift of ten beaver skins, he accompanied with these words:—"I am not surprised that my sons from New England wish to dwell with thee, nor that they have caught thine own spirit; we should long ago have done as much had we known the happiness of belonging to the Great Captain. We shall always greet as our brothers those who come from him, and particularly these our restored kinfolk, *who will take with us the place of our sons slain by the Iroquois.*" In making the last gift of ten beaver skins, he spoke as follows:— "Do not count our gifts, my brother; it is all we have left. The Iroquois have stripped us of everything, but we offer thee our hearts, hoping that in the spring we may be able to give thee greater tokens of our love and gratitude."[18]

The practice of adoption to replace a deceased kinsman or chief by symbolic reincarnation was psychologically very supportive during a period of personal grief or village mourning and unquestionably had deep roots in the cultures of the Indians of the Plains and Northeastern United States. I do not know of a more detailed example of Indian ritual for the Midwestern United States of the seventeenth century than that described in this anonymous *Relation*, and although the example was initiated by the French and the account no doubt written to reflect favorably upon La Salle in the eyes of the French ministry for which the total *Relation* was prepared, the details are consistent with Indian practice.

LA SALLE TRAVELS TO THE GULF

December of 1681 saw La Salle returned from travel to Montreal and Fort Frontenac and newly arrived on the Mississippi where it is joined by the Illinois. In addition to Henri de Tonty and other Frenchmen, La Salle was accompanied, as we already know, by eighteen New England Indian men with their wives and children. Some or all of these may have come from among those encamped near Fort Miami. The Indians had agreed to participate in La Salle's expedition for one hundred beaver skins each and had agreed to give the French half of the game they killed for food. There at the mouth of the Illinois the Indians constructed canoes of elm bark and after twelve days waiting for the ice to clear the Mississippi, the party began its journey south, retracing the route of Jolliet and Marquette in 1673 but going beyond to the Gulf of Mexico.

Jolliet and Marquette did not venture beyond the villages of the Quapaw or Arkansa tribe in the state of that name. La Salle's canoes arrived among the Arkansas in March of 1682. Although the Quapaws initially feared that they were being attacked, they quickly recovered from this fear, exchanged calumets with La Salle, and the following day all engaged in the more formal Calumet ceremony or "danced the calumet" (chapter 1). We have a description of this meeting of the French and Arkansas in the words of Nicolas La Salle, a young man who bore the same name as the explorer purely by coincidence (he was otherwise unrelated):

> They brought two calumets adorned with plumage of all colors, and red stones full of tobacco.—These were given to the chiefs. These chiefs and the warriors have gourds full of pebbles and two drums, which are earthen pots covered with dressed skins. The first began a song accompanied by the chime of their gourds. These having ended, others struck up the same thing; then those who have done brave deeds go to a post set in the midst of the place and smite it with their tomahawks. And, after relating their gallant achievements, they gave presents to M. de La Salle, for whom they made the festival. If anyone striking the post told lying stories, he who knew it would go to the post and wipe it with a skin, saying that he was wiping away the lie.[19]

It was this Indian practice of challenging overly boastful stories that James Fenimore Cooper was referring to when in *The Last of the Mohicans* Cooper had his character Hawkeye criticize Europeans for their custom "to write in books what they have done and seen, instead of telling them in their villages [as did the Indians], where the lie can be given to the face of a cowardly boaster, and the brave soldier can call on his comrades to witness for the truth of his words."[20] The act of striking the post as each deed was proclaimed was known as 'counting *coups*': "Meanwhile the chiefs are smoking the calumet and are having it carried to everyone in succession to smoke. M. de La Salle received fifty or sixty oxhides. The Frenchmen, with the exception of M. de La Salle, also struck the post, related their valorous deeds, and made gifts from that which M. de La Salle had given them for that purpose."[21]

What the early French descriptions do not make explicit, and what the French themselves may often have not clearly understood, was that the Calumet ceremony was an adoption ceremony. The underlying theme of the ceremony was a ritual of adoption, originally or prototypically as part of mourning, to symbolically reincarnate a deceased tribesman in the person of someone received to take his place in the spiritual sense. In other words, the action taken by La Salle the previous spring in assuming the identity of the deceased Miami chief Ouabicolcata, reincarnating him in a figurative sense, was parallel in significance and function to the act of being adopted in the Calumet ceremony.

When La Salle reached the territory of the Taensa Indians, the Taensas told his party some frightening stories of what might be expected of their neighbors to the south. At this point four of the New England Indians elected to remain behind. The rest of the party continued on and were received by the Natchez Indians, with apprehension at first and then in a more friendly fashion. Further along the French would soon discover an omen that gave credence to the Taensas' warnings. Nicolas La Salle recorded that there they saw some Indians fishing. Seeing the strangers coming from upstream, the Indians abandoned their activity and fled, leaving behind a basket containing "a fish, a man's foot, and a child's hand, all smoke-dried."[22]

Still farther below the Natchez the French caught sight of a canoe with three Indians in it who beached their craft and also fled in fear. In the canoe the French found some smoked alligator meat and a rack of ribs, which the French took, leaving a bit of cloth as a token payment. They found the alligator to be edible but not as tasty as the ribs. They agreed that the ribs were tastier than the alligator meat but soon agreed also that the rib meat was human and gave the ribs to the Indians to finish.[23]

In *La Salle and the Discovery of the Great West* Francis Parkman re-created the climactic scene of La Salle's expedition in a way that dramatizes vividly the colossal presumptuousness of the French in claiming the valley of the Mississippi as their own while ignoring the rights of the Indian populations occupying it even then, not to mention the conflicting claims of the Spanish:

> And now they neared their journey's end. On the sixth of April the river divided itself into three broad channels. La Salle followed that of the west and Dautray that of the east; while Tonty took the middle passage. As he drifted down the turbid current, between the low and marshy shores, the brackish water changed to brine and the breeze grew fresh with the salt breath of the sea. Then the broad bosom of the great gulf opened on his sight, tossing its restless billows, limitless, voiceless, lonely as when born of chaos, without a sign of life.
>
> La Salle, in a canoe, coasted the marshy borders of the sea; and then the reunited parties assembled on a spot of dry ground, a short distance above the mouth of the river. Here a column was made ready, bearing the arms of France and inscribed with the words, "LOUIS LE GRAND, ROY DE FRANCE ET DE NAVARRE, RÈGNE; LE NEUVIÈME AVRIL, 1682."

The Frenchmen were mustered under arms, and while the New England Indians . . . looked on . . . they chanted the *Te Deum*, the *Exaudiat*, and the *Domine salvum fac Regem*. Then, amid volleys of musketry and shouts of "*Vive le Roi*," La Salle planted the column in its place and, standing near it, proclaimed in a loud voice:

"In the name of the most high, mighty, invincible, and victorious Prince, Louis the Great, by the grace of God King of France and of Navarre, Fourteenth of that name, I, this ninth day of April, one thousand six hundred and eighty-two, in virtue of the commission of his Majesty, which I hold in my hand, and which may be seen by all whom it may concern, have taken, and do now take, in the name of his Majesty and of his successors to the crown, possession of this country of Louisiana, the seas, harbors, ports, bays, adjacent staits, and all the nations, peoples, provinces, cities, towns, villages, mines, minerals, fisheries, streams, and rivers, within the extent of the said Louisiana, from the mouth of the great river St. Louis, otherwise called the Ohio . . . as also along the river Colbert, or Mississippi, and the rivers which discharge themselves thereinto, from its source beyond the country of the Nadouessioux . . . as far as its mouth at the sea, or Gulf of Mexico, and also to the mouth of the River of Palms, upon the assurance we have had from the natives of these countries that we are the first Europeans who have descended or ascended the said river Colbert; hereby protesting against all who may hereafter undertake to invade any or all of these aforesaid countries, peoples, or lands, to the prejudice of the rights of his Majesty, acquired by the consent of the nations dwelling herein. Of which, and of all else that is needful, I hereby take to witness those who hear me, and demand an act of the notary here present."

Shouts of "*Vive le Roi*" and volleys of musketry responded to his words. Then a cross was planted beside the column and a leaden plate buried near it, bearing the arms of France, with a Latin inscription: *Ludovicus Magnus regnat*. The weather-beaten voyagers joined their voices in the grand hymn of the *Vexilla Regis*:— "The banners of Heaven's King advance, The mystery of the Cross shines forth;" and renewed shouts of "*Vive le Roi*" closed the ceremony.[24]

La Salle's little company of venturers had not exactly been journeying through a wasteland inhabited only by small bands of nomadic hunters and food collectors. The French had, in fact, been astonished by some of the Indian towns that they had just visited or viewed— towns that were unlike any they had seen in Canada. When La Salle sent Henri de Tonty and Father Membré to visit the Taensa capital, they were received by the Taensa chief in what amounted to a royal court, so

in claiming the whole Mississippi valley for Louis XIV of France La Salle was displaying gall unmitigated by the possibility of any claim of innocent ignorance. The Taensa and Natchez chiefs were kings in their own right.

The Taensa chief's lodge was forty feet square with a high, vaulted roof covered with cane mats. Its thick walls were twelve feet high, made or faced with sun-dried clay. The chief awaited the French delegation in an alcove on a litter, while facing him were sixty white-cloaked elders and the headmen of eight surrounding towns dependent upon the Taensa capital. Opposite this palace or council house was a temple, containing a kind of altar, on whose roof were images of three eagles facing the rising sun. Within this temple burned the sacred fire of the Taensa nation.[25]

The scene that Tonty and Membré encountered was hardly unique for the area. Hernando de Soto's Spanish chroniclers had described many such temple towns and regal residences visited while traveling through the southern United States in 1540–1541 (chapter 18), and Frenchmen who followed La Salle left for us detailed and firsthand accounts of the Natchez Indians and their semidivine leader, whom the Natchez called the Great Sun. Even so, because of introduced European diseases, the sun of the Natchez was already setting and would scarcely outlive that of Louis XIV, who died in 1715 styling himself *le roi soleil*, the Sun King.

Shortly after beginning the return voyage, three hundred Indians attacked the venturers at night by land and water. La Salle's party kept up a return fire with their muskets until daybreak, when the attacking Indians departed, abandoning the bodies of two of their number. These the French scalped, leaving their heads impaled on stakes. La Salle's Indians are said to have planned to consume the bodies of these unfortunates, but La Salle objected. To keep La Salle in good humor his Indians settled for merely taking the hearts, "which they dried, in order to show in their country that they had killed men."[26]

On June 1, 1682, La Salle arrived once more among the Taensas. Four Frenchmen were dispatched to escort home a Taensa rescued while floating on a piece of wood after escaping from captivity by nearby Indians. The Frenchmen were quartered in the lodge of the chief, who was seated in one corner on a mat upon a platform a foot high. The chief's lodge, the temple, and seven or eight lodges "of the elders" are described as surrounded by a wall or stockade line of posts upon which were set human heads. This enclosed area defined a sacred precinct that was guarded day and night. The temple was said to be oval, twelve by thirty feet on the inside, painted in red, with earth-covered walls and a mat-covered roof of dome shape.

After earlier suffering days of starvation the exploring

party now found itself so heavily burdened with gifts of food that they had to throw some overboard to lighten their canoes. They soon reached once more the Quapaw village where they had left the four New England Indians who had remained behind out of fear of the Indians downriver. Only two of these were willing to return with La Salle to the Illinois country. The others were crestfallen at seeing the dried hearts of the slain Indians carried by their friends as tokens of their successful combat and vowed not to return home themselves until they could wipe away their shame with victories of their own, or so I interpret the record. They were, indeed, disheartened at learning of the successes of their less cautious comrades, and they felt that under the circumstances they could not yet return.

La Salle and Tonty divided the party and proceeded at different paces up the Mississippi and Illinois Rivers, meeting again at Michilimackinac in the locale where the upper and lower peninsulas of Michigan face each other across the strait of Mackinac. The New England Indians remained on the upper Illinois River near a village abandoned by the Kaskaskia-Illinois during the great Iroquois raid of 1680. This village was located at the point where rapids and low water impede traffic by canoe up the Illinois River, and arriving late in July the river was low.

The Illinois village was a scene of horrible devastation. The Kaskaskia themselves had avoided destruction by negotiations with the Iroquois promoted by Henri de Tonty, who had been there at the time, but they had burned their own lodges before departing and leaving the village to the Iroquois. No longer able to direct their fury at the living Illinois, the Iroquois had compensated by attacking the dead. They had dug up graves and placed the skulls on stakes. They had torn down the scaffolds on which the bodies of the recent dead were being exposed before burial in the earth. They had burned some of the corpses and thrown others to the pleasure of the starving dogs remaining in camp.[27]

Now, after two years, the raucous calls of the carrion-eating crows had finally been stilled. The Frenchmen and New England Indians stopping at the site of the Kaskaskia village in July of 1682 found the charred wooden ribs of Illinois wigwams inhabited only by the disembodied spirits of the disturbed dead, an ill-omened reacquaintance with a location that La Salle intended to become the northern bastion of a fur-trading empire extending south to the Gulf of Mexico. During the following winter of 1682–1683 La Salle would erect the palisade walls of his Fort St. Louis on a nearby sandstone crag. There on *le Rocher*, the Rock, with the Illinois River still swirling at its foot, archaeologists would three centuries later sift the hand-wrought iron nails of Fort St. Louis from the ashes of its eventual destruction, like hard teeth that have resisted the years in a grave that has consumed all else.[28]

3 / The World of the Earth Divers

FRANCIS PARKMAN is not most noted for writing contemporary history. He is best known for his histories of the early colonial wars in America between France and England and their Indian allies—wars that ended three generations before Parkman was born—but Parkman walked the same forest trails walked by his heroes and villains. There in his mind and emotions he could sense the historic presence of the frontiersmen and armies whose stories filled his books.

Parkman's first book was different from those that followed. In 1846, while still in his twenty-second year of age, Francis Parkman followed the settlers' trail westward across the Plains to the foothills of the Rocky Mountains. In his later books he was looking back over his shoulder at history that had gone before; in his first book, *The Oregon Trail*, Parkman was himself flowing with the stream of history.[1] He wrote it as a narrative journal of his personal experiences, but those experiences also informed his writing in later years.

When Parkman was describing the seventeenth-century Illinois prairie rumbling with herds of snorting buffaloes, he was reliving his own experiences in the American West. When in his histories Parkman commented on Indians, he was undoubtedly influenced by views and attitudes formed during his western travels, and I suspect that Parkman was not the only one to draw upon those early experiences to shape images for later books. In *Northwest Passage* the novelist Kenneth Roberts describes his Stockbridge Indian character Captain Jacobs with these words: "His head was shaved; the base of his scalp-lock was wrapped tightly, to the height of five inches, with a rattlesnake skin. Thus the top of his scalp-lock sprayed out above the snakeskin like a ragged shaving brush. Among the hairs of the scalp-lock were bound the rattles of several rattlesnakes."[2]

This is such a specific image that I long wondered where Roberts might have gotten the idea for it, at least until I read Parkman's *The Oregon Trail* and realized that Roberts had surely read it, too, drawing as heavily as he must have upon Parkman's writings for back-ground on the frontier experience. This is how Parkman described a certain Kansas Indian: "His head was shaved and painted red, and from the tuft of hair remaining on the crown dangled several eagle's feathers and the tails of two or three rattlesnakes."[3]

PARKMAN'S QUEST AT STARVED ROCK

Parkman traveled to Illinois in 1867 while preparing the book he first called *The Discovery of the Great West*.[4] While in Illinois Parkman visited the fortress rock upon which La Salle had his agents build Fort St. Louis. We know the location as Starved Rock within Starved Rock State Park near Utica, Illinois. Parkman's visit was itself a historic occasion for the local citizens of La Salle County and was fondly remembered twenty years after the event by Colonel Daniel Hitt in a newspaper account published locally: "Mr. James Clark of Utica, now dead, and I took the historian all over the place, and it's curious, but he told us what we should see every time before we got there."[5] Parkman had drawn upon early French accounts of the Starved Rock area to anticipate the lay of the land.

It was Parkman who identified Starved Rock for later generations as the location of La Salle's fort. Local residents, at least those who were familiar with the story of La Salle's explorations, had until then assumed that Fort St. Louis was built upon Buffalo Rock farther to the east and upon the north side of the Illinois River. Parkman changed that, and in doing so he was correct. Archaeological excavations have since then demonstrated the seventeenth-century French presence on the summit of Starved Rock.[6]

Parkman was not always right. Parkman also identified what he thought was the cemetery of the Kaskaskia-Illinois Indians of La Salle's day, and in that he was wrong. The same James Clark of Utica told Parkman of "great quantities of human bones" that his tenant plowed up each year on Clark's farm at Utica.[7] This was the Utica archaeological site, two groups of burial mounds that the Illinois Archaeological Survey much later coded as its site Ls-1. The Utica site has since been demonstrated to predate the historic Kaskaskia village by perhaps fifteen hundred years and to belong to the Hopewell phase of the Havana tradition and the Middle Woodland period of midwestern prehistory. In Parkman's day there was no concept of Hopewell or of Havana or of Middle Woodland. Parkman assumed that the burial site on Clark's farm was historic in age and Kaskaskia-Illinois in origin.

Like so many archaeological sites in Illinois, little of the Utica site remains intact. Where it once existed, visitors today can only see deep scars on the landscape where gravel mining operations after 1930 carried away all but a few traces of the burial mounds recorded by archaeologists. The archaeological investigation was begun by Percy Hodges in 1929 under the direction of Warren K. Moorehead of Phillips Academy, Andover, Massachusetts. It was continued during the ensuing winter and spring by Peter Stewart of Utica, Illinois, under the direction of Arthur R. Kelly of the University of Illinois. A detailed report of the excavations was published by the Illinois Archaeological Survey in 1965 under the authorship of Harry C. Henriksen of the University of Illinois Museum of Natural History in Urbana.[8]

The Utica mounds were circular in outline and the burials typically placed within rectangular grave pits excavated by the Hopewellian Indians into the earth before the mound was built above. In one mound of the Utica group, and twenty inches above the floor of the mound, the authors of the mound had laid a mosaic of hundreds of rocks in the pattern of a snake or of the head and neck of a long-necked bird. This mosaic was almost identical to the motif trailed as a design onto the clay of a pottery vessel placed in the subfloor burial pit of the same mound.[9]

BLACK MUD AND WHITE CLAY

The excavation of the Utica group in 1929–1930 also brought to light other evidence whose significance was as enigmatic at the time as the snake-like bird head mosaic:

> Noteworthy was the custom of surrounding the bodies in the grave beneath the mound with a very black, sticky, mud, almost peat-like in consistency, color, and appearance. . . . The "black burial mould," as we have described it in these mounds at Utica, is blacker than any soil that can be found anywhere along the river or in the fields, with the possible exception of some of the bog or marsh earth in the low-lying stretches of ground between the mound-covered terrace and the river. This peat or marsh earth might have been the source of the peculiar earth found enveloping the bodies, filling the

graves, and mantling the immediate grave vicinity. . . . There is no doubt in the minds of the archaeologists in charge of the exploration at Utica that the earth around the burials was deliberately chosen and put around the bodies for some definite reason.[10]

The use of special black organic soils in or over Hopewellian grave pits was found to be so common that by 1945 James Griffin described it as a culture trait typical of northern Illinois Hopewell.[11] It was in one case described as smelling like "bog land muck."[12] In Wisconsin Will C. McKern wrote that Indians building effigy mounds—mounds in the form of birds and land animals—had sometimes used dark mucky soil of a type "characteristic of marsh sand occurring in swampy sections of the near-by creek and lake shore" or gray-white sand of a kind "found in the near-by creek bed and in swampy areas."[13] Wisconsin effigy mounds were made more recently than Hopewell mounds but still average well over a thousand years old. In any case, the important thing came to be that burial mounds in parts of Illinois, Wisconsin, Iowa, Minnesota, Michigan, and even more widely were sometimes constructed using special soils associated with wet, mucky, lake-bottom or riverside locations.[14]

In his report on the Utica mounds Henriksen expressed the opinion that the use of this river- or marsh-associated soil had symbolic significance, related somehow to the life-giving river.[15] Nancy Lurie of the Milwaukee Public Museum suggested to me that the use of mud from beneath bodies of water could have had something to do with the mud from which the earth was created in many North American Indian origin myths.[16] This was mud brought from beneath a body of water by one or another species of mythical Earth Diver—a muskrat, crawfish, water beetle, or duck. Could the mythical mud and the archaeological mud be related?

In excavating Mound 4 of the Ryan group in northeastern Iowa archaeologists found that on the floor of the mound the prehistoric builders had placed five patches of a black mucky soil in a pattern (figure 3.1d). In one of these patches there was a bundle burial containing four human long bones accompanied by a long native copper awl. The pattern of the mud was a quincunx, consisting of a central patch surrounded by four others equally spaced around it.[17] This was a pattern of mud that I recognized. It was the pattern in which five sods were cut from the earth in the Cheyenne Sun Dance to represent lumps of mud brought from beneath the primordial sea by a mythical Earth Diver to create the earth (figure 3.1a–c). The dating of Ryan Mound 4 is unfortunately not well understood, but it could date to before 500 B.C. or as late as A.D. 500.[18]

White marly clay was puddled over Hopewell burials in mounds east of Newville, Wisconsin, which is located at the outlet of Lake Koshkonong, and liquid white clay was applied to the faces of two burials in another Middle Woodland mound excavated near the outlet of Lake Monona, south of Madison, Wisconsin. The Potawatomis believed that when drowned persons were found with white clay in their mouth, nostrils, and eyes that it was a sure sign that the horned water panthers had drowned them. The story of such a drowning is said to be a reason that the Potawatomis were afraid of Lake Koshkonong. Lake Wingra in adjacent Dane County had a depth of only fourteen feet in 1916, but beneath this, a bottom deposit up to thirty feet thick of white marl. Marl is more easily accessible just beneath the peat formations in many Wisconsin bogs. The Winnebagoes believed that their horned water spirits dwelled in dens carved out of shining white clay.[19]

The Earth Diver theme is relatively recent in the Americas, as themes of folklore and mythology go. There can be little question that its origin was in Asia, but in the New World the theme is pretty much limited to America north of Mexico. Mythical associations like that between the constellation Orion and a mutilated or injured individual are found worldwide and must have spread around the globe as it was populated by our species. The theme of Earth Diver is distributed from Finland and the Balkans eastward across Russia to Mongolia and then into Canada and the northern United States, except for the Pacific Northwest and the Eskimos.[20] It is unknown in Mesoamerica.

The basic theme is that of an animal that dives into the depths of a sea to retrieve mud that then expands to create the land. There may be attempts by several different animals, but one finally succeeds with the mud clinging to his little paw or foot. In Asia the earth-diving animal is typically a bird, but an earth-diving bird is featured in North America only in the northern Plains. The Cherokee Earth Diver was a water beetle; a muskrat for the Ojibwas, Ottawas, Foxes, and Onondagas; a crawfish for the Shawnees and Osages; a duck for the Arikaras; a mudhen for the Cheyennes; and a red-headed duck and a turtle together for the Arapahoes.[21]

The Arapaho Sun Dance origin myth, as recorded by George Dorsey, begins at a time when there was only water and the mud deep beneath the water. A man was walking on the water carrying a pipe. To provide a place of safety for the pipe the man decided that there should be an earth, and he invited all the creatures of the world to locate some land for him. Only Turtle knew where there might be some, and that was located beneath the water. The man then invited the creatures of the world to dive for the earth, and although many

tried none had the endurance to accomplish the task. Finally, the man announced that he and Turtle would make the attempt.

The man embraced his pipe to his left shoulder, then to his right shoulder, then back to the left and again to the right, and finally he drew the pipe to his breast. With this last action the Flat-Pipe turned into a red-headed duck and became his body. The duck and Turtle then dove into the water and remained there while the other animals watched and waited. On the seventh day the bubbles announced their return and they emerged, each with a small piece of clay. The duck reverted to the form of the man with his pipe, that is represented by the Arapaho Flat Pipe. The lumps of clay are represented in the Arapaho Sun Dance by a certain two sods which are cut for the altar. The man placed the lumps of clay on the pipe, spread them thin, and waited for them to dry thoroughly. When they were dry, he took pieces of the clay and sent them toward the southeast, the southwest, the northwest, and the northeast, and land appeared in each direction as far as the eye could trace the paths of the clay.[22]

During the Arapaho Sun Dance, which would be more precisely called the Ceremony of the Offerings Lodge, a sod is placed on either side of a painted buffalo skull as part of the altar. These sods were cut in a round outline from a swampy place, usually near a spring, and on them were stuck many small sprigs of 'rabbit bush', which represented 'hair'.[23] In the metaphoric language of Indian ritual, vegetation was often referred to as 'hair'. Aside from representing the mud brought from beneath the sea from which the earth was created, these two sods, one slightly larger than the other, represented (in the order of the larger and smaller) the future earth and the present earth, Father and Mother (sky and earth), "the hands of the father and mother for the Arapaho race," scalps, and still more, depending upon who was being asked.

The Cheyenne origin myth, as recorded by George Grinnell, begins with a man floating on a vast expanse of water. Around him were ducks, geese, swans, and water birds of every description. For no reason stated in the story as received, the man requested these birds to dive beneath the water to find earth, but none succeeded except the mudhen or coot, which the story describes as a small blue duck. The mudhen then brought the mud in his little beak to the man, who "worked the the wet earth with his fingers until he had made it dry. Then he put little piles of the earth on the water at different places near him, and these became land which spread out and grew until, as far as could be seen, all was solid land. Thus was created the dry land—the earth."[24]

The Cheyenne Sun Dance is more correctly called the New Life Lodge. There has never been a ceremony

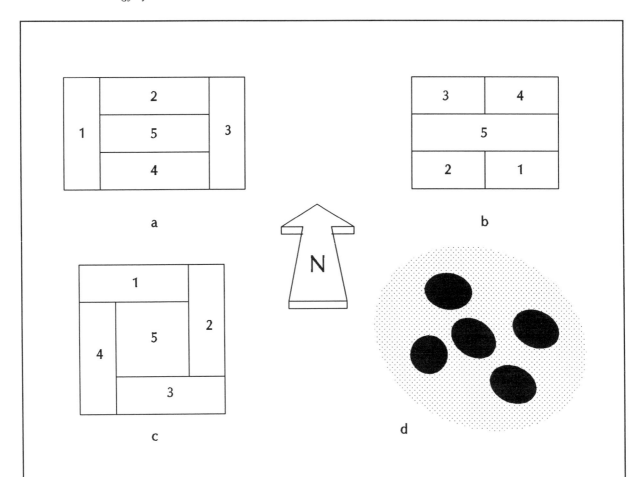

Figure 3.1 Patterns and orders in which sods were cut for the Cheyenne Sun Dance altar (*a–c*) and pattern of muck patches in Ryan Mound 4, Allamakee County, Iowa (*d*): *a*, after Grinnell (1972, 2:257); *b*, after Powell (1969, 2:780); *c*, after Dorsey (1905a, fig. 64); *d*, after Logan (1976, fig. 19), the black ovals representing black muck and the shading indicating an area of yellow sandy soil stained red.

precisely called the Sun Dance. The name is a convenience that historians, travelers, and ethnologists have fallen back upon to refer broadly to a range of midsummer tribal ceremonies common in the short-grass Plains of the United States and Canada, which usually took place within a circular enclosure at the center of which was a pole. The name Sun Dance comes from the ceremony of the Sioux or Dakota, one part of which was called the Sun-Looking Dance or Gaze-at-Sun Dance.[25] In the ceremonies of some tribes those participating might allow themselves to be suspended from ropes attached to wooden skewers inserted into the skin of their backs or chests, or they might drag heavy buffalo skulls attached to their backs by skewers and ropes.

The details of the ceremonies and even the motivations for the ceremonies varied greatly from tribe to tribe. The original Sun Dance of the Crow—the one described by Robert Lowie—was a mourning ceremony. That of the Cheyennes was a World Renewal ceremo-

ny, and that of the Teton Dakota often served to secure supernatural aid or powers to the individual vowing to give it.[26] Quite aside from the explicitly stated motives for any one ceremony, the Sun Dance helped to integrate Indian groups that were often scattered through much of the year. The historic Assiniboine, Teton Sioux, Crow, Blackfoot, Cheyenne, and Arapaho peoples were basically horse nomads who relied upon hunting bison for their livelihood. There were few opportunities during the year for large assemblies to meet except at the midsummer Sun Dance.

There was also another range of ceremonies, related in one way or another to the Sun Dances of the short-grass Plains tribes, which have been thought of either as precursors of the Sun Dance or as eastern derivations of them, depending upon one's perspective on Plains culture history. These were ceremonies of the farming tribes living in semipermanent villages on the eastern prairies (the long-grass Plains) and also along the mainstem of the Missouri River in the Dakotas.

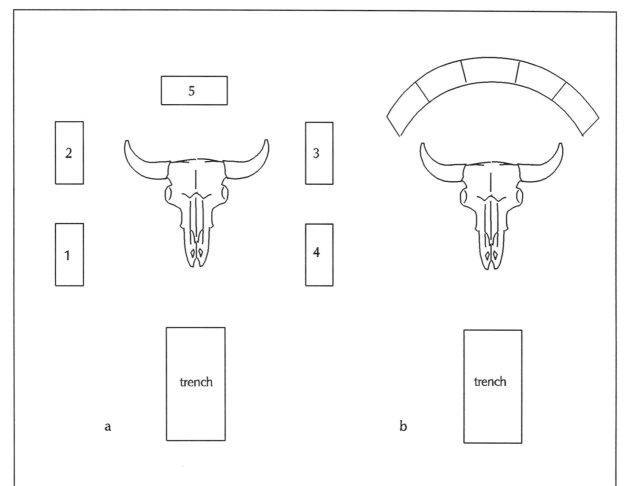

Figure 3.2 Relationship of sods to the buffalo skull and trench on the Cheyenne Sun Dance altar: *a*, initial positions of the sods, after Dorsey (1905a, fig. 69); *b*, positions of the sods when relocated during the ceremony, after Liberty (1967, fig. 2) and Powell (1969, 2:782). The buffalo skull faces east.

The Mandans were an agricultural tribe living in earthlodge villages in North Dakota. They performed a midsummer ceremony called the Okipa (George Catlin's O-Kee-Pa), which celebrated the subsidence of the waters of a primordial flood and other events of tribal history, promoted the fertility of the buffalo herds, and provided an opportunity for adolescent boys to have a vision and be initiated into manhood.[27] The boys were suspended by ropes attached through their flesh until they became unconscious and then were cut down. This aspect of the Okipa was related closely to the self-torture of some versions of the Sun Dance.

The Hidatsas had their earthlodge villages and gardens near the Mandans during the past century. The Hidatsa equivalent of the Sun Dance was the NaxpikE ceremony. The NaxpikE originated as a ritual reenactment of torture undergone by a mythical character called Spring Boy but thwarted by his twin brother Lodge Boy. The twins had made themselves unpopular with the local gods, especially Spring Boy, who was taken to the sky by a sky chief named Long Arm. Lodge Boy rescued Spring Boy, and in the process they threatened to cut off one of Long Arm's hands, or perhaps, in earlier versions of the story, they actually did cut one off. The person impersonating Spring Boy in the NaxpikE danced with the dried left hand of an enemy hanging on his back from a cord about his neck, according to one account, or tied to his right wrist, according to another.[28] Long Arm's hand is believed to be represented in the sky today by the constellation Orion, the 'Hand Star'. The Oxheheom is a ceremony that George Dorsey called the Cheyenne Sun Dance, but to the Cheyennes themselves it was the Lodge of the Creator. The altars of the Cheyenne and Arapaho Sun Dance circles are very similar, and it was the Sun Dances of these tribes that Leslie Spier saw as the prototype of the Sun Dance in his 1921 comparative study of these Plains rituals.[29]

Mud does not appear in earth origin myths only in the context of the Earth Diver theme. The Earth Diver is a fairly new arrival in North American mythology but still may be thousands of years old. Earl Count thought that the theme postdated the beginning of the Christian era, but I am not alone in thinking that it is older.[30] A more important point is that the ritual use of mud in archaeological contexts need not always imply the presence of the Earth Diver theme.

In Osage cosmology the earth origin tradition of one large tribal division (Wazha'zhe) contained the Earth Diver theme, and that of another (Ho^nga) did not. In both versions the people originally lived in the sky and arrived below to find only water. When the elk called to the winds of the four quarters, the winds blew toward the center and gathered the waters together and sent them skyward. In the Ho^nga version only a small island of rocks appeared at first and the land remained hidden. This problem was solved when a muskrat, loon, beaver, and crawfish were sent below the waters to find land. All died in the attempt, but the tiny claws of the crawfish had adhering to them a little mud, and from this the earth was formed. The Wazha'zhe version contains the following account:

> [The Wazha'zhe] came to earth, but found it covered with water. They could not return to the place they had left, so they wept, but no answer came to them from anywhere. They floated in the air, seeking in every direction for help from some god; but they found none. The animals were with them, and of all these the elk was the finest and most stately, and inspired all the creatures with confidence; so they appealed to the elk for help. He dropped into the water and began to sink. Then he called to the winds and the winds came from all quarters and blew until the waters went upward as in a mist. Before that time the winds traveled only in two directions, from north to south and then back from south to north; but when the elk called they came from the east, the north, the west, and the south, and met at a central point, and carried the water upward.
>
> At first only rocks were exposed, and the people traveled on the rocky places that produced no plants, and there was nothing to eat. Then the waters began to go down until the soft earth was exposed. When this happened the elk in his joy rolled over and over on the soft earth, and all his loose hairs clung to the soil. The hairs grew, and from them sprang beans, corn, potatoes, and wild turnips, and then all the grasses and trees.[31]

It seems to me quite possible that Earth Diver had intruded into an Osage cosmology within which he had originally been absent and that the two versions of the creation represent stages in an evolution of a new cosmology. If that is actually the case, then what of the earth origin myths of the Cheyennes and Arapahoes in which Earth Diver also figures? If the cultural background of the Cheyenne and Arapaho Sun Dances really goes back a thousand, or two thousand, or even more years, then what was the ritual and tradition into which the Earth Diver theme intruded? What may have been the original significance of those sods, or the sods that may have been represented by the pattern of muck patches in Ryan Mound 4?

In the Cheyenne Sun Dance the five sods were cut from the earth in the pattern of a quincunx, which was also the pattern of the muck patches in Ryan Mound 4, four patches around a central patch. Then they were arranged around the buffalo skull—two on one side, two on the other, and the fifth behind the buffalo skull. In this position they were said to be symbolic of "the four medicine-spirits and the sun" (figure 3.2a). Then soon afterward "the priests began working down the pieces of sod . . . , so that they caused the inner ends to meet and thus form a complete semi-circle around the skull" (figure 3.2b).[32]

The arrangement of sods around the buffalo skull in a pattern of two on one side, two on the other, and the fifth behind, equally spaced, recalls to my mind a familiar natural pattern. The sods represented mud taken from the feet of the Earth Diver, which was a mudhen in the case of the Cheyennes but commonly a muskrat among many related Algonquian-speaking tribes to the east in the woodlands. The muskrat has five toes. Mud removed from each toe of one paw would provide five lumps of mud. If the sods originally represented the toe pads themselves of an animal paw, say that of a bear or muskrat, or even a human hand, then the myth of the Earth Diver could have easily been adapted to the paw symbolism already existing, and that is what I believe happened.

The muskrat has five toes, as does the beaver, mink, skunk, otter, fisher, wolverine, bear, raccoon, coati, badger, and human. Dogs, coyotes, wolves, mountain lions, bobcats, foxes, and weasels have four. The bison, elk, caribou, moose, deer, antelope, mountain goat, and bighorn sheep have two. In the case of the four- and five-toed animals there is also a central plantar pad that has various forms from trapezoidal and triangular to one resembling the human foot, as in the case of the bear.

The sods in the Cheyenne and Arapaho Sun Dances explicitly represent lumps of mud brought from beneath the primordial sea by mythical Earth Divers and have explicit associations with toes. The importance in northern midwestern Woodland burial mound architecture of mud and sediments from watery environments implies that Woodland mound ceremonialism may have had a hitherto unrecognized relationship to World Renewal ritual. These mortuary and World Renewal connections lead in several directions.

In front of the buffalo skulls on the Cheyenne and

Arapaho Sun Dance altars can be found certain rectangular pits or trenches (figure 3.2). I will show evidence (chapter 7) that these trenches may have originated as symbolic graves, corresponding to the grave area in the Hidatsa Sun Dance. And I will give evidence (chapters 12 and 15) that the Cheyenne and Arapaho Sun Dance altars relate as well to certain symbolic earth entrances represented two thousand years ago in Hopewellian art and ritual structures, some in the form of a bear paw, others more explicitly sexual. What is a grave but a portal to the netherworld by which one returns to the womb of the Earth Mother?

4 / Spirit Bundles, Soul Release, and the Ghost Lodge

SINCE I FIRST SAW SOUTH DAKOTA in 1947 two entire generations have grown to maturity that have never seen the bottomlands of the Missouri upriver from the Fort Randall dam near Lake Andes. I did not spend enough time in the Black Hills of South Dakota to become overly sentimental about their three-dimensional landscapes, but I do sentimentalize from time to time about the cottonwoods that once grew on the bottoms and islands of the Missouri.

The Great Depression of the thirties was very good for archaeology, even if it was good for nothing else. Government make-work projects were needed that would create employment for the jobless without taking work away from those who already had it. Archaeology was ideal for this. An archaeological project could consume thousands of man-hours of unskilled labor in areas where such digs had never before been seen. During the Depression archaeological projects thrived in the South as the dams were constructed that now provide hydroelectric power for the Tennessee Valley Authority. With the resumption of dam construction after World War II the archaeological projects were resumed also—this time not primarily to put men back to work but to salvage the cultural heritage that would otherwise be destroyed as the reservoirs filled behind the dams. The precedent had been established during the thirties that archaeological sites should not be submerged in reservoirs without at least some attempt to evaluate and preserve the human history they contained. Fort Randall itself was one of the sites that came to be threatened and studied in the forties and fifties. Others were sites that each represented some unique chapter of American Indian culture history.

THE WHEELER BRIDGE MOUNDS

The Wheeler bottom is no more. It is submerged beneath the water impounded behind Fort Randall dam. The old iron bridge that crossed the Missouri at Wheeler is no more. I understood that it was to be dismantled before the reservoir filled, perched on a barge, and floated somewhere for another existence and purpose. The Wheeler Bridge mounds are no more as we knew them then, but they still exist in more than memory. They have been transformed into notes, sketches, and photographs archived in South Dakota and Washington, D.C.

My first professionally directed field experience was the investigation of two mounds on the Wheeler bottom. These were circular earthen rises about forty to fifty feet in diameter and less than four feet high. Years of plowing had reduced their height and spread them horizontally to the dimensions we found. The artificial nature of the mounds was evident from a prepared floor of bluish clay that marked the separation between the original undisturbed bottom soil and the overlying fill of one mound.[1]

At the base of each mound a rectangular burial pit had been excavated by the Indians responsible for the mounds. Each was about five to six feet across and a foot deep. Within one there remained vestiges of bark and a whitish mold or niter to show where poles or logs had once covered the burial chamber. As the logs decayed the weight of the overburden had collapsed the mound into the pit so that the traces of log that we found followed the contours of the mound floor and pit like limp rags.

Each pit contained the bones of several secondary burials. Primary burial would have been indicated if the bones had been found in correct anatomical order and all bones were present. These bones were disarticulated and some bundled together with many bones missing. This would happen when the primary burial had been elsewhere, such as on a platform or in a tree, and the bones gathered together for reburial as we found them in the mounds. In the log-roofed burial chamber the long bones of one bundle showed evidence of modification after death; holes had been drilled into the marrow cavities. Our party excavated the mounds in the late summer of 1947, but it was almost thirty years before I discovered what purpose the drilled holes in the long bones might have served.[2]

We were a small group, as archaeological investigations go. The senior member of the group was Paul Cooper with J. Joe Bauxar next in charge. I was one of two students along for the summer as 'expert labor'. The other was Warren L. Wittry. The dig was one of many that summer sponsored by the Missouri Valley Project of the Smithsonian Institution River Basin Surveys operating out of a field headquarters in Lincoln, Nebraska. Our own particular mission for the summer was to make a preliminary estimate of the extent of the threat to archaeological sites in the reservoir area between Fort Randall in the south and Fort Thompson in the north—the 170 square miles of today's Lake Francis Case.

No artifacts were found in the mounds on Wheeler bottom that had been intended to accompany the dead reburied there. Some thick fragments of cordmarked pottery were found as accidental inclusions in the earth used to construct one mound. That suggested that the earth used was obtained in an area that at the time or earlier had been occupied by Indians of the Woodland period, but no village or camp site could be located that might have been occupied by the builders of the mounds. Also found in the fill of one mound were a few perforated, flat, round disks made of shell that looked like washers. Such items could have been worn on a garment as brooches, but they also would have made fantastic eyes in masks, like the washer-shaped tin eyes in modern Iroquois wooden masks. A large-stemmed projectile point was found inside a skull in the other mound.

Burial mounds of the same general type as those at Wheeler bridge, with log-covered subfloor burial pits, are typical of the Havana tradition in the prairie areas of the Midwest during the Middle Woodland period, which climaxed with a Hopewellian phase around 100 B.C. to A.D. 300. By the beginning of the Late Woodland period, which followed shortly after A.D. 400, mounds of similar construction were beginning to appear in the eastern Dakotas. This spread of burial practices probably represents only the diffusion of an idea and not an actual movement of people.

Elmer Ogden, who lived not far from Havana, Illinois, discovered what Havana tradition mounds sometimes contain. He learned this when part of the mound on which his farmhouse was constructed collapsed beneath it.[3] Below the house there once had been a large log-covered tomb built maybe two thousand years earlier. Through time the logs had decayed to powder but the hard earth above had remained as a natural monolithic arch until Ogden began digging a cellar beneath the house. Eventually the property was purchased by the State of Illinois to add to the grounds of the Dickson Mounds branch of the Illinois State Museum. The Ogden house was removed and the

mound stabilized and returned to the appearance it had for so many centuries before the arrival of white settlers in the Spoon River country. The Ogden Mound is exceptional because of its enormous size, 175 by 200 feet. Thousands of smaller mounds simply disappear by inches each year while most people are unaware even of their existence.

A radiocarbon date from one of the Wheeler mounds indicated an age within the range of A.D. 600 to 840.[4] A single such date is not as trustworthy as a series of dates would have been, but this one is at least consistent with the evidence of the bones themselves. The practice of drilling or punching holes into the marrow cavities of human long bones turns out to fall in the same time period for sites in Minnesota and northwestern Wisconsin that are much more accurately dated. Radiocarbon dating was not available in 1947 when the Wheeler mounds were excavated, but material from the excavation was archived and available when the technology became available. There was no way of knowing in 1947 that the principle of anything like radiocarbon dating would someday be discovered.

A reconstruction of the history of the mounds would follow along lines something like these. The dead were originally buried on scaffolds or platforms in trees for a period of time until only bones remained. Primary burial cannot be easily scheduled beforehand, and death may not always be in convenient locations. Reburial can be scheduled for the convenience of the seasonal routine of the band and for an appropriate location. At the right time the skull and long bones of the arms and legs were retrieved, tied into a bundle, and wrapped in a hide for their protection. The ribs, axial skeleton, and foot and hand bones were not saved. Such a bundle was small and light enough that it might be carried for a year or more until the time was appropriate for reburial.

Near some base camp of the band a circular area was cleared of vegetation and organic soil. Clay was brought to the area, or subsoil clay exposed, and trod to produce a hard, flat, dust-free surface. A rectangular pit was excavated into the center of the prepared area and sections of log cut to size and readied for use as a cover to protect bundles to be enclosed in the pit, a practice traceable to Hopewellian burial customs that diffused out onto the Plains from the heartland of the Havana Hopewell tradition. After a ceremony of mourning to dispatch the souls of the deceased along the spirit trail, the bundles were placed in the pit and covered. Other bundles followed in later years. When the time came for the band to move to another location for an extended period, the prepared area and its log vault were covered with a dome of earth. This reconstruction of events is partly speculative, of course, but based also upon ethnographic analogy and the evidence of other archaeological sites.

LAKOTA SOUL KEEPING

Father Louis Hennepin left a written record of mourning by a historic Indian people, which we can use to get some feeling for what a pre-Columbian mourning ceremony may have been like. Speaking of the Santee Dakota chief who became his father by adoption in 1680, Hennepin says that this Aquipagnatin

> had with him the Bones of one of his deceas'd friends, which he kept very choicely in the Skin of a Beast adorn'd with several red and black Lists [bands] of a Porcupine's [quills]. He would be from time to time assembling his Followers to make them smoke; and then would he send for us one after another, and oblige us to cover the Bones of their Deceas'd with some of our *European* merchandise, in order to dry up the Tears which he had shed for him and his Son, who had been kill'd by the *Miami's*[!].
>
> To appease the crafty old Savage, we strew'd on the Bones of the Deceas'd several pieces of *Martinico*-Tobacco, Hatchets, Knives, Beads, and some Bracelets of black and white Porcelain. . . . He gave us to understand, That what he had thus demanded of us, was not for himself but for the Dead, and to give the Warriors that he brought with him; and indeed he distributed amongst them whatever he took from us.[5]

Here Hennepin was speaking of an event that had occurred while he was a prisoner of the Santees on the shore of Lake Pepin, which is a broad expansion of the Mississippi River between Minnesota and Wisconsin. On another occasion Hennepin speaks of the Santees using his chasuble (one of his vestments) "to cover the Bones of their Dead."[6]

The treatment given such bone bundles by the Eastern Dakota in 1680 should sound familiar to some readers. Except for the nature of the bundle honored, this description would hold for the attention given 'soul bundles' by Dakotas of a later century. Only the nature of the soul differed. In later historic times the soul bundle contained a lock of hair of the deceased in which the soul was believed to linger after death. Gifts of needles, awls, knives, tobacco, belts, moccasins, leggings, and pipes were given to the soul keeper for distribution when the soul was finally released. It is not hard to imagine similar attention for bone bundles of the Late Woodland period. Such a scenario would have called for the bone bundles to be kept and honored during a period of mourning and then buried after the proper ritual to release the soul of the deceased for its journey to the spirit world.

Soul Keeping or Spirit Keeping is the English name by which we know the Dakota version of a more widespread mourning practice that climaxed with the release of the soul after an extended period of mourning. The practice is not limited to the Dakota as a people or even to Siouan speakers; it is well described for the Menominees, who are Algonquian speakers living in eastern Wisconsin. Father Hennepin is the only European who may have seen a soul bundle containing bones to represent the soul rather than a lock of hair, but Samuel Barrett and Alanson Skinner did not hesitate to regard as soul bundles the pre-Columbian bone bundles they reported on in eastern Wisconsin (below).

It is impossible to generalize at this late date on the attitude of the pre-Columbian keepers of the bone bundles toward those bundles once the souls had been released. Speaking of more recent Oglala practices in *The Sacred Pipe*, Black Elk remarked simply that "once the soul has left the bundle containing the lock of hair, it is no longer especially *wakan* [holy], but it may be kept by the family, if they wish, as something of a remembrance."[7] This suggests that bone bundles would have been respected after the soul release ceremony—that goes almost without saying—and perhaps even retained and passed on as heirlooms, but also that the bones might no longer have been considered to be actually sacred or to be objects of veneration. After describing an Oglala soul release ceremony she witnessed in 1882 Alice Fletcher wrote that once the lock of hair was returned to the mother she might keep it or bury it.[8]

Commonly in former times—and to some extent still today—a Dakota "filled with grief at the death of a near relative, might prolong his period of mourning by 'keeping the spirit' for several months or a year, and then 'letting it go' by means of a certain ceremony." So wrote Frances Densmore in her report on Teton music.[9] Her account of Spirit Keeping was based on Hunkpapa practice observed on the Standing Rock Reservation which straddles the North Dakota–South Dakota state line. The Hunkpapas and Oglalas are both divisions of the Tetons, known also as the Lakotas or Western Dakotas.

Alice Fletcher's firsthand observations from 1882, published in 1894, constitute a literary pearl but concentrate on detailing the ritual as viewed by an attentive but nonparticipating spectator. Black Elk's account conveys more of the feeling of participation, emphasizing words and thoughts rather than procedure and action. Soul Keeping was more often done in mourning for a child than for a grown person. Black Elk says that at first only the souls of a few of the great leaders were kept and later the practice was extended to the souls of all good people. The case of Spirit Keeping that Black Elk described in detail was that for a child, but his more general statement might apply to some of the bone bundles of pre-Columbian times.

Soul Keeping was not undertaken without serious consideration of the responsibilities entailed. The soul keeper could not hunt, engage in warfare, participate actively in social functions of the tribe, eat dog meat, take a knife or any other weapon in his hand, run, or even make a quick motion that would disturb the air, such as shaking a blanket. No one could pass in front of him or touch him. He was required to distribute gifts generously at the feast during which the soul would be released—generously to the point of impoverishing himself and his family. To be able to fulfill this responsibility he was helped by friends and relatives who contributed gifts toward that end.

During the period of the Spirit Keeping the spirit keeper's behavior was supposed to be exemplary, both for the good of his people and for his own well-being, because it was believed that the habits followed during this period of special mourning would remain with him for the rest of his life. The spirit bundle keeper and his wife were expected to allow only the most charitable thoughts to cross their minds when thinking of their fellow tribesmen. The spirit keeper was expected to forget old grudges or injuries. Unkind words by anyone were forbidden in the lodge in which the spirit bundle was kept. The act of Soul Keeping was a way of publicly honoring the dead, expressing affection for the deceased, reducing grief, expressing devotion to traditions of one's forefathers, and acquiring personal distinction.

The dead child lay dressed in its best clothing with its face painted red. The lock of hair is cut from the child's head by a man whose life was unstained by dishonor. He first purifies his hands and the knife in smoke from a pinch of sweet grass placed on a glowing coal on a buffalo chip. The knife is guided three times toward the lock of hair and withdrawn three times, then allowed to touch and cut the hair only after a fourth movement.

After a prayer directed to *Wakan Tanka*, the Great Spirit, the lock of hair is held in the purifying smoke of the smoldering sweet grass, spoken to as one would to a living person, and then enclosed in a piece of red cloth or tanned hide painted red. This small bundle and a skein of sweet grass are then placed within a larger "spirit wrap" of buckskin embroidered with colored porcupine quills and that wrapping, in turn, is enclosed in an outer wrapping of red cloth or red-painted hide. When on display a buffalo robe especially made for the occasion may be draped over the bundle and its stand, the hair side outside.

Densmore says that on occasion an object other than a lock of hair might might be used that had been in close contact with the child: "Thus Weasel Bear said that when keeping the spirit of his little girl, he used the ornaments which she had worn on her hair as the central article in the spirit bundle."[10] It was believed that the spirit lingers around such items as clothing and personal belongings.

With the spirit bundle thus prepared and held in his arms as if it were the child itself, the spirit keeper rode around the camp circle to give public notice of the charge he had assumed in his grief. This done, the spirit bundle was placed on a red-painted tripod several steps from the door of a specially erected tipi, which was then known as the spirit lodge or ghost lodge. A decorated packbag of tanned leather was placed near the spirit bundle thus displayed. In it were placed gifts by people sympathetic to the grief of the spirit keeper, for him to distribute during the gift giving that took place on the occasion when the soul was finally released.

The place of honor in any tipi was on the far side, opposite the entrance. At night and during bad weather the tripod and spirit bundle were brought inside and set in that special location by hands previously purified in the fragrance of a smudge of sweet grass. Entering, the carrier turned left and proceeded clockwise to the back of the tipi. Between the place of honor and the fire at the center of the tipi a circular area was consecrated or prepared for its special use and in it placed two flat wooden tools and a buffalo chip. When sweet grass smoke was needed the two paddles were used to bring a hot coal from the fire and place it upon the buffalo chip. The sweet grass could then be sprinkled upon the glowing coal. No one could pass between the bundle and the fire or return in a counterclockwise direction. To leave, one was obliged to pass behind the bundle and continue in clockwise fashion to the entrance.

It was especially gratifying to the spirit keeper when he could obtain a white buffalo hide robe to spread over the place of honor for the bundle and tripod to rest upon. The only persons allowed to touch such a robe with their bare hands were holy men known to be qualified for such an activity and children who had been through the Hunka ceremony. The Hunka was a ceremony of a kind only indirectly related to the rites of Spirit Keeping and spirit release among the Dakotas but integrally connected with them among some neighboring tribes to the east, like the Menominee.

The soul keeper was free to ride with hunting parties, but it was his role to sit by himself on a nearby hilltop with his pipe, praying for the welfare of his people and the success of the hunt. If a buffalo were killed near him, he could claim it. He could not himself butcher it because he was restricted from touching knives or blood, but he could transport the butchered meat and buffalo hide back to camp. There the meat was cut into thin slices, dried, and later pounded with chokecherries and bone marrow to make *wasna*, which most people know by its Cree name *pemmican*.

The activities of Soul Keeping required the services of a woman as well as a man. It was she who prepared the *wasna* from the buffalo meat and saw to it that the bundle was returned to the tipi if sudden winds arose or thunder or other loud disturbances threatened the peace when the bundle was on public display. If the keeper of the spirit died before the time for its release, it was his wife who completed his unfinished obligations and then kept the soul bundle of her husband as well.

The releasing of the soul ordinarily took place after a year among the Dakota, although a longer period might be needed if the required number of gifts had not yet been accumulated. Several souls might be released on the same occasion if the timing was appropriate. For each such spirit a man was appointed who had previously himself been a keeper of a spirit bundle. One of this man's duties was to prepare a spirit post in the spirit lodge.

After purifying his hands and knife with sweet grass smoke he whittles a stake from willow or cottonwood, about three feet long for a child but proportionately larger if it is for an adult. The stylized features of the honored dead person are created with beads on a piece of leather wrapped around the top of the post. The face thus made is painted in some pattern that the person had in life earned the right to use. The post is then dressed with the same garments which the person had worn in life. If he was a warrior, his feathered war bonnet is placed on the top of the post and his bow and arrows and other equipment leaned against it. The spirit is now fed for the last time with food that has been previously purified in the smoke of sweet grass. The food is held in the air before the spirit post, a blessing is asked, and the food then buried in the ground within the specially prepared area between the bundle and the hearth.

The climax of the whole process of Soul Keeping was reached when the day arrived for the actual release of the soul. Fletcher describes a scene of excitement and festivity. All signs of mourning are now a thing of the past. The near relatives now braid their hair for the first time since the death, and everyone is gaily dressed. More than eight hundred people gather for the event. Forty-two huge kettles are steaming and simmering. The air is scented with the mingled aromas of beef soup, dog stew, freshly ground coffee, and the sagebrush being carried to the ghost lodge. Girls giggle as they chat while carrying water from the creek or peel turnips. Men compare their memories of previous such events as they admire the thirty-two snorting and whinnying pinto ponies to be given away that day.

The activities this day are especially well attended because nine spirit bundles are being opened. The bundles represented three men, three boys, two girls, and a woman:

The interior of the ghost lodge is arranged in the following manner. The space occupied by the packs [spirit bundles] is marked off in an oblong, the sod removed and the ground spread with Artemisia [sage]. The figure having the mellowed earth in which the offerings of food have been buried each day, is covered with a red cloth. On the centre is laid a disk of shell; eight live coals, four on each side, are arranged outside the figure, and sweet grass laid on them. Four buffalo chips are outside of these at the corners. The different packs are loosened from the initial pack and each one fastened to sticks about four feet long. . . . The [nine] sticks are bound with hide, and an oblong piece of hide, ornamented and having on it a face rudely outlined in paint, is hung in front of each pack. Upon the packs belonging to the young men are fastened eagle feather war bonnets. These effigies are arranged in a semicircle on the south side of the tent, the sticks being thrust into the ground, and the gifts contributed by the relations of the dead person piled about his effigy.[11]

Weasel Bear told Densmore that the bundles were opened in four stages with a "brief discourse" between these acts. Only when the fourth and final wrapper was unfolded about an hour before sunset was the spirit believed to have departed. Black Elk says that the keeper of the bundle advanced from the lodge in four stages, timing the last stop to be outside the spirit lodge door. As soon as the bundle passed outside the lodge, the spirit it contained departed along the spirit road. The accumulated gifts were then distributed in a mood of rejoicing.

MENOMINEE DEATH BUNDLES

Samuel Barrett and Alanson Skinner were able to bring to archaeology the special knowledge they had acquired working among the living Indian peoples in Wisconsin and elsewhere. On the Menominee Reservation they conducted a series of archaeological excavations assisted by local Menominees, especially Valentine Satterlee, who also conducted some excavations on his own. Satterlee's Indian name translated as Little Medicine Man. The Menominee names of Barrett and Skinner translated as Medicine Bundle and Little Weasel.

In various parts of the reservation these men found evidence of pre-Columbian reburials. Barrett and Skinner saw a close relationship between the pre-Columbian practice of reburying bone bundles and the then-contemporary practice among traditionally oriented Menominees of keeping a 'death bundle', containing a lock of hair of the deceased, which was later buried following a memorial service (chapter 8). Barrett and Skinner placed this interpretation in their archaeological report in the form of a fictional dialogue between a young Menominee boy they named Little Wolf and a grey-haired Menominee whom the boy addressed as Grandfather. The dialogue went like this:

"Oh hwa kina, Nase! Alas, my Grandchild, anciently we were a real people. By the long ago ancestors—of whom I only am left—things were better arranged. Eh, ceremonies were properly conducted—nothing was omitted, the rituals were recited entire and perfectly. Our medicines, consequently, were stronger, there was more game and fish, and our enemies trembled.

"It is different now. We eat impure food; our young men devote themselves to chasing women and desert the gods of our ancestors. We are become a degenerate race. You are a member of the Medicine Lodge, and you will know that our ancient master Mä'näbus was a demi-god, a half human. On earth, he was engaged in fighting our wrongs, and in killing or driving off the monsters who preyed upon us. You will also recall that these monsters in revenge slew his younger brother Onápaxtäo, or Muhwäsê, the Little Wolf, whose namesake you are.

"When Mä'näbus learned that his younger brother had been killed, he made war on the Powers Beneath, until they feared that he would exterminate them, and, in their extremity they sent back Little Wolf, restored to life. But, as Onápaxtäo had been dead for four days, he stank, and the flesh fell from his body, and Mä'näbus would have none of him, but sent him on to govern the realms of the dead.

"Therefore, as you well know, when one of our fellow brethren of the Medicine Lodge dies, he goes to 'Nápatäo[!]. When he has remained there a year, we, the survivors, raise up some one of the same age and sex to take his place. At that time the soul of the dead man is called back temporarily from the other world, and enters the body of the candidate. When our memorial services and the initiation of the new brother are over, the soul of the dead man is dismissed in order to return to Onápaxtäo. After this, the clothing of the dead man, hitherto up to this day, kept wrapped around a lock of the dead man's hair to form the Death Bundle, becomes the property of the new brother, who has been dressed in it during the ceremony, and the lock of hair that it contained is buried in the earth.

"Now in ancient times, eh, even yet when I was a young man, this thing was done in full form, with nothing omitted. Then, when a man had been dead for six or eight moons, his body was dug from the earth, and the bones stripped and cleaned, or even burned, and the bones or their ashes were kept wrapped in the death bundle until the time appointed, and then deposited in a mound of earth made of the same size and shape as the ground plan of the Mitäwi'komĭk, the Medicine Lodge Building. This was a monument to

the dead, and a sign that he had trodden the path that all the brethren and fellows had walked before him. Hauka, sometimes in those days the mourners deposited their dead in trees or scaffolds, until the flesh rotted from the bones, and then buried them at the Jebai-nokêt, the Memorial service. . . .

"It is true that there be those among our warriors today who boast proudly that they have killed one of the foe and eaten his heart, or a little of the flesh of his body, and therefore, claim to be of the nature of men. But then, when I was young, we made nothing of such trifles. We ate the whole body of a foe at the victory feast. . . .

"Alas, no longer of this nature are our people! It is no wonder that our medicines are weak and we are easy prey to the enemy! . . . No longer do our priests pay attention to our rituals and ceremonies. Everything is cut short, and our people have even forgotten why our forefathers built the mounds. Eh, oh hwa! Ap'apenisi-wûk!"

. . . In the timber an owl hooted, and somewhere, afar off, the shivering howl of a wolf sent a thrill down every canine spine in camp, causing puppies to shiver, and old tooth scarred dogs to bristle and growl. . . . In a remote wigwam someone was preparing for a medicine hunt on the morrow, and the throbbing of the waterdrum sounded like a heavy heartbeat throughout the settlement, far beyond the range of the voice of the singer who accompanied it. Day had changed to night during the old man's narration.

Little Wolf thoughtfully removed the redstone bowl of his pipe from its stem, and rose to his feet. The ancient was too wrapped in his thoughts of the glorious past, when all ceremonies were held in full, in the right way, as they ought to be held, to notice that his companion of the younger careless generation had bidden him farewell and gone to his own mat wigwam.[12]

The Menominee keeping of the death bundle is in many ways the same as the Dakota practice of keeping the soul bundle. In each case the bundle contained a lock of hair of the deceased referred to as the soul or spirit. In each case, the spirit was dismissed at the end of a period of time to continue to the next world.

Barrett and Skinner were only making an educated guess that in the pre-Columbian past there were death bundles that contained bones for reburial after the ceremony. This is still only an educated guess, but it is one that fits comfortably with both the archaeological and the historical facts. I infer that they also believed that the pre-Columbian sites that they excavated on the Menominee Reservation could have been those of the pre-Columbian Menominees themselves. Barrett and Skinner conducted their archaeological fieldwork in

1919 and 1921. Archaeologists of the time neither had much comprehension of the great depth of culture history represented by the material found nor much awareness of the significance of the cultural variation present.

By 1942 Will C. McKern had made a formal distinction between the manifestations of pre-Columbian mound-building cultures on the reservation and another pre-Columbian culture without mounds, which he named the Keshena focus and regarded to be ancestral to the culture of the Menominees.[13] Even this opinion must now be reconsidered because the Keshena focus, as he defined it, contains a mixture of traits now known to belong to different time periods, leaving a pre-Columbian culture for the Menominees yet to be recognized and defined. In late pre-Contact times the Santee Dakota were the only known close neighbors to the west of the Menominees.

RELEASING THE SOUL

Perforated human bones have not been found in eastern Wisconsin. They were, however, found by Will McKern in Burnett County in northwestern Wisconsin in bundle burials placed in mounds of the Clam River focus, possibly by the pre-Contact ancestors of the Santees. These were not burials placed within log-covered submound pits. These were burials added to layers or strata of circular earth mounds that rose as a sort of accretional cemetery. Some burials in each of two mounds excavated by McKern in 1935 and 1936 contained long bones with holes punched into one or another end.[14] Fragments of bone were still visible in some holes, so it was not believed that the holes had been made to obtain marrow from the bones. That had been a suggestion made by Lloyd Wilford to explain holes similarly found in bones with burials placed in mounds of the Laurel culture in Minnesota.

Wilford excavated Mound 4 of the Smith Group in Koochiching County, Minnesota, in 1933. This mound was almost the same size as the Wheeler mounds—fifty feet in diameter and about five feet high. Unlike the Wheeler mound, Smith Mound 4 contained no subfloor pit. Some 113 burials were found in several groups and strata above ground level, mostly secondary burials consisting only of skull, mandible, and long bones. A majority of the long bones with marrow cavities—which would mean the femora, tibiae, and humeri—appear to have had holes battered into the marrow cavities, usually near one end.

Restudying the materials from Smith Mound 4 forty years later, James Stoltman came up with a suggestion that has a lot of explanatory power: "Motivating such practices could have been a cosmology that demanded the release of the soul or spirit from certain bones after death or that encouraged survivors to partake of the flesh of the deceased to ensure or enhance their own powers."[15] We have seen that there is much support for the idea of soul release from what we know of historic customs. There is no similar support for the suggested alternative of funerary cannibalism. The Smith mound has been assigned by Stoltman to a Smith phase that represents the latest expression of Laurel culture with an estimated time placement within the range of A.D. 500–900, which means that they were partly coeval with the Clam River mounds.[16]

Punching or drilling holes into the marrow cavities to release the soul would imply a mental association of the marrow with the soul. That is exactly what J. N. B. Hewitt came up with in his 1894 study of the Iroquoian concept of the soul, that is, that the animating soul was believed to reside in the marrow of the bones.[17] He tells us that the Iroquois believed that every individual possessed an animating or sensitive soul, which resided in the bones, and one or more reasoning or intelligent souls, which resided in the head. The Jesuit Father Paul Le Jeune obtained this explanation from a Huron Indian which he reported in his Relation of 1636:

> Returning from this [Huron Feast of the Dead] with a Captain who is very intelligent, and who will some day be very influential in the affairs of the Country, I asked him why they called the bones of the dead Atsiken. He gave me the best explanation he could, and I gathered from his conversation that many think we have two souls, both of them being divisible and material, and yet both reasonable; the one separates itself from the body at death, yet remains in the Cemetery until the feast of the Dead,—after which it either changes into a Turtledove, or, according to the most common belief, it goes away at once to the village of souls. The other is, as it were, bound to the body, and informs, so to speak, the corpse; it remains in the ditch of the dead after the feast, and never leaves it, unless some one bears it again as a child. He pointed out to me, as a proof of this metempsychosis, the perfect resemblance some have to persons deceased. A fine Philosophy, indeed. Such as it is, it shows why they call the bones of the dead, Atsiken, "the souls."[18]

While our English word 'spirit' is derived from a Latin root word meaning 'breathe' or 'breath', the Hurons and other Iroquoians similarly relate 'soul' to 'bone', including them in the same semantic set. Any people who also related the soul with bone or marrow in thought could come up with the idea of releasing the soul by opening the cavities of those bones in which marrow was most evident. At least one thousand years separate the period of the Wheeler mounds, the Clam River mounds, Smith Mound 4, and the burial complex of the Keshena focus from any modern observation of spirit bundles and the ghost lodge. Lost within the shadows of this time gap there may be some stain in the soil here or a speck of charcoal there to provide a clue to the change of outlook that led one pattern of mourning to replace another.

The round shell disks found in the fill of one of the mounds on the Wheeler bottom: were they items of personal adornment accidentally included in the mound or some integral part of the ritual of soul release that preceded the sealing of the tomb and the raising of the mound itself? If the shell disks from the Wheeler mound were only lost or discarded personal ornaments that had found their way into the mound accidentally within the basketloads of earth used as mound-fill, then they would not necessarily have been sacred. If the disks were like those used on the altar in front of the soul bundle in the soul release ceremony of 1882, then they might be considered sacred. In this case the Wheeler mound disks did not resemble the particular one illustrated for the Spirit Keeping ceremony because that one had two small holes, such as would be used for attaching a gorget to a cord, rather than a single, large hole.[19]

There was no single consistent set of beliefs about souls that held for all Indians in all times, except that all believed in souls and that such spirit bodies could survive death. Whether there was one or two or more, whether they remained with the bones after death or passed on to a spirit world, whether they could be reborn into new bodies—these things varied from tribe to tribe.

Despite initial government opposition, the practice of Spirit Keeping has persisted in modified and more subtle forms among the Lakotas right into the present day. Speaking through an interpreter in the era of the Vietnam War, R. Clyde McCone asked a Pine Ridge Lakota whether the custom of Spirit Keeping was still active. "Yes," the Lakota told him, "we still do that today," and then went on to explain how when a Pine Ridge soldier was to be buried, the American flag was draped over the casket, and how when the casket was lowered into the ground the flag was removed and folded and given (like a soul bundle) to the father or mother or sister of the dead soldier for keeping. A year later, when the anniversary day of the burial came around, a big feast was held. The flag was unfolded, raised, and allowed to flutter open in the sky. The symbolism of soul release can change through the generations into forms that new generations find more meaningful.[20]

5 / Remembering the Honored Dead

THE DEATH AND MOURNING of an individual can be a private affair or it can be a public affair. The death of an important person almost always calls for a community response in proportion to the degree to which the person's death has disrupted the community, but even the deaths of 'little people' can be made matters of community involvement. The Feasts of the Dead in the Great Lakes area were occasions for entire communities to honor the memory of their dead in a single periodic act of group mourning. That was one kind of response to death. Another kind of response to death was to take to the warpath, although neither response excluded the other. Taking the life of an enemy never served purely to indulge a warrior in the selfish satisfaction of blood revenge. It was widely believed necessary to obtain the spirit of an enemy as a servant for the mourned kinsman while on the spirit trail (chapter 8). It was also widely believed that a spirit freed by death could not rest until someone had been adopted to replace its loss, often taking the name of the deceased (chapters 4, 6, and 8). The person adopted did not have to be a member of the tribe of the deceased, so warfare for the purpose of taking captives was sometimes a part of the mourning process.

THE FATE OF IROQUOIS AND HURON PRISONERS

In his book *The Death and Rebirth of the Seneca* Anthony F. C. Wallace introduces his readers to the onetime Iroquois practice of adopting captives both prior to and as an alternative to torture and death. Adoption with naturalization was a practice hardly limited to the Iroquois, of course, but it became an especially important factor in Iroquois demographics, as many as two-thirds of the Oneida Iroquois, for instance, being said to have once been adoptees.[1] Adoptees chosen to live were not condemned to a life of slavery but enjoyed the same respect and privileges as native-born Iroquois, a happy condition that contrasted dramatically with the fate of prisoners not adopted or adopted but not chosen

to live. These were often subjected to prolonged and agonizing forms of torture. Examples on record typically involved burning coals, red-hot iron, and such other cruelties as fancy and opportunity suggested, ending with the victim's death and not infrequently with a feast in which the captive was eaten.

As for the Hurons, Wallace cites the classic case of Joseph, a Seneca-Iroquois warrior captured in 1637 by the Hurons, a non-League Iroquoian nation. Joseph was initially received warmly to fill the place of a Huron who had recently been killed in battle, but the severity of Joseph's injuries eventually obliged a change of heart on the part of the Huron chief to whom he had been given. The chief then announced his tearful decision and assigned Joseph's head, liver, and one arm to the persons whose pleasure it would be to feast on them after Joseph's death.[2] A puzzling aspect of Iroquois and Huron torture was that the victims were often adopted and addressed by kinship terms. In her *An Ethnography of the Hurons, 1615–1649*, Elisabeth Tooker says: "Each captive was bound, both arms and feet, and was naked except for a wampum collar around his head which designated him as a victim. . . .[3] After the captive had arrived at the village he was adopted by someone who had lost a son in war. This adopted parent was charged with 'caressing' [torturing] the prisoner. . . .[4] The adopted father might approach the captive with a necklace in the form of a hot iron and say, 'See here my son; you love, I am sure, to be adorned, to appear beautiful. . . .'"[5]

Armed Iroquois encounters with the French had motives complicated by Iroquois alliances with the English and the status of English-French relations. Armed Iroquois conflicts with neighboring Indian nations increasingly had motives complicated by territorial considerations, good beaver-trapping lands becoming scarce in the Iroquois home territory. Aboriginally, and to some extent at all times, war parties served the purpose of obtaining revenge for deaths incurred by other tribes. Wallace says:

Generally speaking, whatever economic or political considerations might be involved in the tensions that led to war, the actual formation of war parties was either inspired by or rationalized by the obligation to avenge dead relatives. . . . One might, indeed, regard the Iroquois war complex as being, psychologically, a part of the mourning process.[6]

The common aim of all war parties was to bring back persons to replace the mourned-for dead. This could be done in three ways: by bringing back the scalp of a dead enemy (this scalp might even be put through an adoption ceremony); by bringing back a live prisoner (to be adopted, tortured, and killed); or by bringing back a live prisoner to be allowed to live and even to replace in a social role the one whose death had called for this "revenge."[7]

The relations of the Iroquois with their Indian and French neighbors during the colonial period were punctuated with periodic episodes of peace and war. The destruction was rather out of balance in favor of the Iroquois with Algonquian and non-League Iroquoians suffering losses sometimes extending to the disappearance of entire tribes from the pages of history. In proportion to what some of their Indian trading partners suffered, the French did not fare badly.

The worst reversal of fortune suffered by the French directly at the hand of the Iroquois was the Iroquois attack on the settlement of La Chine near Montreal in 1689. Would-be rescuers, arriving too late and too few in number, could only watch the fires of the fifteen hundred Iroquois warriors encamped for the night on the opposite shore of Lac St-Louis, all too aware of the scenes that the flames probably illuminated. The historian Francis Jennings disparages Francis Parkman's figure of two hundred settlers killed and 120 carried off as prisoners from La Chine, saying that at worst only sixty-four were killed on the scene at La Chine, not counting any who met death among ninety-two captives taken away.[8] Whether the higher or lower figure is closer to correct in this case would seem to be academic quibbling, although I am not sure that my ancestor Sicaire Deguire would have considered it academic quibbling, had he been able to give much thought to the subject, preoccupied as he would have been with other considerations, as he was being led from La Chine by his Iroquois captors in 1689.[9]

THE ADOPTION OF MARY JEMISON

The autobiography of Mary Jemison describes her capture by the Shawnees as a thirteen-year-old girl in 1755 in western Pennsylvania and her subsequent life as an adopted Seneca-Iroquois. The language of this ac-

count is that of James Everett Seaver, who prepared the published story of her life, and some of the account is necessarily a projection into the past of her later experience as a Seneca. Mary Jemison could not speak Seneca when first captured, so the text of speeches made at the time of her adoption must be taken as approximations of what might have been said, but they are useful records even so.

After her capture, Jemison was taken by the Shawnees to Fort Duquesne, a French outpost on the site of present-day Pittsburgh. There she was fed, her hair combed, and her face and hair painted red. The next day she was given to two Seneca women by her Shawnee captors and taken down the Ohio in a canoe. Jemison's canoe was preceded by another in which the mounted scalps of her mother and father were displayed on a pole held by an Indian at the stern. On the way the party passed a Shawnee town where she was horrified at the sight of a wooden rack from which roasted and blackened heads, limbs, and other human body parts were suspended over a fire still smoking. The destination of Jemison's party was a small Seneca town downstream from the fort, and it was at this village that she was formally adopted.[10]

> Having made fast to the shore, the squaws left me in the canoe while they went to their wigwam or house in the town, and returned with a suit of Indian clothing, all new and very clean and white. My clothes, though whole and good when I was taken, were now torn to pieces, so that I was almost naked. They first undressed me, and threw my rags into the river; then washed me clean and dressed me in the new suit they had brought in, in complete Indian style; and then led me home and seated me in the center of their wigwam.
>
> I had been in that situation but a few minutes before all the squaws in the town came in to see me. I was soon surrounded by them, and they immediately set up a most dismal howling, crying bitterly, and wringing their hands in all the agonies of grief for a deceased relative.
>
> Their tears flowed freely, and they exhibited all the signs of real mourning. At the commencement of this scene, one of their number began, in a voice somewhat between speaking and singing, to recite some words to the following purport, and continued the recitation till the ceremony was ended; the company at the same time varying the appearance of their countenances, gestures, and tone of voice, so as to correspond with the sentiments expressed by their leader.
>
> "Oh, our brother! alas! he is dead—he has gone; he will never return! Friendless, he died on the field of the slain, where his bones are yet lying unburied! Oh! who will not mourn his sad fate? No tears dropped around him: oh, no! No tears of his sisters were there! He fell

in his prime, when his arm was most needed to keep us from danger! Alas! he has gone, and left us in sorrow, his loss to bewail! Oh, where is his spirit? His spirit went naked, and hungry it wanders, and thirsty and wounded, it groans to return. . . .

"Oh, friends, he is happy; then dry up your tears! His spirit has seen our distress, and sent us a helper whom with pleasure we greet. Deh-he-wä-mis has come: then let us receive her with joy!—she is handsome and pleasant! Oh! she is our sister, and gladly we welcome her here. In the place of our brother she stands in our tribe. With care we will guard her from trouble; and may she be happy till her spririt shall leave us."

In the course of that ceremony, from mourning they became serene,—joy sparkled in their countenances, and they seemed to rejoice over me as over a long-lost child. I was made welcome among them as a sister to the two squaws before mentioned, and was called Deh-he-wä-mis; which, being interpreted, signifies a pretty girl, a handsome girl, or a pleasant, good thing. That is the name by which I have ever since been called by the Indians.

I afterward learned that the ceremony I at that time passed through was that of adoption. The two squaws had lost a brother in Washington's war, sometime in the year before, and in consequence of his death went up to Fort Duquesne on the day on which I arrived there, in order to receive a prisoner, or an enemy's scalp, to supply their loss. It is a custom of the Indians, when one of their number is slain or taken prisoner in battle, to give to the nearest relative of the dead or absent a prisoner, if they have chanced to take one; and if not, to give him the scalp of an enemy. On the return of the Indians from the conquest, which is always announced by peculiar shoutings, demonstrations of joy, and the exhibition of some trophy of victory, the mourners come forward and make their claims. If they receive a prisoner, it is at their option either to satiate their vengeance by taking his life in the most cruel manner they can conceive of, or to receive and adopt him into the family, in the place of him whom they have lost.[11]

Readers of Mary Jemison's account do not learn why her captors might have had any special reason to paint her face and hair red after her capture, or why her captors also painted the hair of her mother's and father's scalps red, as well as the edges of the attached skin. Jemison otherwise goes into considerable ethnographic detail in describing the preparation of the scalps of her mother and father for mounting on wooden hoops. Although Jemison believed that her initial captors were Shawnees, we may compare Jemison's account with the reported Iroquois practice of adopting scalps as well as living captives.[12] We may also take a

clue from the comment of French explorer-trader Nicolas Perrot that it was a general practice for the Indians of the upper Great Lakes area in the late 1600s to paint the face and hair of the dead red.[13] In a roughly contemporary account by Louis Deliette the face and hair of an Illinois warrior being prepared for burial was said to have been painted red, and even in the late 1800s the face of a Lakota child being mourned was painted red. For whatever reason, the status of Jemison as a captive being made available for adoption was equated symbolically with that of the scalps of her parents as trophies and the status of a dead person being mourned.

Individuals being adopted in the Calumet ceremony of the midcontinental United States were also reclothed and their faces painted red, with examples from the Lakota, Omaha, Osage, Pawnee, and Plains Apache (chapters 6 and 10). The practice of painting the faces of adoptees red in the Calumet ceremony would thus seem to have been derived from the idea of adoption as symbolic reincarnation or resuscitation of the dead and then continued as the mourning function of adoption in the early Calumet ceremony became dissociated from the adoption function, as it must have in the Pawnee Hako.

IROQUOIS CONDOLENCE COUNCILS

When one speaks of 'the Iroquois', one is usually speaking in particular of the several nations of the League of the Iroquois. The Iroquoian family of languages is very extensive, including Seneca, Cayuga, Onondaga, Oneida, Mohawk, Tuscarora, Huron, Petun, Neutral, Erie, Susquehannock, and Cherokee, but only the first five of these comprised the original League or Confederacy. Being related in language and culture did not prevent the Iroquois from waging all-out wars against the Hurons, Eries, and others. The military and political influence of the League Iroquois came from their mutual alliance and the developing of mechanisms to suppress conflict among members.[14] The Tuscarora joined the League in 1722 or 1723, accounting for subsequent references to the Six Nations. The confederacy is believed to have been founded in the era of A.D. 1400–1600 with an original council of fifty chiefs whose names were not allowed to die. The names of the original fifty founding chiefs have been transferred to all chiefs subsequently holding these positions, except for that of Hiawatha, whose name was retired, so to speak.[15]

The organization and affairs of the League were and remain rich in symbolism. The Senecas—the westernmost of the Five Nations—were designated the keepers of the western door of the League, conceived in metaphor as a longhouse of five fires running from east to west across New York. The Mohawks, being the east-ernmost of the Five Nations, were designated the keepers of the eastern door. Each of the five original League tribes was conceived as occupying a compart-ment in this longhouse and to have its own fire, al-though the central fire, representing the Onondagas, was given primacy, making Onondaga the capital of the confederacy and its foremost chief, the chief of the confederacy. The smoke from the Onondaga fire was seen to rise skyward in a pillar that pierced heaven itself. This was a metaphor that was extended to the confederacy as a whole, seen as a mighty white pine rising over Onondaga with great roots stretching out to the four directions.[16]

Another symbol is that of the antlers of office. When a chief is installed into his office, after being nominated by the matriarchs of the clan within which the title descends, he metaphorically acquires the deer antlers that represent his office. When chiefs of the League meet in council or to dance, they are said to be rubbing antlers. When a League chief is close to death, he is dispossessed of his title and metaphorically de-horned, so that no title will go to the grave.[17] When a chief does die, a new chief is 'raised up' to replace him during a Requickening Rite that forms part of a Condo-lence Council. Condolence Councils can only be held in late fall after the crops are in or in the winter season because of the harm to growing crops that might accompany a ceremony associated with death.[18] Burial rites are necessarily performed in any season as needed, but mourning is scheduled.

The Iroquois Requickening Rite is a mourning rite for chiefs involving the transfer of a name to keep it alive in the person of a new chief, but it does not involve adoption. Name transfer, with or without adoption, as a part of mourning, probably has a deep history in Iroquoia that can be approached through practices of neighboring non-League Iroquoians. The idea of 'raising up' a chief can be better understood from the writings of Father Gabriel Sagard, who de-scribed such a rite for the Neutrals of the early seven-teenth century. Once a warrior was chosen to resusci-tate another, Sagard wrote that those participating

> all stand upright, except the one who is to raise the dead; on him they impose the name of the deceased, and all, placing their hands down low, feign to raise him back to life in the person of this other man. The latter stands up, and after loud acclamations from the people he receives the gifts offered by those who were present, who repeat their congratulations at many feasts and thenceforth regard him as if he were the deceased person whom he represents. Thus the memory of good persons, and of worthy and valorous captains, never dies among them.[19]

What Sagard described was the simulation of the actual raising of a deceased warrior from his tomb, which we know from Huron examples was followed by gift giving accompanied by rhetoric phrased with the appropriate metaphors: "May these grasp the arm of the deceased, to draw him from the grave" and "May these support his head, lest he fall back again."[20]

One of the most provocative comments that I have found on the requickening aspect of the Condolence ceremony is that made by the Tuscarora anthropologist J. N. B. Hewitt, to the effect that the Requickening Address details the calamitous effects of death on the health and welfare of the whole "mourning sisterhood of tribes" and that "it [the Requickening Address] counteracts these evils and restores to life the dying people in the person of their newly installed chief."[21] This is an observation or interpretation that coincides beautifully with an idea that I attempt later to develop (chapter 7) to the effect that mound burial in the Midwest once involved a conflation of World Renewal ritual with mourning ritual such that the earth awaiting rebirth in the spring was identified with the person symbolically reincarnating the deceased, who in early times would sometimes have been a chief being mourned.

THE HURON FEAST OF THE DEAD

In the Iroquois Condolence ceremony the assembled chiefs are said at one point to be symbolically carrying the bones of the dead chief on their backs, "as if they brought him back from a distant field, removing him for burial to the cemetery behind the new council house."[22] This conjures up images of the Huron Feast of the Dead, which did literally involve the carrying of the bones of the dead upon the backs of the living for reburial in an ossuary or large common grave. There is another parallel that is less obvious, and it is a particu-lar cry, or lament, or call of *hai hai* that comes into use both in the Huron Feast of the Dead and in the Iro-quois Condolence ceremony. These two ceremonies are too distinctively different for any direct comparison. Ossuary burial does not occur in New York, for exam-ple. But at some time in their pasts the Hurons and New York Iroquois must have shared a common body of beliefs regarding mourning and spirits, and these beliefs are thought to be at the root of the call *hai hai*.

The Requickening Address is but one part of the proceedings of a Condolence Council. It is preceded by a eulogy to the founders of the League, which takes the form of a recitation or roll call of the names of the fifty original chiefs whose names are not allowed to be forgotten. This eulogy is also known as the Hai Hai because of the conspicuous use of that expression in the orations. The word *hai* is sometimes translated as 'hail', but the word has a strong association with the idea of a journey, especially a journey of souls, and may relate to a root word meaning 'to take up a path'. In the case of the Hurons, it is said to be the cry of souls on the march from their burial platforms to an ossuary.[23] In the case of the Iroquois, "the reason for using this particular cry is that it is reputed to be that made by spirits when moving from place to place. But it was believed that should this cry be omitted in the rituals the displeasure of the departed spirits would be manifested in an epidemic disease affecting the spine and head."[24] This compares closely with the Huron notion that if the bearers of bundles of souls (i.e., bones) did not cry *haéé, haé* as they journeyed to the site of an ossuary, they would suffer from backache until the day of their death.[25]

The classic description of a Huron Feast of the Dead is that written by Father Jean de Brébeuf in 1636. Not only is it a detailed description, but it also reveals an appreciation of the metaphorical expression used by the Hurons in talking of the feast, which they referred to only as 'the kettle', so that "in speaking of hastening or of putting off the feast of the Dead, they speak of scattering or of stirring up the fire beneath the kettle; and employing this way of speaking, one who should say 'the kettle is overturned,' would mean that there would be no feast of the Dead."[26]

The Feast of the Dead was an occasion for the reburying of skeletons and even recently interred bodies in a common grave pit. It took place at intervals of eight to twelve years for any one village and was a major event in which other villages were invited to participate. Elisabeth Tooker has inferred that the timing of feasts may have been occasioned by a decision to move the village, eight to twelve years being the interval known to space such moves. Among the Iroquois proper Ghost Dances are known to have been held "to inform the dead whose bones lay in the adjacent cemetery that the band was leaving."[27]

After being disinterred, the bones of the Huron dead were cleaned, placed in bags, wrapped in robes of beaver fur, and carried on the backs of their mourning relatives to the site of the feast, their bearers now and then and as they approached the host village "imitating the cry of souls . . . *haéé haé*."[28] At the host village a large ossuary pit had been prepared about ten feet deep and more than twenty-five feet across, and surrounding it a scaffold or stage nine to ten feet high and about fifty feet wide with poles above to which the bone bundles could be hung. In the early afternoon a crowd of two thousand persons examined the decorated bone bundles and accompanying gifts arrayed on display in the village square or plaza, and then at a signal the mourners climbed the scaffold on ladders and suspended the bundles of 'souls' on the poles awaiting them.

In the late afternoon the bottom and sides of the communal grave pit were lined with forty-eight newly made fur robes, each one made of ten beaver skins. The whole bodies of the recently deceased were placed within the pit at once around three large kettles. The plan was for the bone bundles to be placed within the pit the following morning, as Brébeuf describes the event he witnessed, but during the night or early morning one robe-enclosed bundle on a weak cord broke loose and fell into the robe-lined pit with a noise that is supposed to have awakened the entire community. What I have to imagine hearing in my mind's ear is a bundle falling with a soft, cushioned thud, then one and a second and a third nearby dog startled into barking until every one of their bony companions in the entire village has joined them in a single yapping chorus, and finally the irritated voices of the dogs' masters within their longhouses arousing themselves to learn the reason for the commotion. Brébeuf describes the next scene as "nothing less than a picture of Hell" with all the mourners rushing to the pit to throw their bundles into the pit for fear that there would not be enough room for them all, the whole spectacle illuminated by the flames of fires brought to life for light and resounding with a confusion of voices and cries. The pit was soon filled to within two feet of the top, the robes on the edge folded over the bundles, and earth and other debris packed over the whole.[29]

The Feast of the Dead served to reconfirm friendships and alliances for Indians who believed "that as the bones of their deceased relatives and friends were united in one place, so they would live together in the same unity and harmony."[30] The Huron Feast of the Dead did not survive into the second half of the seventeenth century, however, because of the near-destruction of the Huron nation by the Iroquois in the period 1647–1649. Huronia was abandoned by the Hurons. Nor did Father Brébeuf himself survive. He was tortured and put to death by the Iroquois in 1649. His torture is reported to have included scalding with boiling water in mockery of baptism.[31]

THE ALGONQUIAN FEASTS OF THE DEAD

Although Jacques Cartier had found Iroquoian speakers on the site of the future Montreal in 1535, they had vanished when it was revisited by Champlain in 1603. The entire Algonquian language family takes its name from the Algonquin tribe living in the seventeenth century along the Ottawa River and its tributaries west of Montreal. As French explorers and missionary fathers eventually pushed still farther west, they encountered Iroquoian speakers, such as the Hurons on the eastern shore of the lake of that name, and beyond them only Algonquian speakers—the Ottawas, Nipissings, Saulteaux, and others—until they came to the western end of Lake Superior and the Lake Michigan basin, where Siouan speaking tribes were encountered, such as the Sioux themselves and the Winnebagoes.

The Jesuit *Relation* of 1642 contains an account by Jérome Lalement of a Feast of the Dead on the order of those practiced by the Hurons but hosted by the Nipissings. In today's terms, this was a multicultural celebration, with Nipissings, Hurons, and other nations participating. As in the case of the Huron feast described by Brébeuf, about two thousand persons participated, those from a distance making a grand entrance:

> Those of each Nation, before landing, in order to make their entry more imposing, form their Canoes in line, and wait until others come to meet them. When the People are assembled, the Chief stands up in the middle of his Canoe, and states the object that has brought him hither. Thereupon each one throws away some portion of his goods to be scrambled for. Some articles float on the water, while others sink to the bottom. The young men hasten to the spot. One will seize a mat, wrought as tapestries are in France; another a Beaver skin; others get a hatchet, or a dish, or some Porcelain beads, or other article,—each according to his skill and the good fortune he may have. There is nothing but joy, cries, and public acclamations, to which the Rocks surrounding the great Lake return an Echo that drowns all their voices.[32]

The remaining gifts are put on exhibit and the chief of each visiting nation presents his personal gift to the host nation, "giving to each present some name that seems best suited to it." What followed the presentations was described as nothing less than a "ballet danced by forty persons" to the sound of singing and a drum. This was the first of a three-part performance and amounted to a choreographic dramatization of a war party of the kind called a Discovery Dance that among Algonquian speakers in the upper Great Lakes area frequently figured in funeral ceremonies:

> The dance . . . represented various encounters of enemies in single combat,—one pursuing his foe, hatchet in hand, to give him the deathblow, while at the same time he seems to receive it himself, by losing his advantage; he regains it, and after a great many feints, all performed in time with the music, he finally overcomes his antagonist, and returns victorious. Another, with different movements, fences, javelin in hand; this one is armed with arrows; his enemy provides himself with a buckler that covers him, and strikes a blow at him with a club. They are three different personages, not one of whom is armed like the others; their gestures, their movements, their steps,

their glances,—in a word, everything that can be seen, is different in each one; and yet in so complete accord with one another that it seems as if but one mind governed these irregular movements.[33]

Nearly sixty years ago W. Vernon Kinietz remarked on the resemblance of the Discovery Dance and Calumet Dance, each portraying as it did a war party seeking out, discovering, and attacking an enemy in ballet-like pantomime.[34] This resemblance became one basis for seeking the relationship to mourning for the Calumet Dance that I have pursued in recent years and elaborated on in the present work. The presence of this ritual drama in the Nipissing Feast of the Dead strikes me as a vestige of the Algonquian background upon which elements of the Huron Feast of the Dead may have been superimposed to create an Algonquian Feast of the Dead. The Nipissing feast differed in another important way from the Huron feast, and that was in the presence of a pole-climbing contest:

> A Pole of considerable height had been set in the ground. A Nipissierinien climbed to the top of it, and tied there two prizes,—a Kettle, and the skin of a Deer,—and called upon the young men to display their agility. Although the bark had been stripped from the Pole, and it was quite smooth, he greased it, to make it more difficult to grasp. No sooner had he descended, than several pressed forward to climb it. Some lost courage at the beginning, others at a greater or lesser height; and one, who almost reached the top, suddenly found himself at the bottom.[35]

No one could climb the pole until finally a clever Huron made the top by using a knife to cut notches in the pole, allowing him to attach a rope with which he raised himself by increments until he could claim the prizes. With much hooting and shouting the audience expressed their disapproval, obliging the Hurons as a group to come up with a gift of beads to mitigate the behavior of their tribesman, which was said to have caused the souls of the deceased to weep. After the pole climb there took place what the missionary fathers described as an election of Nipissing chiefs "followed by the Resurrection of those persons of importance who had died since the last feast; which means that in accordance with the custom of the Country, their names were transferred to some of their relatives, so as to perpetuate their memory."[36]

The feast continued with displays of the bone bundles wrapped in beaver robes festooned with belts of beads, feasting, wailing, gift giving, and dancing within a specially constructed cabin "about a hundred paces long." This 1642 account does not make any mention whatever of the final disposition of the bone bundles.

There is no mention of ossuary burial or burial of any kind. This deficiency is made up in a description of an Ottawa Feast of the Dead observed by Antoine de la Mothe Cadillac:

> They erect a hut about one hundred and twenty feet long, with new bark which never has been used before. They set up a maypole at each end and another in the middle, taller than the others. These poles are oiled, greased, and painted; at the top of each is a prize, which belongs to the person who can first reach it and touch it with his hand. They then enter this new hut, in which there are several tiers, and bring the bones of their relatives, in small bags or wrapped very neatly in strips of bark. They set them out then, from one end to the other, and heap gifts upon them of all their finest and best possessions, and generally whatever they have got together in the previous three years. . . .
>
> [After several days and nights of drumming, "howling," and other activities offensive to the ear of Cadillac] they make presents to those who have been invited to the feast of all that belongs to the dead, that is, of all the booty with which the bones were covered. When this has been distributed they go out for the last time and surround the hut, uttering great howls; they fall upon it with heavy blows with sticks and poles, making a desperate clatter, and break all the bark in pieces. When that is done, the women are ready with faggots of fir-branches, and they put a layer of them on the ground from one end to the other of the place where the hut was. At the same time they kill a large number of dogs, which are to them what sheep are to us, and are valued by them more than any other animal, and make a feast of them. But, before eating they set up two great poles and fasten a dog to the top of them, which they sacrifice to the sun and the moon, praying to them to have pity and to take care of the souls of their relations, to light them on their journeys, and to guide them to the dwelling place of their ancestors. . . .
>
> The feast being thus concluded, each takes the bones of his relations; they carry them all in their hands and take them to stony places, hollow, rugged, and unfrequented; they leave them there, and that is the end of the ceremony.[37]

In his own description of the Algonquian Feast of the Dead, Nicolas Perrot indicated that three cornstalks could be substituted for the three poles in the house constructed for the feast. The main idea shared by the Algonquian and Huron Feasts of the Dead would seem to have been the use of rites to honor the dead as a basis for, or as an excuse for, a ceremony to establish, reestablish, or consolidate friendly relationships between villages or between nations. Until its abandonment at the end of the seventeenth century the Feast also served as a means of mobilizing great quantities of beaver robes and other goods of value and providing an opportunity for the exchange of these items as gifts. The Algonquian feast was possibly held annually, but at no single location more than once every six or seven years. Harold Hickerson attributes the abandonment of the Algonquian Feast of the Dead in great part to the loss of native hegemony in the fur trade. Once the French were able to trade directly with the nations of the far interior rather than through the Ottawas and other native middlemen, the need for cooperation among the native peoples west of Montreal was diminished.[38]

THE AZTEC FEASTS OF THE DEAD

Poles figured widely in North American Indian ritual, including mortuary and mourning ritual. One close parallel with the pole climb of the Algonquian Feast of the Dead was the pole climb in the Aztec month known as Xocotlhuetzi or Hueymicailhuitl. The former name translates as Fall of the Xócotl and the second, Feast of the Great Dead or Great Feast of the Dead. Xócotl translates literally as 'fruit' but refers to the pole itself. Preparations for the feast started twenty days earlier, immediately following the feast that concluded the month of Huicailhuitontli, the Feast of the Small Dead or Small Feast of the Dead.[39] At that time a large tree was sought out, chopped down, and brought in with great ceremony, as was the case in the Plains Sun Dance. The pole was erected immediately, stood for twenty days, was lowered with care on the day before the feast of Xocotlhuetzi, which took place on the twentieth or last day of the month Hueymicailhuitl, was raised once more on the feast day itself, and then was sent crashing to the ground at the conclusion of the feast.

The pole was said to have been 150 feet high with a crosspiece thirty feet long tied crosswise near the top. The ends of the few branches and foliage allowed to remain at the top of the pole were gathered together and bound to the crosspiece with a rope. With ropes also attached to the crosspiece and hanging down, the Xócotl thus looked strikingly like the Sun Dance pole of the Teton Dakotas.[40] In one reported example the top of the Xócotl pole was fitted with an effigy made of amaranth seed described by the sixteenth-century Spanish missionary Fray Bernardino de Sahagún as being in the form of a man decorated with strips of white paper, some of which had on them images of a sparrow hawk, but he also described the image as being in the form of a bird. The missionary Fray Diego Durán also described the effigy as being a bird. These differences are compounded by an illustration of the Xócotl pole in the Codex Borbonicus, which clearly shows the image to have been created in the form of a death bundle or mummy bundle.[41]

The ropes on the Xócotl were used by a number of high-born young men in a competitive free-for-all to climb to the top and retrieve pieces of the amaranth dough image or weapons that accompanied it—a spear-thrower and its darts—and throw to the people below pieces of the image. Being first to the top was a great honor and was rewarded with special privileges. In the Plains Sun Dance, of course, the ropes were used to suspend men from wooden skewers inserted into holes in their skin. I feel justified in making these comparisons of the Xócotl pole and Sun Dance pole because of the role I see for mourning in the background of the Sun Dance (chapter 7), quite aside from the role of pole climbing in the Algonquian Feast of the Dead and in mourning ceremonies elsewhere.

A distinctive aspect of the Aztec Great Feast of the Dead was a fire sacrifice during which slaves were hurled into a deep bed of burning coals, retrieved while still alive, and then dispossessed of their beating hearts by priests with stone knives, after which their bodies were thrown at the feet of an idol representing Xiuhtecuhtli, the fire god. By contrast, in the Plains of the eastern United States a man wishing to please a deity would typically humble himself and perhaps make a sacrifice of his own blood or a morsel of his own flesh or even a finger, if the need were pressing. Autosacrifice was abundant in Mesoamerica, frequently involving the drawing of blood from one's tongue or penis, but captors were more generous in spilling their captives' life fluids than their own.

The mourning associations of the Aztec Feasts of the Dead would have to be considered minimal to judge only from contemporary descriptions, but this impression may be deceptive because within two generations of the Conquest these Aztec feast days had been incorporated by local Indians into the Roman Catholic holy days known as All Saints' or All Hallows' Day on November 1 and All Souls' Day on November 2, with departed children being remembered on November 1 and departed adults on November 2. These observances comprise today's *Fiesta de los Muertos*. The remembering of deceased children on November 1 must have been a Mexican innovation because the day was intended by the church to honor martyred saints.[42]

MAGIC, HISTORY, AND SCHEDULED DEATH

There is no indication that Aztec warfare had any motive related to vengeance for personal losses, as in America north of Mexico: Aztec warfare appears to have been controlled as a matter of religious ideology and state policy, i.e., to obtain captives for sacrifice or for service as slaves and to maintain Aztec authority by punishing insubordinate vassal states. In the eastern United States the decision to take the life of a captive or spare it, the decision to submit him to agonizing torture or grant mercy, was sometimes controlled by the recency of the captor's personal misfortunes. Compassion did not well up in the breast of a person who had only recently lost a husband or sister or father or daughter to an enemy. The fate of a prisoner is said to have often been a matter of personal decision for the Iroquois. By contrast, the initial decision to take to the warpath to avenge a death was seldom a purely personal decision. For one thing, any life taken would lead to a response from the enemy that would then lead to the need for further vengeance, and the cycle would never end.

Who, as an individual, had caused a death was irrelevant. A death could be avenged by taking the life of any individual of the offending tribe. This means also that an individual seeking satisfaction from the enemy could put the entire village or tribe at risk, so there was peer pressure to avoid hasty reactions to a death. Any wife, mother, or sister hoeing corn outside the village would forever be at risk of capture or death. Vengeance killing was especially disruptive within a village or tribe, so there was the greatest of pressure to settle such affairs by negotiation. The League of the Iroquois became known to its members as the Great Peace because the original five participating nations extended the same attitude toward the League as a whole. The five nations were conceived to be the equivalents of five families occupying compartments in a longhouse of five fires, and all were encouraged to settle homicides by negotiation and compensation rather than by blood revenge.

The Condolence Councils of the Iroquois became occasions to reinvigorate and basically to reinvent the League by retelling the history of the formation of the League and reciting the roll of its original founding chiefs. The councils were called for the purpose of mourning recently deceased chiefs and installing their successors. These rites may have been practiced long before the creation of the League, because intertribal mourning and the raising of chiefs was also a feature of the Algonquian Feast of the Dead based in great part upon the Huron Feast of the Dead.

The Huron and Algonquian Feasts of the Dead used a shared concern for mourning the dead to establish and maintain intertribal friendships or alliances. The feasts also served to motivate individuals and families into the production of vast quantities of material goods that were either buried with the dead or given away by the host villagers to the point of self-impoverishment. Mourning that would normally have been a matter of private or village concern was elevated to a level of intervillage or intertribal concern to provide a mechanism for intergroup consolidation. It is a thesis of this book that, in like manner, spirit adoption in mourning was long utilized in the midcontinental United States as a mechanism for creating bonds of fictional kinship between the leaders of bands and tribes and, thus, a mechanism for intertribal peace that appeared in history as the Calumet ceremony.

The Algonquian Potomacs of Virginia believed that the spirits of the dead climbed a tall tree to gain access to heaven, the kind of story that provides a logical association between pole climbing and mourning.[43] Climbing contests would have helped the deceased in their task to climb to heaven by the effect of imitative magic. We may also too innocently repeat the explanation that a sacrifice was meant to 'honor' a deity when the sacrifice may have actually been part of a ritual or drama to magically vitalize the present by re-creating the past, or by 'reactualizing' the past, as Jacques Soustelle would say.[44] As will be seen (chapter 11), the Skiri Pawnee sacrifice to Morning Star was a reenactment of an event from the time of creation. It was imitative magic made more effective by putting the primary actors in contact with sacred relics of the deities they represented in the drama. Betty Ann Brown has developed the thesis that "one purpose of Aztec sacrificial ceremonies was to recall, and to symbolically refight, those wars that were important in the history of the formation and growth of the Aztec empire," and that one event in particular was commemorated by sacrifices, ritual combat, and other activities during the Aztec month of Ochpaniztli that followed Xocotlhuetzi.[45]

The relationship of the Discovery Dance in mourning ceremonies in the Midwest to the Calumet Dance is not difficult to recognize, and it is not too difficult to see a relationship of both to the gladiatorial sacrifice of the Aztecs as choreographed performances (chapters 1, 10, 11), but the relationship of the North American and Mesoamerican rites could be attributed to coincidence were it not for the fact that the victims of the Aztec sacrifice also sometimes became the adopted sons of their captors and were mourned as such after their deaths. I must thank Jill Furst for calling my attention to the fact that the practice of warriors fighting in staked and tethered 'no-retreat' situations, as in the gladiatorial sacrifice, extended from Mexico into the northern Plains of the United States, although in the Plains it was voluntary. The ranks of Aztec warriors included some who were obliged to fight without thought of retreat, but in Mexico tethering was for sacrificial victims.[46]

Natural deaths cannot easily be scheduled. Mourning and memorial rites can be and were scheduled in ancient America to fit seasonal rounds of activities and often became the basis for activities serving purposes beyond the remembering and honoring of the dead, such as World Renewal ritual and the reaffirming of alliances. Like mourning ceremonies, the deaths of captives or slaves can also be scheduled to fit seasonal rounds of activities, if this be desired. The deaths of captives in the eastern United States—and the Iroquoians were hardly unique in putting captives to death—served immediate psychological needs in the passion of the moment. The prospects for Aztec captives were no less fateful but were scheduled to serve perceived community needs that obviously were felt to have a higher priority than the mitigation of personal emotional distress. What the Aztecs did was to schedule death itself to serve some needs met in North America by scheduled mourning.

The Feast of the Dead of the Great Lakes Algonquians was, as we have seen, an occasion not only for consolidating intertribal relations but also for symbolically reincarnating deceased tribesmen by transferring their names to others, much as dead founders of the Iroquois League were symbolically reincarnated by transferring their names to their successors during Condolence Councils. Among the Winnebagoes, and presumably more widely in the Great Lakes area and beyond, a person believed to have been reincarnated was said to have 'shed his skin', which is a metaphor obviously drawn from observation of snakes that periodically slough off their old skins and emerge, seemingly reborn, with new skins.[47] When the Mexica Aztecs desired to transfer the name and identity of the earth goddess Toci to the daughter of the king of Culhuacan, they did so not symbolically but by causing her quite literally to shed her skin and then dressing a priest in her flayed skin.

THE MYSTERY OF THE FLAYED CULHUA PRINCESS

A little-understood episode in the history of the Mexicas, the Aztecs that established Tenochtitlan, present-day Mexico City, relates to the death of the daughter of Achitometl, king of Culhuacan. What is agreed upon is that the princess was sacrificed, her body flayed, her father invited to an event during which a priest dressed in the dead girl's skin appeared in front of the outraged king, and that the Mexicas were then driven from the area by the infuriated father and his followers. There is less agreement on the reason for the performance.

The received version is that after a series of adversities the Mexicas found themselves in a wilderness infested with poisonous snakes as the unhappy guests of the ruler of Culhuacan and at his mercy. This ruler granted the Mexicas the privilege of trading and intermarrying with the Culhuas. The Mexicas' war god Huitzilopochtli was supposedly unhappy with the resulting peace and harmony and instructed the Mexicas to ask the king of Culhuacan for his daughter for the service of this god and as their queen, to be called the Woman of Discord. She was also to be known as Toci or Grandmother, a manifestation of the earth goddess, and would be the bride of Huitzilopochtli. This apparently started out with the objective of being a symbolic union of the Mexica and Culhua peoples because just as Huitzilopochtli was the patron deity of the Mexicas, so was Toci the divine patroness of the Culhuas.[48]

If one takes these post-Conquest histories literally, the flaying of the princess was a deliberate attempt by the Mexicas, or some Mexica faction, to infuriate their hosts, the Culhuas, at the instigation of the Mexica war god Huitzilopochtli, the logic being that Huitzilopochtli feared that the Mexicas were becoming too complacent in the Kingdom of Culhua and would soon become disinclined to continue migrating to the location where their destiny was to establish a capital of their own. The incident forms a central role in Susan Gillespie's book *The Aztec Kings: The Construction of Rulership in Mexica History*, wherein she relates the princess's originally proposed temporal role of (a) bringing a legitimacy of rule to the Mexican tribe in the person of a Culhua princess, cum Mexica queen, who was an heir to the heritage of the ancient Toltec kings and who would be accepted by the Mexicas also as the living personification of a goddess, the consort of their war god Huitzilopochtli, and (b) the princess's evolved role of becoming part of a pattern of legitimizing by mythologizing the backgrounds of future Mexica royal families.[49]

I find it easy to believe that the god Huitzilopochtli's supposed wishes, undoubtedly expressed through his priests, could actually have been the wishes of a political faction, which led to an action justified by being attributed to Huitzilopochtli himself. For a later stage of their migrations, history is more explicit in stating that there was a faction that wanted to remain where the

Mexica later came to be, at Coatepec, rather than continue their migrations.[50] I also find it possible to believe that the Mexicas could have been following a line of protocol familiar to the Culhuas but turned into a macabre parody of the form.

After the Culhua princess was flayed her skin was worn by a priest in the manner of persons representing the Mesoamerican god Xipe Totec, Flayed Lord, who in that guise is believed to have represented the earth reincarnated, its skin shed, as it were (chapter 19). Far to the north, beyond the Mesoamerican frontier, beyond the semi-arid Chichimeca, within the river valleys of the North American plains and prairies, the Osage, Pawnee, Omaha, and other farming villagers also celebrated the reincarnation of the earth personified, but within the context of the Calumet ceremony, peacefully and without bloodshed. The child honored in the Pawnee Hako and related Calumet ceremonies was symbolically reconceived, physically reclothed, socially redefined, and made a new link in a chain of simulated kinship connecting two otherwise unrelated bands or villages. When danced the Calumet of the Captain in their honor (chapter 10), strangers were not only symbolically reborn but figuratively reclothed with mantles of honorary leadership, reprising in their persons roles earlier filled by members of a cast of honored dead.

Viewed against the background of eastern North American ceremonialism, many Mesoamerican rituals have the look of sanguinary transformations, for whatever reasons, of practices originally meant to be figurative. The circumstances that might allow a priestly elite to transform metaphor into fatal reality on a grand societal scale pose problems to ponder.[51]

6 / Mourning and Adoption

WILLIAM JONES was born in 1871 on the Sac and Fox Reservation in Oklahoma to an English mother and a father who was half-Fox and half-white. William Jones's mother died when he was only a year old, and he spent the next eight years living with his Fox grandmother. In 1889 he went to Hampton Institute in Virginia and from there to school in Andover, Massachusetts, and then to Harvard University. At Harvard he was introduced to anthropology by Frederick Ward Putnam. Jones graduated from Harvard in 1900 and went on to receive a Ph.D. in anthropology from Columbia University. Being fluent in Fox, or Mesquakie, as a native speaker, Jones specialized in fieldwork among Central Algonquian speaking Indians and produced classic papers and monographs on the Sac and Fox, Kickapoo, and Ojibwa.[1]

MESQUAKIE AND OSAGE SOUL RELEASE CEREMONIES

In 1906 William Jones joined the staff of what was then known as the Field Columbian Museum of Chicago, today's Field Museum. The same year, at the Fifteenth International Congress of Americanists held in Quebec, Canada, "le Docteur" William Jones presented a paper titled "Mortuary Observances and the Adoption Rites of the Algonkin Foxes of Iowa." The content of this paper is relevant well beyond the tribe whose beliefs were being described:

> After the fourth day [following death] the soul is said to return to the spirit world where it wanders about restless and without contentment. Frequent are its journeys back to this world, where it often stays for long periods of time. It abides by the burial place during the light of day, but at night it passes among the living. It is freed from this uncertain state of existence if the ceremony of *adoption* is held within four years; but if not till after that period, then the soul becomes an owl to wander forever in sadness.

Thus the practice of the *adoption* rests in the belief that the soul will be denied a life of happy existence in

the spirit world unless its mortal remains have received full funeral rites within a period of four years; therefore its special object is to *liberate the soul* and send it on its joyful way to the spirit world. And the prominent feature of the ceremony is that the family of the bereaved adopts an individual to take the place left vacant by death. If the dead man had been a son, then the adopted one is a son; in like manner run other relationships. There are two requirements lived up to in making the adoptions: one is that the adopted shall be of the same sex as the dead; and the other is that both must have been companions in life. A boon companion always takes precedence. Hence it is that a child is adopted for a child, a girl for a girl, a boy for a boy, a maiden for a maiden, a youth for a youth, and so on with the older people.[2]

The Fox adoption rite was known by a name literally translated as "throwing away the dead," but which Jones glosses as "setting free the dead." In other words, the Fox adoption ritual was a ceremony of soul release. There was feasting and gift giving, and games were played that were the favorites of the deceased. The adoptee was reclothed in a new costume, as was also the case of the person whose body hosted a returned soul in the Menominee Ghost Lodge ceremony (chapter 8). When the adoptee departed the feast the soul was believed also to start its final journey to the afterworld, and it was "common for the sponsor to lead the pony ridden by the adopted for some distance toward the west as a symbol that the soul is accompanied on its journey homeward."[3]

Mary Alicia Owen translated into a narrative form the beginning of the ghost journey of a Mesquakie man observed toward the end of the nineteenth century. The deceased was named No-chu-ning, and the person adopted to replace him in the family's emotions was given his name. He was the 'ghost-carrier':

> When the chief saw that the sun was almost out of sight, he climbed down from his place opposite the

father, and in a loud voice commanded the ghost-carrier to go to the Happy Hunting Ground, and in a lower tone reminded him that the light necessary for the journey would soon fail.

At once the ghost-carrier dropped to the ground and stalked to a group of young men, who, mounted on their best ponies, awaited him with a fine steed saddled with a new saddle, its mane and tail ornamented with beads and ribbons, its face painted, its sides concealed under bundles made up of all No-chu-ning's personal property not buried with him. Before he could mount, all the mourners ran to him, clung to him calling him by his new name, "No-chu-ning," and entreated him not to leave them. He stood rigid and silent, while the friends, softly chanting the virtues of No-chu-ning and his fitness to enjoy the delights of the Happy Hunting Ground, loosened their hands and led them away.

The moment he was free, the ghost-carrier sprang on his horse and galloped toward the west, followed by the mounted young men.

I was told that the ghost rode with the ghost-carrier who had taken his name. . . . When the ghost-carrier had ridden a few miles, he made a detour and returned with his escort to the place from whence he started, taking care to arrive after nightfall. He was welcomed by the clan-chief and the mourners as one returned from a long journey. Everyone called him "No-chu-ning" instead of "Pa-che-quas," the name by which he had formerly been known. After he returned the greetings, he divided the bundles he had carried among the young men who rode with him; but the horse he reserved for himself. . . .

No-chu-ning's father and mother went back to their own wigwam, where in a few days, the new No-chu-ning, the ghost-carrier, visited them, bringing them presents of meal and meat and announcing at the door that he was No-chu-ning, their son, who would care for their old age. He went home to his own parents after a short call, but both the adopted parents who called him No-chu-ning, and his parents of the blood who continued to call him Pa-che-quas, felt that he was pledged to a son's duty to the adopted ones, should they ever need his services.[4]

The most poignant moment in Owen's account comes when, before his death, No-chu-ning's mother pleaded with him to sing his death song in the traditional farewell of a doomed Mesquakie. Now fast dying of tuberculosis, No-chu-ning shook his head "no." As Owen explained, "No one raises the death-song now. When a man died in battle or succumbed to his wounds after, as No-chu-ning's grandfather did, strength somehow came in the last hour to boast of deeds of prowess and defy the foe; but why should the failing breath be wasted to tell of a few horse-races won, or quickened

to defy the tribe's relentless enemy, consumption?"[5]

The form of the mourning ritual prescribed for a warrior was called the Crow Dance, according to Jones. This designation had nothing to do with the Crow Indians as a tribe. The crow was a sometime scavenger that picked the bones of dead warriors after a battle. When the Mesquakie individual being mourned was one killed in battle, the mourning observances involved more than what was sufficient for an old soldier succumbing to the infirmities of age. The man adopted to requicken the deceased was obliged to vow to avenge the death. He painted his face red on one side to signify 'war' and black on the other to signify 'fasting'. Dressed as a warrior he climbed to the roof of a bark-covered summer lodge and standing there sang a song to each of the four directions. "On coming down from the roof, the man makes straight for home, and as he starts the soul of the dead is said to begin gladly its journey westward, gladly because of the assurance that the mortal remains will be avenged."[6]

The mourner waited until winter to begin his actual fasting and then continued his fasting and vigil until he had the necessary dream to assure that he would be successful when setting out on the war trail to seek an enemy to kill. The last time that adoption was used for this purpose is said to have been in Kansas around 1854. This was to avenge the death of a Fox at the hands of the Osages.

The Osages themselves, of course, required that a death be avenged by a death, so that there was no real end to the chain of deaths, each death requiring another in return. As Frank Speck explains, for the Osage, "The belief is that the human soul after death remains in a sort of sleep until some one of the people on earth discharges the obligation imposed upon him by invoking the supernatural powers for aid and going off at the head of a band of warriors to kill an enemy and secure his scalp as a payment offering. When the ceremony has been completed and the payment offered, it is believed that the dormant soul is ransomed, as it were, and allowed to enter the realm of spirits."[7]

A member of the family of the slain Osage appointed a male relative as the mourner. The mourner fasted and then participated in a ceremony conducted in a special lodge covered with brush and containing a center pole, for which reason this War Dance, as he called it, has sometimes also been called a Sun Dance. The ceremony concluded when the mourner, although weakened from his fasting, led a successful war party and was able to hold aloft the scalp of an enemy, sing a victory song, and address the shadow of the warrior for whose benefit he underwent this ordeal. The last time such a ceremony was conducted in its full form was May of 1873. At that time the scalp of a Wichita chief was taken in Oklahoma. After this event the Osages came to realize that the world to which this ceremony belonged no longer existed.[8]

WILLIAM JONES'S DEATH IN THE PHILIPPINES

As a staff member of the Field Museum, William Jones did some collecting among the Fox Indians of Tama, Iowa, but his major assignment came to be field research among the Ilongot[9] people of northern Luzon in the Philippine Islands. There he found that vengeance killing was still an active pursuit. The idea of a death for a death was not simply a memory of times past. In his field notes for September 5, 1908, Jones gave the hypothetical example of a person from the district of Tamsi with the desire of avenging a death: "When a person leaves Tamsi [for instance] to pay back the score [of an earlier killing] it is likely to be a long time after the killing, at a time when the memory of it begins to wane in the other district. The point is to take a man off his guard. His bolo is asked for to look at, or to cut something with; one is asked to sit and chew the betel nut that is offered. Then in an opportune moment the person is cut down."[10]

Little did Jones know that he would himself become the victim of such a deception on the last day of his field work among the Ilongots, as he was preparing to leave. His interpreter describes the event: "Then the Doctor told the other Ilongotes to take the balsa [raft] and leave, and then it was when Palidat came near the Doctor as though to tell him good-bye, and promising to bring the other balsas the following day, and all at once he drew his bolo and hit the Doctor in the head with it and the other Ilongotes arose and took their bolos from their sheaths and began to attack the Doctor."[11]

Jones was slashed on the head and both arms and speared in the abdomen by four Ilongots. Jones and his interpreter responded with Jones's pistol, but Jones was fatally wounded and he died shortly afterward. That was March 29, 1909. One of the four assailants was shot and killed by Jones's interpreter with Jones's gun. The other three freely admitted their responsibility to the investigating officials and were probably surprised when the government was unwilling to accept two pigs and three bolo knives in compensation for Jones's death. Rather, they were tried May 27, 1909, before Judge Isidro Paredes for the crime of *asesinato* and condemned to death. A year later, however, March 22, 1910, the *Manila Times* carried the headlines "Ilongots Saved from Noose by Court. Death Penalty for Slaying of Scientist is Commuted." The Supreme Court had reduced the punishment to seventeen years in prison and a fine of one thousand pesos each to Jones's heirs, holding "as an extenuating circumstance, the fact that the defendants were members of a wild tribe, ignorant of the law and

civilization, and as such not criminally responsible, in the same degree as would be persons of a higher order of intelligence."

Some years ago I participated in a symposium on ancient human skeletal remains held in Des Moines, Iowa. The Native American and anthropological communities were both well represented. When the time came for a summing up of the symposium and the preparation of a statement of consensus, one of the Indian representatives began by saying—and I am paraphrasing—"Perhaps we can begin by agreeing on a statement about the soul. Are we agreed on the existence of the soul?" There was an awkward moment of silence. 'Soul' is not something many anthropologists recognize the reality of in the usual religious sense of the word. This does not mean that there is *no* basis for consensus on the idea of 'soul' between anthropologists and American Indians, but there was none agreed upon at the time.

The Indian concept of 'soul' encompasses a range of ideas that in English are represented by quite separate ideas—'shadow', 'breath', and 'name' among them. On a wall of the Field Museum a plaque cast in bronze helps to keep William Jones's name alive (figure 6.1). Human lives seldom exceed a century in length, but a name can live for many centuries, and many persons of stature cast shadows that will reach far beyond their own generations. Persons are truly lost to death only when their very existence has been forgotten and their words in life can no longer be heard. Jones's description of the Fox soul release and spirit adoption ceremony was one of the early and classic descriptions of ceremonies of that kind. Jones was murdered, but his words remain and still have the power to inform the research of his successors. Just as in Indian belief the spirit of the deceased may briefly occupy the body of the person adopted to symbolically reincarnate him and take his name, the spirit of William Jones can survive in the persons of those who keep his words alive.

MOURNING IN THE BACKGROUND OF THE SUN DANCE

The tribe called the Cheyenne today actually has in its background a merger or blending of two distinct peoples related in that they both spoke languages of the Algonquian family. The original Cheyennes were those who called themselves Tsistsistas and were living in southern Minnesota during the seventeenth century. Moving westward into the Plains the Tsistsistas encountered the Suhtais, who then lived in eastern South Dakota. The Suhtais had an important ceremony called the Oxheheom or Lodge of the Creator, which was a ceremony of new life or of world renewal.

The Oxheheom is the ceremony that George Grinnell called the Cheyenne Medicine Lodge and George

Dorsey, the Cheyenne Sun Dance. In the physical appearance of their altar areas, the Cheyenne and Arapaho Sun Dances resemble each other most closely, and it was the Cheyenne and Arapaho Sun Dances that Leslie Spier saw as the original nucleus of the Sun Dance in his 1921 comparative study of these Plains rituals.[12] The Cheyennes and Arapahoes are both Algonquian-speaking tribes. Of the two the Arapahoes appear to have had a longer residence in the Plains.

In comparing elements of the various Sun Dance rituals Spier noted a parallel between the altar of the Arapahoes and a particular area of the Hidatsa Sun Dance, if we may call it that—the NaxpikE or Hide Beating ceremony. A certain pair of round sods used in the Arapaho ceremony, with twigs of rabbit bush stuck in them, corresponded in concept, although not especially closely in actual appearance, to two small hills of earth that figured in the Hidatsa ceremony, which also were stuck with sprigs of vegetation. These small mounds were erected for the ceremony on either side of an area that represented the grave meant for Spring Boy after his torture by a sky chief called Long Arm. Spring Boy was rescued, but the element of the grave was sufficiently important to be retained in the ceremony, which was acquired from Long Arm by Spring Boy and Lodge Boy.[13] In neither the Arapaho nor the Cheyenne Sun Dance is there any explicit symbolism of a grave pit. In both there are pits in the earth, but they do not explicitly represent graves, and in both there are cut sods, but they primarily represent the mud retrieved from beneath the sea by the mythical Earth Divers at the time of creation (chapter 3).

The Hidatsas are closely related by language to the Crow tribe, with whom they shared a common history at some time five or more centuries before the opening of history on the northern Plains.[14] The Hidatsas and Crows are Siouan speakers. The Crows share myths of Long Arm, but these myths are not known to figure in the Crow Sun Dance in any way. I am speaking of the original Crow Sun Dance, which is no longer practiced; that performed in recent years was acquired from the Shoshonis.[15] The old Crow Sun Dance was a mourning rite to assist a warrior in obtaining a vision of the death of an enemy to avenge the death of a Crow, much like the Osage War Dance just described.

The Hidatsa Hide Beating ceremony could only be pledged by the owners of certain sacred bundles, and it could be undertaken only by men who were acquiring their father's bundle. Only Hide Beating ceremony bundle owners could obtain visions from the sun. A man who wished to perform the ceremony would say, "I want to raise your house, Sun. I want you to help me to conquer the enemy and let me have plenty of food and get along well." In both the Hidatsa and original Crow Sun Dances, then, the objective was to acquire a vision or the power to obtain a vision, but the Crow vision did not provide a blessing from the sun; it was a vision to guarantee the death of an enemy and assure vengeance for the death of a Crow. The Crow warrior pledging to conduct the ceremony and pledging to obtain the vision was in effect the chief mourner. He never proceeded, however, without the guidance of a tutor or ritual sponsor who possessed a medicine-doll bundle believed to have special powers to assist the efforts of the pledger, who was called the Whistler in the parlance of the ceremony. The doll bundle owner who accepted the appeal of the Whistler became the Whistler's 'father' and the Whistler, his 'son'.[16]

The so-called Sun Dances of the Plains tribes were typically, and are still performed, in a temporary circular enclosure with a central pole. The old Crow Sun Dance was different in that it was performed in a structure with a conical, tipi-like frame made of twenty sturdy pine poles. There was no center pole. The participants undergoing self-torture were suspended instead from the outer poles. The lodge was said to resemble the Tobacco Society adoption lodge except for being larger, the adoption lodge having only ten poles. The right to plant and cultivate the tobacco species sacred among the Crows (*Nicotiana multivalvis*) could be obtained only by being adopted by a member of the Tobacco Society. The relationship of the adopter and the adopted was spoken of as that of parent and child, and membership was not limited to men.[17]

The Whistler, who was the pledger and mourner in the Crow Sun Dance, was treated as though he were an inanimate object and through most of the ceremony behaved as such—as though he were himself dead! There was no reported, explicit Crow explanation for this behavior, but it does make sense in the broader comparative context of mourning ritual, which the old Crow ceremony, after all, was an example of. In the traditional mourning ritual of the Fox or Mesquakie tribe of the upper Midwest, for instance, the man selected as chief mourner sought a vision to guarantee success in a raid to avenge the death of a friend or

> In Remembrance of
> ## WILLIAM JONES PH.D.
> Ethnologist
> Who Was Assassinated March 29, 1909
> While Making Ethnological Investigations
> For Field Museum
> Among the Ilongot of the Philippine Islands

Figure 6.1 Text of a plaque in the Field Museum, Chicago, Illinois, commemorating the death of William Jones.

relative slain in battle, much as among the Crows, but the Mesquakie mourner was himself adopted to symbolically replace—and so in a sense to symbolically reincarnate—that slain warrior![18] I have long suspected that the mourner or Whistler in the Crow Sun Dance represented, or at one time in the distant past represented, the Crow slain in battle for whom the Whistler as pledger-mourner was seeking a vision of vengeance. The details of the Crow ritual support this idea very well.

The Whistler was painted from head to foot with white clay by his ritual father and a white-painted plume tied to the top of the Whistler's head. White clay was used at one time in mourning ritual for a large block of tribes in the central and northern Plains, among them the Mandan, Atsina, Blackfoot, Eastern Dakota, Western Dakota, Assiniboine, Omaha, Ponca, Kansa, and the Crow—all of these being speakers of Siouan languages except the Atsina and Blackfoot. William MacLeod has said that in the Plains "the use of white [paint in mourning] appears to belong to a level of culture earlier than the use of black, and to be receding before the use of black."[19]

White clay was also used to paint the entire body of the pledger—the Spring Boy impersonator—in the Hidatsa Sun Dance. This painting was done in the area that symbolized Spring Boy's grave in the Hidatsa Sun Dance. Once the Hidatsa pledger was painted white, a design was painted on his face in black which was the same motif as that painted in blue on the face of the person adopted in the Plains Calumet ceremony. The Hidatsa motif combined a black arc painted across the forehead, extending down to each cheek, with black paint on the nose. The Hidatsas called this arc a 'new moon'. The Texas Hasinai painted a black arc on the face of Martín de Alarcón in 1718 when they honored him with a Calumet ceremony to make him their honorary chief, and the Pawnees painted the arc blue and related it to the vault of heaven, the line down the nose representing the path of the breath of life descending to the nose of the adoptee, who was thus conceived anew.[20]

When the Whistler was dressed he remained passive and did not even touch the garments; all was done by the hands of others. A bed was made for the Whistler in the Whistler's own lodge such that he was lying on his back, arms downs, palms up, with his feet toward the hearth and his head toward the place of honor. A buffalo skull was placed behind the Whistler's head facing the entrance, as would the Whistler if he were to sit up. The ritual father positioned the son's body and limbs as though the son could not do it for himself and then covered him with a robe. The son was required to sleep on his back through the entire night as positioned by his father, and as though dead, I will add. In other words, the location of the inanimate son and his bed in

relation to the buffalo skull and the lodge was the same as that of the oblong rectangular pits in front of the buffalo skulls in the altar arrangement of the Cheyenne and Arapaho Sun Dance lodges. The pledger (Spring Boy impersonator) in the Hidatsa Hide Beating ceremony was similarly painted and dressed by another (the Long Arm impersonator).[21]

The floor of the Arapaho altar trench was painted black on one half and red on the other. On the floor of the trench sagebrush branches were laid on which the Lodge-Maker stood and danced during the ceremony. On the long north and south sides of the trench short sections of cottonwood poles were placed and referred to by the same name (nahuatech) given to the poles used to define the positions of the sleeping mats in the lodges. Implicitly, this combination gave the trench itself something of the character of a bed, and the trench did, of course, occupy the same relationship to the buffalo skull as the bed of the Whistler in the Crow Sun Dance, who slept on his back, slept with his arms at his sides—slept as one sleeps who sleeps the sleep of death.

The ritual of the preparation lodge was continued through four days, during which time the Whistler fasted and after which the Sun Dance enclosure was constructed. On the last night of the Whistler's preparation a cedar tree was planted behind the buffalo skull and to it was tied a wooden hoop with the Doll attached to its center. A second buffalo skull was placed next to the first. The hanging of the hoop on the cedar recalls the hanging of the sacred hoop by the buffalo skull on the altar of the Arapaho Sun Dance.

When the Crow Sun Dance lodge was completed, a new bed was prepared for the Whistler in the rear and white clay added to the area of the bed "in the form of a little ridge."[22] No better description of the "little ridge" is given, although Martha Beckwith says that in the Hidatsa Sun Dance after the enclosure was erected the builders "gather up the earth into a ridge on the north side and stick bog bush into it, beginning at each end and leaving a place vacant between. They used to leave this space so that when the boy died his body could be laid there. Today that is where they lay the sacred weasles [sic] or other animals used in the ceremony." She also says that the Spring Boy impersonator slept at night using the ridge of earth as a pillow. In the origin myth of the Hidatsa Sun Dance it was said that at the conclusion of Spring Boy's ordeal on the tree of sacrifice his body would be placed "on the ridge."[23]

At the height of the public performance of the Crow Sun Dance twenty or more white-painted men might be suspended from thongs in their flesh, but this ordeal was spared the Whistler. The Whistler's great moment came when he was slowly raised to his feet by his ritual father, repainted, replumed, and an eagle bone whistle placed in his mouth. The Whistler now became a whistler in fact, hardly moving at first, then raising his heels and picking up the pace, dancing progressively faster and faster until he was blowing his whistle with every step from his panting alone and the vigor of his actions. Soon songs of jubilation were sung and gifts distributed. All the while the Whistler continued dancing until so completely exhausted from the exercise and lack of food and water that he eventually lapsed into unconsciousness and was taken to his bed, there to receive the revelation he sought of an enemy killed and so to guarantee success in avenging the slain Crow for whose benefit the Sun Dance was being performed.

The origin of the Menominee and Potawatomi Medicine Lodges was tied closely to the death of the Great Hare's wolf companion at the hands of certain supernatural powers. The Great Hare was taught the medicine ceremony by his companion's slayers in compensation. The origin of the Hidatsa Sun Dance was tied to the planned death of Lodge Boy's maverick brother Spring Boy at the hands of a certain supernatural. The grave was already prepared when Spring Boy was rescued, and the two were taught the Sun Dance by the would-be slayer. These related elements of plot are thus shared by the Medicine Lodges of the Algonquian-speaking Menominees and Potawatomis with the Sun Dance of the Siouan-speaking Hidatsas.[24]

The seeking of a vision was a common element in the Sun Dance, related to mourning and to the seeking of supernatural blessings. Varying in intensity from tribe to tribe, self-sacrifice was a common element, but blood offerings were used both in humbling oneself before the sun when seeking his blessing and in expressing grief upon a death.

Adoption was a means by which mortal Indians could legitimize the transfer of knowledge or aid to their adoptive 'sons'. Adoption was a means by which the sun or other supernatural powers were believed to bestow the favor of their spirit guardianship upon those who sought it in a vision quest. Adoption was a means by which the psychological trauma of a death might be softened in its impact. Adoption was the means by which the avenger of a slain warrior might be formally installed. If I am correct in believing that the Whistler, as mourner and chief avenger in the old Crow Sun Dance, also represented the deceased himself, as in the Fox Crow Dance, then the Sun Dance moves a step closer to explanation and should aid our understanding of Calumet ceremonialism and adoption in the context of mourning.

7 / Calumet Ceremonialism and the Honored Child

ALICE FLETCHER'S career goals in 1881 did not include becoming an ethnologist. She was forty-three years old, unmarried, and supporting herself by giving public lectures to women's groups on popular topics ranging from highlights of travel in Europe to the mysteries of the ancient mounds in the Ohio valley. Finding that her lectures on ancient America were especially well received, she began acquiring information to expand her offerings in that direction and considered the possibility of living among some Indian group for what the experience could offer. Two years earlier she had met the Ponca chief Standing Bear and his interpreter Susette La Flesche, a young Omaha Indian woman who was accompanied east by her brother Francis and future husband Thomas H. Tibbles. Meeting Susette La Flesche and Tibbles again in 1881, she told them of her plans and later in the year was invited by the couple, now married, to join them in Omaha, after which they would accompany her into Dakota Territory where she could then proceed on her own and begin her firsthand acquaintance with Indian life as untainted by white influence as it was then possible to observe in the area.[1]

From Omaha, Nebraska, the party first traveled by wagon eighty miles north to the Omaha Reservation and Susette's family. The Omahas were not Indians living in anything like their aboriginal condition. The buffalo was now gone. The Omahas had always been farmers as well as hunters, but plow cultivation was now starting to replace hoe gardening. The Omahas had always lived in settled communities, but frame houses were now starting to replace skin tipis and earthlodges. Another three hundred miles by wagon took the party to their destination, the Rosebud Agency on the Great Sioux Reservation in present-day South Dakota.

At Rosebud Fletcher experienced what must be called 'culture shock' when attending a dance and feast in her honor. It was one thing to meet Indians on a one-to-one basis in a familiar setting, but she was distressed to have all of her senses suddenly and unexpectedly assaulted by the unfamiliar voices and gestures of a host of scantily clad Indians stomping to the beat of a drum in the close confines of a tent. Her immediate reaction was one of "intense fright" fed by a flashing recollection of every account of Indian attrocities she had ever heard. Culture shock can be disabling, but Fletcher soon recovered with the thought that this was, after all, what she had come west to experience, generally at least. Alice Fletcher had traveled west with the more specific objective of studying women in American Indian society. She was a founding member and, for several years, secretary of the Association for the Advancement of Women. The episode at Rosebud, disorienting as it was, sparked in her a special attraction to Indian music and ceremonies.[2]

From Rosebud Fletcher traveled to Fort Randall on the Missouri, where she met and talked with Sitting Bull, then to the Yankton Agency farther downstream, then on to the Santee Agency, and back to the Omaha Reservation. There she was well received, as before, as someone who not only wanted to learn about their traditional way of life but who also wanted to help the Omahas adjust to their current conditions. The Omahas had recently discovered that allotments of land they had been apportioned by the Bureau of Indian Affairs within their reservation did not in fact give the receivers title to that land because the distribution had not been approved by Congress. Their close relatives the Poncas had only four years earlier been evicted from their Nebraska Reservation and obliged to relocate to Indian Territory in present-day Oklahoma.

Fletcher reacted to the concerns of the Omahas by assisting them in compiling information for a petition to the United States Senate requesting clear land title for the assignees of the allotments. The petition told of each Omaha family's needs and the improvements each had made on the land to date, by way of documenting the community's advance toward goals that the Senate might endorse. Fletcher was able to mail the signed petition to Washington on December 31, 1881, little more than three months after her first reception by the Omahas.[3] She afterward spent three months lobbying for a favorable decision in Washington, where she successfully arranged for an amendment to a bill then in Congress for sale of part of the Omaha Reservation to whites. As amended and finally passed on August 7, 1882, the act "declared that each Omaha man, woman, and child was to be given a portion of the tribal land, secured to him or her by a patent held in trust by the federal government for twenty-five years during which time the land could not be encumbered or sold."[4] The following April Alice Fletcher was appointed to be the agent responsible for putting the provisions of the act into effect and would arrive with Susette La Flesche's brother Francis as her interpreter.

> The Omahas, overjoyed, awaited her arrival with eagerness. "When will they come? . . . Soon?" they kept asking. . . . Some of the older members of the tribe met in council. How could they best express their gratitude to this white woman who had labored for their cause with such success? They decided to pay her one of their highest tribal honors, perform for her the ancient calumet, or adoption ceremony, breaking their traditions by giving it informally.
>
> She came on May 12. The people were called to assemble, and many came together in a big earth lodge. The calumets, sacred pipes decorated with duck heads, were set up in their appointed places. When Miss Fletcher entered as the honored guest, the people fell silent. Three men rose and picked up the calumets and the lynx skin on which they rested; then, standing side by side, they sang softly the opening song, after which, turning to face the people, they moved from right to left, singing a joyful song and waving the sacred pipes over the heads of all in the assembled circle.
>
> "Song after song they sang for their friend," Frank reported long afterward, "of the joy and happiness that would follow when men learned to live together in peace. When the evening was over they told Miss Fletcher that she was free to study this or any other of their tribal rites."[5]

Alice Fletcher's and Francis La Flesche's collaboration did not stop with the Omaha allotment program. In time each became an ethnologist working for the Bureau of American Ethnology of the Smithsonian Institution, but their joint work among the Omahas climaxed with the publication of a full-scale, 672-page ethnography entitled *The Omaha Tribe*, which accompanied the Twenty-seventh Annual Report of the Bureau of American Ethnology in 1911. When they began working together Fletcher (1838–1923) was almost twice as old as La Flesche (1857–1932), but a kinship of spirits developed through their work on the reservation for which they sought some formality. The relationship agreed upon was that of mother and son. Adoption of adults was an established institution in Indian culture.

Many are the anthropologists whose entrée into an Indian community was facilitated by their adoption by some elder, but this was an adoption in the reverse direction. The white woman took the Indian man as her son and provided for him in her will as such. Francis balked at a formal, legal adoption because it would have meant changing his name.[6] Actually, the names were quite close to start with—Fletcher or 'arrowmaker' and La Flesche or *la flèche* 'the arrow'.

THE OMAHA WA'WA^N

What Alice Fletcher lacked in formal training in ethnology she made up in the prompt and conscientious reporting of her observations. She was honored by the Wa'wa^n or Omaha Calumet ceremony in 1883 and published a detailed description of the ceremony in 1884. Taking a step on the route to becoming an ethnologist in his own right, Francis La Flesche published his own description in 1885.[7] Together, Fletcher and La Flesche included an extended description of the Wa'wa^n with their 1911 ethnography.

What one cannot learn from this ethnography, however, is that someone else, James O. Dorsey, also published a description of the Wa'wa^n in 1884, using many of the same sources, including Francis La Flesche's father Joseph and Joseph's brother Frank. Fletcher and La Flesche do not even mention Dorsey's work among the Omaha in their ethnography, using the excuse, as Francis subsequently wrote, that Dorsey's monograph contained errors that they did not want to mention and criticize as such when he was not available to defend himself, Dorsey having died in 1895.[8] The Rev. James O. Dorsey had begun his professional life in Dakota Territory as a missionary to the Poncas, whose language he learned while living with them from 1871 to 1873. Dorsey began a second career in 1878 as an ethnologist for the Smithsonian Institution with an assignment to collect linguistic texts and other materials of ethnographic interest among the Omaha, whose language was very nearly identical to Ponca. He remained on the reservation for two years and acquired the information that appeared in his *Omaha Sociology*. One must draw upon Dorsey's, La Flesche's, Fletcher's, and Fletcher and La Flesche's accounts of the Omaha Wa'wa^n to obtain a full description of the ceremony, or as full as will ever be known for that tribe.[9]

Dorsey's and Fletcher and La Flesche's accounts of the Wa'wa^n are in fair agreement, but they do differ in one unexplainable and puzzling way. By the time Fletcher and La Flesche published their ethnography of the Omahas with its description of the Wa'wa^n, for instance, they were already quite aware of the important role of the ear of Mother Corn in the Hako, the Calumet ceremony of the Pawnees, but they also had to be aware that a generation earlier Dorsey had illustrated and described in detail the use of an ear of Mother Corn in the Omaha rite, yet they explicitly declared that the ear of corn was absent and had no place in the Omaha ceremony.[10] Alice Fletcher, most of all, owed some explanation to her readers because in describing the Omaha Wa'wan in 1884 she *herself* had not only described but illustrated and commented upon the corn ear, giving its name as Wa-ha-ba, "ear of corn, white, without blemish and very full, and called the mother. A green band is painted around the middle from which four stripes extend to the top of the ear. The ear of corn thus decorated, like the gourd and bladder pouch, is tied around the middle by a buckskin thong to a stick about a foot and a half long and painted red. . . . The figure drawn upon the tobacco pouch, the two gourds, and ear of corn, is the cross, indicating the four corners [of the earth]."[11]

The Wa'wan was basically a rite of adoption used to establish a bond of kinship between two respected individuals of different clans and usually of different villages or tribes. Although the adoption was between individuals, the selection of the person to be honored was a community decision and the ceremony required support from the community and extended family in the form of gifts to be accumulated for the event. The ceremony served to create friendly alliances between otherwise unrelated villages and bands but also provided a mechanism for exchange of economic goods because horses, blankets, and other items were exchanged in great number. A man could refuse the honor without losing face only if he was in mourning or if he could not assemble the twelve or more horses required as return gifts. This form of adoption between communities contrasted with that within a community that was associated mainly with mourning. Dorsey says that this form of Omaha adoption was called "'ciégidĕ' *to take a person instead of one's own child*," saying, "This is done when the adopted person resembles the deceased child, grandchild, nephew, or niece, in one or more features. It takes place without any ceremony."

The man receiving the honor in the Wa'wan was referred to as the Son and his party, the Sons. The man doing the adopting and leading the visiting party was called the Father and his party, the Fathers. This practice leaves some confusion in the matter of who it was that was actually being adopted because it is also obvious that a child who figured in the ceremony—the son or daughter of the Son—was itself also regarded as the adoptee. Dorsey states, on the one hand, that the man who does the adopting is called "'wáwan aká,' the dancer of the calumet dance, which is also the title of those who assist him" and that the man "for whom the dance is made . . . becomes the adopted son of the other man" but, on the other hand, that the "child is

ever after treated as the first-born, taking the place of the real first-born, who calls him . . . *elder brother*. The wáwan aká shares his property with this adopted son, giving him presents, and never refusing him anything that he may ask of him. In like manner, the real father of the child makes presents to the real son of the wáwan aká, just as if he were the child's father."[12] In other words, the man who danced the calumet and the man who received the honor each treated the other's real children as their own, as would brothers in societies with an Omaha-type kinship system.[13]

The ceremonial objects necessary for the Wa'wan were a pair of calumets, a 'wild-cat' skin covering or wrapper for the pipes, two gourd rattles, and a bladder tobacco pouch, to which was attached a braid of sweet grass, an eagle bone whistle, and three plumes of eagle down. The 'wild cat' was evidently a bobcat, to judge from the shortness of the tail as illustrated. The rattles and tobacco pouch each had a circle of blue painted around their widest part with four blue stripes extending from the band to the top, in the case of the rattles, or to the bottom, in the case of the tobacco pouch, to represent the earth horizon and the paths of the four winds. Fletcher describes the ear of corn as being decorated in a like manner, but with the stripes being green rather than blue.[14] Dorsey merely says that the top half of the corn ear was painted green with the lower half [remaining] white.

The two calumets had the character both of smoking pipes and of arrows. The stems were made of ash wood and round in cross section with a hole through their entire lengths for the passage of breath. Each was as long as seven spans of the thumb and forefinger stretched apart. These stems were thought of as smoking pipes and had much of the function of sacred pipes, but they had no bowls. Where a bowl would have been expected on a smoking pipe, or a point on an arrow, there was, instead, the head (Dorsey) or the head, neck, and breast (Fletcher and La Flesche) of a mallard duck. Behind the duck attachment on each shaft was a cluster of owl feathers and midway along the shaft the stem was fletched with three wing feathers from a golden eagle, split, trimmed, and glued in place like the feathers on an arrowshaft.

The calumets were always used in pairs, one, with its stem painted sky blue, representing the female element in nature and the other, with its stem painted grass green, the male element (figure 7.1). The female aspect of the blue-painted stem was provided by a fan of ten feathers from the tail of a mature golden eagle, mottled and dark in color overall. The male aspect of the green-painted stem was effected by the use of a fan of seven feathers from a young golden eagle, whose tail feathers are mostly white with black tips. The two calumets together thus represented the opposition or pairing of

Figure 7.1 Paired calumets as used in the Pawnee Hako and Omaha Wa'waⁿ ceremonies: *a*, calumet with green-painted (earth-colored) stem and seven white eagle feathers that represent male elements; *b*, calumet with blue-painted (sky-colored) stem and ten brown eagle feathers that represent female elements. Revised from Hall (1983, fig. 5*a*). Note that not only were calumets used in pairs representing the oppositions sky and earth, day and night, male and female, but the same oppositions were represented within the symbolism of each individual calumet.

male and female in nature, but each calumet individually also contained the same pairing of male and female aspects. The pipes were also decorated with additional attachments of dyed horse hair, streamers, ribbons, and bird heads with various symbolic loads, and a red-painted groove ran along the length of each stem, representing the path of life.

A man could not undertake to organize a Wa'waⁿ party until he himself had been honored four times by other parties. Even then he had to obtain permission from a council of chiefs and to obtain the cooperation of a dozen or more tribesmen to accompany him, to bring gifts for the recipient and his party, and to participate in the associated ritual. Fletcher and La Flesche describe the gifts as "eagle-feather bonnets, bows and arrows, red pipestone pipes, embroidered tobacco bags, otter skins, robes, and, in later years, brass kettles, guns, and blankets. . . . The return gifts were horses (in earlier days burden-bearing dogs), bows and arrows, pottery, robes, and skin tent-covers."[15]

After preliminaries to give formal recognition to the intended recipient—the Son—and to obtain a formal welcome into the host village, the party of Fathers, containing one to three dozen individuals, was given lodging and additional formalities of welcome and thanks.

> At the conclusion of the thanks the pipe bearers arose and the pipes were taken up ceremonially. The movements simulated the eagle rising from its nest and making ready for flight. There are no words to the songs used to accompany these movements. These songs were repeated four times. The beauty of this part of the ceremony was greatly enhanced when the pipe bearers were graceful and could imitate well the flying, circling, rising, and falling of the bird. The feather appendages moved like wings as the pipes were swayed and both the eye and the ear were rhythmically addressed. . . . The fire was always replenished just as the pipes started, so that the flames as they leaped filled the lodge with light and the shadows cast by the moving feathered stems seem to make real their simulation of the eagle's flight.[16]

Other songs followed with words that described some of the significance of the event. When the pipes were finally put down, the feast was served and the guests departed around midnight. Additional songs, gift giving, and feasting continued through the second and third days, but the fourth and final day was a day without song and without food. This was the day of the ceremony honoring the child of the Son or host.

On the fourth day the Father or leader went to the home of the Son or host carrying new garments to reclothe the child and skin pouches with red and black paint. After the child was clothed it was painted by a member of the Wa'waⁿ party who had won honors in defensive warfare. Singing as he painted, he colored the face of the child red and then used black paint to put a horizontal stripe across the forehead of the child and then four additional vertical stripes. One stripe descended down each cheek from the ends of the horizontal stripe, one descended from the center down to the end of the nose, and one vertical stripe went down the back of the head. The total effect of the horizontal and vertical stripes was to create the same symbolism as the markings on the gourd rattles and the tobacco pouch—the horizon and the paths of the winds from the four corners of the earth—a connection that Fletcher and La Flesche state specifically.[17]

Once the child was painted and the associated songs sung, a downy eagle feather was tied on the top of the head of the child. This was followed by songs in which warriors recounted their honors in defensive warfare, after which the child was carried on someone's back to the lodge where the ceremony continued:

> [T]wo young men, holding the feathered stems high above their heads, with a light leaping step danced in two straight lines to and from the east, simulating the flight of the eagle. . . . As the young men leaped and danced—a dance that was full of wild grace and beauty—it might happen that a man would advance and stop before one of the dancers, who at once handed him the pipe. The man recounted his deeds and laid the pipe on the ground. The dance and music ceased, for the act was a challenge and the pipe could be raised only by one who would recount a deed equal in valor to that told by the man who had caused the pipe to be laid down. This stopping of the dance often led to spirited contests in the recital of brave deeds. While the dancing was going on, the ponies were led by the children of the donors to the leader and the little Huⁿ'ga stroked the arm of the messenger in token of thanks.[18]

WHO IS THE HUⁿ'GA?

The name Huⁿ'ga given the adopted child was said to mean the 'ancient one' and 'ancestor', although the child itself was said to have a symbolism looking forward rather than backward in time: "Among the Omaha as with the Pawnee, the child represents the coming generation, the perpetuation of the race; but the Omaha emphasize the innocent character of the child, the absence of warlike spirit."[19] Actually, the name Huⁿ'ga has no accepted etymology in any language of the Siouan family. The meanings in each language are not so much literal translations as glosses or glossings that have no obvious relationship to its derivation, much as the name Big Dipper refers to the Ursa Major constellation but is not a translation of Latin *Ursa Major* (literally 'greater she-bear'):

DAKOTA (SANTEE) **huŋ-ka′** (Riggs orthography). "A parent or ancestor; an elder brother is often so called—*mihuŋka*; *one who has raised himself or herself in the estimation of the people so as to be considered as a kind of benefactor or parent of all; the sun is sometimes so called from his munificence*." ho-huŋ′-ka′ "*a mother fish, i.e., an old fish.*"[20]

LAKOTA (TETON) **huŋka′** (Buechel orthography). "An ancestor."[21]

LAKOTA (TETON) **hųka′** (Boas and Deloria orthography). "To become a principal in the *hųka′* ceremony; the Sun."[22]

OTO **huŋga** (Whitman orthography). "Beloved child"; but also, as an Elk Gens name, **hu′ŋɛ**, **hu′ŋemi**, "Child Beloved (I cannot translate this name. It is the term used for the child honored in the Peace Pipe ceremony. I have heard it called 'Child Beloved', 'The Good' [member of Elk Gens speaking]."[23]

WINNEBAGO **huŋk'a** (Radin orthography). 'Chief'; *Tconaŋke huŋk'a*, personal name glossed as First Chief; *Tconaŋk-huŋk'a*, personal name glossed as Bear Chief (*Tconaŋk* literally means 'blue back' and may have once been a ritual name or term of respect for the bear); **Huŋk'uniga**, personal name 'He who is made chief'; **huŋk wohą**, 'chief feast'; **Huŋk**, 'chiefs', name sometimes used for the sky division, the moiety from which the chief was chosen; **huŋka**, the principal or 'chief' peyote button.[24]

OSAGE **hoⁿ′-ga** (La Flesche orthography). "The-sacred-one. Personal name." "The name of one of the two great tribal divisions of the Osage Tribe, the division representing the earth with its water and dry land. The word signifies sacred or holy, an object that is venerated. It is also the name of a subdivision representing the dry land of the earth. The dark-plumed eagle is spoken of by this term, because of its symbolic use; a child chosen as an emblem of innocence in a peace ceremony is called Hoⁿ′-ga. The origin of the word, being obscure, can not be analyzed."[25]

OMAHA **hoⁿ′ga** (Fletcher and La Flesche orthography). 'Leader'. "The term Hoⁿ′ga is sometimes combined with another word to form the title of an officer, as Nudoⁿ Hoⁿ′ga, 'war leader' or 'captain'." "Hoⁿ′ga means 'leader,' or 'first,' and implies the idea of ancient, or first, people; those who led. . . ." Moiety or tribal half representing the earth and its water, e.g. Hoⁿ′gashenu division or 'Earth people'.[26]

OMAHA **huⁿ′ga** (Fletcher and La Flesche orthography). 'Ancient one'. 'The one who goes before'. 'Leader'. "Peace as symbolized by a little child." The child honored in the Omaha *Wa′waⁿ* or Calumet ceremony.[27]

Fletcher and La Flesche suggested that Hoⁿ′ga was the name by which the Omaha, Ponca, Osage, Kansa, and Quapaw were known when they constituted a single community many years ago and that Huⁿ′ga was simply a variation of Hoⁿ′ga. The languages of these peoples comprise the Dhegiha division of the Siouan language family, and each of these tribes has a Hoⁿ′ga clan, moiety, or other major kinship group with some variation in the pronunciation. Fletcher and La Flesche's suggestion is a possibility that cannot be dismissed out of hand, of course, but their explanation does little to account for the full range of meanings of the name, and there is an alternative interpretation that does relate the use of the name as a kinship grouping, as a name for the child honored in the Calumet ceremony, and as a name for chief, while also providing a logical etymology. But before considering the possible etymology of Hunka, Hunga, and Honga, as I will Anglicize the terms for convenience, we must standardize the phonetic transcription to make comparison easier (see table 1).

The root words $h\mu$ and $h\phi$ are found in bound form in kinship terms such as Lakota *nihu* and Osage *ðihǫ́* 'your mother', but also uncombined as metaphorical extensions of the idea of mother, such as Osage and Omaha *hǫ* 'night'. In Osage belief Night was the mother of Day, and rather widely the night sky was perceived to be the equivalent of the dark interior of the earth as primal Mother. The reconstructed Proto-Siouan term for mother is *$h\mu$*.[28] The elements *–ka* and *–ga* are found as suffixes modifying $h\mu$ and $h\phi$ to produce kinship terms such as Osage *ihǫ́ga* 'mother's sister' from *ihǫ́* 'mother'. The reconstructed Proto-Siouan suffix is *–ka*.

As a suffix *–ka* conveyed the notion of 'rather, almost, not quite, somewhat, pretty much, kind of, not really' and is known largely as a verb suffix. In addition to many other examples of contemporary verbal use, Franz Boas and Ella Deloria give Teton *hé báka* 'he rather blames that one' with *ba* by itself meaning only 'blame', but also, and without explanation or comment, the use of *–ka* as a noun suffix in deriving *čayúka* 'a fool' from *čayú* 'lungs'.[29] The use of *–ka* in the Sioux language as a noun suffix of qualified comparison is clearer in *hoká*, for which Stephen Riggs's dictionary gives the Teton (Lakota) dialect meaning 'eel' but the analytical and descriptive Santee (Eastern) Dakota dialect meaning 'a kind of fish'.[30] The use of the suffix *–ka* as noun qualifier for generating kinship terms has been mentioned and extends well beyond the Central Siouan languages. The suffix appears also in color terms for generating, quite literally, shades of meaning, such as the Biloxi terms translating 'a sort of black' to indicate 'dark brown', 'a kind of blue' to indicate 'gray', and 'a sort of red' to indicate 'purple'.[31]

For argument let us derive Hunka, Hunga, and Honga from Proto-Siouan *$h\mu ka$* with the original meaning 'a kind of mother'. What kind of mother would that be? In what sense could the mother also be a chief and an ancestor? One clue comes from the use of Honga among the Osages and Omahas to designate the moiety or tribal half that represents Earth as opposed to Sky. The earth is a metaphorical mother and in the Hako or Pawnee Calumet ceremony the ear of Mother Corn also symbolizes the earth. During the Hako the identity of the Mother Corn as Earth is in effect ritually transferred from the corn ear to the child being honored by adoption, making the child 'a kind of mother'. Being a language of the Caddoan family, Pawnee does not use any variant of the word Hunka in its ritual, but the word 'mother' is used to refer to the ear of corn in the Hako as in the Omaha Wa'waⁿ.

In the Wa'waⁿ or Omaha Calumet ceremony the pattern of lines painted on the forehead, cheeks, and back of the head of the child was explicitly compared to the patterns painted on the two gourd rattles, on the tobacco pouch, and on the ear of Mother Corn used in

be your life and your issue many."[33] The child was believed to be standing "in the center of the life-giving forces," representing, as the lines did, the paths of the four winds. The child then walked four steps toward the sun and the ceremony was over.[34]

In the Pawnee Hako the ceremonial leader touched the child on the forehead with the ear of Mother Corn and then proceeded to stroke the child with the ear—down the front, down the right side, down the back, and down the left side. He then joined the two calumets and used them to repeat the pattern of strokes upon the child—on the forehead and down the front, the right, the back, and the left. The face of the child was shortly afterward painted entirely red, over which a pattern of lines was then painted in blue—an arc beginning on one cheek, continuing over the forehead and then down the other cheek, with a vertical line extending down to the tip of the nose from a point at the center of the arc. Following this a handful of eagle

DAKOTA (SANTEE)	huŋ-ka'	(Riggs)	=	huŋká	(standardized)
LAKOTA (TETON)	huŋka'	(Buechel)	=	huŋká	(standardized)
LAKOTA (TETON)	huŋka'	(Boas and Deloria)	=	huŋká	(standardized)
OTO	huŋga	(Whitman)	=	húga	(standardized)
WINNEBAGO	huŋk'a	(Radin)	=	húkʰa	(standardized)
OSAGE	hoⁿ'-ga	(La Flesche)	=	hóga	(standardized)
OMAHA	hoⁿ'ga	(Fletcher/LaFlesche)	=	hóga	(standardized)
OMAHA	huⁿ'ga	(Fletcher/LaFlesche)	=	húga	(standardized)

Table 1 Cognates of Lakota Hunka in the orthographies of various sources together with a standardized orthography. Note that Greek eta (η) is used here to represent the velar nasal eng (ŋ).

the ceremony—lines representing the horizon of the earth and the paths of the winds coming from the four corners of the world.[32] After painting the child, the painter placed the two pipes together and used them to make a gesture down the four sides of the child. This was described as a blessing. More details are known of this aspect of the ceremony from a description given of the Ponca version.

In the Ponca ceremony the two calumet pipes were placed together and wrapped in a wildcat skin, the pipe bundle raised high over the head of the child and then slowly lowered, touching the forehead of the child, and then passed down the front of the child until the mouthpiece rested on the child's toes, after which the pipe bundle was placed flat on the ground extending away from the child. This act was repeated three times until the pipes had been passed down the front, back, and each side of the child and had been laid on the ground in all four cardinal directions. Each time the child was told, "Firm shall be your tread upon the earth, no obstacle shall hinder your progress; long shall

down was allowed to fall on the head of the child, a downy eagle plume was retrieved from a location near the owl feathers on the stem of one of the pair of calumets, and the plume tied onto the head of the child. These were all symbolic acts.[35]

The cosmic associations of the Mother Corn were defined by painting the tip of the ear blue (seen supported in a vertical position) to represent the sky, from which four blue lines descended representing "the four paths along which the powers descend to minister to man." On the tip of the ear a downy eagle plume was attached, representing (1) white clouds in the sky, (2) the Pawnee supreme being Tira'wa or Tirawahat, (3) the male principle, (4) the tassle on top of the corn plant, and (5) the breath of the white eagle as father of the child.[36] The act of touching the child on the forehead with the Mother Corn was said to provide a "promise of fruitfulness to the child and its generation." The stroking of the child with the Mother Corn was said to make the child receptive to the powers descending upon it. The four motions on the sides of the child corresponded to the four vertical blue lines on the Mother Corn itself and the eagle plume on the child's head corresponded to the eagle plume on the tip of the Mother Corn. The child became a counterpart or analogue of the Mother Corn.

The red face paint on the child was said to symbolize the brightness of the sun. The line of blue paint making an arc over the child's face symbolized the dome of the sky and the vertical blue line, the breath of Tirawahat, descending from the zenith to the nose of the child and from the nose to the heart. And the touch of the bundled pair of calumets on the head of the child symbolized "the breath of promised life" touching the child. These acts of the Pawnee Hako are described as a 'symbolic inception', which we may read as a 'symbolic conception' because of the equivalence of breath and spirit in Indian belief. We may read it as a sky-earth union as well because the Mother Corn was said to symbolize the earth. The child received a breath of life from the sky father and symbolic rebirth, and the earth was simultaneously reborn as well.

The pattern of black lines on the head of the Omaha child duplicated that on the Mother Corn in that the four vertical lines were located on the front and back of the head and on each cheek (figure 7.2*a*). The line on the forehead was straight and horizontal and represented part of the line that encircled the Mother Corn. The pattern painted on the Pawnee and Osage children (figure 7.2*a–b*) was a forward-looking semicircle, i.e., it faced forward rather than upward so that the center of the circle, if it had been complete, occupied the tip of the nose rather than the top of the head.

The Osage motif was half of the cross-in-circle design known to the Osage as Ho′-e-ga (*hóega* in our standardized phonetic orthography), a name that translates as 'snare' and 'bare spot' but ritually represented a wider range of things—the center of the forehead of the elk that summoned the four winds in the Omaha earth origin myth, the earth itself, and the Osage camp when ceremonially organized. The painting on the head and the strokes on the body of the child were explicitly designed to make the child receptive to the fertilizing breath. The Pawnee saw this as opening the sides of the child to receive the powers from above. The Osage placed on the head of the child a pattern associated in myth with the convergence of the winds that prepared the earth for habitation. The Ho′-e-ga motif was nearly identical with the Teton (Lakota) sacred hoop as a 'wind center' representing the convergence of the four winds within the circle of the horizon.[37]

The Hunka face painting described by Frances Densmore for the Hunkpapa Sioux in her 1918 study *Teton Sioux Music* duplicated that of the Pawnee in being half of a circle facing forward with a vertical line

down the nose, but that described by Black Elk in *The Sacred Pipe*, published in 1953, was a full circle facing forward with additional lines on the cheeks, chin, and forehead. The nose thus coincided with the 'wind center' of a sacred hoop in an optimal position to receive a quickening breath, and Black Elk is explicit in saying that an Oglala thus painted had been born anew. The pledger or 'reproducer' in the Cheyenne Sun Dance was similarly painted with a ring around the face

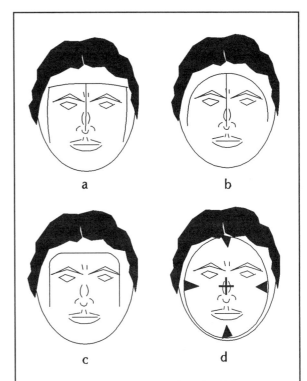

Figure 7.2 Face painting used in the Calumet ceremony and Cheyenne Sun Dance: *a*, motif on the Omaha Hunga, after Fletcher and La Flesche (1972, fig. 89); *b*, motif on the Pawnee Child, after Fletcher [and Murie] (1904, fig. 179); *c*, motif described for the Osage Honga, after La Flesche (1939, 243–244, cf. pl. 5*a*); *d*, motif on the face of the Cheyenne Sun Dance pledger, after Grinnell (1972, 243; cf. Black Elk 1953, 111, for the Oglala Hunka).

and marks on the forehead, chin, and each cheek (figure 7.2*d*).

In Densmore's account the downy eagle plume placed on the head of the child or Hunka was taken from beneath a calumet pipe. In Black Elk's account the plume was removed from the end of the sacred ear of corn, enhancing the parallel being created between the Mother Corn and the Hunka, which I see as an act of ritual 'identification' in the sense used by Gladys Reichard in her book *Navajo Religion*. In a 1660 Plains Apache Calumet ceremony called to my attention by

Donald Blakeslee the eagle plume placed on the head of a Spanish trader was also taken from the end of an ear of corn.[38] In various Navajo chants or rites a subject is identified or made one with a deity in a sand painting when sand from the painting of the deity is applied to the subject of the cure, from foot to foot, from hand to hand, and so on for all corresponding body parts.[39]

La Flesche gives no etymology for the name Ho'-e-ga by which the Osages knew the quartered circle motif, but one is obvious. Ho'-e (*hóe*) by itself means 'mortar'. This was a mortar of the kind made by charring and scraping hollow one end of a log set vertically in the ground. The act of crushing corn in such a mortar with repeated thrusts of a wooden pestle is an unmistakably sexual metaphor that La Flesche may have been alluding to when he called Ho'-e-ga "an enclosure in which all life takes on bodily form."[40] Ho'-e-ga was the Osage ritual name for the earth, which was itself a female metaphor. The suffix of qualified comparison –ga (the Osage reflex of Proto-Siouan *–ka*) would provide the literal meaning 'rather like a mortar'. It is not difficult to see the further comparison between a round, hollow mortar and the bare interior of a camp circle, especially since one of the meanings of Ho'-e-ga is 'bare spot'.

Extending our frame of reference beyond the Plains to the Southeast, the comparison is even stronger between a mortar with its pestle and a Creek or Cherokee town square or Busk ground with a tall central post for the single-pole ball game. The comparison is strengthened when we consider the name by which the Yuchis knew the grassless, bare area used by them as a public square—Rainbow. In addition to 'bare spot', Osage Ho'-e-ga translated as 'snare', and 'snare' or 'trap' was a common Plains name for the rainbow because rain disappeared when the rainbow appeared. Consider, for example, Lakota *wi* 'sun' and *igmuŋke* 'snare, trap', but *wigmuŋ'ke* 'rainbow', and Cheyenne *no nŭn' o* 'snare, trap, fishline, rainbow'.[41]

After the Pawnee ritual leader or Ku'rahus tied the downy eagle plume on the head of the child, the child was told to look into a bowl of water. Alice Fletcher's Pawnee source explains: "The running water symbolizes the passing on of generations, one following another. The little child looks on the water and sees its own likeness, as it will see that likeness in its children and children's children."[42]

A conceiving spirit-breath was widely symbolized by a feather or arrow. Both symbols were used in the Pawnee Hako. The pair of calumet pipes took the form of arrows and were considered to be windpipes as well as pipestems. The plume placed on the head of the child was stored before use on one of the pipes next to the owl feathers, and we know from Francis La Flesche's description of Osage calumet pipes that the owl feathers

represented deer lungs.[43] The soul was also believed to be manifested in reflections on water used as mirrors. The Hako was not the only occasion on which Pawnee children looked at their mirror images:

> In olden times, when the [Pawnee] Indians killed a badger, the older people took the badger and kept it till in the night, when the moon was bright, then skinned it and poured the blood into a wooden bowl. Then they would call their children to the bowl of blood, and tell them to look at themselves in the blood by moonlight. When they looked at the blood they saw their image. If the children saw themselves in the blood with gray hair, the people knew that the children would live to old age; if any child saw its picture in the blood as a very dark and indistinct thing, the older people knew that the child was to die from sickness; if the child did not see its picture in the blood, then the people knew that that child would live and be killed by the enemy.[44]

Among the Aztecs there were women diviners called *tetonaltique* who evaluated the condition of a child's soul by examining its image reflected in a jar of water. If the reflected image was light, then the prognosis of the child's illness was favorable. If the image was dark, then the prognosis was equally dark and the remedy required that the missing soul be located and returned, and more than health might be at risk because the word *tonalli* or *tonal* used for 'soul' was also understood to mean 'fate' and 'fortune'. The diviner exercised a certain amount of control over the prognosis because if the child were placed with its back to the light, its reflection would be dark, and the reverse if placed facing the light.[45]

Farther to the south, the ancient Mayas used the metaphor of 'mirror' in their glyphic writing to signify the idea of 'succession to office'—a son succeeding to the office of his father. This idea brings us back to the Pawnee child looking into his face reflected in the bowl of water during the Hako and seeing in it the faces of his children and children's children.[46] And it brings us back to the words Hunka, Hunga, and Honga as they relate to the ideas of ancestor and chief. And it brings us back to the central purpose of the Calumet ceremony, which was adoption and the creation of bonds of kinship.

The ritual of adoption took the form of symbolic conception and rebirth, but it was directed toward a child. The Omaha, Osage, Oto, Pawnee, and Teton gave the prospect of long life to the child, although by adopting the child, the adoptive father simultaneously became a relative of the actual father of the child. This was important for fostering friendly interband and intertribal relationships. I have argued for years, however, that the basis for the practice of adoption described for Calumet ceremonies in the past century is to be found in adoption as part of mourning ceremonies and that originally the adoptee was an adult who symbolically reincarnated a dead leader by taking his name. This form of the Calumet ceremony was known during the early colonial period as Dancing the Calumet of the Captain (chapter 10). Several lines of evidence point toward this particular interpretation, including the names Hunka, Hunga, and Honga in the sense of chief and ancestor.

DEEPER ROOTS OF THE CALUMET CEREMONY

The style of the painting of the child among the Omaha was called hu^n'$ga\ kio^n$ 'Hu^n'ga painting' and is said to have been the same as that sometimes used on the dead of a subdivision of the I^{n}ke'çabe clan "for entrance into the life after death."[47] This presumably would have included a painting of the face red overall in addition to the pattern of lines. The face of the Omaha Hunga was painted red, as was the face of the Osage Honga, the Lakota Hunka, and the Pawnee and Plains Apache honorees in their versions of the Calumet ceremony.[48] The significance of the red face paint may be inferred from the same practice described for a dead Lakota child being prepared for burial prior to the beginning of the long vigil of Soul Keeping.[49] The painting of the face of the honoree/adoptee red appears to have been a practice transferred from the painting of the dead to the painting of the persons who represented the dead person in a mourning ritual.

A variation of the patterned face painting on the adopted child was used by the Hidatsas on the pledger in their Hide Beating ceremony, also called the Hidatsa Sun Dance. The pledger impersonated a mythical twin called Spring Boy whose station during the ceremony was a location identified as a grave.[50] The pledger in the original Sun Dance of the closely related Crows—the Sun Dance described by Robert Lowie—was effectively the chief mourner for a slain friend or relative whose role it was to obtain a vision of the death of an enemy tribesman to satisfy the need for vengeance.[51] The Spring Boy impersonator was painted with white clay overall but had the semicircle of black painted from one cheek over the forehead to the other cheek and the nose painted black. I have already (chapter 6) compared the Spring Boy impersonator, as pledger in the Hidatsa Sun Dance, to the Whistler, as pledger in the Crow Sun Dance, and noted that the bodies of each were painted with white clay, which was a practice noted by William MacLeod among mourning rites for ten northern and central Plains tribes, and to these I would add one mention for the Hidatsa.[52] The covering of bodies with white clay upon burial is

occasionally found in the Woodland period of the upper Midwest (chapter 3).[53]

Vengeance was an important part of the mourning process quite widely in North America, with obtaining vengeance sometimes incumbent upon the person who reincarnated the dead tribesman by taking his name. Speaking of Indians in seventeenth-century Quebec, the Jesuit Father Barthelemy Vimont reported back to his superiors in France:

> It has often been said that the dead were brought back to life by making the living bear their names. This is done for several reasons,—to revive the memory of a brave man, and to incite him who shall bear his name to imitate his courage; to take revenge upon the enemies, for he who takes the name of a man killed in battle binds himself to avenge his death; to assist the family of a dead man, because he who brings him back to life, and who represents him, assumes all the duties of the deceased, feeding his children as if he were their own Father—in fact, they call him their Father, and he calls them his children. . . . He who brings back the dead to life makes a present to him who is to take his place. He sometimes hangs a collar of Porcelain beads around his neck. If the latter accept, he takes the name of the deceased, and begins to dance before all the others, as a mark of rejoicing.[54]

The probable derivation of the Hako, Wa'wa^n, and other Calumet ceremonies from mourning ritual is understandable because of the widespread relationship of adoption to mourning. What is less obvious is why the child adopted should be given an identity with the earth, or with the Mother Corn symbolic of the earth, until one considers that the earth itself undergoes an annual rebirth. The evidence here points to the remoter past, to the time known to archaeologists as the Burial Mound or Woodland period in the eastern United States. The evidence is for an association of burial mound ceremonialism—not everywhere, but in the Midwest at least—with a World Renewal ritual similar to that of the Cheyenne Sun Dance and with ritual identification of the dead reincarnated by adoption with the earth re-created during the course of mound construction.[55] The earth and the honored dead were reincarnated simultaneously.

One mental block to exploring the origins of calumet ceremonialism has been the common association of calumet ceremonialism with pipes. The particular 'pipes' used in Calumet ceremonies of the Hako type were treated as pipes but were, in fact, more like ceremonial wands and were in the form of highly decorated arrows. They often did not have bowls, and some did not even have a hole for the passage of breath. East of the Mississippi valley friendly intertribal relations were mediated not by exchanges of calumets but by exchanges of shell beads. The cacica of Cofachiqui did not greet Hernando de Soto with a calumet; she did give him a string of pearls from around her own neck. Because pearls, wampum, and other shell beads have mythological associations with saliva and other bodily effluvia,[56] honoring someone with a string of pearls may well have been the symbolic equivalent of the weeping greeting that so revolted Nicolas Perrot (chapter 1). Aside from the behavior of mollusks that reveal their buried locations in tidal flats by spitting into the air through their siphons (cf. Wampanoag *sickissuog* 'clam that spits'),[57] Spitters appear in both the United States and Mesoamerica in the mythical role of conceiver (chapter 19), which provides a nice parallel to symbolic conception mediated by a calumet.

ALANSON B. SKINNER was an anthropologist employed by the American Museum of Natural History (1907–1915), the Museum of the American Indian (1915–1920, 1924–1925), and the Milwaukee Public Museum (1920–1924).[1] Skinner was not himself an Indian, but he was formally adopted by a Menominee and given the Thunder clan name of Sekó'sa 'Little Weasel'. After his marriage to Dorothy Preston, a member of the Wyandot tribe, Skinner also received the Wyandot Deer clan name of Tronyetase 'Round the Sky'. Although he was known in New York early in his career as an archaeologist, he is best known in the Midwest as an ethnologist for his studies of the Iowa, Prairie Potawatomi, Sauk, and Eastern Dakota, and in particular of the Menominees.

Skinner has left several accounts of his field experiences that tell us much of the method and care by which sacred lore was transferred between generations. One of these concerns his acquisition of information on the Menominee Medicine Dance or Medicine Society—the Mitäwin. This material Skinner obtained from John Baptist Perrote or Sabatis (from French Jean Baptiste), whom Skinner describes as the last great Menominee shaman. Sabatis was grand master of the Medicine Dance, a leader of the Dream Dance society, and a United States Indian court judge. Judge Perrote, or Sabatis, was born about 1840 near the limestone ledge overlooking the east side of Lake Winnebago.[2] His father's home was near the rocky cliff location in Menominee mythology where the Thunderbird clan originated.

SABATIS INSTRUCTS HIS NEPHEW LITTLE WEASEL

Skinner gives us the following story of his relationship to Judge Perrote. It begins on a day in 1913 on the Menominee Reservation when Skinner had attended a ceremony of the Dream Dance, of which he was a member. This event was held at the dance ground on the Neopit road where Chickeny Creek crosses the highway a ways west of Keshena. The area around the sacred enclosure was dotted with the tents of visitors, including many Winnebagoes from Wittenberg. Missing Judge Perrote and learning that the judge's brother-in-law Pitwäskum had recently died, Skinner left the grounds to search him out at his home. His account runs like this:

> Leaving the dancers behind, Capt. Satterlee and I toiled on foot over the hill and down the wooded trail to Perrote's cabin. Here, heralded by the barking of the judge's black and white dog, Anamäk, ('rotten fish'; I think the name also contains a merry pun on Änäm 'a dog'), we were admitted to the loghouse, where the old couple were at work on their daily tasks.
>
> A bundle suspended from a nail driven into the wall attracted our attention, although Satterlee and I were both entirely familiar with its significance. It was composed of a complete suit of male attire, formerly belonging to *Pitwäskum*, or purchased since his death for this very purpose. It contained a lock of the hair of the departed, and was called "the Death Bundle." It was to be kept a year and then, at a special rite of the Medicine Lodge Society, it would be opened, and the garments placed upon a person of the same age and sex as the deceased, selected by the mourners to represent the dead man, while the Master of Ceremonies would invoke the warder of the realms of the dead, Na˟patäo, brother of the hero-god Mä'näbus, to release the soul of the dead man from his domaine.
>
> The soul, freed for the occasion, would come down from the western heavens, enter the body of the substitute, and animate him until the end of the ceremony, when it would be released to return to Elysium forever.
>
> During the interval between the funeral and these ceremonies, however, the Death Bundle is kept in the house of the chief mourner, where it is regarded as a living thing. Food is offered to it, and it is addressed and spoken to as if it were the deceased himself.
>
> Stopping to talk to the Bundle and offer it tobacco, Satterlee and I then seated ourselves and lit our pipes

preparatory to a long chat with Perrote. Our conversation on this visit had to do principally with my work of collecting data and specimens among the Menomini. Perrote was very anxious to learn what I had obtained in the way of sacred articles, such as war and hunting bundles, medicine bags, and the like. At last he turned to me: "My friend," said the good old man, "have you yet gathered the ritual of our Medicine Dance?"

"No," I replied. "I've tried hard these many years, yet no one has been willing to tell me. I have about decided to give up. It seems impossible."

Judge Perrote beamed in his kindly fashion. "My friend, I believe you can be trusted. You have never betrayed anyone who has sold or told you a sacred thing even to me, and we have known each other well these many years. This ritual is mine, I bought it when I was young, and now I am the leader here. I will instruct you. Now is a good time when all the people are dancing. Come tomorrow and bring the price of a horse, and we will begin."

Now the price of a horse meant about $75.00 worth of blankets, calicoes, food, and, of course, many pounds of tobacco. Yet this was very cheap compared with what an Indian has to pay to receive instruction. The next morning's sleepy sun found Satterlee and me, deep in the shaded trail, with our packs of goods on our backs. Half a mile from our destination we left the path, gingerly stepping on stones to break our trail, then we returned to the road and walked backwards, so that prying Indians would think that we had come from, not to, the Judge's lodge. These precautions were really necessary. He would have been in danger of his life, had the fact that he was telling an outsider these things ever become known. Later on, when Judge Perrote was sole head of the Medicine Lodge, it was an open secret, no longer guarded, and the members looked upon me as one of their number.

Arrived at Perrote's place, we found him waiting. He had constructed a rude shrine in one corner, and there we saw his water drum and its crooked stick, now mine, his snake skin medicine bag, his gourd rattles, and his redstone pipe. This last was a remarkable object. Its four foot wooden stem was carved cork-screw-wise and inlaid with silver, and etchings of thunder-birds adorned the huge catlinite bowl. Here we deposited our tobacco, food and presents and squatted down, I with notebook in hand, to wait the elder's pleasure. For a while we were kept all silent, then Perrote motioned to Satterlee to fill and light his pipe, while he began a prayer of invocation.

First tobacco was offered to *Mä'näbus*, founder of the lodge, then to the Sun, who was once regarded as the Great Spirit, the Thunder-birds, and all the gods of the four tiers of Heaven and the corresponding strata of the Underworld. The various manitous on the earth's surface came in for their share also, and finally, when all the Powers had been invoked by name, the old man announced to them that in order to obviate any difficulty which might arise from his telling these sacred things to a white man, he then and there adopted me as his nephew (his sister's son) so that thereafter they and all the world were to know me as Little Weasel (*Sekó'sa*), nephew of Judge Perrote. The Gods being thus pacified, the old man dismissed them, and began his discourse.

. . . [T]he narration and the transcription of [the lengthy myths], and the lodge ritual, took many days of hard work for the three of us. Nor did we fail to suffer interruption. Once Mrs. Perrote, long since gathered to her fathers, poor soul, ran in to tell us that a terrible thunder storm was approaching. We hastened out, and, indeed, an ominous black cloud was bearing down out of the west. Facing the coming storm, with breeze blowing through his long hair, Judge Perrote addressed a hasty prayer to the Thunderers, begging them to be moderate, and bless us with a gentle rain. He explained again that they had been mentioned in our talks for good purpose, and he offered them tobacco. Scarcely had he finished speaking when the clouds broke and a pleasant shower fell upon us, the dark clouds parting and going by on either side. Beyond us, at Keshena, the storm was of extreme violence, and did much damage.

On another occasion a step was heard on the threshold. Hastily casting a blanket over the little shrine, Perrote cleverly launched into the middle of a comical folktale of no importance concerning the adventures of the trickster, Raccoon. The visiting Indian entered, listened a while all unsuspicious, and departed, satisfied that our errand was trivial.

Through the old man the writer obtained a complete set of the paraphernalia of the lodge, with instructions as to their use. A year before his death the judge was prevailed upon to sing into a recording phonograph a group of the more notable songs of the Medicine Lodge, and the texts of these with their translations, were also gained. This was the old man's last important contribution to science. . . .

In May and June, 1920, when on the Reserve, I found Judge Perrote quite ill. In April he had caught a severe cold wading in the icy shallows of the swamps setting and inspecting his muskrat traps. A short visit was paid him at his home, at which time he presented the writer with a beautiful belt of woven beads. We last met at Keshena, on the occasion of the Corpus Christi procession, when, though pagan, the old man came in to see the celebration.

When the writer left, he was ill in bed, with bronchitis, it was thought, but this turned into galloping consumption, and, on July 10th, with a letter from his beloved white nephew in the east clasped in his hands, he closed his eyes, and his spirit feet turned westward on the Road of the Dead, which winds skyward over the Milky Way to the realms of Na[x]patäo. People said of him that he had never had even an evil thought in his life.[3]

THE GREAT RABBIT'S TEARS ARE DRIED

Skinner did not reveal the name of his Menominee mentor until 1921 and after Judge Perrote's death. Perrote's account of the origin myth of the Medicine Society will outlive him by the lengths of many lifetimes. It begins by telling how long ago, in the time of beginnings, Mä'näbus, the Great Rabbit, was given the earth to guard and protect. He became lonesome, however, as he had no friends, so he was provided a companion in the form of a pure white wolf. Mä'näbus was delighted to have the wolf as a companion, and he called him his little brother. His name was Na[x]patäo. The wolf served Mä'näbus well, hunting and providing him food as well as companionship.

One day Mä'näbus told Na[x]patäo that there were no gods on the earth except them. He said this in his pride because the earth was his responsibility, but there were other gods in that day who had not yet taken their places in the tiers of the underworld, the Beneath, and they were offended. The gods overheard Mä'näbus make this boastful statement and tattled to the White Bear gods who lived in the fourth and deepest level of the underworld. The bear gods replied, "Do now as you wish, using your power and ours." It was decided to murder Mä'näbus's brother.[4]

Because of Mä'näbus's nature as a god he was able to overhear the plotting and warned his wolf companion of the danger. Despite his precautions, the Powers Below thwarted Mä'näbus. They arranged for one of their number to leave tracks leading Wolf on a chase that lasted all day and past sunset, luring Wolf far from Mä'näbus's lodge and onto the opposite side of a great body of frozen water. There Wolf made the fateful decision to chance a shortcut across the ice to save time returning, not knowing what awaited:

So he started and ran, and when he got to the center he heard a great noise and roaring. Then the ice broke up in chunks, the water heaved and roared, the whole sea began to stir. He sprang from one cake to another, and yet they still grew smaller. Then, when he saw his end was near, he cried: "*He!* Mä'näbus! You have said that you were one of the gods! You have promised to help me, and now I am going to be lost! I shall die! Remember your promise to me!"

When Wolf said this, Mä'näbus was seated in his lodge, yet he heard all these words easily, as though they were uttered nearby. Mä'näbus glanced at the sun, and it had already set. Then he started, running toward where he heard the cries. Halfway there he was interrupted by hearing all the little birds who had gathered in a flock to sing, and this attracted him, so when he reached the shore his little brother had been taken down. The bubbling of the water had ceased and it was too late. He looked, listened, and wondered, but he saw and heard nothing. "*Ápapénisiwûk!*" he cried, "I am undone! Those Dwelling Beneath have made away with my little brother! They have prevailed over me."[5]

Mä'näbus sobbed and wept in his grief but decided to mourn four days before seeking his vengeance on the gods who had deprived him of his companion. The gods of the first tier of the Above overheard Mä'näbus making his plans and said to themselves, "Oh my! Something is happening! It must be that the Powers Below have done something to Mä'näbus, who was left to care for the surface of this earth. Let us tell the Great Power (Mätc Häwätûk) what we have heard him saying, and that we believe that the Powers Below have injured him. We believe that they have grievously wronged him. Something very serious must have been done," they reported to Mätc Häwätûk, "for his distress shook the earth and all the Powers."[6]

The Powers Below acknowledged their guilt and were told by Mätc Häwätûk that they would have to make amends for their action or Mä'näbus would kill them with the powers he had been given as a god. Mätc Häwätûk said that if the Powers Below would give Mä'näbus some of their medicines as a gift, perhaps that would make him forget the loss of his companion, and this the Powers Below decided they would have to do. Here, then, at the time of beginnings, when the earth was still young, the Great Power created the precedent for the giving of gifts to dry the tears of someone in mourning.

The Powers Above and the offending Powers Below held a council and decided first to build a long lodge of poles and mats and then to invite Mä'näbus to come "to receive something to wipe out his sorrow." There would be two doors, one in the east and one in the west. Blue paint was daubed here and there on the lodge poles and was used to color the trail around the interior of the lodge. The Power in the north roofed the north half of the lodge in pure white, while the Power in the south provided a red covering for that side of the roof. The Powers Below seated themselves along the north wall and the Powers Above, along the south wall, just as the Menominees would later seat themselves on the north or south side depending on whether the medicine bags they possessed represented an animal of the lower world or the upper world.

An otter delivered the invitation for Mä'näbus to

come to see the lodge which the Powers had built for him, the *mitäw'ikomĭk* or 'medicine lodge'. When Mä'näbus arrived he was seated between the first and second leaders and was addressed by the leader. Sabatis's narrative now continues, quoting the Powers as they addressed Mä'näbus:

> Do you see this lodge—its shape, height, condition, and the way it is laid out? This has been made for you alone. It is given to you; it is yours, with all that is in it. This we have done to relieve the sadness that now oppresses you. . . . This is all brought here for you to see and to have, from all the Grandfathers. Both sides, Above and Below, have consented to it. They wish to give all this to you, for you to own, to cheer you in your sorrow because they have destroyed your little brother. They beg you to accept this as recompense; then you alone will have profit and reward from it. It will be something great. Take it without fail. . . . When you do accept it, it will be a great means of favor and help for your parents, the people, from now on forever.[7]

Mä'näbus did accept the lodge and the gifts from the Powers, which were given him specifically to console him in his grief for the death of his little wolf brother. He was then and there instructed in the secrets of the lodge and taught to use his otter skin medicine bag to shoot medicine arrows. He was told that the gifts he was being given were to aid in prolonging life, and he was given the secret of a clever trick, a 'sacred amusement', the better to impress the initiates with the powers of the Mitäwin. Mä'näbus then traveled to the Menominee River where he met the people, the Menominees, and instructed them in the manner of constructing a lodge for the conducting of the ceremony, bending poles, securing them with basswood bast twine, and covering them with woven cattail mats. Initiation into the Mitäwin was believed to benefit the candidate with health and long life. A second benefit came at the end of the member's days. This was a memorial service both to honor the deceased and to release the mourners from their obligations.

The Medicine Society created to dry Mä'näbus' tears was not primarily a society with mortuary or mourning functions. Members of the Menominee Medicine Society or Mitäwin could nevertheless count on the attention that the organization gave to burial and mourning observances. In that sense the Mitäwin was a fellowship organization, like a Masonic lodge, which did not exist for mortuary observances but which provided them when needed and in so doing had a supportive role for the survivors at a time when emotional support was needed most. Like a Mason also, a *mitäo* or member of the Mitäwin received esoteric knowledge and could be initiated through several degrees of membership.

The Menominee Mitäwin corresponded to the more widely known Midewiwin or Grand Medicine Society of the Ojibwas but also differed from it, as did the medicine societies of the Winnebagoes and other tribes that were derived from the Midewiwin as its concepts diffused through the upper Great Lakes area and into the Plains. The overriding theme of these medicine societies was the gift of long life and health, with conjuring or jugglery and curing given more emphasis among the Ojibwas, memorial services among the Menominees, and so forth.

All these related medicine societies have a 'shooting' rite in which members 'shoot' one another with magical missiles, usually referred to as 'arrows' but actually consisting of stone pebbles (Omaha), bi-pointed objects cut from shell (Wahpeton Dakota), or, most commonly, marine cowry shells of the species *Cypraea moneta* obtained from traders (Menominee, Ojibwa). The 'shot' members fall 'dead' but quickly revive. The shooting is typically done with special medicine bags made of the skins of animals, the otter being a favorite.[8]

THE SACRED AMUSEMENT

Although the shooting of medicine arrows itself amounts to jugglery, in the sense of being simulated actions or trickery, other shamanistic performances also have their special role in the proceedings of the Medicine Society. One of these was the *pa'pewin* or 'sacred amusement' of the Menominees. This sacred amusement was special because according to the origin myth of the Mitäwin it was given directly to the culture hero Mä'näbus by the Powers Above and the Powers Below when the Mitäwin was first instituted. The sacred amusement was intended for use on the occasions of funeral ceremonies and was said in the origin myth to be intended to impress candidates for initiation into the Mitäwin with the powers of the members of the lodge.[9]

According to Skinner only four Menominees in 1913 were masters of the sacred amusement with the power to use it—Pitwäskûm, Judge Perrote, Kesóapomesao, and Ka'sikäo. The basic element of the trick was for the performer to hold a flat rectangular cloth bag at the two upper corners and while singing to the beat of a water drum to make a pair of heads slowly emerge from concealment inside of the bag and then later slowly sink back into the interior of the bag. The heads were those of loons, snakes, mink, dolls, or the like.[10]

Late one summer I was visiting Keshena to attend the Menominee Fair, which that year was to feature an evening pageant on the history of the Menominees in the Woodland Bowl, a small outdoor amphitheater created in a stand of tall pines next to the fairgrounds.

During the day I was invited by my cousin Raymond Lawe to accompany him while he looked for a hickory sapling from which to make a new band of wood to secure the leather head on his water drum. It was for a performance he was to give that evening during the pageant, but I had no idea what the performance was to be.

The pageant was designed along nontraditional lines, to say the least. Performers advanced from the shadows to stage front costumed now as Indians, now as British soldiers, now as American soldiers, while the stage lighting brightened and dimmed and a public address system provided an amplified commentary. Then, Raymond appeared at the front of the pine-needle covered stage with a flat, rectangular cloth bag held by the two upper corners. As a companion drummed, Raymond sang, and as he sang, two heads slowly rose out of the bag as if by magic the animals had been made to materialize inside of an empty bag. Above the top edge of the bag the heads nodded and bobbed as if alive and then slowly descended, leaving the impression that the bag was once more empty. Too few in the audience realized what an unusual privilege they had been granted to witness this 'sacred amusement' given to Mä'näbus by the gods themselves.

HOSTING THE GHOST

The Jebai Noke was a private memorial service in the home for the rank and file of the Mitäwin. There was also a public ceremony called the Uswinamikäskou or Obliteration ceremony in the lodge and adjacent cemetery for leaders and men of importance in the Mitäwin. The private ceremony lasted a night and a day and consisted of calling the shade of the deceased back from the land of spirits to receive sacrifices, after which he was dismissed to return. The dead person was represented in the ceremony by someone of the same sex close in age to the deceased. The chief mourner hosted the event. A society elder was invited to attend and relate the origin myth of the ceremony, which was not included in the myth provided to candidates at the time of their initiation. This expansion of the origin myth tells how the drowned wolf brother of Mä'näbus appears to him as a spirit, "like a shadow cast by the moonlight," and is commanded to prepare a road to the west, where he is to rule over the land of the dead. Later Mä'näbus himself visits the shade of his brother Na^xpatäo and on leaving gives him additional charges:

> The people who are to come [to you in the land of spirits] shall be good, and they shall have descendents who may be good too, and they shall receive shades as you did, and shall come to you to be accepted and admitted into your beautiful lodge to live with you. In

the meantime they shall have left behind some dear ones who shall mourn them, and they shall occasionally perform a medicine dance, and in it shall have a separate sacrifice to the one who left, and is living with you. When they do that, you must hear them entreat you, and when this occurs, dear little brother, dismiss the shade that is called for, and allow it to go back to the earth to receive the sacrifice. Let it be there long enough for that, and when you do that, you will be very good and wise, and you too will receive a share in the offering: goods, tobacco, and feast.[11]

The person animated by the shade recalled from the west in effect *became* the deceased, and he was addressed by the name of the deceased. The service began in the evening, ended with a feast, and then commenced again the next morning. At that time the guest of honor, personifying the deceased and animated by his spirit, was reclothed—a new suit, hat, and shoes were given him and a new blanket tied around his waist. A new feast was laid and consumed in honor of the *tcibáiwinini* or ghost man.

When the feast was over, the master of ceremonies then repeated what he had said before and turned to the ghostman, saying:

> "You have now finished, and you are dismissed to return." He helps the guest of honor to arise and leads him to the center, still holding him, and faces him to the west. "You have now seen the feast and eaten it, and you have now seen your own relatives who begged for you. Your relatives from beyond, who came here with you, shall start back with you, and you shall all take back what was given you here. You are well provided; your arms are filled with food and tobacco. Take it along now, and before you go you must thank your own relatives who obtained this privilege for you. Do not tarry when you return; go straight home and be contented, and do not be angry at your relations, but appreciate it and thank them."[12]

After this was said the guest of honor was taken outside and faced to the west. The spirit of the deceased animating him was then dismissed and bidden to return to the realm of Na^xpatäo, Mä'näbus's little wolf brother. In one such service Judge Perrote became the ceremonial husband of Mrs. Naiätowa'pomi, "since he was raised in her husband's place." Mrs. Robert Pämo'-pämi was similarly adopted to reanimate Mrs. Peter Fish, deceased.[13]

The Obliteration Rite was the more elaborate public performance of the memorial service. The origin myth of the service was apparently the same as that in the private ceremony with the addition of some admonitions and instructions from Mä'näbus for the time when people drop their medicine bags, a figure of speech meaning 'die'. The guest of honor might also be a non-member of the lodge who was initiated into the lodge during the service. When that happened the initiate was afterward addressed by the relatives of the deceased with the same kinship terms they had previously used for the deceased. This was in effect an *adoption* in which the guest of honor not only ritually replaced but also became a symbolic reincarnation of the deceased, whose spirit had occupied the guest of honor's body during the service. The reclothing of the guest of honor can be seen as a metaphor reinforcing this symbolism.

During the feast on the last day of the Obliteration ceremony the carved wooden spoon and bowl of the deceased were present but turned upside down. At the conclusion of the ceremony these items were turned right-side-up, a song was sung that referred to this act, the guests all rose and danced, and the guest of honor was 'shot' with their medicine bags. The honored guest's bowl was filled with food, and he ate in memory of the deceased he represented. All present then left the lodge through the western door—used at no other time except during a memorial service—and proceeded to the grave. The guest of honor was led to graveside where a song was sung to the rhythm of the water drum; the lock of hair from the death bundle of the deceased was buried in the grave; and the guest of honor as the impersonator of the deceased was dismissed. The scene afterward reflected the joyous mood of a period of mourning terminated.[14]

PLEDGING A SPIRIT TRAIL SERVANT

Walter James Hoffman was a medical doctor who had been initiated into the mysteries of the Midewiwin during the period of 1887–1890 by the Ojibwas of Red Lake and White Earth, Minnesota. During the winter of 1889–1890 several members of this Ojibwa Medicine Lodge went on tribal business to Washington, D.C., where they happened to have rooms in a house where there was also a delegation of Menominee Indians from Keshena. There the Menominees learned of Hoffman's activities among the Ojibwas and of his making a record of the Ojibwa rite.

The Ojibwas told the Menominees of their action in allowing Hoffman to record the ritual and story of their medicine society, which were to be published by the Smithsonian Institution. This would assure that future generations would know of the ancient beliefs and the history of Manabush and the Grand Medicine Society, the Ojibwas explained.

Three of the Menominees were themselves leaders of the Menominee society. They agreed that Hoffman should be invited to Keshena, where a council could convene to decide whether to admit him to their ceremonies so that Hoffman could make a record of them, as he had done for the Ojibwas. Hoffman went in the spring of 1890 and received the unanimous approval of his project. It was agreed that Hoffman should be admitted as a member of the society, after which he could ask any questions and receive information without fear of supernatural retribution.[15]

Hoffman describes the ceremonial structure or *mitäw'ikomik* itself as usually sixty or seventy feet long and about twenty wide with a frame consisting of two parallel rows of poles, each two to three inches at the base arched together and tied with basswood bast cord. When covered with rush mats, birch bark, or canvas the appearance was that of a half-cylinder lying on the flat side. Branches of cedar were laid on the floor of the lodge, except in the seating area around the sides, where woven mats were placed. He says that when an Indian was going to be initiated to replace a deceased member, the structure was ideally erected a short distance east of the grave so that members could walk west to the grave, the direction in which spirits departed this earth. Hoffman paints a word picture easy to visualize in the mind:

> By Saturday afternoon . . . the vicinity of the mitä'-wikŏ'mik became a scene of great animation. Wagons bearing the families, tents, and cooking utensils of members of the society began to arrive from various directions. The young men and boys came on horseback, clad in their best and gaudiest attire; children ran hither and thither while chasing one another in play; and the scene was occasionally enlivened by a rush toward a particular spot to witness or to stop a dog fight, as numerous and various specimens of gaunt, snarling curs had congregated from all parts of the reservation.
>
> The members of the society were yet in their hastily erected lodges preparing themselves for public exhibition; but as the sun began to sink, eight of the most prominent members of the society, together with the chief mourner or giver of the feast and his family and relations, proceeded westward to the grave, distant about 200 yards, around which they formed a circle, while Shu'nien stepped nearer toward the head of the grave box, and produced the mä'tshida'qtokwan, or ceremonial baton. . . . Shu'nien, after taking the baton at the sharpened end, struck the grave box with the other end, and spoke as follows:
>
> "There were two brothers, Mä'näbŭsh [Mä'näbus] and Na'qpote [Na^xpatäo], the Wolf. Mä'näbŭsh lived to mourn for Na'qpote, who was destroyed by the evil underground beings, but who now abides in Tshi'pai-a'qki, the final resting place, where he awaits the arrival of the shades of the dead. The dance to be held at the bottom of the hill is held for Na'qpote, that he

may return and transport the shade of this dead one to the mitä′wikŏmik, where we shall have our ceremonies this night. All the aged whiteheads are invited to it. While Mä′näbŭsh was still on this earth he said that he [Naˣpatäo] should build a fire in the northwest, at which the Indians would always be enabled to obtain warmth for themselves, their children, and their successors. He said that afterward he should go to the place of the rising sun, there to abide always and to watch over the welfare of the Indians. He said if the Indians desired to hold a meeting of the Mitä′wit [Mitäwin], that they must first have a feast at the head of the grave. We will now sit and eat."

The mitä′ᵛ women, assisted by relatives of the deceased, then spread a tablecloth upon the ground, and deposited thereon various kinds of meats, vegetables, bread, and pastry . . . but nothing was so eagerly sought after as the green cucumbers, which were peeled and eaten raw.

After the feast, Shu′nien, the chief priest and master of ceremonies, again took the ceremonial baton, and handing it to one of his assistants, requested him to make an address. The speaker first struck the grave box, and during the time of his remarks frequently struck the box, as if to emphasize his words. The address made by him and his three successors related to exploits performed by them at various times, particularly during the civil war, when most of them had served as soldiers in the Union Army. This digression was prompted because the deceased had been one of their comrades.[16]

Here Hoffman either missed or understated one of the most interesting aspects of the mourning service. The Union veterans tapping what Hoffman called a 'ceremonial baton' on the grave box were undoubtedly recounting coups on Rebel soldiers they had killed and dedicating their spirits to the deceased to assist him on his journey from and back to the land of souls. Describing funeral rites of the Sauk and Fox in 1827, Thomas Forsyth wrote: "Previous to closing the grave one or more Indians who attend the funeral will make a motion with a stick or war-club called by the Indians Puc-ca-maw-gun speaking in an audible voice, 'I have killed so many men in war, I give their spirits to my deceased friend who lies there (pointing to the body) to serve him as slaves in the other world.' " The concept of spirit trail servants was widespread in the Mississippi valley and Great Lakes area.[17]

The Menominees not only participated in the Civil War, but following the war the Menominees had the only all-Indian post of the G.A.R. or Grand Army of the Republic. This was a veterans' organization formed after the Civil War much as the American Legion was formed after World War I. Thirty-eight of the 106

enlisted men in Company K of the 37th Wisconsin Volunteer Infantry were Menominees, to mention a single unit. The last survivor of the Menominee G.A.R. post is said to have been a Joseph Davis, who died around 1937.[18]

Before participants retired to the medicine lodge for the night's ceremony, a gravepost was planted in front of the wooden box erected over the grave. This was a flat stick with marks for eight notable exploits during the life of the deceased and a totem animal drawn head down.

The songs of the medicine ceremony were difficult to record because the singer usually insisted on singing them to the accompaniment of a drum or a rattle because it was believed that otherwise the gods would be angered. The understanding of the songs was further hampered by the insertion of a refrain of nonsense syllables whose purpose was to make the songs unintelligible even to a native speaker, thus to add to the mystery of the songs and impress the uninitiated. Skinner said that just to say the word *mitäw′ikomik* 'medicine lodge' the singer might actually have to develop the following combination of words:

> Mitähe, he, he, mitähi, hi, hi,
> Mitäho, ho, ho, mitäha, ha, ha,
> Mitäwi hi, hi, hi, mitäwi, hi, hi, hi
> Mitä, he, he, he, mitä, hi, hi, hi,
> Mitäw ′ikomĭk hi, mitäw ′ikomĭk ha,
> We ho, ho, ho, ho.[19]

The difficulty of understanding a song or story was further increased by the use of euphemisms, ritual names, and circumlocutions for otherwise common terms. The earth, *akiŭ*, might instead be referred to as 'Our Grandmother'. The color blue might not be used in its usual descriptive sense but in the sense of 'holy' or 'consecrated'. The common Menominee word for 'bear' was *äwä′sĕ* (probably literally meaning 'the animal', according to Skinner), which was already a circumlocution for the more general Algonquian word *makwa* or *mukwa* and was further mystified by being replaced in sacred songs by a term such as *ko′skĭnawäo* 'the scratcher'. A snapping turtle might become *okem-a′uwinĭni* or 'chief man'.[20]

For the candidate there was the additional burden of having to purchase the right to hear songs and myths, and since he had to learn them verbatim he had to pay for repeated tutoring sessions. This cost was supported by religious tradition that asserted that the teachings would not be of use if they were not highly valued. Horses, guns, clothing, blankets, food, and the like were given to the teacher in exchange for the knowledge acquired. In time the student could recoup his expenses by passing on the same knowledge to others for a price,

Menominee Casualties in Company K during the Battle of the Crater

On July 30, 1864, Union and Confederate armies were facing each other outside of Petersburg, Virginia. Petersburg was an important railroad hub twenty-three miles south of Richmond, capital of the Southern confederacy, and was defended by troops dug into a ring of trenches, underground bunkers, artillery emplacements, and barricades of every description. To aid in breaching this defense, former coal miners of the 48th Pennsylvania Volunteer Infantry Regiment dug a tunnel more than five hundred feet long to a point directly beneath the Southern picket line. Before daylight on the morning of July 30 Lt. Col. Henry Pleasants of the 48th entered the tunnel and touched a ninety-eight-foot-long fuse that began sputtering its way toward 320 kegs of black powder packed into the far end of the mine—eight thousand pounds of explosives.

As someone in blue shouted, "There she goes!" the earth shuddered silently for a brief moment and then erupted into a roaring geyser of smoke and dust, heaving skyward a dense plume of gun carriages, Rebels, revetment timbers, sand, and great blocks of clay. At least 278 Southern soldiers died in the blast.

Union batteries immediately began a deafening artillery barrage to amplify the shock effect of the detonation. When the Northern troops finally advanced to the scene of destruction they found a yawning crater two hundred feet long, fifty feet wide, and up to thirty feet deep studded with broken bodies and implements of war. The Federal troops that entered the breach had some initial success in penetrating the Confederate lines but were soon forced back into the trench left by the exploding mine. Here the regrouping Union regiments were crowded together against regiment after regiment of supporting troops still advancing into the trench. Most of the latter were regiments recruited from freed slaves who were given no mercy as the Confederate infantry now rimming the trench fired into the unprotected Union soldiers filling it. This Battle of the Crater resulted in thirty-five hundred dead from the North and fifteen hundred from the South.

The 37th Wisconsin Volunteer Infantry was one of the regiments immediately to the left of the crater that were giving support to the attempted advance through the crater. Of 250 men from the regiment who went into battle that day only ninety-five remained to answer rollcall that evening. Many of these casualties were Menominee Indians from Company K recruited in Shawano County:

Corp. Seymour Hahpahtakwahnoquette, killed in action;

Priv. Jerome Kahtotah, wounded in action;

Priv. Meshell Kennosha, killed in action;

Priv. Meshell Mahmakawit, wounded in action;

Priv. Amable Nahshakahappah, killed in action;

Priv. Joseph Nahwahquah, killed in action;

Priv. John B. Pahpoquah, taken prisoner, still hospitalized when regiment mustered out;

Priv. Peter Paponotniew, captured, died a prisoner of war March 20, 1865, Danville, Virginia;

Priv. Jacob Pequachnaniew, wounded in action;

Priv. August Piahwahsha, captured, died a prisoner of war March 20, 1865, Danville, Virginia;

Priv. Benjamin Rubber, wounded in action, died August 8, 1864, Douglas Hospital, Washington, D.C., buried Arlington National Cemetery;

Priv. Meshell Shaboishakah, Jr., wounded in action and taken prisoner;

Priv. Meshell Shaboishakah, Sr., wounded in action;

Priv. John Shapahkasic, absent, sick since action of July 30;

Priv. Dominekee Teco, taken prisoner;

Priv. Joseph Wahsahwequon, taken prisoner, died of wounds April 7, 1865, Cumberland, Maryland;

Priv. Felix Wahtownut, taken prisoner, still hospitalized when regiment mustered out;

Priv. Paul Weieriskasit, captured, died a prisoner of war February 8, 1865, Salisbury, North Carolina.[21]

but this was forbidden until he had "seen his own white hairs."[22]

When Judge Perrote died in 1920, he was buried with the honors appropriate to his positions as grand master of the Medicine Lodge, a leader of the Society of Dreamers, and federal judge.[23] Nineteen twenty was also the year in which Skinner published the sacred text of the Menominee Medicine Dance which he had received from Judge Perrote. There are sure to have been Menominees who noted the additional coincidence that, at half his age, Skinner followed Perrote in death by a scant five years.

9 / *The Winnebago Medicine Rite*

THERE WAS QUITE LITERALLY a world of difference between the views of Indians and those of Europeans in
the matter of religion, and much of the oral tradition of
Indians was of a religious nature. Europeans openly
revealed the teachings of their own religions and actively promoted their acquisition by Indians. Scriptures and
hymns were translated into Indian dialects from the
time of the first generation of Indian-white contacts in
many cases. This openness of whites about their sacred
knowledge contrasted greatly with Indian attitudes in
earlier historic times and contrasts even today with
those of many Indians. The white man has taken so
much from the Indians through five centuries of contact
that there is an understandable reluctance on the part
of Indians to part with the last things to which anyone
can have a claim of ownership, the thoughts in one's
own mind.

JASPER BLOWSNAKE'S MISSION

Sam Blowsnake, a Winnebago Indian, described in his
autobiography the fatal consequences he was told to
expect if he revealed the secrets of the Winnebago
Medicine Rite: "When we got to [the wilderness], we
found a place where the ground had been cleared in the
outline of a dance lodge. There they preached to me
and they told me that the most fearful things imagin-
able would happen to me if I made public any of this
affair. The world would come to an end, they said.
Then again they told me to keep everything secret, and
that if I told anyone, I would surely die."[1]

The Ojibwa Medicine Society was a ritual and
ceremonial organization that developed among Central
Algonquian speakers in the upper Great Lakes area
during the eighteenth century and strongly influenced
the development of the Winnebago Medicine Rite. One
clue to this influence, as Paul Radin has noted, is that
the songs of the Winnebago rite were "to a large extent" in some Algonquian language.[2] Revealing the
secrets of the rite was regarded by its practitioners as a
mortal sin, yet Radin did come to know these secrets

because of a set of circumstances uniquely favorable for
that purpose. Radin arrived at Winnebago, Nebraska, in
the summer of 1908 for the purpose of doing an ethnographic study of the Winnebago. He arrived at a time
when a new religion, the peyote religion, was becoming
accepted by the Winnebagoes, and when members of
the Medicine Rite were falling away from their former
beliefs.

Peyote is a species of cactus containing the halluci-
nogen mescaline. Visions have or have had a place in
the religions of all North American Indians but normally required days of deprivation of food and water to
produce and were typically acquired by individuals in
isolation. Visions were sought in such rites as the Sun
Dance and the quest for a guardian spirit. Ingesting
peyote, communicants of the peyote religion receive
visions during a single night's session and within a
supportive group. Peyote is regarded as a sacrament, and
peyotists see an analogy between the eating of a peyote
button and the eating of a bread wafer in the Christian
Eucharist, a comparison that Christian clergy have been
less disposed to accept. Many peyote groups are now
incorporated under the name Native American Church.

The peyote religion was introduced to the Winnebago by John Rave, a Winnebago who had been initiated into the use of peyote while on a visit to Oklahoma in 1893–1894. At first the peyote was used by the
Winnebagoes more or less in the context of the old
religious ways. By 1908, the year of Radin's arrival,
however, Rave had changed the orientation of Winnebago peyotism to a direction antagonistic to the old
Winnebago beliefs. Indian religion is unlike Christianity
in many respects, but especially in the matter of toler-
ance. One cannot become a member of a Christian
church while continuing a practice of Judaism, Islam, or
any other faith. From the point of view of Christian
missionaries one could not properly accept the teachings
and tenets of Christianity while remaining a practi-
tioner of traditional Indian religious beliefs, or 'pagan-
ism', as it is referred to among the Christian Winnebagoes and Menominees. By contrast, Indians believed

that membership or even priesthood by an Indian in one society or cult should not by itself prevent him from full participation in some other religious organization.[3]

John Rave changed this traditional eclectic or tolerant attitude for members of the Winnebago peyote religion. He came to insist that no one could become a member of his peyote church and still believe in traditional Winnebago teachings, such as those of the Medicine Rite. He insisted upon a complete rejection of the former Winnebago way of life. The Medicine Rite became a special target because of its doctrine of reincarnation; John Rave's peyote church denied the possibility of reincarnation. He also preached that all other ceremonies were wrong and advocated the destruction of sacred war-bundles and the medicine bags used by practitioners of the Medicine Rite.[4] A century earlier in 1807, as far away as Chequamegon Bay on Lake Superior, Ojibwa converts of the Shawnee Prophet Tenskwatawa, brother of Tecumseh, had similarly thrown away their sacred medicine bags in response to the Ohio prophet's teachings. The shore of Chequamegon Bay was said to have been literally strewn with sacred medicine bags washed up from the waters into which they had been thrown by Ojibwas following the new religion, a case of sacredness being relative to time, place, and circumstances.[5]

Paul Radin stepped into a very similar situation as an anthropologist with the intention of putting on paper the beliefs and customs of the Winnebagoes. Some prominent members of the Medicine Rite had become converted to the peyote church and no longer adhered to the beliefs of the older Winnebago rite, and John Rave, for his own purposes, wished that a public record would be made of the myths, songs, and procedures of the Medicine Rite, heretofore kept secret under threat of death from the spirit powers that the traditional or 'pagan' faction believed controlled the Winnebago universe.

Radin arrived with little practical knowledge of the Winnebago language but with university training in the phonetic transcription of non-Indo-European languages. This allowed him not only to record in writing the spoken text of stories in Winnebago but also to repeat them back in a manner intelligible to the Winnebago. Radin's coming, at the time he did and with his particular skills, was seen as an omen by the peyotists. Radin thus became quite welcome to the followers of the peyote religion, a person seemingly sent to the Winnebago by god himself, but at the expense of a considerably less enthusiastic reception by the Winnebagoes who still followed the Medicine Rite.

In a surprisingly short time Radin was permitted to make a complete record of the Medicine Rite, considering the years it often takes for an outsider to gain the confidence of an Indian people sufficient to be introduced to the deepest secrets of their religion. The sources were members of the Medicine Rite who had fallen away to join the new peyote church, Winnebagoes who nevertheless had strong personal reservations about the wisdom of the action they were taking, considering the belief that the secrets could not be told without someone dying as a consequence. The fear was not dissipated when shortly someone did die.

The largest part of the rite was recorded from the words of Jasper Blowsnake, Sam Blowsnake's older brother. Jasper Blowsnake did not insist upon or accept gifts, money, or other compensation for his efforts, contrary to the usual practice when sacred knowledge was transferred between individuals. He could thus not be accused of having a purely financial interest in the revealing of the secrets of the rite. The project of transcribing the rite required two months of seven-day weeks, working six hours per day. The day after the recording of the rite in Winnebago was finished, Radin received a telegram saying that his father had become seriously ill with little hope for living. The fateful timing of the telegram could hardly be overlooked by anyone concerned and further work at Winnebago, Nebraska, was necessarily postponed.[6]

Working with a bilingual Winnebago in Washington, D.C., Radin was able to obtain an accurate literal translation into English of the Winnebago text but was left at a loss for the secret meanings of the text. Radin's Winnebago interpreter in Washington was fluent in colloquial Winnebago but was unfamiliar with the ritual use of the Winnebago language. The language used in ritual may contain unfamiliar archaic terms but remains unintelligible more because of the highly poetic and figurative nature of the language. The special meanings would be something unknown to persons not initiated into the rite.

Despite the death of Paul Radin's father, Jasper Blowsnake in time became resigned to the job of completing the task begun and proceeded to interpret the metaphoric sense of the words of the rite. He came to believe that it was his preordained task to provide a record of the Winnebago Medicine Rite for all to know, just as it appeared to many to be Radin's god-given task to put that record on paper. "This must be the work assigned to me by the Creator," Blowsnake thought. "Now I know that the telling and the translation of the Medicine Rite is my mission in life."[7] Because of this, Blowsnake also reviewed the entire transcript for the purpose of correcting any errors since errors in a ritual were regarded as dangerous in themselves. The resulting work was edited and published by Radin as *The Road of Life and Death: A Ritual Drama of the American Indians*, an almost unique document of a way of life that has now passed for so many American Indians.

ORIGIN OF THE MEDICINE RITE

The origin myth was the first aspect of the Winnebago Medicine Rite that was recorded by Radin. Three former members of the Rite agreed to dictate for Radin the most sacred myths of the tribe—those of the origin of the world, the origin of the Indians, and the origin of the Medicine Rite itself. This dictation took from midnight until five in the morning on a summer night in 1908, word by word and syllable by syllable. The recording had been done in secret, but it would seem to have been less of a secret that three former members of the Medicine Rite had accompanied Radin across the Missouri to Sioux City, Iowa, and not returned until the next day. In any case, by the afternoon of that next day the mission was hardly a secret any longer; everyone on the Winnebago, Nebraska, reservation knew of the trip.

Radin immediately came under pressure to give a public reading of the myths for the many members of the tribe who wanted to know those stories. Any number of older Winnebagoes were not members of the Medicine Rite and therefore knew no more of this sacred lore than the younger peyotists. After consulting with the older men, Radin agreed, and more than forty Winnebagoes crowded together for the event. Radin read slowly from his transcribed texts to an audience that uttered not a word while listening in awe and with great respect to sacred knowledge, which until then only the members of the Medicine Rite had known.[8]

After creating the earth, Earthmaker was said to have proceeded to create the birds, beasts, and insects of the fields and finally, the human beings. These humans, made with their creator's final thoughts, were the weakest creatures of all, "not even equal in strength to a fly," and were near the point of extinction by evil spirits when Earthmaker intervened. Earthmaker made four additional men one after another and dispatched them to earth to protect the weak humans. These heroes, one after another, all failed in this task—the trickster Foolish-One, Turtle, Bladder, and He-who-wears-human-heads-as-earrings. Earthmaker then created a fifth one, the one called Hare. Earthmaker charged Hare with protecting the earth and its inhabitants from the evil spirits that were harming them.

On arriving, Hare determined to take on a human form, so he entered the womb of a young woman who was walking down to a river to get water. After the proper period of time had elapsed Hare was born in his human form. "[H]e went out through an opening," the story told, and "Not four days after, the woman died."[9] Hare traveled across the earth and through the sky killing all the bad spirits as he went; he alone had accomplished the task that Earthmaker had assigned to his five special emissaries.

Hare was quite pleased with himself, but he became distressed when he learned from his grandmother, Earth, that the human beings whose lives he had saved were ultimately destined for death despite his efforts, that death was a part of Earthmaker's plan for the world. Without death the world would become overcrowded. Death and decay could not be rescinded. Hare grew increasingly despondent. "My aunts and uncles must not die!" he said. It was in such a manner that Hare spoke of the human beings of the earth, and for that reason that members of the Rite spoke of Hare as He-whom-we-call-our-nephew.

In his anger Hare vowed, "To all things death will come. . . . Then he cast his thoughts upon the precipices and they began to fall, to crumble. Upon the rocks he cast his thoughts and they crumbled. Under the earth he cast his thoughts and all beings that were living under the earth stopped moving and their limbs stiffened (in death). Up above he also cast his thoughts and the birds began to fall down (dead)."[10]

Before long, word reached Earthmaker of Hare's violent reaction to his disappointing discovery that it was not in the plan of things that humankind should be immortal like himself. Earthmaker sent four emissaries one by one to return Hare from the earth. One by one each failed in their turns—Foolish-One, Turtle, and Bladder—except for the fourth, He-who-wears-human-heads-as-earrings.

In his compassion Earthmaker promised Hare a holy teaching with which he could return to earth to benefit the lives of his uncles and aunts. Earthmaker revealed to Hare a long lodge and told him that if the human beings of the earth would only perform the lodge ceremony correctly, they could live more than one life. After death they could be reincarnated in any form they chose, human or spirit, upon the earth or below. To aid him, Hare was told to call upon Foolish-One, Turtle, Bladder, He-who-wears-human-heads-as-earrings, and his grandmother, Earth. Earth took from her breast corn for the people to eat and tobacco, so that the people would always have something to offer when seeking life.[11]

When he returned to earth, Hare built the lodge for the first Medicine Rite. The eight side poles of the lodge he created from yellow female snakes tied with rattlesnakes for bindings. The doorway Hare made from black snakes, the female on the left and the male on the right. He threw reed-grass on the lodge and it became its covering. More reed-grass he threw on the floor, along with the hides of a black bear and a white deer, and they became the lodge's floor mats. At the eastern door he stationed a mountain lion to prevent bad spirits from entering and at the western door, a buffalo bull. When this was accomplished, Hare paused to admire his construction while the animals inside bellowed and roared.[12]

The Winnebago rite shared with the Menominee and Ojibwa medicine rites the all-important element of 'shooting' initiates and members with medicine bags, among which was an especially favored type made from the skin of an otter. One clear difference can be seen in the origin myth, which in the Winnebago rite does not contain any reference to a wolf brother of the Great Hare Manabush, or Manabozho, Nanabozho, Nanabush, Wenebojo, Michabo, and so on, as the Great Hare is variously known among Algonquian speakers. Winnebago Hare would obviously seem to be the counterpart of Menominee Manabush and Ojibwa Manabozho, except that Manabush and Manabozho were both rabbits *and* tricksters. Among the Winnebago the trickster Foolish-One was distinct from Hare, who was the hero of the Medicine Rite. Radin sees in this the borrowing by the Winnebagoes of an Algonquian culture hero and his partial rehabilitation because only certain midwestern Siouan speakers like the Winnebagoes and Iowas, who have been in close contact with Algonquians like the Menominees and Fox, have a Hare character in the roles he has.[13]

In the Winnebago, Menominee, and Potawatomi versions of the Medicine Society origin myth the rite is given to a hero of rabbit name, if not always of rabbit form, while he is despondent over his discovery of death for his people generally (Winnebago) or for his companion/brother (Menominee). In the Omaha Shell Society origin myth a medicine ritual with the power to provide success in hunting was given to a couple by animal spirits in exchange, as it turned out, for their four children, who were mystically killed and then claimed by the waves of a lake.[14] By implication at least, the representative of the animal spirits was an underwater monster, a deerlike creature with a long sweeping tail, a hoofed and antlered Omaha counterpart of the long-tailed Underwater Panther of the Great Lakes tribes. In the related Omaha Pebble Society membership was available to those who had dreamed of water, the pebble used for 'shooting', or a certain long-tailed water monster.[15]

Winnebago Hare killed his mother while bursting from her body at birth.[16] This episode parallels the Iroquois mythical theme of the twin, Flint, killing his mother when he forced himself through her side at birth rather than being born in the usual way. Iroquois Flint and his twin brother Sapling were conceived magically when their mother slept next to a pair of arrows given her by Turtle, Flint being conceived by an arrow with a flint point and Sapling by an unpointed arrow.[17] Hare's responsibility in his mother's death is not spelled out so clearly among the Winnebago and is perhaps another example of Hare's rehabilitation by the Winnebagoes.[18]

The Winnebagoes were never neighbors of any Iroquoian people until the Oneidas moved to Wisconsin early in the nineteenth century. However, during the period of the development of the Medicine Rite in the last quarter of the seventeenth century the Winnebagoes were close neighbors of the Potawatomis and the Fox in eastern Wisconsin, and both of these Algonquian tribes had originally lived in lower Michigan where they would have been regional, although not close, neighbors of the westernmost of the non-League Iroquoian tribes, most notably the Neutrals and the Hurons.

In a letter dated St. Louis, Missouri, January 10, 1847, the Jesuit Father Pierre-Jean de Smet described an origin myth of the Medicine Society that had been narrated to him by "Potogojecs, one of the most intelligent chiefs of the Potawatomi Nation."[19] These were the Potawatomis then living at Council Bluffs, Iowa, only recently removed from their original eastern home. Briefly, the story told how a powerful manitou had come to earth and had quadruplet sons. The first was Nanaboojoo, the second Chipiapoos, whose name was glossed 'man of the dead', the third Wabosso, who fled north and became a white rabbit, and the fourth Chakekenapok, whose name was said to mean 'the man of flint, or fire-stone'. This last-born brother caused the death of his mother.[20]

As the Potawatomi story continued, Nanaboojoo avenged the death of his mother by killing Chakekenapok. Chipiapoos ventured onto the ice of Lake Michigan and was drowned when certain manitous or spirits caused the ice to break up. Nanaboojoo was grief-stricken and was given a medicine lodge and medicine bags and initiated into the Medicine Society for consolation. Chipiapoos returned and was given a burning coal to kindle a fire in the region of the souls but was forbidden to enter the lodge. Nanaboojoo then initiated his family into the Medicine Society and gave them orders to perpetuate the ceremony.

This Potawatomi story follows the Menominee version fairly closely except for the births of the hero and his brothers with the death of the mother. It also differs in interesting details from other Potawatomi versions collected by Alanson Skinner in 1923 or sometime earlier. In one of these stories the Manabush character was known as Wisaka, as he is known among the Fox, and his human mother was a woman of the Fox Tribe.[21]

Wisaka was the eldest, impregnated by a gust of wind, a common element in stories of the birth of Manabush. The younger three were hidden in a rotten log, where in time Wisaka found them. One was called Arrow-Elbows and had arrowheads protruding from his elbows. He stabbed and killed his mother, then fled north where he became a rock of flint by day and a great rabbit by night. Wisaka resolved to kill his brother

Arrow-Elbows for his matricide, and all three of the younger brothers fled. One went south and another west, taking charge in those quarters of the earth. Arrow-Elbows fled north and became known as Kaponka 'The-cold-weather-maker'. Wisaka destroyed Kaponka as flint rock, but Kaponka survived as a white rabbit. This purported Potawatomi story parallels the Winnebago Medicine Rite origin myth in associating a rabbit with the death of his mother. It parallels Iroquois stories associating the death of the mother with a son identified both with flint and with ice and cold.

Walter James Hoffman published a Menominee account of the birth of Manabush that he heard recited during a Mitäwin ceremony in the summer of 1891. The narrator was Neopit, chief of the Menominees and grandson of Chief Oshkosh. In this version Manabush and a brother were twins born to a daughter of Nokomis. One twin and the mother died. These were buried, and the living twin was put under an inverted wooden bowl and forgotten. Four days later the bowl was removed and the twin had become a little white rabbit. After Manabush had grown and accomplished the feats for which he had been placed on earth, the good spirits brought his brother back to life as a companion and named him Naq'pote 'expert marksman'. He was human but hunted in the form of a wolf (Moqwai'o 'Wolf'), much as Manabush could transform himself from human to rabbit form. Wolf was drowned by bad spirits in a frozen lake as in other stories and became ruler of the land of the dead.[22]

During another Mitäwin ceremonial in the same year Hoffman recorded a quite different story of the origins of Manabush and Wolf, this one from the lips of Shunien, chief of one of the Menominee bands. Shunien's version begins with Flint as the daughter of Nakomis as Earth. Flint dipped a bowl into the earth. The earth became blood, and the blood turned into Wabus the Rabbit, who was also Fire. The rabbit grew into human form and became a man who was known as Manabush or Great Rabbit. One day Wolf appeared and announced that he would be Manabush's brother and hunt game for him. Manabush changed Wolf into a man, Wolf was drowned in the lake and became ruler of the land of the spirits.[23]

Versions of Manabush's birth closer to that of the Winnebagoes were collected by the linguist Leonard Bloomfield in the period 1920–1921. These can be synopsized as follows. An old woman had a daughter who conceived when a gust of wind blew up her skirts as she bent over facing north. Manabush was born first and initially put in or under a bowl, then scores of game animals or spirit animals were born, and finally Flint-Rock, whose birth caused the mother's death. Manabush grew rapidly, avenged the mother's death by killing Flint-Rock, and stole fire to restore the flames

that had been extinguished during the births.[24] These versions vary in the identity of the creatures born between Manabush and Flint-Rock, I would think, because in the Menominee language the Algonquian word manitou, widely meaning 'spirit', has come to mean 'game-animal'.

The origin myths of the Medicine Society are diverse enough that they cannot by themselves explain how the rite came to appear where and when it did among the Indians of the upper Great Lakes. Much can be learned by examining the ways in which a person can become a member of a Medicine Society and considering those ways in the context of the shooting ritual. Speaking from his nineteenth-century perspective, Hoffman said that Ojibwas could join the Midewiwin, the Ojibwa Medicine Society, in one of three principal ways: (1) a male child could be designated for future membership at the time he was given a name; (2) if a child thus dedicated for membership in the society died before reaching puberty and receiving initiation, the father (or sometimes the mother if the father was unavailable) could be received into membership in his place. This was done in a Ghost Lodge ceremony and was a soul-release ceremony as well; (3) a person who was sick and received a cure with the aid of the Medicine Society could become a patient-member.[25]

No one ever became a member of the Ojibwa Medicine Society just to replace a deceased member. This, however, was the most common way in which a Winnebago joined the Medicine Rite. A Winnebago could also simply apply for membership and make the required gifts.[26] This was also contrary to Ojibwa practice. The two principal means of acquiring membership in the Menominee Medicine Society were the same as for the Winnebagoes. The chief mourner at a Menominee burial ceremony might address the deceased saying, "Go my brother . . . follow the sun to the place prepared for the shades of the dead, where you will see the fire built by Naq'pote; that will light your course beyond the sun's path. Abide there until the proper time [a certain period of a summer month is usually named], when I shall give a feast and bring a substitute to occupy your place; then shall Naq'pote permit you to return to observe the fulfillment of my promise. Go!"[27] The Ghost Lodge ceremony then followed at the time named.

The purpose of all the Medicine Societies mentioned was to prolong life, to allow one to "see one's own gray hairs," but in the Winnebago Medicine Rite we find the additional unique purpose of offering the prospect of reincarnation—allowing one to figuratively shed one's skin, as does a serpent, and emerge reborn. This is a feature closely related to the idea of adoption in mourning as symbolic reincarnation or reconception, and that ties closely to the universal practice of 'shooting', feigned death, and apparent resurrection found in all variants of the Medicine Rite or Medicine Society.

One element that relates all Medicine Societies is that of the simulated or symbolic 'shooting' of initiates and/or members with small missiles—usually shells but sometimes pebbles, beads, or other small objects—supposedly projected from the mouths of birds or mammals made into medicine bags. Paul Radin studied this element in some detail within the context of the societies and their ritual. He noted that the initiation ritual with its associated shooting appeared to be an intrusive element in the Winnebago Medicine Rite, inserted, that is, into a ceremony that seemed to halt for the initiation and shooting and then to continue afterward.

The initiation with its shooting looked to Radin like a part of another ceremony that had been secondarily associated with some preexisting Winnebago ceremony.[28] He saw the Ojibwa Midewiwin as the source of the combination of initiation and shooting, transmitted probably by way of the Fox and Iowa tribes and incorporated into an older Winnebago ceremony. In the older ceremony Radin saw some not-clearly-defined relationships to a certain Night-spirits' Rite of the Winnebagoes and to a much more explicit expression of Winnebago mourning ritual. The latter is found in the Tear-Pouring ceremony within the Winnebago Medicine Rite.[29]

The Winnebagoes believed that every individual was born with a predetermined measure of years to live and that if a person were to die before his time, the unused remainder of the quota of years could be awarded to his survivors if the ghost requested it of the spirits.[30] The Winnebagoes also believed that a dead person might be reborn into the world of the living from the world of the dead—be reincarnated. This reincarnation was referred to as 'skin shedding'. It was to Hare that the Winnebagoes were grateful for teaching them the mysteries of the Medicine Rite and giving them the power to 'shed their skins' and obtain 'new life'.[31] A Winnebago typically became a member of the Medicine Society to replace a member who had died, so in effect such a member was reincarnated in the person of the new initiate. Within the ceremony, however, the promise of reincarnation was interpreted much more literally.

In the Ojibwa ceremony a person never became a member to replace one who had died. The purpose of the ceremony was basically to publicly acknowledge the transfer of shamanistic knowledge and powers from an older member to the initiate who had studied under him. Radin saw little actual ceremonialism except in the initiation with its shooting. He saw this shooting as an *intrusive* element in the Winnebago rite and as the *climactic* act of the Ojibwa and Menominee rites.[32]

The Menominee rite was intermediate between the Ojibwa and Winnebago rites, emphasizing more shamanistic elements than the Winnebago, but giving great importance to replacing deceased members with initiates, as among the Winnebagoes. A member of the Menominee lodge "is always succeeded by a near relative; and, secondly, not only is the [Medicine Society] connected with the function of insuring the safe passage to the future world, but the ceremony itself begins at the grave of the deceased member as soon as the mortuary rites are over. They may even be regarded as a continuation of the same."[33]

Radin called attention to the practice of 'shooting' in the Shell and Pebble societies of the Omahas, noting that while shooting did not figure in the initiation rites of those societies, the identities of members were bound closely to the element of shooting. Members were known as "Those who shoot with a Shell" and "Those who shoot the Pebble."[34] Radin saw shooting as a ritual element widely spread in the Midwest and even beyond, but incorporated differently from tribe to tribe and from ceremony to ceremony.

In the Winnebago rite the members concealed the shell missile in their mouths and at the appropriate time appeared to cough it up and onto their otter skin medicine bags (figure 9.1). Each would then make four circuits of the ceremonial lodge with the shell in one hand and the medicine bag in the other, singing and accelerating his pace as he went. The shell was held in the palm of the right hand for spectators to see. They then pretended to swallow the shell and at once fell down as if dead. After a few moments they simulated the regaining of consciousness and the coughing up of the shell, which they placed in their medicine bags. They then made another four circuits of the lodge and this time shot four members in each of the five bands into which the society was organized for each ceremony.[35] Each person thus shot feigned death and the return to life and then joined in the procession around the crowded medicine lodge while other participants swayed, sang, shook gourds, and struck the water drum until the rhythms and intensity of the scene in the lodge captured the minds and emotions of the onlookers.

The shells used in the shooting ceremonies by the Winnebagoes were referred to in ceremonies by ritual names, commonly as 'arrows'. From this, Radin inferred that in an older form of the shooting rite genuine arrows were used, and he had in mind something like the arrow shooting that Pawnee illusionists practiced in their ceremony of the Medicine Men or Big Doctor Performance.[36] In the Winnebago ritual the shell was referred to not only as an 'arrow' but also as a 'black hawk'.

Because it has been among the Ojibwas that the Medicine Society has taken its best known, most persistent, most widely distributed, and most elaborate form, it would be hard to find anyone knowledgeable in the known history of Medicine Societies who did not look to the Ojibwas, if not for their origin, at least for their center of diffusion. It would also be unusual for such a complex ritual organization to just appear in the eighteenth century, as it did, without some antecedent noted by seventeenth-century chroniclers who were to some degree at least aware of just about all other aspects of upper Great Lakes area Indian life.

I do not see the classically described Ojibwa Midewiwin simply as an Indian response to Christianity or to European encroachment in the upper Great Lakes area. I do see merit in Harold Hickerson's argument that the Ojibwa/Chippewa Midewiwin can be seen in part as a response to the increasing complexity of the Chequamegon settlement and the need for a mechanism to promote cohesion within the village,[37] but that would hardly explain the diffusion of Medicine Societies so far into the non-Chippewa and even non-Algonquian hinterland, nor the greater role given to mourning in the diffused form of the rite. I do not see mourning ritual as the prime inspiration for the Midewiwin, but I do see it as a substratum of ritual into which the Midewiwin could easily have been incorporated south of the Lake Superior area.

A Band of Sorcerers

The Algonquian Feast of the Dead was a periodic reburial ritual that served to create ties between dispersed bands and tribes by committing the bones of their dead to a common grave. It was an annual event whose location moved from place to place as the host village of one year became a guest village of the next. Intergroup marriages took place, trade relationships were discussed, and political alliances were established or strengthened. Chiefs were raised and names of the dead transferred to the living to keep their memories alive, much as in Iroquois Condolence Rites.[38] This feast was practiced by the

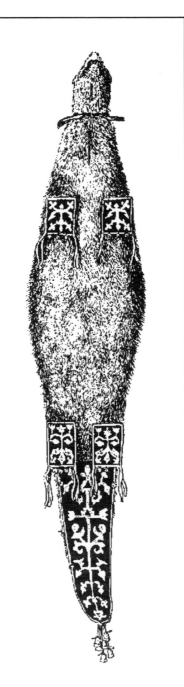

Figure 9.1 Otterskin medicine bag used in the Winnebago Medicine Rite, from Radin (1970, pl. 51*a*).

Nipissings, Ottawas, Saulteurs, and other Algonquian speakers of the Lake Huron–Lake Superior basin. It was derived from a similar ceremony practiced by the Hurons, who were a western, non-League Iroquoian confederacy living on Georgian Bay at the root of the Ontario peninsula (chapter 5).

From the time of a description of such an Algonquian feast by Father Jérome Lalement in 1641 until that of the feast described by La Mothe Cadillac at Mackinac in 1695, no more than two generations passed. This was the brief period during which the Algonquian Feast of the Dead is known from European observation. The original Feast of the Dead necessarily began earlier among the Hurons, but the Huron settlements in the Ontario peninsula were destroyed by the five Iroquois nations of the League by 1649, so the career of the Huron feast was cut short.

Tradition traces the origin of the Medicine Societies to the time of the Creation, when the world was being organized. History is not as generous and allows much less antiquity to these organizations. Despite the number of Europeans in the Great Lakes area available for such observations, the earliest record of a society and performance that Hickerson has accepted as evidence of the existence of the Medicine Society appears in a letter of Antoine Denis Raudot written in 1709.[39] It refers to an event witnessed by Raudot at Sault Sainte Marie among the Saulteurs, who were one of the Algonquian groups that merged to become the latter-day Ojibwas. Hickerson says that the first mention of a Midewiwin ceremony by that name would be that by Jacques de Sabrevois, the French commandant at Detroit from 1714 to 1717, who spoke of a Potawatomi ceremony called the *medelinne* performed by men whom he described as looking "like a band of sorcerers."[40]

Hickerson contrasts the function of the Algonquian Feast of the Dead—maintaining alliances *between* autonomous groups—with that of the Ojibwa/Chippewa Midewiwin—promoting cohesion *within* a group. He sees the situation calling for this cohesion as the appearance of large proto-Ojibwa settlements at Sault Sainte Marie (a locality now split by the Michigan-Ontario boundary along the Saint Marys River) and on Chequamegon Bay on the Lake Superior shore of northwestern Wisconsin. He seconds the statement of the Chippewa historian William W. Warren that the Midewiwin was practiced in its most original form at Chequamegon, adding the qualification that this means only that it was at Chequamegon that "the old shamanistic rites of magic and medicine first became the property of an organized priesthood."[41]

In the controversy over the age of the Midewiwin Hickerson states flatly, "The Midewiwin was in fact a *nativistic movement*, a reaction to contact with Europeans, and not aboriginal. The ceremony represented and reflected new modes of organization, not ancient ones."[42] By referring to a *nativistic movement* Hickerson was invoking the image of a class of ceremonial that commonly arises during a time of stress when older beliefs and practices are reorganized and new patterns of thought emerge, often with the addition of new elements, and often following the inspiration of a holy person. Too little is known of the early Midewiwin among the Algonquians to say that Hickerson is wrong, but I do believe that the roots of the society and ceremonial are older than generally acknowledged.

Felix Keesing saw the gist or kernel of the Midewiwin among the Hurons as early as 1636.[43] In that year the Jesuit Father Jean de Brébeuf mentioned a particular curing ceremonial called "*akhrendoiaen*, inasmuch as those who take part in this dance give poison to one another."[44] He went on to say that the ceremonial had never before been practiced among the Nation of the Bear, by which Brébeuf was referring to the Attignawantan or People of the Bear, the largest of the Huron tribes. The Hurons were a confederacy of four tribes, much as the Iroquois proper were a confederacy of five, later six, tribes or nations.

Brébeuf does not say from what tribe or village the practitioners of the ceremonial came, only that it took a fortnight to assemble the eighty members of the company or society—seventy-four men and six women. He repeats the name of the dance or ceremonial, this time as *Otakrendoiae*, and calls the society *Atirenda* and describes the ritual in these words:

> Let it suffice for the present to say, in general, that never did frenzied Bacchantes of bygone times do anything more furious in their orgies. It is a question of killing one another here, they say, by charms which they throw at each other, and which are composed of Bears' claws, Wolves' teeth, Eagles' talons, certain stones, and Dogs' sinews. Having fallen under the charm and been wounded, blood pours from mouth and nostrils, or it is simulated by a red powder they take by stealth; and there are ten thousand other absurdities, that I willingly pass over.

> The greatest evil is, that these wretches, under pretext of charity, often avenge their injuries, and purposely give poison to their patients, instead of medicine. What is very remarkable is their experience in healing ruptures, wherein many others in these regions are also skillful. The most extraordinary superstition is that their drugs and ointments take pleasure, so to speak, in silence and darkness. If they are recognized, or if their secret is discovered, success is not to be expected.

> The origin of all this folly comes from one named *Oatarra*, or from a little idol in the form of a doll, which [a certain Huron] has asked, for the sake of being cured, from a dozen Sorcerers who had come to see him; having put it into his Tobacco pouch, it began to stir therein, and ordered the banquets and other ceremonials of the dance, according to what they say. Certainly you have here many silly things, and I am much afraid there may be something darker and more occult in them.[45]

A little idol in the form of a doll that stirs and moves inside a pouch and speaks? This sounds familiar. It sounds like the 'sacred amusement' described for the Menominee Medicine Society ceremony and said to date to the origin of the society itself (chapter 8). It is a shaman's illusion Walter James Hoffman witnessed when he was admitted to the society and that he said made such a profound effect on the audience that absolute silence reigned in the lodge except for the singing of the performers.[46] It would not be difficult to add the element of shamanistic ventriloquism to give the additional illusion that the puppets were speaking and giving orders in the manner that Father Brébeuf described. The source of words spoken in a high pitch is exceedingly difficult to determine, and words thus spoken can easily be believed to come from a doll or puppet.

The Jesuit Father Paul Ragenau recorded another possible observation on the ceremony in his *Relation* of 1645–1646. Speaking on the progress of his Huron mission a decade after Brébeuf, Ragenau described "a certain dance,—the most celebrated in the country, because it is believed the most powerful over the Demons to procure, by their means, the healing of certain diseases. Be this as it may, that dance is only for chosen people, who are admitted to it with ceremony, with great gifts, and after a declaration which they make to the grand masters of this Brotherhood, to keep secret the mysteries that are intrusted to them, as things holy and sacred."[47] Reuben Gold Thwaites, editor of

Jesuit Relations, did not hesitate to compare this celebrated dance with the Grand Medicine Society of the Ojibwas as described by Walter James Hoffman.[48]

It is not possible to say that Ragenau's ceremony was the same as that described by Brébeuf, but Brébeuf said enough to describe what are the most important elements of the Midewiwin—a secret society of curers and sorcerers, including both men and women, whose ritual includes the simulated death of members with small objects that they supposedly project through the air at each other. This would be a form of 'shooting', as in the Midewiwin.

No one knows from where the *Otakrendoiae* came, only that it was new to at least one tribe of the Huron Confederacy in 1636 and that it required two weeks to assemble the society to perform its cure. That it required two weeks to assemble the members suggests that they came from entirely outside of the Huron area, perhaps from as much as a week's journey away, calculating five days to a week for notification and five days to a week for traveling. Such a distance would easily extend along water routes to the Tionnontatés, Amikwas, Ottawas, and Nipissings, but it would make special sense to think this particular confraternity originated among the Nipissings. At least, the Nipissings had a widespread reputation for their shamanism. Even the name of this tribe in the Iroquoian languages translates as Nation of Sorcerers.[49] The cultists that Brébeuf described were not simply herbalist curers; Brébeuf tells us that they also had a reputation for occasional *fatal* cures, one might say.

When the Huron villages were destroyed by the Five Nations in 1649, the Nipissings were also attacked and almost disappeared from written history because they moved westward into the Lake Superior area to escape the Iroquois threat. Some are known to have settled by the 1660s among the Amikwas, Saulteurs, and others who together would in later years become known as the Ojibwas.[50] If the *Otakrendoiae* were of Nipissing origin, then this could have put the example of an organized society of curers, illusionists, and sorcerers, with a practice of 'shooting' and simulated death, among the very people who would be developing the Midewiwin, as we know it, through the following generation.

One Frenchman might have known the answer to this riddle. The one European who was thoroughly familiar with the Nipissings and fluent in their language at the time was Jean Nicolet. Nicolet had lived among them for eight or nine years, lived among them *as* a Nipissing, in his own household, with a Nipissing wife and child. Had he not died an untimely death in 1642 we might today know more not only about Nipissing beliefs and practices but also about those of the early Winnebagoes because it was Jean Nicolet who traveled in 1634 as the envoy of Governor Samuel Champlain to the Winnebagoes and became the first European of record to enter the Lake Michigan basin.[51] As it was, Nicolet drowned in the icy waters of the Saint Lawrence River, a victim, the Indians might have said, of the Underwater Panther that angers the river by switching its long tail.

"DRY RICH PRAIRIE," the land surveyor called it, short-ly after Gen. Henry Atkinson crossed Rock Prairie in 1832. General Atkinson was pursuing Black Hawk's band of Sauk Indians at the time, as the Sauks moved up the Rock River from Illinois into Wisconsin. The buffalo had disappeared from Wisconsin prairies by 1832, although there were buffalo grazing on stretches of Wisconsin prairie when Louis Jolliet and Jacques Marquette observed them in 1673. "A rather large number of cows," is what Marquette wrote, having no better way of describing the unfamiliar American bison.[1] Even a century after Marquette wrote, around 1785, the herds of bison crossing the Mississippi River between Wisconsin and the opposite shore could be so dense as to threaten the safety of canoes traveling on that waterway to or from Prairie du Chien.[2] The few buffalo to be seen in Wisconsin today live as guests in zoos or as exotic livestock on private farms like that of David, Valerie, and Corey Heider just south of Janes-ville, Wisconsin. The ruts left by General Atkinson's baggage train crossed Rock Prairie just two miles east of what is now the Heider farm.

WHITE BUFFALO CALF MAIDEN

White buffalo were rare even when buffalo numbered in the millions. They are infinitely rarer today and so much so that when a female white buffalo calf was born on the Heider farm on August 20, 1994, it was the first creature of that description to appear within living memory. It was only a matter of days before American Indians began to arrive at the Heider farm as individu-als, as families, and in delegations to see the miracle, and that is what she was regarded as, and that was the name given to the little calf—Miracle—because that was the form in which one of the most fabled of Indian women was last seen. White Buffalo Calf Maiden is familiar to anyone who has read Black Elk's *Sacred Pipe* or who is otherwise familiar with the traditions of the Teton Dakotas because it is she who is today credited with introducing the sacred pipe–associated ceremo-nies about whom Black Elk and others have spoken.[3]

According to Iśna'la-wića' (Lone Man) of the Hunkpapa Tetons, White Buffalo Calf Maiden first ap-peared to two men of the Sans Arc band who had been sent to scout for buffalo. Lone Man's words were trans-lated by Robert Higheagle and recorded by Frances Densmore for the Bureau of American Ethnology in the period of 1911–1914.[4] As the tradition goes, the two scouts unexpectedly perceived a young woman ap-proaching them, dressed in a buckskin dress, leggings, and moccasins, with a tuft of buffalo hair tied to the left side of her head, and holding a fan of flat sage in her right hand. Her face was painted with vertical red stripes. She announced that she had been sent by the Buffalo People to help them accomplish their mission, but that to do so, the Indians, for their part, must first construct a special lodge in the middle of the camp circle with a buffalo skull altar and other features that she specified. She would then appear the next morning.

While she was speaking, one of the two men had impure thoughts with respect to the woman. A cloud then descended over him, and when it disappeared, only a skeleton remained. The surviving companion hastened back to camp and reported the miraculous events he had witnessed. The band built the lodge as directed and awaited the young maiden, who arrived the next morning as she said she would. She appeared carrying a pipe in her hands, the stem in her right hand and the bowl in her left. She entered the lodge created for her and seated herself in the place of honor opposite the door. She then spoke, saying these things and more:

> I represent the Buffalo tribe, who have sent you this pipe. You are to receive this pipe in the name of all the common people [Indians]. Take it and use it according to my directions. The bowl of the pipe is of red stone—a stone not very common and found only at a certain place. This pipe shall be used as a peacemak-er. The time will come when you shall cease hostilities against other nations. Whenever peace is agreed upon between two tribes or parties this pipe shall be a

binding instrument. By this pipe the medicine-men shall be called to administer help to the sick. . . . Offer sacrifices through this pipe. When you are in need of buffalo meat, smoke this pipe and ask for what you need and it shall be granted you. . . . By this pipe you shall live.[5]

When she had finished speaking, White Buffalo Calf Maiden lit the pipe and raised the stem of the pipe to the sky, then to the earth, and then to the four cardinal directions, addressing each of the six powers in turn and offering them smoke, and then put the pipe to her own mouth. After drawing a puff from the pipe she gave the pipe to the Sans Arc chief, who accepted the pipe on behalf of the whole Sioux nation. While the entire village looked on in silence, White Buffalo Calf Maiden then departed the tent constructed for her and turned into a white buffalo calf. According to Black Elk, the maiden first turned into a red and brown buffalo calf, then into a white buffalo, and then into a black buffalo. According to Arval Looking Horse she changed into four animals, the last of which was a white buffalo calf. Miracle, Janesville's miracle white buffalo calf, herself changed color within a year, and is now brown with a darker face, like most buffaloes, although some people believe that she will cycle through several colors and then turn white again.[6]

The chief who received the pipe was Tataη'ka-woslal'-nažiη (Buffalo Stands Upward, Standing Buffalo) and the possessor of the pipe at the time of Frances Densmore's fieldwork was Red Hair (also known as Elk Head and Old Man Elk Head), who died in 1916 as the eighth keeper of the pipe by the oldest reckonings then on record. The current keeper is Arval Looking Horse, the fourth keeper since Red Hair/Elk Head.[7] This puts the episode considerably closer to the beginning of the nineteenth century than to the "thousands of years ago" that some news media reported for the appearance of White Buffalo Calf Maiden in the wake of the excitement over the birth of the white buffalo calf on the Heider farm.[8]

According to Percy Phillips, a full-blood Teton interviewed by George A. Dorsey on the Cheyenne River Reservation in South Dakota around 1906, the pipe was around nine hundred years old. More important, however, was Phillips's comment that the acquisition of the pipe dated to a time "when the Indians were all living together in the east, near a great lake," living together in a single camp and speaking a single language.[9] If taken at face value, this statement means a time when the Teton Dakotas lived east of the Missouri River because there are natural lakes (as opposed to artificial reservoirs) in the Dakotas only in the formerly glaciated areas east of the Missouri River trench. Ethnohistorians do not believe that the Tetons lived

west of the Missouri until some time in the second half of the 1700s. Arval Looking Horse says that the sacred pipe was received from White Buffalo Calf Maiden on the Cheyenne River Reservation, which is west of the Missouri. This would seem to represent a naturalization of the story of the pipe to the location where the pipe is currently preserved. A recent article in the newspaper *Ho-Chunkwo-Lduk*, quoting Joseph Chasing Horse, says that the sacred pipe bundle was received from White Buffalo Calf Woman two thousand years ago and even farther west, in the Black Hills, and another story in *News from Indian Country* relocates the story of White Buffalo Calf Maiden many days farther west still, to Wyoming, adding also that "the White Buffalo Calf Pipe's sanctuary was in a secret cave on the north side of the Mato Tipi," i.e., Devil's Tower.[10]

References to the appearance of a certain god woman or spirit woman in white mentioned in four different Sioux winter counts between 1785 and 1800, if related, as suspected, to the appearance of White Buffalo Calf Maiden, provide a dating consistent with the dating in winter counts of the initiation of the Hunka ceremony.[11] In his book *The Sacred Pipe* Black Elk indicates that the chief who received the sacred pipe from White Buffalo Calf Maiden was Hehlokecha Najin (Standing Hollow Horn). Black Elk's narrative also credits White Buffalo Calf Maiden with introducing the use of the sacred pipe in seven rites, but this is not the same as introducing the rites themselves. Two of the seven rites, Black Elk admits, were already known to his people—the rite of the sweat lodge and that of the vision quest. The other five were the Keeping of the Soul, the Sun Dance, the Making of Relatives, a puberty rite for young women, and a ball game that is no longer played. Densmore's Hunkpapa band Teton sources mention the Making of Relatives, the rite of Soul Keeping, and the Sun Dance in connection with White Buffalo Calf Maiden. As the Teton Sun Dance has been performed since its reintroduction, following years of being banned, a woman representing White Buffalo Calf Maiden is an important and honored participant.[12]

Pine Ridge Agency physician James Walker wrote his description in the period 1910–1916 when elders willingly provided accounts of the Sun Dance to him fearing that its memory might not long survive their generation. Walker's many Oglala sources do not mention a white buffalo cow in connection with any ceremony except the girls' puberty rite, despite the volumes of records Walker made of Oglala ritual and mythology while being formally instructed as a holy man with the blessings of the elders. Walker's informant Finger, an Oglala holy man, tells the story of the gift of the pipe from a mysterious woman but identifies her as Wohpe, a divinity variously said to represent a meteor, the earth, the smoke of the sacred pipe, and the feminine principle. His informant Thomas Tyon tells of the gift of a Buffalo Calf Pipe from a mysterious woman but does not identify her as White Buffalo Calf Maiden or say she transformed herself into a buffalo on leaving. According to a winter count in the possession of one Black Thunder, the ritual of Making Relatives was first held by the Hunkpapa band of Teton Dakotas in 1801. The differences in the dates attributed to the gift of the sacred pipe from White Buffalo Calf Maiden, and the ceremonies with which it was associated, possibly result from the popular diffusion of oral tradition.[13]

The rite of Making Relatives is the Teton equivalent of the Calumet ceremony. In the Hunkpapa and Oglala rites, as in the rites of the Pawnee, Osage, and Oto, the Hunka is first ceremonially attacked or captured as an enemy and is only then adopted. This relates the ceremony to the widespread practice of adopting captives. There is the interesting contradiction, however, that Black Elk's story of the origin of the rite indicates that it was the Sioux who invented the ceremony, but also that it was the Sioux who were treated as enemies by the Arikaras in the first or original ceremony and were adopted by them. This would indicate that it was the Arikaras who were introducing the ceremony to the Sioux and not the other way around, and this interpretation is consistent with other evidence that Caddoan tribes—Wichita, Pawnee, Arikara—had a central role in the diffusion of the Calumet ceremony.[14]

The idea of deriving the Lakota Hunka ceremony from the Arikaras dwelling along the Missouri is supported by earlier observations of J. L. Smith that the nature of the Sacred Calf Pipe bowl itself indicates a likely origin among the farming 'river tribes', such as the Arikara, who were dwelling in earthlodge villages along the Missouri when the Sans Arc Tetons were coming into contact with them as the Tetons moved west to the Missouri and beyond.[15] The pipe bowl that Thomas illustrates as that of the sacred pipe is of red pipestone or 'catlinite' and is of a style that has been found archaeologically along the Missouri in what was originally Arikara territory in South Dakota (figure 10.1*a*).

In commenting on the adoption of the Ottawa chief Sinagos by the Santee Dakotas in 1665–1666 with a Calumet ceremony, Nicolas Perrot wrote, "The savages believe that the sun gave it [the calumet] to the Panys [Pawnees], and that since then it has been communicated from village to village as far as the Outaoüas." The Skiri band of Pawnees claim that their ceremony was originated by them, but that the ceremony of the Chawi and other Pawnee bands was borrowed from the Wichitas. The Chawi say their ancestors received the ceremony in a vision. Mildred Mott Wedel has commented that in the earliest seventeenth-century histori-

cal records *Pani* referred to the Wichitas while in eighteenth-century French usage *Pani* became a generic term for a slave of any tribe. The Hako ceremony described by Alice Fletcher and James Murie was that of the Chawi band.[16]

WHEN THEY WAVED HORSES' TAILS

What appears to have happened is that the story of the White Buffalo Calf Woman, originating among the Sans Arc Teton band, has served as a catalyst for the formalization or systematization of much Teton ritual and belief well beyond the Sans Arcs themselves. It has

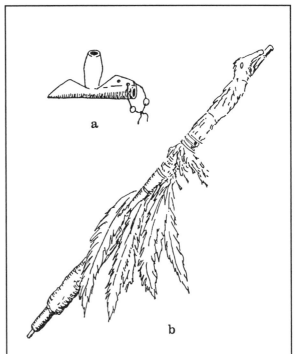

Figure 10.1 The catlinite bowl (*a*) and stem (*b*) of the Sacred White Buffalo Calf pipe, after J. Smith (1967) and Thomas (1941, pl. 2).

provided a focus for the formation of a canon of Teton belief and illustrates the dynamic character of Indian tradition. Speaking of the rite of Making Relatives or Hunka Lowanpi, George Sword, one of James Walker's Oglala sources, told him, "This ceremony has been practiced among the Oglalas for many years. There is a year named for the time when it was given the present form. It was practiced before that time. The name of this year is When They Waved Horses' Tails over Each Other [1805]."[17]

Afraid of Bear told Walker that in the Year They Waved Horses' Tails over Themselves "the Man from the Land of Pines came to the shamans . . . and taught them how to perform this [Hunka] ceremony right." Afraid of Bear learned of the incident from his father, who was three years old when the Man from the Land of Pines came and was told of it from his father. Afraid of Bear indicated that the Hunka ceremony was actually ancient, dating to the time when the Sioux came from the Land of Pines, meaning "from the north," but that anyone could perform it, and they were told that that was not right by the mysterious man.[18] In other words, the rite was old but the present form is new. If this is correct, then what is new, and what was the old rite like? The Santee Dakotas obviously had a version in 1665 that we may suspect was the Calumet of the Captain (below).

What I perceive is that the newer form of the Hunka Lowanpi conforms to the pattern of the Pawnee Hako ceremony in being more forward-looking, placing an emphasis on the living, while the earlier form of the Hunka Lowanpi grew up in the context of rites for mourning and requickening the deceased and the compensatory killing of an enemy. As it was explained to Frances Densmore:

[Looking Elk speaking:] The great result of this ceremony is that the man who performed it was regarded as a father by the child for whom he performed it. He made a solemn vow taking that child under his protection until one or the other died. He became like a brother to the man whose children he sang over and painted with the huŋka stripes. In all the great ceremonies of the Sioux there is not one that binds two men together so strongly as this.[19]

[Robert P. Higheagle speaking:] It is strictly believed and understood by the Sioux that a child is the greatest gift from Wakaŋ'taŋka, in response to many devout prayers, sacrifices, and promises. Therefore the child is considered "sent by Wakaŋ'taŋka.". . . During the period of youthful blessedness the father spared no pains to let the people know of his great love for his child or children. This was measured by his fellow men according to the sacrifices or gifts given, or the number of ceremonies performed.

In order to have a standard by which this love could be shown, the first thing taken into consideration and adopted was the White Buffalo Maiden, sent to the Sioux by the Buffalo tribe. The impression left upon the people by the Maiden and her extraordinary good qualities were things that were much admired by every parent as a model for his children. This maiden was pure white, without a blemish—that was the principal desire of the father for the character of his child. . . .

It had been told by the Maiden that good things would come to the people by means of the pipe, so it seemed necessary that there be a ceremony, having connection with the Maiden and with the pipe. For this reason the essential article in the Alo'waŋpi cer-emony is the "Huŋka Ćanoŋ'pa," a decorated wand, which represents the pipe given to the Indians by the Maiden.[20]

It is obvious in this Hunkpapa account that the feathered Hunka 'wand' represented the 'pipe' given by White Buffalo Calf Maiden. There was no pipe separate from the wand. On the other hand, Black Elk's account of the Oglala ceremony mentions the sacred pipe but makes no mention of the wand, and Walker's account of the Oglala ceremony mentions both pipe and wand. What was this feathered Hunka wand? It was the Teton counterpart of the Pawnee, Omaha, and Osage round-stemmed calumet already described, referred to as a pipe and representing a pipe stem but in its form, a symbolic arrow. All resemblance to an arrow had disappeared by the time the Calumet ceremony diffused to the Iroquois and was assimilated as the Eagle Dance.[21]

The Buffalo Calf pipe was a specific pipe with a specific origin in place and time, although pipes used in ceremonies today are considered to stand for the Buffalo Calf Pipe and to receive power from the Buffalo Calf Pipe. Individuals bring their personal pipes to the keeper of the sacred pipe to be blessed.[22] There were other smoking pipes presumably used by the Sioux before, but their authority was apparently superseded by that of the pipes legitimated by the White Buffalo Calf Maiden story. The wand arrived among the Sioux with a late version of the Calumet ceremony and apparently survived into the twentieth century but was replaced by the middle of this century by the Buffalo Calf pipe with its greater authority, as the ceremony was remembered.

An important difference between the Hunka Lowanpi and the Pawnee Hako and related Calumet ceremonies was that the latter could only be performed between clans or villages or bands or tribes. They were for external use only, so to speak. The Hunka Lowanpi had its origin in cementing intertribal peace, according to the Black Elk story, but, as described, mainly served to create bonds of fictional kinship within a community, much as did adoption in connection with mourning. Walker provides an example of an exhortation by the ritual leader to two men who had just been bonded by the Hunka ceremony that includes the comment, "If he is killed in war you should not be satisfied until you have provided a companion for his spirit," i.e. by killing an enemy to provide a spirit trail servant.[23] In the example of the Fox spirit adoptions already given (chapter 6), the person who was pledged to avenge the death did so upon adoption *after* the death. In the case of the Sioux Hunka, the vengeance was pledged *before* any need. This amounts to a kind of insurance policy with the potential for greatly reducing internal conflicts. One is less likely to kill someone if another someone is already on record as pledged to avenge the death.

Walker's informant No Flesh provided the doctor with a story of the origin of the Hunka Lowanpi that relates it specifically to adoption as part of mourning. The story related to ancient times when all the Sioux camped together. As the story goes, there was a head chief with four sons who were members of the Kit Fox society and two were stake holders. The stakes were the sticks used to support the drum off of the ground when it was in use and were considered part of the regalia of the society, the other items being the drum itself, the drum sticks, the rattle, certain feathered crook staffs or lances, whips, and so on. Carrying such an item of society regalia entailed the responsibility to conduct oneself with special bravery and honor and to carry out a set of responsibilities if the camp were to be attacked by an enemy. It was this chief's misfortune that the two stake-holder sons were killed while defending their camp and the other two sons, who then assumed the roles of stake holders, were subsequently killed while on a war party.[24]

The chief was despondent and sought help from Tate, Spirit of the Winds, who sent his son Yomni, Whirlwind, to counsel the chief. Yomni advised the chief to travel toward the pines and when he found a lone tipi to enter and return with what he found inside. This the chief did and returned with a baby boy and girl, whom he took for his son and daughter. The community celebrated the chief's new fortune with a feast and by smoking willow bark in a 'mysterious pipe' not otherwise identified. A shaman asked the chief, "What was the last word Yomni said to you?" to which the chief replied "Hunka." The shaman then said, "This boy and girl are Hunka, and you are Ate [father]." In time it was agreed that the practice should continue of people accepting each other as Hunka and Ate "when anyone wished to do a great favor to another," and this they did "until the missionaries taught them that this was wrong." The story thus accounts for the origin of the Hunka ceremony and mourning and its subsequent transformation into a rite of ceremonial kinship.

THE CALUMET OF THE CAPTAIN

Sometime in the winter of 1685–1686 the French trader Nicolas Perrot was visited at his fort on the upper Mississippi River by a party of Iowas returning from a winter hunt. Accompanying them to their village, Perrot was honored by a Calumet ceremony in which he said that "they chose him, by the calumet which they left with him, for the chief of all the tribe." In 1700 the Jesuit father Jacques Gravier was offered the honor of receiving the Calumet of the Captain by the Quapaws (the Arkansas) while traveling down the Mississippi, but Gravier declined and pressed on down-stream. While among the Quapaws Gravier did learn that Father Jacques Marquette's arrival among them in 1673 was still remembered, at least to the extent of the chief's remembering a Frenchmen dressed in black like Father Gravier to whom they danced "the Captain's calumet" so long before that he could not count the years, as he said. Gravier understood that this was "a special honor which is done but rarely, and only to persons of distinction," and thanked the chief, but declined the honor for himself, a rejection which the Quapaws found "scarcely agreeable."[25]

If Gravier had accepted the calumet offered him in this non-Christian ritual, his superiors would probably have been quite lenient in their opinion of his behavior. The calumet was well known to the Jesuits and the ceremony itself, a matter less of religion than of hospitality and etiquette between French and Indians along the Mississippi. This was not the case for Captain Diego Romero, a Spaniard of New Mexican birth trading out of Santa Fe in 1660. I am indebted to Donald Blakeslee for recognizing the significance of Romero's experience and sharing his interpretations with me.[26]

It is possible that no one of authority would have heard of Captain Romero's experience except for his bragging, which eventually reached the always receptive ears of the Spanish Inquisition over five hundred miles away in Mexico City. Romero stood before a court of the Inquisition on May 5, 7, and 11, 1663, not being asked so much to explain or defend his behavior—which he little understood the real significance of and the court, even less—as simply to confess his guilt for participating in a heathen ritual. I suspect Romero's spirit will find small comfort in knowing that the testimony of witnesses and depositions used by his prosecutors contained a wealth of ethnohistorical information on a custom that had never before been described in such detail—the Calumet of the Captain.

With respect to the Calumet of the Captain, it is purely a matter of coincidence that Diego Romero was a captain. The Spanish term *capitán*, like the French *capitaine*, meant chief or leader as well as the military rank, and it was so used in many American Indian contexts. Romero was leading a pack train eastward from Santa Fe several hundred miles into the southern Plains with its destination a settlement of the Plains Apaches. This was officially a business trip on behalf of the Spanish governor, but the business probably related to merchandise for trading carried by the pack animals and to the buffalo hides that would be available from the Apaches. This, however, was not all. Romero had his personal mission. Years before, in 1634, Romero's father had also visited the Apaches, and they had honored him by making him their 'captain' in some sense. Romero desired the same honor for himself and was not disappointed.

One evening after arriving at the Apache encampment, a delegation of Apaches came to Romero and announced that they were going to make him "chief captain of the entire Apache nation," or so one witness testified. The Apaches laid Romero face down on a new buffalo hide and did the same to the leader of a group of Pecos Pueblo Indians who traveled with Romero's party and who were well known to the Apaches. In this situation they were hoisted on the shoulders of their hosts and carried to the encampment. There the two were seated on hides, grasped by the shoulders, and rocked or swayed back and forth as the Apaches chanted. A scalp was then brought in attached to a pole, which was erected in front of them, and near it was placed an ear of corn.

The corn was referred to by an Apache term that translated as 'chief captain' and reminds us of the word 'chief' used in reference to the 'chief peyotes' or principal peyote buttons in peyote services, except that this was the Apache counterpart of the corn ear featured in the Teton Hunka and Pawnee Hako ceremonies—the Mother Corn. As a matter of fact, the kind of especially large and perfect specimen of peyote that is placed on the altar in the Winnebago peyote rite is referred to in Winnebago as the Hunka, which is translated as 'chief'.[27]

The next phase of the rite began when forty or fifty Apaches armed with weapons began a mock combat while a single Apache armed only with a stick fought back at them. Shortly afterward Romero was laid flat on his back, face up like a dead man to represent his death, as he said at his trial. After an unspecified period of time he was raised back up, as though he were being revived, he explained, and participated in the smoking of a tobacco pipe with a long wooden stem, which readers will at once recognize as a calumet-pipe. Now requickened, a white feather was placed on his head that had previously been attached to the ear of corn. This was, of course, a climactic part of the Teton Hunka and the Pawnee Hako ceremony. The mock combat corresponds to that represented both in the Calumet Dance and in the Discovery Dance, the latter of the two being a feature of mourning ceremonies in the Great Lakes area. The total affair was Romero's misfortune but none of our own because the record of his reception of the Calumet of the Captain is strong evidence that the prototype for the ceremony was a requickening rite to symbolically raise a deceased chief in the person of the person being honored.[28] His treatment as a dead person recalls also the similar treatment of the Whistler or pledger in the (original) Crow Sun Dance, which was a mourning ceremony (chapter 6).

Captain Romero was participating in a kind of trading arrangement that was serving the French well in New France, despite the ever-present clergy. The historian Bacqueville de La Potherie said of Nicolas Perrot's reception by the Potawatomis at Green Bay in very nearly the same year that "he was careful not to receive all [the proferred] acts of adoration, although he accepted these honors so far as the interests of Religion were not concerned."[29] La Potherie does not specify which acts of adoration Perrot did not accept, although we know that Perrot did once decline to be carried on the shoulders of his hosts.

That Perrot was carried at all is important. There were no horses in Wisconsin when Perrot was trading there, so we cannot accept Romero's explanation that this act among the Apaches was a pantomime for traveling by horseback. Romero explained that the Apaches who seated him on a hide, held his body, and swayed him back and forth did so to indicate that he would go and come to trade with them. La Potherie says that Perrot was seated on a hide and then held in the arms of three Iowas who kept in motion with the cadence of the songs being sung, as did the calumets in the hands of the singers.[30] In 1687 the Caddo in Arkansas similarly rocked Robert La Salle's older brother, the Abbé Jean Cavelier, during a Calumet ceremony in his honor: "The singing began again; the women joined in this music, and the concert was accompanied by means of hollow gourds in which were some large bits of gravel to make a noise, which the savages beat, keeping time with the music of the choir, and, what was most pleasant, one of them placed himself behind M. Cavelier to hold him up while making him move with a swinging motion from side to side with movements regulated to the same cadence."[31]

When Father Jean François Buisson de St. Cosme was met by the Quapaws with a calumet in 1699, he was similarly rocked to the rhythm of gourd rattles, but Buisson de St. Cosme was quite disgusted by the practice and enlisted a stand-in whose pleasure it was to be rocked all night in Buisson de St. Cosme's place.[32]

The Yankton Dakotas—in this case a band of the Yanktonai branch—also carried the Connecticut-born trader Peter Pond on a skin when they honored him with a calumet as winter approached in the year 1774. This took place nine days by canoe up the Minnesota River westward from Pond's cabin, which was located somewhere not far upstream from where the Minnesota joined the Mississippi:

I perceived five persons from the camp approaching—four was employed in carrying a beaver blanket finely painted—the other held in his hand a calumet or pipe of peace—very finely dressed with different feathers with painted hair. They all sat by me except the one who held the pipe. They ordered the pipe lit with a great deal of ceremony. After smoking a few whiffs the stem was pointed east and west—then north and south—then upward toward the skies—then to ye earth after which we all smoked in turn and appeared very friendly. I could not understand one word they said but from their actions I supposed it to be all friendship.

After smoking they took off my shoes and put on me a pair of fine moccasins or leather shoes of their own make wrought in a curious manner—then they laid me down on the blanket—one [taking] hold of each corner and carried me to the camp in a lodge among a very venerable assembly of old men. I was placed at the bottom or back part which is esteemed the highest place. After smoking an old man rose up on his feet with as much gravity as can be conceived of he came to me—laid his hands on my head and groaned out—I—I—I three times—then drawed his right hand down on my arms feigning a sort of a cry as if he shed tears—then sit down—the whole followed the same example which was twelve in number.

There was in the middle of the lodge a raised piece of ground about five inches in height five feet long two and a half broad on which was a fire & over that hung three brass kettles filled with meat boiling for a feast. While we were employed in this ceremony there was waiting at the door four men to take me up and carry me to another feast. At length an old man took up some of the victuals out of one of ye kettles which appeared to be a sort of soup thickened with pounded corn meal. He fed me with three spoonfuls first and then gave me the dish which was bark & the spoon made out of a buffalo's horn to feed myself. As I had got a good appetite from the fatigues of the day I ate hearty. As soon as I had got through with my part of ye feast I was desired to step out the door which I did. The people in waiting then took me and laid me on another skin and carried me to another lodge where I went through the same ceremony. There was not a woman among them—then to a third after which I was taken to a lodge prepared for me in which they had put my people and goods with a large pile of wood and six of their men with spears to guard it from the crowd. At four o'clock I commenced a trade with them.[33]

Pond's narrative, written with quite inventive spelling (modified above for clarity), may be the earliest recorded mention of a calumet decorated with dyed horsehair. At least the Yanktonais whom Pond encountered were traveling by horse, and he mentions that the "Callemeat or Pipe of Pece" was decorated with "Panted Haire." This predates by thirty-one years the Oglala winter count telling of the year 1805 "When they waved horses' tails over each other" (above). The Oglala were, of course, a band of the Teton or Western division and the Yanktonai, of the Central division of the Sioux.

PEACE AND THE INNOCENCE OF THE CHILD

The purpose of the Hako, the Pawnee Calumet ceremony, was to bring the honored individuals "the promise of children, long life, and plenty" and to create bonds of kinship between two otherwise unrelated groups of people. It also facilitated intertribal trade.[34] There was no explicit relationship to mourning, although there were many vestiges of the inferred earlier association with mourning. The adoption was not a spirit adoption in the sense that the spirit of the deceased was believed to occupy the body of the adoptee during the ceremony (chapter 8), only the breath of Tirawahat or Tirawa, but the adoptee was scouted out as by a war party and, when discovered, coups were counted over him or her. The child was not treated as a dead person but was carried in a blanket, much as was Diego Romero when he was representing a dead person. In the Osage Calumet ceremony all persons who were in mourning were asked to end their mourning. All such persons rose and participated collectively in a final shedding of tears, after which they threw away the ragged garments worn as mourners, and the men cut their hair and painted their faces as they had done before their sorrow.[35]

The soft-edged symbolism of the Hako is probably no better illustrated than by the rite of the nests. In this rite the Ku'rahus or priest uses his toe to inscribe four circles in the floor of the earthlodge to the northwest, northeast, southeast, and southwest of the hearth, filling the outline with downy feathers as he proceeds:

The circle represents a nest, and is drawn by the toe because the eagle builds its nest with its claws. Although we are imitating the bird making its nest, there is another meaning to the action; we are thinking of Tira'wa making the world for the people to live in. If you go on a high hill and look around, you will see the sky touching the earth on every side, and within this circular inclosure the people live. So the circles we have made are not only nests, but they also represent the circle Tira'wa atius has made for the dwelling place of all the people. The circles also stand for the kinship group, the clan, and the tribe. . . .

Now a robe is spread on the ground and the child is placed on it with his feet and legs projecting beyond the edge. Four men are appointed to carry the child. One goes on each side and takes hold of the robe and lifts it; a man at the back of the child steadies it as it is raised and carried, while the fourth man holds another robe over its feet and legs.

The chief and Kura'hus precedes the child to the circle at the northwest, where it is held over the nest so that its feet rest within the circle. The chief puts his hands under the robe held over the child's legs and drops the oriole's nest within the circle so that the child's feet rest on it. No one but the chief and the Kura'hus know what is being done beneath the robe. The chief takes up the nest, concealing it from view, and goes to the circle at the northeast, to which the child has also been carried, and in the same way places its feet on it. The same act is repeated at the circles in the southeast and the southwest.

The child represents the young generation, the continuation of life, and when it is put in the circle it typifies the bird laying its eggs. The child is covered up, for no one knows when a bird lays its eggs or when a new birth takes place; only Tira'wa knows when life is given. The putting of the child's feet in the circle means the giving of new life, the resting of its feet upon the oriole's nest means promised security to the new life.[36]

In the corresponding part of the Osage rite the child's feet are placed upon four balls of mud that represent the earth. There is no symbolism of a nesting bird. The symbolism is, rather, that of the first four steps of the child in its new life. The use of balls of mud should call to mind also the sods used in the Arapaho and Cheyenne Sun Dances, representing as they do the lumps of mud brought from beneath the primordial sea by the Earth Diver to create the earth (chapter 3), and taken as they were from the feet of the Earth Diver.[37]

THE GIFTS OF THE PLUMED SERPENT

A volume of Pawnee traditions collected by James Murie for George Dorsey contains one on the origin of the Skiri calumet or 'pipe-stick', narrated by Cheyenne Chief, the son of Pipe Chief, a prominent Skiri chief and priest.[38] The Hako ceremony described by Fletcher and Murie was that of the Chawi band. In the Skiri story the pipe-stick and its ceremony was the gift of a water monster that appeared to a Skiri in a dream. The Skiris made a representation of this monster in connection with their annual Medicine Lodge or Doctors' Lodge performance, a serpent almost sixty feet long with a split tail, constructed in a circle around the interior of the lodge. Water serpents in the Midwest are also described or illustrated as having tails divided at the end.

The water monster seen in the dream was enormous with a white something on the top of its head. The man awoke not knowing what to do but eventually journeyed to the big river he had seen in the dream. In time the water monster appeared to him and drew him into the water with its breath and into a large animal lodge. The monster announced that the animals would teach the people the mysteries of all the animals, but first the man must return and build a lodge with an

image of the monster in it and seek dreams so that the monster could appear to him.

The man constructed the lodge as told, and an image of the water serpent as well, but did not know what to do about the thing on the top of the head because this was a time when the Skiris did not yet know about eagles or other birds and did not recognize feathers. The water serpent appeared to the man in a dream and instructed him in the way to build an eagle trap to obtain eagle feathers, one of which could be put on the top of the head of the monster's image. During a second dream the monster gave the man a pipe stem and instructed him to hang eagle feathers from it. The man had various encounters with different animals after that and learned that the water monster that gave him the pipe stem was Tirawa. Evening Star gave the man an ear of corn, told him how to plant it, and instructed him to place an ear on a stick. In time he acquired all the necessary paraphernalia for the Calumet ceremony and the proper materials to decorate them, along with the necessary songs:

> The man was also taught on the third night they must take a child and decorate it in such a way that it would represent Tirawa. The painting of the child with the red paint about its face represented that the sun had touched the child. There was to be a mark upon the face of the child which was to represent the picture of Tirawa. At last the child was to be placed on the nest of an oriole. The two priests were to hold the child up while the leader of the pipe-sticks placed the nest under its feet. Then the priests stood the child up on the nest. This was to teach that the child should grow up to be either a man or woman and that its life's pathway would be hard, but it would grow up, for the powers of Tirawa were now upon it. The oriole makes its nest high up in the trees.[39]

This story follows a widespread pattern of Indians being given various powers by water monsters, and it accounts for the importance of the serpent effigy in the Doctors' Lodge performances, which were highly shamanistic, but the greater part of the story was an origin myth of the calumet and its associated paraphernalia and ritual. The greatest surprise is the story's identification of Tirawahat with a plumed water serpent. Tirawahat is the supreme being of the Pawnees and more than a god, a creator of gods, but his associations are typically with the sky. Gene Weltfish calls him The Expanse of the Heavens. Fletcher and Murie say that Tirawa's abode is in the sky. Tirawa's association with the water monster as well indicates that Tirawa must be more than just the creator of the universe. His presence must pervade and be the essence of the universe.[40] In the symbolism of Plains camp circles the circle represents the horizon defining the earth's boundaries but represents as well the arch of the sky and the path of the sun along the ecliptic, the two circles being conflated and sometimes personified by a hoop representing a serpent, as does the hoop associated with the altar in the Arapaho Sun Dance.[41]

CULTURAL PROCESSES

The evolution or transformation of the Calumet ceremony is an indication that diffusion was not the only cultural process at work. The Hako type Calumet ceremony created a bond of kinship between two men by virtue of the adoption by one of a child of the other. This placed an emphasis on peace and friendship associated with brotherhood and the innocence of the child—like the *compadre* relationship between the father and godfather of a child in Hispanic custom.

The parallels to be observed between the Pawnee Hako and the Morning Star sacrifice (chapter 11) become more meaningful when compared with the ritual associations of the scaffold or arrow sacrifice in Mesoamerica—spring renewal of the fields, planting, agricultural fertility and, among the Maya apparently, rites of royal succession.[42] The Hako includes a mirror rite related to succession of the generations that parallels Maya associations of the mirror with royal succession, and the Hako has roots in ceremonies for the symbolic resurrection of the deceased—in the case of the Calumet of the Captain, a deceased leader—and the symbolic rebirth of the earth. In both the Hako and the Morning Star sacrifice the honoree/victim was given a ritual identity with the earth, as Karl Taube indicates was the case for victims of the scaffold sacrifice in Mesoamerica.[43]

In trying to explain the identity of White Buffalo Calf Maiden, individual Tetons have fallen back on frames of reference relevant to their particular backgrounds, perhaps Wohpe if one has had a traditional upbringing, or the Virgin Mary if one has had strong contacts with missionaries.[44] Such interpretations can be supportive. Explanations are more convincing if they involve perspectives that individuals find relevant in their personal worlds. By contrast, few Lakotas could be expected to find satisfactory any explanation of White Buffalo Calf Maiden today that requires a source outside of their personal worlds, least of all when it does not account for the apparent actual physical manifestation of a god woman in white.

"THE LAST SUN OF SEPTEMBER had dipped as a lurid orange-colored disk beyond the horizon of the great grass plains of Oklahoma, which never had been shorn by man," he said, "and the glowing cloudless sky was fast passing into a still darkness studded with brillant stars, as a party of five ethnologists consisting of two Americans, two Germans and one Englishman, drove through the small town of Pawnee to witness the Morning Star ceremony of the Skidi Branch of the Pawnee tribe." So spoke the renowned British anthropologist Alfred C. Haddon, addressing the Antiquarian Society of Cambridge, England, May 27, 1907. The companions of which Haddon spoke were Eduard Seler and Paul Ehrenreich of Berlin and George Dorsey and William Jones of Chicago.[1] Dorsey of the Field Museum was hosting the group, accompanied by Jones, who had recently joined the museum staff. Jones was a graduate of Harvard and Columbia universities but was then in home territory, being both a native Oklahoman and a Fox Indian (chapter 6).

THE MORNING STAR SACRIFICE 1506–1906

The ceremony that this group had assembled to observe was one of Mesoamerican origin that no one could have observed in central Mexico, certainly, since the Spanish conquest of 1519–1521, and no one would have known this better than Eduard Seler, a Mesoamericanist of heroic academic stature. In earlier years the ceremony would have included human sacrifice, which had not been practiced by the Pawnee since 1838, and then only by the Skiri band when they felt compelled to do so to by the command of Morning Star himself. There was no element of revenge involved, much less sadistic pleasure; it was believed to be necessary for the welfare of Skiri society.

Not everyone has agreed that the Skiri sacrifice was of Mesoamerican origin. As a later staff member of the Field Museum, Ralph Linton was quite unimpressed by the Mexican credentials of the Pawnee rite and in 1926 published his opinion that most of the elements of the ritual were in accord with Skiri ceremonial patterns and that the remaining elements could have simply diffused to the Nebraska homeland of the Skiri Pawnees from the southwestern and southeastern United States, but certainly not directly from Mexico.[2] Those who accepted the idea of a more direct Mexican origin pointed to the striking similarity of the manner in which the victim died—tied to a vertical pole frame and pierced with arrows. This is an image amply represented in painted Mesoamerican books such as the *Codex Zouche-Nuttall*, *Codex Telleriano-Remensis*, *Codex Fernández Leal*, *Historia Tolteca-Chichchimeca*, and *Codex Profirio Díaz*, and scratched on a wall in Guatemala at the Mayan site of Tikal.[3]

Linton was reacting in part to a 1916 article by Clark Wissler and Herbert Spinden, Plains ethnologist and Mesoamerican archaeologist, respectively, in the *American Museum Journal*. These professional colleagues of Linton were much more impressed by the Mexican connections of the Skiri sacrifice, but they were unwilling to recognize the practice among the Aztecs in particular before A.D. 1506, feeling that it could have been invented by the Aztecs in that year or—and this they believed more likely—that it was borrowed by the Aztecs at that time from some source to the south of the Aztecs. They explained that an early Spanish annotator of the *Codex Telleriano-Remensis* wrote under the symbol for the Aztec year Ce Tochtli (1 Rabbit), our 1506, that "in this year Moctezuma shot with arrows a man in this fashion [referring to the accompanying illustration], say the old men, because for two hundred years there had always been hunger upon the year One Rabbit."[4]

It was the nature of the Aztec and other Mesoamerican calendars that a year with the name 1 Rabbit would recur each fifty-two years, and it was the nature of Mesoamerican belief that events repeated themselves in cycles related to the calendar. The calendar lent itself to such interpretations because Aztec years were not numbered in an ever-continuing, linear sequence. There were fifty-two possible year names and these repeated themselves after fifty-two years, each year taking its name from the name of the last day but five within each 365-day year. The 360th or name day of the year 1 Rabbit of the *Codex Telleriano-Remensis* corresponded to January 22, A.D. 1507, in the Julian calendar in use by the colonial Spanish of the time, but since the name day fell near the end of the Aztec year, the bulk of the year corresponded to Julian A.D. 1506.[5]

The observed motions of the sun, moon, planets, and stars would have also contributed to the Mesoamerican mind-set of cyclicity in historical events. Venus, for instance, rises as a morning star about a week after inferior conjunction with the sun (the time varying from a few days in midwinter to two weeks or more in midsummer) and remains visible before sunrise in the east for about 240 days. During this period Venus moves increasingly farther ahead of the sun until it reaches greatest elongation—forty-seven degrees on the average from the sun—after which it seems to turn its path and return to the sun until disappearing in the brightness of the sun for about ninety days as Venus enters and leaves superior conjunction, finally emerging in the west just after sunset as evening star, remaining visible in the west for about 240 days, and returning to inferior conjunction once more. The total cycle averaged 584 days. Because five such Venus periods of 584 days exactly equaled eight Mesoamerican solar years of 365 days, this meant that every eight years Venus would emerge as the morning star on close to the same day in the tropical year—if, say, on August 17, 1497, then on August 22 in 1505, eight years later. There would be four first risings of Venus as morning star in between, but not in August.[6]

What would have been in the sky during the Aztec year 1 Rabbit that might be a clue to the astronomical associations of the Morning Star sacrifice? Knowing that the Aztecs conducted a sacrifice during the year 1 Rabbit does not tell us when during the year. On August 8, 1505 *Julian*, Venus entered inferior conjunction with the sun and would have been visible as a morning star from late August 1505 until the middle of April 1506. It would then have been visible as an evening star until early in March of 1507. There was a solar eclipse visible with a magnitude of 0.686 at Tenochtitlan on July 20, 1506, and a conjunction of Venus and Mars on October 7, 1506.[7]

Although there is no agreement over whether the Morning Star of the Skiri Pawnees was Venus, Mars, or Jupiter (any one of these planets can be seen as a 'morning star' or as an 'evening star' at one time or another, plus Mercury and Saturn), no one disputes that the preeminent morning star in Mexico was Venus. There seems to be no question that the star the Skiris called 'Bright Star' was Venus as an evening star. The problem of identifying the Skiris' 'Big Star' as Venus in

its morning star phase has been confused by Pawnee references to the Big Star as red, but this hardly eliminates Venus. The Mayas, for instance, called Venus Chak Ek, which translates both as Big Star and as Red Star. Mars may be red, but it is not big. It would appear, however, that Skiri skywatchers could have become less and less discriminating through the years in their identification or choice of morning star for purposes of the ceremony. This is understandable because the decision to conduct the ceremony often depended both upon the presence of a morning star, whatever its identity may have been, and upon a warrior having a dream telling him to do so.[8] This introduces a factor hard to assess from the disadvantage of our late-twentieth-century perspective.

The Bright Star or Evening Star of the Skiris represented the earth's fertility or vital force, and the sacrificial victim herself—usually herself but sometimes himself—was in effect transformed during the ceremony into a cosmogram of the earth, just as the adoptee in the Pawnee and other Calumet ceremonies—male or female—was given a symbolic identity with the earth. The windmill-like splayed orientation of the arms and legs of the scaffold sacrifice victims mimicked the splayed pattern of the elements of the Ollin glyph that represents the earth as the central motif of the Aztec Stone of the Sun (figures 11.3, 14.3g). Ollin translates as 'movement', as does the Pawnee word *awari*, which in Pawnee songs can be found as a gloss for Evening Star, which the victim of the Pawnee sacrifice represented (chapter 12).[9]

The sacrifice among the Pawnees commonly took place in the spring as a fertility rite, but the ceremony was technically not part of the seasonal round of ceremonies and could be performed whenever the situation called for it and the conditions were right. Among the Aztecs the corresponding sacrifice was associated with the corn goddess Chicomecóatl (7 Serpent) and with the god Xipe Totec (Flayed Lord). Xipe's rites in particular related to the spring season. We know from the evidence of the Skiri rite that the sacrifice was supposed to take place when the morning star was visible. Within the year 1 Rabbit Venus would have been visible as morning star only from the end of January until the middle of April because the Aztec year 1 Rabbit began on January 28, 1506. The principal feast days for the god Xipe Totec were the first and last (first and twentieth) days of the Aztec month Tlacaxipeualiztli (The Skinning of Men), which in the year 1506 fell March 9–28 *Julian*, corresponding to March 19–April 7 *Gregorian*. This would have been the most logical time in the tropical year and in the ritual calendar for a ceremony being conducted to forestall a year of bad crops.[10]

Wissler and Spinden said the arrow sacrifice "evidently" took place during the month of Tlacaxipeualiz-tli, apparently inferring the relationship from the *Manuscrit du Cacique,* which shows the sacrifice by arrows and the gladiatorial sacrifice side by side, each performed on the same day and with the sacrificial victims each dressed with identical red clothing and headgear. The gladiatorial sacrifice is explicitly related to the month Tlacaxipeualiztli by both Durán and Sahagún.[11] The name of the month derives from the Aztec practice of flaying or skinning the victims sacrificed to Xipe whole and then dressing men in the raw skins for a period of twenty days. Priests representing Xipe are illustrated wearing flayed human skins with the hands flopping loosely at the wrists and with one or two vertical lines painted on their cheeks behind each eye.[12]

Xipe was a god of fertility, but he was also strongly related to warfare. His principal sacrifice was in the form of gladiatorial combat. During the gladiatorial sacrifice a captive was tethered by a rope to a large stone platform, armed with a wooden club set with feathers, and obliged to fend off the attacks of a series of pirouetting Aztec jaguar and eagle knights with clubs set with blades of chipped volcanic glass. This should remind us of the tethered warriors of the Plains (figure 19.5*a*), the Apache warrior in Romero's calumet ritual who used a wooden stick in mock combat with a multitude of other Apaches with real weapons, and the warrior in the Calumet Dance who used a feathered wand to simulate combat with dancers flourishing lethal weapons.

A sacrifice is known to have been scheduled by the Skiris for the spring of 1817, but it was thwarted by the rescue of the young maiden by the son of a chief in an episode that gained national attention. A Mexican boy was dedicated for sacrifice in 1818 but was ransomed and the ceremony aborted. A Cheyenne maiden who was scheduled for sacrifice in 1827 was rescued but was tragically killed with an arrow as she was being led away on April 11. An Oglala girl was sacrificed on April 22, 1838, the last known ceremony with death as the climax. Numerous ceremonies without the element of sacrifice were celebrated in later years, so that the ceremony in October of 1906 was part of a cultural continuum transmitted through the generations reasonably intact and included a remarkable 276 songs.[13] The result is that more details are known of the scaffold sacrifice from the Plains of the United States than from Mexico, where it was only a fading memory when the likes of Sahagún and Durán wrote their commentaries on Aztec religious practices.

YOUNG EAGLE'S LEGACY

It is ironic that much of what we know of the religion of the Aztecs, Mayas, and other Mesoamerican peoples we owe to the efforts of Spanish priests who recorded the information so that the clergy could be more informed in their efforts to suppress the practices. Ironically also, much of what we know of the the oral literature and ritual life of the Pawnee, Osage, Omaha, Fox, Kickapoo, Dakota, Iroquois, and others has flowed from the pens of writers who themselves—while not denying or rejecting their Native American heritage—had taken advantage of opportunities for schooling in an alien Euro-American culture and were not 'traditionalists' in orientation. The mixed cultural perspectives of mixed-blood Indians such as James Murie, Francis La Flesche, William Jones, Ella Deloria, Ely Parker, and others led directly or indirectly to a body of published literature that the Indian nations would sorely miss were it not for their efforts. So much has been lost already.[14]

While Haddon, Seler, Ehrenreich, Dorsey, and Jones sat as guests in solemn silence, witnessing a Pawnee ceremony little diminished in 1906 by the elimination of a finale that had proved to be unappealing even to the Pawnees by 1817, James Rolfe Murie sat as one of the priests. Murie was born in Grand Island, Nebraska, in 1862 before the move of the Pawnees to Indian Territory—today's state of Oklahoma. Murie's mother was a traditional Pawnee of the Skiri band and his father, an American army officer who commanded a company of Pawnee Scouts. When Murie was still small, his father abandoned his wife and child, after which Murie's mother went with young James, or Young Eagle as he was known to the Skiris, to live with her brother, who had adopted the ways of the white man. Murie attended various local Indian agency schools in Nebraska and Indian Territory, picking up a useful command of English as he did so, and by 1879 was enrolled at Hampton Institute in Virginia with other Indian children.[15]

After graduating from Hampton in 1883, Murie occupied himself for a number of years as clerk, bookkeeper, teacher, farmer, and interpreter, until in the period of 1898–1902 he became a collaborator of Alice Fletcher (see chapter 7) in her effort to make a record of the Pawnee Calumet ceremony, or Hako ceremony, as she called it, for the Bureau of American Ethnology. Fletcher's source was Tahirussawichi, a septuagenarian member of the Chaui band of Pawnees, who spoke and sang into a phonographic recorder to produce dozens of wax cylinders from which a record of the rite was transcribed and translated by Murie.[16] In the period of 1902–1909 Murie worked with George A. Dorsey of the Field Museum, extending his acquisitions of traditional knowledge to include much of Arikara (Ree) as well as Pawnee mythology and ceremonialism. Arikara is a Caddoan language closely related to Murie's native Skiri dialect of Pawnee. During the period of 1910–1921 he worked both independently for the Bureau of American Ethnology and as collaborator of Clark Wissler of the American Museum of Natural History. When Murie died in 1921 he left behind a remarkable legacy of published and manuscript records of Pawnee and Arikara life. As Douglas Parks has written:

> [W]ere it not for James R. Murie, the unusual wealth of ethnography that we now possess for the Pawnee would in all likelihood not exist. He lived at a particularly strategic time, when Pawnee ceremonialism and most of the old culture had nearly ceased. Because the old ways were virtually gone, the priests, doctors, and others who had participated in that way of life were at least willing and, perhaps, happy that those customs be recorded. Had it not been for those circumstances, those same Pawnee would undoubtedly have strongly resisted the revelation of what they held sacred. . . . We shall forever be in debt for [Murie's] perseverance and dedication.[17]

After the occasion of 1906 the Skiri Morning Star ceremony was conducted one last time, in October 1915. This time it was led by James Murie himself. One by one the Pawnees with the knowledge to participate in the ceremony had become fewer. Sadder still, the Pawnees who chose to identify with the ways of the past were becoming fewer. Murie had begun his investigations of Pawnee ceremonialism as an outsider with respect to the esoteric knowledge he was often seeking. Looking back now from the end of the same century, it is difficult for anyone to think of Pawnee ceremonialism without thinking of James Murie. Anytime that we read the words that Murie wrote, we are doing more than keeping bright the spark of life in Pawnee traditions; we are also keeping alive all those Pawnee elders, long dead in the physical sense, whose voices we can still hear echoing as we read.

THE MORNING STAR COMMANDS IT

The legend of the Morning Star sacrifice tells how ages ago Morning Star overcame a series of obstacles to defeat and mate with Evening Star in a union that produced a girl, born during the winter (conceived in spring?). The sun and moon soon followed suit and produced a boy, born during the summer (conceived in fall?). Until these acts men and women had been separated and did not interact, the men stars remaining in the eastern skies, where Big Star ruled, and the women stars in the western skies, the two domains separated by the Milky Way (figure 11.1). The sacrifice is said to have been claimed by Morning Star as a reward for his effort in bringing about the conditions for marriage and fertility, except for which the world of the

Pawnees would not exist. In many ways the ceremony amounted to a reenactment of the legend with the sexual penetration of Evening Star by Morning Star represented by the arrow penetration of the sacrifice victim.[18]

The sacrifice was not held annually, only when a man had dreamed that Morning Star commanded him to do so and then only if the man wakened to find the Morning Star rising. This was hardly a dream to be desired, but it could not be ignored. The dreamer and the Morning Star priest each broke into tears on learning of the dream and confirming the dreadful demand it made. The message from Morning Star might be, "You people have forgotten about me. It is now time to offer a human sacrifice to me. I am watching over your people."[19]

Before a Skiri warrior set out to capture a victim for the Morning Star sacrifice, a priest painted the warrior's face in a particular pattern. Dipping his fingers in red paint, the priest drew two streaks down the left side of the warrior's face and then two down the right (figure 11.2b). Had Seler seen this part of the ceremony he would have immediately caught his breath in unfeigned surprise and then whispered to himself as he slowly resumed breathing, "Xipe!" No surprise in Mexico. The sacrifice by arrows was part of the cult of Xipe Totec and the faces of Xipe impersonators were similarly marked (figure 11.2c–h).[20]

Many weeks might elapse between the capture of the girl and the concluding ceremony, all the while great care being taken to treat the girl with respect. A priest watches the morning sky to determine when it is time for the ceremony proper. On the first day of the ceremony four rings are inscribed on the floor of the ceremonial lodge with the toe of a moccasin and filled with down feathers, one each to the northwest, northeast, southwest, and southeast of the fireplace. A fire is laid in the fireplace fed by the ends of four long poles arranged in an equal-armed cross pattern. Each pole represents one of the four semicardinal directions and is taken from a tree appropriate to that direction, chosen from cottonwood, elm, box elder, and willow. The Morning Star priest presides. The first song begins. The Evening Star bundle is opened and the Mother Corn ear inside exposed to view. The singing begins: "My mother now sits inside the lodge. . . . Earth now sits inside the lodge." The Mother Corn represents both Earth and Evening Star. After the third song the Evening Star impersonator is painted completely red.[21]

During the second day's activities a warrior takes up the northeastern pole burning in the hearth and points it at the girl's right side and then at her left side. He then picks up the southwest pole and points it at her, and so on with all the poles in their turn, never actually touching the girl. This ritual basically duplicates the

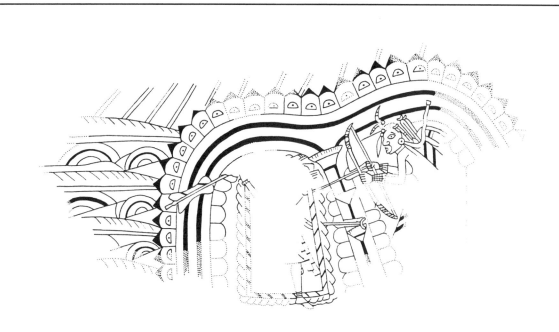

Figure 11.1 Arrow Sacrifice represented on a Spiro site shell bowl, from Phillips and Brown (1984, pl. 165). This engraved *Busycon* bowl from the Craig Mound at the Spiro site, Le Flore County, Oklahoma, contains the only known depiction of an arrow sacrifice by a native artisan in America north of Mexico. This image is especially fascinating because it appears to represent an activity in the night sky rather than on earth.

The scene is surrounded by a petaloid border with each 'petal' containing a stylized eye believed to represent a star (Brown et al. 1995). The scene is divided into two panels, that on the left representing the victim and that on the right, the archer. These two panels correspond to the halves of the night sky west and east of the Milky Way, which in Skiri Pawnee mythology were originally occupied by female stars ruled by Evening Star and male stars ruled by Morning Star. The Skiri Morning Star sacrifice dramatized the conquest of the Evening Star by the Morning Star. Copyright 1984 by the President and Fellows of Harvard College.

effect of that part of the Calumet ceremony in which the identity of the Mother Corn ear is transferred to the child being adopted (chapter 7), except that the identity is being transferred from the hearth, the four poles from the hearth representing the four semicardinal directions in the same way that the four lines painted on the Mother Corn ear represented the world quarters. On the third day the poles are obtained for the scaffold, the directional symbolism of the trees being maintained in their selection—elm for the northeast, box elder for the southwest, cottonwood for the northwest, and willow for the southeast. The scaffold is erected and a rectangular pit excavated beneath to represent the Garden of the Evening Star (chapter 12).

On the fourth day the singing continues. The chief priest dances around the interior of the earth lodge and one by one destroys the circles of feathers constructed on the first day, first that on the northeast, then that on the southwest, scattering the feathers with his feet, then that on the northwest, and finally that on the southeast: "Each time the leading priest wipes out a ring, there is a grunting sound through the lodge as if

they were attacking an enemy. It means that the dancer, like a warrior, goes around the earth and through the timber."[22] As the priest touches the circles with his feet he is performing a ritual act that parallels in some ways that part of the Hako in which the child's feet are placed within the circles of feathers, and that part of the Osage Calumet ceremony in which the child's feet are placed, one at a time, on the four lumps of mud (chapter 10). These circles were created in the same way as were those in the Hako, inscribed first with the toe and then filled with feathers. The use of the circles is peaceful in the case of the Calumet ceremony, but it is warlike in the Morning Star ceremony.

The time is now fast approaching for the sacrifice. The girl's body is painted black on her left side and red on her right. Because she will be tied to the scaffold facing east, the colors will correspond to the directional symbolism of the Pawnees in which black represents north and red, south. This nearly completes the maiden's symbolic transformation into the earth. She approaches the frame, hesitates, and is encouraged to continue, stepping first on the bottom rung, which is elm. Then she continues to ascend the scaffold, stepping in turn on the box elder, cottonwood, and willow poles, which, with the elm pole, represent the northeast, southwest, northwest, and southeast quadrants of the world. Her wrists and ankles are now bound to the pole frame with arms and legs extended. She stands on a willow pole and has another willow pole above her. The two vertical side poles are cottonwood. Other participants are concealed in a nearby ravine. Out of the ravine come two priests representing owls and carrying burning torches representing certain fires said to be visible on either side of the sun in winter. They stand next to the victim, one to the north side and one to the south side. The one on the north then touches the victim's left armpit and groin with his torch while the priest on the south does the same to the victim's right side.[24]

The sky is now lightening. The entire village is present for this aspect of the ceremony—men, women, children, and even tiny infants in their mothers' arms. The fluid blackness that constitutes night is quickly draining away, being swallowed, in Mesoamerican belief, by the Xiuhcocoa, the fire serpents whose jaws bracket the entrance to the earth's interior.[25] With his planet rising into the sky, Morning Star emerges from his concealment in the ravine. The climax is near. He raises his bow, aims, and releases an arrow that passes through Evening Star's side and into her heart. It is done. According to Murie, this arrow represents the arrow that allowed Morning Star to overcome the Evening Star by touching and killing a certain corn plant that was growing in Evening Star's vulva preventing Morning Star from having intercourse with Evening

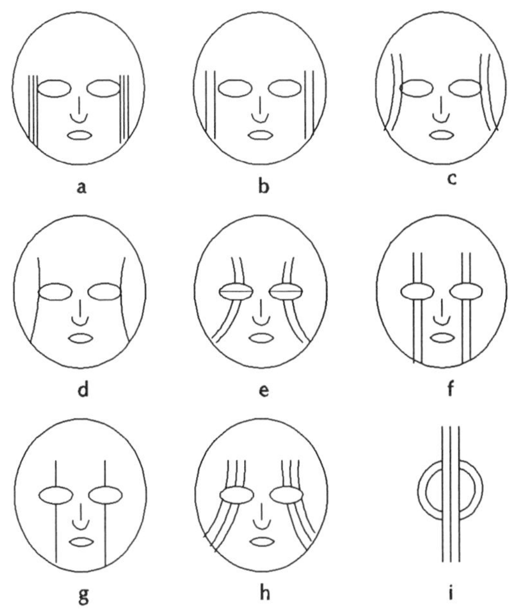

Figure 11.2 Selected modes of face painting shared by persons figuring in the Lakota Calumet ceremony and Skiri Morning Star sacrifice, compared with selected modes of face painting in Mesoamerica representing Xipe Totec: *a*, hunka stripes on the face on a spirit post representing a person mourned in a Lakota soul-keeping ritual, after Densmore (1918, pl. 8); *b*, as described for the pledger in the Skiri sacrifice (Murie 1989, 116, cf. 64); *c*, on a Xipe priest in the *Codex Laud*, after Saville (1929, fig. 48); *d*, on Xipe figures in the *Codex Borgia*, after Díaz and Rodgers (1993, pls. 25, 61) and on a Xipe sculpture from Texcoco, after Saville (1929, fig. 44); *e*, on a ceramic vessel from Monte Albán, after Nicholson (1976, fig. 9); *f*, on a glyph from Monte Albán, after Nicholson (1976, fig. 7); *g*, on a ceramic Xipe head from El Salvador, after Nicholson (1976, fig. 13); *h*, on a head incised on an Olmec jade plaque, after Joralemon (1971, fig. 233); *i*, bisected circle motif representing an atlatl grip, from examples of Preclassic age in Mexico and Middle Woodland age in the Mississippi valley (chapter 14).

Star.[26] And what kind of arrow would kill a corn plant by touching it? A frost arrow. In Aztec belief Morning Star was a god of frost and his arrows could wilt corn.[27] Frost is a phenomenon of the coldest part of a morning when the morning star makes its appearance.

A priest takes a flint knife from the Morning Star bundle and makes a small incision over the victim's heart, slips his fingers into the cut, and marks his face with her blood.[28] Some blood is allowed to fall on buffalo meat and a buffalo heart and tongue held below her, but none is allowed to fall on the down feathers filling the Garden of the Evening Star. A warrior with a war-club then feints four blows at her body, touches her heart with the fifth stroke, and shouts a war whoop, after which her spirit is believed to rise into the sky and become a star. The victim's body is laid face-down on the prairie with her head to the east, and there she will complete her transformation into the earth, in time becoming the earth in fact, as earlier she had become the earth as symbol.[29]

In the legend behind the Morning Star sacrifice the union of Morning Star and Evening Star produced a baby girl. This was no ordinary baby girl. It appeared on earth as an ear of corn wrapped in the skin of a buffalo calf. The woman emerged from the ear of corn, and the calfskin took on its own life and ran away as a yellow buffalo calf.[30] Because of the parallels between the Pawnee Calumet ceremony and Morning Star sacrifice, it is difficult not to be reminded at this point of White Buffalo Calf Maiden, making her appearance as she did with vertical red stripes on her face, and associated as closely as she was with the appearance among the Lakotas of the Hako-type

Calumet ceremony with its corn ear, both apparently acquired from the Arikara cousins of the Skiri Pawnees. The corn ear is an anomaly in the Calumet ceremony of the Lakotas, who were not known to practice farming in aboriginal times.[31]

Among the Skiris the wrapper of the Evening Star bundle was made from the skin of a winter-born buffalo calf, a rarity said to have a peculiar yellowish fur. Within the Evening Star bundle, among other things, were ears of Mother Corn, symbolizing the winter-born woman child born of Evening Star, the Pawnee's Bright Star.[32] This may recall to some the Arikara Mother Corn's departure scene, during which she turned into an ear of corn wrapped in the buffalo robe that she had been wearing: "Then the priests took Mother-Corn and the robe to the river, and threw her into it. For many years she did not return, but one fall, when [the Arikaras] were having their bundle ceremonies, a mysterious-looking woman entered the lodge where the bundle ceremony was being given and they finally recognized her as Mother-Corn. She taught them some more bundle ceremony songs and before daylight disappeared, and was never seen again."[33]

Skiri Ritual and Mesoamerican Cosmology

The arrow piercing of the maiden corresponds to the gesture in the Hako by which the calumets, as symbolic arrows, were used to mediate a symbolic earth-sky union or conception by introducing a quickening spirit or breath from Tirawahat. Like the captive maiden, the honored child in the Calumet ceremony had previously been given an identity with the earth.

In the prototypical Calumet ceremony the adopted person, adult or child, symbolically reincarnated a deceased tribesman. In the ritual language of the Winnebago Medicine Rite (chapter 9) we know that reincarnation was referred to as 'skin shedding'.[34] This is easy to understand from the example of serpents that shed their skin periodically and emerge symbolically reborn. It is but one short step to actually shedding the skin of a sacrificial victim to represent rebirth in the manner of Xipe Totec. It was Seler who first suggested that the wearing of human skins in Aztec Xipe worship represented the new vegetation of the earth. This interpretation is quite compatible with the evidence of the Calumet ceremony and Morning Star sacrifice because of the great likelihood that in the prototypical Calumet ceremony the adoptee quickening the deceased also represented the earth reborn (chapters 7 and 17).[35]

Considering the act that was to follow, I interpret the symbolic attack on the four circles during the Skiri sacrifice to represent the conquests of the four quarters of the earth that the legend says preceded the conquest of Evening Star herself. The attacks on the four circles also have a parallel in the destructions of the first four suns in Aztec cosmology because each of those suns was implicitly associated with one of the world quarters.[36] These destructions were to be followed eventually by the destruction of the fifth sun of the Aztecs, Nahui Ollin or 4 Movement, and as already mentioned, the form taken by the victim in the Pawnee sacrifice resembled that of the Ollin glyph (figure 11.3). I feel that this comparison is more than justified by an additional comparison that can be made to the five circular altars constructed for the Ponca Sun Dance or Sun-Seeing Dance.

The known details of the Ponca Sun Dance are limited in number, but one feature is unique. The Ponca Sun Dance differed from other Sun Dances in that four secret tipis of preparation were constructed rather than the single one usual in the Sun Dance. These tipis, placed inside the large camp circle with one to the southeast, one to the southwest, one to the northwest, and one to the northeast of the center, were numbered one to four by George Dorsey.[37] The main activity in these tipis of preparation is said to have been the construction in each of a circular altar on the ground made with a design traced with dry-color paints. Dorsey was only able to witness the activities in the fourth tipi, whose altar, he was told, represented "the sun's symbol of one of the four medicine worlds." These Ponca activities would thus parallel certain proceedings in the Cheyenne Sun Dance, where "the making of successive 'earths'" was carried out in the single tipi of preparation used by the Cheyenne.[38] Among other activities that took place in the fourth Ponca tipi of preparation, the world symbol was destroyed by the officiating priest using a bunch of sagebrush dipped in a cup of water. This is a point of special interest, because the world of the fourth Aztec sun (4 Water) was also destroyed by water.

It is not known what activities transpired in the other three secret tipis of preparation, but the three remaining altars logically represented the three other mentioned 'medicine worlds' of the sun. Altar 2, containing a design representing, among other things, the paths of the four winds, would seem to have corresponded to the world of the second Aztec sun (4 Wind), destroyed by wind. Altar 3, representing the sun and the nest of the thunderbird, would seem to have corresponded to the third Aztec sun (4 Rain), destroyed by a rain of celestial fire. Altar 1 resembled altar 4 in that it consisted of concentric circles, but the symbolism is not known.

A very large fifth circular altar was constructed inside the Ponca Sun Dance enclosure between the buffalo skull and the pole, and this corresponded in its location to the altars in the Arapaho and Cheyenne Sun Dance enclosures that contained the sods representing the origin of the current world. It is reasonable to assume that the circular worlds in Ponca tipis of preparation 1 to 3 were also destroyed, although not necessarily in the same manner as that in tipi 4, and this would make the Ponca rituals of preparation analogous to the destruction of the four circles during the secret preparatory rites for the Skiri Morning Star sacrifice, which led up to the public rite involving the maiden transformed into a living cosmogram.

No interpretation in pure astronomical terms has yet been offered for the four conquests that preceded that of Evening Star herself. Yet, if we grant that Morning Star in the Skiri legend was originally Venus, however much that identity may have later shifted to morning stars of convenience through time, then it is possible to infer the possible significance of the four conquests. In Pawnee thought there was a mental equation between the concept of season and world quarter, so that an activity that was said in ritual parlance to have taken place in each of the world quarters might have been understood to have taken place in each of the four seasons of the year. If we were to conclude an eight-year Venus cycle with the heliacal or first visible rising of Venus ahead of the sun in mid-August of A.D. 1505 *Julian*, for example, then it would have been preceded by heliacal risings in spring of 1499, fall of 1500, summer of 1502, and winter of 1504, which would put a heliacal rising in four different seasons of the year and therefore, symbolically, in four different world quarters.[39] Consider the relationship of time and space in what Gene Weltfish says of a particular Pawnee wooden hoop: "The circumference of the wheel represented the horizon and it was marked off into twelve sections with bunches of feathers that were fastened at equal intervals. Each section represented the thirty-day lunar month of the twelve-month year. The four seasons of the year were marked off on the hoop with a different color for each quarter-arc. The winter

quarter was white, the spring quarter light green, the summer quarter darker green, and the autumn, reddish-yellow."[40]

The important thing here was the conception of the circle of the horizon as a year with the world quarters as seasons. Venus could rise heliacally in four different seasons and in effect could have entered four different quarters of the world in doing so, before rising heliacally the fifth time to complete a solar-Venus cycle of eight years or five Venus synodical periods.

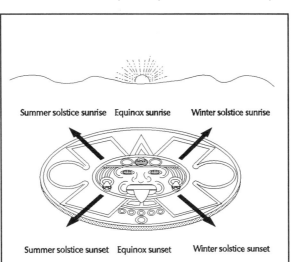

Summer solstice sunrise Equinox sunrise Winter solstice sunrise

Summer solstice sunset Equinox sunset Winter solstice sunset

Figure 11.3 The Ollin glyph at the center of the Aztec Stone of the Sun, representing the earth as symbolized by the handle of an atlatl of the twin-fingerloop type, split and splayed so that its four wings face the summer and winter solstice sunrise and sunset positions. An atlatl dart enters the earth in the west and emerges in the east, tracing the course of the night sun, with the face at the center of the Ollin glyph representing either the sun god Tonatiuh or the earth goddess Tlaltecuhtli. In the Skiri Pawnee Morning Star sacrifice the pose of the Evening Star impersonator, representing the fertility of the earth, compares to the splayed form of the Ollin glyph both while tied to the scaffold frame and while laid on the prairie in death.

The fires seen by the Pawnees on each side of the sun were sun dogs, an atmospheric phenomenon caused by the sun's light being refracted through ice crystals in high-altitude clouds. Sun dogs resemble patches or small arcs of rainbow, but, unlike rainbows, sun dogs are only seen while facing the sun. In Aztec ritual practice these sun dogs were represented by certain torches representing Xiuhcocoa, turquoise serpents or fire serpents. A pair of Xiuhcocoa accompanied the sun in the sky, as do sun dogs, and a pair of their likenesses formed the perimeter of the Aztec Stone of the Suns. The two Pawnee men with torches standing to the north and south of the captive maiden, now given a ritual identity with the earth, nicely parallel the image of the two Xiuhcocoa on the Stone of the Sun, one to the north and one to the south of the Ollin glyph representing the earth. In the iconography of the Classic period central Mexican site of Teotihuacán there is a well-known association of owls with warfare and with Venus, although not with anything recognizable as sun dogs, unless there was an association of Venus and Mercury with sun dogs that has not yet been recognized.

Sun dogs or parhelia are commonly seen when the sun is low on the horizon and there are high-altitude clouds with ice crystals $22\frac{1}{2}°$ to the right and/or left of the sun. Sun dogs can sometimes, but rarely, also be seen 45° away from the sun, sometimes combined with a halo, and sometimes above the sun. These degrees of separation from the sun so closely approximate the degrees of greatest elongation of the planets Mercury and Venus from the sun, 26° and 47°, respectively, on the average, as to raise the question of whether Mesoamerican skywatchers might not also have been aware of the coincidence. Dennis Tedlock has inferred that certain owl messengers in the *Popol Vuh* of the Quiché Maya represent Mercury in the astronomical symbolism of that epic, suggesting to him that the four owls of Xibalaba, the Quiché underworld, represent Mercury, two of them in Mercury's morning star aspect and two in its evening star aspect. This fits elegantly with the idea of a relationship of Mercury at maximum elongation to sun dogs, because there can be two sun dogs seen after dawn 22½° away from the sun and two seen just before sunset at the same distance.[41]

The Aztec word for fire serpent was Xiuhcóatl (plural Xiuhcocoa) with the Náhuatl noun root *cóatl* translating as 'serpent, twin' and surviving in modern Mexican Spanish in the word *cuate* 'twin, companion, pal', an *aztequismo*. How better to think of a phenomenon that rises and sets with the sun, always at the sun's side, like Don Quixote's Sancho Panza or Batman's Robin? The idea apparently also appears in Pawnee mythology. James Murie recorded a myth of the Pawnee Two Lance Society that told of a journey of Paruxti, the Wonder Being, to the earth. To provide him with 'companions' (Murie's choice of word, not mine) for this exploration the council of stars created a rainbow, which they broke into two halves. The North Star and the South Star each provided a man to carry one of the rainbow halves.[42] This corresponds very nicely with the idea of the two Pawnee men, one to the north and one to the south of the sacrifice victim, holding torches representing the little segments of rainbow seen on either side of the sun.

In Skiri belief Evening Star represented the fertility of the earth, and in her final transformation the Evening star impersonator effectively became the earth itself, laid as she was upon the ground with her black-painted side to the north, her red-painted side to the south, her arms and legs corresponding to the semicardinal directions, her head to the east, and her generative parts to the west, coinciding there with the location of the Garden of the Evening Star.

DIFRASISMO is a term used by the Mexican scholar Ángel María Garibay to describe a characteristic of the Náhuatl language, the language of the Aztecs. *Difrasismo* refers to a mode of expression in which a single idea is expressed by the conjunction of two or more words that are synonyms of, metaphors for, or express two qualities of the subject, such as 'flower and song' meaning 'poetry', 'skirt and blouse' meaning 'woman', 'arrow and shield' meaning 'war', and 'water and mountain' meaning 'city'.[1] The logic is somewhat like that behind the rhyming slang of the English as found in the East End district of London, in which 'my storm and strife', for example, means 'my wife'. *Difrasismo* also includes the redundant combination of phrases (hence *difrasismo*) that are complementary in meaning or are synonyms, e.g.:

Lady of our flesh, Lord of our flesh;
she who is clothed in black, he who is clothed in red;
she who endows the earth with solidity,
he who covers the earth with cotton.[2]

The reference is to Ometéotl, the Aztec god of duality, who was both mother and father of the gods as well as the personification of earth and sky and of night and day. In these several lines we find the equations mother-earth-night-black and father-sky-day-red plus the additional equation of those two series within a single divinity. The idea 'mother' contrasts with that of 'father', but each idea represents an aspect of a single being. This idea of duality should by now sound familiar to attentive readers. Each calumet of the Hako type contained male and female, sky and earth, elements within itself, but each calumet was also one of a pair with the same contrasting associations (chapter 7). Tirawahat is said to represent the vault of heaven but appears in one tradition as a water serpent (chapter 10). The handle of one variety of atlatl appears in Panama carved in the form of a crocodilian with a bird head and again in Veracruz in the form of a bird with a crocodilian head (chapter 14), the combinations appearing to represent the intermeshed duality of sky versus earth and water.[3]

The aspect or quality of redundancy in *difrasismo* can be found in English literature. Scores of examples assault the reader in *The Song of Hiawatha* published by Henry Wadsworth Longfellow in 1855:

By the shores of Gitchee Gumee,
By the shining Big-Sea-Water,
Stood the wigwam of Nokomis,
Daughter of the Moon, Nokomis.
Dark behind it rose the forest,
Rose the black and gloomy pine-trees,
Rose the firs with cones upon them;
Bright before it beat the water,
Beat the clear and sunny water,
Beat the shining Big-Sea-Water.[4]

The redundancy exhibited in this English example combines what in the craft of poetry are known as 'parallelism' and 'epanaphora'. The latter means the reiteration or repetition of a word or phrase at the beginning of two or more lines of verse. The former means the repeating of a thought or reference in some alternate form for a rhetorical or poetic effect.[5] In Longfellow's verse the repetition of "By the . . ." helps to define the parallel ideas, or equation, of "Gitchee Gumee" with "Big-Sea-Water." Other equations are "Nokomis" with "Daughter of the Moon," "forest" with both "black and gloomy pine-trees" and "firs with cones upon them," and "water" with "clear and sunny water" and "shining Big-Sea-Water."

Poetics aside, *The Song of Hiawatha* tells the story of the Ojibwa culture hero Manabozho, including the now familiar story of the plot of the evil spirits to destroy Manabozho's companion and the gods' gift of the Medicine Lodge and the secrets of the Medicine Society to console Manabozho (chapters 8, 9, 19), although Longfellow unforgiveably gave his mythical Ojibwa hero Manabozho the name of the historical Iroquois hero Hiawatha:[6]

IN those days the Evil Spirits,
All the Manitos of mischief,
Fearing Hiawatha's wisdom,
And his love for Chibiabos,
Jealous of their faithful friendship,
And their noble words and actions,
Made at length a league against them,
To molest them and destroy them.

. . . .

Then the Medicine-men, the Medas,
The magicians, the Wabenos,
And the Jossakeeds, the Prophets,
Came to visit Hiawatha;
Built a Sacred Lodge beside him,
To appease him, to console him,
Walked in silent, grave procession,
Bearing each a pouch of healing,
Skin of beaver, lynx, or otter,
Filled with magic roots and simples,
Filled with very potent medicines.[7]

SKIRI POETICS

Repetition is a characteristic of many Indian songs in North America, sometimes only a word or phrase being repeated again and again. When lines are repeated with the variation of a single word between lines within a single song, this can be a clue that the words are in some sense synonymous. This would be another example of parallelism defined in part by the reiteration of the other words of the sentence. In one Skiri Pawnee song there is an evident equation between 'earth', 'Evening Star', and 'mother'. This can be seen in the text below provided by James Murie and Douglas Parks:

A	hi	hura·ru	ra·'a [ha a]
	There	the earth	comes.
B	hi	awari	ra·'a [ha]
	There	Evening Star	comes.
A	hi	hura·ru	ra·'a [ha]
	There	the earth	comes.
B	hi	awari	ra·'a [ha]
	There	Evening Star	comes.
C	hi	atira	ra·'a [ha]
	There	my mother	comes.
C	hi	atira	ra·'a [ha]
	There	my mother	comes.[8]

The implied correspondences are awari, hura·ru, and atira, with the translated or glossed meanings of 'Evening Star', 'the earth', and 'my mother'. These are all related ideas. Even in English we speak of Mother Earth, but the relationship of Evening Star is not as

obvious. Among the Pawnees Evening Star represented not merely the planet Venus but also the fertility or reproductive power of the earth. Awari was a word that when used as a noun translates as 'Evening Star' but whose etymology relates more particularly to the idea 'movement, life' (one part, a-, meaning 'being' or 'living', and the second part, -wari, meaning 'to go actively about').[9] The extended semantic equation that I infer is thus 'earth' ≈ 'Evening Star' ≈ 'my mother' ≈ 'movement, life'. Weltfish provides the following song from the same Skiri planting ritual as that from which Murie and Parks give the song above, and in it the relationship of 'earth' and 'movement' implied by the parallel structure in the poetry is evident:

A	huraru		ra·a
	earth		the one that is coming
B	hi	awari	ra·a
	there	movement	that is coming[10]

SACRED METAPHORS

In the ritual of the Skiri Pawnee Morning Star sacrifice the girl who impersonated Evening Star also came to be identified with, and impersonated, the earth itself. She was tied to a frame with arms raised and all four limbs spread apart representing the four semicardinal directions—northeast, northwest, southeast, and southwest. This was the same arrangement, on the same kind of frame, used in the ancient Mexican sacrifice by arrows. This was the same pattern as that of the butterfly-shaped Aztec day sign Ollin, which translates as 'movement' and is commonly glossed as 'earthquake'.[11] The corresponding day among the Yucatec Mayas was called Caban, which meant 'earth'. So, in Mesoamerica, as among the Pawnees, there was also a set of mental associations that included the ideas 'earth' and 'movement'. The parallelism of 'earth' and 'movement' in Pawnee thought are evident again in the tenth song of the ritual of the Skiri Morning Star sacrifice:

A	awari		tara·ru·hu' [u hu]
	Movement (i.e., life)		she is giving you.
B	hura·ru	tara·ru·hu [ri]	tara·ru
	Earth	she is giving you;	she gives you.
C	awari	tara·ru	
	Movement	she gives you.	
B	hura·ru	tara·ru·hu [ri]	tara·ru
	Earth	she is giving you;	she gives you.
C	awari	tara·ru	
	Movement	she gives you.	
B	hura·ru	tara·ru·hu [ri]	tara·ru
	Earth	she is giving you;	she gives you.
C	awari	tara·ru	
	Movement	she gives you.	

B *hura ru*   *tara·ru·hu [ri]*   *tara·ru*
   Earth   she is giving you;   she gives you.
D *awari*
   Movement.[12]

A Pawnee earthlodge was constructed with its floor excavated beneath the general level of the ground surface. This added to its warmth in winter and its coolness in summer. The lodge's skeletal frame was formed of heavy, peeled, cottonwood tree trunks with ribs of lighter cottonwood poles interlaced with willow

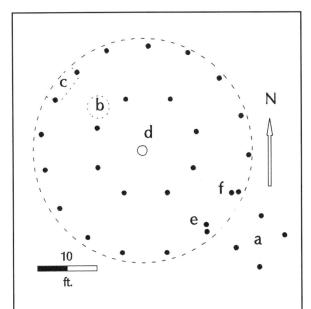

Figure 12.1 Plan view of a South Band Pawnee earthlodge from the Hill site, Webster County, Nebraska, after W. Wedel (1936, fig. 4), showing the entrance passage (*a*), a cache pit (*b*), altar platform (*c*), fireplace (*d*), and interior support posts for the entrance passage (*e–f*), which in the symbolism of Skiri Band Pawnees, according to Murie (1902b), would have represented (*e*) the errand man of the Red Star of the southeast and (*f*) the errand man of the Big Black Star of the northeast.

switches. Its flesh and skin were a covering of grass and earth. In the roof was a small opening to allow smoke to pass out, and on the eastern side was a long, covered entrance passage to allow its inhabitants to pass in. This entrance ideally faced directly east and toward sunrise at equinox time, although one archaeological excavated lodge used for ritual purposes by the Republican band of Pawnees around A.D. 1800 faced to the southeast and sunrise at winter solstice time (figure 12.1).

The number of central support posts was ordinarily four for common dwellings but eight for those of chiefs. If eight, then four of the eight retained special associations with the four semicardinal directions and were

painted with the colors associated with those directions by the Pawnees—northeast *black*, southeast *red*, southwest *white*, northwest *yellow*.[13] At the center of the floor of the lodge and beneath the smoke hole was the hearth. That part of the lodge opposite the entrance was the location of honor for seating purposes.

In lodges used for bundle rituals there would have been a small raised platform opposite the door upon which a buffalo skull was set. The sacred bundle hung from a rafter over the skull. On the top of the buffalo skull and behind the eyes there was painted a rectangular figure that represented the Garden of the Evening Star. According to George Dorsey and James Murie, it was "Upon this rectangular space, or garden, the sun descends and gives light and understanding to all men, for it is in this garden that the sun goes to renew its magic potency."[14] The rectangle was approximately twice as long as it was wide and would have been oriented with the long axis north-south when the skull was facing the east, as it normally was.[15] In the center of the earthlodge was a circular fireplace with a raised rim. Between the fireplace and the buffalo skull altar there was a sacred area used for a variety of purposes.[16] In front of the small platform for the buffalo skull sacred bundles were opened and their contents displayed. Between that area and the hearth in Skiri band lodges there was a shallow square pit which represented in a different form the now familiar Garden of the Evening Star,[17] but this pit was itself also thought of as a hearth or fireplace even though not actually used as one:

> In front of the altar place there is dug a place about a foot deep and nearly square. This is called a bed or fireplace, skararu [*sic*]. This place is put in the lodge because the altar in the heavens where the old men sit is such a place. That is why the bed is placed in front of the altar. The people were told that in time they would go through a great ceremony where they bring the [ceremonial] bundles, unwrap them, and get from each two ears of corn; one of them would be tied upon a stick and is supposed to be a male deity, the other ear of corn being a female. In this excavation they placed the ears of corn on the sticks along side the walls of the square and placed the others at the bottom. Now they call it a place for new birth of power, and it resembles and is symbolic of that place in the west where the Evening-Star created all things [the Garden of the Evening Star].[18]

South of the Skiri villages were those of other Pawnee bands. These differed from the Skiris in language and in aspects of belief important for this chapter. The South bands did not share the Skiri concept of Evening Star nor of her garden,[19] and consequently the archaeological manifestations of features in the sacred area before the buffalo skull may be expected to differ in some way. The Hill site two miles south of Red Cloud, Nebraska, is believed to have been a village of the Republican band, one of the South bands, and the village visited by Lieutenant Zebulon Pike in 1806.[20] In 1930 the Nebraska Archaeological Survey excavated a large earthlodge at this site that had a platform in the place of honor on which a buffalo skull may once have rested. Between that platform and the central fireplace there was a large bell-shaped storage or cache pit of the kind used for food. Because this was not a place where cache pits were normally located, the contents of this pit were possibly quite special—perhaps sacred seed corn, parfleches of dried buffalo meat for ritual use, or the like.

Facing eastward as it did, the entrance of a Skiri band lodge used for ritual purposes would receive rays of light from the morning star because the planets in their orbits followed close to the course of the sun. These rays would pass into the interior of the lodge and touch the Garden of the Evening Star: "As [Morning Star] rose every morning he sent his beam into the long entryway of the house and lit the fire in an act of procreation, symbolizing his first union with Evening Star in the times of the great creation when he had to fight off the guardians of night with which the Evening Star surrounded herself. . . . The house was at the same time the universe and also the womb of a woman."[21]

The drilling of fire by friction for the New Fire ceremony also symbolized the sexual union of Morning Star and Evening Star.[22] The lower fire board or hearth board in such cases represented Evening Star; the fire drill symbolized Morning Star. The fireplace used for the New Fire ritual was not round but a rectangular pit, three by five feet in dimensions, oriented north-south, like the Garden of the Evening Star created for the Morning Star sacrifice, and was another manifestation of the Garden.[23] This hearth and the actual fire drilling were located in a specially prepared temporary enclosure outside of the village. The New Fire ceremony was war-related and not a part of the agricultural cycle as in the southeastern United States.[24]

Well to the north of the Pawnees in North Dakota, the Hidatsa Indians once excavated pits of the same size and proportion as the Garden of the Evening Star anticipating that metaphors of the sun would descend down to them. These were the pits excavated for the trapping of eagles. Such eagle trapping pits were large enough to allow a man to lie within them on his back and so would also have been useful as grave metaphors (chapter 19 and figure 19.6). The pits were covered with sticks and branches to conceal the trapper who waited below for an eagle to descend upon a dead rabbit fastened to the branches as bait. When an eagle had settled upon the bait, the trapper would reach through the branches to grasp the feet of the eagle.

In the temporary Hidatsa lodges used while eagle trapping, the hearth was made in a rectangular form, about two by four feet in size and oriented north-south like the Garden of the Evening Star, just a foot smaller in each dimension than the hearth created in the form of the Garden for the Skiri New Fire ceremony. This Hidatsa hearth explicitly symbolized an eagle trapping pit and was excavated in front of a buffalo skull altar. On each side of the hearth there was a long pole representing a snake. These two 'snake poles' have no stated function in the eagle ritual, but the combination of poles and rectangular hearth pit in front of the Hidatsa buffalo skull nicely parallels the rectangular pit bracketed by two wooden poles found in front of the buffalo skull in the Arapaho Sun Dance lodge, which corresponds in location to the grave for Spring Boy in the Hidatsa Sun Dance and the white clay bed for the Whistler in the old Crow Sun Dance.[25]

This all becomes relevant to Calumet ceremonialism when it is remembered (a) that the prototype for the Calumet ceremony may have been a Woodland period burial mound ritual combining mourning and symbolic reincarnation with the person standing for the reincarnated person also representing the earth reborn (chapter 7), and (b) that the motif used to paint the face of the Spring Boy impersonator was the same as that used to paint the face of child adopted in the Pawnee Calumet ceremony (chapter 6). A person lying in a grave-like eagle trapping pit, capturing an eagle, would have been an appropriate metaphor upon which to model a ritual dramatizing a sky-earth union, which, after all, was one of the meanings of the symbolic conception mediated by the eagle feather–draped calumets. Such an interpretation would help to explain the derivation of the Iroquois and Cherokee Eagle Dance from the Calumet ceremony by going beyond the simple comparison of gestures with feathered calumets to eagles swooping.

THE QUARTERED CIRCLE

The north-south–oriented pit beneath the scaffold for the Skiri Morning Star sacrifice was regarded as an expression of the Garden of the Evening Star.[26] There is also a feature beneath the scaffold for the corresponding sacrifice as depicted by pre-Columbian Mixtec artists in southern Mexico (figure 12.2a), but the Mixtec feature is not a long rectangular pit. It is a variant of the quartered circle motif of the kind called a 'turquoise glyph' by the Mexican archaeologist Alfonso Caso. This glyph is a circle divided into quarters, often with a central circle as a fifth element that makes the total design a 'quincunx'.[27]

Beyond the Mixtecs the quincunx was used by the

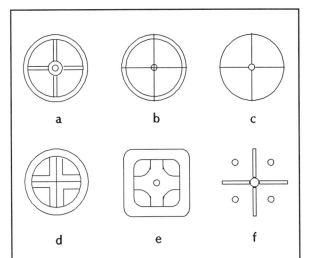

Figure 12.2 Variations on the quartered circle theme in Mesoamerica and the United States: *a,* the glyph upon which blood is flowing from the wounds of the victim in an arrow sacrifice scene from the *Codex Zouche-Nuttall,* after Nuttall (1975, 84); *b,* Maya map of northern Yucatan from the perspective of Merida (Tihoo) in 1618, after Roys (1967, fig. 27) and Edmonson (1986, 195); *c,* sacred hoop or wind-center motif constructed as part of the altar in the Lakota Sun Dance lodge, after Black Elk (1953, 89); *d,* sacred fire (hearth and logs) motif on a Mississippian shell gorget from New Madrid, Missouri, after Holmes (1883, pl. 61, no. 1); *e,* Maya Kan cross, abstracted from sculptured examples at the Palenque site, Chiapas, Mexico, after Thompson (1971, fig. 45, nos. 7–8); *f,* earth image between the buffalo skull and central pole in the Cheyenne Massaum lodge, after Grinnell (1972, 2:294).

Mayas as a symbol of the earth divided into four quarters as seen from a community that regarded itself as the center of the world (figure 12.2*b*).[28] To the north of the Pawnees the Lakotas refer to the identical sign as the 'sacred hoop' and as a 'wind center' (figure 12.2*c*). The outer circle was the surrounding horizon. The four lines quartering the circle were the paths of the winds from the north, south, east, and west, and the central circle was the location of reference, the 'here'.[29] To the southeast of the Pawnee was the Osage Nation. The Osage called the quartered circle Ho′-e-ga (chapter 7) and used this name also for the half-circle motif painted on the face of the child in the Osage Calumet ceremony (figure 7.2*c*). The related design in the Pawnee Hako (figure 7.2*b*) was oriented on the face in a similar manner so that the nose was at the center of the circle, had the circle been complete. It was at that point that a conceiving breath was believed to enter the child's body. In the Omaha ceremony the motif (figure 7.2*a*) was oriented so that the center was on the top of the head, also a significant location for a conception.

On a newborn baby the top of the head is the location of the anterior fontanel or soft spot. The fontanel is in the form of an equal-armed cross or star and is created by the incomplete union of the bones of the forepart of the skull, which is not yet closed in bone but covered with a membrane thin and soft enough to allow the fontanel to pulsate with the heart beat (figure 12.3*b*). Ho′-e-ga was used by the Osage with the ritual meaning 'earth'. The word fontanel comes to English from Middle French *fontenele* 'little fountain' in the sense of 'little spring of water'. The Lakota words for fontanel are *pe′wiwila* and *peówiwila*, both meaning 'little spring on the top of the head'.[30] The Náhuatl or Aztec word for fontanel was *atl* 'water'.[31]

In Indian belief springs were earth openings through which animal spirits could enter the earth or leave the earth and become materialized. This is illustrated by the following excerpt from a Cheyenne myth:

> As the sun went down, all the village began to look toward the spring. After a time, as they watched, they saw a four-year-old bull leap out. He ran a little distance and began to paw the ground, and then turned about and ran back and plunged into the spring. After he had gone back, a great herd of buffalo came pouring out of the spring and all night long they could hear them. No one went to sleep that night, for the buffalo made too much noise. Next morning at sunrise the earth, as far as they could see, was covered with buffalo.[32]

Some Indians explicitly associate the fontanel with the seat of the soul or a passage by which the soul enters or leaves the body. According to Frank Waters, the Hopi believed that the body had several 'vibratory centers': "The first of these in man lay at the top of the head. Here, when he was born, was the soft spot, *kópavi,* the 'open door' through which he received his life and communicated with his Creator. For with every breath the soft spot moved up and down with a gentle vibration that was communicated to the Creator. At the time of the red light, Tálawva, the last phase of his creation, the soft spot was hardened and the door was closed. It remained closed until his death, opening then for his life to depart as it had come."[33] The Shawnees similarly believed that the soul entered the body of a fetus through the fontanel, jumping through the mother's vagina and through the fontanel just before birth.[34]

The Huichols of western Mexico, who belong to the Uto-Aztecan language family, also associate the soul with the fontanel. The Huichols make a variety of yarn cross or god's eye called the *tsikúri* which resembles a rectilinear Ho′-e-ga on a stick (figure 12.3*a*). The *tsikúri* combines the symbolism of the "four-directional universe and the sacred center" but also by its string winding represents the "'life thread' that holds the essential life force to the fontanelle. Structurally, however, it is indistinguishable from the Huichol tüwe, or 'jaguar,' which functions as a kind of a spirit trap or barrier designed to keep the recent dead from re-entering the community of the living at inopportune times."[35] Here again is a cosmogram associated with the idea of 'snare' or 'trap', the gloss of Ho'-e-ga.

During Calumet ceremonies, as described for the Pawnee, for instance, the identity of the Mother Corn ear was transferred to the child. But, because the Mother Corn also represented the earth, the child was

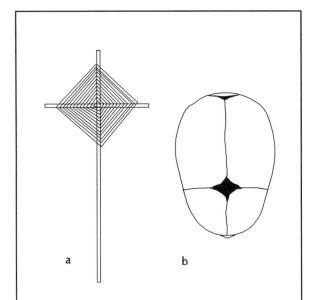

Figure 12.3 *Tsikúri* or yarn cross (*a*), after Furst (1975, fig. 6), used by the Huichols of western Mexico as a protective device for children, representing the four directions of the universe and the sacred center with the string symbolizing the life thread that holds the life force to the fontanel or soft spot (*b*) on the cranium of a newborn.

simultaneously also given an identity with the earth and, because the Mother Corn ear was explicitly believed by the Pawnee to have the character of 'snare' and 'trap', the child received those characters as well, being thus "[made] open to receive the powers" about to descend upon it.[36] This is now becoming a familiar semantic set—earth, snare, trap. The eagle plume on the Mother Corn ear and on the child's head represented Tirawahat, the male principle, and a corn tassel.

Much the same semantic set can be found expressed in a well-known Maya bas relief carved panel in the Temple of the Foliated Cross at the Palenque site, Chiapas, Mexico. The essence of the design is a world tree cum maize plant of cross form growing from the

head of an earth monster with a so-called kan cross (figure 12.2e) in its forehead. Kan (Yucatec *k'an*) basically means yellow but, by various extensions of meaning, also ripe or mature, maize, and precious. Kan's near homophone *k'aan* denotes cord and net.[37] The Kan cross is essentially another form of Caso's turquoise glyph and the Osage Ho'-e-ga motif. Aside from being the name for a motif painted on the forehead of the child in the Osage Calumet ceremony, Ho'-e-ga was also the name for a bare spot on the forehead of the elk, the animal that helped to create the earth in the Osage tradition by summoning the winds from the four directions. There would seem to have been only a small semantic difference between the Plains idea of snare/trap and the Maya concept of cord/net, related as they both were not only to the quartered-circle motif but also to the forehead. The fontanel was a spirit trap.

The Lakotas traditionally created a sacred hoop or wind center design in the ground within the enclosure used for the Sun Dance.[38] A related design was formed in front of the buffalo skull used in the Cheyenne Massaum ceremony, except that earth from the central spot was distributed into four equal-sized mounds between the four arms of the cross (figure 12.2f). The design represented the earth and these mounds represented "the four hills supposed to hold up the earth, in each of which lives one of the powers of the four directions."[39]

In the Sun Dances of the Cheyennes and Arapahoes the feature in front of the buffalo skull was a rectangular trench (figure 3.2), like the garden of the Evening Star. Those officiating at the Sun Dances of these tribes created tiny arbors of arched sticks over these pits—the 'rainbow sticks'.[40] Because 'rainbow' also meant 'snare', the rectangular trenches that formed part of the buffalo skull altar for the Cheyennes and Arapahoes were thus equivalent in meaning to the Osage Ho'-e-ga (snare, trap) motif.

If you can visualize all of the discussed features as verbal expressions, and all of their ritual contexts as similarly having verbal form, then you can find analogies to the poetic devices mentioned at the beginning of this chapter. The buffalo skull altars of the Pawnees, Cheyennes, and Arapahoes are equivalent to the reiterated phrases introducing many lines in Longfellow's *Song of Hiawatha* or within the Pawnee songs given. The features in front of the skulls are equivalent to the phrases that followed the reiterated phrases, phrases that were different yet equivalent in meaning, being examples of parallelism of expression. If Longfellow had been more informed on comparative religion he might have expressed it this way:

There before the buffalo skull
lies the cosmic center to which winds blow;

There before the buffalo skull
lies the grave-like trench with the rainbow snare;
There before the buffalo skull
grows the fabled Garden of the Evening Star.

There beneath a wooden frame
find the turquoise sign of earth and water;
There beneath a wooden frame
find the earthly womb from which life springs;
There beneath a wooden frame
in the western Garden of the Evening Star.

There within the earth life stirs
as in a woman bearing a child;
There within the earth life throbs
with the rhythmic beat of a living heart;
There within the earth life thrives

as death begets life and life follows death
in the sacred Garden of the Evening Star.

The captive maiden prepared for death over the Garden of the Evening Star was a visual metaphor of the kind of dualism expressed in the Náhuatl poem with which this chapter began. The left side of her body was painted in black to represent night and earth. This was her north side as she faced the east. Her right side was painted red to represent day and sky. In death her four limbs would extend to the four semicardinal directions as she lay facedown with her head to the east.[41] Her body would shortly become part of the earth and in death would generate new life. Her example would stimulate the earth itself to produce through the principle of imitative magic.

13 / Sacred Poles and Sacred Trees

FRANCIS LA FLESCHE began his ethnographic work by assisting Alice Fletcher and James Owen Dorsey in their studies of the Omahas. He had an appointment as a clerk with the office of the Commissioner of Indian Affairs in Washington, D.C., beginning in 1891 and received a law degree from the National University in 1893. He began work for the U.S. Bureau of American Ethnology in 1910 and continued there until his retirement in 1929 at the age of 72. He died in 1932.[1]

RECORDING THE SAYINGS OF THE OLD MEN

In Washington Francis La Flesche happened to make the acquaintance of Saucy Calf, a member of a delegation of Osages visiting the Commissioner of Indian Affairs in Washington on tribal business. Saucy Calf became intrigued in talking with La Flesche and spent some time discussing the similarities of customs of the Omahas and those of his own tribe: the two tribes had a common history and separated perhaps as recently as ten centuries ago. A friendship developed and Saucy Calf brought up a suggestion that would affect the balance of Francis La Flesche's career. After contemplating his words in silence for a few moments, Saucy Calf said to La Flesche:

> Many of the sayings of the No$^{n\prime}$-ho^{n}-zhi^{n}-ga ['old men'] who lived long ago have come down to us and have been treasured by the people as expressions coming from the men who had been in close touch with the Mysterious Power whom the people had learned to worship and to reverence. Moreover, the men who uttered these sayings had long since departed for the spirit land and were regarded by their descendents as Wa-ko$^{n\prime}$-da-gi, that is, as sacred and mysterious persons. These sayings had been transmitted in ritual form and during the passage of years had been jealously guarded against desecration by those persons who had succeeded in memorizing them and had taken care to teach them only to such pupils as manifested a proper spirit of reverence for things sacred.

> My people, particularly those of the younger class, are becoming indifferent to these old-time rites. Those who still have an interest in them and manifest a desire to be initiated in the various degrees of the rites are becoming fewer and fewer. It looks as though the sayings of the ancient men will soon be lost and forgotten. Perhaps some day you will come to Oklahoma and then I can recite to you the rituals of my own To$^{n\prime}$-wo^{n}-gtho^{n} (gens) for you to write them upon paper and that much of our tribal rites can be preserved. I know that it is not the practice of the No$^{n\prime}$-ho^{n}-zhi^{n}-ga to teach a person these things without the prescribed formalities or without fees, but, in seriousness, I think that some, at least, of the rituals ought to be put on paper, so that Osage men and women of the future may know what their ancestors thought and said and did.[2]

It happened that not long after Saucy Calf left to return to Oklahoma La Flesche was asked by the Bureau of American Ethnology to begin a study of the Osage tribe. La Flesche agreed to the proposal, but not without many thoughts of the difficulties he would probably encounter trying to secure information on Osage religious affairs. In the end La Flesche knew that he could rely on at least one Osage contact who considered this kind of documentation to be an important and worthy project.

In Oklahoma La Flesche did renew his acquaintance with Saucy Calf and began the recording of what would become "The Rite of the Wa-xo'-be," the record of a major Osage ritual published in the Forty-fifth Annual Report of the Bureau of American Ethnology.[3] And the pair did encounter objections to their collaboration. Although this ritual was Saucy Calf's by purchase to perform and he had the traditional right to teach it to a friend, Saucy Calf was made to feel uncomfortable by persons who disagreed with his doing so. At La Flesche's suggestion the pair continued their work in Washington and completed the recording of the Rite of the Wa-xo'-be.

This accomplished, Saucy Calf indicated his desire to continue by recording all the rituals to which he had the right to repeat by purchase and by virtue of his membership in the clan that owned them. First, however, he wished to return to Oklahoma to refresh his memory. He returned to Oklahoma, but there, in February 1912, Saucy Calf died unexpectedly—murdered and his home burned.

One must guess at the effect this death had upon La Flesche because this was the second time he had lost a father under similar circumstances. At Saucy Calf's suggestion he and La Flesche addressed each other with the kinship terms father and son, as was customary between an elder teaching a rite to an initiate. With Saucy Calf's death La Flesche thus lost a ritual father, but La Flesche had lost his real father years earlier under similar circumstances while recording the legend of the Sacred Pole of the Omaha tribe, something that might have deterred another person.

THE OMAHA SACRED POLE

Francis La Flesche's father was Joseph La Flesche, the son of a French trader and an Indian woman of the Ponca tribe. He was a *metis* (French 'mixed') with a French father and thus could not belong to one of the traditional clans of the Omaha in which descent was patrilineal or through the male line.[4] As a mixed-blood Joseph La Flesche had the opportunity to learn something of both white and Indian ways and in time chose to identify with the Omahas. He was adopted by Big Elk, the principal chief of the Omahas, and upon the death of Big Elk became, himself, the principal chief, an office passed down through the male line.

For twenty-five years Francis La Flesche cooperated with Alice Fletcher in researching and writing an ethnography of the Omaha tribe, culminating in a joint report published in 1911 as the Twenty-seventh Annual Report of the Bureau of American Ethnology.[5] During the course of this study Fletcher acquired for Harvard University some of the most sacred objects of the Omaha tribe for preservation in Harvard's Peabody Museum of Archaeology and Ethnology. Because they were so sacred, these objects presented a special problem to the Omahas.

For generations the three sacred tents of the Omaha and their contents had been essential in tribal ceremonies and were symbolic as well of the authority of the chiefs. They represented a way of life that had passed, however, and there was no longer the prospect of continuity in the proper guardianship of these holy relics. They were objects of fear that few people could touch or even go near. If an unauthorized person, an animal, or even an inanimate object such as a tent pole came into accidental contact with the objects, the offending being or thing had to be cleaned ceremonially to prevent supernatural retribution for the sacrilege. There naturally was concern among the Omaha leaders for the proper care of these objects when their traditional caretakers died, as there were no qualified successors. The leading men of the tribe came to the decision that the objects should be buried with their caretaker.

Fletcher and La Flesche considered it equally unfortunate that the sacred objects of the Omaha might be lost to the tribe along with the associated sacred history that would die with the keepers. With the help of Joseph La Flesche certain sacred objects were eventually acquired for the Peabody Museum, among them the Sacred Pole of the Omaha. In September of 1888 Smoked Yellow or Yellow Smoke, the last person knowing the legend of the Sacred Pole, came to Joseph La Flesche's house to tell the story so it could be added by Alice Fletcher and Francis La Flesche to the permanent history of the Omaha tribe.

Still uneasy about what he had agreed to do, Smoked Yellow continued only after Joseph La Flesche agreed to accept for himself any divine punishment that might follow the revealing of this sacred knowledge. The interview lasted three days. The recording session was hardly over when Joseph La Flesche fell sick with a fatal illness and within two weeks lay dead in the very room that the sacred legend of the Pole had been recited.[6] A more superstitious person would not have continued the seemingly life-threatening occupation of studying Indian religion. On an earlier occasion Joseph La Flesche lost a leg, a misfortune that was attributed by some old men of the tribe to Joseph's opposing the performance of a particular ceremony related to the Sacred Pole.[7] But Francis La Flesche did continue and thirty-eight years later, in 1926, was awarded an honorary Doctor of Letters degree by the University of Nebraska for his accomplishments in preserving the traditional knowledge of Indian peoples. Fletcher and La Flesche give extracts of the legend of the pole in two versions as follow:

> A great council was being held to devise some means by which the bands of the tribe might be kept together and the tribe itself saved from extinction. This council lasted many days. Meanwhile the son of one of the ruling men was off on a hunt. On his way home he came to a great forest and in the night lost his way. He walked and walked until he was exhausted with pushing his way through the underbrush. He stopped to rest and to find the "motionless star" for his guide when he was suddenly attracted by a light. Believing that it came from a tent the young hunter went toward it, but on coming to the place whence the welcome light came he was amazed to find that it was a tree that sent forth the light. He went up to it and found that the

whole tree, its trunk, branches, and leaves, were alight, yet remained unconsumed. He touched the tree but no heat came from it. This mystified him and he stood watching the strange tree, for how long he did not know. At last day approached, the brightness of the tree began to fade, until with the rising of the sun the tree with its foliage resumed its natural appearance. The man remained there in order to watch the tree another night. As twilight came on it began to be luminous and continued so until the sun again rose. When the young man returned home he told his father of the wonder. Together they went to see the tree; they saw it all alight as it was before but the father observed something that had escaped the notice of the young man; this was that four animal paths led to it. These paths were well beaten and as the two men examined the paths and the tree it was clear to them that the animals came to the tree and had rubbed against it and polished its bark by doing so. This was full of significance to the elder man and on his return he told the leading men of the mysterious tree. It was agreed by all that the tree was a gift from Wakon'da and that it would be the thing that would help to keep the people together. With great ceremony they cut the tree down and hewed it to portable size.[8]

The Omahas were closely related to the Poncas, with whom they probably formed a single tribe in the recent past. Both the Poncas and Omahas have legends about the Sacred Pole, suggesting that it was part of their common history. Ponca and Omaha legends agree that they were living near a lake at the time the pole was found and that the tree from which the pole was made grew near a lake some distance from the village. The pole was also said to have been discovered at a time when the Omahas and Poncas were in council with the Cheyenne, Arikara, and Iowa tribes trying to come to an agreement "on terms of peace and rules of war and hunting, and to adopt a peace ceremony."[9] The following is a second version of the legend of the Sacred Pole, another Omaha version, which was said to date to this time:

During this time a young man who had been wandering came back to his village. When he reached his home he said, "Father, I have seen a wonderful tree!" And he described it. The old man listened but he kept silent, for all was not yet settled between the tribes.

After a little while the young man went again to visit the tree. On his return home he repeated his former tale to his father about the wonderful tree. The old man kept silent, for the chiefs were still conferring. At last, when everything was agreed upon between the tribes, the old man sent for the chiefs and said: "My son has seen a wonderful tree. The Thunderbirds come

and go upon this tree, making a trail of fire that leaves four paths on the burnt grass that stretch toward the Four Winds. When the Thunderbirds alight upon the tree it bursts into flame and the fire mounts to the top. The tree stands burning, but no one can see the fire except at night."

When the chiefs heard this tale they sent runners to see what this tree might be. The runners came back and told the same story—how in the night they saw the tree standing and burning as it stood. Then all the people held a council as to what this might mean, and the chiefs said: "We shall run for it; put on your ornaments and prepare as for battle." So the men stripped, painted themselves, put on their ornaments, and sent out for the tree, which stood near a lake. They ran as in a race to attack the tree as if it were a warrior enemy. All the men ran. A Ponca was the first to reach the tree, and he struck it as he would an enemy. . . .

Then they cut the tree down and four men, walking in line, carried it on their shoulders to the village. The chiefs sang four nights the songs that had been composed for the tree while they held a council and deliberated concerning the tree. A tent was made for the tree and set up within the circle of lodges. The chiefs worked upon the tree; they trimmed it and called it a human being. They made a basketwork receptacle of twigs and feathers and tied it about the middle. Then they said: "It has no hair!" So they sent out to get a large scalp lock and they put it on the top of the Pole for hair. Afterward the chiefs bade the herald tell the people that when all was completed they should see the Pole.

Then they painted the Pole and set it up before the tent, leaning it on a crotched stick, which they called imog^nthe (a staff). They summoned the people, and all the people came—men, women, and children. When they were gathered the chiefs stood up and said: "You now see before you a mystery. Whenever we meet with troubles we shall bring all our troubles to him [the pole]. We shall make offerings and requests. All our prayers must be accompanied by gifts. This [the pole] belongs to all the people, but it shall be in the keeping of one family (in the Hon'ga gens), and the leadership shall be with them. If anyone desires to lead (to become a chief) and to take responsibility in governing the people, he shall make presents to the Keepers [of the Pole] and they shall give him authority." When all was finished the people said: "Let us appoint a time when we shall again paint him [the Pole] and act before him the battles we have fought." The time was fixed; it was to take place in "the moon when the buffaloes bellow" (July). This was the beginning of the ceremony of Waxthe'xe xigithe . . . and it was agreed that this ceremony should be kept up.[10]

James O. Dorsey says that in Ponca tradition it was a Ponca who found the pole and a Ponca who first reached the pole in the mentioned race, but that Ponca tradition was denied by two of Dorsey's Omaha sources, Joseph La Flesche and Two Crows.[11] As a practical matter, the history of the pole as known to the Omaha should be separated from the history of the associated legend because archaeological evidence from Oklahoma suggests that the legend was shared by Caddoan peoples

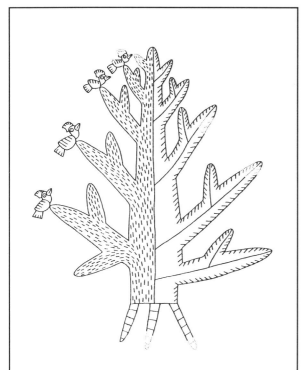

Figure 13.1 A tree with birds engraved on a *Busycon* shell bowl from the Craig Mound at the Spiro site, Le Flore County, Oklahoma, from Phillips and Brown (1984, pl. 236). This image appears to represent in condensed form the elements of the story behind the Omaha Sacred Pole. The half of the tree on whose branches the birds are sitting is rendered differently, as though glowing. Copyright 1984 by the President and Fellows of Harvard College.

in the southern Plains almost a thousand years ago (figure 13.1). Dorsey gives the following short version of the Omaha legend of the pole that leaves out the more supernatural aspects of the story entirely:

At the first there were no chiefs in the gentes, and the people did not prosper. So a council was held, and they asked one another, "What shall we do to improve our condition?" Then the young men were sent out. They found many cotton-wood trees beside a lake, but one of these was better than the rest. They returned and

reported the tree, speaking of it as if it were a person. All rushed to the attack. They struck the tree and felled it as if it had been a foe. They then put hair on its head, making a person of it. Then were the sacred tents made, the first chiefs were selected, and the sacred pipes were distributed.[12]

THE SACRED OMAHA WHITE BUFFALO HIDE

The Omaha Sacred Pole was one of three sacred objects guarded in separate tents occupying special places in the Omaha camp circle. A second was the Sacred White Buffalo Hide and the third, the Sacred Shell. The camp circle was normally set up with its entrance to the east. The Sacred Tent of War was erected near one tip of the horn thus formed, just inward from the south side of the entrance. This tent contained sacred paraphernalia relating to war and thunder, but especially a pouch with the Sacred Shell, half of a river mussel of the species *Unio alatus*. The other two tents were located midway along the south side of the camp circle and a little toward the center of the circle with the tent containing the Sacred White Buffalo Hide on the west and that containing the Sacred Pole on the east. In 1884 the last hereditary keeper of the Sacred Tent of War relinquished its sacred objects for transfer to the Peabody Museum of Archaeology and Ethnology, saying:

These sacred objects have been in the keeping of my family for many generations; no one knows how long. My sons have chosen a path different from that of their fathers. I had thought to have these articles buried with me; but if you will place them where they will be safe and where my children can look at them when they wish to think of the past and of the way their fathers walked, I give them into your keeping. Should there come a time when I might crave to see once more these things that have been with my fathers, I would like to be permitted to do so. I know that the members of my family are willing that I should do this and no others have a right to question my action. There are men in the tribe who will say hard things of me because of this act but I think it best to do as I am doing.[13]

The Sacred Pole followed in 1888 and remained in the Peabody Museum until returned in 1989, a century and a year later, received by the Omahas of our day and by their chairman, Doran Morris, the great-great-grandson of Yellow Smoke, the last hereditary keeper of the Sacred Pole.[14]

The Sacred White Buffalo Hide was scheduled to be transferred by its keeper to the Peabody Museum in 1898, but before this could happen, it was stolen from its tent when its custodian was away on business. The name of the thief was soon learned along with the information that it had been sold to a buyer in Chicago. For years the hide was on loan from its buyer to Chicago's Academy of Science in Lincoln Park, but because the hide was only on loan the Academy did not have the authority to return it directly to the tribe. Eventually, the buyer reclaimed the hide and it was not seen again until recently, when it was discovered in the collections of the Museum of the American Indian, the Heye Foundation, in New York, where it had been stored for more than half a century unrecognized for what it was. The White Buffalo Hide, like the Sacred Pole, has now been repatriated to the Omahas, but a century too late to give comfort to its keeper.[15] Speaking to Francis La Flesche in 1898, and addressing him with a term of ceremonial kinship, the aged keeper Wako^n'mo^{n}thi^n said:

> "My eldest son, . . . The men with whom I have associated in the keeping and teaching of the two sacred houses have turned into spirits and have departed, leaving me to dwell in solitude the rest of my life. All that gave me comfort in this lonely travel was the possession and care of the Sacred Buffalo, one of the consecrated objects that once kept our people firmly united; but, as though to add to my sadness, rude hands have taken from me, by stealth, this one solace, and I now sit empty handed, awaiting the call of those who have gone before me. For a while I wept for this loss, morning and evening, as though for the death of a relative dear to me, but as time passed by tears ceased to flow and I can now speak of it with some composure."

At this point [La Flesche now speaking] I passed the pipe back to the priest and he smoked, keeping his eyes fixed upon the ground as if in deep meditation. When he had finished smoking, he resumed his address, cleaning the pipe as he spoke:

"I have been thinking of the change that has come over our people and their departure from the time-honored customs, and have abandoned all hope of their ever returning to the two sacred houses. No one can now with reason take offense at my giving you the songs of the Sacred Pole, and I am prepared to give them to you. As I sit speaking with you, my eldest son, it seems as though the spirits of the old men have returned and are hovering about me. I feel their courage and strength in me, and the memory of the songs revives. Make ready, and I shall once more sing the songs of my fathers."

It took but a few moments to adjust the graphophone to record the songs for which I had waited so long. As I listened to the old priest his voice seemed as full and resonant as when I heard him years ago, in the

days when the singing of these very songs in the Holy Tent meant so much to each gens and to every man, woman, and child in the tribe. Now, the old man sang with his eyes closed and watching him there was like watching the last embers of the religious rites of a vanishing people.[16]

THE HE'DEWACHI POLE

The He'dewachi ceremony was a midsummer ceremony under the control of the I^{n}ke'çabe Gens. It was a subgens of this gens that had the red ear of corn as a tabooed food and had the responsibility of providing the sacred ears of red corn. These ears were shelled to provide four kernels of seed for each Omaha family at planting time. It was believed that these kernels, mixed with the regular seed preserved by each family, had the power to quicken that seed and bring it to life at planting time.[17]

The pole selected for the ceremony was either cottonwood or willow and was obtained in a manner reminiscent of the ritual procurement of Sun Dance poles. It was scouted out as one would scout out the enemy, was referred to as the enemy, and was charged and attacked like an enemy. Once fallen, it was stripped of bark and branches except for a tuft at the top, again like a Sun Dance pole. It was painted with red and black paint, like a Sun Dance pole, but with bands alternating red and black to represent, as they said, the alternation of day and night.[18]

The objective of the He'dewachi ceremony is not clear, except that it was an occasion for distributing gifts and related strongly to "the vital force in union not only for defense but for the maintenance of internal peace and order," with the pole as "a symbol of life and tribal unity." There must once have been more. Fletcher and La Flesche explicitly say that women used the occasion to wail for children or relatives who had recently died, but they also describe activities during the He'dewachi ceremony that related closely to mourning among the Omahas. During the He'dewachi a group of four young men cut willow wands, stripped them of their bark and leaves, except at the ends, painted these stems red, and gave them to the principal men of the tribe. After this, boys and other men rather generally sought out willow branches and made similar wands because all participants in the ceremony—men, women, boys, and girls—were expected to carry one of these painted sticks, each stick being said to symbolize a person of the tribe. At one point in the ceremony these sticks were all thrown at the foot of the pole.[19]

In times past, when an especially respected Omaha died, whether man or woman, it was a custom for young men to make two cuts in the skin of their upper arms and into these slits to insert a small willow twig trimmed, like those in the He'dewachi ceremony, and to leave a spray of leaves on the end. After singing a funeral song a relative of the deceased withdrew the sticks and threw them on the ground.[20] The Iowas had a similar practice but used sticks whittled to produce a tuft of shavings on the end. More is known of the custom of the Otoes when a chief died. We are told that dogwood branches were peeled, tufts of shavings whittled on one end, and these sticks then inserted into a pair of cuts made on the lower arm. A person was later delegated to withdraw these skewers, the red blood coloring the white wood, and take them to where the body of the chief lay. After burial the red sticks were tied to the grave pole.[21] These peeled and whittled sticks, though smaller, would have resembled the so-

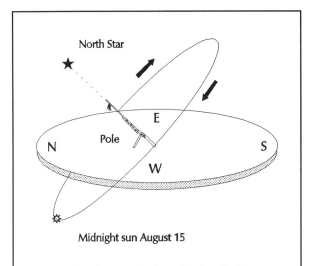

Figure 13.2 The Omaha Sacred Pole, which was traditionally erected so as to lean in a direction and at an angle that would have caused it to point almost directly at the North Star, Polaris.

called 'brave sticks' inserted next to graves by the Forest Potawatomi of Wisconsin and similar sticks once used in mourning rites by the Menominees.

The dogwood ('red willow') sticks, red with blood, tied to the grave pole in the Oto funeral ceremony, and the willow sticks painted red at the base of the red and black He'dewachi pole in the Omaha ceremony, are basically ethnographic accounts that extend our understanding of a funeral practice reported almost two centuries ago for the Indians of the Illinois Country. It was said that for a war chief a pole about forty feet tall was painted red and black and to it was tied a bundle of sticks representing the number of men he had killed.[22] One implication is that the Omaha He'dewachi pole and its ceremony were nineteenth-century survivals of a ceremony that in an earlier century was a community mourning rite.

SACRED TREES AND COSMIC AXES

The Omaha Sacred Pole represented the unity of the tribe and the unity of the Council of Seven Chiefs.[23] The relationship of the Omaha Sacred Pole to chieftainship is a matter that may help us to understand another detail in the story of its origin. In one of the origin traditions the warrior who found it did so while looking for 'the motionless star', i.e. the north star, our Polaris. Later, after the Sacred Pole had become part of Omaha religious practices, and when the Omahas still lived in buffalo hide tipis arranged in a camp circle while on the hunt, it was the practice to set the pole up at a point on the south side of the camp circle, leaning northward at an angle of about forty-five degrees. The astronomer Edwin C. Krupp has noted that the pole was thus pointed almost directly at the north star (figure 13.2).[24] While the Omahas do not explicitly relate the north star itself to chieftainship, some of their close neighbors do. For the Pawnee of Nebraska the north star was the Star-that-does-not-move and was the chief of all the stars. The chief of the Pawnees on earth was the earthly counterpart of the north star, just as the various Pawnee villages were the counterparts of particular stars or asterisms in the night sky. Pointed as it was toward the north star, it is hard to believe that at one time the Omahas did not account for this relationship more explicitly in their traditions.

The Senecas, one of the Six Nations of the Iroquois, believed that before the earth was created there was only a world above the vault of the sky, which was believed to be solid. There was also no sun, moon, or stars. Light was provided by a tree that glowed with a light part of the time and remained dark part of the time, producing the effect of day and night.[25] The tree was not next to a lake, but when the tree was uprooted a hole was left in the sky through which the bride of the chief who owned the tree was pushed, falling down to a sea that existed below. In other respects this Seneca tree of light, which other Iroquois tribes also spoke of in their origin myths, was not like the Omaha Sacred Pole, but the alternating glowing and dark nature of this tree of light does match a similar characteristic of the Omaha Sacred Pole, its red and black bands representing day and night, as they do. The pole thus contained the symbolism of alternating glowing and dark phases, like the tree from which the Omaha Sacred Pole was cut in its origin myth.

The tree trunk used in the bear sacrifice ceremony of the Algonquian Mahican-Munsee, now in Ontario, Canada, similarly had no explicit links to the north star or to chieftainship but did have some implicit links to polar stars. The house in which the ceremony took place was regarded as a projection of the constellation Big Dipper (Great Bear) upon the earth.[26] When the

Big Dipper is seen as a bear in American Indian mythology, it is only the four stars of the dipper bowl that are seen as the bear; the three stars of the handle are considered to be hunters following the bear.

The skin from the sacrificed bear was hung on the large centerpost of the house, where it represented the sacrificed bear as the earthly counterpart of the Sky Bear, renewed each year by the sacrifice, just as the Sky Bear rises in the sky each spring, seemingly renewed, and the earthly bears emerge from hibernation each spring, seemingly reborn from the earth. The post itself was imagined to project upward into the heavens straight to the hand of the Creator. If we consider this centerpost to be a material symbol of the imaginary axis around which the stars of the night sky revolve, then the projection of this post would lead directly to Polaris, the north star, just as did the Sacred Pole of the Omahas. The analogy is strengthened when we consider the Mahican-Munsee pole in the context of the skin of the sacrificed bear, nailed to it, and the context of the Sacred Pole of the Omaha in the Sacred Tipi next to that of the Sacred White Buffalo Hide. The poles and the hides were integral parts of their respective ceremonies.[27]

AUTOSACRIFICE

It is hard to separate the origin of the Sacred Pole ceremony from the political needs of the time, mentioned in the origin myth, and hard not to see the Sacred Pole and its ceremony as a fresh reformulation of time-proven symbols needed to affirm the authority of the chiefs in a critical period of Omaha-Ponca history. In this sense tradition was fallen back upon to provide or amplify a mystery adopted as a symbol of the unity of the tribe and the authority of the chiefs. In the southwestern United States it was once a practice of

weavers to unravel machine-woven blankets acquired in trade from whites and then to reweave the threads into new patterns suitable to Indian tastes and needs. So also were the elements of sacred Indian myth and ritual often recombined and reused in fresh forms to meet the needs of new situations.

It is sometimes difficult to recognize the parallels that may exist between practices in unfamiliar settings. Alanson Skinner recognized the relationship between Iowa arm piercing, "the object of which was to secure the direct passage of the soul of the deceased to heaven" and "the Menominee and other Central Algonkian practices when four braves, after counting their coups, appoint the spirit of those they have slain to guide the ghost of the dead to its destination."[28] He might have made the further comparison between those four braves and the four young men in the Omaha He'dewachi who cut the willow wands that were distributed to the tribal leaders (above). One more comparison is possible. The midwestern practice of blood autosacrifice and the placing of the bloodied skewers at graveside was related to the desire to assist the spirit of the deceased to reach the next world. An almost identical custom was practiced in ancient Mexico for an almost identical purpose.

One of the common functions of human sacrifice in Mexico was to provide strength for the sun to rise into the sky each morning. It was believed that the sun died each evening and was reborn daily, spending the night in the underworld. This rebirth was aided by offerings of human hearts to the sun, but autosacrifices were also made. On the feast day or name day of the sun—the day 4 Movement in the sacred 260-day year—young Aztec warriors skewered themselves and offered the bloody sticks to the sun in much the same way as did Oto and Iowa men. They cut slits in the skin of their left arms, passed sticks through the wounds, and threw them in front of an image of the sun.[29]

THE ATLATL is a weapon that is believed to have been used in North America for eleven thousand years and more, yet if one were to judge from Indian oral tradition alone, the atlatl never existed north of Mexico. North of Mexico the bow and arrow replaced the atlatl among Indians by around A.D. 500, and all references to the atlatl in Indian myths and folktales were simply changed to accommodate the new weapon system. During three years of exploration from Florida to Arkansas in 1540–1543 Hernando de Soto's party encountered an atlatl only once, and that was on the Gulf of Mexico at the mouth of the Mississippi. In Mexico the history of the atlatl was quite different; the atlatl was well known even in the time of Cortez and the Spanish *entrada*. The atlatl was the weapon of choice for warriors in central Mexico, and Spanish *conquistadores* discovered to their dismay that iron chain mail armor was insufficient defense against spears hurled by an atlatl. The atlatl is a spearthrower.[1]

Atlatl is the Náhuatl or Aztec name for the spearthrower. In the United States the name 'atlatl' is so familiar to anyone who has ever had a course in American archaeology that some students may remember *atlatl* if they remember nothing else of American Indian technology. There is today an annual atlatl throwing event that draws participants and observers from many states. I have even seen a vanity auto license plate reading ATLATL. But for most North American Indians of this century, the atlatl is a weapon as foreign as the flintlock musket was to their ancestors at the time of European contact.

In its simplest form the atlatl was a stick about two feet long with a peg, hook, or 'spur' at the far end that inserted into the nock end of a spear shaft made or left concave for that purpose. In South America, Central America, Mesoamerica, and the southern United States atlatl spears or 'darts' were made with mainshafts of cane, i.e., American bamboo, so the spur fitted into the natural cavity of the material. The handle or grip part of the atlatl consisted of a single hole into which the forefinger could be inserted, or a pair of loops into which the thumb and forefinger could be inserted, or a short crossbar or a stop of animal form to prevent the hand from slipping when the arm and atlatl were thrust foreward to propel the spear. The atlatl aided the arm in applying thrust to the dart.[2]

ATLATLS AS COMPOSITE TOOLS

Spearthrowers were sometimes composite tools. In Australia one form of spearthrower used by the Arunta tribe is made with its wooden shaft wide and concave to provide a bowl when one is needed. On the handle end a sharp piece of flint is glued to provide a cutting tool. The edge of this spearthrower is used as a fire saw to produce fire by friction when rubbed vigorously against the wood of a shield. In other words, this is a Swiss army knife of a spearthrower with four separate functions. The Murngin tribe makes one practical spearthrower that can also be used in warfare as a club and as a parrying stick to fend off incoming spears and a second ceremonial type, symbolic of the morning star, that was used by tribal elders as a baton during dances. There is a severe limit to the amount of equipment that any person living as a nomadic hunter can carry from camp to camp. Making a composite tool that served more than one purpose is an economy of effort.[3]

In America there were also spearthrowers of multiple functions. One ancient atlatl found near Lake Winnemucca, Nevada, had an antler tool for flaking flint mounted on its handle end. Single-hole atlatls as a group puzzled me for years until the day I needed a wrench for straightening a cane dart shaft that I was making. I was about to drill a large hole into a flat board to improvise a shaft wrench when I realized that I already had a shaft wrench. A single-hole atlatl that I had made earlier that year served the purpose beautifully. Having a spearthrower that could also straighten a warped dart shaft would have been a great convenience and would have added no weight to what a hunter or warrior normally had to carry. Shaft wrenches for arrows found archaeologically in the Plains are made of buffalo ribs. A wrench for the mainshaft of an atlatl dart has a hole proportionally larger.[4]

Atlatls served functions beyond the purely technological. When you read of an atlatl found in the grave of a man, you are inclined to accept it without further thought as a weapon used by the deceased in his lifetime. When an atlatl is found in the grave of a woman, then one begins to think of additional, nontechnological functions that the atlatl might have served to account for this association because hunting and warfare did not figure importantly in the daily routines of most women. Were there *social* or *magical* functions of the atlatl beyond the technological? What was the *symbolic* load carried by the atlatl?

THE BANNERSTONE CONTROVERSY

Indian Knoll is an occupational and burial site of the Middle Archaic period in Kentucky dating to around 4000 B.C. The site consists of a long artificial mound of earth and river mussel shells built up or accumulated along one bank of the Green River and containing hundreds of Indian burials. Clarence B. Moore brought Indian Knoll to the attention of science in 1915 when he excavated 298 skeletons from the site under the auspices of the Academy of Natural Sciences of Philadelphia. Moore chugged to the site on his own river steamboat called *Gopher*, which served also as living quarters and laboratory.[5] The operation was important for several reasons. For one thing, this was the first major site in the area that could be well examined and determined to predate the manufacture of pottery. This may not seem to be much of a landmark event, but it was. In 1915 American archaeology was just on the verge of becoming aware not only of the deep time-depth of the Indian occupation of the Americas but also of the variety of pre-Columbian cultures that occupied any one area through time. Even today, it is difficult for many people to conceive of Indians who did not have the bow and arrow, corn and beans, pottery, and the other things that Indians of the United States had when they first met Europeans.

Indian Knoll was visited again by archaeologists in 1939 and 1940 as an activity of the WPA or Works Progress Administration established by Franklin Roosevelt. The principal objective of the project was to provide work for the local unemployed during the Great Depression, but this objective served archaeology as well. Some 880 additional burials were excavated, and additional observations could be made of the relationships of artifacts. Moore had made conjectures as to the use of certain artifacts found but had not reported on their relationships, one to another, when found in the same grave.

Moore had found objects made from deer antler prongs carved to provide a hook on the distal end like the hook on a crocheting needle. He suggested that these 'needles' were used in making fiber nets and that other objects of stone or antler found in the same contexts were used for 'sizing' the openings in the nets. The stone objects were of a class that had come to be known as 'bannerstones' and that collectors believed were mounted on staffs to serve some symbolic function.

Byron Knoblock published a book titled *Banner-stones of the North American Indians* in 1939 that emphasized an inferred ceremonial function of bannerstones. William S. Webb published a summary report on Indian Knoll in 1946 that proposed the contrasting utilitarian interpretation that "all of these antler hooks are the distal ends of atlatls. All of the antler sections are handles, attached to the proximal end of the atlatl, and the 'banner' stones, subrectangular bars, and composit[e] shell artifacts are all atlatl weights." These interpretations defined poles of opinion that were argued between amateurs and professionals for years afterward. In a sense, the argument continues because atlatls did indeed have some symbolic functions unrelated to throwing spears, and bannerstones did not serve any indispensable technological function as 'atlatl weights', although Basketmaker atlatls preserved under dry conditions in the Southwest are known to have had one, two, and three stones tied to them for whatever reason. Webb was a professor of physics and was able to argue a mechanical function for bannerstones as atlatl weights.[6]

For nineteen aged and sexed skeletons accompanied by atlatl parts, excavated by Moore, five were adult males, three were adult females, four were adults of indeterminate sex, and seven were children. For forty-two aged and sexed skeletons accompanied by atlatl parts, excavated by Webb, nineteen were adult males, seven were adult females, and sixteen were subadult males or females. In other words, a substantial number of females and children from both excavations were accompanied by atlatls.[7] Why? No one knows for sure. Webb gave reasons for believing that the atlatls buried at Indian Knoll were not just ceremonial in function. My own contribution to the controversy has been the observation, first, that atlatls must have had a symbolic as well as a technological function because long after the atlatl was replaced in its weapon function by the bow and arrow in the United States, the atlatl survived in form as a staff or club of ritual function (figure 14.1). Second, although the atlatl was a weapon presumably used mainly by males, the atlatl was itself, basically, a female metaphor. And, third, one of the derived or secondary functions of the single-hole atlatl was that of holder for tube pipes used for ceremonial smoking and it was in this capacity that the form of the atlatl survived in the flat-stemmed calumet-pipe of later times (figures 14.8, 19.2).

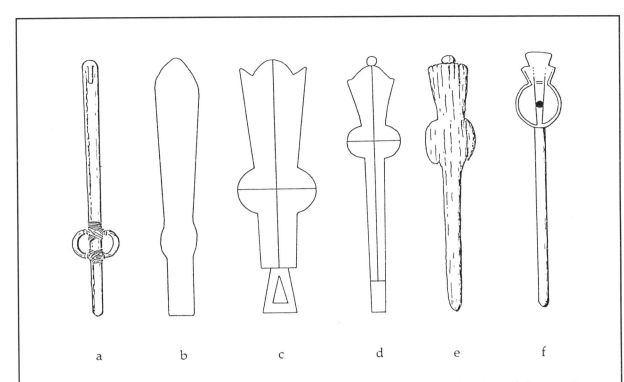

Figure 14.1 The spearthrower and mace and objects based upon their pattern. The twin-fingerloop atlatl or spearthrower shown in *a*, after Ekholm (1968, fig. 2), provided the prototype for the short-handled and long-handled Mississippian maces or ceremonial clubs shown in *b* as a miniature copper cutout found with a Historic period burial of the Oneota culture in northeastern Iowa, after Bray (1961, pl. 2*d*), and in *c* and *d* as details from engraved shells from the Spiro site, Oklahoma, after Phillips and Brown (1978, pls. 55, 66). The mace, in its turn, provided the prototype for the catlinite disk pipe illustrated by *f*, after Fletcher and La Flesche (1972, fig. 64). The disk pipe shown is that belonging to the Omaha sacred white buffalo hide but with a pipe stem added to make the relationship to maces clearer. The long-handled wooden mace illustrated in *e*, after Gilliland (1975, pl. 81*b*), was found preserved by water immersion at the Key Marco site, Florida. Not to scale.

MACES AND MARKS OF HONOR

The artifact called a 'mace' by archaeologists in the eastern United States was a club of wood or stone with the outline of a spearthrower of the twin-fingerloop type. No clubs of this kind are known from post-Contact times. All belong to a period of around A.D. 1000–1400, and most are known only from illustrations engraved on shell, as pendants cut from thin sheets of 'native' (naturally occurring pure) copper, or as monolithic clubs or batons of chipped and polished flint. Three miniature mace cutouts are illustrated by Fletcher and La Flesche as tattoos on the hand of a Ponca girl between symbols for 'day' and 'night', and this tattooing provides a clue to some of the symbolism of the atlatl and to one of the social functions of the atlatl as a symbol (figure 14.2).[8]

The Omaha Hon'hewachi was a society of honorary chieftainship whose members had to their credit at least one hundred achievements that were in the nature of gifts or acts of goodwill that benefited the tribe. The Omaha man who was received into this society had the privilege of selecting a girl of unblemished character to receive certain tattoos that were marks of honor. The miniature maces tattooed on the hand of the Ponca girl were just such marks of honor but were not recognized as maces by Fletcher and La Flesche or by the Poncas themselves.[9] What is significant is that the mace or atlatl symbol was among those tattoos that could be placed on young girls, so that the putting of actual physical atlatls in the graves of women and children at the Indian Knoll site in a much earlier era was not a great departure from the kinds of social acts in which the symbolism of the atlatl was involved in later days.

The honors counted by a candidate were of a certain sort, such as giving food and clothing to a beggar, saving the life of a comrade in an armed conflict, preventing someone's capture by an enemy, giving gifts to put an end to a period of mourning, and contributing gifts to someone about to carry the calumet to another village—acts of bravery or generosity that helped to maintain harmony in the tribe and with its neighbors. When the time came the candidate brought out a hun-

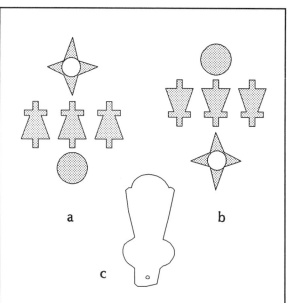

Figure 14.2 The mace form in copper and as a tattoo: *a*, drawing by a Ponca of the tattoo on the hand of a Ponca girl, said to be emblems of day and night and of children, after Fletcher and La Flesche (1972, fig. 106); *b*, the same design reversed top for bottom to show the sun above and the star below, the relationship for these symbols when tattooed as marks of honor on Omaha girls (cf. Fletcher and La Flesche 1972, fig. 105), the children now becoming maces representing the earth with day above and night below; *c*, a sheet copper cutout from the Oneota culture, representing a mace, showing the motif that was reinterpreted as a child on the Ponca tattoo, Walker-Hooper site, Green Lake County, Wisconsin, after Hall (1962, pl. 80*i*).

dred willow sticks about a foot long and counted his deeds aloud as he put down a stick for each.

Only women who had received the mark of honor could dance at the meetings of this society of honorary chiefs. Even the male members themselves could not dance because the society "was one in recognition of Night, of the feminine force or principle." The maiden receiving the mark of honor was referred to as a Woman Chief. "So great were the requirements demanded of a man for admission to the Hon'hewachi that the successful candidate was said to have been 'pitied' (compassionately helped) 'by Night,' as otherwise he could not have accomplished the tasks required."[10]

The tattoo featured cosmic symbols of night and day. In the case of the Ponca tattoo a star symbolized night, a circle representing the sun symbolized day, and three maces lay between. Night was especially honored because it was the mother of Day. In Omaha belief Night gave birth to Day. The maces had been reinterpreted in modern times as 'children', and the tattoo as

a whole was called "an appeal for the perpetuation of all life and of human life in particular."[11] The mace, however, was a relic of the form of the twin-fingerloop atlatl, and the atlatl itself was a cosmic symbol that symbolized the earth and the path of the sun across the earth. The placing of the mace figures between the symbol representing day and that representing night is consistent with the idea that night and day were reversed in the underworld, i.e., when it was day above the earth island it was night below and vice versa.[12]

THE OLLIN GLYPH

In central Mexico, where atlatls were used as weapons until the Spanish conquest, the handle of a twin-fingerloop atlatl served as the symbol of the day Ollin (Movement or Earthquake). The equivalent day in the Maya calendar was Caban or Earth. The atlatl grip symbol was used by the Aztecs and the Mixtecs (figure 14.3*c–d*, *g*), and it was featured as the central glyph of the familiar Aztec *Piedra del Sol* or Stone of the Sun, popularly called the Aztec Calendar Stone. This stone was actually a cosmogram that represented, among other things, the path of the sun entering the earth at the west and continuing beneath the earth to the east where it emerged near a glyph 13 Acatl or 13 Reed.

The day 13 Reed represented the birth of the sun both for the Aztecs and the Mayas. The path of the sun was represented by an atlatl dart on the Stone of the Sun, and because in Indian belief the underworld was believed to correspond to the night sky, when the sun emerged in the east it was equivalent to Night giving birth to Day. Typically, the Movement (atlatl grip) glyph was painted in one color on one half and in another color on the other half.

The day sign Acatl or Reed represented not just any stick but specifically cane, the bamboo from which atlatl darts were manufactured, and atlatl darts could symbolize beams of sunlight or starlight. Far to the north, Osage warriors counted their war honors using a set of thirteen sticks that symbolized thirteen rays of the rising sun.[13] In other words, the symbolism of the Mesoamerican day 13 Reed was shared by the Mayas, Aztecs, and Osages, however the idea may have originated for each. This much can be said. The twin-loop atlatl grip as a symbol was shared by Indians of Mesoamerica and Indians of the Mississippi valley two thousand and more years ago. This opens the possibility of rivulets of diffusion north and south over a much greater period of time than most archaeologists have been willing to acknowledge.

The Utica mound group excavations were described in chapter 3, but much remains to be learned of the symbolic value of the mounds and their contents. I have mentioned the pottery vessel with the snake-bird

Figure 14.3 The Aztec Ollin glyph and related motifs: *a*, atlatl and dart motif from a Preclassic pottery stamp, Tlatilco, Mexico, after Field (1967, fig. 29); *b*, atlatl grip motif from a Preclassic pottery vessel, El Trapiche site, northern Veracruz State, Mexico, after García Payón (1950, pl. 12); *c, d*, atlatl grips as Mixtec variants of the Mesoamerican day sign Movement, after Nuttall (1975, 35, 81); *e*, bisected circle motif from a Havana-Hopewellian pottery vessel from the Utica mound group, La Salle County, Illinois, after Henriksen (1965, fig. 30*a*); *f*, Havana-Hopewell bisected circle motif from Klunk mound 1, Calhoun County, Illinois, after Perino (1968, fig. 9); *g*, glyph for the day Nahui Ollin (4 Movement), from an Aztec wooden drum, Mexico, after Krickeberg (1961, fig. 26); *h*, Marksville-Hopewell bisected circle motif, after Ford (1952, fig. 23, no. 37).

motif found in one mound and related it to examples of the same design found at another Hopewellian site, the Crooks site in Louisiana (chapter 3, note 9). Another Utica site jar has its counterpart at Crooks as well. This vessel was found in the largest of the Utica mounds, a mound ten feet high from top to base.[14]

The characteristics of the two pots that concern us most—the pot from Utica and that from Crooks—are (1) the use of rocked dentate (toothed) stamps rather than color to fill in or texture background areas of the design, and (2) the trailing of a design into the clay of the body of the jar with a motif consisting of two (or three) large concentric circles bisected by (two or) three vertical parallel lines (figure 14.3*e*). This is a pattern of associations found not only in Havana-Hopewell in the

northern Mississippi valley and in Marksville-Hopewell in the southern Mississippi valley but also in the pottery complex of El Trapiche, an early Middle Preclassic site in Veracruz, Mexico (figure 14.3*b*). This was a parallel noted in print by James B. Griffin in 1966.[15]

The El Trapiche site may date to around 1200–1000 B.C., which is about a thousand years earlier than the Hopewellian horizon in the eastern United States. There was no pottery to speak of in the eastern United States contemporary with El Trapiche, and the pottery that was there bore no resemblance to that of the Mesoamerican Preclassic. This results in a dilemma unless one considers that the bisected circle motif and dentate rocker stamping need not have been restricted to pottery. Dentate rocker stamping can be used to decorate

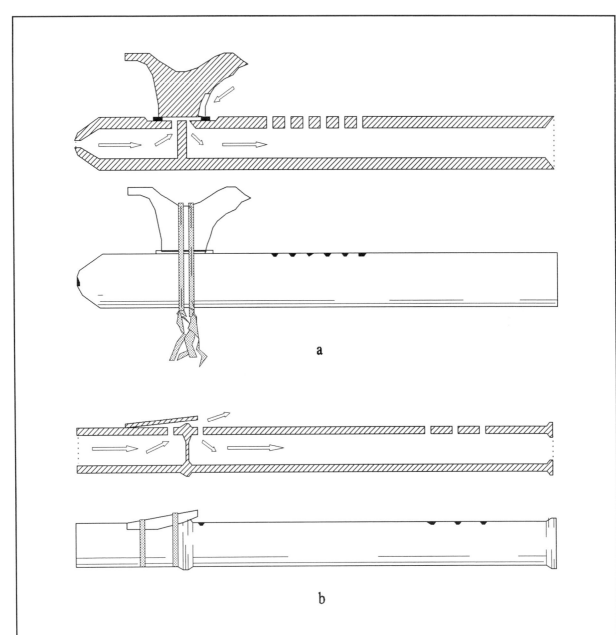

Figure 14.4 Flutes of the vortsatz type shown in cross-section and profile views: *a*, an eastern Woodlands courting flute of cedar with six stops, carved in two halves and assembled with glue, with an adjustable wooden slide of 'birdstone' form for tuning over a carved air deflector, after McIntosh and Shell (1987, figs. 115–122); *b*, a Brazilian flute of taboca reed with three stops, a sound orifice partly covered with an adjustable strip of reed, and a natural air deflector created by leaving a septum intact at one node of the reed, after Izikowitz (1935, fig. 206). Horizontal scale shortened for both; directions of arrows indicating air flow are those of the above-cited authors.

gourds on the vine when they are ripe but not yet dry. I have done so with bottle gourds (*Lagenaria*) using a scallop shell with its outer edge ground at an angle to raise a set of sharp teeth. Walking the shell edge across the gourd produced the same effect as a dentate stamp rocked back and forth on a clay surface. The effect is enhanced as the gourd dries.

Another early Middle Preclassic site is that of Tlatilco, which was located within a brickyard near Mexico City when it was discovered. A pottery stamp found at Tlatilco was made with a design consisting of three parallel lines bisecting a set of concentric circles but with one additional feature. The central line of the three lines was barbed to represent an atlatl dart, which shows that the central line represented the dart itself, the two lines bracketing it represented the outline of the atlatl shaft, and the two concentric circles represented a set of fingerloops attached to the shaft of the atlatl, each loop being of semicircular form (figure 14.3*a*).[16]

The full length of the atlatl was not represented on the Tlatilco stamp. In other words, the design was an early Preclassic prototype of the Ollin glyph, indicating a continuity in Mexico of around twenty-five hundred years for the design or the associated cosmological symbolism, beginning with the Middle Preclassic or Olmec period. In the later, Aztec form of this glyph the atlatl handle was splayed so as to represent the directions of the sun's rays toward the earth's center (the ethnocentric 'here') from the directions of the summer and winter solstice sunrise and sunset positions. In this splayed form the Ollin glyph represented the motions of the sun across the earth through the course of a full year.[17]

BIRDSTONES AND COURTING FLUTES

The 'birdstone' is a class of polished stone objects found most commonly in the eastern United States toward the end of the Late Archaic and at the beginning of the Early Woodland periods, in other words, within a span of centuries centered around 1000 B.C. William Mangold has noted that the so-called birdstones looked more like dogs than birds because when feet were actually represented they were four in number (figure 14.5*e*).[18] Strange birds!

Visiting the Mujica Museum of Gold near Lima, Peru, Robert Ritzenthaler was impressed by the strong similarity between birdstones and certain wooden objects used as handles on pre-Columbian atlatls found in the coastal region of Peru (figure 14.5*c–d*). The dry conditions of the Peruvian coast preserved the wooden atlatls in a way not possible in the eastern United States except, oddly enough, under the waterlogged conditions encountered by Frank Cushing in excavating on Key Marco, Florida.[19] Ritzenthaler was so impressed that he became convinced that birdstones were, in fact, atlatl handles. There had been no better explanation; birdstones were classed as 'ceremonials' or 'problematicals' because their function could only be guessed at.

To Ritzenthaler's surprise, Earl Townsend had several years earlier written a chapter titled "The Atlatl Handle Grip Theory" in his *Birdstones of the North American Indians*, and Townsend illustrated atlatls from Peru with birdstone-like handles. Ritzenthaler wrote in support of the idea, saying that he viewed his role "not as a discoverer, but as a reviver and perhaps as a reinforcer of what seems to me the most logical theory accounting for the function of the birdstone."[20]

The greatest support for the Townsend-Ritzenthaler hypothesis is to be found in an area midway between South America and the eastern United States. At the Sitio Conte archaeological site in Panama a bone atlatl was found that had as a handle a composite animal that

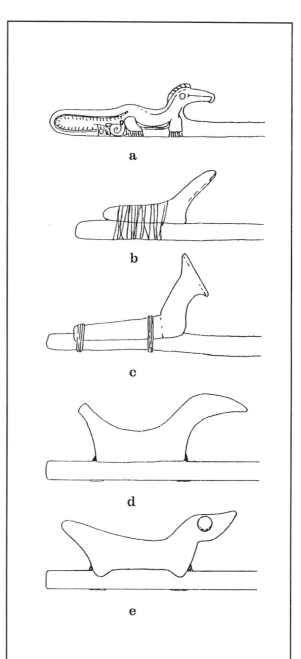

Figure 14.5 Atlatl grips of the birdstone and related types: *a*, composite animal with bird head and crocodilian body, carved in one piece with the bone atlatl arm, Coclé, Panama, after Lothrop (1937, fig. 66*a*); *b–c*, from Peru, with wooden atlatl arms and bindings as found, after Townsend (1959, pl. 32*a–b*); *d–e*, 'birdstones' from Michigan, with reconstructed atlatl arms, *e* with the body of a quadruped, after Hinsdale (1925, pl. 20, no. 5, and 21, no. 3*a*). Scale variable.

was a combination bird and crocodilian or a lizard. Call it a dragon. The body was that of a reptile with four feet and the head, that of a bird (figure 14.5*a*). The function of this dragon was indisputable. It was the handle of an atlatl. This solved the puzzle that William Mangold had posed. If birdstones truly represented birds, why did some have four feet? Well, perhaps they were originally bird-crocodiles or bird-caymans.[21]

Another example of the dragon atlatl grip was found in Veracruz on the Gulf coast of Mexico. This one was preserved because it was a ceramic flute made in the form of an atlatl. Its character as an atlatl was clear because it had both a grip of the twin-loop variety *and* one of the dragon variety, except that in this dragon the crocodilian and bird parts were reversed. The head and body were those of a crocodile and the tail was that of a bird. The crocodile is the only genus of crocodilian found in Veracruz. Alligators were found only in the United States and caymans (as archaeologists use the term) were confined to Central and South America.[22] The widespread presence of a crocodilian or dragon on the handle of an atlatl explains the apparent association of the atlatl with the earth and its nature as a female metaphor because the earth was widely believed to have reptilian associations—being turtle-related in North America and cayman-related in Mesoamerica.

One of the early interpretations of birdstones was that they represented the carved wooden, bird-like sliding parts of courting flutes (figure 14.4a). Charles Willoughby in 1935 pointed out the resemblance of birdstones to these slides that were used to regulate the sound of flutes of this kind.[23] The courting flute is such a well-known element of the culture of the Indians of the Eastern Woodlands that it is hard to imagine that it could be evidence of contacts with cultures far to the south. If birdstones were really part of the handle of an atlatl, how does this affect Willoughby's idea about birdstones and courting flutes? If a flute in ancient Veracruz could be made in the form of an atlatl, could not the courting flute have originally been meant to represent an atlatl as well?

The design of the body of the courting flute requires that a piece of cedar wood be split and hollowed, except for a narrow septum left beneath the hole over which the slide will be tied, and then glued back into one piece (figure 14.4a). This does not have to be done if the flute is made of cane (figure 14.4b). Cane (American bamboo) is already hollow, and holes need only be drilled above and to each side of the natural septum within one of the many nodes. Karl Gustav Izikowitz calls this kind of instrument a Mataco whistle when it does not have additional holes or stops to produce other tones. With the addition of stops he calls it a duct flute. With the additional use of some moveable object to partly cover the hole over the septum, for use in adjusting the flow of air over the septum, the instrument is called a vorsatz-flute by Izikowitz, following the terminology of Curt Sachs.

Vorsatz-flutes made from cane are reported from the

southwestern United States to the Amazon basin. In these the sound orifice over the septum is covered only with a thin, adjustable piece of leather, leaf, or reed. Varieties with a large carved object to adjust the flow of air appear to be limited to eastern North America and to be made of a solid wood such as cedar or sumac rather than cane. In other words, the courting flute is a specialized variation of the vortsatz-flute adapted to an area without cane and distinguished from cane flutes of the same principle by having the adjustable part made of a large carved object rather than a thin membrane.[24]

It is difficult to imagine the invention of the courting flute in the absence of the widely distributed

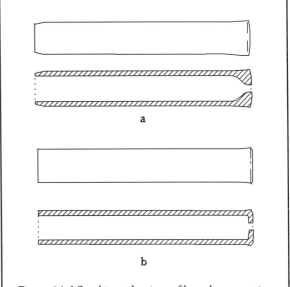

Figure 14.6 Smoking tubes in profile and cross-section views: *a*, stone blocked-end tube pipe, Late Archaic–Early Woodland, Manchester, New Hampshire, after Willoughby (1973, fig. 50*j*); *b*, cane tube shown cut for use as a smoking-tube as in pre-Columbian Meso-america.

prototype made of cane, but I also find it difficult to imagine the evolution of the courting flute in the absence of the atlatl with a birdstone handle as a model upon which to base the carved slide. A slide of birdstone size and shape is not necessary for the function of the flute as a musical instrument. Through the greater part of the distribution of the vorsatz-flute outside of the United States there is no parallel example of a slide of this type or size, with the possible exception of one example that may be illustrated on the *Codex Becker* in Mexico.[25] I am not suggesting that birdstones were used on flutes after all. I am saying that the courting flute was probably *modeled after* an atlatl of the kind with a bird-crocodile or bird-cayman handle for some reason associated with the function of the flute.

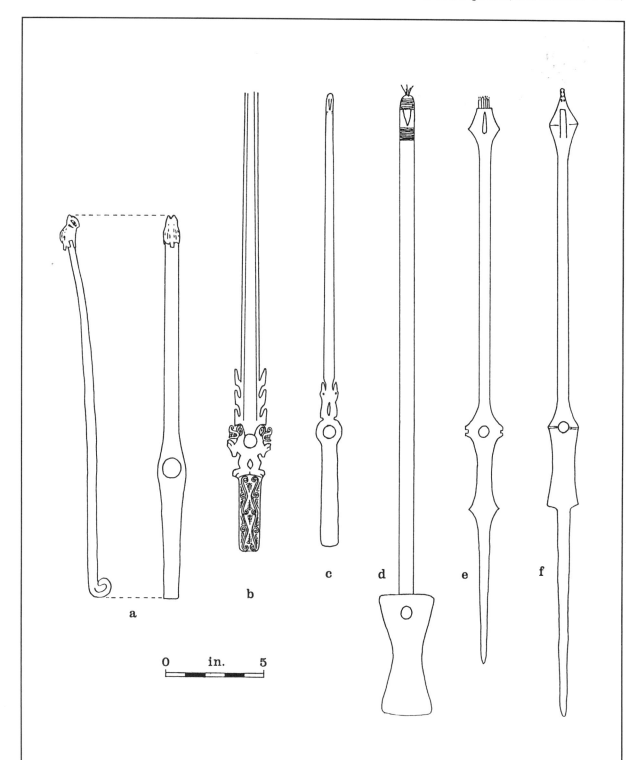

Figure 14.7 Single-hole spearthrowers: *a*, wood, from Key Marco site, Florida, after Cushing (1897, pl. 32, no. 3) and Gilliland (1975, pl. 83); *b*, bone, from Coclé, Panama, after Lothrop (1937, fig. 66*b*); *c*, wood with mother-of-pearl spur, from Nieveria, valley of Lima, Peru, after Townsend (1959, pl. 28*d–f*); *d*, wood, from the upper Xingu valley, Brazil, after Lévi-Strauss (1948, fig. 34*c*; redrawn from Steinen 1894); *e*, wood, spur missing, from Antioquia district, Cauca valley, Colombia, after Bahnson (1889, fig. 13, no. 2*a*); *f*, wood, spur missing, Colombia, collections of the Field Museum, Chicago.

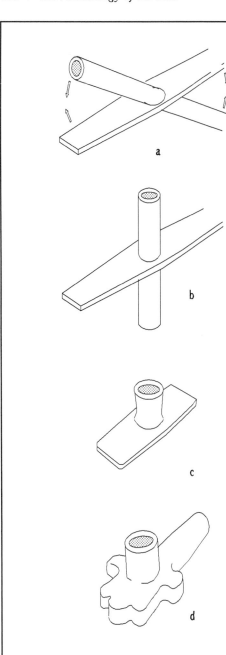

Figure 14.8 The relationship of the plain platform pipe to the single-hole atlatl: *a*, the way in which a single-hole atlatl could have been used as a wrench to straighten the mainshafts of atlatl darts; *b*, the way in which a single-hole atlatl could have been used as a holder for a cane smoking-tube; *c*, the Hopewellian plain platform pipe suggested to be a translation into stone of a flat-stemmed atlatl of the single-hole type holding a smoking tube; *d*, pottery pipe in the form of a mace, a combination that gives support to the idea of a flat atlatl as the prototype of the flat calumet because the mace itself has the atlatl as its prototype, Glenwood culture, western Iowa, after A. Anderson (1961, fig. 35*b*) and photographs supplied by D. Anderson.

Izikowitz mentions an example of a vortsatz-flute without stops from the eastern United States that is made of cane and whose slide is of the thin, flat kind rather than the large, carved type. This flute was part of a Winnebago war bundle. Paul Radin twice mentions flutes associated with Winnebago war bundles. He says, "When blown during a fight, they were supposed to paralyze the running powers of the enemy and thus make him an easy prey," and elsewhere, "The flute represents the voices of musical birds. When an enemy hears them it paralyzes him and he can not run."[26]

In 1824 Charles C. Trowbridge recorded an account of Shawnee traditions in whole or great part from the words of the Shawnee Prophet Tenskwatawa, brother of Tecumseh. Of flutes this early record says:

> *Anciently the flute was used exclusively by young men who were desirous of raising a war party. The leader, or he who wished to distinguish himself by setting afoot an expedition of this kind, would take his flute & retire a short distance from the village, where he would begin to play. The young men around, at the sound of the music, assembled around him, and heard his declarations. If they chose to join him they pledged themselves upon the spot & joined in the song, but if they thought the project rash & inexpedient they retired as they came. The instrument is not exclusively used, by young men in love, tho' few in that situation fail to charm their mistresses with its sounds.*[27]

The functions of the flute of the 'courting' type would thus seem to have once included the wooing of young men to join a war party and not merely the wooing of young maidens for romance. Under these circumstances, with flutes related to war, it is easy to imagine the innovation of a flute in the form of the atlatl—a weapon of war.

ATLATL-FLUTES AND ATLATL-PIPES

Atlatl-flutes, if I may call them that, probably played an important role in the evolution of the calumet-pipe. The word 'calumet' in English has come to refer to any especially ornate Indian smoking pipe with a long stem. The word is not Indian. It is French, the French of the Normandy peninsula, and in that dialect simply meant 'reed'. The word 'calumet' was applied in New France to certain long-stemmed smoking pipes that were so common in the upper Great Lakes and Mississippi valley when the French traders arrived during the seventeenth century (chapter 1). Of these the most well-known was the round-stemmed calumet used in the Calumet ceremony. There were flat-stemmed calumets as well (figure 14.9), but many of these were clan or tribal pipes with their own purposes and ceremonies.

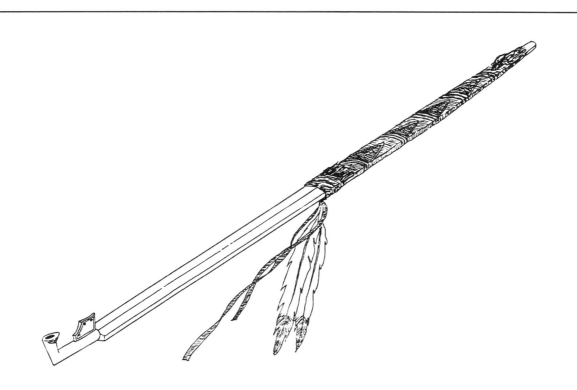

Figure 14.9 Flat-stemmed calumet-pipe. Sacred pipe of the Male Buffalo gens of the Iowa tribe, after Skinner (1926, pl. 39, no. 3, and pl. 31, no. 2). The flat calumet stem is forty inches long and wrapped for eighteen inches with porcupine quills died black, yellow, red, and orange, or left in their natural color, braided in the proper sequence to produce a pattern of buffalo tracks when wrapped. A green ribbon is wrapped around the stem near the point of attachment of two tail feathers of a golden eagle. The scalp and bill of a female ivory-billed woodpecker is tied to the stem near the mouthpiece with the bill opened and turned back. At this point a tuft of hair died red is also attached to the stem.

I use the word 'calumet' to distinguish the feathered stem itself from the combination of long, ornate stem and smoking pipe bowl, which I call a 'calumet-pipe'. Jordan Paper uses the term 'sacred pipe' in much the same sense that I use 'calumet-pipe' and restricts the idea of 'calumet' to the feathered wand, sometimes fitted with a bowl, used in ceremonies similar to the Pawnee Hako, which was the premier example of the Calumet ceremony of the Contact period in the greater Mississippi valley. For Paper the defining characteristic of the 'Sacred Pipe' was its separate stem.[28] Tobacco originated in South America, but stone and pottery smoking pipes originated in eastern North America. In Mesoamerica tubes of cane stuffed with tobacco and smoked by the indigenes were called *cañas de humo* by the Spanish. The difference between a stone tube pipe, a cane smoking-tube, a cigar, and a cigarette lies in the nature of the device containing the tobacco and the degree to which the outer container or wrapper is consumed during the smoking or remains intact.

The transformation of a cane tube of tobacco into a tube pipe of stone was merely a shift of materials, and the blocked-end tube pipes of the terminal Late Archaic and Early Woodland Indians of the eastern United States (ca. 1000–500 B.C.) resemble tubes of cane that were copied in stone (figure 14.6). The expanded end of this kind of cane tube pipe was simply the node of the cane or cane tube cut off immediately behind the node.[29] I had thought that this was an original idea of my own inspiration, but I was anticipated by more than fifty years by Edmund Carpenter.

Carpenter commented as follows on a find he made in western Pennsylvania in 1941, which was "a nine inch section of cane, *Arundinaria gigantea* (Watt) Chapm., covered with cut scraps of comparatively pure, thin, evenly hammered, native sheet silver. . . . The whole was wrapped in a spongey bark and this in turn coated with mud or soft clay. This remarkable specimen had been made by cutting a section of cane, roughly one inch in diameter, below one of the nodes and directly through the next joint, thus creating, intentionally or otherwise, *a natural prototype for the blocked-end tube*."[30] This find was made in Irvine Mound 1, Warren County, and was attributed to the Middle Woodland period by William Mayer-Oakes, who mistakenly classified the cane tube as part of a panpipe.[31]

Smoking pipes of the elbow type with short stems made as a unit with the bowl originated in the eastern United States and diffused southward into Mesoamerica.[32] South of the United States the functional equivalent of the calumet-pipe or long-stemmed smoking pipe was a cane smoking-tube or cigar inserted into a long wooden holder.[33]

It has long been my belief that the detachable flat stem of the flat-stemmed calumet-pipe originated two thousand or more years ago as the body of a wooden atlatl, in other words, that the flat-stemmed calumet-pipe of modern times was a transformation of an atlatl-pipe of Hopewellian age. Hopewellian Indians in Ohio used a local pipestone to carve distinctive smoking pipes called 'platform pipes' (figure 14.8c). The platform part is thin and flat and projects in front and behind the bowls. The path for the smoke passes from the base of the bowl back though the platform. Platform pipes with bowls in the form of short, vertical tubes were called 'monitor pipes' by earlier generations of archaeologists because they resembled the iron-clad Union gunboat *Monitor*, which fought a classic naval battle with the Confederate iron-clad *Virginia* (the rechristened *Merrimack*) on March 9, 1862, during the American Civil War. The part of the *Monitor* visible above the water looked like a round washtub perched upside down on a surfboard.

When the bowls of platform pipes were made in the form of animals, the pipes were called effigy platform pipes.[34] My argument is that Hopewellian (Middle Woodland) plain platform pipes evolved from the use of long and flat atlatls of the single-hole type as holders for stone tube pipes or cane smoking-tubes by Early Woodland Indians of the area. Archaeological specimens of the single-hole atlatl have been found in Peru, Colombia, Brazil, Panama, Mexico, and even in the eastern United States, where one example was found a century ago preserved in a waterlogged site on Key Marco, Florida (figure 14.7).[35] It is another thing to explain how in the United States there came to be a further evolution of the tube and atlatl holder into an atlatl-pipe, and subsequently into the calumet-pipe, by the innovation of a path for the smoke through the atlatl handle itself. The answer is provided by the example of the atlatl-flute that was, as I have argued above, the prototype of the courting flute of modern times.

In the Early Woodland flute of atlatl form the breath passed through the length of a tube representing an atlatl. In the atlatl-pipe the breath would have similarly passed through a long wooden stem that represented the atlatl. The area of distribution of smoking pipes with long separate wooden stems is fairly concentric with the area of distribution of vorsatz-flutes of the courting flute type. Looked at this way, the mental association of 'atlatl' and 'flute' influenced the innovation process

leading to a long-stemmed atlatl-pipe. It would be an example of the operation of a psychological mechanism common in dream formation, but in waking thought also in the process of innovation. The association of atlatl and tube for breath was merely transferred from the atlatl-flute to the atlatl-pipe (figure 19.2).

There still remains the question of why anyone would think to insert a cane tube of tobacco into the eye of a single-hole atlatl in the first place, but that question almost answers itself. If the eye of the single-hole atlatl was used as an atlatl dart shaft wrench, then there was a preexisting mental association between the atlatl and a length of cane. Inserting a cane smoking-tube of tobacco rather than a cane dart shaft was simply inserting a shorter length of cane into the eye of the atlatl (figure 14.8a–b). This explanation is nicely supported by Bernardino de Sahagún who described an Aztec ritual held by the merchants in which smoking-tubes explicitly represented atlatl darts: "The tobacco server . . . bore the tobacco [tube] in his right hand. . . . And he went bearing the bowl for the tobacco tubes in his left hand. First he offered one the tobacco tube. He said: 'My beloved noble, here is thy cane of tobacco.' Then [the guest] took it up; he placed it between his fingers to smoke it. *This denoted the spear thrower or the spear*; war equipment; valor. And the bowl stood for the shield."[36]

ANALOGUES OF THE CALUMET-PIPE

In the eastern United States the Hako-type calumet served to mediate a symbolic rebirth as part of an adoption ceremony to create fictional bonds of kinship between unrelated individuals and hence, indirectly, the social groups to which they belonged. The flat-stemmed calumet and many other sacred pipes served, among other things, as clan or tribe symbols, giving body to the identity of some kinship group. These are functions associated with certain analogues of calumets and sacred pipes in Mesoamerica and South America as well. In lowland eastern Colombia, in the region of the Vaupés River, a tributary of the Amazon, that analogue was a cigar held in a specially carved wooden cigar holder of fork shape (figure 14.10a). The cigar itself symbolized the penis of a mythical anaconda. The real-life anaconda is a snake of enormous size that haunts the waters of the Amazon basin. The mythical anaconda is regarded as a group ancestor. This mythical anaconda ancestor is symbolically returned to life periodically by the assembling of certain sacred objects representing its body parts, large cigars representing the anaconda's penis.[37]

One of the objectives of this symbolic reincarnation was to provide an occasion for the ancestral anaconda to adopt a class of boys as part of a puberty ritual. As explained by Stephen Hugh-Jones for the Barasana, the

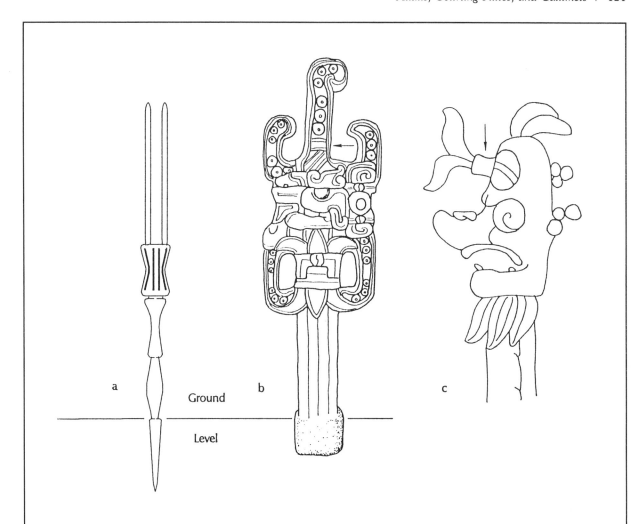

Figure 14.10 Central and South American images relating to cigars and smoking tubes: *a*, carved wooden cigar holder from the area of the Río Tiquié tributary of the Río Vaupés, Colombia, after Koch-Grünberg (1909–1910, pl. 160), shown erected in the ground upon the spike end designed for that purpose; *b*, Preclassic Maya sculpture from Santa Cruz Quiché, Guatemala, from Hall (1983a, fig. 3a), after Gendrop (1985, fig. 222b) and Kidder et al. (1946, fig. 141c); *c*, head of Maya God K as represented on the distal end of a manikin scepter on a bas-relief sculpture from the Temple of the Inscriptions, Palenque site, Chiapas, Mexico, from Hall (1983a, fig. 3c) after Robicsek (1978, fig. 115). The arrows point to short tubes inserted into the glyph for *nen* 'mirror'.

succession of generations was likened to leaves accumulating on the forest floor, the initiations providing opportunities to "squash the pile" and bring the latest generation into contact with their ancestors, thus reestablishing the mythic order and its powers. The cigar in its holder was also passed from hand to hand among members of out-marrying kinship groups to reaffirm their alliance.[38] The cigar in its holder thus figured both in an adoption ritual related to a symbolic reincarnation but also in ritual to affirm alliances. These were the functions of calumets. These Amazon basin carved wooden cigar holders appear to be a rather unique class of artifact, but the physical objects themselves and their symbolism relate to sacred pipes and to atlatls as well. The fork shape of the cigar holders is

explicitly related to a pair of thighs, and the cigar represents, of course, a penis. Even among the Creeks of the southeastern United States the (ritual?) words for tobacco and penis are said to have once been the same or related and the tobacco plant itself believed to have originated in a location in the forest where a couple had lain in intercourse.[39]

The Amazon cigar holders are constructed with pointed bases designed to be inserted into the earth and are carved with two or more objects of bow-tie or hourglass shape along the shaft. These objects have no technological function, but they correspond in shape and location to the handles of a class of spearthrower once known from western Colombia to eastern Brazil.[40] This might be only a coincidence, except that two examples of such a spearthrower from the Antioquia district in Colombia also have pointed ends that serve no purpose on the objects as spearthrowers but would have allowed them to be stuck into the ground in the manner of the forked Amazonian cigar holders (figures 14.7e–f, 14.10). The spearthrower in question also has a hole carved into the hourglass element that is probably too small to allow its use for finger insertion but is large enough to allow its use as a shaft wrench for atlatl darts of the size of cane-shafted arrows. Spearthrowers of the same form, with the hourglass-shaped handle and hole, are reported from eastern Brazil but without the spike end (14.7d). This encourages me to believe that the fork-shaped cigar holder is derivative and based upon an earlier use of the spearthrower with a handle adapted to use as a shaft wrench for cane-shafted darts and secondarily used as a holder for cigars, in the case of the Amazon, or tobacco-filled cane tubes of tobacco, in the case of Mesoamerica (figure 14.8).

The eastern Colombian cigar holders were designed to be stuck into the ground. The mentioned western Colombian atlatls were constructed so that they could have been stuck into the ground, but is there any evidence to suggest that they actually might have been stuck into the ground? The evidence for that is circumstantial but convincing. No one questions the fact of longtime contacts between Colombia, Panama (which until this century was a province of Colombia, after all), Costa Rica, and other parts of Central America right into the Maya area of Mesoamerica. So the presence in Guatemala of a stone sculpture representing a spearthrower erected upright in the ground does not fall outside of an acknowledged pattern of pre-Columbian contacts. The sculpture in question is one that once stood in front of a Maya temple at Santa Cruz Quiché, Guatemala, and is of a 'silhouette' style also known from the Guatemalan site of Kaminaljuyu, where the style is said to date to the late Preclassic period (figure 14.10b).[41]

The Santa Cruz Quiché sculpture is well known and widely published but is typically said only to represent a long-nosed Maya deity, perhaps Itzamna. The particular variety of atlatl represented is that with twin finger-loops that resemble eyes bracketing the shaft, which could then be seen as the long nose. Indeed, there is no reason to discount an association between Itzamna and the atlatl. I have already mentioned atlatls from Veracruz and Panama whose handles were fashioned with representations of a composite bird-crocodile. The very name Itzamna translates as Iguana House and refers to Itzamna's identity with the sky and earth as a cosmic house, an identity that could be shared by a composite (sky-related) bird and (earth-water–related) crocodile. Beyond this, however, there is an association of the Santa Cruz Quiché sculpture that is generally overlooked, and that is its relationship to the Classic period Maya deity known to archaeologists as God K.

God K is himself a long-nosed deity and is one also associated with an atlatl, or at least, with an analogue of the atlatl in the form of the so-called God K manikin scepter (figure 14.10c). God K can be recognized by the presence of a smoking tube inserted into his head within an area containing the Maya glyph representing *nen* 'mirror'.[42] At the top of the Santa Cruz Quiché sculpture there is a clear representation of a head on whose forehead there is a mirror glyph into which is inserted a short tube out of which a smoke-like plume is rising. The manikin scepter is basically a short staff, often representing a serpent with the head at the handle end and with a God K head at the tail end. It resembles an atlatl of the single-hole type with a smoking cane of tobacco inserted into the eye of the atlatl. In other words, it would seem to be a Maya version of the coeval Hopewellian atlatl-pipe and the more recent, ethnographic cigar holder of the Vaupés River region with the smoking cigar in place.[43]

Among other things, the Mayas associated God K with kingship and with royal lineages. God K was patron deity of royal lineages.[44] This kind of association reminds us of the Vaupés cigar as a symbol of the tribal anaconda ancestor and the use of the cigar in reconfirming kin group alliances. It is not difficult to imagine a situation in which an egalitarian ancestor to which all traced their descent could become restricted during the course of sociopolitical evolution to one that was ancestor and patron of one particular elite lineage, the royal lineage. There is a possible parallel in the southwestern United States use of small crook-shaped pahos or prayer sticks (given to young boys by the Hopi and larger crook-shaped staffs used by girls in their puberty rites by the Apaches) with a progressive restriction of crooks to use as tribal, clan, military society, and leadership symbols as one moves across the Plains and into the Midwest, where there was a strong institutionalization of leadership among Mississippian cultures beginning around A.D. 1000 (chapter 18).[45]

Francis Robicsec emphasizes the relationship of the smoking tube to the mirror glyph in the forehead of God K; Linda Schele and David Freidel speak of the object inserted into the mirror more often as a smoking celt or smoking ax.[46] Neither recognizes the relationship of the idea of 'mirror' to water or liquid. Before there were polished obsidian, magnetite, or mosaic pyrite mirrors in Mesoamerica, there were bowls of water, pools of water, and springs in which reflections could be seen. The mirror glyph is located on the head of God K almost exactly at the location of the soft spot or fontanel (Náhuatl *atl* 'water') on a baby's head (figure 12.3b).[47] The God K mirror was also located at the spot where the child in the Calumet ceremony was touched to introduce a spirit. The child had previously been given an identity with the earth represented by an ear of Mother Corn and its face or head painted with a whole- (Lakota, Omaha) or half- (Pawnee, Osage) quartered circle motif. While this motif did not resemble the Maya *nen* or mirror glyph, it was almost identical with the Mesoamerican Kan glyph, which can also occur in the forehead in Mayan iconography.[48]

The touching of the forehead of the Hunka in the Calumet ceremony with a pair of calumets, spoken of as pipes, would logically have been the ritual equivalent of the insertion of the smoking cigar into the mirror glyph or eye in the manikin scepter handle. This act in the Calumet ceremony was a symbolic conception signifying the rebirth of the Hunka and was part of the act of adoption. I have spoken of the bivalent symbolism of the adoption in the Calumet ceremony, rooted ultimately, as it was, both in a ritual to return to life a deceased ancestor or leader and a ritual to aid the earth to return to life. The Calumet ceremony thus related both to continuity between generations and to continuity of earth fertility. The Pawnee Hako variant of the Calumet ceremony even provided an occasion for the adoptee to peer at his or her reflection in a bowl of water used as a mirror, with comments on the symbolism of the child's reflection for continuity through the generations, much as Linda Schele and Jeffrey Miller have argued for the relationship of mirrors to succession in kingship among the Mayas.[49] The atlatl passed from use as a weapon fifteen hundred years ago in the United States, but the symbolic load of the atlatl has continued until the present day in the sacred pipe.

15 / The Sweat Bath and Related Female Metaphors

THE SWEAT BATH has become one of the most persistent elements of American Indian religion. The sweat bath has become one of the most irreducible elements of Indian religion. Many once-common elaborate tribal rituals have been abandoned and their songs forgotten. The meanings of ceremonies have lost significance for younger generations, and elders have died without passing on their sacred knowledge, but the sweat bath persists. The sweat bath was not so much a religious observance in itself as a preparation for an encounter with the sacred, like confession for a Roman Catholic. Steam bathing was believed to clean the soul as well as the body. Even so, sweat bathing is something that an individual Indian can do that is traditional and part of a religious act. It does not presume or require the acquisition of an extensive body of sacred lore from elders or the cooperation of a large corps of participants.

In his study of the sweat bath Ivan Alexis Lopatin pointed out that the steam bath is logically an evolved form of a sweat bath that originally relied upon dry heat alone.[1] A person can develop a sweat within a heated enclosure without the need for steam, and the use of dry heat seems to have an older distribution. For most Indians—for most people—the sweat bath is a steam bath, however, much like the Finnish sauna. Stones are heated and water sprinkled on them to create steam in a confined space, after which the participant may leave the steam room to plunge into the snow or a stream or a cold shower. There is no question that the sweat bath was used in both Europe and North America before the days of Columbus. The principle of the sweat bath could well be thousands of years older still.

Since the origin of fire itself, fire and heat have been necessarily associated with transformations. Food is transformed into a more edible form by cooking. Long before the invention of pottery it was known that heated clay became solid and that heating flint improved its chipping characteristics and its aesthetic qualitities.[2] Eggs incubated in a nest became transformed into birds, and the gestation of a human baby in the womb was not unlike the incubation of a bird's egg.

The association of heat and cooking with transformations must have created a mental association that was ages ago transferred from the material world to the world of social relations because heating and cooking became part of the metaphor and ritual of many social transformations or *rites de passage* in the words of Arnold Van Gennep. This idea is incorporated in the title of Claude Lévi-Strauss's book *The Raw and the Cooked.*[3]

SCARFACE AND NANAHUATL

Scarface was a Blackfoot boy who wished to marry the daughter of the chief. Having no desire to marry a boy with an ugly scar, the girl told Scarface that she would marry him when the scar disappeared from his face. Scarface was much offended but decided to seek the help of the sun. Scarface traveled toward the house of the sun but before reaching it met a young man who turned out to be Morning Star, the son of the sun. Together they went to Sun. There Sun spoke to Morning Star saying, "My son, do you wish this young man for a companion?" Morning Star said that he did indeed. "Well," said Sun, "you must make a sweathouse." This he did and soon Morning Star, Scarface, and Sun were enclosed within the sweat lodge. When the covers were raised from the lodge frame, the two boys looked so much alike that Morning Star's mother could not tell them apart.[4]

Clark Wissler seemed to think that this story was "highly original" and had no parallel in other folklore.[5] Consider, however, two Mesoamerican myths of the origin of the sun. The Huichols and Aztecs were both related by language—both were speakers of Uto-Aztecan languages. For the Huichols the sun originated when the lame and one-eyed son of the moon was thrown into a hot oven. The disfigured boy was consumed by the heat but revived and after five days running beneath the earth, rose as the sun.[6] For the Aztecs the sun originated when Nanahuatl, a man disfigured by boils, leaped into the coals of a flaming hearth at Teotihuacan and was consumed but then rose as the sun. As in the Huichol story, the Aztec sun did not rise immediately, leaving the gods to wonder where and when he would emerge from beneath the earth.[7]

The Aztec story has a variant put on paper by Hernando Ruiz de Alarcón in 1629 in which the point is made that the disfigured man emerged from the fire with his pustular and scabby features made beautiful and shining and then "threw himself into a pool of very cold water." This so clearly parallels the practice of jumping into cold water after a sweat bath that my comparison of the Blackfoot and the Aztec stories seems fully justified, the more so because in John Bierhorst's translation of the Legend of the Suns the term usually translated as 'sacred hearth' is rendered as 'spirit oven'. The sacred hearth in the Aztec story was a sweat bath enhanced by storytellers or state mythologizers until it was transformed into something beyond anyone's normal experience.[8]

My approach to reinterpreting the Legend of the Suns is hardly unique. Stephen Houston has shown that certain small rooms associated with the three temples of the Cross group at the Maya site of Palenque were probably constructed to represent the sweat baths in which were born the three gods of the Palenque Triad.[9] It is conventional to refer to these three gods either by the names of the days on which they were born, i.e., the calendrical names 9 Ik (9 Wind), 13 Cimi (13 Death), and 1 Ahau (1 Lord), or by the arbitrary code names GI, GIII, and GII. GII is the god also known as God K and the Smoking God (chapter 14).

In the Blackfoot, Huichol, and Aztec stories a disfigured boy or man entered a place of great heat and emerged transformed into the sun or the likeness of a star. One Old World equivalent of this theme would be found in those stories telling of the birth of the sun from an egg. In the Finnish *Kalevala* epic the sun was formed from the yellow yolks of teal duck eggs laid in a nest built upon the knee of the Mother of Waters as she floated in an endless sea. As the duck incubated her eggs, the heat grew hotter and more painful until the Water Mother convulsively jerked her knee and shattered the eggs. The earth was then formed from the lower parts of the egg shells, the sky's vault from the upper halves, the moon from the whites, and the sun from the yolks. Ancient Egyptians believed that the sun emerged from a goose egg, and among Australian aborigines there was a belief that the sun was created from the egg of an emu.[10]

THE SWEAT BATH AS A UTERINE METAPHOR

The North American sweat bath lodge was a uterine metaphor within which one sat in a fetal position and could be given new life. American Indian folktales commonly have as a theme the placing of a body or

skeleton in a sweat lodge, where the bones first begin to stir and then slowly to move and groan and then miraculously come to life.[11] In one such tale from the Lakotas, Stone Boy obliges the god Iya to tell him how he can restore to life certain people who have been flattened like dry hides by a rolling stone. He is told:

> You must skin the bear and the coyote and stretch their skins over poles so as to make a tight tipi. Then you must gather all the pieces of the broken living stone. You must make a fire of the wood of the snake tree and heat these stones over this fire. Then place the stones in the tipi. Then get one of the flattened people off the poles of my tipi and place it in the tipi you have built. Then place the hot stones in the tipi and pour water over the stones. When the steam rises onto the flattened persons, they will be as they were before.[12]

The skins of the bear and coyote would not make a covering of the size of a regular tipi with its tall conical form, so Stone Boy made a small, low, dome-shaped sweat lodge. He then followed the directions of Iya, and the flattened people were restored to their former condition.

In describing a Bear sweat lodge ceremony of the Ojibwas, Ruth Landes adds stories of marvelous events reported by those who have participated in this rite. They tell how the sweat bathers came to appear to each other like the fierce bears they were honoring and how even the sweat lodge itself "came to resemble the cavernous insides of a great bear."[13]

Lopatin was very impressed by the similarities between the steam bath of the North American Indians and the northwestern European sauna. In both areas water was poured over heated stones to generate steam in an enclosure, switches were used to beat the body to stimulate circulation, herbs were sometimes placed on the hot stones for the pleasing or therapeutic effects of the fumes produced, and the participants plunged into water or rolled in the snow afterward. Steam baths of this type were found broadly across the North American continent from north to south and east to west with few exceptions, but in Eurasia such steam baths have any great antiquity only in Scandinavia, Finland, and adjacent parts of Russia.

Lopatin deduces from its distribution that the steam bath originated in northern Europe and spread to the North American Indians across the Atlantic, directly or by way of Iceland.[14] He might have considered the reverse route if he had been aware of the maritime efficiency of ancient Indians on the Atlantic Coast of North America from Maine to Labrador. This Maritime Archaic culture dates from around 3000 to 1000 B.C. and was at least as well oriented toward exploiting sea resources as the contemporary cultures of northwestern Europe.[15] Nothing is known of the specific kinds of boats these Indians used for traveling and hunting sea mammals, but the abundant presence of stone ax, adze, and gouge blades indicates that they possessed a woodworking technology easily capable of making boats suitable for limited open-sea travel. The earliest occurrence of the steam bath in Europe was thus within an area accessible by sea from the continent with the broadest early distribution of the steam bath. A minimum antiquity of two thousand years for the sweat bath in North America is suggested by the similarity of the plan of the Lakota sweat lodge to certain symbolic motifs already present in Ohio Hopewellian culture two thousand years ago (below).

The Lakotas constructed a sweat bath lodge with a frame built of twelve to sixteen arched willow poles formed into a dome with an opening to the east, or to a direction indicated to the maker in a dream, or in the direction of a sacred feature of the landscape. At the center of the lodge a circular basin was excavated to hold the heated stones. The earth from this hole was deposited as a circular earth mound east of the lodge entrance along a route known as the 'sacred path'. Just east of the mound a fire was built to heat the stones that were carried along the sacred path to the basin at the center of the lodge.[16] This is a ground plan that was very nearly duplicated in the construction of the enclosure for the Four-Pole ceremony of the Skiri Pawnees (figure 15.1*a, c*). In the case of the Skiris a larger and more elaborate enclosure was built with its edge actually constructed of earth raised into a circular ridge with an opening to the east. At the center a circular hearth was constructed and the earth deposited in a small oval mound east of the entrance. The same ground plan was used by the Skiris for the special enclosures constructed for a fall harvest ceremony and for a preliminary part of the Morning Star sacrifice.[17]

In the mystical language used by the Winnebagoes in the ritual of their Medicine Society, the heated stone of the steam bath was 'grandmother' and the heat and vapors rising from it, 'grandfather'. The poles of the lodge were 'boys'. The sweat lodge as a whole was visualized as "a dark-furred, grizzled and awe-inspiring bear" of great size who seized the 'boys', thrust them into the ground, and bent their bodies to make a frame for the sweat bath. Water was applied to the heated stone with a braid of grass seen as the hair of our 'grandmother', and the sound of the steam hissing was heard as the breathing and moaning of Turtle, who represented water in the ceremony.[18]

As Paul Radin explains, "The imagery here is also supposed to indicate how the vapor-bath lodge is really enclosed within the body of a spirit, a spirit of fierce demeanor and threatening claws and teeth. Into this

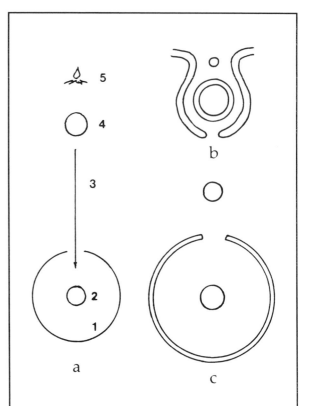

Fig. 15.1 The Lakota sweat lodge compared to other female metaphors. The Lakota sweat lodge is illustrated by *a*, showing (1) the lodge outline, (2) the pit for the heated stones, (3) the path for the heated stones, (4) the *unchi* or earth mound, made of earth removed from the stone pit, and (5) the fire in which the stones are heated, after Black Elk (1953, 33). This plan compares closely both to that of the earthen enclosure used in the Skiri Pawnee Four Pole ceremony (*c*), after Murie (1989, fig. 17), and to the Hopewellian vulviform portal motif (*b*) as the entrance to a Hopewellian earthwork enclosure in Butler County, Ohio, after Squier and Davis (1848, pl. 8, no. 1).

animal-spirit those who are to take the vapor-bath must enter. They must be terrified and yet strong enough in purpose to overcome it."[19] The sweat lodge was also an earth metaphor and by logical extension, a female metaphor that one entered almost as one returning to the womb and from which one emerged physically and ritually cleansed or reborn.

THE HAND AND PAW AS FEMALE METAPHORS

George Catlin sketched the participants of the Mandan Okipa ceremony on the upper Missouri River in 1832. These paintings show several Mandans with body paint that included special designs on the ankles, knees, hips, wrists, elbows, shoulders, around the eyes, and at the rear of the jaws. Catlin says that in addition these men

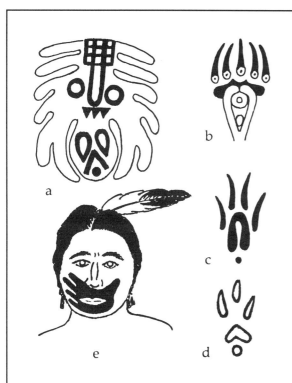

Figure 15.2 Hands and paws as symbolic portals: *a*, bas-relief design from an Adena tablet on which an agnathic animal head like that in figure 15.4 has been transformed with its maxillary teeth elongated and splayed to resemble spider legs, a paw pad portal motif engraved on the tongue, and the nose and eyes rendered as stylized male genitalia, after Webb and Baby (1957, fig. 32); *b* detail from an engraved human femur from the Hopewell mound group, Ross County, Ohio, showing a bear paw with a vulviform portal motif substituting for a paw pad portal motif, after Willoughby (1917, pl. 6*l*); *c*, claw and paw pad motif cut into a copper tube found in a Hopewell mound near Helena, Arkansas, after Ford (1963, fig. 21*b*); *d*, trailed motif on a Hopewellian pottery bowl from the Crook site, La Salle Parish, Louisiana, showing a claw and paw pad motif, after Ford and Willey (1940, fig. 29*b*); *e*, Omaha warrior with painted hand centered over his mouth to indicate a war honor, a mode of face painting found through the U.S. Plains and in pre-Columbian Mexico, after Fletcher and La Flesche (1972, fig. 63) and Howard (1968, fig. 6).

had the same designs on each joint of their fingers and toes.[20] Many of these places were locations near which a pulse, i.e. motion and life, could be felt. The Mandan designs were sets of double concentric circles. More than two thousand years earlier Adena artisans in the Ohio valley represented human and animal figures with a very similar design in exactly the same locations, and in the palms of the hand as well. The Adena design was a dot within a circle or 'nucleated circle'.[21] What

is represented is something known generically as a 'joint mark', which symbolizes a soul or that part of the soul believed to have its seat in the locations represented.[22]

Of special concern are the marks found on the palms of the hands that can symbolize points at which a spirit or power may enter or leave the body. In Adena art these were nucleated circles. In art of the late Mississippi period in the eastern United States, say A.D. 1200–1500, the designs were eyes, quartered circles, and 'ogives', as American archaeologists use that term. In Mexico the eye and quartered circle were common, but a spiral was also used. In one Olmec Preclassic example five oblong rectangles enclosed on three sides a staple-form element that may have been meant to represent a cave entrance.[23] Both in Mexico and in the Plains of the United States it was the practice to indicate certain war honors by painting a human hand over the face in such a way that the mouth occupied the center of the palm (figure 15.2*e* and the Afterword). All of these motifs found in the palm of the hand can carry the symbolism of 'entrance'. Some motifs are purely abstract, like the nucleated circle and double concentric circle, and others are natural, like the eye or mouth.[24]

In the *Popol Vuh*, a Quiché Maya epic, the lords of the Quiché underworld killed Hun Hunahpu and hung his head from the branch of a gourd tree or calabash tree. No tree of this kind had ever borne gourds until Hun Hunahpu's head was hung in it. While Hun Hunahpu's head hung in the tree, the daughter of a lord of the underworld stood before the tree. Blood Woman was her name. She stretched out her right hand. Hun Hunahpu's head spat into its palm and the spittle disappeared. Soon she came to realize that there was life within her body and in time she gave birth to the set of twins whose names were Hunter and Jaguar Deer.[25]

The hand was a female symbol in the *Dresden Codex*. In this prehistoric Maya illustrated book, the hand, cupped upward, was used to represent the hearth board or female firestick in which a god was twirling a fire drill. Among the Skiri Pawnees the hearth board represented the Evening Star; the fire drill represented the Morning Star; and the drilling of fire symbolized the intercourse of the Morning and Evening Star in the days of the Creation. Hun Hunahpu's relationship to the hand of Blood Woman in the *Popol Vuh* was the same as that of the Skiri Morning Star to Evening Star and that of the fire drill to the hand in the *Dresden Codex*.[26] As an organ that can receive and enclose, the human hand was a natural female metaphor in Mesoamerica and, I would argue, in the United States as well.

The pattern of three toe pads and a more naturally shaped plantar pad was found decorating a pottery bowl of Marksville-Hopewellian type from the Crooks site in

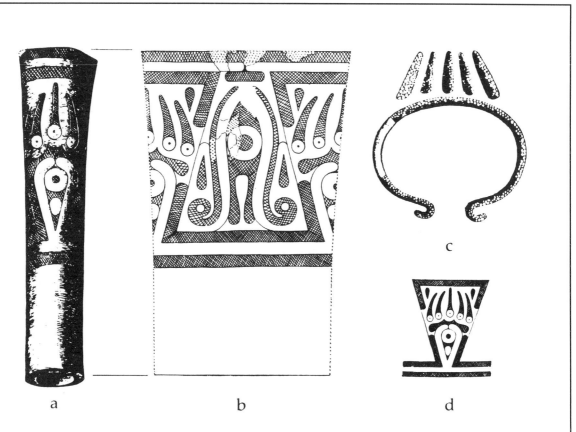

Figure 15.3 Hopewellian representations of the bear paw as a female metaphor. Because of its nature as a receiving and enclosing organ, the human hand serves as a natural female metaphor, as can a bear paw, by analogy. This metaphor is reinforced on an engraved human femur (*a–b*) from the Hopewell type site, Ross County, Ohio, which shows a bear paw (*d*) with a vulviform portal motif in the palm area, from Willoughby (1917, pl. 6*i*, *k–l*). The Hopewellian perception of a bear paw as a female metaphor is illustrated also by the plan (*c*) of a stone enclosure on Black Run, Ross County, Ohio, which is in the form of a bear paw 250 feet wide with a well-defined entry, from Squier and Davis (1848, pl. 30, no. 4).

Louisiana (figure 15.2*d*). This vessel in addition had a large dot to the rear of the plantar pad that corresponds to no natural feature of an animal paw, but then, there is no natural mammal in North America with three toes.[27] A pattern of four long-clawed toes and a long wicket-shaped plantar pad was found cut into a tube of copper from the Helena Crossing site on Crowley's Ridge in Arkansas (figure 15.2*c*). A dot occurs in the same location relative to the plantar pad as on the Crooks site bowl.[28] The Helena Crossing site was also Hopewellian. The copper tube was found with a burial in a submound grave pit.

A pattern of two toes and a plantar pad with the enigmatic dot occurs on the Gaitskill stone tablet from the Ohio valley (figure 15.2*a*).[29] This is an object belonging to a late phase of the Adena culture, but the pattern is more highly stylized than the paw pad patterns mentioned that were of Hopewellian age. On the Gaitskill tablet the foot pad pattern occurs on what could be taken to be the abdomen of a spider, or perhaps the lower part an elaborate mask of some kind.

What this appendage actually represents does not become clear until it is compared with an engraved design on a bone tube found in the year 1801 in a mound in Cincinnati, Ohio (figure 15.4*a*).[30] What on the Gaitskill stone tablet appeared to be something like the abdomen of a spider, on the Cincinnati engraving was obviously the extended tongue of a carnivore. The total design of the Gaitskill stone tablet was a highly simplified and stylized version of the design on the bone tube. The two patterns together comprise a sort of Rosetta Stone of Adena-Hopewell iconography.

Where on the Gaitskill stone tablet there was the stylized paw pad pattern, on the Cincinnati tube there was a design that was called to my attention by Eloise Gadus in 1980 as a Hopewellian emblem. This was a pattern which I took then and still today believe to be a stylized rendering of features of the female genital area and representing metaphorically a grave, cave opening, spring, or other kind of earth entrance. This vulviform motif was definitely used as the pattern for the entrance to a Hopewellian ritual enclosure with earth walls near

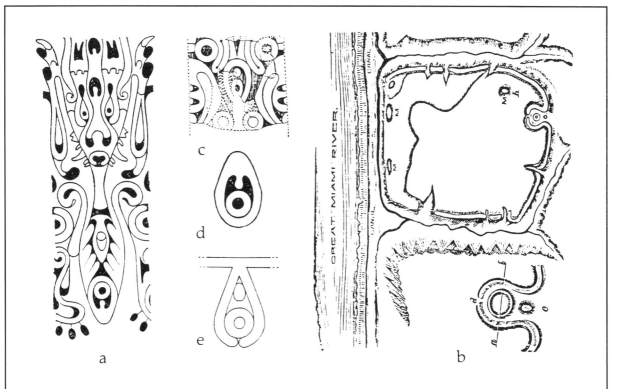

Figure 15.4 Examples of the vulviform Hopewellian portal motif. The use of the vulviform motif as an entrance to a Hopewellian earthen enclosure (*b*) in Butler County, Ohio, from MacLean (1893, fig. 52), supports the interpretation of this motif as a symbolic portal. The symbolic value of the vulviform motif (*d*) as a portal is further supported by its appearance within the mouth of a carnivore (*a*) engraved on a bone found in a mound in Cincinnati, Ohio, in 1801, from Willoughby (1917, pl. 7*i*). The foregoing examples may be compared with a third (*c*) on an engraved human ulna from the Turner mound group, Hamilton County, Ohio, after Willoughby (1917, pl. 7*c*), and a fourth (*e*) on an engraved human femur from the Hopewell mound group, Ross County, Ohio, after Willoughby (1917, pl. 1*g* and 6*l*).

Hamilton in Butler County, Ohio (figures 15.1*b* and 15.4*b*).[31] I interpret the presence of the female symbols within the mouth to be an Adena-Hopewell convention indicating that the maw of the animal—the mouth and throat—was being equated with an entrance into the earth as a female metaphor.

We have already reviewed some of the female sexual associations of the human hand, which I believe extend to the animal paw. In the examples above there is an implicit parallel between the paw pad pattern, female sexuality, and the open mouth of a carnivore, this last being reminiscent of the mythical theme of the *vagina dentata* in the Skiri Pawnee creation story. One of the obstacles that Morning Star had to overcome before mating with Evening Star in the Skiri Pawnee creation story was the set of teeth that she had arranged to discourage intercourse. These were teeth provided by rattlesnakes—venom-delivering teeth selected to inflict the most excruciating pain.[32]

The spatial relationship of the paw pads and explicit female symbols to the Adena-Hopewell animal mouths is the same as that of the trenches to the buffalo skulls in the Cheyenne and Arapaho Sun Dance altars. We have already seen that these trenches carried a symbolism equivalent to that of the Mesoamerican turquoise and Kan glyphs. The sods in the Cheyenne and Arapaho Sun Dances represent lumps of mud brought from beneath the primordial sea by mythical Earth Divers. The sods have explicit associations with toes. Those for the Cheyenne Sun Dance were cut from the earth in the pattern of the turquoise glyph and then arranged around the buffalo skull initially in a pattern like that of five toe pads (figures 3.1, 3.2*a*). It is my belief that the iconography of the Gaitskill stone tablet and the Cincinnati tube represents the ideology from which the buffalo skull altar of the Plains Sun Dance eventually evolved and that the theme of the Earth Diver was assimilated to it.

This interpretation requires a continuity of thought and belief for more than two thousand years, but, then, exactly such a continuity can be demonstrated for the vulviform Hopewellian portal motif. The pattern of this emblem survived into the past century as the plan of the earthen enclosure for the Skiri Pawnee Four Pole ceremony and lives even today within the plan of the Lakota sweat bath lodge, which surrounds its occupants like the body of a great black bear with arched wooden bones.[33]

In constructing both the Lakota sweat bath lodge and the lodge for the Pawnee Four Pole ceremony the earth from the hearth pit is/was deposited east of the lodge proper in a small mound. In the case of the Four Pole ceremony the hearth pit was actually for a fire, and in the case of the Lakota sweat bath lodge the pit is only to contain the stones heated glowing-hot elsewhere (figure 15.1a, c). The Pawnees deposited the earth just outside the entrance to the enclosure, while the Lakotas make the mound at a slightly greater distance. The Pawnee enclosure was outlined with a low earth wall, while the Lakota enclosure is defined by

15.5). He adds that the Arapaho call this earth mound *thi'äya*, "the same name being also applied to a memorial stone heap or to a stone monument. It is always surmounted by a buffalo skull, or in these days by the skull of a steer, placed so as to face the doorway of the lodge. The *thi'äya* is mentioned in several of the Ghost-dance songs, and usually, as here, in connection with crying or lamentation, as though the sight of these things in the trance vision brings up sad recollections."[35] I am grateful to Bea Medicine for the information that buffalo skulls may sometimes in our own day be seen on the earth mounds in front of sweat lodges.

Arval Looking Horse, hereditary keeper of the sacred Lakota Buffalo Calf Pipe, has said of the sweat lodge,

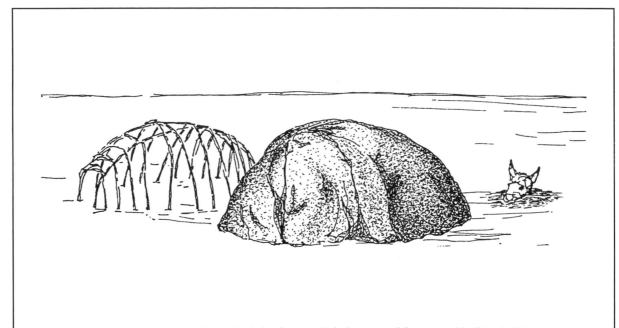

Figure 15.5 Kiowa sweat lodges. Left to right: lodge framework; lodge covered for use; and buffalo skull facing entrance, resting on a small earth mound. After Mooney (1896, pl. 121).

a bower of slender poles. The Lakotas refer to their earth mound as unchi, *uŋci'* in Father Buechel's orthography for the Lakota dialect and *uŋ-ċi'* in that of Reverend Riggs for the Santee dialect.[34] Both agree that 'unchi' means grandmother, but Buechel gives the ritual meaning as 'earth, mother earth', while Riggs gives it as 'the sun'. For Riggs's gloss to make sense, the sun would have to be female, although this was the case, of course, among many tribes in the southeastern United States.

To what we know of the sweat lodge from native sources of this century James Mooney adds some valuable additional details. In his 1896 report on the Ghost Dance Mooney, comments that the Kiowa, Sioux, and Arapaho placed a buffalo skull on the earth mound and illustrates one built by the Kiowa (figure

"It is the mother's womb. They always say when they come out of the sweat lodge, it's like being born again or coming out of the mother's womb."[36] When you superimpose the Pawnee enclosure outline upon the stylized Hopewellian animal paw patterns, the mound unchi corresponds to the enigmatic dot for which paws have no natural equivalent.

COSMIC SWEAT BATHS

As we are now justified in suspecting, the prototype in oral tradition for the sacred hearth from which Nana-huatl emerged reborn as the fifth Aztec sun, 4 Ollin, was the chamber of a sweat bath, much as in Huichol belief the sun emerged from an oven. We can enlarge upon this identification by examining the glyph 4 Ollin that is central to the Aztec Stone of the Sun, a glyph that consists of the glyph Ollin bracketed by four dots for the numeral four. The particular form of the Ollin glyph that appears on the Stone of the Sun is the handle of an atlatl splayed into a butterfly-like form so that segments are directed toward the summer and winter solstice sunrise and sunset directions (figures 11.3, 14.3g). Through this glyph, which represents the earth, there is an arrow entering from the west and emerging in the east near a glyph for the name day 13 Acatl or 13 Reed of the year in the Aztec calendar in which the sun was born. This arrow follows the path of the sun during the spring and fall equinox.[37]

Central to the Ollin glyph is a circle containing the face of the daytime sun, as was once most commonly assumed, or the earth goddess, as Ulrich Köhler, Richard Townsend, and C. Navarrete and Doris Heyden have proposed, or the dead, midnight sun in the interior of the earth, as Cecilia Klein has proposed.[38] The sun was born in the Aztec year 13 Reed but did not start its celestial travels until its name day, 4 Ollin or 4 Movement, which comes four days after 13 Reed.[39]

Returning to the sweat bath chambers of the gods at Palenque, I will note that God GII, God K, was born on a day 1.18.5.4.0, 1 Ahau 13 Mac, in the Classic Maya calendar, which would have been November 6, 2360 B.C., in the Gregorian calendar as projected back into the pre-Gregorian era.[40] This date falls five days short of the antizenith day for the day of first zenith passage of the sun at the latitude of Palenque. The antizenith day would have been the day on which the declination of the sun was $-17°$ 30', as compared with $+17°$ 30' for the day of first zenith passage six months earlier, the latitude of Palenque being $+17°$ 30' north. In other words, the sun at midnight of that November 6 was approaching nadir in the underworld, nearly directly below the Temple of the Foliated Cross, the god's birthing place, much as on a day of zenith passage the sun would have been directly overhead, as it is on May 10. Zenith passage occurs when the declination of the sun matches the latitude of the point of observation and in the tropical latitudes occurs once before and once after the summer solstice each year, except on the Tropic of Cancer in the northern hemisphere and the Tropic of Capricorn in the southern hemisphere, where the sun is exactly overhead only on the day of the summer solstice.[41]

The sweat baths of the Palenque Triad were small rooms in the three temples of the Temple Group and were given the name *pib na* in the inscriptions. In the Yucatec dialect of Maya *na* means house and *pib* refers to a sweat bath used by women who have given birth and to a pit oven or underground oven for baking food. The Temple Group *pib na* are thus believed to have represented in the world of the eighth-century Mayas the cosmic *pib na* in which the gods were actually born in mythic time.[42] Within the yearly cycle the antizenith sun is related to the darker months of the year in much the same way that the midnight sun is to night and the netherworld during the daily cycle.

'RITUAL CLOWN' is a name that requires a bit of explanation. A 'clown' in modern English usage is a purely comic character, a buffoon. The ritual clown among the pueblo-dwelling Indians of the southwestern United States had both comic functions and others that were more serious, not the least of which were social control and the management of some important ceremonial events. The combination is much like that of the trickster in folklore who may be a vulgar comedian and comic character as well as a divine transformer.

SACRED CLOWNS

The pueblo clowns were sacred clowns. They included the Koyemshis or 'mud-heads' of the Zuñis and the Koshares of the Rio Grande pueblos. The Koshares are painted white with horizontal black stripes and black rings around their eyes and mouth, and they have two vertical horns made by wrapping corn husks around long hanks of their hair. The variety of costuming and functions is almost as great as the number of pueblos, but the clowns share several traits of behavior: during public ceremonies when the occasion calls for their activities, the clowns burlesque both common and sacred aspects of behavior, they say the opposite of what they mean, and they mock, often obscenely, persons and things that they would not ridicule under other circumstances.

In addition to the clowns of the practicing clown societies there is also belief in individual gods or groups of gods who are the archetypal or prototypical clowns of pueblo cosmologies. The original Koshares were divine spirits "living in the east at the house of the Sun."[1] In the beliefs of the Keresan pueblos Paiyatemu is a son of the sun conceived when a beam of sunlight fell upon a sleeping mortal woman. He is a companion and deputy of the sun and carries the sun's blazing shield, and he is a musician who plays music on a flute, but he is primarily a trickster and clown.[2] One aspect of clown behavior is reverse speech—saying the opposite of what is meant. Thus, as Frank Cushing tells it, Paiatuma, the

Zuñi equivalent of Paiyatemu responded in the following way when asked to search for the corn maidens: "'Oh, *that's all* is it? The corn maidens are not lost, and if they were I would not go to seek them, and if I went to seek for them I could not find them, and if I found them I would not bring them, but I would tell them you "did not wish to see them" and leave them where they are not—in the Land of Everlasting Summer, which is not their home. Ha! you have no prayer-plumes here, I observe,' said he, picking up one each of the yellow, blue and white kinds, and starting out with the remark—'I come.'"[3] Cushing calls Paiatuma the God of Dew and the Dawn, who freshens seeds with his breath. Flute playing was one of his typical activities.[4]

PLAINS CONTRARIES

Among the Sioux the ritual clown was called a Heyoka. This means that the person was a personification of the Thunderbird god Wakinyan in his more amiable, alter-ego form of Heyoka.[5] A person became a Heyoka from an overpowering fear of lightning or as a result of having seen the Wakinyan in a dream. Heyoka clowns spoke with reverse meanings, saying the opposite of what they meant, and acted in ways contrary to nature—backing out of a tipi, wearing a buffalo robe and sitting next to a fire on hot days, going without adequate clothes in winter, resting their legs against a tipi with their back on the ground, and in a thousand other ways. Heyoka clowns also showed disdain for heat—picking meat from boiling kettles with their bare hands and frolicking by splashing boiling hot water on each other—without being harmed by their acts. Heyokas were credited with great powers as curers.[6]

Among the Cheyennes the equivalent of the Sioux Heyoka clowns were the funmakers of the Contrary Society. Like the Heyoka clowns, the members of this Cheyenne society practiced reverse speech and reverse behavior, plucked meat from boiling kettles without harming themselves, were especially frightened by lightning, and conducted themselves absurdly during ceremonies to the delight of observers. In addition, there was also the Contrary warrior who practiced reverse speech and behavior but who was pledged to certain roles in warfare. This was a more serious commitment, and lonely as well, because a Contrary warrior could mingle with other Cheyennes only in battle. He could associate freely only with another Contrary warrior, and there was normally only one or two others in the tribe at any one time.[7]

East of the Dakotas were the Ojibwas and Menominees. Among these Algonquian speakers the Plains clowns had no counterparts as clowns, but they did as curers and handlers of fire. The members of the Ojibwa and Menominee Wabano or Wabeno cults did not belong to an organized society but practiced their arts as individuals, usually in response to visions obtained as youths. Their name connotes Men of the Dawn or Men of the East. They were said to have been able to handle burning coals and dip their hands in boiling water or maple syrup without harming themselves.

The stunt of fire handling was once found widely among the Central Algonquian tribes but only now and then and, only incidentally, involved plucking meat from a boiling pot. The latter idea appears to have been an elaboration emphasized by neighboring tribes and to have spread through the central and northern Plains tribes, with the Pawnees and Sioux being especially prominent in this diffusion. In the Plains the meat trick became joined to the activities of the Contraries. Fire handling by itself is not limited to the Central Algonquians. It is found also in parts of California with revealing associations. Among the Pomos it was a special ability or trick of 'ash ghosts' who represented the ghosts of the cremated dead in mourning ceremonies known as Ghost Dances. Such ghosts entered ceremonial chambers backward, used reverse speech (saying east for west, and so on), and held contests of endurance in sweat lodges. Among the Arapaho of the northern Plains, walking over hot coals with bare feet was an activity of crazy-dancers, who also spoke in reverse and engaged in clowning, but only during crazy-dances and while wearing certain owl-feather headbands. Owls are associated widely not only with night, of course, but also with death.[8]

REVERSE BEHAVIOR AND THE UNDERWORLD

The Hopis, as did or still do many other Indian peoples, believe in the reversal of day and night between the upper world and the underworld. When it is day in the upper world, it is night in the underworld, and vice versa. Among the Hopis this concept of reversal has been translated into behavior that has been well noted and reported. Maski, the Hopi land of the dead, is a land of opposites. Not only are day and night and

winter and summer reversed in Maski, but the inhabitants of Maski also do things contrariwise to what would be normal in the land of the living. Ruling Maski is Maasaw, the death spirit or God of Death. Maasaw wears over his left shoulder what a living Hopi would drape over his right shoulder. In the story of the emergence of the ancestral Hopis from the world below, it was Maasaw's left arm that was offered to the Hopis to help them in their emergence, tellers of the story take care to note, and Maasaw carries his club in his left hand rather than in his right: "Whatever the Hopi does, Maasaw reverses. For instance, upon entering the kiva, Maasaw will descend to the lower floor portion by going around the west side of the entrance ladder. A Hopi, on the other hand, goes around the east side of the ladder to reach this level."[9]

If you remember that the night sky is the equivalent of the underworld in Indian thought, then you can find a marvelous example of reverse behavior for the Skiri Pawnees in the ritual of their Morning Star sacrifice. During the course of the preparation of the captive for the sacrifice, the Skiri priests took the four burning logs from the hearth, one at a time, and made gestures with them toward the captive. First, the log from the northeast, then that from the southwest, then those from the northwest and southeast in that order—northeast, southwest, northwest, southeast. Later in the ceremony a priest danced to each of four circles made of down feathers in four quadrants of the lodge and destroyed them in the same order of semicardinal directions. This symbolized the conquest of four beasts guarding Evening Star before her own conquest in the origin myth of the ceremony. It is curious, however, that these acts were performed in the exact reverse of the order in which these directions are followed in the sequence of leadership of the ceremonial bundles that figure in the seasonal agricultural rituals. For these the order of directions is northwest, southwest, northeast, southeast. The difference, as I see it, was that the Morning Star sacrifice represented an event that took place in the mythic past among the stars in the night sky before the stars colonized the earth below. The agricultural rituals took place in current time. The night sky being equivalent to the underworld, the order of directions was reversed.[10]

Among the Osages there was reverse behavior of a sort in everyday life, regulated by clan membership. All Osages were born into clans belonging within one or another of two grand divisions or moieties determined by their relationship to an east-west axis dividing camp circles and villages into northern and southern halves. Honga division clans comprised the right or southern half of the Osage camp circle, whose entrance normally faced the east, and a Tsizhu division comprised the left or northern half. When an Osage Honga division member put on his moccasins in the morning, he put the right one on first, while a Tsizhu division member would put the left one on first. A ceremonial gourd rattle used by the Puma clan of the Honga division contained small stones representing teeth from the right side of a puma jaw, and the handle represented the right foreleg of a puma. Division membership also determined whether a man hung his medicine bundle on the right or the left of the lodge. The Osage Honga division corresponded to that of the Omaha Earth People and the Osage Tsizhu division, that of the Omaha Sky People, so in this respect, the mentioned examples of Osage behavior were reversed between right and left depending upon whether a person's clan had a Sky or Earth association.[11]

The underworld is the realm of the sun during the night. The sacred clowns of the Southwest have a number of connections to the sun. The original Koshares were spirits who lived with the sun. Paiyatemu was conceived by the Sun and carried the sun's shield. He was the sun's deputy. The southwestern clowns are sometimes referred to as the 'sons of the sun'. The Pawnees have a tradition of an organization known as the Children-of-the-sun Society, which has not existed for generations. In tradition the members of the society are supposed to have practiced reverse or contrary speech; they said the opposite of what they meant. Where the Cheyenne and Sioux contraries had relationships only to the Thunderers, this Pawnee contrary group was related to the sun, as were contrary-speaking clowns of the Southwest.[12]

CONTROL OF THE SPIRIT WORLD

If we consider the groups mentioned so far as basically related, from the Southwest to the Great Lakes, then there seems to be an underlying relationship to the sun or the underworld sun or the house of dawn for the Southwest generally, for the Pawnee example given, and for the Wabeno cult of the Ojibwas and Menominees, but to the Thunderers for the Western and Eastern Sioux and Cheyennes. We can ask, why do the Cheyenne and Sioux Contraries comprise such an exception in being so strongly related to the Thunderers? The clowns of the Southwest were related importantly to seed germination, fertility, and weather magic. At Oraibi "a dream of clowns dancing is a sign of rain." The Koshares of Laguna administer cures for lightning shock:[13]

> One of the foremost sanctions at Zuñi is drought; if you break a taboo, rain will not fall on your field. The flood-sending water serpent in the Rio Grande valley has a punitive character [much as clowns are punitive in their behavior]. So it is quite consistent that the

clowns should be associated with [as controllers of] the water serpent and with rain-sending and crop-bringing kachina. But the clown groups have direct weather-control and fertility functions, they themselves impersonate kachina or other supernaturals who live in springs or lakes.[14]

The Pueblo war groups or chieftaincies have disintegrated more than any other part of the social organization, due to the passing of war. But there are still positive relics or memories in some pueblos of the sometime war or associated war activities of the clowns. The K'ashale of Acoma, now [1934] almost extinct, were managers of the Scalp ceremony and the Gumeyoichi today act as scouts in the dramatization of the fight with the kachina.[15]

Even the war functions of the southwestern clowns were indirectly related to weather control because it was believed that enemy dead could become rainmakers. In pueblo Indian belief the spirits of the dead followed the sun west after death and then returned as clouds and rain bearers. The pattern of cloud-bringing winds was from west to east. Quite widely in the United States it was believed that the spirit of a slain warrior was controlled by his slayer. This relationship was reinforced by adoption. Enemy scalps obtained by Hopis were referred to as the 'sons' of their takers.[16] Iroquois warriors torturing captives commonly referred to them by kinship terms during their torture, and the custom of adoption might be extended also to the scalps with which they returned when on the war trail (chapter 5).[17] As we have already seen, Bernardino de Sahagún reports that captives of the Aztecs about to be sacrificed in gladiatorial combat were referred to as 'sons' by their captors and were mourned as such after death, and for certain other sacrificial victims their clothing and locks of hair from their head were preserved in a reed box by the victims' sponsors, very much like a Lakota or Menominee death bundle.[18]

REVERSE ELEMENTS IN MESOAMERICAN COSMOLOGY

In a footnote to *The Sacred Pipe: Black Elk's Account of the Seven Rites of the Oglala Sioux*, the editor, Joseph Epes Brown, explained that normal Oglala circumambulation was 'sun-wise', that is 'clockwise', but that occasionally "the counter-clockwise movement is used in a dance or some occasion prior to or after a great catastrophe, for this movement is in imitation of the Thunder-beings who always act in an antinatural way and who come in a terrifying manner, often bringing destruction."[19] Clockwise would be normal for North America north of the Tropic of Cancer (23½° N. Lat.) because at those higher latitudes the sun is never seen in the northern half of the sky at noon (figure 16.1), but there are exceptions for the direction seen in North America as 'sun-wise'.

In describing a Ghost Dance or Feast of the Dead of the Six Nations Iroquois in Ontario, Canada, William Fenton and Gertrude Kurath took careful note of the motions and movements of the participants. It was clear from their observations that circuiting movements were meant to be clockwise in that particular death-associated event, as, for example, when passing food, but that participants occasionally lapsed into the counterclockwise movements normal for the Iroquois and had to be coached to move in a reverse or clockwise direction, which was said by participants to be proper for the Ghost Dance.[20] Counterclockwise would logically be seen as normal south of the Tropic of Cancer in Mexico, where from sometime in May until sometime in August the sun can be seen to rise, transit the meridian, and set entirely in the northern half of the sky. The pattern of motion observed by Fenton and Kurath was curiously Mesoamerican.

Association of the underworld and spirit world with reverse behavior was not limited to North America. Describing ritual behavior among the Mixe Indians of Oaxaca, Mexico, Frank Lipp says that "the movements of personnel in Mixe ritual is [*sic*] in a sinistral fashion, starting from the east, except for those carried out for Mɨku', the lord of the underworld, which are in a clockwise movement."[21] Elsewhere in Mesoamerica other kinds of reversals were taken advantage of to create mythic environments or legitimate ideology.

In 1924 Herbert Spinden observed that 1508 Maya 'vague years' of 365 days precisely equaled 1507 of our tropical years of 365.2422 days and inferred that the Mayas utilized this knowledge.[22] The accuracy of this figure to four decimal places was partly fortuitous: it was a fortunate coincidence that twenty-nine Maya calendar rounds of 18,980 days each (a calendar round contains fifty-two years of 365 days) exactly equaled 1507 tropical years. Because the Maya year added no leap-year days, the Maya calendar would move ahead of our calendar by about one day each four years, but after 1508 vague years the same day of the 365-day calendar would once again exactly coincide with the same day of the tropical year. Munro Edmonson calls this period of 1507 tropical years or 1508 Maya vague years a 'solar era'. It is the length of time it takes for the Maya year of 365 days to depart from synchronization with the tropical year and its seasons and then to return to synchronization once more.[23]

Spinden observed that exactly midway through a period of 1508 vague years a day in the Maya year that originally had coincided with a summer solstice would then coincide with a winter solstice and vice versa. Although Spinden's observation of this reversal of the

seasons has been in the literature for more than seventy years, there has been very little interest in utilizing the information for interpreting Mayan hieroglyphic inscriptions beyond observing (a) that the dates of the birth of the gods at the Palenque site in Chiapas State, Mexico, referred to a year in the Mayan mythical past when the seasons were exactly reversed from those that obtained in the first year of the Maya Era, and (b) that the events took place one-half solar era after the first year of the Maya Era base.[24]

The Maya Era was a period of more than 5,125 years counted from a base date of August 11, 3114 B.C. *Gregorian*. The midpoint of a solar era was possibly viewed by the Mayans as having the same relationship to the total solar era as midnight to the daily cycle of the sun. At night the sun rules the underworld of many American Indian cosmologies. In other words, the midpoint of a solar era appears to have been the equivalent in Maya time to the underworld in space, a spirit world of mythic origins. The first day of first zenith passage of the sun at the latitude of Palenque after the beginning of the Maya era would have occurred at noon of May 10, 3113 B.C. on a day 16 Mac in the Maya 365-day vague year. Because of the 0.2422-day difference in the lengths of our year and the Maya year, the day 16 Mac did not again fall on or near May 10 until 1606 B.C., when it fell on May 11, but midway through that solar era the day 16 Mac fell on November 9, 2360 B.C., when the sun was not directly above Palenque at noon, as it would have been on a day of zenith passage, but very nearly directly below at midnight. November 11 was the antizenith day or day of nadir passage of the sun at the latitude of Palenque, when the sun was directly below Palenque at midnight (figure 16.2). This was the midcyclical epoch to which the birth of the Palenque triad of gods was assigned, their births falling on October 19, October 23, and November 6, 2360 B.C.

The example above is hardly unique. The day of first zenith passage of the sun for San Andrés Tuxtla, Veracruz, Mexico, varies between May 13 and May 14, depending upon the year of observation. San Andrés Tuxtla was near the location of discovery a century ago of a jade statuette inscribed with a Long Count number of 8.6.2.4.17 and a short text in an Epi-Olmec script. Taking a clue from the calendrics of the birth of the Palenque gods, if one counts from May 14, 3113 B.C., as the first day of first zenith passage of the sun after the beginning of the Maya Era, and moves forward by the length of what I have defined as a Tuxtla cycle (a period of sixty-three calendar rounds or 4 × 365 × 819 days), one arrives at a date of March 13, 162 A.D., the Christian-era equivalent of the Maya Long Count number inscribed on the Tuxtla statuette. The midpoint of that particular Tuxtla cycle is a day 8 Manik 0 Kankin, April 13, 1476 B.C. On the evenings of April 12 and September 1 at the Copán site in Honduras the sun sets directly behind Stela 10 when viewed from Stela 12 four miles away. Sylvanus Morley believed that the April 12 event signaled the beginning of a new agricultural year on the following morning, a day of annual renewal, so to speak.[25]

If one counts forward by one Maya Era (13 × 20 × 20 × 360 days) beginning with the Maya Era base date of August 11, 3114 B.C., one arrives at December 21, the winter solstice in the year 2012 A.D. This is a date occasionally touted in the tabloid newspapers as that of the end of the world. The midpoint of the Maya Era is a day with a Long Count number of 6.10.0.0.1, which reduces to April 18, 551 B.C. *Gregorian*. This was the New Year day of the year of inauguration of the Long Count, by the most recent determination of that event. The Long Count was apparently designed so its year of inauguration would fall midcycle in the Maya Era and the 360th or name day of that year would be a day 13 Ahau concluding a calendar round on April 12.[26]

RABBIT LORDS OF THE LAND OF SPIRITS

In 1946 Margaret Fisher said of the Manabush (or Michabo or Nanabozho) myths that, "Even the earliest of the available versions have a composite character, and the writer inclines to the belief that 'Nanabozho', as known to us, is not a really old Algonkian concept, but rather a synthetic figure growing out of the reworking of various older Algonkian myths, possibly under Iroquois influence."[27] In other words, she believed that the heroic hare evolved from the less heroic trickster hare within a substratum of Algonquian folklore. Quite the opposite was believed by Daniel Brinton who expressed his belief in 1868 that Manabush as a trickster rabbit was a "low, modern, and corrupt version" of the original, godlike hero, but he did find it "passing strange" that an animal as insignificant as the rabbit should have been chosen as the model for a god.[28]

There is no consistency among tribes in the story of Manabush's birth or in the number, character, and names of his brothers, when he has brothers. In the Menominee version you are already familiar with, Manabush was introduced to the secrets of the Medicine Lodge by the gods to console him for the death of his wolf companion or brother, who became the lord of the land of spirits. In a Potawatomi version it was a brother by the name of Chipiapoos who was killed and came to rule the dead, but Chipiapoos translates as 'corpse rabbit'.[29] This suggests that in some earlier tradition it was the rabbit himself who died and became the ruler of the land of spirits!

In seventeenth-century Virginia, Jopassus, who was the brother of the chief of the Potomacs, said that the Potomac tribe had "five gods in all," the principal god appearing in the likeness of "a mighty great hare," the other four having no visible form, being the four winds. The dwelling place of the Great Hare of the Potomacs was in the direction of the rising sun, and it was to this place that the shades of the dead traveled after ascending into the sky by means of a high tree. There they lived in the east with the Great Hare until they grew old once more, died, and were reborn into the world from which they had originally come. In other words, the Great Hare of the Potomacs himself ruled the land of the dead. The story of this Great Hare parallels that of Manabush slightly in that a great deer that was a

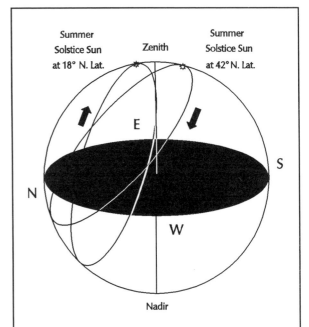

Figure 16.1 Paths of the sun when viewed at midday on the day of summer solstice from the latitude of Tabasco, Mexico (18° N), and from that of Nebraska (42° N).

special creation of the Great Hare was killed by other gods out of jealousy. This compares with Manabush's special friend the wolf who was killed by other gods out of jealousy.[30]

The Potomacs were Eastern Algonquians located on the Atlantic coast and were geographically quite peripheral to the Central Algonquians who developed the Medicine Society. I see in this situation the possibility that the Potomacs preserved an Algonquian tradition that came to be replaced farther to the west as the character of Manabush developed. The earliest hint of anything like a Medicine Society for the Algonquians was among the Nipissings, who were close neighbors of the Iroquoian-speaking Hurons (chapter 9).

The Potomac association of their Great Hare with

the direction of the rising sun is quite consistent with the etymology of Algonquian words for hare or rabbit. The words 'rabbit', 'white', 'east', and 'dawn' are typically cognate, as, for example, Ojibwa *waaban* 'it is dawn', *waaban* 'in the east', *waabooz* 'rabbit, snowshoe hare', *waabimanoomin* 'white rice'. In 1643 Roger Williams provided the following from the Narragansetts, an Eastern Algonquian tribe living in Rhode Island: *wompan* 'dawn, day', *wompanand* 'the Eastern God', *wompi* 'white, bright', *wampom* 'white shell beads'.[31] You will recognize the last, of course, in its Anglicized form of *wampum*, and do not forget the Wabenos

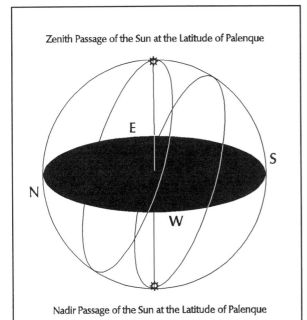

Zenith Passage of the Sun at the Latitude of Palenque

Nadir Passage of the Sun at the Latitude of Palenque

Figure 16.2 Position of the sun when viewed at Palenque, Chiapas, Mexico, at midday of May 10, the day of first zenith passage of the sun for that latitude, and at midnight of November 11, the antizenith day or day of first nadir passage of the sun.

(above), the fire-handling Men of the Dawn among the Great Lakes Algonquians.

Early Woodland artisans of the Adena culture have left us at least two carvings of humanoid beings with either rabbit ears or plumes resembling rabbit ears. These can be seen on the objects known as the Gaitskill Clay Tablet and Lakin A Tablet, each found in the Ohio valley. Each shows an anthropomorphic being standing erect with hands up and palms outward. William Webb and Raymond Baby identified these beings as shamans, one dancing, and saw the heads as masks.[32] They did not mention seeing any resemblance of the head on the Gaitskill tablet to that of a rabbit or the head of the Lakin A figure to that of a sacred

clown. The two horn- or ear-like projections on the tops of the heads are quite distinctive and would call 'clown' to the mind of a southwesternist immediately.

The rabbit in Algonquian folklore was a trickster whose name was cognate with dawn and whose behavior reversed the order of nature as it was originally created, causing problems for those who followed. In the story of the Potawatomi Medicine Society the land of the dead was ruled by Chipiapoos, whose name translates as Corpse Rabbit. The Potomac Great Hare ruled the land of spirits and dwelled in the east where the sun rose. Recall the Koshares of the Rio Grande pueblos, sacred clowns, divine spirits, living in the east in the house of the sun. Recall the reverse behavior of Maasaw, Hopi ruler of the Land of the Dead, and that of Paiyatemu of the Keresan pueblos, trickster and clown, who carries the sun's shield and plays music on a flute. Recall Paiatuma, the Zuñi god of dew and the dawn, a flute player, who freshens seeds with his breath.

It may be that what we know of the trickster hare from history, folklore, ethnography, and archaeology in the Eastern Woodlands is just one reflection of the deeper, pancontinental mythological background out of which also emerged the sacred clowns of the Southwest and the contraries of the Plains. To this might be added certain attendants at rituals honoring the Mesoamerican god of the hunt, Camaxtli, who painted black circles of soot around their eyes and mouth in the manner of the Koshares and images of Maasaw.[33]

SEASONAL RETURN TO THE PRIMAL ERA

Sam Gill has nicely summarized a pattern of seasonal reversal of behavior exhibited in the traditional culture of the Kwakiutl Indians of the Pacific Northwest coast. For the Kwakiutls summer was a time for hunting and fishing, when families were often dispersed and out of contact. Winter was the time of year when families settled down in their permanent villages and directed their attention to a series of ceremonials:

> During the winter, *the entire order of human existence is reversed.* The people represent another form of being. They take winter names and corresponding experiences and actions to effect and express this reversal. *Winter is the time for return to the primal era* when human beings had animal forms, and the people are organized into animal societies corresponding with varieties of spiritual or mythic beings.[34]

[A] relationship of reciprocity lies beneath the interdependence of human beings and animals. This reciprocity is completed by the role reversal of hunter and game animal as the seasons change. In summer the animals undergo death. In the winter, by means of the Winter

Ceremonial, it is the human beings who descend into darkness and death, thus restoring the animal spirits.[35]

SOCIAL CONTROL AND CONTROL OF FERTILITY

Generalizing from examples such as the foregoing, I see an origin of the antinatural behavior of ritual clowns in the reverse behavior of ritual performers associated in one way or another with the underworld, the land of spirits, the night sky, the sun at night, and winter as the seasonal equivalent of the underworld. I see contrariness in clowning activity as the behavioral equivalent of the oppositions of spirit world and world of the living, earth interior and world above, night and day, mythical time and contemporary time, death and life, winter and summer, wild nature and domestic life, animal nature and human. In the case of the southwestern pueblos, the potential of clowning for social control may have been elaborated hand in hand with the *need* for social controls as large and permanent, socially complex communities evolved, and the clowns *did* manage and police many social events.[36]

The broader associations of those practicing reverse or contrary behavior may, nevertheless, be, or may once have been, with control of fertility in nature. The reputation of a chief or shaman on the Northwest Pacific coast was enhanced, for example, by his perceived ability to intercede with the dead, who were believed to have powers of control over the natural food supply.[37] The underworld is where germination takes place. It is where the spirits of the game dwell until they manifest themselves on the earth's surface, and it is the world in which the sun passes the night before its daily rebirth. Rituals for fertility and world renewal re-created the settings of creation and origins. The fertility associations of the clowns in the southwest ranged from control of weather and management of seasonal rituals to the gross sexual humor of the clowns' antics.

Studying the cult of the dead in Mesoamerica, Hugo Nutini has made some observations that have an important bearing on the possible former pancontinental distribution of belief in the relationship of the dead to human fortunes and fertility in nature. Nutini observes that there were numerous kinds of deaths and as many different afterworlds for persons dying specific deaths—persons who drowned went to the domain of Tlaloc, the rain deity, for instance, and warriors who died in battle accompanied the sun in its journey. He goes on to infer and suggest that "every feast in honor of the gods entailed the cult of their dead servants as a means to achieve the protective, propitiatory, intensifying, or any other aim implicit or explicit in the rites and ceremonies."[38] Especially relevant is the apparent distribution of occasions to honor the dead through the agricultural year such that the dead might act as intercessors with their patron deities at different critical seasons.

Nutini's connections between the cult of the dead and the averting of seasonal crises (drought, hail, frost, and so on) are largely but not entirely inferential. I see the possibility that connections with mourning could have been stronger before the elaboration of the Mesoamerican pattern of human sacrifice, which would have obviated much of the need for seeking the aid of those who had died during warfare or from accidents and natural causes, if that was indeed done. I suggested in chapter 5 that human sacrifice in Mesoamerica as 'scheduled death' could have replaced scheduled mourning for some purposes. I have elsewhere suggested that in the midwestern United States "the introduction of new and corn-related fertility ritual (Green Corn ceremonialism, as an example) could have caused a dissociation of mortuary ritual and mound-associated World Renewal ritual formerly tied to the renewal of nature quite broadly and could have led to the discontinuance of mound burial."[39] The Green Corn ceremony or Busk of the southeastern United States does not contain the element of human sacrifice, as we know the Busk, but the evidence is tantalizing that around A.D. 1000 midwestern Indians of the Early Mississippi period may have had a form of the human sacrifice that in Mexico honored Xilonen, the Green Corn goddess.[40]

I have suggested that the Cheyenne Sun Dance is a survival of the World Renewal aspect of a mound burial ritual once related to mourning the dead. The Cheyenne Sun Dance was originally the possession only of the Suhtais, closely related Algonquian speakers met by the Tsistsistas or original Cheyenne as the latter entered the Plains from a homeland along the Minnesota River. Each group had a certain sacred object: the Suhtais had a buffalo cap and the Tsistsistas, a bundle of four medicine arrows. And each group had an important tribal ceremony: the Suhtais had the Sun Dance and the Tsistsistas, the Massaum or Crazy Dance. This Sun Dance was a World Renewal ceremony that served to renew all of nature by repeating the acts that created the earth at the time of origins (chapter 3). The Massaum was oriented toward hunting and remembering the gift of game animals to two young men for the benefit of the Cheyenne from a mysterious couple dwelling inside a blue mountain who owned and controlled the spirit animals living within the earth.[41]

The Massaum was a reenactment of the story of the two men and the couple in the magic mountain and involved both a symbolic drive of all manner of game animals toward the temporary Massaum lodge and the pretended hunting of the animal impersonators by ritual clowns of the Contrary or Hohnuhka society representing Thunder Spirits. The bodies of these clowns were painted white, and black rings were painted around their eyes and mouths. Fray Diego Durán describes an almost identical sixteenth-century Festival of the Hunt for the provinces of Huexotzinco and Tlaxcala in central Mexico: hunters with white-striped bodies and with black circles around their mouths and eyes drove all manner of real game toward a temporary shrine or "bower" where they killed or captured alive all they could. This was a ritual honoring Camaxtli, their god of the hunt, who was a variant or transformation of the Mesoamerican god also known as the Red Tezcatlipoca and Xipe Totec (chapters 11, 19).[42]

The hunters in the Mesoamerican event are not described as clowns or contraries, but in appearance they must have resembled not only the Cheyenne Contraries in the Massaum but also many of the clowns of the pueblos in the American Southwest. The story of two boys obtaining or releasing game animals from a cave within a mountain is so widespread in the eastern United States that it surely must date back three thousand years or more and to the Archaic period or earlier.[43] This does not mean that the particular ways in which the story elements were used by different tribes all date back that far. We cannot even say if the ritual drives in Mexico had any basis in a similar story.

The animal drive and hunt among the Huezotzincans and Tlaxcalans occurred during the month of Quecholli. The Aztecs also had a ritual animal drive and hunt during Quecholli, an event that honored Mixcoatl, a related deity, and they used the same month to honor their war god and tribal or patron deity Huitzilipochtli and to mourn the dead, placing miniature atlatl darts on their graves.[44]

I do not see the evidence to argue for anything like an ancient pancontinental cult of the dead per se, but there does seem to be reason to believe in a former widespread use of death- or other-world–associated ritual performers characterized by reverse or antinatural behavior with functions originally related to fertility in nature and later to agricultural fertility as farming appeared and became important. And I see the basis for that practice to be the mental association relating the spirit world of humans and the spirit world of plants and animals. Trick fire handling would seem to have once had similar associations.

The public performances of the Wabeno shamans of the Great Lakes area included displays of disdain for fire and hot water and exhibitions of the shaking tent or conjurer's lodge. A less obvious function of the Wabeno shamans was the utilization and transmission of traditional knowledge relating to fertility in nature and the renewal of nature's bounty. As Thor Conway tells us, "The Wabeno were responsible for celestial and lunar time-keeping, using calendar sticks and related notational devices" to direct "a series of seasonal transition rituals [that] occurred at specific intervals, including the solstices and equinoxes . . . duties concerned with the harmonious balance between man, the animate landscape, the spirit world, and the band's food and medicinal resource needs." The Wabeno shaman's lodge not only represented the Pleiades constellation, perceived as the portal to the spirit world above the dome of the night sky, it was also a vehicle that allowed the shaman to travel to that spirit world.[45]

17 / Sleeping, Sleeping, Sleeping on the Hill

EDGAR LEE MASTERS (1869–1950) created a town, a cemetery, and the former citizens of that town who slept in the cemetery. He called the mythical town Spoon River, but he modeled it after two quite real small towns that he knew firsthand—Lewistown in Fulton County and Petersburg in Menard County, Illinois. Petersburg faces the Sangamon River, which flows west to join the Illinois River, and Lewistown lies a short distance from the Spoon River, which flows east to the Illinois. Petersburg was platted in 1836 by a young deputy surveyor named Abraham Lincoln whose home was less than two miles away at New Salem.

Edgar Lee Masters returned his community to life in fiction, but many authors have done that. What Masters did that was unusual was to create his community through the words of its dead citizens, spoken from the grave. Masters put into poetry the thoughts that those dead citizens might have written themselves, as epilogues to their own lives, had they been given the opportunity.

UNCHISELED EPITAPHS

Masters's *Spoon River Anthology* was an anthology of *epitaphs*. There is a cynical thread that unites many of the poems in *Spoon River Anthology*—and an unflattering image of rural, small-town America—but each poem reads as though it could, indeed, express the final thoughts of the character for whom it was meant to be an unchiseled epitaph. No one passes though life expecting to escape the grave, unless in some other form of existence that our beliefs hold out to us. It is very human, however, to want later generations to know, "I was here. I lived. I existed." American Indians often sought to guarantee the memories of honored tribesmen by transferring their names to worthy recipients in later generations, "to keep their names alive."

Nelly Sachs (1891–1970) shared a Nobel Prize for Literature in 1966. Her most serious writing dates to the period after 1940 when she left Germany for Sweden to escape being sent to a forced labor camp as a Jew. One collection of poems written after World War II she titled *Grabschriften in die Luft Geschrieben*—"Epitaphs Written on the Wind." In this title Sachs invokes the image of the smoke from the ovens of the Nazi death camps into which the lives of their victims were transformed.[1] With this smoke were written the epitaphs of the Peddler, the Ballerina, the Puppeteer, and others, but it is Sachs who is speaking, not the victims. The poet addresses each with the familiar *du*. Masters's poems create words for the dead with which they address the living:

Hod Putt

HERE I lie close to the grave
Of Old Bill Piersol,
Who grew rich trading with the Indians, and who
Afterwards took the bankrupt law
And emerged from it richer than ever.
Myself grown tired of toil and poverty
And beholding how Old Bill and others grew in
    wealth,
Robbed a traveler one night near Proctor's Grove,
Killing him unwittingly while doing so,
For the which I was tried and hanged.
That was my way of going into bankruptcy.
Now we who took the bankrupt law in our respective
    ways
Sleep peacefully side by side.[2]

Knowlt Hoheimer

I WAS the first fruits of the battle of Missionary
    Ridge.
When I felt the bullet enter my heart
I wished I had staid at home and gone to jail
For stealing the hogs of Curl Trenary,
Instead of running away and joining the army.
Rather a thousand times the county jail
Than to lie under this marble figure with wings,
And this granite pedestal
Bearing the words, "*Pro Patria*."
What do they mean, anyway?[3]

The Hill

. . . .

Where are Uncle Isaac and Aunt Emily,
And old Towny Kincaid and Sevigne Houghton,
And Major Walker who had talked
With venerable men of the revolution?—
All, all, are sleeping on the hill.

They brought them dead sons from the war,
And daughters whom life had crushed,
And their children fatherless, crying—
All, all are sleeping, sleeping, sleeping on the hill.[4]

. . . .

There have been many other Spoon River residents with no Edgar Lee Masters to put their tortured lives into words and many other victims of genocide with no Nelly Sachs to write their epitaphs in verse. There are, for example, pre-Columbian American Indian cemeteries in the Spoon River country that are next to unknown in literary circles but whose stories are every bit as poignant as those from the graves to which Edgar Lee Masters and Nelly Sachs called attention.

One prehistoric Indian cemetery is preserved on the grounds of what is today called the Dickson Mounds Museum near Lewistown. The Indians buried in this cemetery belong to what archaeologists call the Spoon River tradition, or to the Spoon River variant of the Mississippian tradition. No archaeologist can say, for sure, what language these Spoon River Indians spoke or knows, for sure, who their descendants might be, but these Indians speak to the living in their own way. The Spoon River Indians created this cemetery almost exactly a thousand years ago on a hill overlooking the valleys of the Spoon and Illinois Rivers. Their village was originally at the foot of the hill on a location now called the Eveland site.

In time, as the local Indian community expanded, there came to be about three thousand Indians buried on the hill overlooking the Eveland site as well as additional residential areas. One of these was the Larson site just a mile away, a large permanent village built around a central plaza with a temple elevated upon a platform mound of earth. The whole temple town was surrounded by a log palisade for defense. These were Indians with a 'Mississippian' level of social and political organization, as archaeologists call it. Mississippian towns were organized with stronger central political controls and more pronounced social rankings than those exhibited by the egalitarian tribes found in the Illinois country by the earliest French explorers or at any time later.[5]

The Dickson cemetery has had a very complex history. It was neither a typical mound nor a simple cemetery. A 'mounded cemetery' would be the more accurate term, and this would have been an 'accretional mound', not one constructed in a single season but one built upon and added to as needed to bury the community's dead through the years and from generation to generation. The first burials had been interred in pits excavated for each on the bluff edge overlooking the Eveland village. As time went on, at least ten low burial mounds, sometimes overlapping, were erected over the early cemetery burials; individual burials were intruded into these mounds and into earlier burials; and earth was accumulated over the whole to produce an enormous mound that came to contain about three thousand individuals.[6]

As a young man growing up on his father's farm, Dr. Don Dickson took a professional interest in the Indian burials that for years had attracted the attention of relic hunters to the area. Don Dickson was not an archaeologist or even an anthropologist. His interest was originally primarily medical. He was a chiropractor and unlike others was attracted not so much by the pottery vessels that accompanied the burials as by the pathology that many burials exhibited. Because of the nature of chiropractic procedures, chiropractors have a necessary interest in the human skeleton and in skeletal pathology.

Don Dickson began excavations in the spring of 1927 by exposing several skeletons. Others before him had been interested only in the "grave goods"—the pots, ornaments, and other grave accompaniments. In an earlier time one collector had carted pots away literally by the wagon-load. Visitors to Don Dickson's excavation suggested that he leave the skeletons all in place for others to see—the skeletons and what had been placed in the graves. This he did, and when he uncovered more, Dickson made a temporary shelter over the excavation, and then more, and another shelter. Finally, he built a permanent building to enclose a total of 234 burials, and people came to see the burials. In explaining the exhibit to the public through the years Dickson became an interpreter of prehistoric Indian life in the Spoon River valley.[7]

When the State of Illinois acquired Dickson Mounds in 1945 and designated it a state memorial, the Dicksons became state employees to continue the interpretation program for visitors. Additional excavations were conducted by the Illinois State Museum in 1966–1968 at the Dickson Mounds site but just outside of the area of the Dickson cemetery burial exhibit in anticipation of the construction of the present museum building. I directed the excavations during June of 1967.

Another of these ancient Fulton County cemeteries is that known to archaeologists as the Norris Farms 36 cemetery. It is only about a mile from Dickson Mounds in distance and little more than a century younger in time, but other differences are more dramatic. The

Indians responsible for the Norris Farms 36 site belonged to a midwestern cultural tradition called Oneota. The Indians themselves had no such concept as Oneota. The name Oneota is simply one applied by archaeologists for convenience of reference to certain late prehistoric archaeological cultures that shared a certain level of social and political organization, certain economic adaptations, and certain artifact types and styles of pottery manufacture. These were Indians with a level of tribal organization like that found among Indians of the seventeenth century in Illinois and the Midwest.

The Spoon River Indians and Oneota Indians were partly contemporary and they interacted in recognizable ways. In 1969 and 1970 I directed excavations to salvage information and material from a major late Spoon River temple town located on land leased by a large international corporation for testing earth-moving equipment. This was the Crable site about fourteen miles south of Dickson Mounds. Crable was a large village with a temple mound within a plaza ringed by hundreds of residences that were probably once surrounded in turn by a fortification wall. The evidence of our excavation showed that the houses in the residential area were rebuilt upon the same locations time after time. On one spot we excavated a sequence of six houses and nearby, a sequence of seven houses.[8] Radiocarbon dates indicated that the Crable site village was occupied at least until around A.D. 1400.[9] This may actually have been the last stronghold of Spoon River tradition Indians and, in fact, no village of prehistoric Indians of *any* description has been found in the central Illinois valley that dates more than a generation or two later than Crable.

The Oneota (Norton Farms 36) cemetery delivers a message that almost screams to us from the graves. This was a cemetery that was completely excavated by archaeologists in advance of highway construction and so it is a nearly complete record of life and death among the Indians who cared for it. This record speaks not only of tender love but also of warfare. Of almost three hundred individuals buried in the cemetery the skeletons of fifty show evidence of violent death over a period of years. The message is that of intermittent raids upon the associated Oneota village until the village was abandoned following a final devastating attack that culminated years of stressful insecurity.[10]

Sixteen individuals showed evidence of scalping, as indicated by cutmarks incised in locations on the bone around the crowns of the skulls. Twenty-six additional individuals were buried without heads at all, and of these twenty-six, eleven exhibit cutmarks somewhere on the first four cervical vertebrae, showing that the heads had actually been severed from the spine. These figures would attest to trophies of war being taken from the bodies of forty-two victims without regard to age or sex.

Of the scalped individuals ten were adult females; three were adult males and one an adolescent male; two were children.[11] This scalping dates to a period ending no later than A.D. 1450—a century before de Soto traveled through the southern states and longer still before the settlement of New France, New England, and New Netherlands.[12]

Broken arrowpoints were found in the bodies of several of the Oneota burials—four points in chests or pelvic regions, three in contact with spinal columns, one inside a skull, and two in other bones. There was evidence of stone ax or wooden warclub strikes against the shoulder, chest, face, and arms. The wounds on the arms were probably inflicted while the three victims were trying to protect themselves with their arms from anticipated blows. Some skeletons and parts of skeletons were sun-bleached or gnawed by animals, showing that they had been buried only after lying exposed on the surface for a period of weeks or months.

Examined as life sketches rather than as medical postmortem examinations, such tabulations provide mental snapshots of the personal tragedies of mothers, fathers, wives, husbands, and children whose long-forgotten distress still has the power after more than five centuries to shock and embarrass. I say "embarrass" because many Indians give little thought to the extent of Indian-on-Indian violence in North America before the European alliances that set Indian against Indian, making the occupants of many pre-Columbian graves twice martyred—once by the weapons of their enemies and again by the skepticism of their friends—victims of the myth of an idyllic Indian past.

We can never know their names, but like the dead memorialized by Edgar Lee Masters and Nelly Sachs, death has not erased their memories or identities completely. Burial 200: female, age thirty-five to forty, hand fractured, possibly while trying to ward off the blow of a stone ax, skull crushed with a stone ax, scalped, bones subsequently gnawed by animals, recovered, and buried. Burial 27: female age thirty to thirty-five, scalped, survived scalping, possibly died from infection evidenced in the scalped area. Burial 230: infant age twenty-four to thirty-two months, died from a blow to the head, subsequently scalped. Burial 62: male age thirty to thirty-five, four stone ax blows to the head, two arrows in the chest, two arrows through the back and embedded in the sternum, scalped. Burial 91: female age thirty to forty, healed fracture of the left forearm from an early injury, stone ax wound on the shoulder, cuts on the neck vertebrae, head missing, skeleton gnawed by animals before burial.[13]

None of the Dickson Mounds burials is as late as the period of Oneota intrusion into the Illinois valley. The majority of the Dickson Mounds burials belongs to a period of several generations beginning around A.D.

1250, although the cemetery area had been used for as much as a century and a half before that time. Two-thirds of the original total of an estimated three thousand burials were exposed and reburied elsewhere during various earth-moving operations as the Dickson farm was developed a century ago. Of the rest, the 234 of the burial exhibit even today remain where they have lain for over seven hundred years.

Unlike the skeletons found in 1984 at the Oneota cemetery, the skeletons that Dr. Dickson exposed in place for viewing showed little unambiguous evidence of violent death—no evidence of scalping or decapitation for trophy taking in war, no arrow wounds, and only one possible injury from an ax or warclub. This does not mean that there were no threats; Mississippian towns were typically well fortified for defense. The absence of skeletal evidence of violence suggests only that such external threats must have been contained, perhaps by some social mechanism. The danger was surely there, and one skull from the mound found before 1927 exhibited two ax wounds and evidence of scalping. The more common pathology in the Dickson cemetery was that which appears normally in human populations and that many persons can relate to from their own personal life experiences—osteoarthritis, osteomyelitis, osteoporosis, and healed fractures of ribs, arms, and legs.[14]

PERSONALITIES INTERLOCKED BY FATE

Much of the success of the Dickson Mounds Museum operation from 1927 through the 1960s can be attributed to the personally guided interpretation of the burial exhibit by members of the Dickson family. Using examples in the burial exhibit the Dicksons were able to convey the picture of pre-Columbian Indians as human beings who lived in families, loved, laughed, cried, prayed, and believed in a divine creator and an afterlife, and for many white visitors to Dickson Mounds this came as an unexpected revelation. A public interest that had begun as simple curiosity, perhaps even originally as a morbid curiosity, was transformed by the Dicksons for many into understanding and empathy.

In the year 1964 visitors from fifty-six countries received the Dickson family's personally delivered message at the Dickson Mounds State Memorial, but this was the last year anyone could hear it from Don Dickson himself. Dickson died on July 5, 1964. On July 1 of the following year the property was transferred from the control of the Illinois Department of Conservation, Division of Parks and Memorials, to the Illinois State Museum. Twenty-five years later, in 1989, the board of the Illinois State Museum made the decision to close the burial exhibit. The reasons were rapidly diminishing

for maintaining an exhibit of Indian skeletons of this sort when balanced against the express wishes of Native Americans across the country who found displays of this kind racist and disrespectful. I do not question that this was the right action for the museum board to take.

The closing of the burial exhibit was vigorously opposed by residents of the area and was subsequently disapproved by Governor Jim Thompson. American Indians and non-Indian sympathizers then converged on Dickson Mounds to demand that the burial display be closed, as the museum board originally wished, but the final decision to close the display was not made until a new administration was in the Springfield statehouse. An arrangement was eventually negotiated by Thompson's successor Jim Edgar that reconciled as nearly as possible the interests of the museum, the Indians, and area residents. The burial exhibit was closed and sealed and additional exhibits created that emphasized aspects of American Indian spirituality. The refurnished museum opened to the public September 18, 1994.[15]

The resistance of Spoon River area residents to the closing of the Dickson Mounds cemetery exhibit is easy for someone living in the area to understand. For generations, for white inhabitants within an hour's drive of Lewistown, the only firsthand knowledge and contact with any Native American population that they had ever experienced was that which they had had as adults or schoolchildren visiting the Dickson Mounds. There have been no Indians living as a community in the Illinois valley in this century and few even during the last century and a half. For the modern inhabitants of the Spoon River area, the Dickson Mounds Indians were 'our Indians'. When the time came to express their opinions on closing the cemetery exhibit, the modern inhabitants of Edgar Lee Masters's Spoon River sided strongly with the only Indians with whom they had ever had personal contacts—Don Dickson's Indians—rather than with the living Indians who came as strangers, Indians whom they had never seen before and never expected to see again. Indian protesters saw the Dickson Mounds burial exhibit as, at best, the tasteless commercial exploitation of an Indian cemetery to capitalize on the morbid curiosity of tourists.

"One thing about the bone show, though," wrote James Krohe Jr. in Chicago's *Reader*, "it's the truth. After lifetimes of seeing movie Indians played by Jews and Italians and wooden Indians in cigar stores and contemporary Indians who disobligingly dress like cowboys or truck drivers, at Dickson Mounds people saw their first real Indians." Krohe continued:

My own experience has been that the lesson most visitors draw from the graves is not the vanity of Man but the humanness of the Indian. I recall my first sight of the Dickson Mounds burials, more than 20 years ago. I had seen plenty of Indian artifacts before, in conventional museums. Rather than establish a kinship, all those stone axes and beaded garb merely confirmed my sense that their authors were backward and impossibly distant from late-20th-century technological sophisticates like myself. My house may be manifestly superior in every way to their houses, but looking at the Dickson Mounds dead I saw that their bones are my bones. They look no different in their graves than I will look in mine. The vestiges of ceremony still visible speak of sentiments common to anyone who knows what it is to love and respect other humans. Speaking for myself—a deracinated sixth-generation German American—the graves made these people truly human for the first time.

None of this, I realize, relieves the exhibit of taint. Modern Native Americans are not much concerned with how educated whites learn about life or choose their careers—though the testimonials of various archaeologists suggest that any imputation of ridicule or racism is exaggerated, if not imagined. The dismaying fact that it takes something like a Dickson Mounds to remind white people that Indians are human too should be blamed on the living, not the dead.[16]

Edgar Lee Masters began *Spoon River Anthology* in 1914 by writing "The Hill" and then almost at once conceived the idea of portraying a total community by sketching the fortunes and misfortunes of its individual citizens. "Why not," he said, "put side by side the stories of two characters interlocked in fate, thus giving both misunderstood souls a chance to be justly weighed?"[17] Today, the Dicksons themselves lie sleeping on the hill, and the Indians whom Don Dickson roused from seven centuries of sleep have returned to their own slumber. For better or worse, in death as in life, the stories of the Dicksons and the Indians of Dickson Mounds are forever interlocked.

18 / Long-Nosed Gods

MANY AMERICAN INDIAN AUTHORS have contributed to our century's knowledge of Indian culture history, but few readers may be aware that the first American Indian author to write a history of events in any part of the United States did so years before the Mayflower sailed into Cape Cod Bay. What he wrote was very nearly contemporary history, compiled from the words of participants in Hernando de Soto's military expedition through the Gulf states in the years 1539 to 1543. The author of whom I speak, who styled himself 'The Inca', provided readers with vivid descriptions of the temple mound–building cultures of the Southeast in a climactic phase of their development and wrote with a sensitivity to cultural values that puts to shame the efforts of all but a scant few historians of later times. His English translators, John Grier Varner and Jeannette Johnson Varner, describe Garcilaso de la Vega as "the first American to attain pre-eminence in literature."[1]

THE FLORIDA OF THE INCA

Garcilaso de la Vega, El Inca, was born in Cuzco, Peru, April 12, 1539, the natural son of a Spanish conquistador, Don Sebastián Garcilaso de la Vega Vargas, and Chimpa Ocllo, niece of the Inca emperor Huayna Capac. Baptized Gómez Suárez de Figueroa, Garcilaso assumed the name Garcilaso de la Vega after he had won a reputation of his own in Spain, fighting as an officer of the Spanish king, and added the epithet El Inca to complement his authorial name when he wrote the two works for which he is best known, *La Florida del Inca*, published in Lisbon in 1605, and his *Historia General del Perú* or *Comentarios Reales*, published in Lisbon in 1609 (part 1) and Cordoba in 1616 (part 2).

Although Garcilaso wrote as a narrative historian describing the actions of others, he did not submerge his authorial presence and American Indian identity. He informed his readers from the start that he felt "under obligation to two races . . . [being] the son of a Spanish father and an Indian mother" and implied that

any merit readers recognized in his works would honor, through him, "all of the mestizo Indians and creoles of Peru."[2] Garcilaso did nothing to conceal admiration for his paternal heritage of Roman Catholicism and European learning, but neither did he hesitate to inform readers of the gallantry, intelligence, and native abilities exhibited by the Indians among whom de Soto's party traveled in the Southeast:

> The companions and friends of Francisco de Aguilar were amazed at what they heard, for they had never dreamed that the Indians were inclined to be so chivalrous as to want to fight singly with the Castilians when they could attack at an advantage [of numbers].[3]

> [The Indian] men and women whom our soldiers had seized for their services, regardless of what province they came from, . . . within two months after they had been speaking with Spaniards, . . . comprehended what their masters said to them in Castilian, and . . . were able to make themselves understood in this same language when they talked of things necessary and common to all. Furthermore, when they had been with the Spaniards for six months, they served as interpreters between their masters and strange Indians. All of the inhabitants of this great kingdom of Florida disclosed this same skill in language and in anything else that they considered worthwhile.[4]

> [T]he facts of history demand that we narrate the brave deeds of the Indians as well as those of the Spaniards, and that we not do injury to either race by recounting the valiant achievements of one by omitting those of the other, but instead tell all things as they occurred and in their proper time and place.[5]

RANKED SOCIETIES IN THE SOUTHEAST

The Indian nations among whom de Soto traveled were the most advanced in North America from the standpoint of political organization and much else. They could be compared to city-states governed by all-powerful hereditary rulers who would have been known as princes had the seats of their authority been located in France or Italy during the same century. To de Soto and his followers they were known as *caciques*, and *cacicas* when women, terms that entered the Castilian language from that of Indians met by Spaniards in the Antilles two generations earlier.

De Soto encountered the cacique and province of Capaha near the Mississippi River in present-day Arkansas. The principal town of Capaha contained five hundred large houses, from which one may estimate that the population could have easily numbered twenty-five hundred, and perhaps twice that. It was surrounded by a moat forty to fifty feet wide that was supplied with water from the Mississippi directed to the town by an artificial canal three leagues long, three fathoms deep, and "so wide that two large canoes went down and came up it side-by-side without the oars of one touching those of the other." This canal was dug in such a way that it protected three sides of the town, the fourth side being defended by a palisade of timbers set in the ground, plastered with clay daub strengthened with grass, penetrated by loopholes for the use of its defenders, and defended as well from bastions or towers constructed at intervals along the wall.[6]

When de Soto entered the Capaha capital, he had been preceded by the cacique Casquin of another Indian province accompanied by a force of armed men. De Soto himself sought no conflict, but benefiting from the advantage of his temporary association with de Soto, Casquin deceived de Soto and sacked the town. He directed his warriors to desecrate the Capaha temple, which, from what we know of other towns of that time and area, would have been located on a high earthen platform or truncated pyramid within or adjacent to the plaza (chapter 2). In any case, the Casquins threw to the ground the chests containing the bones of the ancestors of the cacique Capaha found in the temple, removed from lances set at the temple door the heads of Casquins stuck on them as trophies, and replaced them with the heads of Capaha dwellers killed when the Casquins entered the town. For whatever reason, most of the inhabitants of Capaha had abandoned their capital before de Soto's arrival, allowing the Casquins to kill and behead or scalp 150 Capaha men and take captive a number of women and children.[7]

We may infer from circumstantial evidence that the cacique Capaha inherited his office. He is described as a young man of twenty-six or twenty-seven years, which alone suggests that he did not acquire his position of leadership from many years of experience in council or on the war path, and the bones preserved in the temple sepulchres were said to have been those of his ancestors. The pattern of social and political organization described or implied in the Spanish accounts of the southeastern chiefdoms was of the ranked or stratified type inferred by archaeologists for many cultures of the Mississippi period in the Mississippi, Illinois, Ohio, Arkansas, and Tennessee valleys, and in the Gulf states from Georgia to Texas and described by the French for the historic Natchez tribe of colonial Louisiana.

Natchez children were born into one or the other of two social divisions—the Suns and the Stinkards—much as an Osage or Winnebago was born into a tribal half associated either with the sky or with the earth and water. And, like an Osage or Winnebago, a Natchez youth was obliged to marry someone of the opposite half. There were, however, important differences. The Suns comprised an elite social division, and the Stinkard spouse of a Sun expected to be put to death on the day of burial of the Sun husband's, or Sun wife's, burial. Also, because descent was reckoned in the female line, the children of a Sun woman were also Suns, but not those of a Sun man.[8] There was no such favoritism given to either tribal half among the Osage and the Winnebagoes, and descent for them was patrilineal, i.e., reckoned in the male line. The leader of the Natchez was called the Great Sun, and the title was hereditary but passed not to the Great Sun's son but to a sister's son in accordance with matrilineal rules of descent.[9]

The principal temple of the Natchez was described by Simon Antoine Le Page du Pratz from his acquaintance with the Natchez in the period of 1718–1734. It was built on an earthen mound about eight feet high with the building itself said to measure about thirty feet square with walls ten feet high constructed of logs set vertically in the earth and plastered with mud. These walls supported a roof along whose ridgepole were mounted three large wooden birds facing east. On the inside a wall divided the temple into two parts. As described, the temple would appear to have faced east with a door opening into a room containing the sacred hearth and fire of the nation and a bench four feet high, two wide, and six long, on which was placed a basket of woven canes containing the bones of the most recently deceased Great Sun.[10]

I call the reader's attention to these details because they are part of the basis for inferring, as archaeologists do, that the leaders of ranked societies in the Southeast during the Mississippi period acquired their authority by descent from previous leaders and that this relationship was symbolized by the mortuary aspect of the temple. Mounds of the Woodland period were long considered to be simply burial mounds, but some may have figured importantly in World Renewal ceremonies (chapter 3). Many mounds of the Mississippi period were temple mounds, but the importance of the mortuary aspect of those mounds cannot be minimized, and the rekindling of the sacred fire in the temple was itself a World

Renewal ceremony. The distinction is even further diminished when one considers that some mound-related World Renewal rituals during the Woodland period may have involved adoption as a mechanism to transfer leadership from the deceased to his successor. The distinction is diminished further still when one considers that adoption may have provided a mechanism not only for Hopewellian interactions but for some Mississippian interactions as well, as we will now see.

LONG-NOSED GODS

When I saw it I could hardly believe my eyes, or my good fortune to have been there to see it—a painting of two round eyes within a moon-white face staring out from a hole in a tree trunk. I was in the home of Oscar Howe, the University of South Dakota's highly respected Nakota artist and my former colleague at the university. Still not believing my luck, I asked Oscar what the face represented in his painting. He explained that it was a kind of wood spirit that appears in some Sioux folktales. Feeling rather smug about my own familiarity with the face, I said, "But how did you come to represent the wood spirit with that particular face?" "Well," he replied, "it's really just a small shell mask I happened to see on exhibit in the Stovall Museum." *Of course*, I thought to myself. *How stupid of me! Oscar attended the University of Oklahoma. Why wouldn't he be familiar with the displays at the Stovall?* "Oh, then you know," I said, quite chagrined. "The Long-Nosed God. No one is sure what it represents. Some may be almost a thousand years old. I thought I was just about to learn some secret of the ages from your painting." "You just did," he replied. "You just did. No one else knows where I got the idea for the face."

It was 1956 when Stephen Williams and John Goggin published their definitive paper on the Long-Nosed God mask in the eastern United States. The masks had been known for some time, found here and there throughout the eastern United States from Missouri to Florida, but no one before had characterized their time and place in culture history in as great detail. The consensus was that they must have once related somehow to "an integrated complex spreading across the eastern United States, with the Long Nosed God as its figurehead" within the Mississippi period but preceding what came to be known as the Southeastern Ceremonial Complex (earlier known as the Buzzard Cult or Southern Cult), which was virtually an illustrated catalog of icons of the high cultures of the northern Mississippi valley and southeastern United States around A.D. 1250-1350.[11] The story of marine shell Long-Nosed God mask earrings and their copper counterparts illustrates very well the protracted period of gestation preceding the birth of some archaeological

brainchildren and the value of maintaining collections and records accessible to future generations:

1869. Needing fill to extend its roadbed in St. Louis, the North Missouri Railroad purchases the earth from the Big Mound, a large prehistoric mound of Mississippian construction located northeast of the corner of Broadway and Mound streets. Within months all that is left of the Big Mound is the name Mound Street and St. Louis's nickname of Mound City.[12]

1870. T. T. Richards writes in the *American Naturalist* mentioning the finding of certain copper objects behind the ears of the bigger of two Indians found buried three feet below the summit of the Big Mound at its north end. Dr. Wills De Hass sends photographs of these ear ornaments to F. W. Putnam, editor of *American Naturalist*. The photographs will many years later be discovered by Stephen Williams in the collections of the Peabody Museum, Harvard University.[13]

1877. Henry R. Howland mentions the find of the copper ear ornaments from the Big Mound in an article in the *Bulletin of the Buffalo Society of Natural Science*. This article will many years later come to the attention of James B. Griffin, who will suspect that certain "spoon-like" copper ornaments mentioned were like the copper objects described by Clarence B. Moore and Clarence Webb (below).[14]

1883. In a report on shell art of ancient America appearing in the *Second Annual Report of the Bureau of American Ethnology*, W. H. Holmes illustrates a small shell mask made of shell found in a cave at Mussel Shoals, Alabama.[15]

1894. Clarence B. Moore finds two copper ear ornaments near the base of the Grant Mound, a large burial mound near Jacksonville, Florida, whose excavation is reported in the *Journal of the Academy of Natural Sciences of Philadelphia*.[16]

1933. Samuel Barrett illustrates a pair of copper masks found by him at the Aztalan site, Jefferson County, Wisconsin, in a report of his excavations appearing as a volume of *Bulletin of the Public Museum of the City of Milwaukee*.[17]

1939. Clarence H. Webb and Monroe Dodd Jr. describe and illustrate two copper earrings found at the Gahagan site, De Soto Parish, Louisiana, in an article in the *Texas Archaeological and Paleontological Society Bulletin*. The authors recognize that the earrings have counterparts in earlier discoveries in shell and copper (above) and comment on the distribution of these finds.[18]

1942. Bernard V. Beadle reports and illustrates in *The Minnesota Archaeologist* a small shell mask found on the Diamond Bluff site, Pierce County, Wisconsin.[19]

1946. In a synoptic article on eastern United States prehistory appearing in *Papers of the R. S. Peabody Foundation for Archaeology*, James B. Griffin comments on the distribution and associations of shell and copper Long-Nosed God earrings.[20]

1947. Fred E. Lawshe describes and illustrates the Diamond

Bluff shell mask in a report on the site for *The Minnesota Archaeologist.*[21]

1952. In a report on the Spiro Mound in Oklahoma appearing in *The Missouri Archaeologist* Henry W. Hamilton illustrátes the so-called Big Boy pipe that is in the form of a sculptured male seated cross-legged and wearing earrings in the form of human heads.[22]

1952. In a report on space and time perspectives in Florida archaeology appearing in *Yale University Publications in Anthropology* John M. Goggin lists the occurrence of copper or shell maskettes at six sites and discusses their associations.[23]

1956. Stephen Williams and John M. Goggin publish a comprehensive study of the history and associations of discoveries of copper and marine shell Long-Nosed God earrings in an issue of the *The Missouri Archaeologist.*[24]

1961. In a comment in *American Antiquity* James B. Griffin and Dan F. Morse illustrate a copper-covered wooden Short-Nosed God mask from the Emmons site in Fulton County, Illinois, and a shell Long-Nosed God maskette from a nearby bluff.[25]

1966. Gregory Perino illustrates a pair of shell Long-Nosed God earrings found in St. Clair County, Illinois, in an article on shell ornaments in the *Central States Archaeological Journal.*[26]

1968. In a report to *American Antiquity* Charles J. Bareis and William M. Gardner describe three Long-Nosed God earrings found by local residents in Mound 3 of the Yokem site in Pike County, Illinois, and mention a pair of maskettes found by a collector in the neck region of a burial at the Crable site in Fulton County, Illinois.[27]

1971. In the *Illinois Archaeological Survey Bulletin* Perino reports the finding of a Long-Nosed God mask on the floor of a charnel house in Mound 1 of the Yokem site and also reports radiocarbon ages, uncalibrated, of 760 ± 110 years B.P. for the charnel structure in Mound 3 and 520 ± 100 years B.P. for a charnel structure in Mound 2. These dates would be consistent with a calibrated age somewhere around A.D. 1300.[28]

1974. Illuminated by the beam of his flashlight, a series of paintings are discovered by a schoolboy, Dean Dax, on the wall of what will later become known as the Gottschall site in Iowa County, Wisconsin.[29]

1975. Alan D. Harn reports in *The Wisconsin Archeologist* the discovery of half of a Long-Nosed God maskette found while conducting salvage excavations on the grounds of the Dickson Mounds Museum, Fulton County, Illinois.[30]

1978. Word of the Gottschall site paintings comes to the attention of a summer resident of Iowa County who takes flash photographs of the rock art and shows them to Robert J. Salzer of Beloit College.[31]

1980. Duane C. Anderson describes in the *Iowa Archaeological Society Newsletter* a Long-Nosed God maskette found in northwestern Iowa.[32]

1982. Salzer begins the first of nine seasons of excavations in the Gottschall site, a shallow cave or rockshelter in Iowa County, Wisconsin, whose walls contain painted figures, one of whom Robert L. Hall identifies as a son of the Winnebago mythical hero Red Horn, a.k.a. He-who-wears-human-heads-as-earrings, who Hall believes figured in the mythology behind Long-Nosed God earrings.[33]

1987. Salzer publishes descriptions of the Gottschall site cave and its art in *The Wisconsin Archeologist* and *Wisconsin Academy Review.*[34]

1989. In a chapter of *The Southeastern Ceremonial Complex* (ed. Patricia Galloway) Hall relates Long-Nosed God maskettes to Red Horn as He-who-wears-human-heads-as-earrings and comments on the possible relationship of the Long-Nosed God theme to the bilobed arrow of the later Southeastern Ceremonial Complex and to a much older flute-nosed character engraved on a bone found in Mound 25 of the Hopewell type site in Ohio.[35]

1990. While searching for examples of rock art in eastern Missouri, Carol Diaz-Granados Duncan discovers on the wall of a cave the painting of a human with its face marked with parallel vertical lines and wearing white Long-Nosed God earrings.[36]

1991. In a chapter of *Cahokia and the Hinterlands* (eds. Thomas E. Emerson and R. Barry Lewis) Hall shows how Long-Nosed God earrings could have figured in an Early Mississippian adoption ritual that served as part of the mechanism of the Cahokia Interaction, as Calumet ceremonialism may have done for the Oneota Interaction.[37]

1992. Salzer's excavations at Gottschall climax with the discovery of a remarkable human head sculptured in sandstone, ten inches high, the face marked with parallel, vertical, blue lines, which lends support to Salzer's belief that the rockshelter may have served as a shrine for a cult or sodality related to the Winnebago hero Red Horn.[38]

HE-WHO-WEARS-HUMAN-HEADS-AS-EARRINGS

He-who-wears-human-heads-as-earrings belongs in the category of semidivine Winnebago culture heroes, along with Trickster, Turtle, Hare, Bladder, and the Twins. Paul Radin distinguishes between such 'heroes' and true 'spirits' such as Earthmaker, Disease Giver, Morning Star, Evening Star, Sun, Moon, Earth, the Night Spirits, the Thunderbirds, Cardinal Directions, and Water Spirits. What Radin calls heroes were semidivine, or at least had special powers, and in the case of Hare and Turtle were said to have possibly been deities that became demoted, as it were, and lost much of their divinity as the canon of Winnebago oral tradition came down to Radin's day.[39]

The Winnebago distinguished between a sacred story, or *waikan*, which dealt with the period of the creation and with divine beings and the semidivine heroes, and a *worak*, which dealt largely with the familiar world and told of the activities of human beings. A *waikan* could not be told when the snakes were above ground, which meant that they could only be told during the winter months.[40] The *worak* was a tale that could be told at any time and typically ended tragically, which a *waikan* story never did. The latter dealt, after all, with immortal beings.

The hero of one sacred Winnebago story was He-who-is-hit-with-deer-lungs. This character was the youngest of ten brothers and figures in a Cinderella-like episode within a longer cycle of stories.[41] In this episode He-who-is-hit-with-deer-lungs alone of the brothers must stay at home while his brothers are out hunting bear and deer, and he alone of the ten is not allowed to participate in a race whose winner will be given the hand of the chief's daughter in marriage. As one might anticipate, He-who-is-hit-with-deer-lungs tags along and wins the race, in great part because he is able to transform himself into an arrow and shoot himself along the course. He declares himself too young to marry, however, and offers his would-be bride to his next older brother, who similarly declines and offers her to the next older until finally the oldest of the ten accepts her and marries her.

The next day Kunu, the oldest brother, goes out to hunt and returns with a deer. When dressing the deer he set the lungs aside and his new wife throws them at the little brother because that was what she understood her husband always did to his little brother and how he acquired his name. There follows a discussion about this unfeeling behavior and finally He-who-is-hit-with-deer-lungs speaks up: "'Those in the heavens who created me did not call me by this name He-who-is-hit-with-deer-lungs. They called me He-who-wears-human-heads-as-earrings.' With that he spat upon his hands and began fingering his ears. And as he did this, little faces suddenly appeared on his ears, laughing, winking and sticking out their tongues. Then he spoke again, 'Those on earth, when they speak of me, call me Red Horn.' With this he spat upon his hands, and drew them over his hair which then became very long and red."[42]

Red Horn is sought after by many Winnebago maidens and finally accepts and marries a poor orphan girl who lives outside the village near the dump pile. This is a girl who wears a white beaver skin as a wrap, a sign, Radin felt, that her character may have once been more divine than it was represented to be.[43] Other incidents follow with abundant and colorful detail given to a lacrosse game between Red Horn's village and a challenging team of giants. The giants are defeated, placed in four circles, each of which is destroyed in their turn by lightning bolts from the war club of Red Horn's companion Storms-as-he-walks, a thunderbird. All the giants are destroyed except a female giant with red hair who fell in love with Red Horn and took him on during the game as her special challenge. The red-haired giant thus becomes Red Horn's second wife.

For attentive readers this story should start to have a familiar ring. Red Horn leads his team in defeating the giants, who are placed in four circles that are destroyed one at a time, and then marries the woman who is the champion of the giants' team. This recalls the story of the red-colored Skiri Pawnee Morning Star defeating the beasts guarding the four quarters of the earth, an act represented in the ritual of the Morning

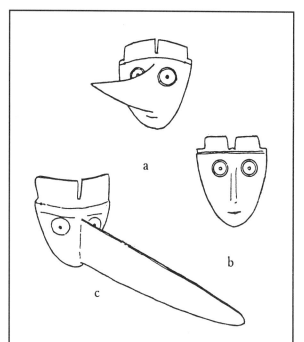

Figure 18.1 Long-Nosed God earrings. These maskettes were made both of shell (*a–b*) and copper (*c*) during the Early Mississippi period and are known to have been used as earrings, giving rise to the belief that the wearers had been given a ritual identity with a supernatural being such as that known to the Winnebago and Iowa as He-who-wears-human-heads-as-earrings: *a*, from the Yokem site, Pike Co., Illinois, after Bareis and Gardner (1968, fig. 2*a*); *b*, short-nosed variant, from the Yokem site, after Perino (1971, fig. 73*c*); *c*, from the Gahagan Mound, Arkansas, after Williams and Goggin (1956, fig. 12*a*).

Star sacrifice (chapter 11) by the destruction of four circles, and then marrying Evening Star. Radin felt that Red Horn was "almost certainly the earthly manifestation of either the evening- or the morning-star."[44]

Red Horn and his fellow villagers subsequently have other contests with the race of giants and defeat them in distance shooting, dice, and staying under the water but are finally defeated at wrestling and put to death. Meanwhile, Red Horn's two wives have become pregnant and given birth to boys, half-brothers, whose lives were spared by the giants. The woman with the white beaver skin wrap gave birth to a boy who was the image of his father with long red hair and little human heads hanging from his ears. The red-haired giant gave birth to a boy with long red hair but with human heads attached to his nipples rather than to his ears.

I had some difficulty viewing in my mind's eye the son with the human heads on his nipples until July 30, 1982, when I received a letter from Robert Salzer of Beloit College enclosing drawings of paintings on the wall of the Gottschall rockshelter in Iowa County, Wisconsin. He asked for my comments. I gave a quick reply the same day telling him that I thought one of the characters was a son of Red Horn or He-who-wears-human-heads-as-earrings. The next day I wrote:

> The character in your Fig. 4 has a pattern around each nipple which resembles the long-nose god maskettes. The face[s] of the maskettes are of the same outline as that found around each nipple on the pictograph. I first interpreted the two parallel lines above the "face" outline as the red horn. I now feel that they represent the long nose of the long-nosed god in a face-on perspective which the artists could not quite handle. That leaves the nipples for the mouth and tongue, and remember that the little faces stuck out their tongues when manipulated. The stone Big Boy pipe from Spiro had long-nose god maskettes on each ear, and I would guess that is what Red Horn also wore on his ears and was the reason he was called He-who-wears-human-heads-as-earrings.[45]

An intriguing point is that the nipples when excited would have become tumescent and, in effect, provide a tongue sticking out from the face tattooed on the breasts, as the story said it should. The cycle of stories continues with considerable detail given to an episode in which the two half-brothers encounter the giants in their village, defeat them, and return with the bones of their father and all his friends. These bones they grind into a fine powder, distribute through various lodges in their village, and magically return to life, providing joyful reunions.

While this story is valuable in itself, it becomes even more valuable when compared with related stories, such as a version collected by Alanson Skinner among the Iowas, close cultural relatives of the Winnebagoes.[46] In the Iowa story Waⁿkx!istowi, a man with human head earrings, was the youngest of ten brothers, as in the Winnebago version, and wins a race around the world, as in the Winnebago version, but the race is against the giants rather than for the hand of the chief's daughter. The defeated giants are slain by Human-head-earrings, assisted by his friends Turtle and Blackhawk. Human-head-earrings then moves on with his two friends, like a small troop of knights-errant, and finds himself at a

place where the local villagers are being tormented by a race of bears. Human-head-earrings, Turtle, and Blackhawk lead the villagers in a lacrosse match against the bears, defeat them in a game played on ice, and put the losers to death—these are the rules of the sport as the bears play it—except, by implication, for a she-bear who was particularly attracted to Human-head-earrings.

In the Iowa story, as it was told to Skinner, Human-head-earrings had a son whose mother is not identified, but because the son had a human head earring on his chest, the son corresponds to that of the red-haired giant in the Winnebago story, whose son had earrings on his chest, and the role of the she-bear during the lacrosse game in the Iowa version corresponds to that of the female giant in the Winnebago version. The presence of a single human head 'earring' on the chest of the son is a story element that does requires some explanation. Understand that about seven hundred years had elapsed between the time that Long-Nosed God earrings were in current use and the time that Skinner collected the Iowa story. The story as recorded probably reflects the later history of Red Horn in Iowa-Winnebago oral tradition. One archaeological expression of this later version would seem to be a certain shell mask gorget or pendant found around 1945 by Dale Henning in Allamakee County, Iowa, with an Oneota burial of historic age. James Collins regards this shell mask gorget to be an evolved form of the shell maskette earrings of the Early Mississippi period, the human face of the earring becoming transformed into a pendant representing a human face.[47]

In the Iowa version the two boy companions are not half-brothers, the sons of He-who-wears-human-heads-as-earrings, but the sons of Human-head-earrings and his friend Blackhawk who would seem to correspond to the thunderbird Storms-as-he-walks in the Winnebago story. Human-head-earrings, Turtle, and Blackhawk are killed by the giants with whom they engage in a wrestling contest and lose, and their heads are cut off and hung up as trophies by the giants. At about age eleven the two young boys inquire of their mothers about their fathers and learn of their fates. They seek out the giants, communicate with their deceased fathers, cause the giants to die spitting blood, return home with the heads of Human-head-earrings, Turtle, and Blackhawk, and magically return them to life.

The Iowa story ends with a moral, as the narrator explains: "Human-head-earrings was only a man like the rest of us, but he said that when he died his little heads should live always. So now when we die the little person invisible to us that dwells in us (the soul) goes to the other world."[48] Put into a more contemporary setting, this conclusion has the elements of a pilot for a television series, introducing the characters and plot elements and raising our expectations for what may follow if the series is picked up by a network—"He said that when he died his little heads should live always." I read the line as an indication that the human head earrings came to figure in a ritual for which the story was the charter myth. It is true enough that human head earrings in the form of Long-Nosed God maskettes appeared over much of the eastern United States. We may make an educated guess at what the ritual may have been.

THE CAHOKIA AND ONEOTA INTERACTIONS

Storms-as-he-walks's destruction of the four circles followed by Red Horn's marriage to the giant has a parallel in the ritual of the Skiri Morning Star sacrifice and to some extent in the Ponca Sun Dance, as mentioned in chapter 11, and lies in the background of Calumet ceremonies of the Hako type. The capture, death, and requickening of adoptees in Calumet ceremonies more generally parallel the capture, death, and requickening of He-who-wears-human-heads-as-earrings in the Winnebago and Iowa stories. He-who-wears-human-heads-as-earrings dies and is returned to life, and how is this done?

In the Winnebago version the bones of He-who-wears-human-heads-as-earrings and those of his dead friends are gathered and ground to a powder by the two half-brothers. In the Iowa version the two boys put the heads of Human-head-earrings and his two friends on the earth and shoot three arrows into the air, after which the owners of the three heads come to life. This recalls the use of the symbolic gesture with arrows—the calumets—to mediate the reconception of the adoptee in the Hako ceremony (chapter 7). More important, it recalls the third name by which Red Horn or He-who-wears-human-heads-as-earrings was known—He-who-is-hit-with-deer-lungs—because the owl feathers attached to the calumets represented deer lungs. The calumet stems represented windpipes as well as arrow shafts, and the combination of windpipe and lungs was believed to introduce a quickening breath into the nose of the adoptee that then descended into his chest and gave him life. Logically, the name He-who-is-hit-with-deer-lungs could derive from a ritual in which an impersonator of He-who-wears-human-heads-as-earrings was symbolically requickened with the calumets.

What I believe is that the Long-Nosed God maskettes may have functioned in the Early Mississippi period of the eastern United States within an adoption ritual much like that of the Calumet ceremony of the Historic period. The difference I see is that the Calumet ceremony served to create bonds of kinship between persons of roughly equal social status, while the maskettes could have functioned within a ritual to create fictions of kinship between the powerful leader of a large polity and his political clients in outlying areas.[49] In historic times in the Plains and Mississippi valley, adoption was used, in the form of the Calumet Ceremony, to extend bonds of kinship to important persons in other villages or tribes and was the basis for an interband trade network whose nature and history Donald Blakeslee has well documented.[50] One would not expect such an egalitarian basis for political alliances in a ranked Mississippian society like Cahokia or even smaller, outlying temple towns such as Aztalan in Wisconsin. Radin has noted that the Winnebago society portrayed in the story of Red Horn was one that appeared to have well-developed ranking, quite unlike the Winnebago as they have been known through the past three centuries.[51]

How exactly does one recognize hereditary status in an archaeological context? One clue is differences in the nature of burials, which usually means the quantity and quality of goods accompanying the body. The high-status burial in Mound 72 at the Cahokia site is a good example.[52] Not only were there great quantities of valuable objects buried with the deceased, including quivers of arrows from half a thousand miles away, but he was also accompanied in death by the bodies of others who may have been killed to provide servants along the spirit trail. Retainer sacrifice is documented both by archaeology and historical record for the Natchez. Le Page du Pratz had the unusual opportunity to have known wives, household servants, and others who were strangled to accompany the brother of the Great Sun in death in 1725. Aside from a detailed description of the funeral itself, Le Page du Pratz provides clues to the endurance of the practice. The men who served as executioners were exempted thereby from being executed themselves upon the death of any other Sun and were raised in rank to boot.[53]

The story of Burial 197 at the Norton Farm 36 Oneota cemetery (chapter 17) is another case in point. Few stories allow us to penetrate the very soul of those Oneota villagers as well as that of Burial 197. This was a three-to-nine-month-old infant buried as though held within the grasp of a pair of adult human hands—the hands alone. This was not a child buried with an adult. There was just a pair of skeletal human hands with the infant nestled between them. Other things were found in the same grave—a shell bead bracelet, a strand of beads, and a set of hawk legs—but nothing that would explain the hands.[54] We can infer, however, that the hands had some special symbolic value.

Gene Weltfish has said of the Pawnees that when "a chiefly infant was born to two high-ranking parents, he was wrapped in a wildcat skin symbolizing the heavens with its panoply of stars and planets."[55] Knowing these things—knowing that a chiefly child might be cradled on birth in a wildcat skin, knowing that the starry night sky had a metaphor in the spotted fur of a wildcat, and knowing that the dome of the night sky could have a metaphor in the cup formed by a pair of human hands, as we know it did for the Zuñi—how can we not suspect that the infant of Burial 197 was itself a 'chiefly infant', found as it was, cradled within a pair of human hands?[56]

I have used the term 'Oneota Interaction' to refer to the network of relationships that resulted in the spread of a pattern of economic adaptions and styles of artifacts throughout the upper Mississippi valley during the Late Mississippi period—the several centuries beginning around A.D. 1275 and concluding with the first European contact in the seventeenth century. What was involved was a process of diffusion both of material objects and ideas that gave an appearance of uniformity to the archaeological cultures of tribes such as the Winnebago, Iowa, Oto, Missouri, and others, in most cases, tribes of Siouan language affiliation. These cultures acquired a common face, so to speak, and were characterized by social and political organization similar to that of tribes in the same area during the post-Contact era. Traces of matrilineality that Radin inferred from Winnebago oral traditions do not fit what is known or inferred about this late Oneota pattern as well as they might some related or antecedent cultures in the same era during the Early Mississippi period of around A.D. 1050–1275.[57] Matrilineality appears to have been more closely associated with intensive corn farming and permanent villages than with cultures exhibiting a balance of gardening, hunting, and fishing, although some Oneota cultures, like the Lake Winnebago phase in eastern Wisconsin, exhibit many characteristics of culture climax and could well have been matrilineal.

I have used the term 'Cahokia Interaction' to refer to the network of relationships within the same area that produced a different set of uniformities during the Early Mississippi period with a nonegalitarian face, reflecting a ranked society with a strong differentiation of elites and commoners. This does not mean that all communities during this period were similarly ranked, only that there was a stratification of social ranks within principal temple towns, such as prehistoric Cahokia (between East St. Louis and Collinsville, Illinois) and a presumption of ranking between communities, with smaller settlements being political dependents of the larger towns or, at the very least, subject to Cahokia cultural hegemony. The Cahokia Interaction had a quite specific center, the Cahokia site itself and the immediately surrounding communities within the American Bottom of the alluvial Mississippi valley. The Oneota Interaction had a more diffuse center of origin encompassing sites within a polygon defined by points at Red Wing, Minnesota, Green Bay, Wisconsin, Blue Island, Illinois, and the Yellow River in Iowa.

Oneota cultures start to appear in the northern Mississippi valley around calendar A.D. 1100, adapted originally to the alluvial valley of the Mississippi and to lake and stream environments within the mentioned core area, then achieve a prairie adaptation, extending across Iowa and Missouri into South Dakota, Nebraska, and Kansas. By contrast, Cahokia Mississippians seem never to have moved beyond an adaptation to the alluvial valleys of large rivers such as the Mississippi and Illinois, with the very conspicuous exception of Aztalan on the Crawfish River of southern Wisconsin, although Cahokia cultural influence was very nearly coextensive with that of the later Oneota expansion. This alluvial valley adaptation of Mississippians apparently lost its advantage by the beginning of the fourteenth century, possibly because of the availability of a maize better adapted to a greater variety of growing conditions and because of the movement eastward of bison herds toward the Mississippi, leading to a less centralized, more egalitarian sociopolitical structure, and with this change of adaptation went much of the archaeologically visible identity of the Mississippians.[58]

When styles of pottery decoration, tool types, and modes of house construction come to resemble each other over broad areas, archaeologists justifiably infer that the peoples involved have been in contact over a prolonged period of time. In the Plains culture area this process is well exampled by the transformation that produced the Coalescent tradition (A.D. 1300–1550) from the Initial Middle Missouri (A.D. 1000–1300) and the Central Plains (A.D. 1050–1400) traditions. I am talking here of the cultural processes that produced the archaeological manifestations of late prehistoric Plains cultures from their earlier antecedents, irrespective of language stock. These changes cut across language and tribe. Donald Blakeslee sees the Coalescent tradition as an expression of a Plains interband trading network facilitated by Calumet ceremonialism,[59] a model that "envisions a rapidly expanding trade network which involved annual visits between various Plains groups, regardless of ethnic identity. The individual links in the trade network regularly involved quite long distances, and a very wide range of goods were exchanged. Furthermore, regular trade visits allowed each group to copy the traits of their trade partners in items of their own manufacture."[60]

Calumet ceremonialism was the de facto mechanism for intergroup trade at the time of contact and was more than just suited to the circumstances of the times. It helped to create the circumstances. A great part of the success of the hierarchical, ranked Mississippian societies is believed to have been the way in which they hedged against economic distress caused by unpredictable aspects of nature, much as the Federal government today can funnel money to aid areas damaged by flood, hurricane, earthquake, fire, or other natural disasters. Crisis management of this sort is an organizational solution. Any technological improvement that would make corn more drought resistant, more resistant to damage from insects, or less susceptible to damage from late-spring and early-fall frosts by virtue of a shorter growing season, would reduce the need for an elaborate, and perhaps repressive, social mechanism to counter environmental risks.[61]

In point of fact, Northern Flint Corn appears on stage in Illinois about the same time that Cahokia begins its descent from political and cultural hegemony. Beans also appear, providing an alternate protein source. And bison are out there in the wings, still west of the Mississippi but ready for their role in making hunting a rewarding, not to mention a possibly more appealing, alternative to grubbing in the soil for subsistence.[62] Viewed this way, the post-Mississippian decline in the northern Mississippi valley was not so much a cultural death as a transition to a mode of adaptation allowing settlement in new areas of the prairies. Here, as in the Plains, nature could still exact a price for settlement, but Calumet ceremonialism provided the mechanism for a new organizational solution suited to the changed circumstances:

The major features of the [Plains interband] trade system, its location on the plains, the importance of food, the redundancy in goods exchanged, and the reticular structure of the system, are understandable if the trade system is viewed as an adaptation to the localized food shortages which periodically occurred on the plains. . . . [E]xchanges of food during times of plenty maintained the acceptability of food as an item of exchange so that it could be obtained when a shortage occurred. Items available for trade in exchange for food were primarily goods available to all plains societies through their own efforts. Redundant exchanges maintained the acceptability of receiving goods of this sort when hungry people came to trade for food, and redundant exchanges during times of plenty maintained the social ties necessary for the functioning of the system. The reticular rather than centralized structure can also be seen as an adaptation to the droughts. A local band or village affected by a localized drought could fission into smaller groups and visit several trade centers. Furthermore, a single central place would eventually be affected by drought itself, making it dysfunctional.[63]

The popular conception of a Hako-type round-stemmed calumet-pipe as simply a sacred smoking pipe obscures its ritual function in mediating a symbolic conception, either as a tube through which breath passes or as a symbolic arrow. Its associated ritual derives from the kind of background one would expect of a ritual based in varying degrees upon spirit adoption in mourning, the story of He-who-wears-human-heads-as-earrings, the Morning Star sacrifice, and World Renewal ritual. Calumet ceremonialism fits the bill as the mechanism of the Oneota Interaction, while Long-Nosed God earrings and tattoos are implicated, at least, in the mechanism of the Cahokia Interaction, much as silver 'peace medals' were given by the British and later by the United States government as material tokens of the recognition by those governments of the favored status of the chiefs on whom the medals were conferred. No Long-Nosed God earrings have ever been found at the Cahokia site itself. They have been found at many sites near and far of the same age and culturally related to Cahokia, but not at Cahokia itself. On the other hand, I do not know of any peace medals that have been found during archaeological excavations in London, England, or Washington, D.C., yet we know that those are places from which they were distributed by the hundreds.

HUNAHPU AS ANCESTORS' DAY

The 260 days of the Mesoamerican sacred almanac calendar are composed of the 260 possible combinations of twenty day names and thirteen numbers, 260 being the product of twenty and thirteen. This sacred calendar originated early in the first millennium B.C. and continues in use even to the present day in many communities of Mesoamerica. There is a strong correspondence between the day names from community to community, although the names themselves are in the local language or dialect and the direct translations do not always correlate well. We have already seen that the Yucatec Maya day name Caban 'earth' corresponds to Aztec Ollin 'movement, motion', which is, however, commonly translated as 'earthquake'. Yucatec Maya Imix corresponds to a dialectical cognate Imox, said to refer to the ceiba tree that stands in each town plaza in Chiapas, while the corresponding Aztec day is Cipactli, a primordial water monster. This relationship is more understandable when one examines Stela 25 from the Guatemalan site of Izapa, depicting, as it does, a crocodilian, head down, with its rear half raised into the air and transformed into a tree or plant.[64]

As the twentieth day, the Yucatec Maya day Ahau 'lord' corresponds in the sequence of day names to the Aztec day Xochitl 'flower'. The seeming contradiction is resolved when one discovers that among the Aztecs the young sun god was called Xochipilli 'flower prince' and the Maya glyph *kin* 'day' was a four-petaled flower. Ahau was a day whose patron was the sun god. Quiché Maya Hunahpu relates in a similarly obscure manner. 'Ahpu' means 'blowgunner' or 'blowgun hunter' and

'Hun' means 'one'. Hunahpu 'one blowgun hunter' does not seem to relate to the idea of sun, flower, or lord until one understands that blowguns were the weapons carried by the hero twins of Maya mythology Hunahpu and Xblanque, who have certain interests in the sun and moon in addition to their primary relationship to Venus. They were also flute players.[65]

Hunahpu and Xblanque, often referred to simply as Hunter and Jaguar Deer, appear in the Quiché epic *Popol Vuh* as the twin sons born of Blood Woman, daughter of a lord of the Maya underworld, conceived when the head of their father, Hun Hunahpu, spit into her hand from the gourd tree in which it had been placed by the lords of the underworld. In later years the young twins outwitted and defeated the lords of Xibalba, the underworld, who had killed their father. There in Xibalba, the realm of the dead, the twins reassembled the bones of their father and returned him to a semblance of life but bade him remain in Xibalba. "You will be prayed to here," he was told. "Your name will not be lost," they said before ascending into the sky.[66]

Andrés Xiloj is a daykeeper in the Quiché Maya town of Momostenango, Guatemala, and the head of his patrilineage. He clarified to Dennis Tedlock, then translating the *Popol Vuh*, the meaning, as he saw it, of the statement "You will be prayed to here." He said that after a death the funeral rites are not considered complete until the keeper of the lineage shrines visits the shrines on a day Hunahpu and offers prayers that will aid the spirit of the dead to descend to Xibalba. He said also that he saw the twin boys' promise to their dead father in Xibalba as the origin of the practice of venerating the dead.[67]

The described episode in the much longer *Popol Vuh* should be familiar. The plot and characters are basically those of the Iowa-Winnebago story of He-who-wears-human-heads-as-earrings—the story of a culture hero who loses his head after a contest with an uncommon enemy but is requickened by the actions of his two sons, one of whose mothers is an enemy woman with red hair. Ball games with the enemy figure importantly in both stories and, lest the reader forget, the Iowa story ends with the remark, "Human-head-earrings was only a man like the rest of us, but he said that when he died his little heads should live always. So now when we die the little person invisible to us that dwells in us (the soul) goes to the other world."[68] Each episode thus ends with a comment on the immortality of the memory of the dead father and reads like the charter myth for a mourning practice. The story of Hun Hunahpu figures in the origin of rites to keep the names of the dead alive among the Quichés. In the United States the story of Red Horn or He-who-wears-human-heads-as-earrings similarly appears to have figured in a rite to keep the name of Red Horn alive and may enter into the background of the Calumet of the Captain, related as it was to rites serving to keep alive the name of the honored dead by symbolic reincarnation.

19 / The Earth Reawakened and the Dead Requickened

ON OCTOBER 12, 1968, while presenting a paper at the Midwest Archaeological Conference in St. Louis, Missouri, I made a not entirely facetious comparison between Christopher Columbus and the pioneer American archaeologist Warren K. Moorehead. Columbus and Moorehead were each born in Italy, where Moorehead's parents were American missionaries, and Columbus and Moorehead each figured in their own ways in the history of midwestern archaeology. In 1892 Moorehead directed a project in Ohio meant to provide exhibit pieces for display at the World Columbian Exhibition to open in Chicago the following year.

DISCOVERING HOPEWELL

One of Moorehead's projects was to excavate a mound on the farm of a Mr. M. C. Hopewell near Chillicothe, Ohio. The mound group on the Hopewell farm became the type site for what was later called the Hopewell culture. Within fifty years variants of the Ohio Hopewell culture were found in Wisconsin, Louisiana, Missouri, Iowa, Michigan, and elswhere, and it was obvious that Hopewell was a widespread phenomenon. I say 'phenomenon' because it was not clear just what Hopewell was. All sites called Hopewell share some part of a long list of distinctive culture traits: burial in log-covered tombs beneath earthen mounds or cremation; well-made pottery decorated with toothed stamps; polished stone smoking pipes of the 'platform' type; certain styles of pottery figurines; construction of grand-scale geometrical earthworks; and various objects made of materials traded from distant regions—earspools and celts hammered from copper mined near Lake Superior; designs cut from mica from the Appalachians; spear-points chipped from obsidian quarried in Wyoming; certain types of projectile points, scrapers, and flake knives of high-quality Indiana, Illinois, and Ohio cherts; river mussel pearls from Illinois; and shark teeth from the Gulf of Mexico.

Was Hopewell a religion that had spread through the eastern United States like the Ghost Dance? Was Hopewell the culture of some Indian people that had multiplied and spread through the eastern states or was Hopewell the culture of a mysterious race of Mound Builders that had preceded the Indians but later vanished? Cyrus Thomas's mound explorations for the Smithsonian's Bureau of American Ethnology had exploded the pre-Indian Mound Builder idea by the end of the nineteenth century. Radiocarbon dating had established the antiquity of Hopewell by the 1950s. Hopewell was two thousand years old! As recently as 1947 opinion was that Hopewell might have lasted until as late as A.D. 1300. The logic of the time was that Indians as highly developed as Hopewellians must have preceded and somehow led into the cultures archaeologists were then calling Middle Mississippi, when actually there was a time gap of well over five hundred years—perhaps as much as six or seven hundred years—between anything that could be called Hopewellian and Mississippi. This intervening period came to be called Late Woodland, preceded by Middle Woodland with a Hopewellian phase and followed by an Early Mississippi period, as exampled by the Aztalan site in Wisconsin and the so-called Old Village levels of the enormous Cahokia site in Illinois.[1]

INTERACTION SPHERES AND GREAT TRADITIONS

In 1961, thirty-one years after his excavation of the Hopewell mounds near Utica, Illinois (chapter 3), Arthur R. Kelly organized a symposium at the annual meeting of the American Anthropological Association in Philadelphia to consider several regional manifestations of 'Hopewell culture'. Joseph R. Caldwell's contribution was a paper entitled "Interaction spheres in prehistory." In it Caldwell characterized Hopewell not as a culture per se but as the material evidence of an episode of interaction between several regional traditions. The concept of a 'sphere' of interaction was implicitly based upon the concept of 'diffusion sphere' coined by Gordon Willey, whom Caldwell acknowledged in the published version of his paper as a source of stimulation. Willey was at the time absorbed with the implications of the spread of certain great art styles in Mesoamerica and Andean South America that bespoke wide-ranging contacts of a religious nature on the very eve of the appearance of civilization in Nuclear America, and Caldwell said of this that "Willey's Great Art Styles and attendant religious ideologies each evidently connected a number of separate societies in the nuclear areas . . . and seem structurally similar to what we have called 'interaction spheres of a religious kind'."[2]

The concept of 'interaction' between regional traditions was less consciously, perhaps, based upon the view of Philip Phillips, James Ford, and James Griffin that the Mississippian pattern of culture had no single center of origin but was the result of parallel developments by regional centers in continuous interaction. Earlier in the year that Caldwell spoke in Philadelphia of Hopewellian interaction he had addressed the problem of Mississippian interaction in a paper presented at a meeting in Bloomington, Indiana. In his Hopewell paper Caldwell did quite explicitly acknowledge stimulation from his University of Chicago professor Robert Redfield for the concepts of great traditions and small traditions, useful because these concepts do not force a distinction between, or an equation of, religion and civilization. Caldwell saw Hopewell as a great tradition that had spread through the eastern United States and had come to be shared by many regional traditions, such as the Havana tradition in the prairie peninsula of the Midwest, the Scioto tradition in Ohio, and Crab Orchard in the Ohio-Mississippi confluence area. Illinois Hopewell is not the same as Ohio Hopewell because each has its base in a different regional tradition. Caldwell saw the spreading and sharing as the result of a religious interaction that fostered the kind of innovation that can follow increased rates of contact between cultures. I have myself preferred to speak of the 'ideology' of the Hopewellian great tradition, choosing not to force a further distinction between the sacred as we see it and the sacred as Hopewellians might have seen it.[3]

When archaeologists are not digging in the earth, they spend a great part of their time just refining the language they use to organize and discuss their ideas and argue their points of view. Archaeology is more than shelved boxes of artifacts; it is also a whole babel of languages by which culture history is described. The Hopewellian *Interaction* is thus the process that saw materials and ideas exchanged or diffused throughout the Hopewellian Interaction *Sphere* as a geographical theater of activity, while the body of shared ideas, values, and formats for material goods constituted the Hopewellian *great tradition* uniting the Havana, Scioto, and other regionally based *small traditions*.

Hunahpu and Xblanque would have understood. While reassembling the bones of their father in Xibalba, they asked him to name his body parts. In this he was only partly successful, being able only to name his mouth, nose, and eyes: "Although his mouth could not name the names of each of his former parts, he had at least spoken again." The implication is for an association of the naming of body parts with the regaining of those parts, much as keeping alive the name of an individual is tantamount to keeping the individual himself alive.[4]

Hopewell appears as a phase in each of the many participating traditions, providing material clues for the archaeological sleuth to a shared episode of interaction during which ideas and things moved without great hindrance over great stretches of the North American continent. The time was in the area of 100 B.C. to A.D. 300. The nature of the ideas moving can be guessed from the nature of the objects moving, from the tasks to which Hopewellians assigned priority when budgeting their energies, and from judicious use of ethnographic analogy. I do not see Hopewellian leaders as merchant princes, even though valuable products were moving great distances. Acquisitiveness was quite remote from any Indian ethic of which I have knowledge for North America; North American Indians gained prestige not from possessing but from giving to others, often to the point of impoverishing themselves. And the *Pax Hopewelliana* was hardly a *Pax Romana* or a *Pax Britannica*, maintained by the strength of an imperial army or navy. I think it unlikely that there was anything in Hopewell that cannot be explained by the workings of processes known from eyewitness knowledge of historic North American Indian customs, the geological doctrine of 'uniformitarianism' applied to culture history, if you will.

The most conspicuous aspect of Hopewell is the great amount of energy expended on the dead, energy expended in the construction of burial mounds and graves and in the manufacture or procurement of objects eventually buried within them. The magnitude of expenditure of energy on elaborate burial practices was once thought difficult to explain in the absence of a well-developed agriculture or hierarchical social structure, but the absence may be the key to the explanation. The elaboration of the mortuary complex may have been some part of an organizational solution to problems of life in a society based upon a mixture of hunting, fishing, gathering wild plant foods, and limited gardening. One useful model is that of Calumet ceremonialism as an adoption ritual.

Calumet ceremonialism was a point of intersection of many aspects of Indian life. It functioned on an intertribal, political level to establish and maintain peaceful relationships between unrelated groups by creating fictions of kinship between the principals involved. It functioned in the area of economic adaptation by cushioning villages or bands against the dangers of crop failures or changes in the availability of game animals, doing so by establishing patterns of friendly exchange with neighbors upon whom one might fall back in time of need. And it functioned at the social level by providing a means by which a capable and worthy person could rise in status through personal achievements. It is not difficult to imagine a similar network of relationships among Hopewellian societies.

When dancing the Calumet of the Captain (chapter 10), a group honored a worthy nontribesman by accepting him as a chief of their nation with the implication from the historic record that he was symbolically resurrecting a dead chief, much as Robert La Salle did when he presumed to reincarnate the Miami chief Ouabicolcata in his own person (chapter 2). In the Great Lakes area the raising of a new chief was often the symbolic reincarnation of a dead chief, with examples from the Condolence Councils of the Iroquois and the Algonquian Feast of the Dead (chapter 5). Spirit Adoption was an integral part of both private and public rites of mourning in the greater Midwest (chapters 4, 6, 8, and 9). The calumet figuring in Calumet ceremonialism was merely the more obvious material aspect of a rite of adoption with strong roots in adoption in mourning. There is much in the archaeological expression of the Hopewellian great tradition that can be explained by mourning ritual designed to involve and honor important people among neighboring villages, bands, or tribes by receiving them as symbolic reincarnations of local leaders.

Spirit Adoption by itself may have provided the mechanism of the Hopewellian Interaction, but the ideology of the great tradition was presumably more complex. Implicit in Calumet ceremonies of the Hako type and more explicit in the Sun Dances of the Cheyenne, Arapaho, and Ponca is the element of World Renewal (chapters 3, 7, and 11). The sacred fires of temple towns in the Southeast were quenched and renewed annually as part of rites of World Renewal, but the sacred fire of the Natchez was also quenched and renewed with the death and raising of a chief known as the Great Sun because the Great Sun and the sacred fire were representatives of the celestial sun on earth. I have long argued that during the Woodland period in the Midwest the person symbolically raising the deceased also represented the earth to be reborn in the spring. I believe that this element of ideology is evident from the Calumet ceremony itself, from interior features of burial mounds, and from the elements of mourning and renewal in the Sun Dance. The pledger in the Cheyenne Sun Dance, for instance, was known as the "reproducer" or "multiplier" because "through him the tribe is supposed to be reborn and to increase."[5] The pattern of face paint of the pledger in the Cheyenne Sun Dance is a variant of that applied to the person adopted in the Calumet ceremony, whom I have argued had his prototype in a person symbolically reincarnating a dead tribesman and symbolically renewing the earth as well.

MODELING A WOODLAND CREATIVE PROCESS

When hiking along a field edge or driving along a highway in midwinter, often the only flash of color that one may see against the snow comes from the stems of the red-osier dogwood, *Cornus stolonifera*, an unobtrusive green in summer but brilliant scarlet red in winter. Also known as 'red willow', the red-osier dogwood and some related species provided many North American Indians with wood for fashioning arrowshafts and for carving tent pegs and skewers, as well as furnishing the makings for a variety of kinnikinnick. The Sioux knew the red-osier dogwood as *caŋśa'śa* 'red wood'.

The botanicals generally lumped under the rubric 'kinnikinnick' were once quite generally regarded by anthropologists and historians as simply a tobacco substitute or as a material to mix with native tobacco to extend it or to dilute its effect. The word is cognate with an Eastern Algonquian word, *kinukkinuk*, meaning 'mixture'. This identification was not very satisfying, however, because it did not account for occasions when one or another variety of kinnikinnick was used by itself for ritual purposes. The Osage, for example, used the leaves of the sumac for smoking during the ceremonies for making the rush mat shrine for the sacred hawk emblematic of the courage of warriors.[6] What might sumac leaves, bearberry leaves, and dogwood shavings have had in common in the traditional worldview of Indians?

The Fox tribe associated the bright-red coloration of sumac leaves in autumn with the blood of a mythical sky bear that was pursued by hunters through the spring and summer and killed in the autumn. This sky bear was the quadrangle of the Big Dipper constellation, *Ursa major*, the Great She Bear, and the hunters were the stars of the handle. The dead sky bear emerged reborn in the spring, much as bears emerge from hibernation in real life, and continued its journey across the sky followed by the tireless hunters. The leaves of the sumac may thus have shared something of the quality of immortality of the bear itself. Quite aside from the bear association of its English name, which I do not know to be shared by any Indians, the bearberry also ties into the theme of immortality or continuity of life. The bearberry is a plant whose leaves turn brown in the winter but do not drop and then turn a vivid green once more in the spring.[7]

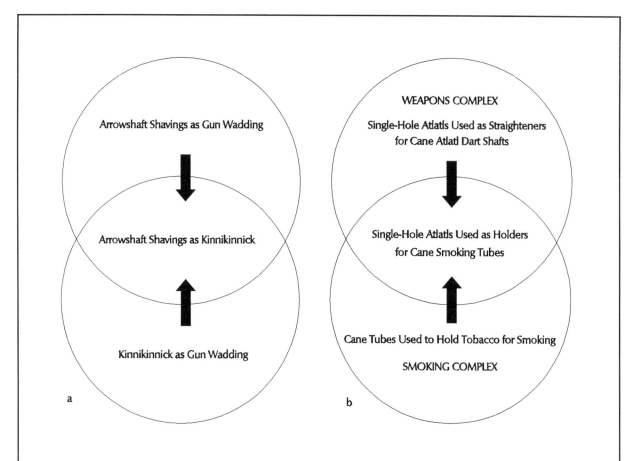

Figure 19.1 Venn diagrams illustrating the role of intersecting mental associations in the processes of inference and innovation: *a*, the inference that 'red willow' bark kinnikinnick was a by-product of arrow manufacture; *b*, the innovation of the use the single-hole atlatl as a holder for cane smoking tubes.

The significance of dogwood kinnikinnick escaped me until one day when I was scraping bark from a dogwood branch to make an arrowshaft. Looking at the pile of scrapings at my feet I realized that I had just duplicated the act of making kinnikinnick that I had done on another occasion. *Do you suppose*, I thought, *that dogwood kinnikinnick originated as a by-product of arrow manufacture?* I had no hint of evidence in support of that notion until I later ran into a Menominee tale of a hunter who had run out of tobacco and who then reached into his quiver, drew out an arrow, and chopped it into fine pieces that were magically transformed into tobacco.[8] The incident would have meant nothing to me if I had not already had in my mind the possible association of dogwood kinnikinnick with arrowshaft shavings. I felt the association was clinched when I later discovered a reference to the Osage using dogwood arrowshaft scrapings as gun wadding (to seat a lead ball firmly in the barrel of a muzzle-loading musket) and then a reference to the Hidatsa using kinnikinnick for the same purpose. Dogwood kinnikinnick did apparently originate as a by-product of arrow manufac-

ture. I was bothered that arrows did not seem to relate very closely to the idea of immortality, but then under *mo*[n] 'arrow' in Francis La Flesche's Osage dictionary I found this entry: "The Osage made their arrows out of a wood they call mo[n]'-ça hi, arrow wood (*Cornus asperi folia*). . . . Two arrows, ceremonially made, are used in some of the Osage tribal rites, one painted black and the other red, to represent night and day, *they being symbols of everlasting life.*"[9]

The sacred associations of tobacco for Indians are well known, but the symbolism shared by many varieties of kinnikinnick had remained unexplored. Seen as something only to mix with tobacco, kinnikinnick's origin would logically have postdated the introduction of tobacco. Seen as a product with its own ritual associations and symbolism tied closely to the natural history of the area of its use, kinnikinnick could logically have preadapted Indians of eastern North America to the smoking of tobacco, as *Nicotiana rustica* diffused into North America from South America by way of Central America and Mexico. It may have been kinnikinnick that was smoldering in the stone tube pipes of cloud-

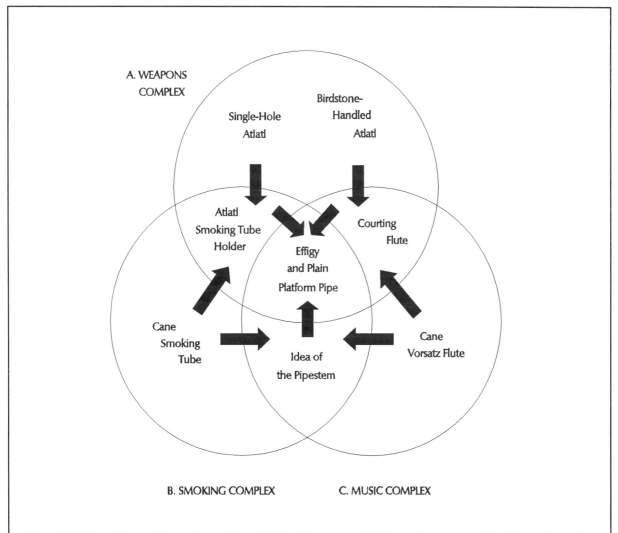

A. WEAPONS COMPLEX

Single-Hole Atlatl

Birdstone-Handled Atlatl

Atlatl Smoking Tube Holder

Courting Flute

Effigy and Plain Platform Pipe

Cane Smoking Tube

Cane Vorsatz Flute

Idea of the Pipestem

B. SMOKING COMPLEX

C. MUSIC COMPLEX

Figure 19.2 Venn diagram illustrating an inferred chain of innovations leading to the creation of the Hopewellian effigy and plain platform pipes.

blower type used by Late Archaic peoples in the Ohio valley during the second millennium B.C., smoked perhaps to generate fumes for ritual smudging of sacred articles and precincts. The appearance of tobacco per se is possibly signaled by the appearance of tube pipes of the blocked-end type during the period of Late Archaic–Early Woodland transition around 1200–900 B.C. (figure 14.6).[10]

There is much value in seeing a relationship between the processes of thought association involved in discovery or attempted explanation, as in the cases above, and the processes of thought association involved in innovation itself. These processes both can be conveniently modeled by the use of Venn diagrams, as in figure 19.1. Figure 19.1a illustrates the convergence of thought associations in the example of discovery just discussed, and figure 19.1b, in an example of innovation discussed in chapter 14. Figure 19.2 models the much more com-

plex process of innovation that I hypothesize for the innovation of plain and effigy platform pipes through the Early Woodland period and continuing into the Middle Woodland period. The thought associations thus modeled were available, are logical, have great explanatory power, and reduce a confusion of inferred relationships and connections to an easily understood pattern. Just as Venn diagrams can be used to model a converging pattern of innovations as thoughts associate, they can also be used to model the shaking out of the components of a pattern through time as conditions change (figure 19.3).

SEEKING WOODLAND CEREMONIAL TRADITIONS

The Hidatsa Sun Dance or Hide Beating ceremony was not considered a mourning ceremony, but it did contain an area designated as a grave. The old Crow Sun Dance

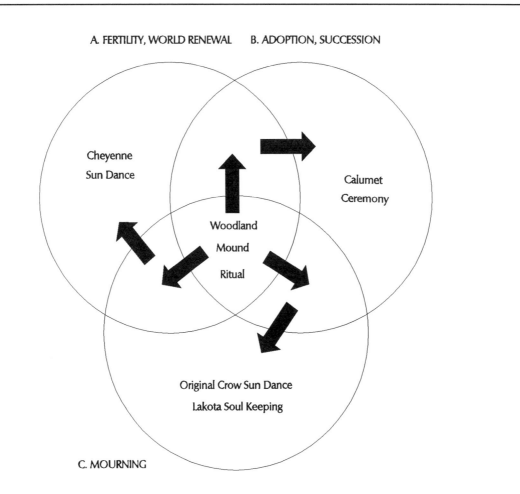

A. FERTILITY, WORLD RENEWAL   B. ADOPTION, SUCCESSION

Cheyenne
Sun Dance

Calumet
Ceremony

Woodland

Mound

Ritual

Original Crow Sun Dance

Lakota Soul Keeping

C. MOURNING

Figure 19.3 Venn diagram illustrating the manner in which components of a Woodland period burial mound ritual complex could have become dissociated to produce Historic period rituals specific to the areas of world renewal, adoption, and mourning.

was a mourning ritual and did not contain any feature explicitly seen as a grave, but it did contain an area that structurally and functionally corresponded to the grave location in the Hidatsa Sun Dance. Because the Crow and Hidatsa are closely related and must have been a single tribe in the not-too-distant past, logic suggests that there was a time in the background of the Crow and Hidatsa Sun Dances when there was a ceremony involving both mourning and a real or simulated grave. Because the chief mourner in the Crow Sun Dance corresponds to the Spring Boy impersonator in the Hidatsa Sun Dance—the person for whom the grave was meant—and the pattern of face paint of Spring Boy is the same as that for the adoptee in the Calumet ceremony, logic suggests that the principals in the prototypical Crow-Hidatsa Sun Dance were originally both the chief mourners and the persons designated to symbolically resurrect the deceased. The Sun Dance can usefully be thought of as the survival of ritual once

associated with Woodland period burial mound ceremonialism, i.e., ritual that outlived the practice of mound construction as part of mortuary ritual. One point of divergence might be the distinction between a rite performed for an actual individual and one representing a rite performed for a character in the mythical past, although the two kinds of rites may coincide.

The old Crow Sun Dance was a mourning ritual closely related to the war complex and the perceived need for personal vengeance for the death of a warrior (chapter 6). It was last performed in 1875. Government and missionary opposition to the Sun Dance coincided with the ebbing of the need for vengeance, as intertribal warfare became a memory of days past. When the Sun Dance was reinstated by the Crows in 1941, it was a version borrowed from the Shoshonis, who are said to have acquired it from the Kiowas, who had learned it from the Crow themselves in an earlier century. During that time the motivation for performing the Crow Sun

Dance had shifted from personal vengeance for a death to the acquisition of the power to alleviate physical or psychological afflictions, to promote tribal welfare, and to satisfy a need for personal identification with tribal history. The symbolism of bloodletting in the Lakota Sun Dance has shifted so far from simulation of the torture of warriors as to include empathy for the pain of childbirth. Greater recognition of the woman's role in Indian society has proceeded apace with the downplaying of warfare as a former aspect of Indian life.[11]

The skewering aspect of the Lakota Sun Dance, however, was more than a display of warrior machismo, however. It was a guarantee of the sincerity of the performer, and it was part of a ritual drama with interesting implications. No one could go through the skewering aspect of the Sun Dance without previously performing successfully in a Buffalo Dance, which was another part of the Sun Dance. Such dancers became Buffalo Men. Buffalo People lived "in the regions under the world" and were "people of the Sun," corresponding in those particulars to sacred clowns who dwelt beneath the earth with the midnight sun. The sun-gazers were relieved of their skewers and thongs when their "captors" feigned discovering that their captives were Buffalo Men. This relates the Lakota Sun Dance to a broad category of ceremonies related to the fertility of nature and to the underworld, and it provides a tie-in to the story of White Buffalo Calf Maiden because she identified herself as representing the Buffalo People (chapter 10).[12]

Bloodletting in the Sun Dance could well have originated centuries ago, during the Middle or Late Woodland period, with self-mortification in mourning—slashing, puncturing, and minor amputations, as practiced in historic times. Although blood and snippets of flesh were offered to the sun in the historical Sun Dance without reference to mourning, the bloodying of peeled wooden skewers was, of course, once a part of mourning practice in a large area of the Midwest to aid the spirit of the deceased in its travel along the spirit trail (chapter 13). It must not be forgotten also that while the flesh and blood offerings in the Sun Dance may be directed to the sun, the same practice in Mesoamerica served the purposed of giving strength to the dead sun, allowing it to be reborn and to rise from the underworld.

While Spirit Adoption related to mourning could have provided the mechanism for much intergroup interaction during the Woodland period, surviving into prototypes of the Calumet ceremony, this does not mean that calumets or calumet-pipes need have been involved in Spirit Adoptions during the Woodland period. Spirits may be introduced in a variety of ways. It is very possible that strands of shell beads or river pearls were used to mediate adoptions by the ancient Hopewellians. The calumet was in the form of an arrow, and while the calumet mediated the conception of the adoptee in the Calumet ceremony, much as the twins Sprout and Flint were conceived in Iroquois creation stories by a pair of arrows, twins in certain Muskogean folktales were conceived by a character known as Bead Spitter. The adoptee in the Tutelo (Atlantic coast Siouan) Spirit Adoption and Reclothing rite, which was also a renaming rite, wore a string of white wampum while impersonating the deceased. Among the Delaware the naming ceremony for a small child required that the child touch a string of white wampum when his name was pronounced, and wampum strings sent out by way of invitation to Requickening rites for a dead Iroquois chief conveyed the message, "the 'name' of the deceased 'calls for a council'."[13]

Rituals are seldom without their origin myth, and the rituals themselves may consist of little more than a dramatic telling or reenactment of the myth itself. The Medicine Lodge rites of the Great Lakes Indians are a case in point (chapters 8 and 9). In the case of burial mound ceremonialism the associated myth could be expected to have been an important part of the ideology of the Woodland people involved, perhaps even a key ingredient of the Hopewell great tradition itself. There are two classes of myth known to have had ties to the Sun Dance and that are at the same time broadly distributed. One of these is the Earth Diver myth, importantly connected with the Cheyenne and Arapaho Sun Dances. This is a myth with a continent-wide distribution in Asia and eastern Europe but limited in the New World pretty much to North America.[14] The Arapaho Sun Dance origin myth relates to the Calumet ceremony as well in that the character of the Earth Diver, a duck, was merged with a pipe, much as the calumet itself was spoken of as a pipe but had a duck's head on the end, either instead of a pipe bowl or just behind it. In both cases the action of the duck-cum-pipe led to the creation or conception of the earth (chapter 3). The ritual of the Ponca Sun Dance preparation tipis apparently related to a succession of earth creations and destructions more akin to those in Aztec cosmology (chapter 11).

The second class of myth is one associated with myth cycles of twins. The twin-related myths have a hemisphere-wide distribution and were possibly part of the oral literature of the earliest peoples in both North and South America, varying locally and through time. Like myths with the Earth Diver theme, those based on the Twins theme have an Old World distribution as well, with easily recognizable counterparts even in ancient Egypt and Mesopotamia.

The Earth Diver theme (chapter 3) is an earth origin myth that came to be incorporated into a rite of World Renewal in the northern Plains. The Twins theme does not relate as directly to the creation of the earth per se, with exceptions like that among the Iroquois, where twin heroes were born following the creation of the earth for their pregnant grandmother. What the twin stories may relate to more directly is the origin of death and mourning—either of the mother or one twin or both the mother and a twin—which may sometimes then tie into the theme of a universal flood and on into renewal. The death of the Maya twin Hun Hunahpu relates to mourning, as does the death of the related Winnebago Red Horn more implicitly (chapter 18). Among Great Lakes area Algonquians the story of the death of Manabush's wolf brother leads, on the one hand, to Manabush's revenge against the water spirits responsible, to the flooding of the world by the water spirits in revenge, and then to the Earth Diver theme.[15] It leads, on the other hand, to consolation of Manabush and the gift of the Medicine rite with its promise of long life (chapters 8 and 16).

The theme of Manabush, the Great Hare, grieving the death of his wolf brother in many ways parallels that of the Mesopotamian Gilgamesh, king of the Sumerian city of Uruk, mourning the death of his wild brother Enkidu. Gilgamesh then sought the secret of everlasting life, learned the story of the flood from Utnapishtim, who was the Mesopotamian prototype of biblical Noah, and received Utnapishtim's gift of a flower whose taste restores youth and guarantees long life. Gilgamesh's flower of eternal youth was subsequently stolen from him by a serpent who "immediately sloughed its skin." Even in the ancient civilization of Sumeria five thousand years ago there was a mental association of the snake with eternal youth because of its ability to shed its skin.[16] This habit of the serpent is so easily observed by anyone living close to nature that the mental association must be worldwide and repeatedly incorporated into myth and ritual, as in the Winnebago Medicine rite: "He-whom-we-call-our-nephew, Hare, secured this Rite for us. It was not a ceremony acquired through a vision. This Rite was taught to two human beings in the first Creation Lodge. He-whom-we-call-our-nephew became a human being in order to succour us. In order to obtain a larger span of life for us, he looked for and obtained the promise of reincarnation, the shedding of our skin, at this Rite. If any member adheres to its teachings meticulously and sincerely, then will he obtain this new life, this shedding of skin."[17]

As for Mesoamerica, as impressive as the cosmologies of Mesoamerica were, they nevertheless emerged from a background ultimately once shared by all native Americans of their day, often cross-fertilized as ideas diffused from area to area. Though appearing in a Maya story, the wife of the god 7 Macaw in the Maya *Popol Vuh* had a name, Chimalmat, that was not of Maya origin. Her name derives from Postclassic contact with Náhuatl speakers. Chimalmat is a name cognate with Chimalman, Prostrate Shield, who became the mate of Mixcóatl in *The Legend of the Suns*.[18] As David Freidel, Linda Schele, Joy Parker, and colleagues read the Maya record, 7 Macaw was the personification of the Big Dipper, and the tree in which the Maya Hero Twins found 7 Macaw in *Popol Vuh* was perceived to be the Milky Way at a time of the year when it was visible running north and south across the sky with the Big Dipper to one side near its northern end.[19] Bernardino de Sahagún identified the deity on top of the pole (read 'tree') in the Aztec Feast of the Dead as Otontecuhtli or god of the Otomies, and elsewhere he refers to Mixcóatl as god of the Otomies.[20]

The Milky Way has been seen as a trail for the spirits of the dead quite widely in the world. We know that the Algonquian-speaking Potomacs of Virginia believed that spirits ascended into the sky by climbing a tree (chapter 16), and to the Potomacs could be added the Winnebago,[21] so seeing the Milky Way as a tree must have required no great leap of logic for ancients pondering their world. Pole climbing in the Feast of the Dead among the Great Lakes Algonquians and in that of the Aztecs can be easily interpreted as being in the nature of imitative magic to aid the spirits in their ascent (chapter 5). Poles once figured in mortuary ritual from coast to coast and could thus have had a logical role in any Sun Dance prototype conducted as a mourning ritual (chapter 13).

Although it did not involve a pole climb, the Hidatsa Sun Dance did have an origin myth in which twin brothers ascended the sky and there lopped (or threatened to lop) the hand from a spirit named Long Arm who ruled a sky world of birds (chapters 3 and 6). Long Arm's arm was said to be so long that it reached from the sky down to earth. For this and other reasons I have sought to identify Long Arm with the Big Dipper.[22] The Hidatsas were close cultural relatives of the Crows, who, according to one source, are said to have acquired the medicine dolls used in their (first) Sun Dance in a vision in which it was conducted by seven men, a possible reference to the seven stars of the Big Dipper.[23]

I do not hesitate to compare the encounter of the Hidatsa twins Lodge Boy and Spring Boy with Long Arm and the Maya Hero Twins' encounter with 7 Macaw. For instance, one of the Hidatsa twins came to have a rattle for a head, which recalls the head of Hun Hunahpu, father of the Maya Hero Twins, hanging in the gourd tree—a father who was himself a twin—and although neither of the Hidatsa twins impregnated a woman with twins by spitting, as Hun Hunahpu's severed head did, they did cause a virgin to conceive without intercourse. Stories of the twin cycle in the eastern United States do, however, include some in which twins are conceived by a character known as Bead Spitter (above). In the eastern United States the second-born twin, representing the personified placenta or umbilical cord, sometimes has a flint association. This conforms agreeably with the implicit identity of Hun Hunahpu with flint, insofar as Hun Hunahpu has a Quiché Maya calendrical name that corresponds to Yucatec Maya Hun Ahau or 1 Ahau, which was the ritual name for the flint chip in the *Ritual of the Bacabs*.[24]

Long Arm's severed hand appears in the sky each year as the Hand Star or Hand Constellation, a part of Orion, with the three stars of the belt of Orion as the wrist.[25] The three stars of the belt are those that make up part of the Aztec Firesticks constellation, presumably the hearth board, into which was inserted the fire drill, represented by Orion's sword ('belt' and 'sword' as the ancient Greeks saw Orion). Sahagún has told us that the Aztec men burned an image of the Firesticks constellation onto their wrists as a precaution against something that might happen to them in the afterworld. Some Shawnees once similarly burned round scars on their forearms in preparation for their eventual journey to the afterworld and the Lakotas burned spots on the wrists of young boys, but for the stated purpose of teaching endurance. Black Elk says that during his youth dry sunflower seeds were placed on the wrists of boys, lit, and allowed to burn down to the flesh. Those resisting or crying out were called women.[26]

The use of the imagery of the belt of Orion as a protective device may have a history in North America extending back at least to 1000 B.C., because in contexts that old in parts of the northeastern United States stone tablets and shell plaques have been found into which were drilled three holes, with one, apparently purposely, a little out of line with the rest, just as is one of the three stars of Orion's belt, although the shell and stone examples may represent the sword rather than the belt. An even more fascinating prospect is that of associating hearth boards generically with wooden-handled whips used by Plains Dog Soldiers. The handles of some of these whips vary in form around a model that has a striking resemblance to a hearth board (figure 19.5).[27]

What can be learned from the above is that there may be a sufficient number of story elements with widespread distributions and ritually relevant associations to permit a fuller reconstruction of the ideology of Woodland period ceremonialism, perhaps even that of the Hopewellian great tradition. Beyond ritual related to the Earth Diver theme, ritual based on the Twins theme has the potential for having ties to the Hopewellian great tradition, with Spirit Adoption possibly related to the death and mourning of a character in a story with the Twin theme.

XIPE, CALUMET CEREMONIALISM, AND DOG SOLDIERS

The relationship of aspects of Calumet ceremonialism to the Skiri Pawnee Morning Star sacrifice, and the relationship of the latter to Xipe worship in Mesoamerica, forced a comparison between Xipe worship and Calumet ceremonialism. The more obvious parallel was between choreographed ritual combat in the Calumet Dance, in which a warrior with a symbolic weapon (the calumet) was pitted against warriors with real weapons, and the gladiatorial sacrifice honoring Xipe, in which a victim with a token weapon defended himself to the death against eagle and jaguar knights with clubs set with obsidian blades. An easily overlooked parallel was the aspect of adoption in each. The victim in the gladiatorial sacrifice effectively became the adoptive son of the person offering him for sacrifice, much as the child in the Calumet ceremony became the adoptive son of the person sponsoring the ceremony. The person sponsoring a victim in other Aztec sacrifices might even preserve what amounted to a soul bundle representing the deceased, a parcel containing the hair and clothes of the victim,[28] much as the Sioux, Menominees, and others preserved in a bundle the clothes of a deceased tribesman together with a lock of hair to represent the soul of the deceased (chapter 4). Such practices reinforce the idea that mourning may lie somewhere in the background of some Mesoamerican sacrifices (chapter 5).

The least obvious parallel between the Calumet ceremony and the gladiatorial sacrifice was the aspect of skin shedding. In Xipe worship the skins of the sacrificial victims were shed quite literally, flayed from the victims' bodies, turned inside out, and worn for twenty days by Xipe impersonators. In the Calumet ceremony the honoree was simply reclothed. In rites of Spirit Adoption as part of mourning, which provided the prototype for both the Calumet of the Captain and calumet rites of the Hako type, the reclothing of the adoptee in garments belonging to the deceased was part of the symbolism of the reincarnation of the deceased. In Winnebago ritual parlance, as we already know, reincarnation was referred to as 'skin shedding', much as in northwest Amazonia "the power to change skins" refers to the potential for rebirth and immortality.[29]

The comparison is made more compelling still because of the similarity of (a) the metaphor of the earth reborn represented by the symbolic reconception in the Hako of a child previously given an identity with Mother Corn and the earth, and (b) the metaphor of the earth reclothed represented by the Xipe personator wearing a flayed skin. The visible sign of the impersonation of the earth may well have been the painting of single or multiple, vertical red stripes, originally through and later to the side of the eye of the impersonator, the combination of eye and stripes often resembling the

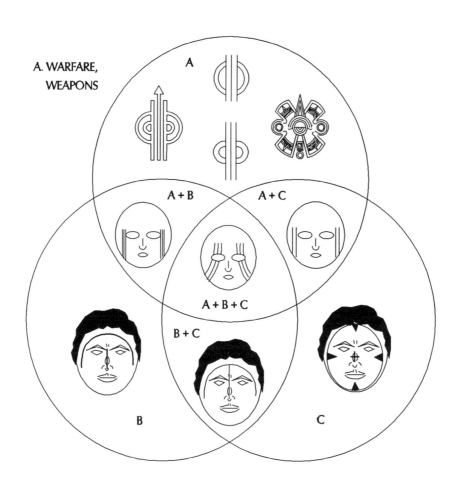

A. WARFARE, WEAPONS

A

A + B   A + C

A + B + C

B + C

B   C

B. ADOPTION, SUCCESSION   C. FERTILITY, WORLD RENEWAL

Figure 19.4 Venn diagram showing the associations of selected motifs of face painting in North America and Mesoamerica, as discussed in the text.

bisected circle motif that represents the grip of an atlatl, which was itself a metaphor of the earth that daily gives birth to the sun (figures 11.1, 14.3, and 19.4). This was the pattern of face paint of Xipe figures in Mesoamerican iconography, of the person adopted in the Lakota Calumet ceremony, and of the warrior pledging the Skiri Morning Star sacrifice. The comparison is made credible by the occasional portrayal of an eye centered within that form of the atlatl grip motif familiar as the Aztec Ollin glyph (figures 14.3g and 19.4a).

The specific identity of Xipe Totec within the natural world continues to elude Mesoamerican scholars, beyond the speculation that his flayed skin represented the husk of an ear of corn, or the hull of a kernel of corn, or a prepuce, or the sloughed skin of a serpent, or the vegetation of the earth renewed. As

Xipe he was not explicitly associated with any particular astronomical phenomenon, although there is a provocative reference in a Náhuatl poem to Xipe as Drinker of the Night, which opens the possibility that Xipe had one identity as a Fire Serpent. The *Codex Zouche-Nuttall* illustrates a Fire Serpent swallowing a ball court, which was a metaphor for the night sky. There is evidence that the darkness of night was thought of as a fluid by some Indian peoples.[30]

If one aspect of Xipe's Mesoamerican identity were to have been as a serpent, and as a Fire Serpent in particular, this association would have much explanatory power, even aside from the obvious association of skin sloughing with renewal. We know already that in the Calumet ceremony of Siouan tribes the child honored by adoption was referred to by the term Hunka or some cognate thereof and that the Omaha term for the child, Hu^n'ga, was a cognate of the name of the Omaha moiety or tribal half called Ho^n'ga, which included those clans related to the earth and its waters. The equivalent tribal half among the closely related Poncas was known by the name that James O. Dorsey renders as Wažáže and that he translates both as Osage and as Snake. Alice Fletcher and Francis La Flesche explain that Wažáže was "an old term . . . said to refer to the snake after shedding . . . [its] old skin and again in full power." The equivalent tribal half of the Osage includes two subdivisions whose names are cognates of both names, Hu^n'ga as well as Wažáže. The child adopted and symbolically reconceived in the Siouan Calumet ceremony could thus be thought to relate inferentially not only to the earth reborn but to the snake renewed as well, giving support to the idea of a serpent aspect for Xipe.[31]

In his Osage dictionary Francis La Flesche relates the Wa-zha'-zhe division, as he spells it, specifically to "the water portion of the earth," saying that it was also a personal name belonging to a gens whose origin myth told of encountering in their wanderings "a man who stood in the midst of the waters" and who declared, "Here stands Wa-zha'-zhe, a person who has made the waters of the earth his body." The man can thus be considered to have been a personification of the waters themselves as well as being a snake, almost like the Hidatsa twin Spring Boy, who as Black Medicine ate part of a large two-headed snake and consequently became Grandather Snake, dwelling in the Missouri River as the chief of water spirits.[32]

The Náhuatl word Xiuhcóatl, which can be translated as Fire Serpent, also translates as Turquoise Serpent with the differences deriving from the several meanings of the root modifier *xiuh-*, which can convey the meanings grass, green, turquoise, and precious, can serve as an intensifying modifier for heat, and can relate the noun root to the idea of year. It is not conventional for Mesoamericanists to think of the Xiuhcóatl in anything but its solar aspect, i.e., as a companion of the sun or as a solar fire–related weapon used by the Aztec tribal deity Huitzilipochtli. I infer that the puzzling sense of 'year serpent' derives from the relationship of the Xiuhcóatl to the circle of the horizon, viewed either as the limits of the blue horizon or as the encircling sea, explaining the 'circle of turquoise' referred to in the cosmology of the *Annals of Cuauhtitlán*, whose iconographic representation I see in the circle of Fire Serpents, i.e., Turquoise Serpents, around the perimeter of the Aztec Stone of the Sun. The circle of the horizon has the association of 'year' among the Sioux and the Pawnees, and presumably in Mesoamerica as well, because of its conflation with the ecliptic and the annual movement of the sun.[33]

Xipe is believed to have been a variant of the god of the hunt known in Huexotzinco and Tlaxcala, Mexico, as Camaxtli, whose temple was renewed every eight years. This suggests a relationship to the planet Venus because eight years is the length of a Mesoamerican sun-Venus cycle (chapter 11). The relationship thus inferred of Camaxtli to Venus is not, however, in serious conflict with any relationship of Xipe to a serpent. One of Venus's most familiar manifestations was as a serpent—as Quetzalcóatl—after all. Moreover, Camaxtli was also a variant of Mixcóatl, and Mixcóatl's name translates as Cloud Serpent with an accepted glossing of Milky Way. Mixcóatl was a god of the hunt for the Chichimecs, the nomadic northern frontier hunter bands out of whose background the Aztecs emerged, and the similarity must not be forgotten of ritual animal drives honoring Camaxtli to those featured in the Cheyenne Massaum ceremony (chapter 16), a renewal ceremony whose origin myth relates to two young men, one of whom, like Spring Boy/Black Medicine, had an encounter with a water serpent.

Myths with the Twins theme may include incidents in which animals are penned or released from pens or caves for the benefit of humanity, as in the story of the Cheyenne Massaum and of the Cherokee Thunder Boys. These stories are important for relating the ideas of earth interior, lightning, and the animals of nature, all things that lie in the background of Plains ritual clowns (chapter 16). These relationships are spelled out more clearly in parts of the Maya area where deified ancestors are believed to live inside mountains where they maintain corrals of the wild animals that are the *naguals* or external spirits of all living people. If a living person commits some misdeed, his animal alter ego may be released and if harmed would automatically cause his human counterpart to come to grief. Such a belief provides a powerful charter for mechanisms of social control related to mourning and respect for ancestors, if not outright ancestor worship.[34]

The accepted relationship of Xipe to the ritual combat of the gladiatorial sacrifice recalls Zelia Nuttall's comparison of the actions of the participants in the gladiatorial sacrifice to the Big Dipper, which wheels nightly around the Pole Star.[35] The victim was similarly constricted in his movements by the short rope that tethered him to the center of the round stone platform on which he stood with his wooden stick. On the North American Plains a member of a soldier society sworn to fight without retreating in defensive combat would often dramatize his pledge by tethering himself to a crook lance stuck into the earth (figure 19.5a). Partly as a demonstration of his personal courage, such a warrior might disdain using weapons that killed at a distance, sometimes to the extent of arming himself only with a distinctive quirt or whip in a wooden

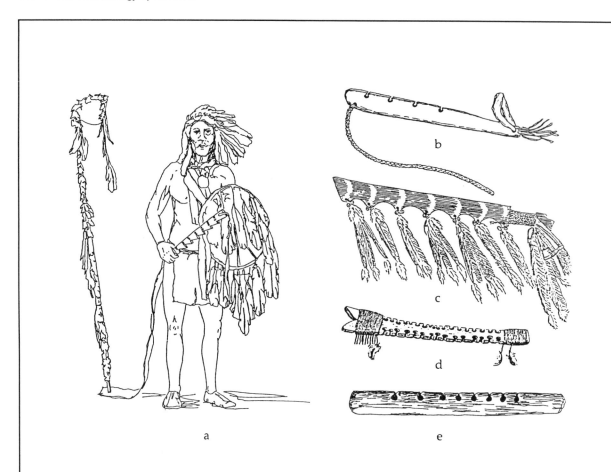

Figure 19.5 Certain fire sticks and Plains men's society regalia and their use: *a,* warrior, after Mails (1973, 48), shown in a no-retreat defensive mode tethered to an Arapaho (Plains Algonquian) crook lance, after Mooney (1896, pl. 122), holding an Arapaho quirt or whip, after Mooney (1896, fig. 94), resembling a notched club used in the Creek Busk or New Fire ceremony (cf. Howard 1968, fig. 23); *b,* Comanche (Shoshonean) quirt, resembling a hearth board, after Rollings (1989, 47); *c,* Arapaho men's society dance wand or sword, resembling a quirt handle, after Kroeber (1983, fig. 56); *d,* hearth board of the Hopi (Shoshonean) Aaltû society, resembling a quirt handle, from Fewkes (1900, pl. IV-1); *e,* Wind River Shoshoni hearth board, after Hough (1928, fig. 9). Not to scale.

handle that was a trademark weapon of such soldiers (figure 19.5).

The crook lances were not lances in the true sense of the word but, rather, standards or banners with wooden shafts in the form of a cane, wrapped with strips of fur or bird skin and embellished with feathers. Linguistic evidence from the Osage, Omaha, and Sioux suggests an original mental association of these crooks with the Dipper constellations. When staked with such a crook lance, the Plains warrior was limited in his movements to the circle of space around the crook, just as the Big Dipper is obliged to circle the Pole Star at the end of the handle of the Little Dipper.[36]

James Walker's Lakota source No Flesh attributed the origin of the Lakota Hunka ceremony, the Lakota version of the Calumet ceremony, to a chief who was mourning the loss of four sons who were members of the Kit Fox Society. This was a men's society or soldier society sworn to a code of chivalry and bravery.[37] I use the word 'chivalry' quite deliberately because the Kit Foxes and many other Plains men's societies had their counterparts in the orders of so-called jaguar and eagle knights among the Aztecs. There must have once been a fairly continuous distribution of such organizations from the northern Plains south into Mesoamerica, although only in Mexico did they come to dramatize combat with the fatal realism of the gladiatorial sacrifice. In the Plains warriors did, however, tether themselves as the quintessential act of defensive warfare.

In Aztec belief and widely in the Americas the night sky was associated with the underworld, so that traditions of descent from the night sky can be tantamount to traditions of ascent from the interior of the earth. The earthly world of the Pawnees was a reflection of a previous world among the stars, for instance, as was that of the Hidatsas. The traditional social organization of the Siouan peoples of the Plains and Midwest drew strongly on the symbolism of seven stars, and because the original homeland of a dozen or so Siouan tribes was specifically said to have been in the far north, the seven stars would more logically have represented a Dipper than the Pleiades. The seven original bands of the Sioux or Dakotas are spoken of even today figuratively as the seven fires, with the more literal meaning of seven 'fireplaces', La Flesche's comments on the Osage cognate supporting the more specific idea of 'fireplaces' as 'fire pits'.[38]

Almost a century ago Zelia Nuttall suggested that a certain seven mysterious caves in the far north, from which emerged the seven tribes of the Chichimec ancestors of the Aztecs, were actually the seven stars of one of the Dipper constellations. These seven caves (Chicomóztoc) were located within a mythical geological aberration whose name and pictorial representations identify it as a mountain with a curved or twisted top (Colhuacatépec), which was represented by a figure of hook shape. Had Nuttall been aware of the inferred relationship of crooks to the Dippers, she would undoubtedly have seen the hook-topped mountain itself as a Dipper. The comparison that she did make might have been taken more seriously had Mesoamericanists known that the Hidatsas saw in the seven stars of the Big Dipper a group of dogs that originated in dens (read 'pits' or 'caves') within a certain butte (read 'mountain') in North Dakota and that these dogs were the forerunners of the Hidatsa dog societies. Undoubtedly, this knowledge would have reawakened interest in the etymology of the name Chichimec itself, which some translate as something like 'lineage of dogs', although not without challenge.[39]

Because of its representation in the Spiro site shell engravings (chapter 11), the Morning Star sacrifice by arrows must have had a presence in the area of the trans-Mississippi Southeast by early Mississippi times. Because of Xipe's association in Mesoamerica with maize agriculture as well as with the arrow sacrifice, it might be logical to assume that the appearance of aspects of Xipe worship in the Plains dates no earlier than the Mississippi period and the beginning of maize agriculture in the eastern United States, but this assumption would ignore the important relationship of Xipe to modes of sacrifice mimicking combat and hunting. Xipe worship in Mesoamerica could profitably be examined as a special-case elaboration, within an area of intensive maize cultivation, of religious practices with wide-ranging and long-standing connections to warfare and hunting, but more particularly to World Renewal ritual in the context of animal resources, and to nature more generally. Referring to the broader context of the arrow sacrifice, Karl Taube says, in fact: "The scaffold ceremony does not appear to be a full-blown innovation by an enterprising elite; rather, it originated long before the emergence of complex Mesoamerican states, an example of a 'little tradition' becoming part of the 'big tradition' of the ruling elite."[40]

The abandoning of mound burial of the type common during the Woodland period could have been brought about by the gradual restricting of mound burial to the elite with the rise of socially stratified societies during the Mississippi period. During the Historic period and probably through the whole Mississippi period renewal of the world in the southeastern United States was accomplished by the New Fire ceremony as part of the Green Corn ceremony or Busk. I have reason to believe that Green Corn ceremonialism was an introduction from Mesoamerica during the period of the Toltec civilization in Mexico, which coincided with the beginnings of the Mississippi period in the eastern United States.[41] The dissociation of mound construction from World Renewal ritual could have led to the replacement of mound construction by cemetery burial for the general population and in time to the emergence of the Sun Dance and Calumet ceremony from elements previously associated with burial mound ceremonialism.

EAGLE TRAPPING AND THE CALUMET CEREMONY

What might an eagle trapper have thought while lying in the solitude of his pit through the day, awaiting the descent of an eagle? The practice was to prepare a pit or trench in which the trapper could sit or lie on his back concealed from the eagle beneath a loose covering. On this cover a dead rabbit was placed to attract the eye of a passing eagle, which was then supposed to swoop down to snatch the bait unaware that the trapper was ready to seize its legs. To increase his prospect of success, the trapper might first perform a ritual meant to snare the spirit of the eagle, using a small symbolic snare of twisted fiber made for that purpose.[42]

Lying on his back, relying on his bare hands for the catch, the trapper must have sensed a certain vulnerability that would not have been shared by a hunter crouching with a weapon. The trapper waited for the eagle to pounce upon the rabbit and then seized the legs of the eagle while its talons were sunk into the flesh of the rabbit, but there was little defense against the beak of the eagle or the talons if there were some misstep at this moment.

What might an eagle trapper have dreamt while sleeping in his eagle trapping lodge through the night? There are few things that can focus one's thoughts as much as lying in a grave, albeit only a metaphorical grave. It would be surprising if this association of eagle

Figure 19.6 The eagle as a sun metaphor soaring over a submound tomb in a Woodland period mound in process of construction. The situation of an eagle trapper lying in a grave-like pit, awaiting the descent of an eagle, may be compared to the symbolism of the adoptee in the Calumet ceremony, undergoing a symbolic reconception mediated by the calumet with its fan of eagle feathers, because of the inferred original status of the adoptee as a person not only symbolically resurrecting a deceased tribesman from the grave but also representing the earth awaiting the fertilizing touch of the sun, which will allow it to be reborn in the spring.

trapping pit and grave did not find some unconscious expression in the waking mind (figure 19.6). The act of trapping itself became a metaphor employed in greeting. Visitors entering a Hidatsa eagle trapping camp would be seized by the ankles to cries of "I have caught an eagle," and the fire pit in the lodge was not round, as might have been expected, but rectangular in shape, and was explicitly meant to represent an eagle trapping pit. The eagle was a common sun metaphor, and fire had a logical connection to the sun that was not overlooked.[43]

The magical snaring of the spirit of the eagle had its counterpart in the Calumet ceremony. In ceremonies of the Hako type the face or head of the child being adopted was painted, as we already know, with one or another variant of the quartered circle motif whose Osage name translates as 'trap' or 'snare'. A pair of calumets with their fans of eagle tail feathers were thrust toward the child's head in a short gesture representing the transfer to the child of a conceiving spirit. The spirit then entered the child's nose and descended to its breast. In Pawnee practice, the child received an identity transferred to it from an ear of Mother Corn representing the earth, an ear of corn referred to also by the ritual term 'snare'. 'Snare' was a term also applied by the Osage to the hearth. When arranged for ritual purposes the hearth with its four logs symbolized the earth and when aflame, amounted to a cosmogram representing earth and sun combined.[44]

How might the subconscious thoughts of an eagle trapper have combined to relate the capture of the eagle as sun metaphor to the snaring of the eagle's soul? How might they have combined to relate hearth pit as eagle trapping pit in metaphor with the metaphor of the trapper in his pit as a body in its grave? How might they have combined to relate the reawakening of the earth by the sun's warmth in spring with the requickening of the dead in the person of a friend animated by the spirit of the deceased during a ghost lodge ceremony? It is only hypothesis that rites of World Renewal were merged with rites of Spirit Adoption by burial mound builders of the Woodland period, but it is difficult in any other way to explain as elegantly the relationship of Spirit Adoption to Calumet ceremony, Calumet ceremony to Sun Dance, Sun Dance as mourning ritual to Sun Dance as World Renewal ritual, and Eagle Dance to Calumet Dance.

[The calumet] is a stick two feet long, as thick as an ordinary cane, and bored through the middle. It is ornamented with the heads and necks of various birds, whose plummage is very beautiful. To these they also add large feathers,—red, green, and other colors,—wherewith the whole is adorned. They have a great regard for it because they look upon it as the calumet of the Sun. . . .

Every one, at the outset, takes the Calumet in a respectful manner, and, supporting it with both hands, causes it to dance in cadence, keeping good time with the air of the songs. He makes it execute many differing figures. . . . Sometimes he offers it to the sun, as if he wished the latter to smoke it; sometimes he inclines it toward the earth; again, he makes it spread its wings, as if about to fly.[45]

AFTERWORD / *Connecting with the Past*

IN *BLACK ELK SPEAKS* Black Elk explains to John Nei-hardt that the spirit world "is the real world that is behind this one, and everything we see here is some-thing like a shadow from that world." The same philos-ophy applies nicely to culture history. The historical past was real, but the evidence that survives of it can be distorted and disconnected, like a shadow cast on a field of rocks. The evidence includes traditions often imperfectly transmitted between generations; ceremonies whose symbolism has changed to become supportive of new values; origin myths naturalized to new locations; ceremonial objects whose full significance was known only to elders who have died; the bones of Indians whose deaths silenced personal stories that still await telling; buried artifacts that speak of technologies long forgotten; and earth constructions that speak of rituals long abandoned.[1]

In 1562 the Spanish missionary priest Diego de Landa sought to hasten the process of converting the Mayas of Yucatan, Mexico, to Christianity by destroying a library of their hieroglyphic, screen-fold books on a blazing pyre along with five thousand 'idols'—all re-garded by him as works of the devil. The world had possibly not seen such a loss of written knowledge since the burning of the library of Alexandria in Julius Caesar's day. Archaeologists, linguists, and art historians have nevertheless made monumental progress in their effort to demonstrate the great degree to which the Mayas enjoyed a literate civilization for fifteen hundred years or more. Deciphered Maya texts illuminate a view of the Maya Creation that was tied not only to a very keen knowledge of the daily and annual motions of the stars and planets but also to a very refined calendar system and philosophy of time. The Mayas had created a theology of awesome sophistication that belies the Spanish portrayal of it as little more than a collection of trickeries of the devil designed to deceive and mislead those not yet enlightened by Christianity.[2]

Landa's burning of the ancient 'codices', as archaeol-ogists call these books, was not an unprecedented act in Mesoamerica, however, nor was historical revisionism a European invention. Less well known than Landa's book burning was that ordered by the Aztec ruler Itzcóatl in A.D. 1427. In that year the Mexicas of Tenochtitlan (today's Mexico City) defeated the Tepa-necs of Azcapotzalco to become the dominant Aztec power in the valley of Mexico. To legitimate the Mexicas' new status as an imperial power, Itzcóatl ordered the burning of records and genealogies in con-flict with Mexica visions of their perceived role and destiny in history. This vision required a social order in which personal abilities demonstrated in war became a basis for upward social mobility, replacing lineage an-cestry as the route to status, and it required creative pruning and grafting of Itzcóatl's family tree to legiti-mate his ascent to power. A mythology was provided that sanctioned the imposing of tribute on other king-doms and made the sacrifice of captives to the sun a mandate. A Mexica political agenda of the day was served by the destruction of the old records, but at the cost of losing whole literatures.[3]

When history is written only by the winners, posteri-ty is the loser. Modern Mexicans identify with a heri-tage that is much more inclusive than the patrimony of Tenochtitlan both in time and space. The benefits de-rived from Itzcóatl's destroying of the records appear fleeting when the history of the valley of Mexico is viewed as something greater than the dynastic history of the Aztecs, and there will be many who will remem-ber Itzcóatl only for what he destroyed, however justi-fiable his motives may have seemed at the time. This comparison can be extended to many other peoples. If this book has a central message it is that the culture history of North America can be compared more to a complex fabric than to a checkerboard. There is no Indian nation whose story does not have some bearing on the stories of other Indian nations, no thread of history for one nation that does not extend beyond its home territory to connect with the history of other nations.

On April 30, 1905, James Murie, himself a Pawnee, made a record of a story of the construction of the first

Skiri Pawnee earthlodge from the words of one Buffalo Skidi. This was the first earthlodge, built in the days of the Creation for the daughter of Morning Star and Evening Star and the son of Sun and Moon. To establish the location for this lodge the all-powerful Tirawahat was said to have caused an ash tree to grow where the center of the lodge should be. When the lodge was completed the Council of Chiefs—which we see only as the constellation *Corona Borealis*—ordered the sun to send down a blaze of fire that consumed the ash tree and left a hole that marked the location for the fireplace in the exact center of the lodge beneath the smokehole in the roof. To someone familiar only with Pawnee history and archaeology the element of the ash tree might be taken as simply a literary embellishment within an origin myth. To anyone with a knowledge of Caddoan ways that extends beyond the Pawnee to their southern linguistic relatives, the Hasinai and Wichita, Buffalo Skidi's account has fascinating relevance.[4]

The construction of Pawnee earthlodges did not require a central post or pillar, although a short ash stick was used to ceremonially mark the centerpoint of the projected lodge during construction. The construction of southern Caddoan grass lodges did require a large centerpost. Buffalo Skidi's story included a detail of house construction that any southern Caddoan of the seventeenth century would have recognized. Hasinai lodges were as much as fifty feet high, thatched with grass and built in a circular, slightly pointed, dome-shaped form. To facilitate construction, a large post was erected in the center of the house location to allow men at the top to draw together and fasten the many poles set into holes at the outer edge of the house floor. Once these vertical rib poles were bent together and securely tied, the center pole was removed and a firepit constructed over the location. Buffalo Skidi could have simply incorporated into his Pawnee story a detail from a southern Caddoan origin story, but more likely the story itself had a southern Caddoan origin in the remote past and may have been only incompletely readapted to the situation of the earthlodge-building Skiris. Such an origin may be betrayed by references to grass lodges in other Skiri stories related to Morning Star and his sacrifice, which did, of course, have an origin far to the south.[5]

Except for surviving knowledge of the mode of construction of southern Caddoan grass lodges, the element of the ash tree in the northern Caddoan story loses much of its significance. Except for the preserving of the northern Caddoan story of the first earthlodge, southern Caddoans would have lost the religious and literary correlate of a detail of their material culture long abandoned. And the lesson may be extended.

The year 1990 marked the two hundredth anniversary of the rediscovery of the Aztec Stone of the Sun or calendar stone. Much of the symbolism of the stone was easily read, but some remained undecipherable to any great degree of satisfaction. Like the sacred hoop of the Lakotas of which Black Elk speaks, the sun stone is a many-voiced cosmogram. Among other things, the stone can be seen as the earth island surrounded by a pair of serpents that in one dimension personify the encircling sea and in another but conflated dimension personify the path of the sun, moon, and planets across the sky. Under certain conditions the serpents represented on the stone were believed to become visible as short arcs of fiery colors—sun dogs—that bracket the rising and setting sun.[6]

On this cosmogram the direction east can be identified by the position of an engraved glyph for the day 13 Reed, which in both Aztec and Maya cosmology was identified with the birth of the sun. The direction west can be identified by the position of the heads of the two serpents, between whose jaws the sun sets daily as it descends beneath the earth. Chiseled adjacent to and above the two serpent heads are two day glyphs that defied satisfactory interpretation for two hundred years. These were the days 1 Rain and 7 Monkey, which are situated on either side of the earth's western portal.

Within the repeating 260-day sacred year of the Aztecs, 1 Rain is the 79th day and 7 Monkey the 111th day. The days are thus 32 days apart, but also 260 + 32 or 292 days apart because of the repeating nature of the sacred year. The period of 292 days is the mean interval between conjunctions of the sun and Venus, which occur twice during the 584-day synodical period of Venus, once at superior conjunction preceding the appearance of Venus as an evening star and once at inferior conjunction just before the appearance of Venus as a morning star. It would thus seem that 1 Rain and 7 Monkey were calendar-based names for Venus in its two aspects.[7]

One of Venus's guises in Aztec cosmology was as the god Xólotl, a god who served as guardian of the portal by which the sun enters the earth nightly in the west. The name 'Xólotl' was glossed to mean male servant, page, messenger, and slave. These functions correspond to the office of errand man of the Pawnee, whose cosmology compares in so many ways to that of the Aztecs, as we have seen. During formal events such errand men sat on either side of the entrance to the lodge, one on each side, like the 1 Rain and 7 Monkey glyphs, as guardians, in effect, of the entrance to the earth (cf. figure 12.1). In Plains Indian thought lodges were metaphors of earth and sky. Except for preservation of knowledge relating to Pawnee errand men, the cosmological significance of the 1 Rain and 7 Monkey glyphs on the sun stone would have gone unsuspected.[8]

Venus was the archetypal warrior. Xólotl's name survives even today as the root for the Mexican Spanish word for male turkey, *guajolote*, an *aztequismo* derived from the Aztec word *huēhxōlōtl*. This relationship of Xólotl to the turkey makes little sense until one considers the clue that in the southeastern United States the male turkey symbolized the warrior with the pendant hairy neck feathers of the turkey seen as trophy scalps and the turkey's gobble heard as a war cry. As a manifestation of Venus Xólotl did, indeed, have warrior credentials. The *Codex Borgia* portrays Xólotl with a hand painted over his mouth, a manner of face painting that was found widely through the Plains to symbolize a war honor and that can be dated in the Midwest back to the Mississippi period: a hand appears over the mouth of a falcon warrior on an embossed copper plate from Malden, Missouri, that dates to that time. The native inhabitants of central Mexico shared much of the symbolism and imagery of warfare found throughout the eastern United States, and it would be unwarranted to say that this sharing resulted simply from northward diffusion. We must look to a pattern of interaction through many centuries, perhaps millennia, that crossed many boundaries defined by accidents of history.[9]

The cultural patrimony of North American Indians and modern Mexicans alike would be the poorer if the Sun Stone had been simply reburied following its rediscovery in 1790. Instead, the stone was moved for display to the atrium of the national cathedral. Cultural objects and preserved traditions can tell stories beyond count when they are approached like respected elders and their mysteries sought out. The prospect is still bright for someone to write a culture history of the plains and plateaus, prairies and woodlands that is a connected narrative of the whole Indian people and not just an anthology of tribal perspectives.

NOTES

PREFACE

1. Bailey 1995; Liberty 1978, 52.
2. Medicine 1981, 281.

ACKNOWLEDGMENTS

1. Tribal Judges 1960.

CHAPTER 1

1. Médard Chouart, Sieur des Groseilliers, was married to Marguerite, the half-sister of Pierre d'Esprit, Sieur de Radisson. Groseilliers arrived in Canada in 1641 and Radisson, ten years later. Radisson wrote an account of their travels in English for the purpose of interesting King Charles II in sponsoring a fur-trading venture with posts on Hudson's Bay. The bay was accessible to the English by sea, and trading there did not interest the French authorities. A manuscript of the account was discovered in 1750 among others being used as wrapping paper by London shopkeepers. In 1670 Charles II did grant a charter for what became the Hudson's Bay Company, still doing business after more than three centuries.

2. The Feast of the Dead was a ceremony found among the Hurons, who were non-League Iroquoians, and their Algonquian neighbors to the west, such as the Ojibwas and Nipissings. The ceremony was held at intervals of about seven years and rotated among villages. It was an occasion for the reburial of the dead from many villages in a common grave and was used to confirm continuing friendly intergroup relationships. See, for example, Hickerson 1960.

3. Radisson 1888, 76–77.
4. Ibid., 77.
5. Skinner 1915, 700–701.
6. Radisson 1888, 83.
7. Ibid., 83.
8. Kellogg 1925, 123. Through the present century it has been widely believed that Jean Nicolet traveled through the Great Lakes until arriving in 1634 among the Winnebago Indians at or near their traditional village on the east shore of Green Bay in Wisconsin. As archaeological knowledge of Wisconsin has become more refined, however, the archaeology has become increasingly difficult to reconcile with the idea of a Green Bay landfall for Nicolet.

It is currently believed possible: (a) that the Winnebago, as known today, are the survivors of a population that until the fifteenth century occupied much of southern Wisconsin and northern Illinois but which had diminished by 1634 to much smaller numbers occupying a territory south of Chicago, represented by the distribution of the Huber culture (a phase of Oneota culture); (b) that it was in this southern Cook County, Illinois, location where Nicolet actually found the Winnebago in 1634; and (c) that the traditional Green Bay village was the location where the Winnebago reorganized their independent tribal life after a period of captivity following a devastating defeat around 1640 by the Illinois, who then moved into the former Winnebago territory in Illinois, where the Illinois were found in 1673 by Jacques Marquette and Louis Jolliet (Hall 1995b). This interpretation finds support in new knowledge of the archaeological identity of the Illinois that suggests that the Illinois had a much shallower history of occupation in Illinois than previously believed and were more likely indigenous to a location in or near the Lake Erie basin than that of Lake Michigan.

9. Hall 1995a; *Jesuit Relations* 54:217; *Wisconsin Historical Collections* (*WHC*) 16:68. A bronze combination sundial and compass was found in 1902 at Point Sable on Green Bay that dates to Allouez's time (Hall 1993b, 25–26; *WHC* 16:opposite 64). The mile of shore between Point Sable and Red Banks to the north contains evidence of several Indian occupations, at least one believed to date to the late seventeenth century (Hall 1993c; Hall 1995b).

10. La Potherie 1911–1912, 368.
11. Ibid., 368–369.
12. Ibid., 369–370; emphasis added.
13. Swanton 1946, 722–733.
14. Wagley 1977, 238.
15. Ibid., vii, citing Jean de Léry, *Le Voyage au Brésil, 1556–1557* (1st ed., 1578), 1927 edition, 258.
16. Wagley 1977, vii, citing Fernan Cardim, *Tratado da Terra e Gente do Brasil em 1665*, describing the Tupinambá.
17. Wagley 1977, vii, citing Abbeville n.d., describing the Tupinambá.
18. Leakey 1973, 5–6.
19. This is not a characteristic of "primitive" reasoning but of the way the brains of all humans are organized. To learn about the underlying principle involved see Frazer (1935, 1:174–214), Hall (1977, 500–502), and Jakobson and Halle (1971).
20. Bergen 1899, 19.
21. Kluckhohn 1944, 18.
22. Nuñez Cabeza de Vaca 1871, 66; Nuñez Cabeza de Vaca 1904, 56.
23. Bushnell 1935, 5.
24. Hewitt 1907, 191.
25. Paper 1989, 88.
26. Fletcher [and Murie] 1904.
27. *Jesuit Relations* 51:47, 53; Kellogg 1925, 154.

28. *Wisconsin Historical Collections* 16:57–58; paragraphing added.

29. Kinietz 1940, 195.

30. Hamilton 1970a, 117; Hamilton 1970b, 47.

31. *Jesuit Relations* 59:106–107.

32. Hamilton 1970a, 161.

33. *Jesuit Relations* 59:129–137.

34. Two of the three Peoria villages mentioned by Marquette have recently been discovered and are the subject of test excavations, one by Larry Grantham of the Missouri Division of State Parks and another by Kathy Ehrhardt of New York University in collaboration with Lawrence Conrad of Western Illinois University. It had previously been thought that these villages were located near Toolesboro, Iowa.

35. *Jesuit Relations* 59:150–151.

36. Ibid., 185–191.

37. Hamilton 1970a, 48, 146–150; Hamilton 1970b, 74–77; *Jesuit Relations* 59:201–205.

38. Hamilton 1970a, 189–195, 196.

CHAPTER 2

1. Brasser 1974, 25; Brasser 1978, 209; Minet 1987, 42n.

2. Tonty 1879, 593–595.

3. Brasser 1974, 1; Brasser 1978, 211.

4. Brasser 1974, 1; Brasser 1978, 211. Note that the Mahicans were members of the Algonquian language family or stock, as were all Indians of New England and eastern Canada during the seventeenth century. By a convention agreed upon by Americanist linguists all indigenous language families on the American continents have been given names with the adjectival ending -an added to the name of a language typical of the family or stock. We thus have Algonquin as the eponymous language of the Algonquian family, Siouan from Sioux, Iroquoian from Iroquois, and so on.

The spellings 'Algonquin' and 'Algonquian' have been used in the present work in preference to Algonkin and Algonkian, following the practice of the Smithsonian Institution in its *Handbook of North American Indians* and that of the Canadian government in, for example, the naming of its Algonquin Provincial Park, Ontario.

5. Brasser 1978, 211; Day 1978a, 149; Hunter 1978, 592; Weslager 1972, 214.

6. Day 1978a, 151.

7. Tonty 1879, 594. Tonty says that eighteen Indian men accompanied the expedition but he gives only seventeen names. The missing name presumably would have been that of La Salle's faithful Ouiouilamec.

8. Parkman 1925, 7–14.

9. The source text says merely 'Bristol,' but Bristol, Connecticut, was not founded until the eighteenth century, so Bristol, Rhode Island, was necessarily meant. See Anderson 1901, 270–271.

10. Anderson 1901, 275.

11. Parkman 1925, 235n. For the fate of other captives, see Anderson 1901, 235–237; and Parkman 1925, 235.

12. Anderson 1901, 275–277. The paragraphing has been changed for this extended quotation here and in later passages.

13. Ibid., 277–279; emphasis added. I have replaced the translator's English 'unwonted' for French *extraordinaires* with the more current 'unusual'. In this passage La Salle is made to appear that he is treating the Miamis to an entirely new experience.

14. Ibid., 279–285; emphasis added. Onontio means 'The Great Mountain' in Iroquois and was the name used to refer to the governor of Canada by Iroquoian and Algonquian speaking tribes alike (Parkman 1925, 156n).

15. Anderson 1901, 251, 261, 285. Parkman 1925, 187.

16. Anderson 1901, 287–289; emphasis added.

17. Kinietz 1940, 202; Trowbridge 1938, 33–37.

18. Anderson 1901, 289–293; emphasis added.

19. Anderson 1898, 19–21.

20. Cooper 1961, 23; see McWilliams (1985, 151) for critical comment on this passage.

21. Anderson 1898, 21.

22. Ibid., 39.

23. Galloway 1982, 37; Minet 1987, 54.

24. Parkman 1925, 306–308.

25. Ibid., 301–303; Tonty 1879, 600–601.

26. Anderson 1898, 51; Minet 1987, 58.

27. Anderson 1901, 223–225; Parkman 1925, 230–234.

28. Hall 1991a.

CHAPTER 3

1. Beginning in February of 1847 Parkman's book was serialized in the *Knickerbocker Magazine* under the title *The Oregon Trail*. It was published as a book in 1849 with the title *The California and Oregon Trail* and in one American edition with the title *Prairie and Rocky Mountain Life* (Parkman 1963, ix).

2. Roberts 1937, 106.

3. Parkman 1963, 11. Another verbal image from Kenneth Roberts may have been influenced by the well-known photograph of the body of Chief Big Foot after the Wounded Knee Massacre of December 29, 1890, in South Dakota. Big Foot's body was found frozen with both arms raised. For a recent publication containing this photograph see D. Brown (1970, pl. 48). This posture calls to mind Roberts's (1937, 187) character Langdon Towne in *Northwest Passage* describing an Abenaki with an arm raised defiantly even in the rigor of death after Major Robert Rogers's attack on the Indian town of St. Francis in Canada. There is no historical basis for Roberts's description in the records of Rogers's expedition.

4. Early editions, beginning with the first in 1867, were called simply *The Discovery of the Great West*. The title *La Salle and the Discovery of the Great West* (Parkman 1925) did not appear until the eleventh edition of 1879.

5. Hitt [ca.] 1887.

6. A brief history of the archaeological investigations on the summit of Starved Rock is given in Hall 1991a.

7. Parkman 1983, 1:835n3.

8. Henriksen 1965.

9. Ibid., 6, figs. 3, 28b. Possible Adena bird prototypes of the Hopewellian snake-bird can be seen in Webb and Baby (1957, figs. 33–35, 37–39, 44–45, 47–49). Examples of the snake-bird from Marksville-Hopewellian Crooks site can be seen in Ford and Willey (1940, figs. 28d–f, 30b–b', 31c–d', 32a–b, 36e, 38, 39a–a'). The snake-bird motif on a Hopewel-

lian bowl is the logo of the Illinois Archaeological Survey. Cf. Swanton 1946, 751; Hudson 1976, 129–130, 133, 340.

10. Kelly and Cole 1931, 326–327.

11. Griffin 1945, 47.

12. Herold 1971, 14–15.

13. McKern 1928, 251; McKern 1930, 442.

14. See Hall (1979, 260) for a longer commentary on special earths used in burial mound construction in the Midwest, including bog and lake-bottom marls.

15. Henriksen 1965, 65.

16. Nancy O. Lurie, personal communication.

17. This pattern of patches of black muck was found in Ryan Mound 4, Allamakee County, Iowa (Logan 1976, fig. 19). Compare with the pattern in Dorsey (1905a, fig. 64), and Grinnell (1972, 2:294).

18. Pottery found in mounds 1, 2, and 4 of the Ryan group was of the type called Lane Farm Cord-Impressed. The necks of vessels of this type have the individually impressed twisted cord designs of much Late Woodland pottery in the upper Midwest, especially that associated with effigy mounds in Wisconsin. The bodies of vessels of Lane Farm Cord-Impressed were in addition decorated overall with a so-called dentate rocker stamping otherwise mainly found on pottery of the preceding Middle Woodland period. My own guess date for the pottery would be A.D. 400–600.

The pattern of muck patches was created within an area defined by coloration with red ocher. With the bundle burial there was an awl or rod of native copper 15.5 inches long. This has created a dilemma because the presence of red ocher staining, utilitarian copper, and certain diagnostic flint blades has suggested an affiliation with the Red Ocher culture of Illinois and adjacent states, which fell toward the end of the Late Archaic period and dates no later than about 500 B.C. There was no information recorded by the excavator (Ellison Orr in the mid-1930s) on the relationships of the small pot within Mound 4.

19. The Newville mounds were excavated in 1877 by W. C. Whitford and W. P. Clarke of Milton, Wisconsin. These mounds comprised the Rock River Group of Arlow B. Stout and Halvor L. Skavlem (1908, 50, 51). The burials were described by Clarke (1884) in print and in correspondence preserved in the Charles E. Brown papers in the State Historical Society of Wisconsin, Madison (B. J. C. 1876). Hall (1962, 112–113, 115) reports testing of a stratified woodland refuse midden at an adjacent village area. The Outlet Site burials with white facial clay were excavated by A. H. Whiteford (1949) in August of 1948 and were described by Charlotte Bakken (1950, 51–53).

The Potawatomi and Winnebago accounts are found in Skinner (1924, 47–48; Skinner 1927, 397–398), and Bergen (1896, 52). Related beliefs of the Menominees can be found in Skinner and Satterlee (1915, 455). Marl or 'bog limestone' is a calcium carbonate sediment with minute lacustrine snail shells. See Martin 1916, 262.

The covering of Adena burials with clay is discussed by Webb and Snow (1945, 73) and called "a fairly common practice."

20. Count 1952.

21. Barnouw 1977, 68; Blackbird 1887, 77; Dorsey 1903, 198; Dorsey 1904a, 11; Erdoes and Ortiz 1984, 105–107;

Fletcher and La Flesche 1972, 1:63; Grinnell 1972, 2:337–338; Hewitt 1903, 181–182; Howard 1981, 185, citing Trowbridge 1939, 60–64; Hudson 1976, 133; Owen 1904, 37.

22. Dorsey 1903, 191–200.

23. Ibid., 119–120.

24. Grinnell 1972, 2:337–338. The Cheyenne blue duck was identified by Grinnell, from details of its description, as "the coot or mud-hen, *Fulica*," which would necessarily be the American coot, *Fulica americana* (Grinnell 1972, 2:338n2).

25. Grinnell 1972, 2:211; Walker 1917, 61.

26. Dorsey 1905a; Lowie 1915; Lowie 1956; Walker 1917. For some critical, theoretical, and comparative commentary on ceremonies subsumed by the rubric Sun Dance see Bennett 1944; Brown 1989, 193–199; Clements 1931; Dorsey 1910; Jones 1967; Jorgensen 1972; Schlesier 1990; Spier 1921; Wilson 1981.

27. Bowers 1950, 111–163; Catlin 1976.

28. Beckwith 1969, 38–43; Bowers 1965, 317, 349, 359. In the Hidatsa versions of the experiences of Long Arm and the twins, as reported, Long Arm was only threatened with the loss of his hand but did not actually lose a hand or arm. In the Crow versions of the same story Long Arm was both killed and mutilated (Lowie 1918, 92–93, 98). In view of the use of a human-hand trophy in the Hidatsa ceremony dramatizing the torture and rescue of Spring Boy, I would guess that the origin myth of the NaxpikE had originally included the mutilation of Long Arm.

Lowie (1919, 415) says that Hidatsa *naxpiké* (in his orthography) is "said to mean something like 'hide covering'," but the word would seem to contain more than the single root word for 'hide'. Washington Matthews's (1874) Hidatsa dictionary gives *dahpi* 'pelt, robe' and *diki* 'beat'. In Hidatsa and Crow there is no sharp distinction between *n* and *d*. The Hidatsa name for the ceremony is thus possibly a contraction of the words for 'hide' and 'beat'.

29. Spier 1921, 453.

30. Count (1952) proposes a post–Christian Era and, therefore, a late dating of the Earth Diver theme in North America, and this belief is also expressed in his doctoral dissertation (Count 1935).

31. Fletcher and La Flesche 1972, 1:63. The authors' note calls attention to the personal name I'batsetatse (Winds Coming Together) of the Sho'ka subdivision of the Hoⁿ'ga division of the Osages. Note also the similarity of the concept to that of the wind center of the Lakotas (Densmore 1918, 12n1, 122).

32. Dorsey 1905a, 136–140, figs. 63–70.

CHAPTER 4

1. Wedel 1948, 17–20; Wedel 1961, 167; Wheeler Bridge Mounds 1947.

2. Hall 1976.

3. Cole and Deuel 1937, 10–11; Marion Dickson, personal communication 1965.

4. Based upon an uncalibrated age of 1230 ± 120 B.P. (I-562) reported in Trautman (1963, 71–72).

5. Hennepin 1903, 1:241; Wallis 1947, 34.

6. Hennepin 1903, 1:255.

7. Black Elk 1953, 29–30.

8. Fletcher 1953, 575–576.

9. Densmore 1918, 77.

10. Ibid., 78.

11. Fletcher 1953, 575.

12. Barrett and Skinner 1932, 494–499.

13. McKern 1942, 155–156.

14. McKern 1963, fig. 56.

15. Stoltman 1973, 11. Also see Torbenson et al. (1992).

16. Ibid., 117–118; Stoltman 1974, 88.

17. Hewitt 1894.

18. *Jesuit Relations* 10:287.

19. Fletcher 1884, 305, fig. 3*b*.

20. McCone 1968, 307.

CHAPTER 5

1. Wallace 1972, 103.

2. Ibid., 104–107. The eating of human flesh is said to have been officially prohibited under the articles of the Iroquois League (Hewitt 1920, 541), and it certainly would have been, between League members, although cannibalism directed at non-League members continued into the 1700s. In 1649 some of the flesh of Father Jean de Brébeuf was roasted and eaten by the Iroquois while he was still alive and being tortured at his mission station in Huronia (*Jesuit Relations* 34:31–35).

Richter (1992, 303n11) provides the sources for much documentation of Iroquois cannibalism. Algonquian neighbors to the east of the Iroquois referred to them by variations on a name meaning 'man-eaters', which has entered our general vocabulary as Mohawk (Fenton and Tooker 1978, 478; Jennings 1976, 161).

3. Tooker 1964, 32–33, citing *Jesuit Relations* 15:185–187. Note that the white dog designated to be burned during the Iroquois Midwinter or New Year celebration also wore a necklace of wampum (Morgan 1901, 202).

4. Tooker 1964, 33, citing *Jesuit Relations* 18:31.

5. Ibid.

6. Wallace 1972, 101.

7. Ibid., 102.

8. Jennings 1984, 195.

9. Parkman 1983, 2:133–134. I am descended directly from Sicaire Deguire's brother François Deguire (also called Larose) and am therefore a collateral descendant of Sicaire Deguire (also called Laprairie). Sicaire's body was never found, and there is no known report of him from captives who were later repatriated from the Iroquois.

I learned the fate of Sicaire Deguire from the research of his collateral descendant Frère René Desrosiers, Drummondville, Quebec, conveyed in a letter of October 11, 1989, to Lu Ann Elsinger of Stevens Point, Wisconsin, which she has shared with me as a fellow descendant of François Deguire.

10. Seaver 1856, 55–56.

11. Ibid., 56–60; paragraphing modified. The 'Washington's war' mentioned by Jemison refers to the opening engagements of the French and Indian War near present-day Uniontown, Pennsylvania, involving George Washington as an officer of the Virginia militia.

12. For detail from the Cheyennes on the art of preparing a scalp, see Grinnell 1972, 2:37–38.

13. Fletcher 1953; Pease and Werner 1934, 357; Blair 1911, 78.

14. The culture history and relationships of the Iroquoian peoples are discussed in detail by contributors to volume 15 of the *Handbook of North American Indians* (Trigger 1978). A keystone of Confederacy policy was avoiding the destructive force of blood revenge among League members. Relatives of homicide victims were encouraged at all costs to settle grievances by accepting wergild in the form of wampum belts, twenty for a man and thirty for a woman (Tooker 1978a, 423).

15. Tooker 1978a, 424.

16. Fenton 1975, 142–143; Hewitt 1920, 542; Tooker 1978a, 429.

17. E.g., Fenton 1946, 123, 127.

18. Hewitt 1916, 165; Hewitt 1944, 66.

19. Kinietz 1940, 119, citing Sagard 1632, 289–290. See also Tooker 1964, 45–46, citing Sagard in Wrong 1939, 209–210; and *Jesuit Relations* 17:242n7.

20. *Jesuit Relations* 23:167–169; Tooker 1964, 46.

21. Hewitt 1916, 166.

22. Fenton and Kurath 1951, 144; Tooker 1964, 135n58.

23. Bruyas 1862, 23; Fenton 1950, 26, 47.

24. Hewitt 1920, 544.

25. Tooker 1964, 137.

26. *Jesuit Relations* 10:279.

27. Fenton and Kurath 1951, 143–144; Tooker 1964, 135n58.

28. *Jesuit Relations* 10:289, 291.

29. Ibid., 293–301.

30. Tooker 1964, 139–140.

31. *Jesuit Relations* 34:31–35.

32. *Jesuit Relations* 23:211.

33. Ibid., 213.

34. Kinietz 1940, 194. The particular example Kinietz was writing of came from the Miami.

35. *Jesuit Relations* 23:215.

36. Ibid., 217.

37. Cadillac n.d. cited in Kinietz 1940, 283–284; emphasis and paragraphing added.

38. Blair 1911, 86–87; Hickerson 1960, 81, 87, 98–99.

39. One of the primary sources of information on these feasts was Fray Bernardino de Sahagún (1948, 302–305; Sahagún 1971, 106–112), who designated them in Spanish *Fiestecilla de los Muertos* and *Fiesta Grande de los Muertos*, which translate as Little Feast of the Dead and Great Feast of the Dead. Sahagún's younger contemporary, Fray Diego Durán, referred to the former by terms translating both as Little Feast of the Dead and Feast of the Little Dead.

40. Densmore 1918, 114

41. Durán 1971, 203–206; Sahagún 1971, 108–112. Compare the illustration of the effigy on top of the Xócotl pole in *Codex Borbonicus* with that of a death bundle in *Codex Magliabecchiano* (Caso 1958, 71, 96).

42. Durán 1971, 204n1, 206n2, 441, 441n1. Carmichael and Sayer (1991) detail the background of the celebration of the Feast of the Dead in Mexico from pre-Spanish times into the present day.

43. Strachey 1849, 98–100, cited in Swanton 1946, 749.

44. Soustelle 1984, 4.

45. Brown 1984, 195.

46. Hassig 1988, 100.

47. Radin 1945, 112, 154, 264, 337n31.

48. The incident of the flayed princess occurred several hundred years before the arrival of the Spanish and entered European recorded history in the late sixteenth century—years after the Conquest—described by Durán (1867–1880; Durán 1964) and Alvarado Tezozomoc (1878, 28). Woman of Discord is a translation for the title Yaocihuatl, which derives from Náhuatl *yāō-* 'war' and *cihuātl* 'woman'.

49. Gillespie 1989, 59–60.

50. Ibid., 65, 68.

51. Joseph Gabel (1975) proposes that persons with serious mental disturbances, such as schizophrenia, may be illustrating in their personal delusions the kind of false consciousness provided on the societal level by ideologies as collective delusions, and that the delusions of the schizophrenic, for instance, may be thought of as a mode of adaptation. Ideologies are themselves modes of adaptation in that they organize perceptions of the world and suggest guides to action that may relieve anxieties caused by circumstances over which a society has no control. Such circumstances may be real (crop-killing droughts or unpredictable late frosts) or imagined (space aliens living among us).

In an introduction to Gabel's book Kenneth Thompson cites from Eugene Minkowski the example of a schizophrenic terrified each morning by the delusion "that he would be tortured to death that evening, the certainty of which was never shaken by its failure to happen the previous day" (Gabel 1975, xi). This personal delusion compares to the Aztec fear that the sun could not rise each morning unless strengthened by the blood of human sacrifices, a belief that presumably was not allowed to be challenged by any history of the sun rising before the practice of daily human sacrifice (see Afterword).

CHAPTER 6

1. For a full-length biography of Jones, see Rideout (1912). A brief biographical sketch and biobibliography of William Jones is given in Jones (1939, vii–ix, 115). The Fox are a tribe distinct from the Sauk or Sac but for years have been treated with the Sac as a single tribe, the Sac and Fox, by the Federal government for administrative purposes.

2. Jones 1968, 269–270; emphasis added.

3. Ibid., 271–272.

4. Owen 1904, 84–86.

5. Ibid., 78.

6. Jones 1968, 274.

7. Speck 1907, 168.

8. La Flesche 1939, 141–142.

9. The Ilongot referred to here are a mountain people of northern Luzon and are not closely related to the people called Ilongo who occupy some of the smaller Philippine islands.

10. Jones 1908, 4.

11. Dumaliang 1909.

12. Spier 1921, 453.

13. Bowers 1965, 306, 316, fig. 2.

14. As calculated by Headley (1971), using the method of glottochronology and published vocabularies, the proto-Mandan and proto-Hidatsa-Crow languages as a group separated from other Siouan speakers about 150 B.C., followed by the separation of Mandan from Hidatsa-Crow about A.D. 350, and Hidatsa from Crow about A.D. 1150. These are linguistic separations, but they imply loss or infrequency of contact.

Relying on one informant for each dialect, Pierce (1954) found a greater time depth for the separation of Hidatsa from Crow. Using the method of 'dialect distance', he estimates that Hidatsa and Crow communities spoke a single dialect about 14 B.C. and, using the method of glottochronology, that Hidatsa and Crow speakers formed a single speech community around A.D. 771. The method of dialect distance is based upon failure of understanding, which breaks down faster than failure of recognition of cognate words by an expert linguist. The average date of separation of Hidatsa and Crow generated by glottochronology would be A.D. 960.

15. The original Crow Sun Dance was abandoned in 1875. The Shoshoni Sun Dance was introduced in 1941 (J. E. Brown 1989, 197–198; Voget 1984).

16. Lowie 1919, 421; Lowie 1956, 304, 307.

17. Lowie 1956, 280, 317. The number twenty for the poles of the Crow Sun Dance lodge is that given by Lowie (1956, 313, 321), although the model illustrated by Lowie (1956, fig. 14) just has twelve. In the example given by Lowie only the first pole was cut with the ceremony and symbolism common to the Sun Dance elsewhere, and that pole was left where it fell. The twenty poles used in the lodge were cut without ceremony.

For the purpose of the Tobacco Society adoption ceremony a lodge was constructed that at its center contained a feature called the *arā'ca* in Crow, which Lowie refers to as an altar, for want of any better word in English. The altar was a flat, rectangular area two-and-a-half by five feet in dimensions and was said to represent a tobacco garden. It resembled a bed in that it was sometimes strewn with juniper sprigs and was demarked on its two longer sides by logs (Lowie 1920, fig. 9; Lowie 1956, pl. opp. 290).

The altar in the Crow Tobacco Society adoption lodge also recalls the rectangular trench associated with the altar of the Arapaho Sun Dance in that sage branches were strewn in the trench and on each long side of the trench there were placed poles with the same name given the poles used to define sleeping areas in Arapaho lodges (Dorsey 1903, 120).

18. Jones 1968.

19. MacLeod 1938, 361, 364–365, 384–388, 395.

20. Bowers 1965, 317; Swanton 1942, 181.

21. Bowers 1965, 316–319; Lowie 1956, 306–308.

22. Lowie 1956, 319.

23. Beckwith 1969, 39–40, 43.

24. Karl Schlesier (1990) has recently published a provocative article titled "Rethinking the Midewiwin and the Plains Ceremonial Called the Sun Dance." Perhaps the least provocative of this rethinking is his characterization of the Sun Dance as an "anthropological fiction" or an "anthropological invention" (Schlesier 1990, 1, 23). The name 'Sun Dance' always has been mainly a convenient fiction. Potentially more controversial in my mind is Schlesier's argument that *both* the Midewiwin and the Sun Dance, or what has conveniently been called the Sun Dance, "developed because the old Indian world of the western Great Lakes and the eastern Great Plains was crumbling under the impact of: a) epidemic

diseases. . . ; b) the disorganization of previously existing social, economic and religious systems; and c) the demands of European explorers, fur traders, military personnel and missionaries."

Schlesier sees the Midewiwin and Sun Dance originating as "expressions of revitalization and reorganization." It would be hard to prove that he is wrong, but I am more disposed to seek a more natural birth for the Sun Dance before falling back on the influences of disasters brought on by Europeans. The idea of a 'revitalization movement' has become an explanatory cliché for religious intensification in the shadows of recorded history. The Calumet ceremony and the Southeastern Ceremonial Complex (alias the Buzzard Cult, alias the Southern Death Cult) were once similarly proposed to be 're-vitalization' or 'nativistic' or 'messianic' movements in response to the effects of European contacts, but the suggestions have not survived more careful scrutiny (see Blakeslee 1981; Griffin 1944; Howard 1968, 7; Phillips and Brown 1984; Schlesier 1990, 23; Turnbaugh 1979; Waring 1945).

CHAPTER 7

1. Biographical material on Alice Cunningham Fletcher is taken largely from Mark (1988) and Wilson (1974).

2. Mark 1988, 56–57.

3. Ibid., 70, 73.

4. Ibid., 76.

5. Wilson 1974, 302–303.

6. Mark 1988, 152–153, 207, 346, 348.

7. Fletcher 1884; La Flesche 1885.

8. La Flesche 1913, cited in Mark 1988, 338.

9. Barnes 1984, 11.

10. J. Dorsey 1884, 278–279, 163, fig. 23; Fletcher and La Flesche 1972, 2:379.

11. Fletcher 1884, 310, 310n11, fig. 1g. Omaha *waha'ba* translates as 'ear of corn' (Fletcher and La Flesche 1972, 1:269); 'mother' would be a glossing for the ear in the context of the Wa'wa^n.

12. J. Dorsey 1884, 276, 281.

13. J. Dorsey (1884, 254) says of the Omahas, "My brother's children (male speaking) are my children, because their mother . . . can become my wife on the death of their father."

14. Fletcher 1884; Fletcher and La Flesche 1972, 386.

15. Fletcher and La Flesche 1972, 378.

16. Ibid., 397.

17. Ibid.

18. Ibid., 399–400.

19. Ibid., 379. Cf. Whitman (1969:125) saying, "The huηga may be either a boy or a girl, but a girl, I was told, was more frequently selected for honoring. The reason given was that 'they were the weaker sex.'"

20. Riggs 1968, 152, 157; emphasis in the original. I have used the Greek character eta (η) as an approximation of the phonetic character eng (η) in the original.

21. Buechel 1970, 188.

22. Boas and Deloria 1941, 102.

23. Whitman 1969, 31, 121.

24. Radin 1970, 131, 136, 141, 188, 189, 204. Among the Winnebago the civil or principal chief was chosen from the Thunderbird clan of the moiety representing the sky. For a comment on the history of chieftainship among the Winnebagoes, see Hall (1995b, 23).

25. La Flesche 1932, 65.

26. Fletcher and La Flesche 1972, 40–41, 141, 153.

27. Ibid., 389, 391, 393.

28. Matthews 1959, 256.

29. Boas and Deloria 1941, 55, orthography standardized from the original, boldface added.

30. Riggs 1968, 152.

31. Dorsey and Swanton 1912, 203, 258, 266, 277; Hall 1987, 39n1.

32. Fletcher 1884, 310; Fletcher and La Flesche 1972, 381, 397.

33. Fletcher and La Flesche 1972, 400–401.

34. In the Ponca ceremony the blessing strokes began with front and proceeded in the order of right side, back side, and left side and, since the child was facing east, in the order of east, south, west, and north. The order followed in the Omaha and Pawnee ceremonies was similarly 'sunwise', but the direction among the Otoes was the reverse or countersunwise, i.e., left, back, right, front or north, west, south, east. The Osage blessing proceeded in the sunwise order of right, front, left, back or south, east, north, west, but the instruments used were not the bundled calumet pipes but whisps of sedge grass and bunches of cedar fronds (Fletcher [and Murie] 1904, 206; La Flesche 1939, 250–252).

In the high northern latitudes the sun is perceived to travel clockwise from east to south to west because the sun can never be seen north of zenith at noon. In Mesoamerica, all of which lies south of the Tropic of Cancer, the sun is perceived to travel counterclockwise or east to north to west because through a variable part of the summer the sun rises in the east, is visible at noon north of zenith, and then proceeds to set in the west. The Omaha, Ponca, Osage, and Pawnee perception of 'sunwise' in the blessing ritual was thus northern, while the Oto perception was Mesoamerican.

35. Fletcher [and Murie] 1904, 206–209, 229–241.

36. Ibid., 22, 44, 47, 51, 52, 124, 206, 208–209, 236.

37. Black Elk 1953, 89, 108, 111; Densmore 1918, 120–121; La Flesche 1925, 362–363; La Flesche 1932, 63; La Flesche 1939, 244.

38. Blakeslee 1981, 761.

39. Reichard 1974, xxxvi, 112, 509–510, 583, 708.

40. La Flesche 1932, 63. One is reminded of the visible reciprocating action of the pistons of a steam locomotive that led to its recognition as symbol of a sexual intercourse in Freudian analysis.

41. Buechel 1970, 215, 584, 576; Grinnell 1972, 1:96, 262; Howard 1968, figs. 53a, 55, 56; Speck 1979, 79, 81, 110–112.

42. Fletcher [and Murie] 1904, 241; La Flesche 1939, 254.

43. La Flesche 1939, 254.

44. Dorsey 1969, 351.

45. Ruiz de Alarcón 1984, 155, 161–162, 166, 213, 286.

46. Fletcher [and Murie] 1904, 222, 228–230, 241; Schele and Miller 1983, 14, 94.

47. Fletcher and La Flesche 1972, 397.

48. Black Elk 1953, 111; Blakeslee 1981, 761; Fletcher and La Flesche 1972, 397; Fletcher [and Murie] 1904, 230; La Flesche 1939, 243.

49. Fletcher 1953.

50. Bowers 1965, 317. The motif is described as a black-painted "new [in this case a beginning crescent] moon" on the forehead with the horns extending onto the cheeks and the nose painted black.

51. Lowie 1915; Lowie 1956, 297–326.

52. "Guts was very happy now for he was even with the enemy for killing his two sons. No longer did he fast. He painted his body black and rubbed off the white paint" (Bowers 1965, 243).

53. Hall 1993b, 39.

54. *Jesuit Relations* 22:289.

55. Hall 1979; Hall 1983c; Hall 1987.

56. Hall 1989b, 255, 258–260; Speck 1919, 9.

57. Peters 1992, 25.

CHAPTER 8

1. Harrington 1926.

2. Skinner 1921, 41–43.

3. Ibid., 46–49.

4. Skinner 1920, 28.

5. Ibid., 32–33.

6. Ibid., 35.

7. Ibid., 42–43.

8. Ibid., 47, 61, 140, 165–168, 265, 336n22; Fletcher and La Flesche 1972, 2:529, 530, 566, 581; Hoffman 1896, 100–102, fig. 17, pl. 8. During the first initiation, when Mä'näbus himself was initiated, the various gods of the upper world and nether world removed their animal natures and became men, and the shed skins became the original medicine bags (Skinner 1920, 140).

9. Skinner 1920, 62.

10. Hoffman 1896, 97, fig. 14, pl. 7; Skinner 1920, 62–64, 333–335n15.

11. Skinner 1920, 112–113.

12. Ibid., 121–122.

13. Skinner 1925a, 301–303.

14. Skinner 1920, 123–127.

15. Hoffman 1896, 69–70.

16. Ibid., 72–74. Skinner (1920, 16) says that Hoffman incorrectly used *Mitäwit* for Mitäwin. The latter refers to the society while the former is a term sometimes used to indicate a candidate for the initiation ceremony or Mitäwiwin. Note also that Hoffman, Skinner, and Bloomfield each used different symbols for rendering the spoken Menominee language into print, and that the orthography of Bloomfield 1928 is even different from that of Bloomfield 1975, hence the different spellings, in the order of sources mentioned, Mä'nä-būsh, Mä'näbus, Me'napus, Mɛqnapos.

17. Forsyth 1827 cited in Bushnell 1927, 14; Hoffman 1896, fig. 6, 72–73. As Hoffman describes it, the baton was a stick about an inch thick and thirty inches long made of soft wood with three or four bands of shavings created along its length. These were made by making many long, shallow cuts and allowing the shavings to remain attached at their base. At the base of each band of shavings was a band of red paint an inch wide circling the stick. From accounts of such sticks for other tribes it is clear that these clusters of shavings originally represented scalps, which would also account for the band of red at the base of each (Skinner 1915, 758–759).

Ritzenthaler (1953, 145, figs. 9–10) describes a similar whittled stick for the forest Potawatomis of northern Wisconsin, calling it a 'brave stick' with the Potawatomi name of *yajimo 'kumtɪk*. He says that the red stripes represented blood and also that such a stick was erected by the grave "so that the dead warriors now in heaven will protect and help the soul on its journey to heaven." Skinner (1926) says that Iowa war chiefs had a staff of office called *wirotci pa^xnegr^xri*, which he illustrates (pl. 36, fig. 1) and describes as having four knobs to which shavings were once attached, each bunch of shavings representing a coup in battle.

Paul Radin (1970, 97) says of the Winnebagoes: "It was believed that every warrior was in control of the spirit of an enemy he had slain and he was supposed always to be willing to put the spirit at the service of any member of his tribe who had just died, if the proper offerings were made. At the proper time tobacco was given to the warrior, who, rising, narrated his war exploits, at the conclusion of which he ordered the spirit of the enemy he had slain to take charge of the deceased."

18. Jones 1938[?], 1–2; State of Wisconsin 1886, 2:628–631.

19. Skinner 1920, 20.

20. Skinner 1925a, 291.

21. A history of the 37th Wisconsin Volunteer Infantry is provided in Eden 1865. For the personal histories of members of K company, I have used the published roster in State of Wisconsin 1886 (2:628–631) supplemented and corrected by manuscript regimental rosters compiled by the Adjutant General of Wisconsin now in the Archives of the State Historical Society of Wisconsin. I identified Menominees in Company K as Menominees when their enlistment was in Keshena and their family names were obviously Indian, except for Dominekee Teco, who enlisted in Keshena and, like those with recognizably Indian family names, was described as having dark eyes, black hair, and dark complexion. Rubber is a patronymic derived from the given name of Wechanequaha 'The Rubber' (*Wisconsin Historical Collections* 3:280, 7:284n). For the Civil War Battle of the Crater, see Davis et al. 1986, chapter 3.

22. Skinner 1920, 22.

23. Skinner 1921, 41, 49. A photograph of Sabatis Perrote in full ceremonial dress appears as the frontispiece of the April 1921 issue of *The Wisconsin Archeologist*.

CHAPTER 9

1. Radin 1963, 20.

2. Radin 1911, 168.

3. John Moore (1974, 9–10) comments on this difference for the Cheyenne, giving the example of a Cheyenne acquaintance who was baptized a Mennonite and though joining the Catholic church later, and active on a committee of a Catholic mission school, was a lay Mennonite minister and had danced two times in the Sun Dance. His son was both a Mennonite and a Mormon, though baptized a Catholic.

4. Radin 1963, 48n123.

5. Edmunds 1983, 52; Mooney 1896, 679.

6. Radin 1945, 42–43.

7. Ibid., 48, 49.

8. Radin 1970, 302. The full version of the rite published by Radin in 1945 presented the origin myth in two forms, one essentially the same as that given here, first published in 1923, and another differing in several potentially important details. In the latter, Earthmaker made one set of Island-Anchorers, which he set in the four corners of the earth, and a second set, "four very white and awe-inspiring waterspirits" which he oriented "all in a row, facing the east, right underneath our grandmother, Earth." In other words, the second set of four would seem to have been laid in the earth parallel to one another.

9. Radin 1970, 304.

10. Ibid., 306.

11. Ibid., 306–308. Tobacco is not actually mentioned by name in this particular text, but it was obviously meant to be, except for an obvious copyreading error, as one may easily see by comparison with the text of the origin myth given by Radin later (1945, 27).

12. Radin 1970, 308–309.

13. Radin 1948, 34–35.

14. Fletcher and La Flesche 1972, 2:509–516.

15. Ibid., 2:565.

16. Radin 1945, 303.

17. For the birth of Flint and Sapling, see Hewitt 1903, 185–188; Tooker 1964, 151–155.

18. Radin 1948, 35.

19. Chittenden and Richardson 1905, 3:1080–1083.

20. In a classic study of Algonquian mythology Margaret Fisher (1946, 231) comments that "Even the earliest of the available versions [of the Manabozho or Nanabozho myths] have a composite character, and the writer inclines to the belief that 'Nanabozho,' as known to us, is not a really old Algonkian concept, but rather a synthetic figure growing out of the reworking of various older Algonkian myths, possibly under Iroquois influence." I see this as especially apparent in the names and characters of Manabush and his brothers.

Manabush, Manabozho, Nanabozho, and so on, are Anglicizations of names that are contractions of the Algonquian words 'great' and 'rabbit', yet in the Potawatomi versions it is a brother that is explicitly a rabbit, not the hero. This paradox is further compounded by the etymology of the name of the brother Chipiapoos or Chibiabos, which is a contraction of the words 'corpse' and 'rabbit', as I am informed by the Canadian linguist Paul Proulx. Chibiabos was the ruler of the land of the dead. He is not only *not* a rabbit in the Potawatomi stories, but he also corresponded to the wolf brother of the Menominee Manabush who became the ruler of the after-world. Manabush's brother or companion Little Wolf was also referred to in the Menominee stories by an epithet Na^xpatäo 'Expert Marksman', which appears cognate to the name Napatâ by which the same character was known in a Potawatomi Medicine Lodge origin collected by Skinner (1920, 327–330, 340n53) from Mrs. John Shawano, an Ojibwa married and living among the Potawatomis at Carter's Siding, Wisconsin.

The ruler of the land of the dead was, indeed, a rabbit in the mythology of the Potomacs, who were an Algonquian tribe living on the Atlantic Coast. He was also a "*great* hare" to whose dwelling place in the east the souls of the dead traveled (Strachey 1849, 98–100, cited in Swanton 1946, 749; emphasis added). It would seem that the name of the Potawatomi Chibiabos could be one survival of a period in Algonquian mythology when the land of the dead was ruled by a great rabbit, the Potomac myth being a more explicit example of the same.

21. Skinner 1924, 212–217. It is also not clear where or when this story was gathered. Skinner attributes "the bulk" of his information on the Potawatomis to a Samuel Derosier (Wapuka or 'Watching') of the former Wabash River (Indiana) band of Prairie Potawatomis, living at the time of Skinner's fieldwork on a reservation near Mayetta, Kansas, but the only source Skinner mentions specifically for the Medicine Society was a John Nu'wi (M'jikwus or 'Eldest One'), a Prairie Potawatomi living in Arpin, Wisconsin.

22. Hoffman 1896, 113–115.

23. Ibid., 87–88.

24. Bloomfield 1928, 132–153.

25. Hoffman 1891, 163–164, 278–286. Ritzenthaler (1953, 184) writes that among the Wisconsin Chippewas the "Midewiwin is now so dominated by the curative aspect that sickness is actually a pre-requisite for membership."

26. Radin 1970, 312.

27. Hoffman 1896, 68–69.

28. Radin 1911, 183, 185, 186.

29. Radin 1945, 74, 75–76.

30. Radin 1911, 194; Radin 1945, 33, 99, 103, 129, 145, 161, 167.

31. Radin 1970, 266–268, 307, 378; Radin 1945, 112, 154, 264, 337n31.

32. Radin 1911, 180, 187.

33. Ibid., 190.

34. Ibid., 179, 182.

35. Ibid., 158. The five bands represented the east, west, north, south, and the ancestor host. Membership in the bands changed from meeting to meeting depending upon who took the initiative for the ceremony and the order in which others were invited to participate. The title of the ancestor host in Winnebago was *x'okera*, which was a designation derived from *x'okê'* said to literally mean 'root' and metaphorically 'ancestor' (Radin 1911, 151, 154). The *x'okera* was the initiator and as such would seem to correspond in title to the *xo'ka* or initiator in the Osage tribal rite (La Flesche 1932, 219).

36. Radin 1945, 75, 197, 281, 282, 339n9; Weltfish 1977, 296–301. For shells Menominees and Chippewas used cowries of the species *Cypraea moneta* (Hoffman 1891, 220, 251, and pl. 11; Skinner 1920, 336n22). The Omahas used shells of the species *Olivia nobilis* and *Olivia elegans* (Fletcher and La Flesche 1972, 2:519–520).

37. Hickerson 1963, 78.

38. Ibid.; Day 1978b, 788, citing *Jesuit Relations* 23:209–223. My synopsis of the Algonquian Feast of the Dead is based largely upon Hickerson's paper.

39. Hickerson 1963, 76, citing Kinietz 1940, 329, referring to Raudot 1710a in Margry 1876–1886, 6:9–10.

40. Hickerson 1963, 76, citing *Wisconsin Historical Collections* 16:367.

41. Hickerson 1963, 77; Warren 1885, 78–80.

42. Hickerson 1970, 63, emphasis added.

43. Keesing 1987, 49.

44. Brébeuf in *Jesuit Relations* 10:205–207.

45. Ibid., 10:207–209; new paragraphing added.

46. Hoffman 1896, 97, pl. 7, fig. 14.

47. *Jesuit Relations* 30:23.

48. Ibid., 303n1.

49. Day 1978b, 790–791; *Jesuit Relations* 5:218.

50. Day 1978b, 789.

51. The Winnebagoes were known to the Hurons as the Aweatsiwaenrrhonon, or the A8eatsi8aenrrhonon in the French orthography of the *Jesuit Relations*. It appears that the peace that Nicolet arranged with the Winnebagoes in 1634 was already broken by 1636. In that year the Amikwas three days from the Hurons reported two of their men killed and eaten by the Aweatsiwaenrrhonon (*Jesuit Relations* 10:82–83). Thwaites (*Jesuit Relations* 10:32n7) said that the name Aweatsiwaenrrhonon in this report referred not to the Winnebagoes but to the Nipissings, but Day (1978b, 706) does not include the Nipissings within the designation Aweatsiwaenrrhonon, and Trigger (1976, 2:488) attributes the assault on the Amikwas in 1636 to the Winnebagoes.

CHAPTER 10

1. "Nous n'auons veu ny gibier, ny poisson, mais bien des cheuëils et des vaches en assez grande quantité" (*Jesuit Relations* 59:106).

2. Brisbois 1882, 291–292. The particular episode in question occurred at the time of an unusually great flood on the upper Mississippi that may have been that of April 1785.

3. Black Elk 1953; Densmore 1918; Row 1994; White buffalo calf 1994.

4. Densmore 1918, 63–78.

5. Ibid., 65–66.

6. Associated Press 1994; Black Elk 1953, 9; Jones 1995; Looking Horse 1987, 69.

7. Densmore 1918, 66; J. L. Smith 1967, 6–9 and chart; J. L. Smith 1970, 88–89. I have used Smith's (1967) tabulation of four sets of countings of the keepers of the pipe made during the period 1916–1934, one of which makes Red Hair/Elk Head the seventh, two the eighth, and one the ninth keeper of the pipe, with considerable disagreement between the names on the lists, some of which is probably due to multiple names for the same individual, some alternate names possibly being counted as those of different persons. The current keeper is the fourth since then yet is considered to be the nineteenth keeper (Looking Horse 1987, 67; cf. Lame Deer and Erdoes 1972, 255). He acquired the honor at the age of twelve in 1966.

8. Joseph Chasing Horse is quoted, for instance, as saying that the story of White Buffalo Calf Woman has been talked about "for thousands of years" (*The Week* 1994). By comparison, the Tetons claim to have lived in the Black Hills from time immemorial, although the Teton discovery of the Black Hills dates to A.D. 1775–1776 according to the winter count record begun by the grandfather of American Horse, an Oglala of the Pine Ridge Agency in South Dakota interviewed through an interpreter by Garrick Mallery (1886, 129, 130, pl. 34). Winter counts are records painted on buffalo hide in which the individual years are represented by pictographs that serve as reminders to the record keeper, who must memorize the significance of each picture. The pictograph on the American Horse winter count for 1775–1776 shows an Indian holding a tree branch and represents an Oglala named Standing Bull who returned to his camp from the Black Hills with a specimen of tree his people had not seen until his visit there.

9. Dorsey 1906, 326.

10. Chasing Horse 1994; C. Hamilton 1994; Looking Horse 1987, 68. The Tetons are not believed to have been in the Black Hills area in sufficient numbers to have challenged Crow, Kiowa, and Kiowa-Apache control of the area much before the date the American Horse winter counts indicates (Henning 1982, 58–59; Sundstrom 1989, 74–75). Although various Sioux bands were ranging as far west as the Arikara villages on the Missouri River at the time of the explorations of Pierre Gautier de Varennes, Sieur de la Vérendrye in 1742–1743 (Robinson 1914), Vérendrye saw no Sioux west of the Missouri, even though he traveled as far west as the Black Hills.

11. J. L. Smith 1967, 5–6.

12. Amiotte 1987, 76, 85; Black Elk 1953, 7n12; Medicine 1987, 163, 167, 168.

13. Densmore 1918, 69; Walker 1980, 35, 39, 109–112, 148–149, 249; Walker 1983, 181. Walker's instruction by the elders and his initiation into the Buffalo Society is mentioned by Elaine A. Jahner in her introduction to Walker's (1983) *Lakota Myth*.

14. Black Elk 1953, 101–115; Blakeslee 1975.

15. J. L. Smith 1967, 27–29; J. L. Smith 1970, 88–89; Thomas 1941. The bowl illustrated by Thomas compares closely with two illustrated by Hurt (1951, 35, fig. 7, nos. 17a and 17b) from Brule County, South Dakota.

Jordan Paper (1988, 11, 137) identifies the pipe illustrated by Thomas as of an "archaic Sioux style" but apparently infers this from its White Buffalo Calf Woman pipe bundle association. Lame Deer (and Erdoes 1972, 255) and Thomas (1941) have each seen the contents of the pipe bundle, although Lame Deer's account of the pipe and stem, as transmitted through Richard Erdoes, differs in saying that the stem is made from the lower leg bone of a buffalo calf, while that illustrated by Thomas appears to be made of wood, as might be expected. It would be inconsistent with tradition to think that the bowl itself were made of bone because early accounts of the story of the pipe say it was made of red pipestone.

Lame Deer and Thomas agree (a) that the stem is decorated with red eagle feathers, four small scalps, and bird skins, (b) that "the pipe" (bowl?) was cushioned with buffalo wool and wrapped in red flannel, and (c) that the Elk Head family caring for the pipe bundle also had a second pipe bowl of pipestone that is of a style common among the Lakotas. Lame Deer's account, again as transmitted through Erdoes, does not specifically describe or refer to the bowl of the Buffalo Calf Pipe except indirectly by saying that it was the *other* pipe bowl that has provided the model for subsequent Lakota sacred pipes.

16. Blair 1911, 1:186; Fletcher [and Murie] 1904, 148; Murie 1989, 154; M. Wedel 1973. Murie (1989, 154) indicates that the name Hako that Alice Fletcher and James Murie (1904) gave to the Pawnee Chawi band Calumet ceremony is derived from a Wichita word for pipe.

17. Walker 1980, 198. Walker (1917, 122–123) interprets an unnamed Oglala winter count as indicating that the rite of Making Relatives was first performed in 1805. This date closely approximates that of 1801 on Black Thunder's winter count. Clark Wissler (editorial comment in Walker 1917, 123n1) has also pointed out that since the ceremony was referred to as Waving Horsetails Over One, the ceremony would not have had that name before the introduction of the horse.

18. Walker 1980, 200–202. The movements of the Sioux proper and their more closely related Siouan relatives over the centuries was more westward and northward than southward, from the general area of Minnesota west into the Dakotas and north into Canada, but mythic traditions of many Siouan speakers reflect a once more widespread ancient substratum of origin stories related to seven stars, which would account for traditions of a northern origin. Although the Pleiades constellation has seven stars visible to the naked eye under the most favorable of conditions, it is only the seven stars of the Big Dipper that can be seen in the northern sky from the latitude of the northern Mississippi valley.

The Lakotas today trace their origin to an emergence from the interior of the earth out of Wind Cave in the Black Hills of South Dakota, which is a naturalization to the Black Hills of an origin story once located elsewhere (e.g., M. N. Powers 1986, 50). For a more detailed consideration of Siouan origins in the northern night sky see Hall (1993b, 28–30). It should be remembered also that because the night sky was commonly equated with the underworld, stories of origins in the night sky do not seriously conflict with stories of emergence from the earth. Groups tracing their origin to caves in mountains are fairly widespread, thus providing a comparative framework in which to examine any single story (chapter 19).

19. Densmore 1918, 70.

20. Ibid.

21. Fenton 1953.

22. J. L. Smith 1967, 5, 27–29; Looking Horse 1987, 69.

23. Walker 1980, 237. Walker comments editorially in parentheses: "The exhortation to provide a companion for the spirit alludes to the custom of killing an enemy in the name of one who has been killed in war, when the spirit of the enemy killed must accompany the spirit of the one in whose name he was killed and serve it on the spirit trail and forever be as a captive to it."

24. Walker 1980, 193–195, 267, 304n11.

25. Gravier 1902, 128–129; *Jesuit Relations* 65:117–125.

26. Blakeslee 1981; Kessell 1978; Kessell 1979.

27. Radin 1970, 341.

28. Blakeslee 1981.

29. *Wisconsin Historical Collections* 16:34–35.

30. La Potherie 1911, 369–370; *Wisconsin Historical Collections* 16:34–36, 43–44.

31. Margry 1875–1886, 3:416–419, cited in Swanton 1942, 180).

32. Shea 1902, 71–72.

33. *Wisconsin Historical Collections* 18:348–349, spelling modified and paragraphing added.

34. Fletcher [and Murie] 1904, 280; Blakeslee 1975.

35. Fletcher [and Murie] 1904, 203, 244; La Flesche 1939, 232–233.

36. Fletcher [and Murie] 1904, 244–245.

37. La Flesche 1939, 245–249.

38. Dorsey 1904c, 6; Dorsey 1906, 52–56; Linton 1922, 5; cf. Murie 1989, 290.

39. Dorsey 1906, 56.

40. Fletcher [and Murie] 1904, 233; Weltfish 1977, 64.

41. Dorsey 1903, 13. The conflation of horizon and ecliptic is especially obvious in the camp circle of the Omaha, representing, as it does, the sky and earth, with the Deer Head (Pleiades) clan at the center of the semicircle representing the sky (chapter 13).

42. Taube 1988.

43. Schele and Miller 1983; Taube 1988.

44. DeMallie and Parks 1987, 14; Walker 1980, 111.

CHAPTER 11

1. Duke 1989; Murie 1902a. The spellings 'Skiri' and 'Skidi' for that branch of the Pawnee Nation vary because of the difficulty of representing the exact pronunciation in standard English orthography.

2. Linton 1926. Archaeological evidence for the presence of the scaffold sacrifice by arrows in Oklahoma during the Mississippi period (Phillips and Brown 1984, 164–165) and historical evidence for its presence among the Natchez of French Louisiana in the early eighteenth century (Le Page du Pratz 1972, 355) does not preclude diffusion of the sacrifice from Mesoamerica; it merely indicates that that sacrifice was once more broadly distributed.

3. Nicholson 1971, fig. 36; Krickeberg 1961, pl. opp. 112; Maler 1911, fig. 10; Nuttall 1975, 84; Taube 1988, fig. 12*a-c*; Thompson 1966, fig. 2; Thompson 1970, 178; Wissler and Spinden 1916, 49, 52, 53, 54.

4. Wissler and Spinden 1916, 51.

5. The Aztec calendar is described in Edmonson 1988, 142–144. Drucker (1987) and Kelley (1980, S2–S3) comment on the correlation of the Aztec and Mayan calendars.

6. See Aveni (1980, 83–86, 150) for comment on the Venus cycle.

7. Eclipses and conjunctions have been calculated using the microcomputer program LodeStar by Zephyr Services of Pittsburgh.

8. Clark Wissler editorial note in Murie 1989, 181n60.

9. Eduard Seler (1963, 1:131–132) suggested that the posture of the victim during the sacrifice was based upon the posture of a female during intercourse, which I do not find as credible as simulation of the Ollin glyph, but I do accept his suggestion that the arrow penetration represented both sexual penetration and planting because the Pawnee victim represented the earth and arrow penetration was also a Pawnee metaphor of planting (Weltfish 1977, 100–101). See also Taube 1988, 331–332. In the miniature diorama representing the sacrifice in the Field Museum the legs of the victim were for some reason placed together by the artist preparing the exhibit, although illustrations of the sacrifice, both in North America and in Mesoamerica, typically show the legs spread.

10. Durán 1971, 227; Murie 1989, 114; Vaillant 1948, table 17. Xipe Totec is an alternate identity of the Red Tezcatlipoca, and the Red Tezcatlipoca is an alternate identity of the Tlaxcalan god of the hunt Camaxtli, whose temple was re-

newed every eight years, implying a Venus identity (Durán 1971, 149). Because Mesoamerican calendars did not utilize the leap year the correlation of any one day in the Mesoamerican year with a day in the Christian calendar will differ by an average of thirteen days every fifty-two years.

11. See Wissler and Spinden (1916, 52) and Krickeberg (1961, pl. opp. 112) for the same in color. Nicholson (1971, 424) says that the gladiatorial sacrifice (Náhuatl *tlahuahuanaliztli*) was the principal mode of sacrifice in Xipe worship, but that the arrow or scaffold sacrifice (Náhuatl *tlacacalaliztli*) was an integral element "at least in the Mixteca-Puebla zone."

12. Krickeberg 1961, fig. 65 (from *Codex Borgia*); González Torres 1985, fig. 14 (from *Codex Borgia*).

13. Chamberlain 1982; Thurman 1970a, Thurman 1970b, Thurman 1983. O'Brien (1987) has noted the contradiction that a male could be sacrificed by the Skiris as an impersonator of the female Evening Star. This need not be a contradiction, considering that the victim underwent a transformation of identity during the course of the ceremony, as did the child honored in Calumet ceremonies of the Hako type. The victims of the scaffold sacrifice in Mesoamerica appear to have invariably been men, to judge from surviving illustrations.

14. E.g., Broda et al. 1987, 17; Jones 1939, vii–ix; Liberty 1976; Liberty 1978; Murray 1974; Parks 1978; Rice 1993, 1–18; Rideout 1912; Tooker 1978b; Whitten and Zimmerman 1982.

15. Parks 1978; Parks 1989.

16. Fletcher [and Murie] 1904, 13–16.

17. Parks 1989, 27.

18. Dorsey 1904c, 6; Linton 1922, 3–5; Linton 1926, 460–461; Murie 1989, 52–53, 112; cf. Taube 1988, 332; Murie 1914, 552.

19. Murie 1989, 115.

20. Ibid., 116. This would have been no surprise to Seler's latter-day compatriot Walter Krickeberg. Krickeberg (1961, 399) recognized the relationship of scalping in the United States to the cult of Xipe. Describing certain events during the Aztec month of which Xipe was patron, Sahagún (1971, 52) wrote, "The captives were killed by scalping them, taking the scalp off the top of the head, which was kept by their owners as a relic."

21. Murie 1989, 126.

22. Ibid., 121.

23. Ibid., 121.

24. Murie 1902b.

25. The image is graphically illustrated by a scene in the *Codex Zouche-Nuttall*, a Mixtec book in which a fire serpent is seen to be swallowing a ballcourt that symbolizes the night sky (Nuttall 1975, 19 of original pagination). The Coras of western Mexico believe, for example, that night exists as a dark liquid below the earth that spills out into the sky each evening from the edges of the earth (Krickeberg 1966, 221). In a folktale of the Apaches it was said that the character Badger carried darkness on his back in a bag. When the trickster Coyote opened the bag, darkness spilled out and spread like night (Goodwin 1939, 164–165). I infer from scattered bits of evidence that in the greater Southwest area the Mexican badger was once something of a night sky metaphor with the white stripe along the length of its back representing the Milky Way.

26. Murie 1989, 123; Murie 1902b.

27. Sahagún (1971, 115) is very explicit in saying that a person representing the male Aztec corn deity Cintéotl wore a peculiar hat of cone shape bent backwards and called "liztlacoliuliqui [!], which means god of frost." It is equally clear that the Aztec Morning Star deity Tlahuizcalpantecuhtli had an identity as Cetl or Frost (Bierhorst 1992, 149; Velázquez 1945, 121, 124, cited in Brundage 1979, 43, 155, and Brundage 1982, 180). Believing Itzlacoliuhqui to translate as 'curved obsidian knife', Seler (1963, 2:202–205) sought to reconcile the contradiction by suggesting that Cintéotl was a deity of mature corn with hard, stony kernels.

Since Seler's day Richard Andrews and Ross Hassig (see Ruiz de Alarcón 1984, 229) have retranslated Itzlacoliuhqui as Everything-has-become-curved-by-means-of-obsidian in the figurative sense of Everything-has-become-wilted-because-of-coldness. This translation has a more logical connection to both frost and to corn and would provide reason enough for both Tlahuizcalpantecuhtli and Cintéotl to wear the hat Itzlacoliuhqui, as they do. The hat frequently has an arrow through it, which makes sense in the context of the Skiri example of Morning Star's killing the corn plant growing in Bright Star's vulva with an arrow because the wearer of the hat also wore over his head the skin flayed from the thighs of a woman sacrificed as personifier of the goddess Toci, mother of Cintéotl.

In the sign language of the Plains Indians certains ideas were conveyed by fairly descriptive representations of the objects or actions concerned. *Scalp*, for instance, was symbolized by a pantomime of the act of scalping, with the left hand holding the hair fast and the right hand making a cutting motion. Other ideas were represented in a more complex manner. The concept of *frost* was represented by the signs, in sequence, for *water*, *night/darkness*, *cold*, *white*, and *earth* (Mallery 1978, 192, 305). The mental association of frost on the ground with night comes into play with the extended association of frost with the morning star seen in the darkness preceding dawn.

28. Murie 1989, 123.

29. Ibid., 124; O'Brien 1991, 58–59.

30. Murie 1989, 52–53.

31. Francis Densmore does not in words indicate more than that the White Buffalo Calf Maiden had vertical red stripes on her face, was the first Hunka, and that red stripes were placed on the face of a Hunka. Densmore does, however, illustrate a wooden spirit post carved to represent a girl whose spirit bundle was kept in a Soul Keeping ceremony and showing three vertical stripes next to each eye that are explicitly identified as Hunka stripes (Densmore 1918, 81–82, pl. 8; Densmore 1935, 186). White Buffalo Calf Maiden is credited with inspiring and providing instructions for the conduct of the Spirit Keeping ceremony.

32. Dorsey 1904c, 6; Murie 1989, 52–53, 112.

33. Dorsey 1904a, 23.

34. Radin 1945, 112, 154, 264, 337n31.

35. Nicholson 1972, 216.

36. Consider also J. E. Brown's editorial comments to Black Elk's (1953) *The Sacred Pipe*: "the buffalo was a natural symbol of the universe" whose four legs "represent the four ages which are an integral condition of creation" (6n8); and

"according to Siouan mythology, it is believed that at the beginning of the cycle a buffalo was placed at the west to hold back the waters. Every year this buffalo loses one hair, and every age he loses one leg. When all his hair and all four legs are gone, then the waters rush in once again, and the cycle comes to an end" (9n15).

37. Dorsey 1905c. George A. Dorsey does not indicate in what way he came to number the four secret tipis of preparation because the activities in each seem to have gone on simultaneously. Dorsey probably numbered them, beginning in the east, in what would have been a 'sunwise' or clockwise direction for most indigenous North American peoples, since the tipis were located, one each, in the four quadrants of the camp circle. This is the order in which James O. Dorsey (1897, 228–229, fig. 36) numbered the positions of clans of a Ponca camp circle, i.e., with number one located south of the east-facing entrance of the circle and then proceeding clockwise to number eight located north of the entrance. See chapters 5, 7, and 15 for commentary on the directionality of rituals.

James O. Dorsey also describes Ponca clans as organized into four phratries identified with fire in the southeast, wind-makers in the southwest, earth in the northwest, and water in the northeast. James Howard's (1965, 87) Ponca sources "vehemently denied" that Ponca clans were ever organized into phratries, but Dorsey's localization of Ponca clans within the quadrants of the camp strongly resembles the symbolism of the four outlying tipis of preparation in the Ponca Sun Dance, which were, of course, located within the four quadrants of the circle.

38. Dorsey 1905a, 183.

39. Chamberlain (1982, fig. 20) suggests that a conjunction of Mars and Venus provided the astronomical model for the mating of Morning Star and Evening Star, partly because the Morning and Evening Stars are treated as distinctly different 'stars' by the Skiris, one male and the other female, and the morning star and evening star aspects of any single planet, like Venus, can obviously never occur in conjunction. Even so, there is evidence from the Kickapoo that the morning star and evening star aspects of Venus were considered to be separate stars (Latorre and Latorre 1991, 267).

Interpreting the ordeals of the Quiché Maya Hero Twins in the *Popol Vuh*, Tedlock (1985, 235, 286, 326–237) suggests that a certain five test houses occupied in sequence by the twins represented five locations in the zodiac, i.e., locations along the path of the ecliptic, corresponding to the position of Venus during its five ninety-day periods centering on superior conjunction of invisibility within an eight-year Sun-Venus cycle. This is tantamount to equating Venus's periods of invisibility with seasons because a season is also about ninety days long.

40. Weltfish 1977, 400.

41. Aveni 1980, 85, 325n14; Carlson 1991 passim (unpaginated) and fig. 2f1; Tedlock 1985, 275, 347, 353, 361. Sahagún (1971, 131, 174) describes the torches representing the fire serpents (or fire serpents made of torches) in the context of the Mexica tribal deity Huitzilopochtli, but he does not relate them explicitly to sun dogs. Aside from the clues provided by the Pawnee accounts, the relationship is implicit in the relationship of fire serpents to the sun as companions

of the sun on its daily round (see Chamberlain 1982; Hall 1991c, 563–568; Lynch 1978.

42. Murie 1914, 561–562.

CHAPTER 12

1. Garibay K. 1940, 112; León-Portilla 1963, 75, 99, 102–103, 113, 147; Sullivan 1983, 16–17.

2. From the *Anales de Cuauhtitlán* (Velázquez 1945:fol. 4) as cited in León-Portilla 1963, 29–30. León-Portilla considers the god of duality to be the "most profound" of all Aztec *difrasismos*.

3. The Aztec god of duality was known as Ometéotl when considered as a composite individual but as Tonacacíhuatl (lady of our subsistence or flesh) and Tonacatecuhtli (lord of our subsistence or flesh) when considered in her/his separate female and male aspects. Tonacatecuhtli was the divine patron of the Aztec day Cipactli or Crocodile and of the *trecena* or thirteen-day week beginning with the day Cecipactli (1 Crocodile) in the 260-day sacred year of the Aztecs (Vaillant 1948, tables 13 and 14). As the first day of the sacred year, Cecipactli or 1 Cipactli was the Aztec equivalent of 1 Imix in the Maya sacred year. Cipactli was the water monster from which the earth and sky were fashioned in Aztec cosmology.

David Kelley (1980) has shown the cosmological equivalence of the Maya day 12 Rabbit (12 Lamat) to the Aztec day 12 Rabbit (12 Tochtli) on which the gods were born of Tonacacíhuatl at the time of creation. Noting that the fifth Aztec sun was born on a day 13 Reed (13 Acatl) which follows 12 Rabbit by 365 days or one solar year, Kelley goes on to suggest that 12 Rabbit was also the calendrical name for the planet Mars because in the 260-day sacred year days named 12 Rabbit repeat at intervals of 260 days, and 780 or 3 × 260 days is the synodical period of Mars. This makes sense because if one counts backward in the sacred calendar with 12 Rabbit as day 1, day 687 will be a day 1 Cipactli, and 687 days is the sidereal period of Mars.

4. Longfellow 1975, 119–120.

5. See, for example, Allen 1966, 325–327.

6. Longfellow at first called his hero by the correct name of Manabozho but after several days settled upon the name Hiawatha. He mistakenly believed that both were the same individual, although Hiawatha, far from being a mythical Ojibwa, was the historic personage who founded the Iroquois League. See Arvin 1963, 136; Tooker 1978a, 422n.

7. Longfellow 1975, 147.

8. Murie 1989, 81.

9. Weltfish 1977, 100.

10. Ibid.

11. Köhler (1982) summarizes the history of scholarship on the Ollin glyph. He concludes that the specific meaning 'earthquake' for *Ollin* 'movement' came about as a shift of understanding, much as the more generic 'quake' in English has come to also have the more restricted meaning of 'earthquake'.

Köhler sees the glyph in its splayed or butterfly-shaped form "as a symbol of the course of the sun around the earth." Rueda Escobar (1971, cited in Köhler 1982, 123) and Tichy (1981) both see a relationship of the limbs of the Ollin glyph to the summer and winter solstice sunrise and sunset positions.

12. Murie 1989, 129.

13. Ibid., 78, fig. 18; Weltfish 1977, fig. 10-1.

14. Dorsey and Murie 1907, section titled "The Ceremonial Lodge and its Symbolism."

15. Skiri Pawnee lodges with buffalo skull altars normally faced east, as would the buffalo skulls facing the entrance from across the lodge in the place of honor. For some ceremonies the buffalo skull was removed and placed north of the fireplace and facing it.

16. The English term 'altar' applies equally to the area in front of the buffalo skull, when and where a sacred bundle is opened, and to the small platform or dais upon which the buffalo skull rests.

17. Murie (1989, 73) describes this pit as rectangular, but Dorsey and Murie (1907) describe it as nearly square. Neither account gives the horizontal dimensions of it. In the full-sized reconstructed Pawnee earthlodge on display at the Field Museum of Natural History in Chicago the Garden of the Evening Star is represented as a small pit about a foot square. In one scaled-down model of a Pawnee earthlodge at the Field Museum, long on exhibit, the Garden is represented as proportionately three or four times larger.

18. Dorsey and Murie 1907, section titled "The Ceremonial Lodge and its Symbolism."

19. Editorial comment by Clark Wissler in Murie (1989, 465).

20. Wedel 1936, 34.

21. Weltfish 1977, 64.

22. Murie 1989, 40, 150.

23. Dorsey and Murie 1907, section entitled "Warrior Bundle: Scalp Sacrifice."

24. The New Fire ceremony associated with the Green Corn ceremony is discussed in Witthoft (1949).

25. Dorsey 1903; Wilson 1928, fig. 8. A litter with serpent-headed litter poles transporting the god Huitzilopochtli is illustrated by Durán (1971, pl. 1). Because the hearth fire was regarded as an earthly representation of the sun in much Indian belief, the snake poles in the Hidatsa eagle trapping lodge could have originated as representations of sun dogs located on each side of the sun, perceived as snakes. When Prince Maximillian observed sun dogs in North Dakota while visiting the Mandans in 1834, he was told that sundogs represented certain spirits accompanying the sun (Hall 1991c, 564, 566; Thwaites 1966, 23:304).

26. Linton (1922, 12) says that the pit below the sacrificial victim was called *kusaru* [*kusa·ru'* 'bed'] and "represented the garden which the Evening Star kept in the west, or, according to another account, the reproductive organs of the Evening Star."

27. One must distinguish between a glyph that represents the mineral turquoise as such and a glyph only conveniently called the turquoise glyph by archaeologists, for want of a better name, because it represents things that are bluish or greenish or that had associations (earth, water, year, grass, green, precious, intense fire) conceptually related in one way or another to turquoise. See Thompson 1962, 66; Thompson 1967.

28. Roys 1967, fig. 27.

29. Black Elk 1953, 89; Densmore 1918, 120n1, 122. Densmore's Lakota or Teton Sioux song no. 137 contains the translated lines, "At the center of the earth I stand . . . at the wind center (where the winds blow toward me from every side) I stand."

30. Buechel 1970, 441, 442, 591.

31. Karttunen 1983, 13; López Austin 1980, 160–162.

32. Grinnell 1972, 261.

33. Waters 1969, 11.

34. Howard 1981, 168.

35. Furst 1975, 43, 49, fig. 6. The yarn-wound cross (popularly called a god's eye or *ojo de dios* in U.S. gift shops) *tüwe* or 'jaguar' protects the approaches to Huichol villages as a trap for unwelcome spirits. Speaking of the Maya village of Chan Kom in Yucatan, Redfield and Villa Rojas (1962, 111–117, 167) say that the four approaches to the villages are guarded from evil winds by *balams*, who are protective spirits not conceived to have any particular form. The name *balam* translates as 'jaguar' but also has been applied by Mayas to shamans, priests, and town officials. Each of the four approaches are also protected by a pair of Christian crosses.

In Chan Kom the tortoise is regarded as sacred, in no small part because of the cross pattern of coloration that appears on his plastron or breastplate. The plastron with its cross is often put around the necks of children to protect them (Redfield and Villa Rojas 1962, 111, 207n2).

36. Fletcher [and Murie] 1904, 22, 44, 47, 51, 52, 156, 158, 206.

37. Freidel, Schele, and Parker 1993, 103, 424n61; Thompson 1971, 74. Dennis Tedlock (1992, 262) says that the Quiché Maya equivalent of the Yucatec day Kan is K'at, which also translates as net.

38. Densmore 1918, 120–122; Walker 1917, 122.

39. Grinnell 1972, 2:292.

40. Dorsey 1905a, 144–145; Dorsey 1975, 32; Grinnell 1972, 2:262.

41. Murie 1989, 124; cf. Weltfish 1977, 114. It is explicitly stated that the victim was placed on the ground facedown with her head to the east. I have assumed that the position of her arms while on the ground would be the same as the position of her limbs while tied to the frame of sacrifice, since those limbs represented the four semicardinal directions.

CHAPTER 13

1. Biographical sketches of Francis La Flesche and evaluations of his work can be found in Bailey (1995), Burr (1933), Liberty (1976), and Liberty (1978).

2. Saucy Calf quoted in La Flesche (1930, 532).

3. La Flesche 1930.

4. Liberty 1978, 51.

5. Fletcher and La Flesche 1972.

6. Ibid., 224; Liberty 1976, 102.

7. Wilson 1974, 44–47, 76.

8. Fletcher and La Flesche 1972, 217–218.

9. Ibid., 218.

10. Ibid., 218–219.

11. Dorsey 1884, 234.

12. Ibid.

13. Fletcher and La Flesche 1972, 453–454.

14. Worthington 1989.

15. Fletcher and La Flesche 1972, 248–250.

16. Ibid., 249, 251.

17. Ibid., 147–148, 251–252, 262.

18. Ibid., 252–254.

19. Ibid., 253, 260.

20. Ibid., 592–594.

21. Skinner 1926, 255; Whitman 1969, 59–60, 59n2.

22. Deliette 1934, 358; Raudot 1710b, 396.

23. Fletcher and La Flesche 1972, 236.

24. Ibid., 141, 217, 224, 233; Hall 1989b, 267; Krupp 1983a; Krupp 1983b, 89–90.

25. Wallace 1972, 86.

26. Speck and Moses 1945.

27. See Hall 1989b, 270–273.

28. Skinner 1915, 706, as quoted in Whitman (1969, 59n2).

29. Durán 1971, 191; Hall 1989b, 276–277.

CHAPTER 14

1. Garcilaso de la Vega 1951, 597–598. Bernal Díaz del Castillo (1956, 130) says of Tlaxcalan warriors in Mexico that during an attack their spears fell so thickly that they lay like corn (in the European sense of 'wheat') on a threshing floor, "all of them barbed and fire-hardened, which would pierce any armour and reach the vital where there is no protection." Kellar (1955, 335) feels that the use of the atlatl in sixteenth-century Louisiana reported by the de Soto expedition was due to reintroduction from the south rather than to survival from earlier times.

2. For some papers and opinions on the nature, occurrence, technology, and functions of atlatls and 'atlatl weights', see Butler 1975; Butler 1977; Dickson 1985; Elliott 1989; Hill 1948; Howard 1974; Howard 1976; Kellar 1955; Knoblock 1939; Kwas 1981; Mason 1885; Nuttall 1891; Patterson 1977; Peets 1960; Spencer 1974; Swanton 1938; Webb 1946; Webb 1981. For atlatl competitions in the contemporary United States, see Cowan 1988.

3. Gould, Koster, and Sontz 1971; Spencer and Gillen 1966, 2:525–527; Spencer and Gillen 1969, 667–670; Warner 1958, 483–485, 525.

4. For the Lake Winnemucca atlatl, see Harrington 1959; Hester 1974; Hester, Mildner, and Spencer 1974, pl. 1a; Mildner 1974, 10. For single-hole atlatls, see Cushing 1897, pl. XXXII-3; Gilliland 1975, pl. 83; Hall 1983a, figs. 1c, 1f, fig. 2a; Lévi-Strauss 1948, 336, fig. 34c; Lothrop 1937, fig. 66b; Townsend 1959, pl. 28. For arrowshaft wrenches, see Cooper and Bell 1936, pl. 23a–b; Griffin 1952, fig. 52i′, fig. 53b′; Prufer and Andors 1967, pl. 4; Spaulding 1956, pl. 4u; W. Wedel 1959, pl. 36a–c; Wood 1967, fig. 8e–f.

5. Moore 1916.

6. Webb 1946, 320, 322, figs. 18–20, 25, 28, 48a, 51d, 55; Webb 1981, 21–25, 37–41.

7. Webb 1946, 329–330.

8. Fletcher and La Flesche 1972, 2: fig. 106; Hall 1962, 2: pl. 80a–b,-d, -h–i, pl. 81i–j; Hall 1983c, fig. 2a–h.

9. Fletcher and La Flesche 1972, 2:493–509.

10. Ibid., 495.

11. Ibid., 507.

12. For a schematic representation of the Osage cosmos, see Bailey (1995, fig. 3.1).

13. La Flesche 1921, 119–120; La Flesche 1939, 90–91. Osage war honors were also symbolized by thirteen footprints of the black bear in two sets of six and seven (La Flesche 1932, 380), just as the thirteen eagle feathers attached to a pair of calumets were divided into sets of six on one calumet and seven on the other.

14. Ford and Willey 1940, fig. 28b, 32d; Griffin and Morgan 1941, pl. 57, no. 2; Henriksen 1965, fig. 30a.

15. García Payón 1950, pl. 12, fig. 4; Griffin 1966, 121–122; Hall 1983a, fig. 5i. For a map showing the distribution of Marksville-Hopewell or 'Louisiana Hopewell', 'Illinois Hopewell' or Hopewell of Havana tradition, 'Ohio Hopewell' or Hopewell of Scioto tradition, and other regional Hopewellian phases see Seeman 1979, fig. 1.

16. For the pottery stamp, see Field 1967, fig. 29; Hall 1983a, fig. 5g; Hall 1983c, fig. 2k. For the Tlatilco site, see Piña Chan 1958; Tolstoy and Paradis 1970; Tolstoy and Paradis 1971; Porter 1953.

17. The character of the Ollin glyph as an atlatl grip is especially evident for the day 12 Earthquake in the top left corner of page 35 of the *Codex Zouche-Nuttall* (Hall 1983a, fig. 5j; Hall 1983c, fig. 2o; Hall 1991c, fig. 2l–n; Nuttall 1975, 35; Waterman 1916, fig. 34m). For the relationship of the Ollin glyph to the motions of the sun through the course of the year, see Chavero (1886), Köhler (1979), Tichy (1981), and Nuttall (1901, 13).

18. Mangold 1973.

19. Cushing 1896; Gilliland 1975.

20. Hall 1983a, 49; Ritzenthaler 1970; Townsend 1959; Uhle 1909.

21. Hall 1983a, fig. 4i; Lothrop 1937, fig. 66a; Mangold 1973.

22. Hall 1983a, figs. 3b, 5c; Von Winning 1968, 207, pl. 278. In regional usage 'cayman' may refer to a crocodile.

23. Willoughby 1973, 109–110, 305, figs. 55, 146.

24. The typology and distribution of flutes is discussed in Izikowitz 1935.

25. Ibid., fig. 210.

26. Radin 1970, 394, 502. See also Radin 1972, 117.

27. Trowbridge 1939, 39; emphasis added.

28. Paper 1989, 9, 12.

29. Hall 1983a, fig.1h–i. For other examples of tube pipes of the blocked-end type, see Dragoo 1964, pl. 1o; Griffin 1952, fig. 15j–k, fig. 31b; Heckenberger et al. 1990, fig. 9; Mayer-Oakes 1955, fig. 22c; Willoughby 1973, fig. 50j; and especially Bache and Satterthwaite 1930, pls. 8–10, 16–17 (plates 8 and 9 of this last are transposed).

30. Carpenter 1956, excerpted from a 1941 typescript field report; emphasis added.

31. Mayer-Oakes 1955, 64–66.

32. Porter 1948, 240. Ford (1969, 83) believed that tube pipe originated in North America and diffused directly to northern South America during the first millennium B.C.

33. Hall 1983a, fig. 2c; Hugh-Jones 1979, 52n6; Koch-Grünberg 1909, 1:281–282.

34. A large assortment of plain and effigy platform pipes from the Tremper Mound, Scioto County, Ohio, is illustrated in Mills 1916. A discussion of the chronology of plain platform pipe styles is given in Seeman 1977.

35. Cushing 1896, pl. 32-3; Gilliland 1975, pl. 83; Hall

1983a, figs. 1c and 1f; Lothrop 1937, fig. 66b; Townsend 1959, pl. 28c-f. One clue to the use of flat-bodied rather than round-bodied atlatls by Adena Indians of the Early Woodland period in the Ohio valley is the finding at various sites of what appear to be six flat atlatl handles. Five of these with late Adena associations have rounded ends and slightly concave sides (Dunnell 1973; Dunnell 1977). One with a middle to early Adena association has slightly concave sides but a rectangular end (Bache and Satterthwaite 1930, fig. A, pl. 23, no. 3. The material of choice appears to have been antler, although one occurs in slate and one is said to be of bone. The interpretation of these objects as atlatl handles is supported by the position and orientation of one relative to an expanded bar gorget that may have been attached to the atlatl (Dunnell 1973, 7).

36. Sahagún 1959, 34; emphasis added. Thompson (1970, 115) says, "Why a tobacco tube should symbolize a spear-thrower is beyond our comprehension, but the aside makes us sorrowfully aware of how much of the allusive imagery of the past escapes us."

37. Hugh-Jones 1979, 154, 249, 293.

38. Ibid., 139, 249; Reichel-Dolmatoff 1971, 118.

39. Among the Creeks in the Southeastern United States tobacco is said to have once been known by a word which translates as 'copulator' (*coeuns*, as John Swanton transcribed it in Latin to protect the sensitivities of his readers). Swanton (1929, 19) provides a Creek origin myth for tobacco which concludes with the comment that "when we smoke we shall call it the same as quum coimus" (Latin *quum coimus* 'when we have intercourse').

40. Hall 1983a; Lévi-Strauss 1948, fig. 34c.

41. Gendrop 1985, fig. 222b; Hall 1983a, fig. 3a; Kidder, Jennings, and Shook 1946, fig. 141c.

42. Robicsek 1978; Schele and Freidel 1990, 78, 231, 236, 245, 343. I believe that Clemency Coggins (1976, 40) is right in seeing the God K scepter as an analogue of the atlatl, but I differ in that I see the scepter as a survival from the Preclassic period rather than as a Classic period introduction from Teotihuacan. The Preclassic silhouette sculpture from Santa Cruz Quiché is evidence for me that the atlatl form was known, if not the atlatl as a weapon, before the period of Teotihuacan expansion.

43. What I see as a Late Classic period equivalent of the Santa Cruz Quiché sculpture can be found painted on a Mayan vase. I have called this item a God K standard because it is shown erected on the ground like the sculpture Hall 1983a, fig. 3b; Robicsek 1978, 189, fig. 213.

44. Schele and Freidel 1990, 143, 343, 414.

45. Bradfield 1973, 2:120, fig. 42; Fletcher and La Flesche 1972, 45, 154–155; Radin 1970, 154–155, 178; Skinner 1926, 240, pl. 36; Titiev 1944, 145.

46. Schele and Freidel 1990; Robicsek 1979. Celts are ungrooved stone ax blades designed to fit into an eye formed in a wooden handle and tapered so that continued use improves the fit. Because of their form some celts may be described as petaloid or cigar-shaped.

47. Buechel 1970, 441, 442, 591, 672, 831; Karttunen 1983, 13; López Austin 1988, 1:150; 2:136.

48. Schele and Freidel 1990, fig. 6:21b.

49. Schele and Miller 1983.

CHAPTER 15

1. Lopatin 1960, 978.

2. Heat treating as I discuss it is analogous to sintering in metallurgy. It has nothing to do with the American folk belief that dropping drops of water on heated flint will produce the pattern of flaking seen on flintwork.

3. Lévi-Strauss 1970; Van Gennep 1960.

4. Wissler and Duvall 1909, 61–66. See also Grinnell 1962, 93–103. The sweat lodge does not figure in the Grinnell version.

5. Wissler and Duvall 1909, 14.

6. Lumholtz 1902, 2:107–108.

7. Sahagún 1953, 5–6. The pueblo-dwelling Hopis of Arizona were speakers of a Uto-Aztecan language closely related to that of the Shoshoni. The sun origin myth of the Hopis begins to resemble that of the Aztecs only at the point where the sun fails to appear above the horizon. As Coyote explained to the Hopis, the movement of the sun into the sky and across it required human deaths; the sun would not move until someone died (Malotki and Lomatuway'ma 1987, 94–96, 96n5). Aztec human sacrifices were intended to assure that the sun should rise and move across the sky.

8. Bierhorst 1992, 147, 148; Ruiz de Alarcón 1984, 71.

9. Houston 1993; Houston 1996. A year after drafting this chapter I participated in a sweat lodge ceremony at the end of a long dirt road forty miles outside of Austin, Texas. Over the heated rocks the leader sprinkled both red willow kinnikinnick and copal gum. This last was by way of recognition for several Maya Indians present who were in Austin for the Seventeenth Maya Hieroglyphic Workshop. In front of the sweat lodge was a pit about three feet deep and four feet across in which a fire had been burning for three hours to heat more than two dozen head-sized igneous rocks until they glowed orange in the dark.

As I stood at the edge of this pit, peering at the bed of hot coals, balancing on one foot to remove my shoes, cold March rain on my back and blistering heat on my face, I very consciously empathized with Nanahuatl, the Ulcerated One, and imagined myself gazing into the sacred hearth at Teotihuacan, deciding whether I would have wanted *that much* to become the Fifth Sun that I would incinerate myself in the fire. The impression was so strong that two nights later I dreamed that I was again attending the sweat but with Nanahuatl as my companion in the person of a Menominee cousin. I know that my cousin represented Nanahuatl because in the dream his face appeared deeply pockmarked, as Nanahuatl's face might have appeared. In addition to that, he was not the Menominee cousin I knew well but rather his son (read 'sun') whom I had communicated with but not actually seen for fifty years or more.

10. Budge 1969, 2:95, 107n1, 108, 110; Kirby 1970, 1:6–7.

11. E.g., Barnouw 1977, 95; Grinnell 1962, 26; Walker 1983, 93, 97.

12. Walker 1983, 149–150.

13. Landes 1968, 27.

14. Lopatin 1960, 989.

15. For a brief summary of the Maritime Archaic, see Tuck 1978, 32–34, figs. 1, 4.

16. Black Elk 1953, 31–43; Grobsmith 1981, 66–67.

Laubin and Laubin (1957, 106–117) describe the lodge and comment that it represented the womb of Mother Earth in Sioux tradition. Because all reservations in South Dakota are to the east of the sacred Black Hills, the entrance to Lakota sweat bath lodges often face west.

17. Murie 1989, 109, fig. 17; Weltfish 1977, 108, 259. The Chaui Band of Pawnees made use of a similar pattern within the plan of their earthlodges: "The entrance of the lodge shall always face the east, for the lodge that you are to build shall breathe as if human. . . . When you make the fireplace, dig up the dirt in the center of the lodge and take it out and place it in front of the lodge in the form of a mound, so that when the sun shall rise in the east he will see that mound" (Dorsey 1906, 14–15).

Note here the idea that light coming from the sun can be inhaled. "Breathing in the sun" is a concept found also among the Navajos (Reichard 1974, 529, 714, 736).

18. Radin 1945, 201–202.

19. Ibid., 339–340n21.

20. Catlin 1976, 54, cover and plates V–VI and IX.

21. Webb and Baby 1957, figs. 33, 38–41.

22. Joint marks are discussed in Hall 1979, 261–262; Rands 1957; Schuster 1951. See also Furst 1995, 69, 129.

23. One spiral form is from a stamp found at San Andrés Tuxtla, Veracruz, Mexico (Anton 1969, 31). Since its discovery this hand has been widely reproduced as jewelry and as a decorative element. The six-element pattern is illustrated in Joralemon (1971, fig. 172).

24. E.g., Howard 1968, figs. 4–5; Rands 1957; Waring and Holder 1945, fig. 2, 4). The painting of a hand over the mouth indicated for the Omahas that the wearer had been struck by the enemy (Fletcher and La Flesche 1972, 1:255, fig. 63; Howard 1968, fig. 6a), and for the Sisseton Dakotas that the wearer was especially brave (Bushnell 1927, 24). For the Winnebagoes a hand painted on the face, body, or blanket indicated that the wearer had taken a captive (Michelson 1935, 447). For the Mandans the painting of a hand on the chest indicated that the wearer had "captured some prisoners" (Thwaites 1966, 23:261). An Iowa named Shauhaunapotinia wore a hand painted over his mouth, an honor that presumably related to his reputation for bravery acquired when, as a teenager, he rode alone into a Sioux camp and killed three Sioux, avenging the death of a close companion (Horan 1982, 308–309).

Certain Aztec slaves who were to be sacrificed to the war god during the month of Panquetzaliztli first left the imprints of their hands in red or blue paint on the door lintels and house posts of their masters and relatives (Sahagún 1971, 128). The Aztec god Xólotl, whose name is glossed as 'slave, page' was sometimes shown with a hand painted over his mouth (Caso 1958, 20). Because slaves were normally captives, this meant that the Aztec slaves, before sacrifice, themselves painted the mark, possibly thus giving notice of the honor to be acquired by their captors or purchasers.

25. Edmonson 1971, 76–77; Hall 1989b, 257–258; Tedlock 1985, 114–115. The calabash tree, *calabazo*, or *totumo* (*Crescentia cujete* L.) in tropical America produces a hard, spherical, head-sized gourd, the *calabaza* or *totuma*. A vessel made from such a gourd was called a *xicalli* by the Aztecs and is today called a *jícara* in Spanish (Kiddle 1944).

26. The symbolism of drilling fire for the Skiri band of Pawnees is given in Murie 1989, 40. In the passage cited the 'hearthboard' is referred to merely as the 'hearth', which has led to some confusion (e.g., Duke 1989, 196, 202n2). The nature of the glyph Manik and its relationship to the fire drill is given in Gates 1978, 27–30, 190–191.

The hand cupped upward was the glyph used for the day Manik in the Maya 260-day sacred year. This Maya day Manik corresponded to the day Mazatl in the Aztec sacred year and Mazatl translates as 'deer', but Manik has no agreed-upon translation. Yucatec Maya 'deer' was *ceh*. Hence, Manik has only been glossed as 'deer' for convenience. The Quiché Maya received Náhuatl *mazatl* as the loan word *mazat*, and it was used with two meanings—'deer' and 'woman's genitals'. This, of course, strongly supports the view that the hand was a female metaphor.

27. Ford and Willey 1940, 29, fig. 29b.

28. Ford 1963, 26–27, fig. 21. Ford believed that the dot behind the plantar pad was made for a pin to hold the copper tube on a staff, but a dot occurs in the same location on the footprint used to decorate a pottery vessel illustrating the Crooks site report he coauthored earlier (Ford and Willey 1940, fig. 29b).

29. Webb and Baby 1957, fig. 32.

30. Willoughby 1917, 495–496, pl. 7g–i.

31. MacLean 1893, fig. 52; Squier and Davis 1848, pl. 8, no. 1; Willoughby 1917, pl. 1f. Gadus (1980) suggests that the emblem more broadly represents both male and female elements.

Mircea Eliade (1965, 47–51) describes a ritual among the Australian aborigines in which a certain dancing area represented the womb of the earth mother and quotes R. M. Berndt (1951, 36), who says: "As the neophytes leave the camp for the sacred ground, they themselves are said to become increasingly sacred, and to enter the Mother; they go into her uterus, the ring place, as happened in the beginning. When the ritual is completed the Mother 'lets them out'; they emerge from the ring place, and pass once more into ordinary life."

32. Evening Star was "opposed to the creation of people" (Marriott and Rachlin 1975, 18; Murie 1989, 31, 39).

33. The plan of the enclosure for the Skiri Four Pole ceremony is shown in Murie 1989, fig. 17. In the ritual language of the Winnebago Medicine Rite the sweat lodge covering can be referred to as a bear (Radin 1945, 201, 339n20).

34. Buechel 1970, 505; Riggs 1968, 484.

35. Mooney 1896, 822, 980, 981, pl. 121.

36. Looking Horse 1987, 72.

37. The butterfly form of the Ollin glyph has been a topic of much discussion through the years with general agreement that the four wings of the glyph tie in one way or another to the four semicardinal directions or their approximations in the summer and winter solstice sunrise and sunset points (Köhler 1982; Tichy 1981). There is much less agreement on what the form of the Ollin glyph is derived from in other respects. My contribution has been to place the glyph in a cross-cultural, pancontinental, and deep-time perspective to show its relationship both in form and symbolism to the atlatl handle as a cosmic symbol (chapter 14).

38. Klein 1975, 77; Köhler 1979; Navarrete and Heyden 1974; Nicholson 1993; Townsend 1979.

39. The eras of the previous four suns lasted integral numbers of calendar rounds of fifty-two years each, namely thirteen, seven, six, and thirteen rounds. If one counts forward by integral numbers of calendar rounds beginning on a day 4 Movement one will always come to another day 4 Movement. Thus, while it is believed that the fifth sun was meant to die on a day 4 Movement, it is less commonly noted that the fifth sun was also necessarily born on a day 4 Movement.

According to the *Annals of Cuauhtitlan* the Fifth Sun was born in a year 13 Reed (Bierhorst 1992, 260). According to the *Legend of the Suns* the sun tarried in the sky for four days before appearing on the day 4 Movement (Bierhorst 1992, 148). The day 4 Movement falls four days after the day 13 Reed, but that would place it within the five-day unlucky period at the end of the year if the day 13 Reed in question were the name day of the Aztec year, which is the 360th day of the year. The day 13 Reed can also occur on the one hundredth day of a year 13 Reed.

40. Kelley 1976, 96–97; Schele and Freidel 1990, 245–251, 413–414. I join others in finding the 584283 calendar correlation more accurate than than the 584285 (see Drucker 1987; Tedlock 1992, 268). The 584285 correlation would put the date of birth of GII two days later, on November 8, the date used by Schele and Freidel 1990.

41. Zenith passage is treated in Aveni 1980.

42. Houston 1993; Schele and Freidel 1990, 239, 470n24.

CHAPTER 16

1. Tyler 1964, 206. Information on clowns considered cross-culturally can be found in Tedlock (1975) and Steward (1931).

2. Tyler 1964, 142–148, 194–208.

3. Cushing 1981, 360.

4. Ibid., 217.

5. Riggs (1968, 289, 487, 514) derives Dakota Wakinyan (glossed 'the Winged One') from *kiŋyaŋ* ' 'fly' with the addition of the prefix *wa-* as a nominalizer. Heyoka has been glossed 'the Restorer' by Walker (1983, 214), but I cannot find an etymology for Heyoka consistent with that glossing.

6. Landes 1968, 57, 182–185; W. K. Powers 1986, 26, 89–90, 183, 203; Walker 1980, 105, 129, 155–157, 187, 230, 277–280; Walker 1982, 126; Walker 1983, 213, 214; Wallis 1947, 111–223.

7. Grinnell 1972, 2:79–86, 204–211.

8. Barrett 1917, 401–420; Hoffman 1891, 156–157; Hoffman 1896, 62, 66, 151–157; Keesing 1987, 48, 50, 214; Kroeber 1983, 188–196; Krusche 1981; McLendon and Lowy 1978, 316; Ray 1945, 95–104; Steward 1991, 29–30.

9. Malotki and Lomatuway'ma 1987, 16. See also ibid., 30, 33; Loftin 1991, 23, 111–113; and Titiev 1944, 139n74, 173–174, 176, 185, 186, 236.

10. Murie 1989, 75, fig. 13; Weltfish 1977, 111, 255. In an editorial footnote to Murie (1989, 182n65), Douglas Parks observes that Murie reported the trees associated with the four semicardinal directions in two different and conflicting ways. These I have tabulated under the intials JM1 from Murie

(1989, figs. 17 and 18; note that NE in fig. 18 is erroneously given as SW) and JM2, also from Murie (1989, 120). To these I have added a still different list as JM3 from Dorsey and Murie (1902):

Trees	JM1	JM2	JM3
Elm	NE	NE	NE
Cottonwood	SW	NW	SW
Willow	NW	SE	SE
Box elder	SE	SW	NW
Elm	NE	NE	NE

You will notice that the sequences of directions of JM2 and JM3 are exactly reversed. If you follow the sequence of trees in column JM2, you will make a figure eight going in one set of directions; if you follow the set of directions under column JM3, you will travel through a figure eight in the opposite direction. This does not look like the product of random error. The difference of context is that the directional associations of trees in column JM2 are for events in the Morning Star sacrifice *within* the ceremonial lodge and for column JM3, *outside* of the lodge. The associations of JM3 are for the poles used as rungs on the sacrificial scaffold. The associations for JM2 are for the logs used as fuel in the sacred hearth in the ceremonial lodge. The associations of trees in column JM1 are for poles erected within the temporary enclosure used in the Four Pole ceremony.

Murie (1989, 109) says that the four trees/poles, ritual bundles, and directional colors in the Four Pole ceremony "represent the powers in the four quarters of the world and also stand for spring, summer, autumn, and winter, *but in no fixed order, the season a bundle represents being determined by the order of the ceremony*" [emphasis added]. Thus, presumably, the same sequence of seasons in two different ritual contexts would result in two different sequences of bundles, and the same sequence of directions within different ritual contexts might also be associated with different sequences of trees.

11. Fortune 1932, 14–15; La Flesche 1916.

12. Dorsey 1969, 57–59, 339n114, 339n115.

13. Parsons and Beals 1934, 494, 495n13.

14. Ibid., 499.

15. Ibid., 497.

16. Malotki and Lomatuway'ma 1987, 33; Parsons and Beals 1934, 511; Titiev 1944, 171, 172, 173.

17. Wallace 1972, 102, 103, 106–107.

18. Sahagún 1959, 67; Sahagún 1971, 76–77.

19. Black Elk 1953, 5n4.

20. Fenton and Kurath 1951, 150.

21. Lipp 1991, 57.

22. Spinden 1924.

23. Edmonson 1988, 112.

24. Cf. Kelley 1976, 51.

25. For the Tuxtla cycle, see Hall (1991d). For the relevance of the April 12 date to the Copán site, see Aveni (1977, 9–14), Morley (1947, 144–146 and fig. 4), and Sharer (1994, fig. 12.11). If one substitutes a solar era for a Tuxtla cycle, the midpoint is again a day 8 Manik 0 Kankin, but much earlier, on November 13, 2360 B.C., seven days after the birth of the last of the three gods of the Palenque triad

and two days after the nadir passage of the sun at Palenque. A Tuxtla cycle is the minimum number of days required for any day in the Maya calendar to repeat on the same day of the 260-day sacred almanac year, the same day of the 365-day solar year, and the same day within a certain 819-day ritual period.

26. The Maya Era base was August 11, 3114 B.C. (the astronomical year −3113) *Gregorian*, when using the preferred Goodman-Martínez-Thompson 584283 constant to correlate the Maya and Christian calendars. This means that the Maya Era base date coincided with Julian Day number 584283 in the original sense proposed by Joseph Justus Scaliger (1540–1609). The Maya Era base was the zero point from which the Mayas counted records of elapsed time in a form Mayanists call the Long Count (LC). The era base date was projected into the mythical past and should not be confused with what I have referred to as the date of inauguration of the Long Count, which was a contemporary event.

For the inauguration of the Long Count, see Hall (1991d and 1994). Long Count numbers are treated as the Maya analogues of western science's Julian Days. The last number in a normal LC number is a count of individual days up to nineteen. The second-to-last number is a count of uinals or twenty-day months up to seventeen. Once a count of uinals and days reaches 17.19, the next day becomes 1.0.0, which represents one tun (360-day year), zero uinals, and zero days. The accumulation of twenty tuns generates a katun and the number 1.0.0.0. After twenty katuns the count of elapsed time generates a baktun and a Long Count number of 1.0.0.0.0, so a number like 7.16.6.16.18 (as Mayanists transcribe sequences of Mesoamerican bar-and-dot vigesimal numbers) would indicate a day that followed the era base by seven baktuns, sixteen katuns, six tuns, sixteen uinals, and eighteen days or kins, which we see as a total of 1,125,698 days.

The first day of the Maya mythological creation has been established by Freidel et al. (1993) as being a day 13.0.0.0.0, 4 Ahau 8 Cumku, coinciding with the base date of the Maya Era and at the beginning of the era rather than in the middle. This apparent contradiction is resolved when it is realized that the Maya Era base is actually the last day of a 13-baktun era preceding the 13 baktuns of the Maya Era, and hence actually the midpoint of two eras totaling 26 baktuns. The number of the day following 13.0.0.0.0 is not 13.0.0.0.1 but 0.0.0.0.1, being the first day of a new period of thirteen baktuns.

27. Fisher 1946.

28. Brinton 1976, 176–178. Rabbits and hares are quite distinct animals to a taxonomist but not to the popular mind. The jackrabbit, for instance, is really a hare. Rabbits belong to the genus *Sylvilagus* and hares to the genus *Lepus*. I am using the names somewhat interchangeably, although rabbits do not have white coloration in the wild, and the snowshoe hare does in the winter.

29. Chipiapoos was glossed with the meaning 'man of the dead' in the source (Chittenden and Richardson 1905, 3: 1080–1083). Paul Proulx called my attention to the etymology of Chipiapoos.

30. Strachey 1849, 98–100, in Swanton 1946, 749.

31. Nichols and Nyholm 1979, 86–87; Williams 1963, 89, 105, 110, 147, 149, 175, 206.

32. Webb and Baby 1957, 90–91, figs. 40–41.

33. Durán 1971, 146, 456; Malotki and Lomatuway'ma 1987 passim.

34. Gill 1982, 125; emphasis added.

35. Ibid., 126.

36. Adams (1991) relates the rise of the Katsina cult in the Southwest to its usefulness as a bonding mechanism in integrating pueblo society.

37. Wike 1952, 99–100; cf. Bierhorst 1976, 238–241; Drucker 1963, 48–49.

38. Nutini 1988.

39. Hall 1993b, 51.

40. Hall 1993a.

41. Grinnell 1972, 2:285–336; Schlesier 1987.

42. Durán 1971, 140–153, 455–456.

43. Mooney 1982, 242–249, 432–433.

44. Sahagún 1971, 122–126.

45. Conway 1992.

CHAPTER 17

1. Sachs 1961, 33–46.

2. Masters 1916, 3; Masters 1992, 89.

3. Masters 1916, 27; Masters 1992, 113.

4. Masters 1916, 1–2; Masters 1992, 87. The hill referred to in this title is the Oak Hill Cemetery in Lewistown, not the Dickson Mounds cemetery, although the latter is, in fact, located upon a hill.

5. For more on the Larson site, see Conrad (1989, 109–110), Harn (1978, 251–252), and Harn (1994). The term 'Spoon River' was first applied to an archaeological entity by Cole and Deuel (1937) when they defined a Spoon River Focus of the Monks Mounds Aspect of the Mississippi Pattern within the structure of the Midwest or McKern taxonomic system. Recognition of temporal divisions in Spoon River resulted in Wray's (1952, 157–158) concept of early, middle, and late Spoon River 'complexes'.

The application of the term 'Spoon River' to an archaeological tradition followed in the 1960s and 1970s as archaeologists moved away from the McKern terminology. Where most *foci* of the older taxonomy became *phases* in the new, Spoon River was recognized as having enough temporal depth to warrant being recognized as a regional tradition divided into sequent phases named Eveland, Orendorf, Larson, and Crable (Conrad 1989; Harn 1980, 78).

For the concept and characteristics of 'Mississippian' see Galloway 1989; B. Smith 1978; B. Smith 1984; B. Smith 1990.

6. Harn 1980.

7. Cole and Deuel 1937, 120–126; Harn 1967; Harn 1980, 1–3.

8. Records of the 1969 and 1970 archaeological field schools of the University of Illinois at Chicago Circle (now the University of Illinois at Chicago), directed by Robert L. Hall. These records are on deposit at the Dickson Mounds (Lewistown, Illinois) branch of the Illinois State Museum. For an early report on the Crable site, see H. Smith (1951).

9. A.D. 1385 ± 55 (Wis-648) and A.D. 1435 ± 60 (Wis-644) as reported in Bender, Bryson, and Baerreis (1975, 124–125), based upon outer-ring charred lodge pole samples from University of Illinois at Chicago excavations.

10. Sharron Santure says, "The location of victims' graves suggests a major mortality episode just prior to the abandonment of the cemetery" (Santure, Harn, and Esarey 1990, 158). For the concept of Oneota, see Gibbon (1972); Gibbon ed. (1982); Green (1995); Hall (1962); Henning (1970); McKern (1945); and M. Wedel (1959).

11. Santure, Harn, and Esarey 1990, 154–158.

12. Nearly contemporary with this cemetery was an improvised grave of 486 massacred Indians found deposited in the fortification ditch of a prehistoric proto-Arikara earthlodge village in South Dakota. Almost every one of the skulls in this mass grave showed indications of scalping (Gregg et al. 1981; P. Willey 1990, 105–106, 149, 176–177; Zimmerman et al. 1981). This is the Crow Creek archaeological site (39BF11) on the east bank of the Missouri River thirteen miles north of Chamberlain, South Dakota. This site is believed to date to around 1325 A.D. The Caddoan-speaking Arikara are related in culture and language to the Pawnee.

Such evidence, along with that of the Norris Farms 36 cemetery and examples from other sites, argues against the popular belief, voiced by many Indians and whites alike and uncritically repeated in the media, that American Indians did not take scalps until they were taught to do so by the colonial English. See also Axtell (1981, 16–35), Gaschet (1969a, 67–168; 1969b, 47–48), and Neumann (1940).

Although the term 'massacre' is value-laden, using a more neutral term such as 'major mortality episode' in the particular case of the Crow Creek site deaths would not have really conveyed the tragedy of a population of almost five hundred individuals so completely and violently destroyed. Predating by two centuries, as it did, the European colonization of mainland America, the Crow Creek massacre calls to question the opinion that pre-Columbian warfare produced few casualties and that examples of 'total war' were responses to European examples (e.g. Jennings 1976, 153, 159). Keeley (1996) addresses the myth of the peaceful pre-Columbian past.

13. Santure, Harn, and Esarey 1990, table 13.2.

14. Harn 1980, 72–75.

15. Newspaper accounts on file at the Dickson Mounds Museum, Lewistown, Illinois.

16. Krohe 1992, 26.

17. Masters 1916, 339.

CHAPTER 18

1. In Gacilaso de la Vega 1980, xxxiv.

2. Ibid. 1980, xxxvii, xlv.

3. Ibid., 422–423.

4. Ibid., 460.

5. Ibid.

6. Bourne 1904, 1:123–124; Garcilaso de la Vega 1980, 436; Phillips, Ford, and Griffin 1951, 356.

7. Garcilaso de la Vega 1980, 435–439.

8. Le Page du Pratz 1972, 326–329.

9. Ibid., 329.

10. Ibid., 333–334. The nature of this temple is known from archaeological excavations. See Neitzel (1965, 74 and figs. 10, 12) and critical comments by Brown (1990).

11. Williams and Goggin 1956, 60. For descriptions and commentaries on the Southeastern Ceremonial Complex, see

Brown 1976; Fundaburk and Foreman 1957; Galloway 1989; Howard 1968; Phillips and Brown 1978; Phillips and Brown 1984; Rands 1957; Waring 1945; Waring 1968; Waring and Holder 1945.

12. Williams and Goggin 1956, 16.

13. Richards 1870; Williams and Goggin 1956, 23.

14. Howland 1877, 206; Williams and Goggin 1956, 9.

15. Holmes 1883, 296, pl. 70, figs. 1–2; Williams and Goggin 1956, 28, 31.

16. Moore 1894; Moore 1895, 485–488; Williams and Goggin 1956, 23–26.

17. Barrett 1933, pl. 69, fig. 25; Williams and Goggin 1956, 28–30.

18. Webb and Dodd 1939; Williams and Goggin 1956, 24, 28.

19. Beadle 1942; Williams and Goggin 1956, 32–33.

20. J. B. Griffin 1946.

21. Lawshe 1947.

22. Hamilton 1952, pl. 27; Williams and Goggin 1956, 32, 35.

23. Goggin 1952.

24. Williams and Goggin 1956.

25. Griffin and Morse 1961.

26. Perino 1966.

27. Bareis and Gardner 1968.

28. Perino 1971, 163, 177, 182, fig. 73c.

29. Salzer 1993, 85.

30. Harn 1975b.

31. Salzer 1993, 85.

32. D. Anderson 1980.

33. Salzer 1993, 86; letters from Salzer to Hall, dated July 28, 1982, and from Hall to Salzer, dated July 30 and July 31, 1982.

34. Salzer 1987a; Salzer 1987b; Salzer 1987c.

35. Hall 1989b, 239–250.

36. Duncan 1993.

37. Hall 1991b, 30–34.

38. Barreca 1992.

39. Radin 1954, 12; Radin 1970, 391–393; Radin 1972, 118.

40. Radin 1972, 118.

41. Radin 1948.

42. Radin 1948, 117.

43. Ibid., 43.

44. Ibid., 41–42, 126.

45. Letter from the author to Robert Salzer dated July 31, 1982. Salzer (1993, 88, lines 2–3) identifies as Red Horn himself the figure I identified as the son of Red Horn by the red-haired giant, although the figure in the cave has no little heads on his ears, as either Red Horn or Red Horn's son by the woman with the white beaver skin wrap could be expected to have had. Salzer earlier (1987a, 450, 465, figs. 20–23) allowed that the same cave figure might be either Red Horn or one of his sons.

46. Skinner 1925b, 456–458.

47. Collins 1995.

48. Ibid., 458.

49. Hall 1986; Hall 1991b, 31.

50. Blakeslee 1975.

51. Radin 1948, 45. John Staeck (1994) has pursued the

idea of matrilineality in pre-Contact Winnebago society and developed some of its implications for archaeology.

52. Fowler 1974.

53. Le Page du Pratz 1972, 334–339; Neitzel 1965, 40–44, 77–85, fig. 10.

54. Santure, Harn, and Esarey 1990, 105, 238.

55. Weltfish 1977, 19.

56. Speck and Moses 1945, 40. See also Hall (1983b, 94). While living at Zuñi pueblo in New Mexico 1879–1884, Frank Hamilton Cushing became fluent in the language of the pueblo and was able to record sayings of a Zuñi priest, which Cushing (1981, 347) rendered into an almost biblical English in these words: "'Behold!' said the Sky-father [addressing the Earth-mother]. He spread his hand high and abroad with the hollow palm downward. Yellow grains like corn he stuck into all the lines and wrinkles of his palm and fingers. 'Thus,' he said, 'shall I, as it were, hold my hand ever above thee and thy children, and the yellow grains shall represent so many shining points which shall guide and light these, our children, when the Sun-father is not nigh.' Gaze on the sky at night-time! Is it not the palm of the Great Father, and are the stars not in many lines of his hand yet to be seen?"

57. For a discussion of Mississippi period chronology in Illinois, see Hall (1991b, 8–14), and Fowler and Hall (1978). For a discussion of some of the problems of Winnebago archaeology, see Overstreet (1993). John Staeck (1993, 1994) addresses the problem of matrilineality for the Winnebago.

58. Gibbon 1972, 176–178; Gibbon 1982; Hall 1991b, 19; Hall 1993b; Henning 1970, 140–162.

59. Blakeslee 1975.

60. Ludwickson, Blakeslee, and O'Shea 1981, 162.

61. Chmurny 1973, 138; Hall 1991b, 21–27.

62. Hall 1980; Hall 1991b.

63. Blakeslee 1975, abstract.

64. Norman 1973, pls. 41–42.

65. The solar aspects of Hunahpu and Xblanque are discussed in D. Tedlock (1992, 263–264).

66. Tedlock 1985, 159.

67. Ibid., 295.

68. Skinner 1925b, 458.

CHAPTER 19

1. Fitting 1978; Greber and Ruhl 1989; Griffin 1952; Griffin 1983; Hall 1980; Hall 1991b; Martin, Quimby, and Collier 1947; Moorehead 1922.

2. Caldwell 1964; Willey 1962. The Hopewell Interaction Sphere is discussed to varying extents in works such as those of Brown (1964, 1965), Hall (1980, 1991b), Seeman (1979), Struever (1964), and Struever and Houart (1972). The relationship of 'great traditions' and 'little traditions' is discussed by Redfield (1955).

The concept of 'diffusion sphere' in an Old World context was introduced to American archaeologists by Christopher Hawkes (1954, 160, 167). The concept was subsequently applied by Gordon Willey (1955, 571) to the network of pancontinental relationships known for the high civilizations of the Americas. Joseph Caldwell (1958, vii, 62, 71; Caldwell 1964) borrowed Willey's use of the term to create a model of cultural relationships within the eastern United States and then transformed the idea of 'diffusion sphere' into that of 'interaction sphere'.

3. Hall 1979. For papers on Mississippian-level culture and its emergence see Brown (1991) and Smith (1990). Discussions of the Mississippian, Cahokia, and Oneota Interactions can be found in Hall (1991b), Kelly (1980), and Stoltman (1991).

4. Tedlock 1985, 295.

5. Dorsey 1905a, 58; Hall 1983c; Hall 1987, 35; Hall 1993b, 51–52.

6. La Flesche 1932, 95.

7. Hall 1977, 513–514; Hall 1983a, 540–541; Jones and Michelson 1911, 873; Marriott and Rachlin 1972, 76–79.

8. Hoffman 1896, 167.

9. La Flesche 1932, 95, emphasis added; Wilson 1928, 229. Cf. Weltfish 1977, 75.

10. Hall 1983a, 41–42; Winters 1969, 68–69.

11. Voget 1984. Those pierced in the Sun Dance as described by Oglala elders to Walker (1917, 116–119) first underwent simulated capture, then were pierced and suspended from skewers inserted into their wounds to simulate torture, while their female relatives wailed in simulated bereavement. This contrasts with a modern interpretation reported by Russell Means to John Wideman (1995, 71) that "piercing is about trying to understand birth." This compares with Ed McGaa's (1990, 93) comment that "a sun dancer has more fully understood a woman's [childbirth] pain by doing the Sun Dance."

12. Walker 1917, 91, 93, 114–115, 116–119.

13. Fenton 1962; Hall 1989b, 258–261; Hewitt 1928; Morgan 1901, 110; Speck 1942, 26; Speck and Moses 1945, xi; Swanton 1929, 2–7, 126–131, 163–164, 172–175, 213.

14. Köngäs 1960.

15. Barnouw 1977, 34–46, 62–69. The wolf brother may also appear as a nephew or simply a companion.

16. Kovacs 1989; Kramer 1959, 150–154, 182–199; Sandars 1964, 83–114. The wild nature of the Sumerian Enkidu was tamed by an association with women and sexual experience. The wild nature of the wilder twin in eastern North America was reduced by loss or removal of something internal—swallowed shells (Hidatsa Spring Boy), his tooth (Pawnee Long Tooth Boy), an internal heart of flint or ice (Iroquois Flint)—(Bowers 1965, 305; Dorsey 1969, 89–90; Fogelson 1980, 144; Hall 1983b, 86, 96; Hewitt 1910, 709–710). The wilder twin in the latter cases was either the second born or implicitly so by being derived from the placenta or umbilical cord of the first born (sometimes from animal blood), although the second born might claim to be first born. The placental twins in North America were frequently associated with flint.

17. Radin 1945, 154.

18. Bierhorst 1992, 149, 153. This relationship implicitly relates 7 Macaw with Mixcóatl, of course. The further comparison can be made between Mixcóatl and Chimalman and the Skiri Pawnee Morning Star and Evening Star.

19. Freidel, Schele, and Parker 1993, 79, 85–89.

20. Sahagún 1948; Sahagún 1971, 124–125.

21. Radin 1945, 171, 263.

22. Hall 1977, 512.

23. Lowie 1956, 302–304.

24. Bowers 1965, 306–307; Roys 1965, 58–63; Thompson 1971, 218. Also see note 13 above.

25. As Ronald Goodman (1992, 219; cf. Goodman 1990, 26–27) interprets the Lakota story of a chief who lost his arm, the appearance of the Hand Constellation (Orion) each fall is said to signal the impending loss of the fertility of the earth, which "the sun dancers hope to renew . . . by voluntarily sacrificing their blood." Neither of these interpretations is part of the original Lakota story as related by Black Elk (cf. DeMallie 1984, 407–409).

26. Coe 1975, 25–26, fig. 7a; Howard 1981, 168; Neihardt 1972, 50; Sahagún 1953, 60. See also Furst 1995, 68.

27. Fewkes 1900, pl. IV-1, -2; Hall 1983b, 89–93, fig. 3; Hough 1928, figs. 9–10; Kroeber 1983, figs. 56–57; Rollings 1989, fig. on p. 47. The relationship of the sword to the belt in the Firesticks asterism in Orion is similar to the relationship of the fire drill to the hearth board, giving the former a male character and the latter a female character, and recognized as such by the Pawnee (Murie 1989, 40, 150). This sexual symbolism may explain the logic of fashioning a club-like wooden whip handle to resemble a hearth board.

Certain wooden clubs in the American Southwest and in Mesoamerica appear not only to have been used as 'fending sticks' to deflect atlatl-launched spears in flight but also to have had certain female, i.e., receptor, associations (Hall 1982; Hall 1989a). The logic would have been to magically enhance the sticks' ability to attract spears, much as Sioux rawhide shields were provided with magical symbols to enhance their ability to attract arrows to themselves and hence to protect their wearer from harm, according to Wissler (1907). With the shift to the bow and arrow from the atlatl and spear, fending sticks possibly remained with modified functions.

The Osage see the nebula in the sword as female and the three stars of the belt as a male named Three Deer. While it is common for the three stars of the belt to be seen as three deer (plural) or other beings (e.g., Tres Marías), seeing the three stars as a single person named Three Deer looks Mesoamerican. At least, Three Deer is a calendar-based name in Mesoamerica, occurring, for instance, as the name of the Jaguar Captain featured on the murals of the Cacaxtla site in the state of Tlaxcala, Mexico (Baird 1989; Carlson 1991, 15, fig. 6a-b).

There may be some value in considering a relationship of Orion with its prominent triple-star asterism to the so-called triple dot–bigotera (Spanish bigotera 'handle-bar mustache') motif representing Tlaloc as the Teotihuacan storm god. This motif occurs on the plantar surfaces of the front paws of a reclining jaguar sculpture from Teotihuacan (Gendrop 1985, fig. 78c, after Covarrubias) but is more commonly found on emblems in combination with the Kan cross or turquoise glyph (Carlson 1991, fig. 13g; Caso 1966, fig. 3).

The hearth board of the Hopi Kwakwantû society at Walpi, as illustrated by Fewkes (1900), has three holes for the drill. The hearth board for the Aaltû society has thirty-three holes and a cord-wrapped handle and resembles Plains whip handles more closely.

28. Sahagún 1971, 76–78, 154–155; Sahagún 1959.

29. Hugh-Jones 1979, 12.

30. Asturias 1968, 67; Garibay K. 1972, 21, 185; Ingham 1984, 387; Goodwin 1939, 164–165; Krickeberg 1966, 221; Nuttall 1975, 19 of original pagination.

31. Fletcher and La Flesche 1972, 1:42–43; Howard 1965, 87–90; Dorsey 1891, 331–332.

32. Bowers 1965, 360, 371; La Flesche 1932, 209–210.

33. Hall 1993c; Karttunen 1983, 324, 326, 327; León-Portilla 1963, 32–33, 48; Walker 1980, 54; Weltfish 1977, 400–401. Note that the north and south halves of the Omaha and Osage camp circles were associated with the sky and the earth, much as in Mesoamerica the cardinal directions followed the sun: sunrise, zenith sun, sunset, nadir sun (Hall 1993c; cf. Bricker 1983; Coggins 1980).

34. Mooney 1982, 242–249, 262, 432, 435, 441; Thompson 1970, 314–315.

35. Nuttall 1901, 10–12.

36. Hall 1989b, 267–268, 272, figs. 4e and 4h. The Omaha referred to a sacred crook as a washaʼbe, which translates as 'dark object', but their linguistic cousins the Osage used the cognate word wathaʼbe as a ritual name or circumlocution for the black bear. The Lakotas call a feathered crook lance waʼpaha, a word cognate with the Omaha name for the Big Dipper or Great Bear constellation, waʼbaha. Beyond this, the crook was associated with leadership, as was the star Polaris, and Polaris is the end star of the Little Dipper constellation, which has the shape of a crook.

Among the Omahas the subclan responsible for the sacred crooks was the subclan also responsible for caring for the sacred white buffalo hide associated with the sacred pole, which was erected in such a way as to point to the North Star (figure 13.2). The relationship of the Omaha buffalo hide to the pole suggests the relationship of the bear hide to the pole in the Mahican-Munsee bear sacrifice, in which the bear skin represented the Great Bear constellation (chapter 13). Among the Winnebagoes crooks of smaller scale were the property of the Bear clan.

Fire or Turquoise Serpents can be distinguished from other supernatural serpents by the crook-shaped objects on their heads, each such object having seven dots representing a constellation with seven stars. These groupings of seven dots on the heads of the Fire Serpents conceivably have a Plains parallel in the small bunch of blue beads attached to the neck of the snake represented by the wooden hoop used for the sacred wheel in the Arapaho Sun Dance, especially since these beads are said to have represented "the sky or the heavens" (Dorsey 1903, 12, 13, 20.)

37. Walker 1980, 193–195. For the code of chivalry see Walker (1980, 262). Vine Deloria Jr. (1995, 127) refers to the Fox Society as "an honorary group that performed a charitable function in Sioux society." The designations 'soldier society' and 'warrior society' relate to functions which have passed with time. Such men's societies continued into the reservation period as charitable associations.

38. Hall 1993b, 28–30; Powers 1977, 4; Walker 1982, 176n22. La Flesche (1932, 167) speaks of "u-dseʼ-the, hearth, fireplace" and "u-dseʼ-the, a place hollowed out in the ground in which to place or kindle a fire. In the Osage tribal organization there are seven fireplaces of the Ṭsiʼ-zhu, of the Wa-zhaʼ-zhe, and of the Hoⁿʼ-ga."

39. Bowers 1965, 196; Coe 1977, 114; Davies 1983, 129; *Historia Tolteca-Chichimeca* 1947, pls. 2, 7; Karttunen 1983, 47, 48; Krickeberg 1966, 223; Nuttall 1901, 29, 57. Bowers (1965, 194) says, "The wide distribution of the Dog society in

the Plains suggests considerable antiquity as well as popularity." Furst (1995, 187) comments on the wide range of peoples in the Americas who have traditions of dog ancestors.

Spinden (1948, fig. 4) asserts that the seven Chicomóztoc caves represented the first seven baktuns or four hundred–year periods of the Maya Long Count, a statement probably based on the belief that the Long Count was designed to have a mythical zero date preceding by seven baktuns the date of actual inauguration of the count. Nuttall's suggested relationship of Chichimec origins to a Dipper conforms not only to related beliefs in the Plains of the United States but also to Old World myths that target the Big Dipper as a place of lineage origins, such as those of the Seven Sages of Hindu tradition.

40. Taube 1988, 351.

41. Hall 1993a.

42. Pepper and Wilson 1908; Wilson 1928.

43. Wilson 1928, 190, 194.

44. Fletcher [and Murie] 1904, 44, 51, 52, 124, 158, 206; La Flesche 1921, 62.

45. *Jesuit Relations* 59:135.

AFTERWORD

1. Neihardt 1972, 71.

2. Sharer 1994, 598–599; Valdiosera Berman 1983, 59–66.

3. Katz 1972, 147, citing León-Portilla 1959, 245.

4. Chamberlain 1982, 159; Chamberlain 1992, 226–227.

5. Bolton 1987, 112–115; Dorsey 1906, 42.

6. Apparently because its great size discouraged any thought of reducing it to rubble as well, the calendar stone lay in the plaza near the demolished great temple of Tenochtitlan following the Spanish conquest until it was ordered buried by Fray Alonso de Montúfar, who was archbishop of Mexico from 1551 to 1559. It was rediscovered in 1790 when the pavement of the plaza was being repaired (Chavero 1886[?], 3–4; Nicholson 1993, 3; Townsend 1992, 10).

The more obvious associations of the calendar stone are with the five creations or worlds in Aztec cosmology, which were named for the suns that ruled the skies at the time. In broader perspective, of course, these five periods of creation correspond to the world quarters and seasons of the year plus the center, or here and now, much as Aztec sacrifices frequently consisted of four men plus one woman (chapters 11 and 19).

I thank Courtney Schmoker for pointing out certain critical points of resemblance of the serpents on the calendar stone to the sky band in Maya cosmology that represents the ecliptic or apparent path of the sun, moon, and planets across the background of the heavens. See also 182n41.

7. Hall 1990.

8. Furst 1978, 240–241; Hall 1991c, 558–559; Karttunen 1983, 330; Klein 1975, 78; Molina 1970; Murie 1989, 11, 92, fig. 34; Sahagún 1969, 219; Weltfish 1977, 131.

The errand runner among the Pawnee would seem to correspond, as a ceremonial messenger, to the *sho'-ka* among the Osage (Fletcher and La Flesche 1972, 1:61–62; La Flesche 1916, 287; idem 1932, 132–133; idem 1939, 83).

The Osage camp circle, divided into a north half representing the sky and a south half representing earth and water, corresponds to the glyphs 4 Wind and 4 Rain on the north half of the Sun Stone, representing sky, and the glyphs 4 Jaguar and 4 Water on the south half, representing earth and water.

9. Caso 1958, 20; Fletcher and La Flesche 1972, 1:255, fig. 63; Hall 1991c, fig. 1a-b, -d; Howard 1968, fig. 6b; Hudson 1976, 130, 415, 477; Karttunen 1983, 85, 330. Also see chapter 15, note 24.

REFERENCES CITED

ADAMS, E. CHARLES. 1991. *The Origin and Development of the Pueblo Katsina Cult.* Tucson: University of Arizona Press.

ALARCÓN, HERNANDO RUIZ DE. 1984. *Treatise on the Heathen Superstitions that Today Live Among the Indians Native to this New Spain, 1629,* trans. J. Richard Andrews and Ross Hassig. Norman: University of Oklahoma Press.

ALLEN, GAY WILSON. 1966. *American Prosody.* New York: Octagon. Reprint of the 1935 American Book edition.

ALVARADO TEZOZOMOC, HERNANDO. 1878. *Crónica Mexicana,* ed. José M. Vigil. Mexico City: I. Paz.

AMIOTTE, ARTHUR. 1987. The Lakota Sun Dance: historical and contemporary perspectives. In *Sioux Indian Religion: Tradition and Innovation,* ed. Raymond J. DeMallie and Douglas R. Parks, 75–89. Norman: University of Oklahoma Press.

ANDERSON, ADRIAN D. 1961. The Glenwood sequence: A local sequence for a series of archeological manifestations in Mills County, Iowa. *Journal of the Iowa Archeological Society* 10 (3):1–101.

ANDERSON, DUANE C. 1980. Long nosed god masks and other items. *Iowa Archeological Society Newsletter* 97:16–17.

ANDERSON, MELVILLE B., trans. 1898. *Relation of the Discovery of the Mississippi River, Written from the Narrative of Nicolas de La Salle, Otherwise Known as the Little M. de La Salle.* Chicago: Caxton Club.

———, trans. 1901. *Relation of the Discoveries and Voyages of Cavelier de La Salle From 1679 to 1681.* Chicago: Caxton Club.

ANTON, FERDINAND. 1969. *Ancient Mexican Art.* London: Thames and Hudson.

ARVIN, NEWTON. 1963. *Longfellow: His Life and Works.* Boston: Little, Brown.

ASSOCIATED PRESS. 1994. Viewing of white buffalo finished until spring. Associated Press news release appearing in *News from Indian Country* 8 (24 [late Dec.]):3.

ASTURIAS, MIGUEL ÁNGEL. 1968. *Poesía Precolombina.* Buenos Aires: Compañía General Fabril Editora, S.A.

AVENI, ANTHONY F. 1977. Concepts of positional astronomy employed in ancient Mesoamerican architecture. In *Native American Astronomy,* ed. Anthony F. Aveni, 3–19. Austin: University of Texas Press.

———. 1980. *Skywatchers of Ancient Mexico.* Austin: University of Texas Press.

AXTELL, JAMES. 1981. *The European and the Indian: Essays in the Ethnohistory of Colonial America.* New York: Oxford University Press.

BACHE, CHARLES, and LINTON SATTERTHWAITE JR. 1930. The excavation of an Indian mound at Beech Bottom,

West Virginia. *The University of Pennsylvania Museum Journal* 21 (3–4):132–187.

BAHNSON, KRISTIAN. 1889. Über Südamerikanische Wurfhölzer im Kopenhagener Museum. *International Archiv für Ethnographie* 2:217–227.

BAILEY, GARRICK. 1995. *The Osage and the Invisible World, from the Works of Francis La Flesche.* Norman: University of Oklahoma Press.

BAIRD, E. T. 1989. Stars and war at Cacaxtla. In *Mesoamerica after the Decline of Teotihuacan A.D. 700–900,* ed. Richard A. Diehl and Janet C. Berlo, 105–122. Washington, D.C.: Dumbarton Oaks.

BAKKEN, CHARLOTTE. 1950. Preliminary investigations at the Outlet site. *Wisconsin Archeologist* n.s. 31 (2):43–70.

BAREIS, CHARLES J., and WILLIAM M. GARDNER. 1968. Three long-nosed god masks from western Illinois. *American Antiquity* 33 (4):495–498.

BARNES, R. H. 1984. *Two Crows Denies It: A History of Controversy in Omaha Sociology.* Lincoln: University of Nebraska Press.

BARNOUW, VICTOR. 1977. *Wisconsin Chippewa Myths and Tales and Their Relation to Chippewa Life.* Madison: University of Wisconsin Press.

BARRECA, ELAINE. 1992. The secret of EB3/47: Meet Beloit's acclaimed discovery, 'Mr. Head,' a most significant stone. *Beloit Magazine* December, 6–7.

BARRETT, SAMUEL A. 1917. Ceremonies of the Pomo Indians. *University of California Publications in American Archaeology and Ethnology* 7 (3):397–441.

———. 1933. Ancient Aztalan. *Bulletin of the Public Museum of the City of Milwaukee* 13.

BARRETT, SAMUEL A., and ALANSON SKINNER. 1932. Certain mounds and village sites of Shawano and Oconto Counties, Wisconsin. *Bulletin of the Public Museum of the City of Milwaukee* 10 (5).

BEADLE, BERNARD V. 1942. A recent find of carved shell effigies. *Minnesota Archaeologist* 8 (4):169.

BECKWITH, MARTHA WARREN. 1969. *Mandan-Hidatsa Myths and Ceremonies.* New York: Kraus Reprint. Originally published as Memoir 32 of the American Folk-Lore Society, Boston, 1938.

BENDER, MARGARET M., REID A. BRYSON, and DAVID A. BAERREIS. 1975. University of Wisconsin radiocarbon dates XII. *Radiocarbon* 17 (1):121–134.

BENNETT, JOHN W. 1944. The development of ethnological theory as illustrated by studies of the Plains Sun Dance. *American Anthropologist* 46:162–181.

BERGEN, FANNY D. 1896. Some customs and beliefs of the

Winnebago Indians. *Journal of American Folk-Lore*. 9:51–54. Reprint, Kraus Reprint, New York, 1963.

——. 1899. Animal and Plant Lore. *American Folk-Lore Society Memoirs*, vol. 7. Reprint, Kraus Reprint, New York, 1969.

BERNDT, RONALD M. 1951. *Kunapipi: A Study of an Australian Aboriginal Cult*. Melbourne: F. W. Cheshire.

BIERHORST, JOHN. 1992. *History and Mythology of the Aztecs: The Codex Chimalpopoca*. Tucson: University of Arizona Press.

BIERHORST, JOHN, ed. 1976. *The Red Swan: Myths and Tales of the American Indian*. New York: Farrar, Straus and Giroux.

B. J. C. 1876. Interesting discoveries at Milton. Typescript news release, October 24. State Historical Society of Wisconsin, Archives, Charles E. Brown papers, archaeology, Rock County 1838–1927, Wis Mss HB, box 38, folder A.

BLACKBIRD, ANDREW J. 1887. *History of the Ottawa and Chippewa Indians of Michigan; a Grammar of Their Language, and Personal and Family History of the Author*. Ypsilanti, Mich.: Ypsilantian Job Printing House. Reprint, Friends of the [Little Traverse Regional Historical] Society, 1977.

BLACK ELK. 1953. *The Sacred Pipe: Black Elk's Account of the Seven Rites of the Oglala Sioux*, ed. Joseph Epes Brown. Norman: University of Oklahoma Press.

BLAIR, EMMA HELEN, ed. and trans. 1911–1912. *The Indian Tribes of the Upper Mississippi Valley and the Region of the Great Lakes as Described by Nicolas Perrot, French Commandant in the Northwest; Bacqueville de la Potherie, French Royal Commissioner to Canada; Morrell Marston, American Army Officer; and Thomas Forsyth, United States Agent at Fort Armstrong*. 2 vols. Cleveland: Arthur H. Clark.

BLAKESLEE, DONALD J. 1975. The Plains interband trade system: An ethnohistoric and archeological investigation. Ph.D. diss., Department of Anthropology, University of Wisconsin-Milwaukee.

——. 1981. The origin and spread of the Calumet Ceremony. *American Antiquity* 46 (4):759–768.

BLOOMFIELD, LEONARD. 1928. Menomini Texts. *Publications of the American Ethnological Society* 12.

——. 1975. Menominee Lexikon, ed. Charles F. Hockett. *Milwaukee Public Museum Publications in Anthropology and History* 3.

BOAS, FRANZ, and ELLA DELORIA. 1941. Dakota Grammar. *Memoirs of the National Academy of Sciences*, vol. 23, 2d memoir.

BOLTON, HERBERT EUGENE. 1987. *The Hasinais: Southern Caddoans as Seen by the Earliest Europeans*. Norman: University of Oklahoma Press.

BOURNE, EDWARD G., ed. 1904. *Narratives of the Career of Hernando De Soto*. 2 vols. New York: A. S. Barnes.

BOWERS, ALFRED W. 1950. *Mandan Social and Ceremonial Organization*. Chicago: University of Chicago Press.

——. 1965. Hidatsa social and ceremonial organization. *Bureau of American Ethnology Bulletin* 194. Reprint, University of Nebraska Press, Lincoln, 1992.

BRADFIELD, RICHARD M. 1973. *A Natural History of Associations*. 2 vols. London: Duckworth.

BRASSER, TED J. 1974. Riding on the frontier's crest: Mahican Indian culture and culture change. *National Museum of*

Man, Ethnology Division, Mercury Series Paper 13. Ottawa.

——. 1978. Mahican. In *Handbook of North American Indians*, vol. 15, *The Northeast*, ed. Bruce C. Trigger, 198–212. Washington, D.C.: Smithsonian Institution.

BRICKER, VICTORIA R. 1983. Directional glyphs in Maya inscriptions and codices. *American Antiquity* 48:346–353.

BRAY, ROBERT T. 1961. The Flynn cemetery: An Orr focus Oneota burial site in Allamakee County. *Journal of the Iowa Archeological Society* 10 (4):15–25.

BRINTON, DANIEL G. 1976. *Myths of the New World: The Symbolism and Mythology of the Indians of the Americas* [cover title, *Myths of the Americas*]. Blauvelt, N.Y.: Multimedia. Originally published in 1868.

BRISBOIS, B. W. 1882. Recollections of Prairie du Chien. *Wisconsin Historical Collections* 9:282–302.

BRODA, JOHANNA, DAVID CARRASCO, and EDUARDO MATOS MOCTEZUMA. 1987. *The Great Temple of Tenochtitlan, Center and Periphery in the Aztec World*. Berkeley and Los Angeles: University of California Press.

BROWN, BETTY ANN. 1984. Ochpaniztli in historical perspective. In *Ritual Human Sacrifice in Mesoamerica*, ed. Elizabeth P. Benson and Elizabeth H. Boone, 195–210. Washington, D.C.: Dumbarton Oaks.

BROWN, DEE. 1971. *Bury My Heart at Wounded Knee: An Indian History of the American West*. New York: Holt, Rinehart and Winston.

BROWN, JAMES A. 1964. The northeastern extension of the Havana tradition. In *Hopewellian Studies*, ed. Joseph R. Caldwell and Robert L. Hall, 107–122, *Illinois State Museum Scientific Papers*.

——. 1976. The Southern Cult reconsidered. *Midcontinental Journal of Archaeology* 1 (2):115–135.

——. 1990. Archaeology confronts history at the Natchez Temple. *Southeastern Archaeology* 9 (1):1–10.

——. 1991. The falcon and the serpent: Life in the Southeastern United States at the time of Columbus. In *Circa 1492: Art in the Age of Exploration*, ed. Jay A. Levenson, 529–534. New Haven: Yale University Press.

BROWN, JAMES A., DAVID H. DYE, and ROBERT L. HALL. 1995. Oral report of the war and weapons subgroup to the Workshop on Southeastern Ceremonial Complex Symbolism, San Marcos, Texas, March 18.

BROWN, JOSEPH EPES. 1989. Sun Dance. In *Native American Religions: North America*, ed. Lawrence E. Sullivan, 193–199. New York: Macmillan.

BRUNDAGE, BURR CARTWRIGHT. 1979. *The Fifth Sun: Aztec Gods, Aztec World*. Austin: University of Texas Press.

——. 1982. *The Phoenix of the Western World: Quetzalcoatl and the Sky Religion*. Norman: University of Oklahoma Press.

BRUYAS, R. P. JAMES. 1862. *Radices Verborum Iroquaeorum (Radical Words of the Mohawk Language)*. Shea's Library of American Linguistics, no. 10. New York: Cramoisy Press.

BUDGE, E. A. WALLIS. 1969. *The Gods of the Egyptians*. 2 vols. New York: Dover. Originally published by Open Court, Chicago, and Methuen, London, 1904.

BUECHEL, REV. EUGENE, S. J. 1970. *A Dictionary of the Teton Dakota Sioux Language, Lakota-English, English-Lakota, with Considerations Given to Yankton and Santee*, ed. Rev. Paul Manhart, S.J. Pine Ridge, S.D.: Red Cloud Indian School, in cooperation with the Institute of Indian Studies of the University of South Dakota, Vermillion.

BURR, ALEXANDER H. 1933. Francis La Flesche. *American Anthropologist* 35:328–331.

BUSHNELL, DAVID I., JR. 1927. Burials of the Algonquian, Siouan and Caddoan tribes west of the Mississippi. *Bureau of American Ethnology Bulletin* 83.

———. 1935. The Manahoac tribes in Virginia, 1608. *Smithsonian Miscellaneous Collections* 94 (8).

BUTLER, WILLIAM B. 1975. The atlatl: The physics of function and performance. *Plains Anthropologist* 20 (68):105–110.

———. 1977. Atlatl, fancy, flex, and fun: a reply to Howard. *Plains Anthropologist* 22 (76, pt. 1):161–162.

CADILLAC, ANTOINE DE LA MOTHE. n.d. Cadillac Papers. *Michigan Pioneer and Historical Collections*, vols. 33, 34.

CALDWELL, JOSEPH R. 1958. Trend and Tradition in the Prehistory of the Eastern United States. *Illinois State Museum Scientific Papers*, vol. 10. Published simultaneously as *American Anthropological Association Memoir* 88.

———. 1964. Interaction spheres in prehistory. In Hopewellian Studies, ed. Joseph R. Caldwell and Robert L. Hall, 133–143, *Illinois State Museum Scientific Papers* 12.

CARDINAL, ELIZABETH A. 1975. Faunal remains from the Zimmerman site, 1970. In *The Zimmerman Site: Further Excavations at the Grand Village of Kaskaskia*, Margaret K. Brown, 73–79, *Illinois State Museum Reports of Investigations*, no. 32.

CARLSON, JOHN B. 1991. Venus-regulated warfare and ritual sacrifice in Mesoamerica: Teotihuacan and the Cacaxtla "Star Wars" connection. *Center for Archaeoastronomy Technical Publication* 7.

CARMICHAEL, ELIZABETH, and CHLOË SAYER. 1991. *The Skeleton at the Feast: The Day of the Dead in Mexico*. Austin: University of Texas Press.

CARPENTER, EDMUND. 1956. The Irvine, Cornplanter, and Corydon Mounds, Warren County, Pennsylvania. *Pennsylvania Archaeologist* 26 (2):89–115.

CASO, ALFONSO. 1958. *The Aztecs: People of the Sun*, trans. Lowell Dunham. Norman: University of Oklahoma Press. Originally published as *El pueblo del sol*, Mexico City, Fondo de Cultura Económica, 1954.

———. 1966. Dioses y signos Teotihuacanos. In *Teotihuacán: Onceava Mesa Redonda*, 249–279. Mexico City: Sociedad Mexicana de Antropología.

CATLIN, GEORGE. 1976. *O-Kee-Pa: A Religious Ceremony and Other Customs of the Mandan*. Lincoln: University of Nebraska Press. Reprint of the 1967 Yale University edition. Originally published concurrently in 1867 by Lippincott of Philadelphia and by Trübner of London.

CHAMBERLAIN, VON DEL. 1982. *When Stars Came Down to Earth: Cosmology of the Skidi Pawnee Indians of North America*. Ballena Press Anthropological Papers no. 26. Los Altos, Calif.: Ballena Press; College Park, Md.: Center for Archaeoastronomy.

———. 1992. The chief and his council: Unity and authority from the stars. In *Earth and Sky: Visions of the Cosmos in Native American Folklore*, ed. Ray A. Williamson and Claire R. Farrer, 221–235. Albuquerque: University of New Mexico Press.

CHASING HORSE, JOSEPH. 1994. The Story of the White Buffalo Calf Woman [as told by Joseph Chasing Horse]. *Ho-Chunkwo-Lduk*, early December, 4. Reprinted from the newspaper *Isthmus*.

CHAVERO, ALFREDO. 1886[?]. La Piedra del Sol: estudio arqueológico. *Anales del Museo Nacional de México*, vols. 1–3 (1882–1886).

CHITTENDEN, HIRAM M., and ALFRED R. RICHARDSON, eds. *Life, Letters and Travels of Father Pierre-Jean de Smet, S.J., 1801–1873; Missionary Labors and Adventures Among the Wild Tribes of North American Indians*. 4 vols. New York: F. P. Harper.

CHMURNY, WILLIAM W. 1973. The ecology of the Middle Mississippian occupation of the American Bottom. Ph.D. diss., Department of Anthropology, University of Illinois at Urbana-Champaign.

CLARKE, W. P. 1884. Ancient earthworks in Rock County, Wis. *American Antiquarian* 6:317–322.

CLEMENTS, F. E. 1931. Plains Indian tribal correlations with Sun Dance data. *American Anthropologist* 33 (2):216–227.

COE, MICHAEL D. 1975. Native astronomy in America. In *Archaeoastronomy in Pre-Columbian America*, ed. Anthony F. Aveni, 3–31. Austin: University of Texas Press.

———. 1977. *Mexico*. 2d ed. New York: Praeger.

COGGINS, CLEMENCY. 1976. A new order and the rule of the calendar: some characteristics of the Middle Classic period at Tikal. In *Maya Archaeology and Ethnohistory*, ed. Norman Hammond and Gordon R. Willey, 38–50. Austin: University of Texas Press.

———. 1980. The shape of time: Some political implications of a four-part figure. *American Antiquity* 45:727–739.

COLE, FAY-COOPER, and THORNE DEUEL. 1937. *Rediscovering Illinois: Archaeological Explorations in and Around Fulton County*. Chicago: University of Chicago Press.

COLLINS, JAMES M. 1995. A shell mask gorget from Allamakee County, Iowa. *Plains Anthropologist* 40 (153):251–260.

CONRAD, LAWRENCE A. 1989. The Southeastern Ceremonial Complex on the northern Middle Mississippian frontier: late prehistoric politico-religious systems in the central Illinois River valley. In *The Southeastern Ceremonial Complex: Artifacts and Analysis—The Cottonlandia Conference*, ed. Patricia Galloway, 93–113. Lincoln: University of Nebraska Press.

CONWAY, THOR. 1992. The conjurer's lodge: celestial narratives from Algonkian shamans. In *Earth and Sky: Visions of the Cosmos in Native American Folklore*, ed. Ray A. Williamson and Claire R. Farrer, 236–259. Albuquerque: University of New Mexico Press.

COOPER, JAMES FENIMORE. 1961. *The Last of the Mohicans: A Narrative of 1757*. New York: Scribner's.

COOPER, PAUL, and EARL H. BELL. 1936. Archaeology of certain sites in Cedar County, Nebraska. In *Chapters in Nebraska Archaeology* by Earl H. Bell, 11–145. Lincoln: University of Nebraska.

COUNT, EARL W. 1935. The Earth-Diver: An attempt at an Asiatic-American correlation. Ph.D. diss., Department of Anthropology, University of California, Berkeley.

———. 1952. The Earth-Diver and the Rival Twins: A clue to time correlation in North-Eurasiatic and North American mythology. In *Indian Tribes of Aboriginal America: Selected*

Papers of the XXIXth International Congress of Americanists, ed. Sol Tax, 55–62. Chicago: University of Chicago Press.

COWAN, JAY. 1988. At long last, an atlatl of your very own. *Sports Illustrated,* November 14.

CUSHING, FRANK HAMILTON. 1896. Explorations of ancient key dwellers' remains on the Gulf coast of Florida. *Proceedings of the American Philosophical Society* 35 (153):329–448.

———. 1981. *Zuñi: Selected Writings of Frank Hamilton Cushing,* ed. Jesse Green. Lincoln: University of Nebraska Press.

D'ABBEVILLE, CLAUDE. n.d. *História da Missão dos Padres Capuchinhos na Ilha do Maranhão* [1614], trans. Sergio Millet. São Paulo: Livraria Martins Editora.

DAVIES, NIGEL. 1983. *The Ancient Kingdoms of Mexico.* Pelican Books edition. Harmondsworth, England: Penguin.

DAY, GORDON M. 1978a. Western Abenaki. In *Handbook of North American Indians,* vol. 15, *The Northeast,* ed. Bruce C. Trigger, 148–159. Washington, D.C.: Smithsonian Institution.

———. 1978b. Nipissing. In *Handbook of North American Indians,* vol. 15, *The Northeast,* ed. Bruce C. Trigger, 787–791. Washington, D.C.: Smithsonian Institution.

[DELIETTE, LOUIS]. 1934. Memoir . . . Concerning the Illinois Country. *In* The French Foundations 1680–1693, ed. Theodore Calvin Pease and Raymond C. Werner, 302–395. *Collections of the Illinois State Historical Library,* vol. 23.

DELORIA, VINE, JR. 1995. *Red Earth, White Lies: Native Americans and the Myth of Scientific Fact.* New York: Scribner's.

DeMALLIE, RAYMOND J., ed. 1984. *The Sixth Grandfather: Black Elk's Teachings Given to John G. Neihardt.* Lincoln: University of Nebraska Press.

DeMALLIE, RAYMOND J., and DOUGLAS R. PARKS. 1987. Introduction. In *Sioux Indian Religion: Tradition and Innovation,* ed. Raymond J. DeMallie and Douglas R. Parks, 3–22. Norman: University of Oklahoma Press.

DENSMORE, FRANCES. 1918. Teton Sioux music. *Bureau of American Ethnology Bulletin* 61.

———. 1935. A collection of specimens from the Teton Sioux. *Museum of the American Indian, Heye Foundation, Indian Notes and Monographs* 11 (1):169–204.

DÍAZ, GISELE, and ALAN RODGERS. 1993. *The Codex Borgia: A Full-Color Restoration of the Ancient Mexican Manuscript.* Introd. Bruce Byland. New York: Dover.

DÍAZ DEL CASTILLO, BERNAL. 1956. *The Discovery and Conquest of Mexico 1517–1521,* trans. A. P. Maudslay. New York: Grove Press.

DICKSON, D. BRUCE. 1985. The atlatl assessed: A review of recent anthropological approaches to prehistoric North American weaponry. *Bulletin of the Texas Archaeological Society* 56:1–38.

DORSEY, GEORGE A. 1903. The Arapaho Sun Dance: The Ceremony of the Offerings Lodge. *Field Columbian Museum Publication* 75, *Anthropological Series* 4.

———. 1904a. *Traditions of the Arikara.* Washington, D.C.: Carnegie Institution of Washington.

———. 1904b. *The mythology of the Wichita.* Washington: Carnegie Institution of Washington.

———. 1904c. *Traditions of the Skidi Pawnee.* Memoir 8 of the American Folk-Lore Society. Boston and New York: Houghton, Mifflin.

———. 1905a. The Cheyenne, Part 2—The Sun Dance. *Field Columbian Museum Publication* 103, *Anthropological Series* 9 (2).

———. 1905b. *Traditions of the Caddo.* Washington, D.C.: Carnegie Institution of Washington.

———. 1905c. The Ponca Sun Dance. *Field Columbian Museum Publication* 102, *Anthropological Series* 7 (2).

———. 1906. *The Pawnee: Mythology* (Pt. 2). Washington, D.C.: Carnegie Institution of Washington.

———. 1910. Sun Dance. In *Handbook of American Indians North of Mexico,* ed. Frederick W. Hodge, 2:649–652, *Bureau of American Ethnology Bulletin* 30.

———. 1969. *Traditions of the Skidi Pawnee.* New York: Kraus Reprint Co. Reprint, *Memoir* 8, American Folk-Lore Society, published for the society by Houghton, Mifflin, Boston and New York, 1904.

———. 1975. *The Cheyenne.* Fairfield, Wash.: Ye Galleon Press. Originally published in 1905 as The Cheyenne, Part 1—Ceremonial Organization. *Field Columbian Museum Publication* 99, *Anthropological Series* 9 (1).

DORSEY, GEORGE A., and JAMES R. MURIE. 1902. Pawnee notes, Morning Star folder, on file in the archives of the Department of Anthropology of the Field Museum of Natural History, Chicago.

———. 1907. The Pawnee: Society and Religion of the Skidi Pawnee. Manuscript notes and drafts on file in the archives of the Department of Anthropology of the Field Museum of Natural History, Chicago.

DORSEY, JAMES O. 1884. Omaha sociology. *Third Annual Report of the Bureau of American Ethnology,* 205–370.

———. 1891. The social organization of the Siouan tribes. *Journal of American Folk-Lore* 4:331–332.

———. 1897. Siouan sociology. *Fifteenth Annual Report of the Bureau of American Ethnology,* 228–229. Washington, D.C.

DORSEY, JAMES O., and JOHN R. SWANTON. A Dictionary of the Biloxi and Ofo languages. *Bureau of American Ethnology Bulletin* 47.

DRAGOO, DON W. 1964. The development of Adena culture and its role in the formation of Ohio Hopewell. In *Hopewellian Studies,* ed. Joseph R. Caldwell and Robert L. Hall, 1–34, *Illinois State Museum Scientific Papers* 12.

DRUCKER, PHILIP. 1963. *Indians of the Northwest Coast.* American Museum Science Book. Garden City, N.Y.: Natural History Press.

DRUCKER, R. DAVID. 1987. The Mexican ("Aztec") and Western Yucatec (Landa) 365-day calendars: A perpetual relation. *American Antiquity* 52(4):816–819.

DUKE, PHILIP. 1989. The Morning Star Ceremony of the Skiri Pawnee as described by Alfred C. Haddon. *Plains Anthropologist* 34 (125):193–203.

DUMALIANG, ROMANO. 1909. Testimony given May 27, 1909, in criminal case no. 69 before Hon. Isidro Paredes, Judge at Large, acting in the Mountain Judicial District, Philippine Islands.

DUNCAN, CAROL DIAZ-GRANADOS. 1993. The petroglyphs and pictographs of Missouri: A distributional, stylistic, contextual, functional, and temporal analysis of the state's rock graphics. 2 vols. Ph.D. diss., Department of Anthropology, Washington University, St. Louis, Missouri.

DUNNELL, ROBERT C. 1973. Late Adena atlatl handle

style. *Central States Archaeological Journal* 20 (1):4–9.
———. 1977. A further note on a late Adena atlatl handle style. *Central States Archaeological Journal* 24 (2):74–76.

DURÁN, FRAY DIEGO. 1867–1880. *Historia de las Indias de Nueva España e Islas de Tierra Firme.* 2 vols., ed. José F. Ramírez and F. Escalante (vol. 1), I. Escalante (vol. 2). Mexico City: J. M. Andrade y F. Escalante.
———. 1964. *The Aztecs,* trans. Doris Heyden and Fernando Horcasitas. New York: Orion Press.
———. 1971. *Book of the Gods and Rites and the Ancient Calendar,* trans. and ed. Fernando Horcasitas and Doris Heyden. Norman: University of Oklahoma Press. Translation of the Mexican edition of 1880.

EDEN, ROBERT C. 1865. *The Sword and Gun: A History of the 37th Wisconsin Volunteer Infantry.* Madison: Atwood and Rublee.

EDMONSON, MUNRO S. 1971. The Book of Counsel: The Popol Vuh of the Quiche Maya of Guatemala. *Tulane University, Middle American Research Institute, Publication* 35.
———. 1988. *Heaven Born Merida and its Destiny: The Book of Chilam Balam of Chumayel.* Austin: University of Texas Press.
———. 1988. *The Book of the Year: Middle American Calendrical Systems.* Salt Lake City: University of Utah Press.

EDMUNDS, R. DAVID. 1983. *The Shawnee Prophet.* Lincoln: University of Nebraska Press.

EKHOLM, GORDON F. 1962. U-shaped "ornaments" identified as finger-loops from atlatls. *American Antiquity* 28 (2):181–185.

ELIADE, MIRCEA. 1965. *Rites and Symbols of Initiation.* Harper Torchbook edition. New York: Harper and Row. Originally published as *Birth and Rebirth,* Harper and Row, New York, 1958.

ELLIOTT, DAN. 1989. Bannerstones of Missouri. *Missouri Archaeological Society Quarterly* 6 (1):8–13, 18–20.

ERDOES, RICHARD, and ALFONSO ORTIZ. 1984. *American Indian Myths and Legends.* New York: Pantheon.

FENTON, WILLIAM N. 1946. An Iroquois Condolence Council for installing Cayuga chiefs in 1945. *Journal of the Washington Academy of Sciences* 36:110–127.
———. 1950. The roll call of the Iroquois chiefs: A study of a mnemonic cane from the Six Nations Reserve. *Smithsonian Miscellaneous Collections* 111(15). Washington, D.C.: Smithsonian Institution.
———. 1953. The Iroquois Eagle Dance, an offshoot of the Calumet Dance. *Bureau of American Ethnology Bulletin* 156. Reprint, Syracuse University Press, 1991.
———. 1962. This island, the world on the turtle's back. *The Journal of American Folk-Lore* 75 (298):283–300.
———. 1975. The lore of the longhouse: Myth, ritual and red power. *Anthropological Quarterly* 48 (3):131–147.

FENTON, WILLIAM N., and GERTRUDE P. KURATH. 1951. The Feast of the Dead, or Ghost Dance, at Six Nations Reserve, Canada. *Bureau of American Ethnology Bulletin* 149. Reprinted in *An Iroquois Source Book,* vol. 3, ed. Elisabeth Tooker, Garland, New York, 1986.

FENTON, WILLIAM N., and ELISABETH TOOKER. 1978. Mohawk. In *Handbook of North American Indians,* vol. 15, *Northeast,* ed. Bruce G. Trigger, 466–480. Washington, D.C.: Smithsonian Institution.

FEWKES, J. WALTER. 1900. The New Fire Ceremony at Walpi. *American Anthropologist* n.s. 2:80–138.

FIELD, FREDERICK V. 1967. Thoughts on the meaning and use of Pre-Hispanic Mexican sellos. *Studies in Precolumbian Art and Archaeology* 3. Washington, D.C.: Dumbarton Oaks.

FISHER, MARGARET W. 1946. The mythology of the northern and northeastern Algonkians in reference to Algonkian mythology as a whole. In Man in Northeastern North America, ed. Frederick Johnson, 226–262, *Papers of the Robert S. Peabody Foundation for Archaeology* 3. Andover: Phillips Academy.

FITTING, JAMES E. 1978. Regional cultural development, 300 B.C. to A.D. 1000. In *Handbook of North American Indians,* vol. 15, *The Northeast,* ed. Bruce C. Trigger, 44–57. Washington, D.C.: Smithsonian Institution.

FLETCHER, ALICE C. 1884. The Wa-wan or Pipe Dance. Omahas. In Fletcher's *Five Indian Ceremonies,* 308–333. Salem, Mass.: Salem Press. Reprint from *16th Annual Report of the Peabody Museum of American Archaeology and Ethnology of Harvard University* in *Reports,* vol. 3, Cambridge, 1883.
———. 1953. A ghost lodge for the dead child. In *Primitive Heritage: An Anthropological Anthology,* ed. Margaret Mead and Nicolas Calas, 567–576. New York: Random House. Originally published in 1883 as "The shadow or ghost lodge" in *Reports of the Peabody Museum of American Archaeology and Ethnology of Harvard University* 3:296–307, Cambridge.

FLETCHER, ALICE, and FRANCIS LA FLESCHE. 1972. *The Omaha tribe.* 2 vols. Lincoln: University of Nebraska Press. Originally published as a paper accompanying the *Twenty-Seventh Annual Report of the Bureau of American Ethnology,* 1911.

FLETCHER, ALICE, [and JAMES R. MURIE]. 1904. The Hako, a Pawnee ceremony. *Twenty-Second Annual Report of the Bureau of American Ethnology,* part 2, 13–368.

FOGELSON, RAYMOND. 1980. Windigo goes south: Stoneclad among the Cherokees. In *Manlike Monsters on Trial,* ed. M. Halpin and M. M. Ames, 132–151. Vancouver: University of British Columbia Press.

FORD, JAMES A. 1952. Measurements of some prehistoric design developments in the Southeastern states. *Anthropological Papers of the American Museum of Natural History* 44 (3).
———. 1963. Hopewell culture burial mounds near Helena, Arkansas. *Anthropological Papers of the American Museum of Natural History* 50 (1).
———. 1969. A Comparison of Formative Cultures in the Americas. *Smithsonian Contributions to Anthropology* 2.

FORD, JAMES A., and GORDON R. WILLEY. 1940. Crooks site, a Marksville Period burial mound in La Salle Parish, Louisiana. *Louisiana Geological Survey, Anthropological Study* 3.

FORSYTH, THOMAS. 1827. Letter dated St. Louis, January 15. In Blair 1911–1912, 2:206–209.

FORTUNE, REO. 1932. Omaha secret societies. *Columbia University Contributions to Anthropology* 14.

FOWLER, MELVIN L. 1974. Cahokia: Ancient Capital of the Midwest. *Addison-Wesley Module in Anthropology* 48. Menlo Park, Calif.: Cummings.

FOWLER, MELVIN L., and ROBERT L. HALL. 1978. Late Prehistory of the Illinois Area. In *Handbook of North American Indians*, vol. 15, *The Northeast*, ed. Bruce C. Trigger, 560–568. Washington, D.C.: Smithsonian Institution.

FRAZER, JAMES GEORGE. 1935. *The Magic Arts and the Evolution of Kings*. 2 vols. New York: Macmillan.

FREIDEL, DAVID, LINDA SCHELE, and JOY PARKER. 1993. *Maya Cosmos: Three Thousand Years on the Shaman's Path*. New York: William Morrow.

FUNDABURK, EMMA LILA, and MARY FUNDABURK FOREMAN. 1957. *Sun Circles and Human Hands: The Southeastern Indians, Art and Industries*. Luverne, Ala.: Emma Lila Fundaburk.

FURST, JILL LESLIE. 1978. Codex Vindobonensis Mexicanus I: A commentary. *Institute for Mesoamerican Studies, State University of New York at Albany, Publication No. 4*.

———. 1995. *The Natural History of the Soul in Ancient Mexico*. New Haven: Yale University Press.

FURST, PETER T. 1975. House of darkness and house of light: sacred functions of west Mexican funerary art. In *Death and Afterlife in Pre-Columbian America*, ed. Elizabeth P. Benson, 33–68. Washington, D.C.: Dumbarton Oaks.

GABEL, JOSEPH. 1975. *False Consciousness: An Essay on Reification*, trans. Margaret Thompson, introd. Kenneth A. Thompson. New York: Harper and Row.

GADUS, ELOISE. 1980. Letter to author, July 22.

GALLOWAY, PATRICIA. 1982. Sources for the La Salle expedition of 1682. In *La Salle and His Legacy*, ed. Patricia K. Galloway, 11–40. Jackson: University Press of Mississippi.

———, ed. 1989. *The Southeastern Ceremonial Complex: Artifacts and Analysis—The Cottonlandia Conference*. Lincoln: University of Nebraska Press.

GARCÍA PAYÓN, J. 1950. Restos de una cultura prehistórica encontrados en la región de Zempoala, Veracruz. *Uni-Ver* 2 (15):90–130.

GARCILASO DE LA VEGA. 1980. *The Florida of the Inca*, trans. John and Jeanette Varner. Austin: University of Texas Press.

GARIBAY K., ÁNGEL M. 1940. *Llave del Náhuatl: Collección de Trozos Clásicos con Gramática y Vocabulario, para Utilidad de los Principiantes*. Mexico City: Otumba.

———. 1972. *Poesía Indígena de la Altiplanicia: Divulgación Literaria*. Mexico City: Universidad Nacional Autónoma de México.

GASCHET, ALBERT S. 1969a. *A Migration Legend of the Creek Indians*, vol. 1., no. 4 of Brinton's Library of Aboriginal American Literature. New York: Kraus Reprint. Reprinted from the 1884 Philadelphia edition of D. G. Brinton.

———. 1969b. *A Migration Legend of the Creek Indians*, vol. 2. New York: Kraus Reprint. Reprinted from the 1889 St. Louis edition privately printed by the author.

GATES, WILLIAM. 1978. *An Outline Dictionary of Maya Glyphs with a Concordance*. New York: Dover. This edition combines the book of the same name, originally published by Johns Hopkins Press, Baltimore, 1931, with the article "Glyph studies" by the same author, originally published in *The Maya Society Quarterly* 1 (4, September 1932).

GENDROP, PAUL. 1985. *Arte Prehispánico en Mesoamérica*. 4th ed. México: Editorial Trillas.

GIBBON, GUY E. 1972. Cultural dynamics and development of the Oneota life-way in Wisconsin. *American Antiquity* 37 (2):166–185.

———. 1982. Oneota origins revisited. In *Oneota Studies*, ed. Guy Gibbon, 85–90, University of Minnesota Publications in Anthropology, no. 1.

———, ed. 1982. *Oneota Studies*. University of Minnesota Publications in Anthropology, no. 1.

GILL, SAM D. 1982. *Native American Religions: An Introduction*. Belmont, Calif.: Wadsworth.

GILLESPIE, SUSAN D. 1989. *The Aztec Kings: The Construction of Rulership in Mexica History*. Tucson: University of Arizona Press.

GILLILAND, MARION S. 1975. *The Material Culture of Key Marco, Florida*. Gainesville: University Presses of Florida.

GOGGIN, JOHN M. 1952. Space and time perspective in northern St. Johns archaeology, Florida. *Yale University Publications in Anthropology* 47.

GONZÁLEZ TORRES, YOLOTL. 1985. *El Sacrificio Humano entre los Mexicas*. Mexico City: Fondo de Cultura Económica.

GOODMAN, RONALD. 1990. *Lakota Star Knowledge: Studies in Lakota Stellar Theology*. Rosebud, S.D.: Sinte Gleska College.

———. 1992. On the necessity of sacrifice in Lakota stellar theology as seen in "The Hand" constellation, and the story of "The chief who lost his arm." In *Earth and Sky: Visions of the Cosmos in Native American Folklore*, ed. Ray A. Williamson and Claire R. Farrer, 215–220. Albuquerque: University of New Mexico Press.

GOODWIN, GRENVILLE. 1939. Myths and tales of the White Mountain Apache. *Memoirs of the American Folk-Lore Society* 33.

GOULD, R. A., D. A. KOSTER, and A. H. L. SONTZ. 1971. The lithic assemblages of the western desert aborigines of Australia. *American Antiquity* 36 (2):149–169.

GRAVIER, JACQUES. 1902. Gravier's voyage down and up the Mississippi in 1700. In *Early Voyages Up and Down the Mississippi by Cavelier, St. Cosme, Le Sueur, Gravier and Guignas*, ed. John Gilmary Shea, 113–163. Albany: Joseph McDonough. Reprint of the 1861 Albany edition of Joel Munsell.

GREBER, N'OMI B., and KATHARINE C. RUHL. 1989. *The Hopewell Site: A Contemporary Analysis Based on the Work of Charles C. Willoughby*. Boulder: Westview Press.

GREEN, WILLIAM, ed. 1995. *Oneota Archaeology: Past, Present, and Future*. Report 20 of the Office of the State Archaeologist of Iowa, University of Iowa, Iowa City.

GREGG, JOHN B., LARRY J. ZIMMERMAN, JAMES P. STEELE, HELEN FERWERDA, and PAULINE S. GREGG. 1981. Antemortem osteopathology at Crow Creek. *Plains Anthropologist* 26 (96, pt. 1):287–300.

GRIFFIN, JAMES B. 1944. The De Luna expedition and the "Buzzard Cult" in the Southeast. *Journal of the Washington Academy of Science* 34 (9):299–303.

———. 1945. The Box Elder mound in La Salle County, Illinois. *American Antiquity* 11:47–48.

———. 1946. Cultural change and continuity in northeastern North America. *In Man in Northeastern North America*, ed. Frederick Johnson, 37–95. *Papers of the R. S. Peabody Foundation for Archaeology* 3. Andover: Phillips Academy.

———. 1952. Culture periods in eastern United States archaeology. In *Archaeology of Eastern United States*, ed. James B.
Griffin, 352–364. Chicago: University of Chicago Press.

———. 1966. Mesoamerica and the eastern United States in
prehistoric times. In *Archaeological Frontiers and External
Connections*, ed. Gordon F. Ekholm and Gordon R. Willey,
111–131, vol. 4 of *Handbook of Middle American Indians*.
Austin: University of Texas Press.

———. 1983. The Midlands. In *Ancient North Americans*, ed.
J. D. Jennings, 243–295. San Francisco: W. H. Freeman.

GRIFFIN, JAMES B., ed. 1952. *Archeology of Eastern United
States*. Chicago: University of Chicago Press.

GRIFFIN, JAMES B., and RICHARD G. MORGAN, ed. 1941.
Contributions to the archaeology of the Illinois River
valley. *Transactions of the American Philosophical Society* n.s.
32 (pt. 1).

GRIFFIN, JAMES B., and DAN F. MORSE. 1961. The short-
nosed god from the Emmons site, Illinois. *American Antiquity* 26 (4):560–563.

GRINNELL, GEORGE BIRD. 1962. *Blackfoot Lodge Tales: The
Story of a Prairie People*. Lincoln: University of Nebraska
Press.

———. 1972. *The Cheyenne Indians*. 2 vols. Lincoln: University
of Nebraska Press. Originally published by Yale University
Press, New Haven, 1923.

GROBSMITH, ELIZABETH. 1981. *Lakota of the Rosebud: A
Contemporary Ethnography*. Orlando: Harcourt Brace.

HALL, ROBERT L. 1962. *The Archaeology of Carcajou Point*. 2
vols. Madison: University of Wisconsin Press.

———. 1976. Soul release as an hypothesis for explaining perforated long bones and crania in Great Lakes area prehistory. Paper presented at the forty-first annual meeting
of the Society for American Archaeology, St. Louis,
Missouri, May 6–8.

———. 1977. An anthropocentric perspective for eastern
United States prehistory. *American Antiquity* 42 (4):499–
518.

———. 1979. In search of the ideology of the Adena-Hopewell
climax. In *Hopewell Archaeology: The Chillicothe Conference*,
ed. David S. Brose and N'omi Greber, 258–265. Kent,
Ohio: Kent State University Press.

———. 1980. An interpretation of the two-climax model of
Illinois prehistory. In *Early Native Americans: Prehistoric
Demography, Economy, and Technology*, ed. David Broman,
401–462. The Hague: Mouton.

———. 1982. A second look at gunstock warclubs. *Wisconsin
Archeologist* 63:246–253.

———. 1983a. The evolution of the calumet-pipe. In *Prairie
Archaeology: Papers in Honor of David A. Baerreis,
University of Minnesota, Special Publications in Anthropology*,
no. 3, ed. Guy E. Gibbon, 37–52.

———. 1983b. A pan-continental perspective on Red Ocher
and Glacial Kame ceremonialism. *In* Lulu Linear Punc-
tated: Essays in Honor of George Irving Quimby, ed.
Robert C. Dunnell and Donald K. Grayson, 74–107,
*University of Michigan, Museum of Anthropology, Anthropo-
logical Papers* 72.

———. 1983c. Some thoughts on afterlife and afterworld. In
The Study of Ancient Human Skeletal Remains in Iowa: A

Symposium. Iowa City: Office of the State Archaeologist of
Iowa.

———. 1983d. Long distance connections of some long-nosed
gods. Paper presented at the eighty-second annual meeting
of the American Anthropological Association, Chicago,
November 17–20.

———. 1986. The mechanisms of the Cahokia and Oneota
interactions. Paper presented at the annual meeting of the
Society for American Archaeology, New Orleans, April
23–27.

———. 1987. Calumet ceremonialism, mourning ritual, and
mechanisms of inter-tribal trade. In *Mirror and Metaphor:
Material and Social Constructions of Reality*, ed. D. W. Inger-
soll and G. Bronitski, 29–43. Lanham: University Press of
America.

———. 1989a. The material symbols of the Winnebago sky
and earth moieties. In *The Meanings of Things: Material
Culture and Symbolic Expression*, ed. Ian Hodder, 178–184.
London: Unwin Hyman.

———. 1989b. The cultural background of Mississippian symbolism. In *The Southeastern Ceremonial Complex: Artifacts
and Analysis*, ed. Patricia Galloway, 239–278. Lincoln:
University of Nebraska Press.

———. 1990. Northern light illuminating the Aztec Sun
Stone. Paper presented at the twenty-third Annual Chacmool Conference, Calgary, Alberta, Canada, November 8–
11.

———. 1991a. The archaeology of La Salle's Fort St. Louis on
Starved Rock and the problem of the "Newell Fort." In
*French Colonial Archaeology: The Illinois Country and the
Western Great Lakes*, ed. John A. Walthall, 14–28. Urbana
and Chicago: University of Illinois Press.

———. 1991b. Cahokia identity and interaction models of
Cahokia Mississippian. In *Cahokia and the Hinterlands:
Middle Mississippian Cultures of the Midwest*, ed. Thomas E.
Emerson and R. Barry Lewis, 3–34. Urbana and Chicago:
University of Illinois Press.

———. 1991c. A Plains Indian perspective on Mexican cosmovision. In *Arqueoastronomía y Etnoastronmía en Mesoamérica*, ed. Johanna Broda, Stanislaw Iwaniszewski, and
Lucretia Maupomé, 557–574. Mexico City: Universidad
Nacional Autónoma de México.

———. 1991d. Algunas consecuencias de las asociaciones astro-
nómicas de las fechas de cuenta larga de la Estela 1 de La
Mojarra y de la Estatuilla de Tuxtla. *La Palabra y el
Hombre* [Revista de la Universidad Veracruzana] 80 (Oct.–
Dec.): 9–18. Xalapa, Ver., Mexico.

———. 1993a. A green card for the green corn goddess; or,
acknowledging Xilonen's legitimate residence in the U.S.
Paper presented at the thirteenth International Congress
of Anthropological and Ethnological Sciences, Mexico
City, July 29–August 5.

———. 1993b. Red Banks, Oneota, and the Winnebago: views
from a distant rock. *Wisconsin Archeologist* 74:10–79.

———. 1993c. What is Mesoamerican directional symbolism
doing in Nebraska? Paper presented at the Midwest Archaeological Conference, Milwaukee, Wisconsin, October
22-24.

———. 1994. Review of *The Book of the Year: Middle American*

Calendrical Systems by Munro S. Edmonson. *Archaeoastronomy* 11:118–121. College Park, Md.: Center for Archaeoastronomy.

———. 1995a. 'The Open Door recognizes a window of opportunity' and other tales of suns turned black. Paper presented at the Midwestern Archaeological Conference, Beloit College, Beloit, Wisconsin, October 25–28.

———. 1995b. Relating the big fish and the big stone: The archaeological identity and habitat of the Winnebago in 1634. In *Oneota Archaeology: Past, Present, and Future*, ed. William Green, 19–30. Report 20, Office of the State Archaeologist, University of Iowa, Iowa City.

HAMILTON, CANDY. 1994. Tribal people received spiritual guidance at Mato Tipi. *News from Indian Country* 8 (22 [late Nov.]): 11.

HAMILTON, HENRY W. 1952. The Spiro Mound. *Missouri Archaeologist* 14.

HAMILTON, RAFAEL N., S.J. 1970a. *Marquette's Explorations: The Narratives Reexamined.* Madison: University of Wisconsin Press.

———. 1970b. *Father Marquette.* Grand Rapids, Mich.: William B. Eerdmans.

HARN, ALAN D. 1967. Dickson Mounds: An evaluation of the amateur archaeologist in Illinois. *Earth Science* 20 (4): 152–157.

———. 1975. Another long-nosed god mask from Fulton County, Illinois. *Wisconsin Archeologist* 56 (1):2–8.

———. 1978. Mississippian settlement patterns in the central Illinois River valley. In *Mississippian Settlement Patterns*, ed. Bruce D. Smith, 233–268. New York: Academic Press.

———. 1980. The prehistory of Dickson Mounds: The Dickson excavation. *Illinois State Museum Reports of Investigations* 35.

———. 1994. Variations in Mississippian settlement patterns: The Larson settlement system in the Central Illinois River valley. *Illinois State Museum Reports of Investigation* 50. Dickson Mounds Museum Anthropological Series.

HARRINGTON, M. R. 1926. Alanson Skinner [obituary]. *American Anthropologist* n.s. 28:275–280.

———. 1959. A two-purpose atlatl. *Masterkey* 33 (2):60.

HASSIG, ROSS. 1988. *Aztec Warfare: Imperial Expansion and Political Control.* Norman: University of Oklahoma Press.

HAWKES, CHRISTOPHER. 1954. Archeological theory and method: Some suggestions from the Old World. *American Anthropologist* 56:155–168.

HEADLEY, ROBERT K., JR. 1971. The origin and distribution of the Siouan-speaking peoples. Master's thesis, Catholic University of America.

HECKENBERGER, MICHAEL J., JAMES B. PETERSON, LOUISE A. BASA, ELLEN R. COWIE, ARTHUR E. SPIESS, and ROBERT E. STUCKENRATH. 1990. Early Woodland period mortuary ceremonialism in the far northeast: A view from the Boucher cemetery. *Archaeology of Eastern North America* 18:109–144.

HENNEPIN, LOUIS. 1903. *A Discovery of a Vast Country in America.* Introd. Reuben Gold Thwaites. Chicago: A. C. McClurg. Reprinted from the 2d London edition of 1698.

HENNING, DALE R. 1970. Development and interrelationships of the Oneota Culture in the lower Missouri River valley. *Missouri Archaeologist* 32.

HENNING, ELIZABETH R. P. 1982. Western Dakota winter counts: An analysis of the effects of westward migration and culture change. *Plains Anthropologist* 27 (95):57–65.

HENRIKSEN, HARRY C. 1965. Utica Hopewell, a study of early Hopewellian occupation in the Illinois River valley. In *Early Woodland Sites in Illinois*, ed. Elaine Bluhm Herold, 1–67. *Illinois Archaeological Survey Bulletin*, no. 5.

HEROLD, ELAINE BLUHM, ed. 1971. The Indian Mounds at Albany, Illinois. *Davenport Museum, Anthropological Papers*, no. 1.

HESTER, THOMAS R. 1974. Supplementary notes on a Great Basin atlatl. In *Great Basin Atlatl Studies*, ed. T. R. Hester, M. P. Mildner, and L. Spencer, 29–31. *Ballena Press Publications in Archaeology, Ethnology and History* 2.

HESTER, THOMAS R., MICHAEL P. MILDNER, and LEE SPENCER, eds. 1974. Great Basin Atlatl Studies. *Ballena Press Publications in Archaeology, Ethnology and History* 2.

HEWITT, J. N. B. 1894. The Iroquoian concept of the soul. *Journal of American Folk-Lore* 8 (29):107–116.

———. 1903. Iroquoian cosmology [pt. 1]. *Twenty-First Annual Report of the Bureau of American Ethnology*, 127–339.

———. 1907. The calumet. In Handbook of American Indians North of Mexico, ed. Frederick Hodge. *Bureau of American Ethnology Bulletin* 30 (pt. 1):191–195.

———. 1910. Tawiskaron. In Handbook of American Indians North of Mexico. *Bureau of American Ethnology Bulletin* 30 (pt.2):707–711.

———. 1916. The requickening address of the League of the Iroquois. In *Holmes Anniversary Volume,* 163–179. Washington: Bryan Press. Reprinted in *An Iroquois Source Book*, vol. 1, ed. Elisabeth Tooker, Garland Publishing, New York, 1985.

———. 1920. A constitutional league of peace in the stone age of America: The League of the Iroquois and its constitution. *Annual Report of the Smithsonian Institution for 1918*, 527–545.

———. 1928. Iroquoian cosmology [pt. 2]. *Forty-Third Annual Report of the Bureau of American Ethnology*, 449–819.

———. 1944. The requickening address of the Iroquois condolence council. *Journal of the Washington Academy of Sciences* 34:65–85.

HICKERSON, HAROLD. 1960. The Feast of the Dead among the seventeenth century Algonkians of the upper Great Lakes. *American Anthropologist* 62 (1):81–107.

———. 1963. The sociohistorical significance of two Chippewa ceremonials. *American Anthropologist* 62 (1):67–85.

———. 1970. *The Chippewa and their Neighbors: A Study in Ethnohistory.* New York: Holt, Rinehart and Winston.

HILL, M. W. 1948. The atlatl or throwing stick: A recent study of atlatls in use with darts of various sizes. *Tennessee Archaeologist* 4 (4):37–44.

HINSDALE, W. B. 1925. *Primitive Man in Michigan.* University Museum, University of Michigan, Michigan Handbook Series, no. 1.

HISTORIA TOLTECA-CHICHIMECA: ANALES DE QUAUHTINCHAN. 1947. Mexico City: Antigua Librería Robredo de José Porrúa e Hijos.

HITT, COL. DANIEL. [ca.] 1887. Newspaper clipping on file with the records of the Starved Rock Archaeological Project at the Illinois State Museum, Springfield.

HOFFMAN, WALTER JAMES. 1891. The Midewiwin or "Grand Medicine Society" of the Ojibwe. *Seventh Annual Report of the Bureau of American Ethnology*, 143–300.

———. 1896. The Menomini Indians. *Fourteenth Annual Report of the Bureau of American Ethnology* (pt. 2), 3–328.

HOLMES, WILLIAM H. 1883. Art in shell of the ancient Americans. *Second Annual Report of the Bureau of American Ethnology*, 185–305.

HORAN, JAMES D. 1982. *The McKenney-Hall Portrait Gallery of American Indians*. New York: Bramhall House.

HOUGH, WALTER. 1928. Fire-making apparatus in the United States National Museum. *Proceedings of the United States National Museum* 73 (14).

HOUSTON, STEPHEN. 1993. Sweatbaths that aren't: Architectural conflation in the Cross group at Palenque. Paper presented at a University of Texas symposium honoring Merle Greene Robertson and Floyd Lounsbury, Austin, March 11–12.

———. 1996. Symbolic sweatbaths of the Maya: Architectural meaning in the Cross Group at Palenque, Mexico. *Latin American Antiquity* 7 (2):132–151.

HOWARD, CALVIN D. 1974. The atlatl: Function and performance. *American Antiquity* 39 (1):102–104.

———. 1976. Atlatl function: A reply to Butler. *Plains Anthropologist* 21 (74):313–314.

HOWARD, JAMES H. 1965. The Ponca tribe. *Bureau of American Ethnology Bulletin* 195.

———. 1968. The Southeastern Ceremonial Complex and its interpretation. *Memoir* 6, Missouri Archaeological Society.

———. 1981. *Shawnee! The Ceremonialism of a Native American Tribe and Its Cultural Background*. Athens, Ohio: Ohio University Press.

HOWLAND, HENRY R. 1877. Recent archaeological discoveries in the American Bottom. *Bulletin of the Buffalo Society of Natural Science* 3:204–211.

HUDSON, CHARLES. 1976. *The Southeastern Indians*. Knoxville: University of Tennessee Press.

HUGH-JONES, STEPHEN. 1979. *The Palm and the Pleiades*. Cambridge: Cambridge University Press.

HUNTER, WILLIAM A. 1978. History of the Ohio valley. In *Handbook of North American Indians*, vol. 15, *The Northeast*, ed. Bruce C. Trigger, 588–593. Washington, D.C.: Smithsonian Institution.

HURT, WESLEY R., JR. 1951. Report of the investigation of the Swanson site 39Br16, Brule County, South Dakota, 1950. *Archaeological Studies Circular* 3. Pierre: State Archaeological Commission.

INGHAM, JOHN M. 1984. Human sacrifice at Tenochtitlan. *Comparative Study of Science and History* 26 (3):379–400.

IZIKOWITZ, KARL GUSTAV. 1935. Musical and other sound instruments of the South American Indians: A comparative ethnographical study. *Göteborgs Kungl. Vetenskaps- och Vitterhets-Samhälles Handlingar*, Femte Följden, ser. A, 5 (1).

JAKOBSON, ROMAN, and MORRIS HALLE. 1971. *Fundamentals of Language*. 3d ed. The Hague: Mouton.

JENNINGS, FRANCIS. 1976. *The Invasion of America: Indians, Colonialism, and the Cant of Conquest*. New York: W. W. Norton. Originally published in 1975 by the University of North Carolina Press.

———. 1984. *The Ambiguous Iroquois Empire: The Covenant Chain Confederation of Indian Tribes with English Colonies from Its Beginnings to the Lancaster Treaty of 1744*. New York: W. W. Norton.

JESUIT RELATIONS. 1896–1901. *The Jesuit Relations and Allied Documents: Travels and Explorations of the Jesuit Missionaries in New France, 1610–1791; the original French, Latin, and Italian texts, with English Translations and Notes. . .*, ed. Reuben Gold Thwaites. 73 vols. Cleveland: Burrows Brothers.

JONES, DAVID E. 1967. The "thunder motif" in Plains Indian culture. *University of Oklahoma Anthropology Club Papers in Anthropology* 8 (1):1–33.

JONES, MEG. 1995. White buffalo still draws crowd. *Milwaukee Journal Sentinel*, May 30, 5B.

JONES, ROBERT R. 1938[?]. Menominee notes. State Historical Society of Wisconsin Archives, file Wis Mss BU.

JONES, WILLIAM. 1908. Book VII of typescript copy of field diary of William Jones in notebook no. 1 of the Robert F. Cummings–Field Museum Philippine Expedition 1907–1909 in Field Museum Anthropology Archives, cabinet B, box 52.

———. 1939. Ethnography of the Fox Indians, ed. Margaret Welpley Fisher. *Bureau of American Ethnology Bulletin* 125.

———. 1968. Mortuary observances and the adoption rites of the Algonkin Foxes. In *International Congress of Americanists 15th Session 1906*, 263–277. New York: Kraus Reprint. Originally published in vol. 1 of *Congrès International des Américanistes, XVᵉ Session, Tenue à Québec en 1906*, Québec, Dussult & Proulx.

JONES, WILLIAM, and TRUMAN MICHELSON. 1911. Pursuit of the bear. Mesquakie linguistic text recorded by William Jones, translated and revised by Truman Michelson, accompanying Jones's "Algonquian (Fox)," in Handbook of North American Indian Languages, pt. 1, 735–873. *Bureau of American Ethnology Bulletin* 40.

JORALEMON, P. D. 1971. A study of Olmec iconography. *Studies in Pre-Columbian Art and Archaeology* 7. Washington, D.C.: Dumbarton Oaks.

JORGENSEN, JOSEPH G. 1972. *The Sun Dance Religion: Power for the Powerless*. Chicago: University of Chicago Press.

KARTTUNEN, FRANCES. 1983. *An Analytical Dictionary of Nahuatl*. Austin: University of Texas Press.

KATZ, FRIEDRICH. 1972. *The Ancient American Civilizations*. New York: Praeger.

KEELEY, LAWRENCE H. 1996. *War Before Civilization: The Myth of the Peaceful Savage*. Oxford: Oxford University Press.

KEESING, FELIX M. 1987. *The Menomini Indians of Wisconsin: A Study of Three Centuries of Cultural Contact and Change*. Madison: University of Wisconsin Press. Originally published by the American Philosophical Society in 1939.

KELLAR, JAMES H. 1955. The atlatl in North America. *Indian Historical Society Prehistory Research Series* 3 (3):281–352.

KELLEY, DAVID H. 1976. *Deciphering the Maya Script*. Austin: University of Texas Press.

———. 1980. Astronomical identities of Mesoamerican gods. *Journal for the History of Astronomy, Archaeoastronomy Supplement*, S1–S54. Reprinted as Contributions to Mesoamerican Anthropology, publication no. 2, of the Institute of Maya Studies, Miami, Florida, 1980.

KELLOGG, LOUISE PHELPS. 1925. *The French Regime in Wisconsin and the Northwest*. Madison: State Historical Society of Wisconsin.

KELLY, ARTHUR R., and FAY-COOPER COLE. 1931. Rediscovering Illinois. In *Blue Book of the State of Illinois 1931–1932*, 318–341. Springfield: Secretary of State.

KELLY, JOHN E. 1980. Formative developments at Cahokia and the adjacent American Bottom: A Merrell tract perspective. Ph.D. diss., Department of Anthropology, University of Wisconsin at Madison.

KIDDER, ALFRED V., JESSE D. JENNINGS, and E. M. SHOOK. 1946. Excavations at Kaminaljuyu, Guatemala. *Carnegie Institution of Washington Publication 561*.

KESSEL, JOHN L. 1978. Diego Romero, the Plains Apaches, and the Inquisition. *The American West* 15:12–16.

———. 1979. *Kiva, Cross and Crown: The Pecos Indians and New Mexico, 1540–1840*. National Park Service.

KIDDLE, LAWRENCE B. 1944. The Spanish word *Jícara*. *Philological and Documentary Studies* 1 (4). New Orleans: Middle American Research Institute, Tulane University.

KINIETZ, W. VERNON. 1940. *The Indians of the Western Great Lakes 1615–1760*. Occasional Contributions from the University of Anthropology of the University of Michigan. Ann Arbor: University of Michigan Press.

KIRBY, W. F. 1970. *Kalevala: The Land of the Heroes*. 2 vols. New York: Dutton. Reprint of the London edition of 1907 published by J. M. Dent, London.

KLEIN, CECILIA F. 1975. Post-Classic Mexican death imagery as a sign of cyclic completion. In *Death and the Afterlife in Pre-Columbian America*, ed. Elizabeth P. Benson, 69–104. Washington, D.C.: Dumbarton Oaks.

KLUCKHOHN, CLYDE. 1944. Navaho Witchcraft. *Papers of the Peabody Museum of American Archaeology and Ethnology, Harvard University* 22 (2).

KNOBLOCK, BYRON W. 1939. *Banner-stones of the North American Indian*. La Grange, Ill.: the author.

KOCH-GRÜNBERG, THEODOR. 1909–1910. *Zwei Jahre unter den Indianern: Reisen in Nordwest-Brasilien, 1903–1905*. 2 vols. Berlin: Ernst Wasmuth.

KÖHLER, ULRICH. 1979. "Sonnenstein" ohne Sonnegott: zur Korrektur einer überkommenen Fehldeutung der bekanntesten aztekischen Steinplastik. *Ethnologia Americana* 16/1, Nr. 91:906–908. Düsseldorfer Institut für amerikanische Völkerkunde.

———. 1982. On the significance of the Aztec day sign 'Ollin'. *In* "Space and Time in the Cosmovision of Mesoamerica," the proceedings of a symposium at the forty-third International Congress of Americanists, Vancouver, Canada, August 11–17, 1979, published in the series *Lateinamerika Studien*, Band 10, ed. Franz Tichy, 111–127. Munich: Wilhelm Fink Verlag.

KÖNGÄS, ELLI KAIJA. 1960. The Earth-diver (Th. A 812). *Ethnohistory* 7 (2):151–180.

KOVACS, MAUREEN GALLERY. 1989. *The Epic of Gilgamesh*. Stanford, Calif.: Stanford University Press.

KRAMER, SAMUEL NOAH. 1959. *History Begins at Sumer: Twenty-seven "Firsts" in Man's Recorded History*. Garden City, N.Y.: Doubleday.

KRICKEBERG, WALTER. 1961. *Las Antiguas Culturas Mexicanas*. Mexico City: Fondo de Cultura Económica.

———. 1966. El juego de pelota mesoamericano y su simbolismo religioso. *Traducciones Mesoamericanistas* 1:191–313. México, D.F.: Sociedad Mexicana de Anthropología.

KROEBER, ALFRED L. 1983. *The Arapaho*. Lincoln: University of Nebraska Press. First published in the *American Museum of Natural History Bulletin* 18:1–229, 279–454, New York, 1902–1907.

KROHE, JAMES, JR. 1992. Skeletons in our closet. *Reader* (Chicago) February 12, 21 (19):1, 16–26.

KRUPP, E. C. 1983a. Climbing the cosmic mountain. Lecture presented at the First International Conference on Ethnoastronomy: Indigenous Astronomical and Cosmological Traditions of the World, September 5–9, Smithsonian Institution, Washington, D.C.

———. 1983b. *Echoes of the Ancient Skies: the Astronomies of Lost Civilizations*. Meridian Book edition. New York: New American Library.

KRUSCHE, ROLF. 1981. The Wabeno cult as an adversary of the Midewiwin. In *North American Indian Studies: European Contributions*, ed. Pieter Hovens, 77–88. Göttingen: Edition Herodot.

KWAS, M. L. 1981. Bannerstones as chronological markers in the southeastern United States. *Tennessee Anthropologist* 6: 144–171.

LA FLESCHE, FRANCIS. 1885. The sacred pipes of friendship. *Proceedings of the American Association for the Advancement of Science* 33:613–615.

———. 1913. The Omaha tribe. *Science* 37:982–983.

———. 1916. Right and left in Osage ceremonies. In *Holmes Anniversary Volume*, 278–287.

———. 1921. The Osage tribe: rite of the chiefs; sayings of the ancient men. In *Thirty-Sixth Annual Report of the Bureau of American Ethnology*, 35–604.

———. 1925. The Osage tribe: rite of vigil. In *Thirty-Ninth Annual Report of the Bureau of American Ethnology*, 31–630.

———. 1927. The Osage tribe: Two versions of the child-naming rite. In *Forty-third Annual Report of the Bureau of American Ethnology*, 23–164.

———. 1930. The Osage rite of the Wa-xo-be. In *Forty-Fifth Annual Report of the Bureau of American Ethnology*, 523–833.

———. 1932. A dictionary of the Osage language. *Bureau of American Ethnology Bulletin* 109.

———. 1939. War ceremony and peace ceremony of the Osage Indians. *Bureau of American Ethnology Bulletin* 101.

LAME DEER (JOHN FIRE) and RICHARD ERDOES. 1972. *Lame Deer Seeker of Visions: The Life of a Sioux Medicine Man*. New York: Simon and Schuster.

LANDES, RUTH. 1968. *Ojibwa Religion and the Midéwiwin*. Madison: University of Wisconsin Press.

LA POTHERIE, CLAUDE CHARLES LE ROY, SIEUR DE BACQUEVILLE. 1911–1912. History of the savage peoples who are allies of New France. In *The Indian Tribes of the Upper Mississippi Valley and Region of the Great Lakes*, ed. Emma H. Blair, 1:275–372, 2:13–136. Cleveland: Arthur H. Clark.

LATORRE, FELIPE A., and DOLORES L. LATORRE. 1991. *The Mexican Kickapoo Indians*. New York: Dover. Reprint with corrections of the 1976 University of Texas Press edition.

LAUBIN, REGINALD, and GLADYS LAUBIN. 1957. *The Indian*

Tipi: Its History, Construction, and Use. Norman: University of Oklahoma Press.

LAWSHE, FRED E. 1947. The Mero site–Diamond Bluff, Pierce County, Wisconsin. *Minnesota Archaeologist* 13 (4):74–95.

LEAKEY, LOUIS S. B. 1973. *White African.* New York: Ballantine Books.

LEÓN-PORTILLA, MIGUEL. 1959. *La Filosofía Náhuatl estudiada en sus fuentes.* 2d edition. Mexico City: Universidad Nacional Autónoma de México.

———. 1963. *Aztec Thought and Culture: A Study of the Ancient Nahuatl Mind.* trans. Jack Emory Davis. Norman: University of Oklahoma Press. English edition of *La Filosofía Náhuatl,* Mexico City, 1959.

LE PAGE DU PRATZ, SIMON ANTOINE. 1972. *The History of Louisiana.* Baton Rouge: Claitor's. Reprinted from the London edition of 1774.

LÉVI-STRAUSS, CLAUDE. 1948. The tribes of the upper Xingu River. In *The Tropical Forest Tribes,* 321–348, *Handbook of South American Indians,* vol. 3, ed. Julian H. Steward, *Bureau of American Ethnology Bulletin* 14.

———. 1970. *The Raw and the Cooked,* trans. John and Doreen Weightman. Harper Torchbook edition. New York: Harper and Row. Originally published as *Le Cru et le Cuit,* Paris, 1964.

LIBERTY, MARGOT. 1967. The Northern Cheyenne Sun Dance and the opening of the sacred Medicine Hat 1959. *Plains Anthropologist* 12 (38):367–385.

———. 1976. Native American "informants": The contribution of Francis La Flesche. In *American Anthropology: The Early Years, 1974 Proceedings of the American Ethnological Society,* ed. John V. Murra, 99–110. St. Paul: West.

———. 1978. Francis La Flesche: The Osage odyssey. In *American Indian Intellectuals, 1976 Proceedings of the American Ethnological Society,* ed. Margot Liberty, 44–59. St. Paul: West.

LINTON, RALPH. 1922. The Sacrifice to the Morning Star by the Skidi Pawnee. *Field Museum of Natural History, Department of Anthropology, Leaflet* 6.

———. 1926. The origin of the Skidi Pawnee sacrifice to the morning star. *American Anthropologist* 28 (3):457–466.

LIPP, FRANK. 1991. *The Mixe of Oaxaca: Religion, Ritual, and Healing.* Austin: University of Texas Press.

LOFTIN, JOHN D. 1991. *Religion and Hopi Life in the Twentieth Century.* Bloomington and Indianapolis: Indiana University Press.

LOGAN, WILFRED D. 1976. Woodland complexes in Northeastern Iowa. *U.S. Department of the Interior, National Park Service, Publications in Archaeology* 15.

LONGFELLOW, HENRY WADSWORTH. 1975. *The Poetical Works of Longfellow.* Boston: Houghton Mifflin. Reissue of *The Complete Poetical Works of Henry Wadsworth Longfellow,* ed. Horace E. Scudder, Houghton Mifflin, Boston, 1886.

LOOKING HORSE, ARVAL. 1987. The Lakota Sun Dance: historical and contemporary perspectives. In *Sioux Indian Religion: Tradition and Innovation,* ed. Raymond J. DeMallie and Douglas R. Parks, 75–89. Norman: University of Oklahoma Press.

LOPATIN, IVAN ALEXIS. 1960. Origin of the native American steam bath. *American Anthropologist* 62:977–992.

LÓPEZ AUSTIN, ALFREDO. 1980. *Cuerpo Humano e Ideología:*

Las Concepciones de los Antiguos Nahuas. Mexico City: Universidad Nacional Autónoma de México.

———. 1988. *The Human Body and Ideology: Concepts of the Ancient Nahuas.* 2 vols., trans. Thelma Ortiz de Montellano and Bernard Ortiz de Montellano. Salt Lake City: University of Utah Press.

LOTHROP, SAMUEL K. 1937. Coclé: An archaeological study of central Panama, part 1. *Memoirs of the Peabody Museum of Archaeology and Ethnology of Harvard University* 7.

LOWIE, ROBERT H. 1915. The Sun Dance of the Crow Indians. *Anthropological Papers of the American Museum of Natural History* 16:1–50.

———. 1918. Myths and Traditions of the Crow Indians. *Anthropological Papers of the American Museum of Natural History* 25 (1).

———. 1919. The Hidatsa Sun Dance. *Anthropological Papers of the American Museum of Natural History* 16:411–431. New York.

———. 1920. The Tobacco Society of the Crow Indians. *Anthropological Papers of the American Museum of Natural History* 21:101–200. New York.

———. 1956. *The Crow Indians.* New York: Rinehart. Originally published in 1935 by Farrar and Rinehart, New York.

LUDWICKSON, JOHN, DONALD BLAKESLEE, and JOHN O'SHEA. 1981. *Missouri National Recreational River: Native American Resources.* A contract report prepared for the Heritage Conservation and Recreation Service, Interagency Archaeological Services–Denver and funded by the U.S. Army Corps of Engineers, Omaha District.

LUMHOLTZ, CARL. 1902. *Unknown Mexico.* 2 vols. New York: Scribner's.

LYNCH, DAVID K. 1978. Atmospheric halos. *Scientific American,* April, 144–152.

MACLEAN, JOHN P. 1893. *The Mound Builders of Butler County, O[hio].* 6th ed. Cincinnati: Robert Clarke.

MACLEOD, WILLIAM CHRISTIE. 1938. Self-sacrifice in mortuary and non-mortuary ritual in North America. *Anthropos* 33:349–400.

MAILS, THOMAS E. 1973. *Dog Soldiers, Bear Men and Buffalo Women: A Study of the Societies and Cults of the Plains Indians.* Galahad Books. Englewood Cliffs, N.J.: Prentice-Hall.

MALER, TEOBERT. 1911. Explorations in the Department of the Peten, Guatemala: Tikal. *Peabody Museum of American Archaeology and Ethnology, Harvard University, Memoirs* 2 (1).

MALLERY, GARRICK. 1886. On the pictographs of the North American Indians. *Tenth Annual Report of the Bureau of American Ethnology.*

———. 1978. A collection of gesture-signs and signals of the North American Indians with some comparisons. In *Aboriginal Sign Languages of the Americas and Australia,* 2 vols., ed. D. Jean Umiker-Sebeok and Thomas A. Sebeok, 1:77–406. New York: Plenum Press. Reprinted from the Smithsonian Institution edition of 1880.

MALOTKI, EKKEHART, and MICHAEL LOMATUWAY'MA. 1987. *Maasaw: Profile of a Hopi God.* Lincoln: University of Nebraska Press.

MANGOLD, BILL. 1973. Birdstone or dog effigy. *Central States Archaeological Journal* 20:146–148.

MARGRY, PIERRE. 1876–1886. *Découvertes et établissements des Français dans l'ouest et dans le sud de l'Amérique septentrionale (1614–1754). Mémoires et documents originaux.* 6 vols. Paris: D. Jouaust.

MARK, JOAN. 1988. *A Stranger in Her Native Land: Alice Fletcher and the American Indians.* Lincoln: University of Nebraska Press.

MARRIOTT, ALICE, and CAROL K. RACHLIN. 1972. *American Indian Mythology.* Mentor Book edition. New York: New American Library. Originally published in 1968 by Thomas Y. Crowell.

———. 1975. *Plains Indian Mythology.* New York: Thomas Y. Crowell.

MARTIN, LAWRENCE. 1916. The physical geography of Wisconsin. *Wisconsin Geological and Natural History Survey Bulletin 36.*

MARTIN, PAUL S., GEORGE I. QUIMBY, and DONALD COLLIER. 1947. *Indians before Columbus.* Chicago: University of Chicago Press.

MASON, OTIS T. 1885. Throwing-sticks in the National Museum. *Annual Report of the Smithsonian Institution for 1883–1884,* pt. 2, 279–289. *Report of the National Museum.*

MASTERS, EDGAR LEE. 1916. *Spoon River Anthology.* New York: Macmillan.

———. 1992. *Spoon River Anthology: An Annotated Edition,* ed. John E. Hallwas. Urbana and Chicago: University of Illinois Press.

MATTHEWS, G. H. 1959. Proto-Siouan kinship terminology. *American Anthropologist* 61:252–278.

MATTHEWS, WASHINGTON. 1874. *Hidatsa (Minetaree)–English Dictionary.* New York: Shea's Library of American Linguistics.

MAYER-OAKES, WILLIAM J. 1955. Prehistory of the Upper Ohio valley: An introductory archeological study. *Carnegie Museum Anthropological Series 2.*

McCONE, R. CLYDE. 1968. Death and the persistence of basic personality structure among the Lakota. *Plains Anthropologist* 13 (42, pt. 1):305–309.

McGAA, ED, EAGLE MAN. 1990. *Mother Earth Spirituality: Native American Paths to Healing Ourselves and Our World.* HarperSanFrancisco.

McINTOSH, W. E., and HARVEY SHELL. 1987. *Indiancraft.* Happy Camp, Calif.: Naturegraph.

McKERN, WILL C. 1928. The Neale and McClaughry mound groups. *Bulletin of the Public Museum of the City of Milwaukee* 3 (3).

———. 1930. The Kletzien and Nitschke mound groups. *Bulletin of the Public Museum of the City of Milwaukee* 3 (4).

———. 1942. The first settlers of Wisconsin. *Wisconsin Magazine of History* 26 (2):153–169.

———. 1945. Preliminary report on the Upper Mississippi phase in Wisconsin. *Bulletin of the Public Museum of the City of Milwaukee* 16 (3).

———. 1963. The Clam River focus. *Milwaukee Public Museum Publications in Anthropology* 9.

McLENDON, SALLY, and MICHAEL J. LOWY. 1978. Eastern Pomo and southeastern Pomo. In *Handbook of North American Indians,* vol. 8, *California,* ed. Robert F. Heiser, 306–323. Washington, D.C.: Smithsonian Institution.

McWILLIAMS, JOHN P. 1985. Red Satan: Cooper and the American Indian Epic. In *James Fenimore Cooper: New Critical Essays,* ed. Robert Clark, 143–161. London: Vision Press.

MEDICINE, BEATRICE. 1981. Native American resistance to integration: Contemporary confrontations and religious revitalization. *Plains Anthropologist* 26 (94):277–286.

———. 1987. Indian women and the renaissance of traditional religion. In *Sioux Indian Religion: Tradition and Innovation,* ed. Raymond J. DeMallie and Douglas R. Parks, 159–171. Norman: University of Oklahoma Press.

MICHELSON, TRUMAN. 1935. Some notes on Winnebago social and political organization. *American Anthropologist* n.s. 37:446–449.

MILDNER, MICHAEL P. 1974. Descriptive and distributional notes on atlatls and atlatl weights in the Great Basin. In *Great Basin Atlatl Studies,* ed. Thomas R. Hester, Michael P. Mildner, and Lee Spencer, 7–27. *Ballena Press Publications in Archaeology, Ethnology and History 2.*

MILLS, WILLIAM C. 1916. Exploration of the Tremper Mound. *Ohio Archaeological and Historical Quarterly* 25 (3): 262–398.

MINET, —?—. 1987. Voyage made from Canada inland going southward during the year 1682. . . , trans. Ann Linda Bell, annot. Patricia Galloway. In *La Salle, the Mississippi, and the Gulf,* ed. Robert S. Weddle, Mary Christine Morkovsky, and Patricia Galloway, 29–68. College Station: Texas A & M University Press.

MOLINA, FRAY ALONSO DE. 1970. *Vocabulario en lengua castellana y mexicana.* Madrid: Ediciones Cultura Hispánica.

MOONEY, JAMES. 1896. The Ghost Dance religion and the Sioux outbreak of 1890. *Fourteenth Annual Report of the Bureau of American Ethnology,* pt. 1, 653–1136. Washington. Reprinted in 1991 by the University of Nebraska Press, Lincoln.

———. 1982. *Myths of the Cherokee and Sacred Formulas of the Cherokees.* Nashville: Charles and Randy Elder–Booksellers. Reprints of the originals appearing as papers in the nineteenth and seventeenth *Annual Reports of the Bureau of American Ethnology.*

MOORE, CLARENCE B. 1894. Certain sand mounds of the St. John's River, Florida. *Journal of the Academy of Natural Sciences of Philadelphia* 10(1-2).

———. 1895. Certain river mounds of Duval County, Florida. *Journal of the Academy of Natural Sciences of Philadelphia* 10 (4):7–59.

———. 1916. Some aboriginal sites on Green River, Kentucky. *Journal of the Academy of Natural Science of Philadelphia,* 2nd series, 16 (3).

MOORE, JOHN. 1974. A study of religious symbolism among the Cheyenne Indians. Ph.D. diss., Department of Anthropology, New York University.

MOOREHEAD, WARREN K. 1922. The Hopewell mound group of Ohio. *Field Museum of Natural History, Anthropological Series* 6 (5).

MORGAN, LEWIS HENRY. 1901. *League of the Ho-De´-No-Sau-Nee of Iroquois,* 2 vols., ed. Herbert M. Lloyd. New York: Dodd, Mead. Reprinted by Burt Franklin, New York, n.d.

MORLEY, SYLVANUS G. 1947. *The Ancient Maya.* 2d ed. Stanford, Calif.: Stanford University Press.

MURIE, JAMES R. 1902a. Ethnographic and linguistic notes,

Morning Star folder. Archives of the Field Museum Department of Anthropology, Chicago.

———. 1902b. Ethnographic and linguistic notes, Pawnee earthlodge notes. Archives of the Field Museum Department of Anthropology, Chicago.

———. 1914. Pawnee Indian societies. *Anthropological Papers of the American Museum of Natural History* 11:543–644.

———. 1989. *Ceremonies of the Pawnee*, ed. Douglas R. Parks. Lincoln: University of Nebraska Press. Originally published as *Smithsonian Contributions to Knowledge* 27 (1981).

MURRAY, J. 1974. Ella Deloria: A biographical sketch and literary analysis. Doctoral diss., Center for Teaching and Learning, University of North Dakota, Grand Forks.

NAVARRETE, C., and DORIS HEYDEN. 1974. La cara central de la Piedra del Sol: Una hipótesis. *Estudios de Cultura Náhuatl* 11:355–376.

NEIHARDT, JOHN G. 1972. *Black Elk Speaks: Being the Life Story of a Holy Man of the Oglala Sioux.* New York: Pocket Books. Originally published in 1932 by William Morrow.

NEITZEL, ROBERT S. 1965. Archaeology of the Fatherland site: the grand village of the Natchez. *Anthropological Papers of the American Museum of Natural History* 51 (1).

NEUMANN, GEORG K. 1940. Evidence for the antiquity of scalping from central Illinois. *American Antiquity* 5 (4):287–289.

NICHOLS, JOHN, and EARL NYHOLM, eds. 1979. *Ojibwewi-Ikidowinan: an Ojibwe Word Resource Book.* St. Paul: Minnesota Historical Society.

NICHOLSON, HENRY B. 1971. Religion in pre-Hispanic central Mexico. In *Archaeology of Northern Mesoamerica*, pt. 1, ed. Gordon F. Ekholm and Ignacio Bernal, 395–445, vol. 10 of *Handbook of Middle American Indians*, ed. Robert Wauchope. Austin: University of Texas Press.

———. 1972. The cult of Xipe Totec in Mesoamerica. In *Religión en Mesoamérica: XII Mesa Redonda*, ed. Jaime Litvak King and Noemi Castillo Tejero, 213–218. Mexico City: Sociedad Mexicana de Antropología.

———. 1976. Preclassic Mesoamerican iconography from the perspective of the Postclassic: Problems in interpretational analysis. In *Origins of Religious Art and Iconography in Preclassic Mesoamerica*, ed. Henry B. Nicholson, 158–175. Los Angeles: UCLA Latin American Center and Ethnic Arts Council of Los Angeles.

———. 1993. The problem of the identification of the central image of the "Aztec Calendar Stone." In Current Topics in Aztec Studies: Essays in Honor of Dr. H. B. Nicholson, ed. Alana Cordy-Collins and Douglas Sharon, 3–15. *San Diego Museum Papers* 30.

NORMAN, V. GARTH. 1973. Izapa sculpture, part I: Album. *Papers of the New World Archaeological Foundation* 30.

NUÑEZ CABEZA DE VACA, ALVAR. 1871. *Relation of Alvar Nuñez Cabeça de Vaca*, ed. and trans. Buckingham Smith. New York: privately printed. Reprinted with the cover title *Relation of Nuñez Cabeza de Vaca*, Readex Microprint Corporation, 1966.

———. 1904. *The Journey of Alvar Nuñez Cabeza de Vaca, and His Companions from Florida to the Pacific, 1528–1536*, ed. and trans. Fanny Bandelier and A. F. Bandelier. New York: Allerton. Reprint, Rio Grande Press, 1964.

NUTINI, HUGO G. 1988. Pre-Hispanic component of the syncretic cult of the dead in Mesoamerica. *Ethnology* 27 (1):57–78.

NUTTALL, ZELIA. 1891. The atlatl or spear-thrower of the ancient Mexicans. *Papers of the Peabody Museum of American Archaeology and Ethnology, Harvard University* 1 (3).

———. 1901. The fundamental principles of Old and New World civilizations: A comparative research based on a study of the ancient Mexican religious, sociological and calendrical systems. *Papers of the Peabody Museum of American Archaeology and Ethnology, Harvard University* 2 (1).

———, ed. 1975. *The Codex Nuttall: A Picture Manuscript from Ancient Mexico*, introd. Arthur G. Miller. New York: Dover. Originally published by the Peabody Museum of American Archaeology and Ethnology, Harvard University, Cambridge, Mass., 1902.

O'BRIEN, PATRICIA J. 1987. Morning star sacrifices: Contradiction or dualism? *Plains Anthropologist* 32 (115):73–76.

———. 1991. Evidence for the antiquity of women's roles in Pawnee society. In Approaches to Gender Processes on the Great Plains, ed. Marcel Kornfeld, 51–64. Memoir 26 of *Plains Anthropologist* 36 (134, pt. 2).

OVERSTREET, DAVID F., ed. 1993. Exploring the Oneota-Winnebago direct historical connection. Special volume honoring Nancy O. Lurie. *Wisconsin Archeologist* 74 (1–4).

OWEN, MARY ALICIA. 1904. *Folk-Lore of the Musquakie Indians of North America.* London: Folk-Lore Society.

PAPER, JORDAN. 1988. *Offering Smoke: The Sacred Pipe and Native American Religion.* Moscow: University of Idaho Press; Edmonton: University of Alberta Press.

PARKMAN, FRANCIS. 1925. *La Salle and the Discovery of the Great West.* Boston: Little, Brown.

———. 1963. *The Oregon Trail.* New York: Washington Square Press. Based upon the 1892 edition with an introduction by James D. Hart.

———. 1983. *France and England in America.* Vol. 1: *Pioneers of France in the New World* [1865], *The Jesuits in North America in the Seventeenth Century* [1867], *La Salle and the Discovery of the Great West* [rev. ed. 1879], *The Old Régime in Canada* [1874]. Vol. 2: *Count Frontenac and New France under Louis XIV* [1877], *A Half-Century of Conflict* [1892], *Montcalm and Wolfe* [1884]. New York: Library of America.

PARKS, DOUGLAS R. 1978. James R. Murie, Pawnee, 1862–1921. In American Indian intellectuals, ed. Margot Liberty, 75–89. *1976 Proceedings of the American Ethnological Society.*

———. 1989. Biography of James R. Murie. In *Ceremonies of the Pawnee*, James R. Murie, 21–28. Lincoln: University of Nebraska Press.

PARSONS, ELSIE C., and RALPH L. BEALS. 1934. The sacred clowns of the Pueblo and Mayo-Yaqui Indians. *American Anthropologist* n.s. 36 (4):491–514.

PATTERSON, L. W. 1977. Atlatl function: commentary on Howard's views. *Plains Anthropologist* 22 (76, pt. 1):159–160.

PEASE, THEODORE CALVIN, and RAYMOND C. WERNER. 1934. The French foundations. *Collections of the Illinois State Historical Library*, vol. 23.

PEETS, O. H. 1960. Experiments in the use of atlatl weights. *American Antiquity* 26:108–110.

PEPPER, GEORGE H., and GILBERT L. WILSON. 1908. An Hidatsa shrine and the beliefs respecting It. *American Anthropological Association Memoirs* 2:275–328.

PERINO, GREGORY. 1966. Short history of some shell ornaments. *Central States Archaeological Journal* 13:4–8.

———. 1968. The Pete Klunk Mound Group, Calhoun County, Illinois: The Archaic and Hopewell occupations. In *Hopewell and Woodland Site Archaeology in Illinois*, ed. J. A. Brown, 9–128. *Illinois Archaeological Survey Bulletin 6*.

———. 1971. The Yokem site, Pike County, Illinois. In *Mississippian Site Archaeology in Illinois I: Site reports from the St. Louis and Chicago Areas*, 149–186. *Illinois Archaeological Survey Bulletin 8*.

PETERS, RUSSELL M. 1992. *Clambake: A Wampanoag Tradition.* Minneapolis: Lerner Publications.

PHILLIPS, PHILIP, and JAMES A. BROWN. 1978. *Pre-Columbian Shell Engravings from the Craig Mound at Spiro, Oklahoma,* part 1. Cambridge: Peabody Museum Press of Harvard University.

———. 1984. *Pre-Columbian Shell Engravings from the Craig Mound at Spiro, Oklahoma,* part 2. Cambridge: Peabody Museum Press of Harvard University.

PHILLIPS, PHILIP, JAMES A. FORD, and JAMES B. GRIFFIN. 1951. Archaeological survey in the lower Mississippi alluvial valley, 1940–1947. *Papers of the Peabody Museum of Archaeology and Ethnology, Harvard University* 25.

PIERCE, JOE E. 1954. Crow vs. Hidatsa in dialect distance and in glottochronology. *International Journal of American Linguistics* 20:134–136.

PIÑA CHAN, ROMÁN. 1958. Tlatilco. *Serie Investigaciones* 1–2. México: Instituto Nacional de Antropología e Historia.

PORTER, MURIEL NOÉ. 1948. Pipas precortesianas. *Acta Antropológica* 3(2).

———. 1953. Tlatilco and the pre-Classic cultures of the New World. *Viking Fund Publications in Anthropology* 19.

POWELL, REV. PETER J. 1969. *Sweet Medicine.* 2 vols. Norman: University of Oklahoma Press.

POWERS, MARLA N. 1986. *Oglala Women: Myth, Ritual, and Reality.* Chicago: University of Chicago Press.

POWERS, WILLIAM K. 1977. *Oglala Religion.* Lincoln: University of Nebraska Press.

———. 1986. *Sacred Language: the Nature of Supernatural Discourse in Lakota.* Norman: University of Oklahoma Press.

PRUFER, OLAF H., and ELLEN ANDORS. 1967. The Morrison village site. In *Studies in Ohio Archaeology*, ed. Olaf H. Prufer and Douglas H. McKenzie, 187–229. Cleveland: Press of Western Reserve University.

RADIN, PAUL. 1911. The ritual and significance of the Winnebago Medicine Dance. *Journal of American Folk-Lore* 24 (92):149–208.

———. 1945. *The Road of Life and Death: A Ritual Drama of the American Indians.* Bollingen Foundation Series, no. 5. New York: Pantheon.

———. 1948. Winnebago hero cycles: A study in aboriginal literature. *Indiana University Publications in Anthropology and Linguistics, Memoir* 2.

———. 1954. *The Evolution of an American Indian Prose Epic: A Study in Comparative Literature.* Part 1. Basel: Ethnographical Museum. Also issued as Special Publication 3 of the Bollingen Foundation.

———. 1963. *The Autobiography of a Winnebago Indian.* New York: Dover. Originally published in 1920 in *University of California Publications in American Archaeology and Ethnology* 16 (7).

———. 1970. *The Winnebago Tribe.* Lincoln: University of Nebraska Press. Originally published in 1923 in the *Thirty-Seventh Annual Report of the Bureau of American Ethnology.*

———. 1972. *The Trickster: A Study in American Indian Mythology.* New York: Schocken Books. Reprint of the 1956 edition with an introduction by Stanley Diamond.

RADISSON, PIERRE D'ESPRIT, SIEUR DE. 1888. Radisson and Groseilliers in Wisconsin. *Wisconsin Historical Collections* 11:64–96. Selections from the narratives of Radisson's third and fourth voyages reprinted from the author's *Voyages of Peter Esprit Radisson, Being an Account of His Travels and Experiences among the North American Indians, from 1652 to 1684* (Prince Society, Boston, 1885).

RANDS, ROBERT L. 1957. Comparative notes on the hand-eye and related motifs. *American Antiquity* 22 (3):247–257.

RAUDOT, ANTOINE DENIS. 1710a. Letter 47, "Of the Saulteur Jugglers," dated Quebec, 1710. In Kinietz 1940, 372–374.

———. 1710b. Letter 63, "The way the Illinois women mourn their husbands, and their interment." In Kinietz 1940, 395–397.

RAY, VERNE F. 1945. The contrary behavior pattern in American Indian ceremonialism. *Southwestern Journal of Anthropology* 1:75–113.

REDFIELD, ROBERT. 1955. The social organization of tradition. *Far Eastern Quarterly* 15 (1):13–21.

REDFIELD, ROBERT, and ALFONSO VILLA ROJAS. 1962. *Chan Kom: A Maya Village.* Chicago: University of Chicago Press. Originally published by the Carnegie Institution of Washington, 1934.

REICHARD, GLADYS A. 1974. *Navaho Religion: a Study of Symbolism.* Bollingen Series, no. 18. Princeton, N.J.: Princeton University Press.

REICHEL-DOLMATOFF, GERARDO. 1971. *Amazonian Cosmos: The Sexual and Religious Symbolism of the Tukano Indians.* Chicago: University of Chicago Press.

RICE, JULIAN. 1993. *Ella Deloria's Iron Hawk.* Albuquerque: University of New Mexico Press.

RICHARDS, T. T. 1870. Relics from the Great Mound. *American Naturalist* 4 (1):62–63.

RICHTER, DANIEL K. 1992. *The Ordeal of the Longhouse: The Peoples of the Iroquois League in the Era of European Colonization.* Chapel Hill: University of North Carolina Press.

RIDEOUT, HENRY MILNER. 1912. *William Jones: Indian, Cowboy, American Scholar, Anthropologist in the Field.* New York: Frederick A. Stokes.

RIGGS, STEPHEN RETURN. 1968. *A Dakota-English Dictionary,* ed. James Owen Dorsey. Minneapolis: Ross and Haines. Originally published as *Contributions to North American Ethnology* 7, by the Department of the Interior, U.S. Geographical and Geological Survey of the Rocky Mountain Region, Washington, 1990.

RITZENTHALER, ROBERT E. 1953. The Potawatomi Indians of Wisconsin. *Bulletin of the Public Museum of the City of Milwaukee* 19 (3).

———. 1970. The theory of the birdstone as an atlatl handle grip, revisited. *Wisconsin Archeologist* 51 (1):31–34.

ROBERTS, KENNETH. 1937. *Northwest Passage*. Garden City, N.Y.: Doubleday, Doran.

ROBICSEK, FRANCIS. 1978. *The Smoking Gods: Tobacco in Maya Art, History, and Religion*. Norman: University of Oklahoma Press.

ROBINSON, DOANE. 1914. La Vérendrye's farthest west. *Proceedings of the State Historical Society of Wisconsin [for 1913]*, 146–150.

ROLLINGS, WILLARD H. 1989. *The Comanche*. New York: Chelsea House.

ROW, HEATH. 1994. Herd mentality? Interest in white buffalo may signify cultural rebirth. *Janesville Gazette* (Wisconsin), September 11, A1, A10.

ROYS, RALPH L., trans. and ed. 1965. *Ritual of the Bacabs*. Norman: University of Oklahoma Press.

———. 1967. *The Book of Chilam Balam of Chumayel*. Norman: University of Oklahoma Press. Originally published by the Carnegie Institution of Washington, 1933.

RUEDA ESCOBAR, OSCAR. 1971. Nuevas consideraciones sobre la Piedra del Sol. Revista ICACH, segunda época, 4 (22):53–84.

RUIZ DE ALARCÓN, HERNANDO. 1984. *Treatise on the Heathen Superstitions That Today Live Among the Indians Native to This New Spain, 1629*, trans. J. Richard Andrews and Ross Hassig. Norman: University of Oklahoma Press.

SACHS, NELLY. 1961. *Fahrt ins Staublose: die Gedichte der Nelly Sachs*. Frankfurt am Mein: Suhrkamp Verlag.

SAGARD THÉODAT, FATHER GABRIEL. 1632. *Le Grand voyage du pays des Hurons, situé en l'Amerique vers la mer douce, ès derniers confines de la Nouvelle France, dite Canada*. Paris: Denys Moreau.

SAHAGÚN, FRAY BERNARDINO DE. 1948. Relación breve de las fiestas de los dioses, ed. and trans. Ángel M. Garibay K. *Tlalocan* 2 (4):289–320. Mexico City.

———. 1953. *Florentine Codex*, pt. 8 of 13. *General History of the Things of New Spain, Book 7—The Sun, Moon, and Stars, and the Binding of the Years*, trans. and ed. Arthur J. O. Anderson and Charles Dibble. *Monographs of the School of American Research* 14. Salt Lake City: University of Utah Press.

———. 1959. *Florentine Codex*, pt. 10 of 13. *General History of the Things of New Spain, Book 9—The Merchants*, trans. and ed. Charles Dibble and Arthur J. O. Anderson. *Monographs of the School of American Research* 14. Salt Lake City: University of Utah Press.

———. 1969. *Florentine Codex*, Pt. 7 of 13. *General History of the Things of New Spain, Book 6—Rhetoric and Moral Philosophy*, trans. and ed. Charles Dibble and Arthur J. O. Anderson. *Monographs of the School of American Research* 14. Salt Lake City: University of Utah Press.

———. 1971. *A History of Ancient Mexico*, trans. Fanny R. Bandelier, from the Spanish version of Carlos María de Bustamante. Detroit: Blaine Ethridge. Originally published by Fisk University Press, Nashville, 1932.

SALZER, ROBERT J. 1987a. Preliminary report on the Gottschall site (47Ia80). *Wisconsin Archeologist* 68 (4):419–472.

———. 1987b. A Wisconsin rock art site. *Wisconsin Academy Review* 33 (2):67–70.

———. 1987c. Introduction to Wisconsin rock art. *Wisconsin Archeologist* 68 (4):277–287.

———. 1993. Oral literature and archaeology. *Wisconsin Archeologist* 74 (1–4):80–119.

SANDARS, N. K. 1964. *The Epic of Gilgamesh*. Baltimore: Penguin Books.

SANTURE, SHARRON K., ALAN D. HARN, and DUANE ESAREY. 1990. Archaeological investigations at the Morton village and Norris Farms 36 cemetery. *Illinois State Museum Reports of Investigations* 45.

SAVILLE, MARSHALL. 1929. The Aztecan god Xipe Totec. *Museum of the American Indian, Heye Foundation, Indian Notes* 6:151–174.

SCHELE, LINDA, and DAVID FREIDEL. 1990. *A Forest of Kings: The Untold Story of the Ancient Maya*. New York: William Morrow.

SCHELE, LINDA, and JEFFREY H. MILLER. 1983. The mirror, the rabbit, and the bundle: "Accession" expressions from the Classic Maya inscriptions. *Dumbarton Oaks Studies in Pre-Columbian Art and Archaeology* 25.

SCHLESIER, KARL. 1987. *The Wolves of Heaven: Cheyenne Shamanism, Ceremonies, and Prehistoric Origins*. Norman: University of Oklahoma Press.

———. 1990. Rethinking the Midewiwin and the Plains ceremonial called the Sun Dance. *Plains Anthropologist* 35 (127):1–27.

SCHUSTER, CARL. 1951. Joint-marks: A possible index of cultural contact between America, Oceania and the Far East. *Mededeling* 94, *Afdeling Culturele en Physische Anthropologie* 39. Amsterdam: Koninklijk Instituut voor de Tropen.

SEAVER, JAMES EVERETT. 1856. *Life of Mary Jemison*, ed. Lewis H. Morgan. New York and Auburn: Miller, Orton and Mulligan; Rochester: D. M. Dewey. Reprint, Garland, New York, 1977.

SEEMAN, MARK F. 1977. Stylistic variation in Middle Woodland pipe styles: The chronological implications. *Midcontinental Journal of Archaeology* 2 (1):47–66.

———. 1979. The Hopewell Interaction Sphere: The evidence for interregional trade and structural complexity. *Indiana Historical Society Prehistory Research Series* 5 (2).

SELER, EDUARD. 1963. *Comentarios al Códice Borgia*. 2 vols. Mexico City: Fondo de Cultura Económica.

SHARER, ROBERT J. 1994. *The Ancient Maya*. 5th ed. Stanford, Calif.: Stanford University Press.

SHEA, JOHN GILMARY, ed. 1902. *Early Voyages Up and Down the Mississippi by Cavelier, St. Cosme, Le Sueur, Gravier and Guignas*. Albany: Joseph McDonough. Reprint of the 1861 Albany edition of Joel Munsell.

SKINNER, ALANSON B. 1915. Societies of the Ioway, Kansa, and Ponca Indians. *Anthropological Papers of the American Museum of Natural History* 11 (9).

———. 1920. Medicine Ceremony of the Menomini, Iowa, and Wahpeton Dakota, with notes on the ceremonies among the Ponca, Bungi Ojibwa, and Potawatomi. *Museum of the American Indian, Heye Foundation, Indian Notes and Monographs*, vol. 4.

———. 1921. Recollections of an ethnologist among the Menomini Indians. *Wisconsin Archeologist* 20 (2):41–74.

———. 1924. The Mascoutens or Prairie Potawatomi Indians: part I, social life and ceremonies. *Bulletin of the Public Museum of the City of Milwaukee* 6 (1).

——. 1925a. Songs of the Menomini Medicine Ceremony. *American Anthropologist* n.s. 27:290–314.

——. 1925b. Traditions of the Iowa Indians. *Journal of American Folk-Lore* 38:425–506.

——. 1926. Ethnology of the Ioway Indians. *Bulletin of the Public Museum of the City of Milwaukee* 5 (4).

——. 1927. The Mascoutens or Prairie Potawatomi Indians: part III, mythology and folklore. *Bulletin of the Public Museum of the City of Milwaukee* 6 (3).

SKINNER, ALANSON B., and JOHN V. SATTERLEE. 1915. Folklore of the Menomini Indians. *Anthropological Papers of the American Museum of Natural History* 13 (3):217–546.

SMITH, BRUCE D. 1984. Mississippian expansion: Tracing the historical development of an explanatory model. *Southeastern Archaeology* 3 (1):13–32.

——, ed. 1978. *Mississippian Settlement Patterns.* New York: Academic Press.

——, ed. 1990. *The Mississippian Emergence.* Washington, D.C.: Smithsonian Institution Press.

SMITH, HALE G. 1951. The Crable site, Fulton County, Illinois. *University of Michigan, Museum of Anthropology, Anthropological Papers* 7.

SMITH, J. L. 1967. A short history of the sacred calf pipe bundle of the Teton Dakota. *Museum News* 28 (7–8). Vermillion, S.D.: W. H. Over Museum.

——. 1970. The sacred calf pipe bundle: Its effect on the present Teton Dakota. *Plains Anthropologist* 15 (48):87–93.

SMITH, MARY ELIZABETH. 1973. *Picture Writing from Ancient Southern Mexico.* Norman: University of Oklahoma Press.

SOUSTELLE, JACQUES. 1984. Ritual human sacrifice in Mesoamerica: an introduction. In *Ritual Human Sacrifice in Mesoamerica*, ed. Elizabeth P. Benson and Elizabeth H. Boone, 1–5. Washington, D.C.: Dumbarton Oaks.

SPAULDING, ALBERT C. 1956. The Arzberger site, Hughes County, South Dakota. *Occasional Contributions from the Museum of Anthropology of the University of Michigan* 16.

SPECK, FRANK G. 1907. Notes on the ethnology of the Osage Indians. *Transactions of the Free Museum of Science and Art* 2. Philadelphia: University of Pennsylvania.

——. 1942. *The Tutelo Reclothing and Spirit Adoption Ceremony.* Harrisburg: Pennsylvania Historical Commission.

——. 1919. The functions of wampum among the Eastern Algonkian. *Memoirs of the American Anthropological Association* 6:3–74. Reprint, Kraus Reprint, New York, 1964.

——. 1979. *Ethnology of the Yuchi Indians.* Atlantic Highlands, N.J.: Humanities Press. Originally published as *Anthropological Publications of the University Museum* 1 (1), University of Pennsylvania, Philadelphia, 1909.

SPECK, FRANK G., and JESSE MOSES. 1945. The celestial bear comes down to earth. *Reading Public Museum and Art Gallery, Scientific Publications* 7.

SPENCER, BALDWIN, and F. J. GILLEN. 1966. *The Arunta: A Study of a Stone Age People.* Oosterhout N.B., Netherlands: Anthropological Publications.

——. 1969. *The Northern Tribes of Central Australia.* Oosterhout N.B., Netherlands: Anthropological Publications.

SPENCER, LEE. 1974. Replicative experiments in the manufacture and use of a Great Basin atlatl. *In* Great Basin Atlatl Studies, ed. Thomas R. Hester, Michael P. Mildner, and Lee Spencer, 37–60. *Ballena Press Publications in Archaeology, Ethnology and History* 2.

SPIER, LESLIE. 1921. The Sun Dance of the Plains Indians: Its development and diffusion. *Anthropological Papers of the American Museum of Natural History* 16:451–527.

SPINDEN, HERBERT J. 1924. The reduction of Mayan dates. *Papers of the Peabody Museum of Archaeology and Ethnology, Harvard University* 6 (4). Reprint, Kraus Reprint, New York, 1969.

——. 1948. Mexican calendars and the solar year. In *Annual Report of the Board of Regents of the Smithsonian Institution . . . for the Year Ended June 30, 1948,* 393–405.

SQUIER, EPHRAIM G., and E. H. DAVIS. 1848. Ancient monuments of the Mississippi valley, comprising the results of extensive original surveys and explorations. *Smithsonian Contributions to Knowledge* 1.

STAECK, JOHN P. 1993. Chief's daughters, marriage patterns, and the construction of past identities: Some suggestions on alternative methods for modeling the past. *Wisconsin Archeologist* 74:370–399.

——. 1994. Archaeology, identity, and oral tradition: A reconsideration of Late Prehistoric and Early Historic Winnebago social structure and identity as seen through oral traditions. Ph.D. diss., Department of Anthropology, Rutgers University.

STATE OF WISCONSIN. 1886. *Roster of Wisconsin Volunteers, War of the Rebellion, 1861–1865.* Compiled by authority of the legislature under the direction of Jeremiah M. Rusk, governor, and Chandler P. Chapman, adjutant general. Madison: Democrat Printing Company, State Printers.

STEINEN, KARL VON DEN. 1894. *Unter den Naturvölkern Zentral-Brasiliens.* Berlin: D. Reimer (Hoefer & Vohsen).

STEWARD, JULIAN H. 1931. The Indian ceremonial buffoon. *Papers of the Michigan Academy of Science, Arts, and Letters,* 194.

——. 1991. *The Clown in Native North America.* New York: Garland.

STOLTMAN, JAMES B. 1973. *The Laurel Culture in Minnesota.* St. Paul: Minnesota Historical Society.

——. 1974. An examination of within-Laurel cultural variability in northern Minnesota. In *Aspects of Upper Great Lakes Anthropology: Papers in Honor of Lloyd A. Wilford,* ed. Elden Johnson, 74–89. St. Paul: Minnesota Historical Society.

STOLTMAN, JAMES B., ed. 1991. New perspectives on Cahokia: Views from the periphery. *Monographs in World Archaeology* 2. Madison, Wis.: Prehistory Press.

STOUT, ARLOW BURDETTE, and HALVOR L. SKAVLEM. 1908. The archaeology of the Lake Koshkonong region. *Wisconsin Archeologist* 7 (2).

STRACHEY, WILLIAM. 1849. The Historie of travaile into Virginia Britannia, expressing the cosmographie and commodities of the country, together with the manners and customs of the people. *Hakluyt Society Publications* 6.

STRUEVER, STUART. 1964. The Hopewellian Interaction Sphere in Riverine–Western Great Lakes culture history. In *Hopewellian Studies*, ed. Joseph R. Caldwell and Robert L. Hall, *Illinois State Museum Scientific Papers* 12:85–106.

STRUEVER, STUART, and GAIL L. HOUART. 1972. An analysis

of the Hopewell Interaction Sphere. *In* Social Exchange and Interaction, ed. E. Wilmsen, *University of Michigan, Museum of Anthropology, Anthropological Papers* 46:47–49.

SULLIVAN, THELMA D. 1983. *Compendio de la Gramática Náhuatl.* Mexico City: Universidad Nacional Autónoma de México.

SUNDSTROM, LINEA. 1989. Culture history of the Black Hills with reference to adjacent areas of the northern Great Plains. *Reprints in Anthropology* 40. Lincoln: J & L Reprints.

SWANTON, JOHN R. 1929. Myths and tales of the Southeastern Indians. *Bureau of American Ethnology Bulletin* 88.

———. 1938. Historic use of the spear-thrower in southeastern North America. *American Antiquity* 3:356–358.

———. 1942. Source material on the history and ethnology of the Caddo Indians. *Bureau of American Ethnology Bulletin* 132.

———. 1946. The Indians of the Southeastern United States. *Bureau of American Ethnology Bulletin* 137.

TAUBE, KARL. 1988. A study of classic Maya scaffold sacrifice. *In Maya Iconography,* ed. Elizabeth Benson and Gillett Griffin, 331–351. Princeton, N.J.: Princeton University Press.

TEDLOCK, BARBARA. 1975. The clown's way. *In Teachings from the American Earth: Indian Religion and Philosophy,* ed. Dennis Tedlock and Barbara Tedlock, 105–118. New York: Liveright.

TEDLOCK, DENNIS, trans. 1985. *Popol Vuh: The Mayan Book of the Dawn of Life.* New York: Simon and Schuster.

———. 1992. Myth, math, and the problem of correlation in Mayan books. *In The Sky in Mayan Literature,* ed. Anthony F. Aveni, 247–273. New York: Oxford University Press.

THOMAS, S. J. 1941. A Sioux medicine bundle. *American Anthropologist* 43:606–609.

THOMPSON, J. ERIC S. 1962. *A Catalog of Maya Hieroglyphics.* Norman: University of Oklahoma Press.

———. 1966. *The Rise and Fall of Maya Civilization.* 2d ed. Norman: University of Oklahoma Press.

———. 1967. Aquatic symbols common to various centers of the Classic Period in Meso-America. *In The Civilizations of Ancient America: Selected Papers of the XXIXth International Congress of Americanists,* ed. Sol Tax, 31–36. New York: Cooper Square.

———. 1970. *Maya History and Religion.* Norman: University of Oklahoma Press.

———. 1971. *Maya Hieroglyphic Writing.* 3d edition. Norman: University of Oklahoma Press.

THURMAN, MELBURN D. 1970a. A case of historical mythology: The Skidi Pawnee Morning Star Sacrifice of 1833. *Plains Anthropologist* 50:309–311.

———. 1970b. The Skidi Pawnee Morning Star Sacrifice of 1827. *Nebraska History* 51:269–280.

———. 1983. The timing of the Skidi-Pawnee Morning Star Sacrifice. *Ethnohistory* 30 (3):155–163.

THWAITES, REUBEN GOLD, ed. 1966. *Early Western Travels.* 32 vols. New York: AMS Press. Originally published 1904–1907 by Arthur H. Clark, Cleveland, Ohio.

TICHY, FRANZ. 1981. Order and relationship of space and time in Meso-america: Myth or reality? *In Mesoamerican*

Sites and World-Views, ed. Elizabeth P. Benson, 217–245. Washington, D.C.: Dumbarton Oaks.

TITIEV, MISCHA. 1944. Old Oraibi. *Papers of the Peabody Museum of Archaeology and Ethnology of Harvard University* 12.

TOLSTOY, PAUL, and L. I. PARADIS. 1970. Early and Middle Preclassic culture in the Basin of Mexico. *Science* 167:344–351.

———. 1971. Early and Middle Preclassic culture in the Basin of Mexico. *In* Observations on the Emergence of Civilization in Mesoamerica. *Contributions of the University of California Archaeological Research Facility* 11, ed. Robert F. Heizer and J. A. Graham, 7–28.

TONTY, HENRI DE. 1879. Enterprises de M. de La Salle, de 1678 à 1683; relation écrite de Quebec, le 14 Novembre 1684. *In Découvertes et établissements des Français dans l'ouest et dans le sud de l'Amérique septentrionale, 1614–1754. Mémoires et documents originaux,* ed. Pierre Margry, 1:573–616. Paris: D. Jouaust.

TOOKER, ELISABETH. 1964. An ethnography of the Huron Indians, 1615–1649. *Bureau of American Ethnology Bulletin* 190.

———. 1978a. The League of the Iroquois: Its history, politics, and ritual. *In Handbook of North American Indians,* vol. 15, *The Northeast,* ed. Bruce C. Trigger, 418–441. Washington, D.C.: Smithsonian Institution.

———. 1978b. Ely S. Parker, Seneca, 1828–1895. *In American Indian Intellectuals,* ed. Margot Liberty, 15–30. St. Paul: West.

TORBENSON, MICHAEL, ARTHUR AUFDERHEIDE, and ELDEN JOHNSON. 1992. Punctured human bones of the Laurel culture from Smith Mound Four, Minnesota. *American Antiquity* 57 (3):506–514.

TOWNSEND, EARL C., JR. 1959. *Birdstones of the North American Indian.* Indianapolis: privately printed.

TOWNSEND, RICHARD F. 1979. State and cosmos in the Art of Tenochtitlan. *Dumbarton Oaks Studies in Pre-Columbian Art and Archaeology* 20.

———. 1992. *The Aztecs.* London: Thames and Hudson.

TRAUTMAN, MILTON A. 1963. Isotopes, Inc. Radiocarbon Measurements III. *In Radiocarbon* 5.

TRIBAL JUDGES. 1960. *Program and Proceedings of the First Annual Conference for Tribal Judges Held at Vermillion, South Dakota, March 2–6, 1959, Sponsored Jointly by the Association on American Indian Affairs, Inc., the State University of South Dakota Institute of Indian Studies and School of Law, and the U.S. Bureau of Indian Affairs.* Vermillion, S.D.: State University of South Dakota Institute of Indian Studies.

TRIGGER, BRUCE G. 1976. *The Children of Aataentsic: A History of the Huron People to 1660.* 2 vols. Montreal: McGill-Queen's University Press.

———, ed. 1978. *Northeast,* vol. 15 of *Handbook of North American Indians,* gen. ed. William Sturtevant. Washington, D.C.: Smithsonian Institution Press.

TROWBRIDGE, C. C. 1938. Meearmeear Traditions, ed. Vernon Kinietz. *Occasional Contributions from the Museum of Anthropology of the University of Michigan* 7.

———. 1939. Shawnese Traditions, ed. Vernon Kinietz and E.

W. Voegelin. *Occasional Contributions from the Museum of Anthropology of the University of Michigan* 9.

TUCK, JAMES A. 1978. Regional cultural development 3000 to 300 B.C. In *Handbook of North American Indians*, vol. 15, *The Northeast*, ed. Bruce C. Trigger, 28–43. Washington, D.C.: Smithsonian Institution.

TURNBAUGH, WILLIAM A. 1979. Calumet ceremonialism as a nativistic response. *American Antiquity* 44:685–691.

TYLER, HAMILTON A. 1964. *Pueblo Gods and Myths*. Norman: University of Oklahoma Press.

UHLE, MAX. 1909. Peruvian throwing sticks. *American Anthropologist* n.s. 11:624–627.

VAILLANT, GEORGE C. 1948. *Aztecs of Mexico: Origin, Rise and Fall of the Aztec Nation*. Garden City, N.Y.: Doubleday.

VALDIOSERA BERMAN, RAMÓN. 1983. *La Maldición de los códices mexicanos*. Mexico City: Editores asociados M., S.A., EDAMEX.

VAN GENNEP, ARNOLD. 1960. *The Rites of Passage*, trans. Monika B. Vizedom and Gabriel L. Caffee. Chicago: University of Chicago Press. Originally published as *Les Rites de Passage*, Paris, 1909.

VELÁZQUEZ, PRIMO FELICIANO, trans. 1945. *Códice Chimalpopoca*. Mexico City: Universidad Nacional Autónoma de México.

VOGET, FRED W. 1984. *The Shoshoni-Crow Sun Dance*. Norman: University of Oklahoma Press.

VON WINNING, HASSO. 1968. *Pre-Columbian Art of Mexico and Central America*. New York: Harry N. Abrams.

WAGLEY, CHARLES. 1977. *Welcome of Tears: The Tapirapé Indians of Central Brazil*. New York: Oxford University Press.

WALKER, JAMES R. 1917. The Sun Dance and other ceremonies of the Oglala division of the Teton Dakota. *Anthropological Papers of the American Museum of Natural History* 16 (2).

———. 1980. *Lakota Belief and Ritual*, ed. Raymond J. De Mallie and Elaine A. Jahner. Lincoln: University of Nebraska Press.

———. 1982. *Lakota Society*, ed. Raymond J. De Mallie. Lincoln: University of Nebraska Press.

———. 1983. *Lakota Myth*, ed. Elaine A. Jahner. Lincoln: University of Nebraska Press.

WALLACE, ANTHONY F. C. 1972. *The Death and Rebirth of the Seneca*. Vintage Books edition. New York: Random House.

WALLIS, WILSON D. 1947. The Canadian Dakota. *Anthropological Papers of the American Museum of Natural History* 41 (1).

WARING, ANTONIO J., JR. 1945. The De Luna expedition and southeastern ceremonial. *American Antiquity* 11 (1):57–58.

———. 1968. The Southern Cult and Muskogean ceremonial. In The Waring Papers, ed. Stephen Williams, 30–69. *Papers of the Peabody Museum of Archaeology and Ethnology, Harvard University* 58.

WARING, ANTONIO J., JR., and PRESTON HOLDER. 1945. A prehistoric ceremonial complex in the Southeastern United States. *American Anthropologist* 47 (1):1–34.

WARNER, W. LLOYD. 1958. *A Black Civilization: A Social Study of an Australian Tribe*. Rev. ed. New York: Harper and Brothers.

WARREN, WILLIAM G. 1885. History of the Ojibways. *Collections of the Minnesota Historical Society*, vol. 5.

WATERMAN, T. T. 1916. The delineation of the day-signs in the Aztec manuscripts. *University of California Publications in American Archaeology and Ethnology* 11 (6).

WATERS, FRANK. 1969. *The Book of the Hopi: the First Revelation of the Hopi's Historical and Religious World-View of Life*. New York: Ballantine Books. Originally published by Viking, New York, 1963.

WEBB, CLARENCE H., and MONROE DODD JR. 1939. Further excavation of the Gahagan Mound: Connections with a Florida culture. *Texas Archaeological and Paleontological Society Bulletin* 11:92–126.

WEBB, WILLIAM S. 1946. Indian Knoll. *University of Kentucky Reports in Anthropology and Archaeology* 4 (3, pt. 1).

———. 1981. The development of the spearthrower. *Occasional Papers in Anthropology* 2. Lexington: University of Kentucky, Department of Anthropology. Copyrighted 1981 but dated 1957 on the cover.

WEBB, WILLIAM S., and RAYMOND S. BABY. 1957. *The Adena People, No. 2*. Columbus: Ohio State University Press for the Ohio Historical Society.

WEBB, WILLIAM S., and CHARLES E. SNOW. 1945. The Adena people. *University of Kentucky Reports in Anthropology and Archaeology* 6.

WEDEL, MILDRED MOTT. 1959. Oneota Sites on the Upper Iowa River. *Missouri Archaeologist* 21 (2–4).

———. 1973. The identity of La Salle's *Pana* slave. *Plains Anthropologist* 18 (61):203–217.

WEDEL, WALDO R. 1936. An Introduction to Pawnee archaeology. *Bureau of American Ethnology Bulletin* 112.

———. 1948. Prehistory and the Missouri Valley Development Program: Summary report on the Missouri River Basin Archaeological Survey in 1947. *Smithsonian Miscellaneous Collections* 111 (2). Washington.

———. 1959. An introduction to Kansas archeology. *Bureau of American Ethnology Bulletin* 174.

———. 1961. *Prehistoric Man on the Plains*. Norman: University of Oklahoma Press.

THE WEEK (Walworth County, Wisconsin). 1994. Giving thanks. November 20, 1, 32–37.

WELTFISH, GENE. 1977. *The Lost Universe: Pawnee Life and Culture*. Lincoln: University of Nebraska Press. Originally published in 1965 by Basic Books under the title *The Lost Universe with a closing chapter on "The Universe Regained."*

WESLAGER, CLINTON A. 1972. *The Delaware Indians: A History*. New Brunswick, N.J.: Rutgers University Press.

WHEELER BRIDGE MOUNDS. 1947. Notes and sketches of the excavation of the Wheeler Bridge Mounds (39CH4). Photocopies in the files of the State Archaeological Research Center of the South Dakota State Historical Society, Rapid City.

WHITE BUFFALO CALF. 1994. White buffalo calf named "Miracle." 1994. *News from Indian Country* 8 (18 [late Sept.]):1.

WHITEFORD, ANDREW H. 1949. A report on the Outlet site on Lake Monona. *Wisconsin Archeologist* n.s. 30 (1):22–35.

WHITMAN, WILLIAM. 1969. *The Oto*. New York: AMS Press. Originally published in 1937 as *Columbia University Contributions to Anthropology* 28.

WHITTEN, RICHARD G., and LARRY J. ZIMMERMAN. 1982.

Directions for Miss Deloria: Boas on the Plains. *Plains Anthropologist* 27 (96):161–164.

WIDEMAN, JOHN EDGAR. 1995. Russell Means. *Modern Maturity* 38 (5 [Sept.–Oct.]): 68–74, 76, 78–79.

WIKE, JOYCE. 1952. The role of the dead in Northwest Coast culture. In *Indian Tribes of Aboriginal America: Selected Papers of the XXIXth International Congress of Americanists*, ed. Sol Tax, 97–103. Chicago: University of Chicago Press.

WILLEY, GORDON R. 1949. Archaeology of the Florida Gulf Coast. *Smithsonian Miscellaneous Collections* 113.

———. 1955. The prehistoric civilizations of Nuclear America. *American Anthropologist* 57:571–593.

———. 1962. The early great styles and the rise of the pre-Columbian civilizations. *American Anthropologist* 64 (1):1–14.

WILLEY, P. 1990. *Prehistoric Warfare on the Great Plains: Skeletal Analysis of the Crow Creek Massacre Victims*. New York: Garland.

WILLIAMS, ROGER. 1963. *A Key into the Language of America, or an Help to the Language of the Natives in That Part of America Called New-England; Together with Briefe Observations of the Customs, Manners, and Worships, etc. of the Aforesaid Natives, in Peace and Warre, in Life and Death. On All of Which are Added Spiritual Observations Generall and Particular. . . .* In *The Complete Writings of Roger Williams*, ed. James Hammond Trumbull, 1:77–282. New York: Russell and Russell. Originally published by Gregory Dexter, London, 1643.

WILLIAMS, STEPHEN, and JOHN M. GOGGIN. 1956. The long nosed god mask in eastern United States. *Missouri Archaeologist* 18 (3):4–72.

WILLOUGHBY, CHARLES. 1917. The art of the great earthwork builders of Ohio. *Annual Report of the Smithsonian Institution for 1916*, 469–480. Originally published in *Holmes Anniversary Volume*, 469–480, Washington, 1916.

———. 1935. Michabo the Great Hare: A patron of the Hopewell Mound settlement. *American Anthropologist* n.s. 37:280–286.

———. 1973. *Antiquities of the New England Indians*. New York: AMS Press. Originally published in 1935 by the Peabody Museum of Archaeology and Ethnology, Harvard University.

WILSON, DOROTHY CLARKE. 1974. *Bright Eyes: The Story of Susette La Flesche, an Omaha Indian*. New York: McGraw-Hill.

WILSON, GILBERT LIVINGSTONE. 1928. Hidatsa eagle trapping. *Anthropological Papers of the American Museum of Natural History* 30 (4).

WILSON, MICHAEL. 1981. Sun dances, thirst dances, and medicine wheels: A search for alternative hypotheses. In *Megaliths to Medicine Wheels: Boulder Structures in Archaeology*, ed. Michael Wilson, Kathie L. Road, and Kenneth J. Hardy, 333–370. Proceedings of the eleventh Annual Chacmool Conference. Calgary, Alberta: University of Calgary, Department of Archaeology, Archaeological Association.

WINTERS, HOWARD D. 1969. The Riverton culture. *Illinois State Museum Reports of Investigations* 13.

WISCONSIN HISTORICAL COLLECTIONS. 1855–1915. *Collections of the State Historical Society of Wisconsin*. vols. 1–10 (1855–1888), ed. Lyman C. Draper; vols. 11–20 (1888–1911), ed. Reuben Gold Thwaites; vol. 21 (1915), index to vols. 1–20, ed. Milo M. Quaife.

WISSLER, CLARK. 1907. Some protective designs of the Dakota. *Anthropological Papers of the American Museum of Natural History* 1 (2).

WISSLER, CLARK, and D. C. DUVALL. 1909. Mythology of the Blackfoot Indians. *Anthropological Papers of the American Museum of Natural History* 2 (1). Reprint, AMS Press, New York, 1975.

WISSLER, CLARK, and HERBERT J. SPINDEN. 1916. The Pawnee Sacrifice to the Morningstar. *American Museum Journal* 16 (1):48–55.

WITTHOFT, JOHN. 1949. Green Corn Ceremonialism in the Eastern Woodlands. *Occasional Contributions from the Museum of Anthropology of the University of Michigan* 13.

WOOD, W. RAYMOND. 1967. An interpretation of Mandan culture history. *Bureau of American Ethnology Bulletin* 198.

WORTHINGTON, ROGER. 1989. Reclaiming a bit of its past culture, tribe celebrates return of totem pole. *Chicago Tribune*, Sunday, August 20, sect. 1:21, 26.

WRAY, DONALD E. 1952. Archeology in the Illinois valley. In *Archeology of Eastern United States*, ed. James B. Griffin, 152–164. Chicago: University of Chicago Press.

WRONG, GEORGE M., ed. 1939. *Father Gabriel Sagard: The Long Journey to the Country of the Hurons*. Toronto: Champlain Society.

ZIMMERMAN, LARRY J., THOMAS E. EMERSON, PATRICK WILLEY, MARK SWEGLE, JOHN B. GREGG, PAULINE GREGG, EVERETT WHITE, CARLYLE SMITH, THOMAS HABERMAN, and M. PAMELA BUMSTEAD. 1981. *The Crow Creek Site (39BF11) Massacre: A Preliminary Report*. Prepared by the University of South Dakota Archaeology Laboratory for the Omaha District, U.S. Army Corps of Engineers.

INDEX

ROBERT L. HALL is a professor of anthropology at the University of Illinois at Chicago, where he has taught since 1968, during ten of those years serving as department chairman. He has published in a wide variety of fields, including comparative studies of North American and Mesoamerican Indian ritual, symbolism, and iconography, Mesoamerican calendar systems, archaeoastronomy, ethnohistory, radiocarbon dating, ceramic chronology, and the archaeology of Mississippian-level societies of the Midwest. Hall comes to his interest in North American Indian culture history through his family background, having lived much of his childhood in a household that included his mother, grandmother, and great-grandmother, who were all enrolled Stockbridge-Munsee tribal members of Mohican, Menominee, and Ottawa ancestry.